juvenile JUSTICE

an introduction

fifth edition

John T. Whitehead
East Tennessee State University

Steven P. Lab
Bowling Green State University

 LexisNexis®

 **anderson publishing**
A member of the LexisNexis Group

Juvenile Justice: An Introduction, Fifth Edition

Copyright © 1990, 1996, 1999, 2004, 2006
Matthew Bender & Company, Inc., a member of the LexisNexis Group

Phone 877-374-2919
Web Site www.lexisnexis.com/anderson/criminaljustice

Library of Congress Cataloging-in-Publication Data

Whitehead, John T.
   Juvenile justice : an introduction / John T. Whitehead, Steven P. Lab--5th ed.
      p. cm.
   Includes bibliographical references and index
   ISBN 1-59345-318-3 (softbound)
   1. Juvenile delinquency. 2. Juvenile justice, Administration of. 3. Juvenile justice,
Administration of--United States. I. Lab, Steven P. II. Title.

   HV9069.W46 2006
   364.36--dc22   2005036776

Cover design by Tin Box Studio, Inc.

EDITOR Ellen S. Boyne
ACQUISITIONS EDITOR Michael C. Braswell

Dedication

to

Pat, Danny & Tim Whitehead

and

Danielle Lab

Foreword

In this Fifth Edition of *Juvenile Justice: An Introduction* we have done several things. First, we have updated all of the materials throughout to make the book as current as possible. In addition, we have included the latest available statistics on juvenile crime and victimization, drug use, court statistics, and corrections, as well as the latest opinion poll data on attitudes toward the police. Second, we have added a new chapter on restorative justice (Chapter 12). We previously had material about restorative justice in the probation chapter but decided that this important topic now merits a separate chapter. In the last chapter we have added excerpts from the recent Supreme Court decision on the death penalty for juveniles to the discussion of capital punishment. In the courts chapter we have added to the discussion of both teen courts and drug courts. In the police chapter we have added a discussion of CompStat as a strategy for improving police operations. Throughout all the chapters we have attempted to add recent research findings including, for example, recent findings on the effectiveness of juvenile aftercare and an evaluation of a community probation program.

An Instructor's Guide is available. It contains test bank questions, suggestions for classroom activities and videos to supplement the text.

We thank all of the people at Anderson for their support of the book. We are especially grateful to Mickey Braswell for his continued support and to Ellen Boyne for her excellent work in editing and producing the final product.

JTW
SPL

Table of Contents

Chapter 1

Introduction—The Definition and Extent of Delinquency

INTRODUCTION

Discussions of the juvenile justice system cannot proceed without a clear understanding of the behaviors that it is tasked to address. As will be seen in Chapter 2, the juvenile court and the juvenile justice system are relatively recent inventions, tracing their history back to the late 1800s. Prior to that time, youths who broke the law were handled in the same system and in the same ways as adults. It was not until the 1800s that crime and misbehavior by youths were redefined as separate and distinct from adult offending. "Delinquency" was born and new mechanisms of social control developed to address problem children.

In the relatively short time period since "delinquency" and the juvenile court were initiated, society has developed a separate system for handling youthful offenders. Youthful offenders who used to be seen as simply young "criminals" have been transformed into "delinquents." The label of delinquent, however, represents a variety of different behaviors and means different things at different places and points in time. It is important to understand the diversity in definitions of delinquency in order to adequately examine the workings of the juvenile justice system.

KEY TERMS

dark figure of crime

delinquency

Index crimes

juvenile

Monitoring the Future (MTF) survey

National Youth Survey (NYS)

offense rate

panel design

PRIDE Surveys

self-report surveys

Short-Nye instrument

status offenses

transfer

Uniform Crime Reports

waiver

Youth Risk Behavior Surveillance System (YRBSS)

DEFINING DELINQUENCY

As already noted, **delinquency** has a number of different meanings. These various interpretations appear both in state statutes and criminological discussions of juvenile behavior. As a result, it is possible to delineate three kinds or types of definitions corresponding to the behavior of the juvenile and the intended use of the definition. These three definitions can be considered as a criminal law definition, a status offense definition, and social/criminological definitions.

Criminal Law Definitions

A criminal law definition of delinquency delineates activity that is illegal regardless of the age of the offender. Delinquency is simply a substitute label for criminal behavior by a juvenile. The only distinction between being a delinquent and being a criminal is the age of the individual.

Criminal law definitions of delinquency typically define a delinquent as someone who violates the criminal laws of the jurisdiction (see Figure 1.1). The key to these statutes is the idea that a juvenile violated the criminal law. The fact that a juvenile committed the offense means that a different label will be imposed (delinquent versus criminal) and a different system will handle the individual (juvenile versus adult). A criminal law definition explicitly extends the criminal statutes to the juvenile population.

Figure 1.1   A Criminal Law Definition of Delinquency

(F)   "Delinquent child" includes any of the following:

(1)   Any child, except a juvenile traffic offender, who violates any law of this state or the United States, or any ordinance of a political subdivision of the state, that would be an offense if committed by an adult;

(2)   Any child who violates any lawful order of the court . . .

(3)   Any child who violates [prohibitions against purchasing or owning a firearm or handgun (Section 2321.211)];

(4)   Any child who is a habitual truant and who previously has been adjudicated an unruly child for being a habitual truant;

(5)   Any child who is a chronic truant.

Source: Ohio Revised Code (2005). Section 2152.02. Anderson Online Docs. Available at: http://online docs.andersonpublishing.com.

Status Offense Definitions

Besides criminal actions that can be committed by a juvenile, there are other behaviors for which only juveniles can be held accountable. These behaviors are usually referred to as **status offenses** because they are only illegal if they are committed by persons of a particular "status." Thus, juvenile status offenses represent acts that are illegal only for juveniles. Adults who take part in these acts are not subject to sanctioning by the formal justice system.

While "status offender" is the most common term for those who violate these acts, a variety of other names are applied to these individuals. Among the more common names are "unruly," "dependent," and "incorrigible," as well as acronyms such as PINS (person in need of supervision) or CHINS (child in need of supervision). One common criticism of status offense definitions is that they are ambiguous and the language is so vague that they allow wide latitude in interpreting what is and is not a violation (see Figure 1.2). Such statutes allow the juvenile justice system to intervene in the life of almost any youth.

Figure 1.2   A Status Offense Definition of Delinquency

Ohio Chapter 2151.022 defines an "unruly child" as:

(A) Any child who does not submit to the reasonable control of the child's parents, teachers, guardian, or custodian, by reason of being wayward or habitually disobedient;

(B) Any child who is an habitual truant from school and who previously has not been adjudicated an unruly child for being an habitual truant;

(C) Any child who behaves in a manner as to injure or endanger the child's own health or morals or the health or morals of others;

(D) Any child who violates a law . . . that is applicable only to a child.

Source: Ohio Revised Code (2005). Section 2151.022. Anderson's Online Docs. Available at: http://online docs.andersonpublishing.com

The behaviors outlined by status offense statutes make virtually any behavior of a juvenile sanctionable by the state. The definitions are all-encompassing and have been criticized for being overly broad (see, for example, President's Commission on Law Enforcement and the Administration of Justice, 1967). Arguments for eliminating such overly broad language have resulted in some courts ruling that the statutory language, such as that referring to "leading an idle, dissolute, lewd, or immoral life," is unconstitutionally vague (*Gonzalez v. Mailliard*, 1971).

Actions that typically fall under the heading of status offenses include truancy, smoking, drinking, curfew violations, disobeying the orders of parents, teachers or other adults, swearing, running away, and other acts that are allowable for adults. All juveniles violate these statutes at one time or another. Normal youthful behavior includes many of these activities. It is possible that all youths could be subjected to system intervention under these types of "status" definitions.

Social/Criminological Definitions

The study of delinquency and juvenile justice often relies on definitions of delinquency that do not conform precisely to the legal definitions of delinquent or status offenses. The definition of delinquency often takes on a specific meaning depending on the interests of the group or individual dealing with juvenile misconduct at any given time or place. The 1967 President's Commission on Law Enforcement and the Administration of Justice took a broad view by defining delinquency as a combination of delinquent and status offense statutes:

> Delinquency comprises cases of children alleged to have committed an offense that if committed by an adult would be a crime. It also comprises cases of children alleged to have violated specific ordinances or regulatory laws that apply only to children . . . (President's Commission, 1967:4).

Cloward and Ohlin's (1960) definition of delinquency depends on the response of the justice system. Delinquent acts are those "that officials engaged in the administration of criminal justice select . . . from among many deviant acts, as forms of behavior proscribed by the approved norms of society" (Cloward and Ohlin, 1960:2-3). This means that the criminal and juvenile justice systems determine which actions are to be considered delinquent. Social control agents, however, are (or should be) responsive to the views and needs of the larger society, and actions chosen for intervention are to be determined by the sentiments of society. This definition limits the discussion of delinquency to those actions that are handled by the justice system. Juvenile behavior which is ignored by the system is not to be considered delinquent.

Most definitions of delinquency present juvenile behavior as either delinquent or nondelinquent, with no middle ground. Cavan and Ferdinand (1981) offer a continuum of behavior that ranges from extreme delinquency on one end to extreme goodness on the other (see Figure 1.3). The shape of the continuum, a bell curve, represents the proportional distribution of juveniles along the continuum. It is assumed that the largest group of youths would fall into the middle category of "normal conformity." The left-hand portion of the curve represent youths who run the risk of being apprehended and labeled delinquent. These juveniles are involved, to varying degrees, in delinquent behavior. Minor underconformity may include such acts as status and victimless offenses while the delinquent contraculture category includes serious acts such as murder and rape and suggests organized involvement in deviance. The right side of the curve represents individuals who do not become involved in delinquency. Few juveniles appear in either of the "contraculture" categories of extreme delinquent or extreme goodness.

Figure 1.3   **Behavior Continuum**

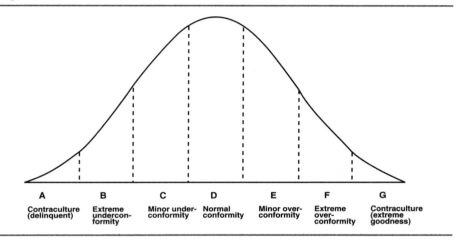

A	B	C	D	E	F	G
Contraculture (delinquent)	Extreme undercon- formity	Minor under- conformity	Normal conformity	Minor over- conformity	Extreme over- conformity	Contraculture (extreme goodness)

Source: Figure 2.1 from *Juvenile Delinquency*, 4th ed. by Ruth Shonle Cavan and Theodore N. Ferdi-nand. Copyright © 1981 by Ruth Shonle Cavan and Theodore N. Ferdinand. Reprinted by permission.

This last view of delinquency more closely represents the type of definition emerging in criminological study. It does not limit the researcher to a simple legal definition or an either/or dichotomy. Instead, it allows the inspection of various types of delinquent activity as well as activity that is highly overconforming. Seen as a continuum, juvenile activity can be subdivided into various parts and phases that change over time and can be compared to one another.

What Is a Juvenile?

In every definition of delinquency there is an implicit assumption of what constitutes a **juvenile**. Interestingly, the legal definition of a juvenile varies from jurisdiction to jurisdiction. This means that persons subject to the juvenile statutes in one location may not be in another place. Table 1.1 presents the age at which the adult court assumes responsibility for the actions of individuals in different jurisdictions. Under these ages the individual is considered a juvenile and is handled in the juvenile justice system. The majority of states (37) and the District of Columbia recognize juveniles as individuals below the age of 18. In three states juveniles are age 15 or younger, and 10 states define juveniles as those under 17 years old.

Table 1.1.   Ages at Which Criminal Courts Gain Jurisdiction over Young Offenders

Age 16	Age 18	
Connecticut	Alabama	Nevada
New York	Alaska	New Jersey
North Carolina	Arizona	New Mexico
	Arkansas	North Dakota
	California	Ohio
	Colorado	Oklahoma
Age 17	Delaware	Oregon
	District of	Pennsylvania
Georgia	Columbia	Rhode Island
Illinois	Florida	South Dakota
Louisiana	Hawaii	Tennessee
Massachusetts	Idaho	Utah
Michigan	Indiana	Vermont
Missouri	Iowa	Virginia
New Hampshire	Kansas	Washington
South Carolina	Kentucky	West Virginia
Texas	Maine	Wyoming
Wisconsin	Maryland	
	Minnesota	
	Mississippi	
	Montana	
	Nebraska	

Source: M. Bozynski and L. Szymanski (2004). "National Overviews." *State Juvenile Justice Profiles.* Pittsburgh: National Center for Juvenile Justice.

Besides setting an upper age for juvenile status, other factors influence whether an individual can be handled in the juvenile justice system. First, some states set a lower age limit in outlining who can be treated by the juvenile justice process. These ages range from age six to age ten (see Table 1.2), although 33 states and the District of Columbia have no lower age limit. In those states with a lower age level, any juvenile below the minimum age who exhibits deviant behavior is simply returned to his or her parents or guardian for handling.

Table 1.2   Lower Age Limits for Juvenile Court Jurisdiction

Age 6	Age 10	No Specified Age		
North Carolina	Arkansas	Alabama	Iowa	Oregon
	Colorado	Alaska	Kentucky	Rhode Island
	Kansas	California	Maine	South Carolina
Age 7	Louisiana	Connecticut	Michigan	Tennessee
	Minnesota	Delaware	Montana	Utah
Maryland	Mississippi	District of	Nebraska	Virginia
Massachusetts	Pennsylvania	Columbia	Nevada	Washington
New York	South Dakota	Florida	New Hampshire	West Virginia
	Texas	Georgia	New Jersey	Wyoming
	Vermont	Hawaii	New Mexico	
Age 8	Wisconsin	Idaho	North Dakota	
	Illinois	Ohio		
Arizona	Indiana	Oklahoma		

Source: M. Bozynski and L. Szymanski (2004). "National Overviews." *State Juvenile Justice Profiles.* Pittsburgh: National Center for Juvenile Justice.

A second age consideration is the termination of the juvenile system's intervention with an individual. Many state statutes allow the juvenile system to continue supervision and intervention with individuals who have passed the maximum age limit (see Table 1.3). In three states the juvenile court retains jurisdiction until the disposition is completed. The most common maximum age at which juvenile court jurisdiction is relinquished is age 20. Maintaining jurisdiction occurs mainly when that person committed his or her act as a juvenile and/or is being handled as an extension of intervention begun when he or she was a juvenile.

Table 1.3   **Maximum Ages at Which Juvenile Courts May Maintain Jurisdiction over Youthful Offenders**

Age 18	Age 20		
Alaska	Alabama	Maryland	South Carolina
Iowa	Arizona	Massachusetts	South Dakota
Kentucky	Arkansas	Michigan	Texas
Nebraska	Connecticut	Minnesota	Utah
Oklahoma	Delaware	Missouri	Vermont
Tennessee	District of	Nevada	Virginia
	Columbia	New Hampshire	Washington
Age 19	Georgia	New Mexico	West Virginia
	Idaho	New York	Wyoming
Mississippi	Illinois	North Carolina	
North Dakota	Indiana	Ohio	
	Louisiana	Pennsylvania	
Age 21	Maine	Rhode Island	
Florida	**Until the Full Term of Disposition Order**		
Age 22	Colorado	New Jersey	
	Hawaii		
Kansas			
Age 24			
California			
Montana			
Oregon			
Wisconsin			

Source: M. Bozynski and L. Szymanski (2004). "National Overviews." *State Juvenile Justice Profiles.* Pittsburgh: National Center for Juvenile Justice. Available at: http://www.ncjj.org/stateprofiles/

A final factor influencing juvenile court jurisdiction involves **waiver** or **transfer** provisions that may send a youth to adult court. Waiver is a process by which an individual who is legally a juvenile is sent to the adult criminal system for disposition and handling. While in the past ages 15 and 16 typically constituted the youngest ages at which waiver could occur, recent years have seen a move toward waiving younger individuals to the adult system. Currently, 22 states and the District of Columbia set no minimum for waiver, two set age 10, three set age 12, and another four states allow waiver of 13-year-olds to the adult court (see Table 1.4).

Table 1.4   Minimum Ages for Transfer to Criminal Court

Age 10	Age 15
Kansas	New Mexico
Vermont	
	No Minimum Age
Age 12	
	Alaska
Colorado	Arizona
Missouri	Delaware
Montana	District of Columbia
	Florida
Age 13	Georgia
	Hawaii
Illinois	Idaho
Mississippi	Indiana
New Hampshire	Maine
New York	Maryland
North Carolina	Nebraska
Wyoming	Nevada
	Oklahoma
Age 14	Oregon
	Pennsylvania
Alabama	Rhode Island
Arkansas	South Carolina
California	South Dakota
Connecticut	Tennessee
Iowa	Washington
Kentucky	West Virginia
Louisiana	Wisconsin
Massachusetts	
Michigan	
Minnesota	
New Jersey	
North Dakota	
Ohio	
Texas	
Utah	
Virginia	

Source: P. Griffin (2004). *National Overviews: State Juvenile Justice Profiles*. Pittsburgh: National Center for Juvenile Justice. Available at: http:www.ncjj.org/stateprofiles

Waiver provisions and processes can take a variety of forms (see Table 1.5). Some of these require a judicial hearing before a youth can be sent to adult court (*judicial waiver*), while others leave the decision to the prosecutor or are mandated by the legislature (*statutory exclusion*). There are even provisions for sending youths back to the juvenile court from adult proceedings (*reverse waiver*). Finally, almost two-thirds of the states have decided that once a youth has been waived to and adjudicated in the adult system, that youth is permanently under the jurisdiction of the adult criminal system, regardless of the future offense (*once/always provisions*). The variations on waiver and transfer are addressed in more detail later in the book. Juveniles who are handled by the adult system comprise a special category of delinquents (or criminals) with which a discussion of juvenile justice must deal.

Table 1.5   States Use of Waiver and Blended Sentencing

	Judicial Waiver			Direct File	Statutory Exclusion	Reverse Waiver	Once/ Always	Juvenile Blended	Criminal Blended
	Discretionary	Presumptive	Mandatory						
Total States	45	15	15	15	29	25	34	15	17
Alabama	x				x		x		
Alaska	x	x			x			x	
Arizona	x			x	x	x	x		
Arkansas	x			x		x		x	x
California	x	x		x	x	x	x		x
Colorado	x	x		x		x		x	x
Connecticut			x			x		x	
Delaware	x		x		x	x	x		
DC	x	x		x			x		
Florida	x			x	x		x		x
Georgia	x		x	x	x	x			
Hawaii	x						x		
Idaho	x				x		x		x
Illinois	x	x	x		x	x	x	x	x
Indiana	x		x		x		x		
Iowa	x				x	x	x		x
Kansas	x	x					x	x	
Kentucky	x		x			x			x
Louisiana	x		x	x	x				
Maine	x	x					x		
Maryland	x				x	x	x		
Massachusetts					x			x	x
Michigan	x			x			x	x	x
Minnesota	x	x			x		x	x	
Mississippi	x				x	x	x		
Missouri	x						x		x
Montana				x	x	x		x	
Nebraska				x		x			x
Nevada	x	x			x	x	x		
New Hampshire	x	x					x		
New Jersey	x	x	x						
New Mexico					x			x	x
New York					x	x			
North Carolina	x		x				x		
North Dakota	x	x	x				x		
Ohio	x		x				x	x	
Oklahoma	x			x	x	x	x		x
Oregon	x				x	x	x		
Pennsylvania	x	x			x	x	x		
Rhode Island	x	x	x				x	x	
South Carolina	x		x		x				
South Dakota	x				x	x	x		
Tennessee	x					x	x		
Texas	x						x	x	
Utah	x	x			x		x		
Vermont	x			x	x	x		x	
Virginia	x		x	x		x	x		x
Washington	x				x		x		
West Virginia	x		x						x
Wisconsin	x				x	x	x		x
Wyoming	x			x		x			

Source: P. Griffin (2004). "National Overviews." *State Juvenile Justice Profiles*. Pittsburgh: National Center for Juvenile Justice. Available at: http:www.ncjj.org/stateprofiles

The varying definitions of delinquency and considerations of what constitutes delinquent behavior have a major impact on any study of juvenile justice. The definition alters the type of behavior with which we are concerned, the practices and interventions used in the treatment of delinquency, and the number of problems and youths who are subjected to intervention and study. It is the effect of the definition of delinquency on the measurement of delinquency to which we now turn.

THE EXTENT OF DELINQUENCY

There are a number of different ways to measure delinquency, each of which produces a different picture of the delinquency problem. The various methods for measuring delinquency result in different absolute levels of delinquency as well as different information on the offense, the offender, and the victim. The two basic approaches to measuring delinquency are the use of official records and the administration of self-report surveys.

Official Measures of Delinquency

Official measures of delinquency are based on the records of various justice system agencies. Consequently, the level of delinquency reflects both the activity of juveniles and the activity of the agency that is dealing with the youths. The degree of detail in the records also varies by agency. The police, courts, and corrections each have different sets of priorities and mandates under which they operate. As a result, the data compiled by the agencies differ from one another. The following pages will consider data from each of these official sources.

Uniform Crime Reports

The **Uniform Crime Reports** (UCR) provide information on the number of offenses coming to the attention of the police, the number of arrests police make, and the number of referrals by the police to the juvenile court. This data is collected yearly by the Federal Bureau of Investigation and provides information on 29 categories of offenses. These counts only reflect crimes known to the police. Actions that are not reported to the police are not included in the yearly crime figures. The UCR is comprised of two offense subgroups. The first eight offenses are known as the Part I or **Index crimes**. Included in this group are the more serious crimes (as delineated by the FBI) of murder, rape, robbery, aggravated assault, burglary, larceny, motor vehicle theft, and arson. All remaining offenses fall within the Part II category.

Extensive information, including demographic data on the victim and offender (if known), circumstances of the offense, the use of a weapon, and the time and place of the offense, is gathered for the Part I offenses. For Part II offenses, only information on offenses in which a suspect has been arrested are tabulated.

Age Distribution. Due to the fact that only about 20 percent of all crimes are cleared by an arrest each year, little information is known about the offender in most crimes. Some idea about the participation of juveniles in delinquent/criminal behavior, however, can be gathered from an inspection of those cases in which an offender can be identified and/or arrested. Table 1.6 presents arrest data for 2003. A total of 9,581,423 arrests were reported to the FBI. Of these arrests, 1,563,149 or 16.3 percent of the total were of juveniles under the age of 18.

A closer inspection of the arrest data reveals the extent to which youths were involved in serious offending. For the violent crimes of murder, rape, robbery, and aggravated assault, youths comprised 15.5 percent of the total arrests. This represents almost 65,000 offenses. More striking is the fact that youths were arrested for more than 328,000 property offenses. This reflects almost 29 percent of all property offense arrests in 2003. Taken by themselves, these figures are large. The problem is exacerbated, however, when you consider that youths between the ages of 10 and 17 (inclusive) make up 11.6 percent of the total U.S. population (U.S. Bureau of the Census, 2005). Youthful offenders are contributing more than their share to the level of arrests in the nation.

Sex Distribution. The UCR routinely presents breakdowns of crime by sex of the offender. UCR data for 2003 show that juvenile females made up 29 percent of all juvenile arrests. Adult females, however, constitute only 22 percent of adult arrests. While males commit a greater percentage of violent crimes than property crimes (81.6% compared to 68.2%), roughly one quarter of both male and female juvenile arrests are for Index crimes. A much greater percentage of males are arrested for every Index offense category, as well as most Part II offenses. The only offenses for which females are more often arrested are prostitution and runaway.

Race Distribution. The UCR also provides information on the race of juvenile arrestees. Table 1.6 presents data on arrests for white, black, native American, and Asian/Pacific Island youths. White youths make up the vast majority of all arrestees (70.6%), and account for more than two-thirds (69%) of the Part I property offenses. Black youths, however, are greatly over-represented in violent personal offenses (murder, rape, robbery, and aggravated assault). This over-representation of blacks in the violent offenses (45%) is even more dramatic in light of the fact that blacks comprise only 14.6 percent of the youthful U.S. population (U.S. Bureau of the Census, 2005).

Table 1.6   Distribution of Juvenile Arrests, 2003

Offense Charged	Number		Percent Under 18	Males	Females	Percent of Juvenile Arrestees			
	All Ages	Under 18				White	Black	Am. Indian or Alaskan Native	Asian or Pacific Islander
Total	9,581,423	1,563,149	16.3	71.0	29.0	70.6	26.6	1.3	1.6
Murder and nonnegligent manslaughter	9,119	783	8.6	90.7	9.3	48.9	48.1	1.3	1.7
Forcible rape	18,446	2,966	16.1	98.0	2.0	64.1	33.4	1.6	0.9
Robbery	75,667	17,900	23.7	91.1	8.9	35.2	62.8	0.5	1.6
Aggravated assault	315,732	43,150	13.7	76.4	23.6	59.3	38.3	1.0	1.3
Burglary	204,761	59,870	29.2	88.2	11.8	71.4	26.1	1.2	1.3
Larceny-theft	817,048	232,322	28.4	60.6	39.4	69.8	26.7	1.5	2.0
Motor vehicle theft	106,221	30,874	29.1	83.1	16.9	56.1	40.3	1.4	2.1
Arson	11,330	5,757	50.8	87.6	12.4	81.3	16.9	0.9	0.8
Violent crimes	418,964	64,799	15.5	81.6	18.4	52.7	45.0	0.9	1.4
Property crimes	1,139,360	328,823	28.9	68.2	31.8	69.0	27.7	1.4	1.9
Other assaults	877,105	170,168	19.4	67.5	32.5	61.4	36.3	1.1	1.2
Forgery and counterfeiting	79,188	3,328	4.2	64.5	35.5	77.2	20.5	0.8	1.5
Fraud	208,469	5,642	2.7	66.9	30.1	66.3	31.6	0.6	1.5
Embezzlement	11,986	826	6.9	59.9	40.1	68.0	29.8	0.4	1.8
Stolen property	89,560	17,184	19.2	85.1	14.9	57.1	40.6	1.0	1.3
Vandalism	193,083	76,042	39.4	86.2	13.8	80.1	17.6	1.2	1.1
Weapons; carrying, possessing, etc.	117,844	27,492	23.2	88.9	11.1	66.0	31.7	0.7	1.7
Prostitution and commercialized vice	51,686	972	1.9	30.6	69.4	50.9	47.2	0.4	1.4
Sex offenses (except forcible rape)	63,759	12,747	20.0	90.7	9.3	71.4	26.5	0.7	1.4
Drug abuse violations	1,172,222	137,658	11.7	83.5	16.5	72.1	26.0	0.9	1.0
Gambling	7,414	1,151	15.5	97.7	2.3	11.6	86.4	0.3	1.8
Offenses against family and children	94,488	4,859	5.1	61.1	38.9	76.7	20.0	1.7	1.6
Driving under the influence	1,005,577	14,570	1.4	79.8	30.2	93.7	3.7	1.7	0.9
Liquor laws	431,912	96,592	22.4	65.0	35.0	91.8	4.2	2.8	1.1
Drunkenness	389,626	12,529	3.2	76.8	23.2	88.7	8.4	2.1	0.8
Disorderly conduct	453,645	136,970	30.1	57.0	43.0	64.0	33.9	1.1	0.9
Vagrancy	20,052	1,594	7.9	74.7	25.3	61.7	37.3	0.5	0.5
All other offenses	2,571,023	266,365	10.4	72.6	27.4	74.4	22.8	1.2	1.6
Suspicion	1,812	390	21.5	76.1	23.9	66.2	33.1	0.8	0.0
Curfew and loitering law violations	95,052	95,052	100.0	69.7	30.3	67.9	30.0	0.8	1.3
Runaways	87,396	87,396	100.0	41.3	58.7	73.4	20.2	1.7	4.7

Source: Compiled by authors from UCR data.

An examination of individual Part I offenses provides a more detailed look at the data. While a greater percentage of white youths commit every offense than blacks, except for murder and robbery (blacks and whites commit almost exactly the same number of murders and blacks commit many more robberies), offending by black youths far surpasses their population representation for all Part I offenses, except arson.

Trends in Delinquency. The trend in youthful crime has changed in recent years. The change in the number of violent offenses since 1986 appear in Figure 1.4. Both arrests for murder and rape have remained relatively stable, while robbery and aggravated assault arrests increased from 1986 to 1995 and have dropped since that time. Data on property crimes (Figure 1.5) show general declines since 1986, except for an increase in larceny arrests in 1995.

Figure 1.4   Trends in Violent Crime, 1986-2003

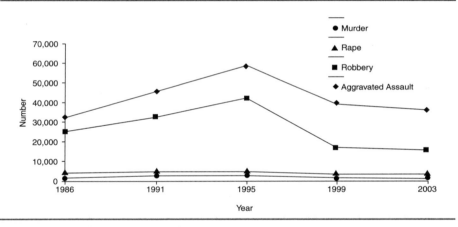

Source: Constructed by authors from UCR data.

Figure 1.5   Trends in Property Crime, 1986-2003

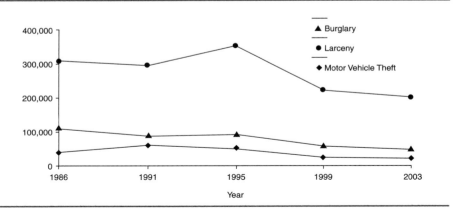

Source: Constructed by authors from UCR data.

Perhaps a better way to examine change over time is to consider the **offense rate** (typically the number of offenses per 100,000), which eliminates the influence of any changes in the number of potential offenders on the delinquency data. Juvenile arrest rates showed a steady increase throughout the 1960s and mid-1970s, leveled off, and showed some decline in the late-1970s and 1980s, increased in the late 1980s and early 1990s, and has abated since the mid-1990s. One thing that is clear in both the raw number of arrests and the arrest rate figures is that official juvenile offending is higher today than 40 years ago, although the recent trend has been toward lower arrests.

A Critique of the UCR. The UCR is the longest running and most widely known and cited method of collecting information on crime in the United States. It began in 1931 and has continued on a yearly basis since that time. Despite this longevity and notoriety, the UCR has a number of flaws that must be considered when using the data (see O'Brien, 1985). The most frequent criticism is the fact that it reflects only those offenses known to the police. Many individuals, for whatever reason, opt not to contact the police when they are a victim or a witness to a crime. This failure to bring crimes to the attention of the police results in an undercount of crime in the United States. The unreported crimes are typically referred to as the **dark figure of crime**.

A second concern with the UCR is that it is voluntary and it relies on the individual agencies to accurately report their data. Each agency tabulates and forwards its own data to the FBI. Political and economic pressures have been known to influence the accuracy of counts submitted to the UCR system. For example, changes in police procedure due to political decisions can alter the amount of attention a police department pays to a certain form of crime. Similarly, the simple reclassification of offenses from one category to another (i.e., listing "rapes" as "other sex offenses" or "aggravated assaults" as "simple assaults") can alter the reported crime rates. Decisions like these can greatly alter the yearly offense counts and have an impact on trend data over time.

Another concern in using the UCR is the lack of information on offenders in much of the data. UCR arrest data reflect only those offenders who were caught in the course of the crime or ensuing investigation. The fact that only about 20 percent of all crimes are cleared by an arrest means that little is known about the offenders in most crimes. It is possible that UCR figures are distorted in terms of the age, race, and sex distribution of the total offending population. The UCR provides no information about the offender in roughly 80 percent of the crimes committed each year.

Another serious problem entails the fact that the UCR counts offenses and not offenders. It would be easy to claim that the number of offenders is equal to the number of reported offenses. Unfortunately, this would provide a highly inaccurate picture. Many offenders commit more than one offense over a period of time. Alternatively, some individuals may commit a single act (such as bank robbery) that legally constitutes more than one offense (robbery, assault, and possibly kidnapping). These problems make it difficult to estimate the number of offenders over any period of time using the UCR. The number of offenders is clearly not equal to the number of offenses.

A variety of other concerns must be considered in using the UCR data. Among these are the fact that legal definitions of crime change over time and vary from place to place. In addition, the methods of data collection have changed over time (particularly from hand to computer tabulation). A further concern is the fact that any selective enforcement of the law or bias in making arrests can result in an overrepresentation of certain individuals (such as lower-class youths) in the UCR figures.

The most problematic aspect of the UCR for the study of delinquency is the combined issue of the dark figure of crime and the failure to identify offenders in the vast majority of all cases. It is due to these problems that alternative methods of unofficial crime and delinquency data have been developed. Before turning to these types of data collection, we will look at two additional official measures of delinquency.

Juvenile Court Statistics

Juvenile court data present a picture of the cases and the juveniles who reach the adjudication stage of the system. The numbers of juveniles who appear in these records are smaller than those found in the UCR police data. This is due primarily to the fact that most juveniles reach the court through contact with the police, who filter and screen cases. Relatively few youths are referred to court directly by their families, schools, or other associates. In 2000, the police referred 84 percent of the cases in juvenile court (Puzzanchera et al., 2004). Table 1.7 presents data on delinquency cases in juvenile court. In 2000, approximately 1,633,000 youths reached the juvenile court for delinquent offenses. This translates into a rate of 51 out of every 1,000 youths. Data since 1960 (not presented) show a steady increase in the rate of youths entering the court. In 1960, the rate was 20.1. The 2000 rate represents a 250 percent increase. In addition to the delinquency cases, an additional 300,403 youths in 35 states appeared in court for status offense violations in 2000; a rate of 13.8 youths per 1,000 (Puzzanchera et al., 2004).

Information on type of offense, sex, and race is also available in the court statistics. Like the UCR data, males dominate throughout the juvenile court statistics. Both the number of male and female delinquency cases increased since 1985. While the number of male cases peaked in 1996-1997 and have fallen since that time, the number of female cases increased from 1985 to 1997 and has remained relatively stable since 1997 (Puzzanchera et al., 2004). The number of person, public order, and drug cases has shown clear increases since 1985, but property crime cases have been decreasing since the mid 1990s after increasing from 1985 and the early 1990s (Puzzanchera et al., 2004).

Table 1.7   Number and Rates of Youths in Juvenile Court—1991, 1994, 1997, 2000

Offense Type	1991	1994	1997	2000
	Number of Offenses			
Delinquency				
Person	278,151	360,574	392,568	375,592
Property	848,896	867,770	847,556	668,588
Drugs	65,422	131,141	194,457	194,187
Public Order	221,051	306,375	385,122	394,975
	Rate per 1,000 Population			
Delinquency				
Person	10.0	12.1	12.5	11.5
Property	30.5	29.1	27.0	20.5
Drugs	2.4	4.4	6.2	5.9
Public Order	7.9	10.3	12.3	12.1

Source: Constructed by authors from data presented by C. Puzzanchera, A.L. Stahl, T.A. Finnegan, N. Tierney, and H.N. Snyder (2004). *Juvenile Court Statistics 2000*. Pittsburgh: National Center for Justice; and A. Stahl, T. Finnegan, and W. Kang (2003). *Easy Access to Juvenile Court Statistics: 1985-2000*. Washington, DC: U.S. Department of Justice.

Similar to UCR figures, court data show that property offenses dominate at about 40 percent of all delinquency cases. Public order offenses (such as disorderly conduct and liquor violations) and offenses against persons each contribute approximately 23 percent to the juvenile court caseload. Not surprisingly, older youths are referred at a much greater rate than are younger youths for delinquency offenses (rate of 111.5 for 17 year olds; 5.1 rate for 10 year olds) (Puzzanchera et al., 2004).

In terms of race, raw court numbers are dominated by white youths (roughly two-thirds of all petitions). Despite the fact that more white youths appear in juvenile court, blacks are overrepresented given their proportion in the population. The 2000 delinquency case rate for white youths is 46.3 per 1,000, while the rate for black youths is roughly double at 95.6, and the rate for other races is 32.5 (Puzzanchera et al., 2004).

Juvenile Corrections Statistics

A third official source of information on juveniles coming into contact with the juvenile justice system is records kept on juvenile correctional facilities. The U.S. Justice Department routinely conducts a census of the population of juvenile facilities. As with juvenile court statistics, the numbers of youths who appear in these statistics are smaller than the UCR and court figures. This is due to the funneling process of the juvenile system whereby fewer and fewer youths are subjected to intervention the further one looks into the system. In addition, the juvenile court may handle youths in a variety of ways that do not involve institutionalization. Figure 1.6 provides a view of how petitions coming to juvenile court in 2000 were disposed. Forty-two percent of the cases that come to the juvenile court are handled without a formal petition being made. Of those petitioned, 41 percent are not adjudicated as a delinquent, although 33 percent of those still receive some form of intervention (either placement, probation, or other sanction).

Figure 1.4   Juvenile Court Processing of Delinquency Cases, 2000

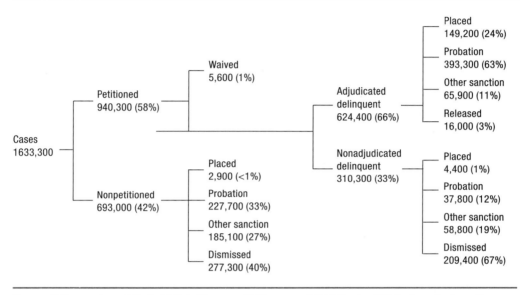

Source: C. Puzzanchera, A.L. Stahl, T.A. Finnegan, N. Tierney, and H.N. Snyder (2004). *Juvenile Court Statistics 2000*. Pittsburgh: National Center for Juvenile Justice.

Clearly, juvenile facilities rely heavily upon the juvenile court for their clients, and few of the youths coming into contact with the court are sentenced to confinement. Therefore, the figures found in data from juvenile facilities represent only a fraction of all the youths having contact with the juvenile system.

Table 1.8 presents data on youths in public and private juvenile facilities in 1999. The data in the table represent a one-day count and the daily totals would vary around these figures. For 1999, public facilities handled more than 77,000 youths, and private institutions dealt with an additional 31,599 on any one day (Sickmund, 2004). Information on the race, sex, and type of offense is also provided in correctional data. Not unlike UCR or court statistics, correctional figures show that most offenders are male. Table 1.8 shows that females make up only 16 percent of the private and 12 percent of the public institutions' clients.

Great differences appear in the institutional populations when you look at the racial composition of the juveniles. Sixty-five percent of the juveniles in public institutions are nonwhite, while only 55 percent of the private facilities' clients are nonwhite. The racial discrepancy may be due to various factors. First, private institutions can select the youths they wish to admit.

Second, wealthier white families can better afford the treatment costs imposed by many private institutions. A final possibility may entail a bias on the part of the court to send black youths to (more punitive) public facilities.

Table 1.8   Characteristics of Juveniles in Correctional Facilities: Average One Day Count—1999

Characteristic	Public Facility	Private Facility
Number of Juveniles	77,158	31,599
Sex:		
Male	68,126 (88%)	26,493 (84%)
Female	9,190 (12%)	4,948 (16%)
Race/Ethnicity:		
White	27,005 (35%)	14,220 (45%)
Black	30,863 (40%)	12,008 (38%)
Hispanic	16,203 (21%)	3,792 (12%)
Other	3,086 (4%)	1,264 (4%)
Reason for Admission:		
Person Offense	28,056 (36%)	9,897 (31%)
Property Offense	22,725 (29%)	9,051 (29%)
Drug Offense	6,819 (9%)	3,054 (10%)
Public Order Offense	7,380 (10%)	3,087 (10%)
Status Offense	1,623 (2%)	3,063 (19%)
Technical Violation	10,557 (14%)	3,447 (11%)

Source: Compiled from M. Sickmund (2004). *Juveniles in Corrections: National Report Series Bulletin.* Washington, DC: U.S. Department of Justice.

Similarly, differences in the reason for admission appear when comparing public and private institutions. The vast majority of the youths in public facilities are there because of committing delinquent offenses (86%). Conversely, more youths in private facilities are there as status offenders (19%), with only 31 percent for personal crimes.

The trend in correctional figures is somewhat interesting. Figures tend to indicate that the number of incarcerated youths has been steadily increasing. The one-day count of youths in public and private facilities increased from 80,091 in 1983 to 99,008 in 1993 (a 24% increase) to 108,757 in 1999 (a further 10% increase). These increases may be due to two factors. First, youths are staying longer in the institutions, thus there is greater overlap in the institutional stays making the daily head count inflate. Second, the increased violence and drug problems in the late 1980s and early 1990s led to larger numbers of youths being incarcerated.

Summary of Official Statistics

Each of the various official measures of delinquency present a slightly different view of juvenile offending. In terms of numbers of offenses, the UCR presents the most disturbing picture due to the large numbers of offenses it reflects. In addition to the number of offenses, the UCR provides detailed information on a variety of demographic and crime-related characteristics. Unfortunately, as noted earlier, this source of data has a number of inherent defects, in particular its reliance upon offenses known to the police, which limit its usefulness.

Juvenile court statistics and correctional facility data also present a picture of juvenile misconduct that is somewhat narrow. A large part of the problem with these figures lies in the fact that they are greatly dependent on the productivity of the police. Most youths entering the courts and institutions initiate their journey by way of police contact. Any failure at the police level, therefore, carries over to these other counts. The increased levels of status offenses in court and correctional data is one point at which discrepancies with the arrest data appear. This is probably due to court referrals from sources other than the police. The problems and differences do not make the information useless. Rather, the data can be used to assess the workings of the institutions over time and provide insight to the juvenile system. They, however, cannot be used to portray the extent of the juvenile crime problem accurately.

Self-Report Measures of Delinquency

Self-report measures attempt to gauge the level of delinquency by asking individuals to tell of their participation in deviant activity. This approach has a number of advantages. First, actions besides just those "known to the police" are considered. Second, it becomes possible to gather information on all offenders and not just those few who are arrested for an offense. Where the UCR data mainly reflect information on those offenses for which an individual has been arrested, self-reports do not need an arrest in order to have information on the perpetrator. Third, self-report surveys can ask a variety of questions designed to elicit information useful in understanding why an individual violates the law. Information routinely collected includes data on family background (such as broken home, parental affection), economic status (occupation, income), education, attitudes (toward school, family, or work), friends' behavior, and many others as well as direct questions about the deviant behavior. This type of information is not available from most official delinquency measures. For these and other reasons, self-report methods have proliferated in recent years.

Self-report surveys have a fairly long history in juvenile justice. One of the earliest surveys was developed by James Short and Ivan Nye (see Figure 1.7). This survey asked youths to note the frequency with which they committed each of 23 items. The items in the scale are dominated by status and minor offenses. The few serious crimes included in the original list (such as stealing over $50) were deleted in subsequent forms of the scales which included only the seven starred items. Dentler and Monroe (1961) offer a similar self-report survey that focuses on minor delinquent offenses.

Figure 1.7   Short and Nye Self-Reported Delinquency Items

Defied parents' authority*
Driven too fast or recklessly
Taken little things (worth less than $2) that did not belong to you*
Taken things of medium value ($2-$50)
Taken things of large value ($50)
Used force (strong-arm methods) to get money from another person
Taken part in "gang fights"
Taken a car for a ride without the owner's knowledge
Bought or drank beer, wine, or liquor (including drinking at home)*
Bought or drank beer, wine, or liquor (outside your home)
Drank beer, wine, or liquor in your own home
Deliberate property damage*
Used or sold narcotic drugs
Had sex relations with another person of the same sex (not masturbation)*
Had sex relations with a person of the opposite sex
Gone hunting or fishing without a license (or violated other game laws)
Taken things you didn't want
"Beat up" on kids who hadn't done anything to you
Hurt someone to see them squirm

*Commonly used items in subsequent self-report studies.
Source: J.F. Short and I. Nye (1958). "Extent of Unrecorded Delinquency: Tentative Conclusion." *Journal of Criminal Law, Criminology and Police Science* 49:296-302.

Self-report scales like the **Short-Nye instrument** invariably uncover a great deal of delinquent activity. Indeed, various studies using these types of scales show that virtually every person is a delinquent. This is due to the type of questions asked in the scale. It is hard to conceive of anyone saying they never committed any of the behaviors asked. Defying parental authority or trying alcohol at some time are pretty universal activities by juveniles. Asking if the individual has "ever" committed an act contributes to the high levels of positive responses. Compared to official counts of delinquency, such self-reports show a great deal more deviance.

More recent self-report surveys, such as the **Monitoring the Future (MTF) survey** (see Table 1.9), include many more serious offenses that elicit significantly fewer positive responses. The MTF project includes questions on hitting teachers, group fighting, use of weapons, robbery, and aggravated assault. The data in Table 1.9 show the great differences in response rates between less serious and more serious offenses. For example, arguing or fighting with your parents is reported by 88 percent of the total

Table 1.9   **Percent Reporting One or More Delinquent Acts in Last 12 Months, Class of 2002—Monitoring the Future Survey**

Delinquent Activity	Total	Sex		Race	
		Males	**Females**	**Whites**	**Blacks**
Argued or had fight with either of your parents	87.7	84.9	91.5	90.2	78.1
Hit an instructor or supervisor	3.0	4.6	1.3	2.8	3.3
Gotten into a serious fight in school or at work	13.7	16.6	9.8	12.3	16.2
Taken part in a fight where a group of your friends were against another group	17.1	19.0	14.3	16.2	17.3
Hurt someone badly enough to need bandages or a doctor	11.7	17.5	5.1	11.6	15.1
Used a knife or gun of some other thing (like a club) to get something from a person	3.2	5.1	0.9	2.6	4.2
Taken something not belonging to you worth under $50	28.8	32.9	24.8	29.7	21.7
Taken something not belonging to you worth over $50	10.1	14.2	5.4	10.0	8.3
Taken something from a store without paying for it	27.9	29.9	25.8	27.2	26.7
Taken a car that didn't belong to someone in your family without permission of the owner	4.9	6.9	2.7	4.0	5.7
Taken part of a car without permission of the owner	4.7	7.0	2.1	4.0	3.6
Gone into some house or building when you weren't supposed to be there	22.6	26.5	18.8	23.7	24.8
Set fire to someone's property on purpose	3.1	4.7	1.2	3.0	4.9
Damaged school property on purpose	11.5	15.8	6.6	12.1	11.5
Damaged property at work on purpose	6.5	11.1	1.6	7.2	5.3
Been arrested and taken to a police station	9.3	13.5	4.3	9.5	9.3

Source: Adapted by authors from K. Maguire and A.L. Pastore (2005). *Sourcebook of Criminal Justice Statistics, 2003*. Available at: http://www.albany.edu/sourcebook

respondents, while only 3 percent report hitting an instructor, using a weapon in a robbery, or setting fire to someone's property. An inspection of the MTF data by sex reveals similar levels of offending by males and females. Only for "arguing or having a fight" with one's parents do more females report offending. Males exceed females by more than 10 percent only for aggravated assault, theft, burglary, and damaging school property. In the remaining offense categories males and females are within 10 percentage points of one another. In terms of racial breakdown, in only one category (arguing or having a fight with parents) do whites and blacks differ by more than 10 percent. For most categories the difference is less than 5 percent.

Although many persons commit various deviant acts, the majority of subjects confine their activity to minor offenses. Indeed, when major, serious offenses are included in self-report scales, there is a great decrease in the level of reported offending. The figures become much more similar to those in official statistics.

One problem with many self-report surveys is the fact that they are one-shot studies. That is, they take a single measurement on one sample of youths. There is no second sample to compare the results to and no repeat measurement taken on the same or similar persons at a later point in time. Several notable exceptions to this are the Monitoring the Future (MTF) project, the **National Youth Survey (NYS)**, the **PRIDE Surveys**, and the **Youth Risk Behavior Surveillance System (YRBSS)**.

Each of these surveys are (or have been) undertaken on a regular basis. The MTF project surveys a national sample of youths and young adults each year, primarily about drug use. While different respondents participate each year, it is possible to examine general trends and changes over time. The NYS used a **panel design**, which means the same set of individuals were interviewed repeatedly over an extended number of years. The NYS began with a group of 11- to 17-year-olds from across the United States and reinterviewed them over a period of years. This allows researchers to compare the number of offenses and changes in offending over time. The PRIDE Surveys are completed annually and gather data on sixth- to twelfth-graders from schools in participating states (21 in 2002). Similarly, the YRBSS, conducted by the U.S. Centers for Disease Control and Prevention, surveys high school students every two years on a number of delinquent and drug use behaviors. Each of these self-report surveys finds high levels of delinquency when minor and less serious behaviors are considered, but reduced levels of serious offenses and behaviors.

Age Distribution

The age distribution of offending in self-report data is greatly dependent on the items included in the survey. Self-report surveys using minor and status offenses reveal that criminal activity is largely a juvenile problem. Indeed, if questions were posed to probe behavior over the past year, adults could hardly be expected to report status offense violations. Similarly, younger respondents tend to report less involvement in serious offenses (such as aggravated assault and felony theft). Older youths report more alcohol and other drug use, possibly due to easier availability of these substances as one grows older. While offending may occur throughout one's life, the trend in self-report data mirrors official data, with offending increasing in frequency as one reaches the later teen and early adult years. After that point in time there is movement toward the commission of fewer offenses.

Race Distribution

Unlike in official data, most differences in offending by race are modest in size. Data from the MTF project show only minor variation between black respondents and white respondents. Similarly, NYS data reveal a greater percentage of blacks involvee in felony assaults, some minor assaults, and robbery, while white percentages exceed black figures for hitting parents, minor theft offenses, damage offenses, and most other categories of crime (Elliott, Ageton, and Canter, 1983). These differences, however, are generally very small and range in the area of one to five percentage points.

Social Class Distribution

Social class is often considered in studies of self-report delinquency. This is possible because the researcher can either ask the respondent questions about his or her social class or can discreetly gather data about each individual who answers the survey. According to the NYS, a slightly greater number of lower- and working-class youths report involvement in most crime categories. Only for some minor offenses do the figures for middle-class youths exceed the figures for the other social classes (Elliott, Ageton, and Canter, 1983). The differences between the social classes, however, are minimal and amount to a few percentage points. Self-report data for Seattle also show little discrepancy in delinquency according to the social class of the individual regardless of the seriousness of the offense (Hindelang, Hirschi, and Weis, 1981).

Sex Distribution

Self-report surveys display sex differences similar to those found in official data. Almost without exception, males report higher involvement in offending than females, although the differences are dependent on the type of behavior. Table 1.9 includes data on the sex differential in the MTF. Like the race and social class findings, many of the differences in the data for males and for females are small and appear mainly in the more serious offenses.

Critique of Self-Report Data

Self-report studies paint a different picture of offending compared to official figures and pose separate problems for researchers. The most common concern with self-report data involves the truthfulness of the respondents. Interestingly, most investigations into the validity of the data show that self-report figures are fairly accurate. This assessment is based on studies that compare self-report results to lie-detector tests, repeated measures, and cross checks with other forms of data (Clarke and Tifft, 1966; Gold, 1970; Hardt and Peterson-Hardt, 1977; Hindelang, Hirschi, and Weis, 1981; Lab and Allen, 1984). The greatest discrepancies between self-report and official figures can be attributed to the different domains of behavior that are tapped by the two methods. Official records focus more on serious offenses, while self-reports often probe more minor offending.

An additional shortcoming of self-report data is the focus on juveniles. Due to the problems of locating accessible groups of adults, most self-report research has been carried out on juveniles. Although the data are rich with information on kids, there is little opportunity to compare the findings to those found on adults. Typical adult samples found in self-report surveys deal with institutionalized adults or young adults in college settings. Neither of these two groups are representative of the general adult population. The method of selecting youths for self-report surveys may also bias the results. The typical use of school students in surveys may inadvertently miss high-rate offenders who are truants or dropouts and not present at the time of data collection.

Despite these shortcomings/concerns, there are great advantages to using self-report data. First, these data provide information on offenses not known by the police. Second, the method is able to probe the number of times each individual commits an offense. Much official data (especially police records) are not readily set up to track an individual over time. Self-reports, however, can simply ask about the number and frequency of offending. Third, self-report surveys often ask a variety of questions about the individual's background, which provides a rich base of information on the demographic and social factors related to delinquent activity. Finally, the richness of the data allows for a more complete discussion of the reasons why an individual acts in a certain way than does the data found in official records.

Comparing the Delinquency Measures

The different types of delinquency measures (official and self-report) show both similarities and differences. In general, they show that delinquency is a widespread problem. It is not restricted to any one group, area, or type of offense. The level of offending increased throughout the 1960s and early 1970s, leveled off and showed some decreases in the late 1970s and 1980s, increased in the late 1980s and early 1990s (particularly in serious personal offenses), and has been decreasing in recent years. There is a clear diversity in offending. Youths are involved in all types of behavior—from status offenses to serious personal crimes. Property crimes dominate in all measures, and personal offenses are the least common.

Most differences in the measures appear in the relative magnitude of offending and by offending subgroups in the population. Self-report measures uncover more offending than do official measures. Official measures themselves differ in magnitude, with police figures leading court and correctional data. In terms of demographics, official figures show a much larger number of black offenders than self-report measures. Self-report statistics find few racial differences in offending. Social class differences also tend to disappear when most self-report data are considered. Similar discrepancies emerge when considering the sex of the offenders. While males dominate in magnitude of offending, official figures show the sexes committing different types of offenses. Self-report data, however, tend to portray the sexes as participating in the same types of behavior.

The differences between the measures are a result of the measurement techniques. Official records provide an ongoing look at the level and change in delinquency from year to year according to the formal justice system. These records reflect offenses that are brought to the attention of the authorities. Actions that are not reported and are withheld from public officials are lost to these records. Self-reports typically portray a larger delinquency problem than official figures. The cause of this is the type of activities probed in the survey. Surveys that inquire about minor status offenses will always find high delinquency levels. When more serious offenses form the core of the questionnaire, however, the number of delinquents falls to lower levels.

No single method of measuring delinquency should be considered better than the others. The usefulness of the measures depends entirely on the question being answered. Each method provides a different set of information about delinquency. Official records are useful for noting change in official processing and handling of youths over time. They also provide a long-term set of data that allows the inspection of changes over time. Official data are also rich in information about various demographic and offense factors not found in other measures. Self-reports provide a measure of delinquency based on the offender's viewpoint. They are capable of addressing behaviors that may not result in arrests and lead to official records. These measures are rich in data on minor crimes, the number of offenses an individual commits, demographics on offenders, and why an individual acts in a certain way.

SUMMARY

The study of delinquency depends heavily on the definition of delinquency and the measurement of the problem. The definition is not clear-cut and varies greatly from one study to another. Delinquency can be limited to those acts that are violations of the criminal code, can signify those actions that are illegal only for juveniles, can represent some combination of both criminal and status offenses, or be molded to fit the criminological question of each researcher.

The outcome of this search for a definition of delinquency is a vast array of different measures of delinquency and resultant claims about the level of delinquent activity. The major methods of measuring delinquency—official and self-report—rely on somewhat different conceptions of what constitutes delinquency. The UCR, for example, is oriented more toward a criminal law point of view and considers only two very broad status offense categories (runaway, curfew, and loitering) among the 29 offense categories. Conversely, self-reports often rely heavily on status offenses in their surveys and include only a few (mostly property) criminal offenses. Throughout this great confusion of definitions and measures there is no clear sign of arriving at a consensus on the issues.

Perhaps the reason behind the great discrepancies in definitions and measures can be found in the history of juvenile justice. The juvenile system has grown quickly over the past century and has seen many changes. Part of this is due to changes in the view society holds of youthful offenders. It may also be attributable to changes in the field of criminology and corrections. The changes in the juvenile system and the impact of various factors on the definition and extent of delinquency make up the substance for the next chapter on the history of juvenile justice.

Discussion Questions

1. You have been appointed to write a definition of delinquency for the state legislature. You can either propose a new definition or rely on the existing definition. What is your definition? Why is it best and why should it be accepted?

2. You have been asked to research each of the following questions or issues. What type of delinquency measure(s) will you use and why?
   —How much delinquency is there in the country?
   —What characterizes the typical juvenile offender?
   —What are some of the causes for delinquency?
   —Has the delinquency rate increased or decreased over the past 15 years?

3. A discussion has arisen over the best measure of delinquency. As an expert on such matters, you are asked to present an unbiased view of the strengths and weaknesses of official and self-report measures. Be as thorough as possible.

Chapter 2

The History of Juvenile Justice

INTRODUCTION

There is no question that juvenile misbehavior is a major concern in modern American society. No matter which definition of delinquency or which form of measurement is used, the level of delinquent activity is high. Any understanding of the juvenile justice system must begin with an analysis of delinquency in a historical framework. Interestingly, the history of juvenile delinquency and juvenile justice is a relatively short one. While deviance on the part of young persons has always been a fact of life, societal intervention and participation in the handling of juvenile transgressors has gained most of its momentum in the last 100–150 years. This chapter will discuss the state of affairs leading to the development of a juvenile justice system and briefly examine the early workings of that system.

KEY TERMS

abandonment

apprenticeship

Chancery Court

child savers

Commonwealth v. Fisher

dowry

Ex parte Crouse

houses of refuge

infanticide

involuntary servitude

Kent v. United States

nullification

parens patriae

wet-nursing

PROPERTY AND PERSON

An understanding of the development of juvenile justice must begin with an understanding of the place of children in society. Throughout most of history, there was no such status as "child." Youthful members of society did not enjoy a separate status that brought with it a distinct set of expectations, behaviors, and/or privileges. Rather, the young were considered to be either property or people. The very young, from birth to age five or six, held much the same status as any other property in society. They were subject to the same dictates as other property—bought, sold, and disposed of according to the needs of the owner. Once the individual reached the age of five or six, he or she became a full-fledged member of society and was expected to act according to the same mandates placed on all "adult" members of society (Aries, 1962).

The state of indifference toward the young and the absence of any separate status are easy to understand within a historical setting. First, the life expectancy of the average person was short. More importantly, the infant mortality rate exceeded 50 percent. The failure to develop a personal, caring attitude for infants, therefore, can be viewed as a defense mechanism. Indifference reduced or eliminated the pain and sorrow that would accompany the loss of the infant. A second explanation for the lack of concern over the young entailed the inability of many families to provide for the young. Families lived from day to day on what they could produce. Each child represented an increased burden to the already overburdened family.

The inability to provide economically for a child led to a variety of practices. **Infanticide**, or the killing of young children, was a common response to the appearance of an unwanted and demanding child prior to the fourth century (and continued in some places into the fourteenth century) (Mause, 1974). Mothers would kill their young in order to alleviate the future needs of providing for the child. The great chances that the infant would die anyway from disease or illness made this practice easier for the parents.

The killing of female offspring was especially prominent. Females were considered more burdensome than males. This was because they would not be as productive as a male if they lived and because of the **dowry** practice, which entailed the provision of goods by the female's family to the groom upon the marriage of a daughter. The basic rationale was that the groom and his family were assuming the burden of caring for a marginally productive female. The dowry practice was especially problematic for the poor, who could not provide a sufficient enticement for a prospective husband. The killing of a female infant, therefore, not only removed the immediate needs of caring for the infant but also eliminated the future need of a dowry.

A practice similar to infanticide was **abandonment**. Parents would abandon their children to die for the same reasons underlying infanticide. Abandonment grew to be the more acceptable practice in the fourth to thirteenth centuries and appeared frequently as late as the seventeenth and eighteenth centuries. Infanticide and abandonment were not restricted to the poor members of society. Historical records show that even the affluent accepted the killing of infants. One prime example of this is the story of Oedipus the king. Oedipus, the son of the Greek king and queen, was destined to kill his father and marry his mother. In order to avoid this fate, the parents had the infant Oedipus bound at the ankles, taken to the mountains, and abandoned.

Another method that appeared for handling youths was **wet-nursing**. A wet nurse was a surrogate mother paid to care for a child (Mause, 1974). Wealthy families would hire other women to raise their children until they reached the stage of "adulthood," at which time the child would return and assume a productive role in the family. Poor women, who assumed the role of wet nurses, would kill their natural offspring in order to save their mother's milk for the "paying" youths. The arrangement served a monetary purpose for the poor while relieving the wealthy of an unwanted responsibility.

Children who survived the first few years of life became subjected to a new set of activities. These new actions, however, reflected the economic concerns that allowed for infanticide and other practices. The inability to provide for the needs of the family prompted the development of **involuntary servitude** and **apprenticeship** for the young. In essence, these actions were nothing more than the sale of youths by the family. The father, by selling the children, accomplished two things. First, he alleviated the burden of having to feed and clothe the child. Second, he gained something of "greater" value in return—money, a farm animal, food, or some other necessity of life. Such practices also were promoted as a means of providing labor for those in need. The rise of industrialization created a need for skilled labor; children learned these skills through apprenticeships.

A second set of reasons behind the apprenticeship and servitude of youths was the general view that individuals who survived the years of infancy were simply "little adults." Indeed, children participated in the same activities as adults. Children worked at trades, drank alcohol, dueled, and participated in sex with adults and other young people. Part of this can be attributed to the lack of distinct expectations for youths. There was no period of schooling or education that separated the young from the actions of adults. Additionally, the living conditions of the family placed all ages within the same set of social conditions. The family home was typically a single room used for all activities. Eating, sleeping, and entertaining occurred in the same place and in view of everyone. The youthful members of society, therefore, learned and participated early in life.

The general view that children were the same as adults extended to the realm of legal sanctioning. Children were viewed as adults and were subject to the same rules and regulations as adults (Empey, 1982). There did not exist a separate system for dealing with youthful offenders. At best, the father was responsible for controlling the child, and his choices for punishment had no bounds. Additionally, society could sanction youths in the same way as adults. The law made no distinction based on the age of the offender. In fact, youths could be (and were) sentenced to death for various deviant actions. While the law allowed for and prescribed harsh punishments, there is some question regarding how frequently the more serious actions were actually used. Platt (1977) suggested that, while many youths could be sentenced to death, few received such a sentence, and most of those who did were never put to death. Similarly, Faust and Brantingham (1979) claimed that a process of **nullification**, or refusal to enforce the law against children, took place because of the lack of penalties geared specifically for juvenile offenders.

Throughout most of history, children held no special status in society. They did not receive any special, protected treatment. If anything, they were subjected to harsher treatment than adults. In terms of legal proscriptions, children could be held liable for the same actions and in the same fashion as adults. There was no legal term of "delinquency" under which the state could intervene with youths. Youths fell under the same statutes and guidelines that were used with adult offenders.

The concept of childhood began to emerge in the sixteenth and seventeenth centuries. It was during this time that medical advancements brought about a lengthening of the life expectancy of youths. Youths also began to be viewed as different from adults. They were in need of protection, assistance, and guidance in order to grow up uncorrupted by the world. This movement was led by clergy and scholars of the time. These leaders saw the young as a source of attack on the immoral and sinful aspects of society. Youths, who were not yet corrupted, had to be shielded from society and trained for their future role in the world. Children were seen as a catalyst for general social change. Childhood came to be seen as a period of time during which the young could receive an education and moral training without the pressures of adulthood.

Table 2.1   Highlights in the Development of Juvenile Justice

16th-17th century	concept of "childhood" begins to emerge
1825	first House of Refuge opened in New York
1838	*Ex parte Crouse* established *"parens patriae"* as basis for state intervention with youths
1841	probation started in Boston by John Augustus
mid-1800s	development of cottage reformatories for juveniles
1892	New York legislation enacted providing for separate trials for youthful offenders
1899	first juvenile court in Cook County (Chicago), Illinois
1905	*Commonwealth v. Fisher*—reaffirmation of *parens patriae* philosophy for juvenile court
1912	U.S. Childern's Bureau established to oversee juvenile justice
1920	all but three states with juvenile court; 320 separate juvenile courts in the United States
1920-1960	growth of juvenile justice system—separate institutions, few legal challenges, new agencies and treatments
1966	*Kent v. U.S.*—beginning of legal challenges to *parens patriae* and juvenile justice processing
1970s-present	increasing growth of due process in juvenile justice and emphasis on punishment in juvenile and criminal justice systems

Accompanying these changes were alterations in how youthful offenders should be disciplined. Responses to misbehavior began to be tailored to fit the age of the offender. In England, youths under the age of seven could not be held responsible for their actions, individuals between eight and 14 could be held responsible only when it could be shown that they understood the consequences of their actions, and youths age 14 and over were considered adults (Empey, 1982). While these types of changes began to recognize the difference between juveniles and adults, the actions taken against offenders remained the same, regardless of the age of the offender.

THE RISE OF JUVENILE INSTITUTIONS

Changes in the methods of dealing with problem youths corresponded to the changes occurring in American society of the early 1800s. During this time, there was a great movement toward the cities. Industrialization was drawing families out of the countryside and to the cities. The cities were growing in both size and density. In addition, the individuals moving to the cities brought with them a variety of outlooks and ideas. This growing diversity in the population was especially true of the cities in the United States, which were attracting immigrants from a wide range of European countries. The promise of a better life in the new world also brought with it a great deal of poverty.

Methods for dealing with problem youths grew out of the establishment of ways to handle poor people in the cities (see Rothman, 1971, 1980). The poor were seen both as a threat to society and in need of help. The primary response for dealing with the poor entailed the training of the poor. It was assumed that these people could be made into productive members of society. Unfortunately, there was little that could be done with the adult poor. They were beyond the training stage and were set in their ways. The children of the poor, however, were viewed as trainable. A key aspect of this training was the removal of the child from the bad influences and substandard training of the poor parents. While this view became prominent in the 1800s, Krisberg and Austin (1978) noted that as early as 1555 the English established the Bridewell Institution in London to handle youthful beggars. The primary emphasis of the institution was the handling of poor and destitute youths, although in practice the institution handled all problem youths, including delinquents. The Bridewell Institution was envisioned as a place where the youths would be trained in a skill that they could use after they were released.

The establishment of institutions in the early 1800s in the United States closely followed the ideas of the Bridewell Institution. The institutions were viewed as places for training those individuals who were not productive and who seemed to pose a threat to society. There was a heavy emphasis on the problems of the poor. The establishment of institutions for the poor and delinquent also reflected a shift in the view of causes of deviance. Throughout most of history, deviance was viewed as a result of problems inherent in the individual. The 1800s, meanwhile, witnessed a growth in the belief that deviance was a result of poor environmental conditions. A change in the environment, therefore, should result in changed behavior. The earlier the individual was placed into a new environment, the better the chances of having a positive impact on the person's actions. The establishment of new institutions also provided the court with an alternative to doing nothing with juveniles or placing them in adult institutions.

Houses of Refuge

The establishment of institutions for children in the 1800s clearly conformed to these ideas. These early institutions were called **houses of refuge** and were envisioned as places for separating the youths from the detrimental environment of the city. The first house of refuge was established in New York in 1825 and was followed by institutions in Boston (1826) and Philadelphia (1828). The rationale and set-up of the houses of refuge closely followed the concern for the poor and the need for training discussed above.

Central aspects in the handling of youths were indeterminate sentences, education, skills training, hard work, religious training, parental discipline, and apprenticeships (Pisciotta, 1983). The use of education, skills training, hard work, and apprenticeships were clear indications that the goal was to produce a productive member of society. Indeterminate sentences allowed the institution to work with each person on an individual basis. Where one youth may benefit from a short period of intervention, another child may require extended work and assistance. The interest in religious training and parental discipline carried over the historical ideas that the best methods of training lay in the realm of the family and the church. The families of the youths in the institution were considered to be lacking in the ability to provide these basic needs. The houses of refuge were envisioned as shelters and sanctuaries that would protect and nurture their wards away from the corrupting influences of the city and the poor family (Rothman, 1971).

The establishment of the houses of refuge also was seen as a means of removing children from the criminogenic influences of the workhouses and adult jails (Krisberg and Austin, 1978). Reformers saw the prior methods of handling youths through the adult system as nothing more than placing poor and problem juveniles in contact with adult criminal offenders. The natural outcome would be "schools for crime" that produced more problems than they solved. The houses of refuge supposedly differed by offering education and training in useful skills within a setting that allowed for control and discipline of the children.

While the rationale and the goals of the houses of refuge were laudable, the daily operations and the impact of the institutions were questionable.

Many of the activities were far removed from the real world. Inmates had little, if any, contact with members of the opposite sex. Military behavior was the norm. This included enforced silence, marching to and from different activities, the wearing of uniforms, and swift and habitual corporal punishment (Rothman, 1971). Apprenticeships often failed to be more than simple slave labor. Many of the apprenticeships were on farms in the country. Problem youths were apprenticed to ship captains and sent to sea. In general, there was no quality control or oversight for the apprenticeships. The institutional labor was often dictated by contractual obligations, which led to exploitation of the youths by the institutional masters. Children were bribed, beaten, and even subjected to extended incarceration if the monetary interests of the administrators were at stake (Pisciotta, 1982).

Besides failing to provide the basic tools that they promised, the houses of refuge also failed in other respects. For the most part, these institutions were nothing but new prisons. They were tremendously overcrowded. This overcrowding was partly due to the admission of persons not suited for the goals of the institutions. The houses of refuge served the poor and destitute, as well as the delinquent youths. At the same time, they handled poverty-stricken adults and adult offenders. The overcrowding of the facilities by such diverse groups of inmates changed the focus of daily operations from the goals of education and training to that of simple custody and discipline. The establishment of institutions like the Lyman School for Boys in 1848 by the state of Massachusetts eliminated the housing of adult and juvenile offenders in the same facility but carried on the tradition of overcrowding and related problems. In general, the early houses of refuge failed to provide their stated goals and settled into a process reminiscent of that of the adult prisons and jails that had previously been the norm for handling youths.

New Reformatories

The failure of the early houses of refuge did not lead to the end of juvenile institutions. The problems of the houses of refuge were well known by the mid-1800s. While the practice of the institutions had failed, proponents argued that the principles underlying intervention were correct. The issue, therefore, was the proper implementation of intervention. Emphasis on education, training, and parental discipline led to the establishment of "cottage" reformatories.

The cottage setup was intended to parallel the family. Concerned surrogate parents would oversee the training and education of a small number of problem youths. Discipline would be intermixed with the care and concern typical of family life. Most of the cottages were located in the country and emphasized work on the farm. This was supposed to separate the youth from the criminogenic features of the urban environment and instill a sense of hard, honest work in him or her. The idea of indeterminate sentencing carried over to the cottage approach.

Other changes in the handling of youths accompanied the growth of these cottage reformatories. Foremost among these features was the development of probation in 1841 by John Augustus. While the early use of probation was centered on adult offenders, by 1869, the state of Massachusetts dictated that the State Board of Charities would participate in, and take charge of, court cases involving youthful offenders (Krisberg and Austin, 1978). Probation officers would assist in the gathering of information on the youths, suggest alternative means of intervention, and oversee the placement of juveniles in reformatories and apprenticeships. Another method of dealing with youths, in accordance with the cottage idea, entailed the "placing out" of juveniles into foster homes. For the most part, these placements were the same as apprenticeships. Such placements were seen as an alternative to institutionalization and allowed for the training of youth in a worthwhile occupation.

These new alternatives for handling youths faced many of the same problems as the earlier houses of refuge. The institutions and cottages became overcrowded to the point that custody became the primary concern. Apprenticeships proved to be little more than slave labor, and youths often fled at the first opportunity. One analysis of 210 apprenticed individuals found that 72 percent of the youths either ran away or returned to the institution (Pisciotta, 1979). The harsh treatment of the youths in the institutions led to running away, the setting of fires, and various sexual problems (Pisciotta, 1982). The inability to handle some youths prompted the establishment of special facilities such as the Elmira Reformatory in 1876. Elmira accepted both juveniles and young adults, thus negating the premise of separating youths from criminogenic older offenders. A final problem with the institutions was the continued mixing of both deviant and destitute youths in the same facilities. The institutions considered that being poor was closely tied to deviant activity and, as a result, intervened in the lives of lower-class individuals regardless of the existence (or lack) of a delinquent or criminal act.

Institutions for Females

Throughout the development of alternatives for handling boys, little attention was paid to females. Problem girls were dealt with in the same institutions as males and adults. Part of the reason for this was the relatively small number of females officially handled by agents of social control. Exceptions to this situation began to appear in the mid-1800s with the establishment of separate institutions for girls. One of the most well-known facilities for females was the Lancaster State Industrial School for Girls in Massachusetts. The girls committed to Lancaster had the same basic background as boys found in other institutions. They were mostly from poor, immigrant families who were faced with the vagaries and problems of the urban environment (Brenzel, 1983). The institutions were setup as family cottages in order to deal with these problems.

The hoped-for end product of the institutions for girls was the production of females capable of fulfilling their place in society. Whereas boys were to become productive laborers, females were to learn how to be good housewives and mothers (Brenzel, 1983). Success with the girls was gauged by successful marriage and parenthood. Much of the concern centered on the plight of future generations that were to be raised by the problem girls and not on the girls themselves. These institutions fared no better than those handling boys. While some girls successfully graduated from the institutions, married, and became mothers, others did not realize the goals set by the institutions. In addition, Lancaster and similar institutions tended to be little more than prisons for youths. They were characterized by overcrowding, lack of treatment, and strict discipline. The differing focus from male institutions did not result in different outcomes.

THE ESTABLISHMENT OF THE JUVENILE COURT

The juvenile court arose in response to the failure of the earlier interventions with juveniles in order to address the issues of the era. The late 1800s continued to experience great levels of immigration by lower-class Europeans to the industrial cities of the United States. Environmental factors remained at the head of the list of causes for deviant behavior. In addition, the emergence of psychological and sociological explanations for behavior suggested that the problems of society could be fixed. Finally, middle- and upper-class individuals (primarily women) were interested in doing something to help the poor and destitute. The new court system utilized many of the earlier intervention ideas. Consequently, the expansion of juvenile justice was subjected to many of the same problems of the earlier interventions, as well as new concerns.

The Growth of the Juvenile Court

The first recognized individual juvenile court was established in Cook County, Illinois, in 1899. While this represented the first official juvenile court, a variety of jurisdictions implemented and experimented with similar institutions. Between 1870 and 1877, the state of Massachusetts established separate court dockets, separate hearings, and separate record keeping for cases involving juveniles under the age of 16 (Ryerson, 1978). New York passed legislation in 1892 that provided for separate trials for juvenile offenders, although they continued to be held in the adult system (Platt, 1977). Similarly, Judge Ben Lindsey of Colorado, a leading advocate of juvenile court, operated a quasi-juvenile court for a number of years prior to the establishment of the court in Illinois (Parsloe, 1978). Regardless of the initial beginnings, by 1920, all but three states had juvenile courts and there were more than 320 separate juvenile courts in the United States (Ryerson, 1978).

The legislation that established the Illinois court reflected a general belief in the ability to alter youthful behavior. First, the court was to operate in a highly informal manner without any of the trappings of the adult court. Lawyers and other adversarial features of the adult system (such as rules of evidence and testimony under oath) were discouraged. The judge was to take a paternal stance toward the juvenile and provide whatever help and assistance was needed. The emphasis was on assisting the youth rather than on punishing an offense. Second, all juveniles under the age of 16 could be handled by the new court. The court was not restricted to dealing with youths who committed criminal acts. Rather, the court could intervene in any situation in which a youth was in need of help. In practical terms, this allowed intervention into the lives of the poor and immigrants, whose child-raising practices did not conform to the ideas of the court. Third, the new court relied extensively on the use of probation. Probation continued to serve both administrative functions for the court as well as supervisory actions with adjudicated youths.

While no two juvenile courts could claim to have the same program, the courts all held the same general principles of providing assistance for the juveniles. Julian W. Mack of the Chicago juvenile court aptly portrayed the role and methods of the court when he stated:

> Most of the children who come before the court are, naturally, the children of the poor. In many cases the parents are foreigners, frequently unable to speak English, and without an understanding of American methods and views. What they need, more than anything else, is kindly assistance; and the aim of the court, in appointing a probation officer for the child, is to have the child and the parents feel, not so much the power, as the friendly interest of the state; to show them that the object of the court is to help them to train the child right . . . (Mack, 1909).

Within this statement, Mack noted the minor concern over the deviant act in the court, the goal of providing assistance to both the youth and the family, the place of probation in the court, and the typical youth who was subjected to court intervention.

The progressive reforms that led to the establishment of the juvenile courts also had other influences. One of the impacts was a gradual widening of the juvenile court's mandate. The original Illinois statute allowed intervention for criminal activity, dependency, and neglect. In 1903, Illinois added such actions as curfew violation and incorrigibility (status offenses) to the situations allowing intervention. A second area of change involved the development of new institutions for handling youths who needed to be removed from their families. One of the first new institutions was the Illinois State School at St. Charles, Illinois, which was funded in 1901 and opened in 1905 (Platt, 1977). These institutions closely followed the family/cottage model used throughout the late 1800s. The greatest distinction was in the administrative unit (the juvenile court vs. the adult court) and not in orientation. A move toward using full-time, paid probation officers also occurred shortly after the court's beginnings. By 1912, the federal government established the U.S. Children's Bureau to oversee the expanding realm of juvenile justice (Ryerson, 1978).

A final major movement coming from the progressive reforms was the institution of court-affiliated guidance clinics. The first of these was established in Chicago by William Healy, a leading proponent of the juvenile court, in 1909. These clinics relied on the new psychological and sociological explanations emerging during this time. Central to these explanations was the need for the expert analysis of each juvenile in order to identify the unique factors contributing to the individual's behavior. Following Healy's example, 232 clinics were established by 1931 (Krisberg and Austin, 1978).

The Legal Philosophy of the Court

Perhaps the greatest challenge to the growth of the juvenile system entailed debate over the philosophy of the court and the question of a juvenile's constitutional rights. Critics of the court and earlier interventions often claimed that the state was subjecting juveniles to intervention without regard for their rights and those of the family. In many instances, the state was forcibly removing a youth from his or her parents' custody. These new interventions were viewed as an abrogation of the family's position in society. The problems of constitutional rights and the new juvenile justice system were deemed inconsequential compared to the possible benefits that could accrue from intervention. Indeed, the state relied on the doctrine of *parens patriae* for justification of its position. Table 2.2 presents key factors in the growth of *parens patriae* and its application to the juvenile court.

Parens patriae, or the state as parent, was based on the actions of the English **Chancery Court**. The Chancery Court was primarily concerned with property matters in feudal England. One aspect of the court's function was to oversee the financial affairs of juveniles whose parents had died and who were not yet capable of handling their own matters. The court acted as a guardian until such time that the youth could assume responsibility. In practice, the court only dealt with matters involving more well-to-do families. The offspring of the poor did not have any property to protect. As an arm of the state, the Chancery Court often converted much of the property to the ownership of the state. There would be little to gain in overseeing the needs of the poor. Regardless of the intention of the Chancery Court, the precedent was set for intervention into the lives of children.

Table 2.2   Factors in the Growth of *Parens Patriae*

English Chancery Court (Middle Ages)	Basis of state intervention for welfare of children, particularly in cases of property rights and orphans
Ex parte Crouse (1838)	Pennsylvania Supreme Court rules that *parens patriae* is sufficient basis for intervening in the lives of juveniles without parental consent
People v. Turner (1870)	Illinois Supreme Court rules against *parens patriae* in favor of parental rights to raise and care for offspring; largely ignored by the courts
Commonwealth v. Fisher (1905)	Pennsylvania Supreme Court rules that the court can intervene without impunity when the objective is to help the youth, i.e., if the intent is good the juvenile court can act
Kent v. U.S. (1966)	*Parens patriae* is seriously questioned in light of the lack of adequate help and treatment provided by the juvenile court coupled with the lack of due process applied in juvenile cases

Movements to intervene into the lives of children in the United States were quick to rely on *parens patriae* for justification. The earliest example of this involved the case of ***Ex parte Crouse***. Mary Ann Crouse was incarcerated upon her mother's request but against her father's wishes. Her father argued that it was illegal to incarcerate a child without the benefit of a jury trial. In rejecting the father's argument, the court denied that the Bill of Rights applied to youths. The Pennsylvania Supreme Court ruled in 1838:

> May not the natural parents, when unequal to the task of education, or unworthy of it, be superseded by the *parens patriae*, or common guardian of the community? It is to be remembered that the public has a paramount interest in the virtue and knowledge of its members, and that of strict right the business of education belongs to it. That parents are ordinarily entrusted with it, is because it can seldom be put in better hands; but where they are incompetent or corrupt, what is there to prevent the public from withdrawing their faculties, held as they obviously are, at its sufferance? The right of parental control is a natural, but not an inalienable one. It is not excepted by the declaration of rights out of the subject of ordinary legislation (*Ex parte Crouse*, 1838).

The *Crouse* opinion set the tone for intervention with juveniles in the United States. In essence, the state could intervene, regardless of the reason, if it found that the child was in need of help or assistance that the parents and family could not provide. The decision relied solely on the good intentions of the state and the need to provide the proper training for the child.

Intervention based on *parens patriae* did not go completely unchallenged. Critics charged that the state was overextending its rights by intervening in many minor matters that should be simply ignored. More importantly, the argument was made that the state provided little more than incarceration and was not providing the education, training, and benevolent care that was required under the *parens patriae* doctrine. In *People v. Turner* (1870), the Illinois Supreme Court stated:

> In our solicitude to form youths for the duties of civil life, we should not forget the rights which inhere both in parents and children. The principle of the absorption of the child in, and its complete subjection to the despotism of, the State, is wholly inadmissible in the modern civilized world.
>
> The parent has the right to the care, custody, and assistance of his child. The duty to maintain and protect it, is a principle of a natural law.

In this instance, the court affirmed the rights of the parent to care for the child. The intervention of the state was to be reserved for instances in which the youth had violated a criminal law and after the application of due process concerns. The good intentions of the state and the needs of the youth were not enough to warrant unfettered intervention into the family unit. Despite this apparent shift in legal concerns, most jurisdictions ignored the opinion and continued to follow the general guidelines set forth in the *Crouse* decision.

The issues of a child's and parent's rights were largely settled in the 1905 case, *Commonwealth v. Fisher*. In this case, the Pennsylvania Supreme Court directly addressed the question of a juvenile's behavior, his or her constitutional rights, and the intent of the juvenile system in intervention. The court said:

> The design is not punishment, nor the restraint imprisonment, any more than is the wholesome restraint which a parent exercises over his child. The severity in either case must necessarily be tempered to meet the necessities of the particular situation. There is no probability, in the proper administration of the law, of the child's liberty being unduly invaded. Every statute which is designed to give protection, care, and training to children, as a needed substitute for parental authority, and performance of parental duty, is but a recognition of the duty of the state, as the legitimate guardian and protector of children where other guardianship fails. No constitutional right is violated (*Commonwealth v. Fisher*, 1905).

The key concern was over the intent of the intervention and not the rights of the juvenile, his or her parents, or the effectiveness of the system. In essence, the child had a right to intervention and not a right to freedom. Moreover, the parents had little, if any, rights in the disposition of the child. The juvenile court was viewed as providing help in the most benevolent fashion possible. The Pennsylvania Supreme Court was granting the juvenile system a free hand in dealing with youths.

The basic constitutionality of the juvenile system went largely unchallenged after the *Fisher* decision. Those cases that did arise were met with the same rationale and outcome of the earlier case. It was not until the mid-1960s that the courts began to alter their views and grant some constitutional rights to juveniles. Indeed, not until 1966 was the benevolent premise of the juvenile system adequately challenged. In the U.S. Supreme Court case of ***Kent v. United States***, Justice Abe Fortas said:

> There is evidence, in fact, that there may be grounds for concern that the child receives the worst of both worlds: that he gets neither the protections accorded to adults nor the solicitous care and regenerative treatment postulated for children (*Kent v. United States*, 1966).

As will be seen in Chapter 8, the constitutional rights provided to juveniles in the last two decades are not equal to those provided to adults. The courts have continued to reserve various powers for the state and treat juveniles as a separate class of citizens with different rights and expectations.

Problems of the Court

Despite the swift adoption of the juvenile court and its related components, the new system was faced with a number of problems and failures. A major problem involved the extent to which the various operations were initiated. Many of the courts and agencies relied solely on untrained volunteers. The number of full-time, paid juvenile court judges, probation officers, and trained clinicians was small. Ryerson (1978) cited one survey (Beldon, 1920) that found that only 55 percent of the courts provided regular probation services and, of those with probation, less than 50 percent of the officers were full-time employees. The same survey reported that there were only 23 full-time juvenile court judges in the United States in 1918 (Beldon, 1920). The child guidance clinics experienced the same shortage of trained professionals. As a result, most youths did not receive any evaluation. Most evaluations that did occur took place after a child was incarcerated (Ryerson, 1978). This lack of adequate staff was accompanied by substandard facilities and resources. While the juvenile court retained the use of institutionalization, the choice of placement usually rested on those institutions that had existed prior to the court's establishment. The problems of these institutions were the same as before. Harsh treatment, military regimentation, lack of training and education, high recidivism, and running away all continued. The new agencies, such as the child guidance clinics, similarly failed to provide the treatment and supervision they promised.

Criticism of the court also focused on its expanded jurisdiction. As noted above, new statutes outlined juvenile behavior that had previously been left to the family for correction. The expanded jurisdiction of the court based on *parens patriae* also led to an increase in unofficial dispositions and handling of youths. There is evidence that many proceedings took place without the presence of a judge or the keeping of records. Such actions were justified on the basis of relieving the burden of the court and the desire to avoid the stigma of a more formal procedure. While these reasons may have been laudatory, they encouraged the handling of more juveniles with very minor transgressions. Many trivial actions such as making noise, sledding in the street, playing in the street, riding bicycles on the sidewalk, and throwing paper into the sewers, became the subject of these unofficial cases (Rothman, 1980).

BENEVOLENCE OR SELF-INTEREST?

The institution of the juvenile court has generally been held as a progressive, humanitarian development. Most historians refer to the time period from about 1880 to the 1920s as the Progressive Era. It was during this time that many laws were passed mandating apparent humanitarian reforms. Actions such as mandatory schooling, regulations on working conditions for both adults and juveniles, concern over the plight of the poor and immigrants, the growth of agencies dealing with health concerns, and the establishment of the juvenile court were listed as examples of the benevolent actions of the reformers and society. Coercion within the juvenile justice system, as well as other forms of intervention, were considered a necessary evil for improving the lot of those who did not know any better (Rothman, 1980). Schlossman (1977) went so far as to label the benevolent movement in juvenile justice as an "exercise in love." He plainly stated that institutions and the court needed to provide the type of love, affection, and concern found in the family setting.

According to other writers, however, benevolence was not the driving factor. Anthony Platt (1977) referred to the persons involved in the development of the juvenile court as **child savers**. The issue he addressed was the rationale for saving the youths. Platt viewed the growth of juvenile justice as a part of larger social movements that attempted to solidify the position of corporate capitalism in the United States. Rather than being a humanistic endeavor to help the less fortunate societal members, intervention through the courts allowed the powerful classes of society to mold a disciplined, complacent labor force. The juvenile court was a means of preserving the existing class system in the United States (Platt, 1977). Krisberg and Austin (1978) essentially made the same argument. They saw the system as a vehicle of the upper classes for controlling the "dangerous" (lower) classes in society.

Both Platt (1977) and Krisberg and Austin (1978) pointed to a variety of factors in support of their contentions. First, the driving force behind the growth of the juvenile system, especially the juvenile court, were middle- and upper-class individuals. Middle-class women formed one key group in the system's development (Platt, 1977). These women were the wives and daughters of the industrialists and landed gentry who controlled production and had the greatest say in government. A second form of support rested on the fact that the system grew during the time when the lower-class ranks were swelling with new, poor immigrants. In essence, the lower class was growing to a point at which it could pose a threat to the status quo. Third, and related to the second, was the establishment of new laws that addressed the activity of the lower classes. Statutes governing youthful behavior primarily addressed the actions of the poor and immigrants. The government extended control over entirely new classes of behaviors in the juvenile justice statutes. A fourth indication of the juvenile system's inherent bias was the exploitive use of children who were incarcerated or under the care of the system. Youths were placed in involuntary servitude, indentured, and apprenticed, all under the argument that they would benefit from learning a trade. Realistically, according to Platt (1977) and Krisberg and Austin (1978), these actions supplied immediate cheap labor and indoctrinated the youths in the capitalistic ideology of the upper classes. It was upon these and similar arguments that various writers questioned the benevolent intentions of those individuals involved in the juvenile justice system movement.

Additional support for the argument that the system lacked the benevolence purported in many studies comes from an evaluation of the treatment of females and blacks. Pisciotta (1983) offered evidence that the juvenile justice system had been both racist and sexist. The author noted that most residential institutions in the early 1800s refused to admit blacks. Instead, black youths were subjected to continued incarceration in adult facilities until special institutions for blacks could be built. One of the earliest separate black institutions was opened in Philadelphia in 1848. Exceptions to this rule of separating whites and blacks were restricted to instances in which the admittance of blacks was economically advantageous to those in charge. Once admitted to an institution, little education was supplied. Intervention with blacks revolved around training them in menial labor and to learn their "proper place" in society. Females were handled in a similar fashion (Pisciotta, 1983). Academic education was minimized while religious, moral, and domestic training was emphasized. This view of proper training for women rested on the expectation that females were to stay in the home and raise the next generation of children (Brenzel, 1983; Pisciotta, 1983).

One possible problem with the proposal that the juvenile court was a self-serving invention of the powerful involves the place of the new professionals in the growth of the system. As noted earlier, the emergence of the new psychological and sociological explanations for behavior played a major role in the direction of the juvenile institutions and court. Why did these professionals not criticize the growth of juvenile justice if, indeed, it was simply a means for the powerful to control the masses? Platt (1977) addressed this issue by pointing out that the professionals received a great deal of benefit from juvenile justice, regardless of the driving forces. These individuals gained the reputation as experts, secured employment as either full-time employees or paid consultants, gained access to data and information otherwise denied to them, and found a forum willing to let them advance their theories and ideas. It was not necessarily that these professionals may not have objected to the biased premise of the system, they simply found more personal benefits in allowing the system to be instituted and advanced.

The debate over the intent of those forming the juvenile court has not been resolved. The usefulness of recognizing the difference in opinion is in opening the way for varied suggestions about dealing with problem youths. Individuals who assume the benevolence point of view turn to a variety of theoretical explanations and their accompanying forms of intervention. Advocates of the self-interest perspective focus on the actions of society and not the individual offender. Instead of looking for ways to help the youth, these writers suggest that changes in the social structure account for variation in the levels of deviance. This approach will be further explored in Chapter 4.

JUVENILE JUSTICE FROM 1920 TO THE 1960S

Most of the great movements and changes in juvenile justice were completed by the early 1920s. By this time, the juvenile court was solidly entrenched as the proper institution for dealing with problem youths. The problems and criticisms directed at the court and its institutions were passed off as the failure to properly implement the programs. The shortcomings were not inherent features of the system. Advocates called for increased resources, time, and patience. Society and the legal system were content to leave the juvenile justice system alone to search for effective interventions, provided the system continued to act in the best interests of its youthful clients. Changes in the handling of youths over the next few decades, therefore, were restricted to generating new theories of behavior, attempting new types of treatment, and evaluating their efforts.

Various new institutions were established for handling problem youths. These were necessitated both by increased numbers of youths entering the system as well as differing approaches to treating youths. Psychological explanations and perspectives led to the growth of various training and counseling (group and individual) programs. Psychotherapeutic interventions gained prominence in the 1940s and led to private and public institutions based on these ideas. The use of such interventions as guided group interaction and peer pressure formed the basis of programs such as the Highfields Project in 1950. Highfields was a short-term, residential facility that allowed the youths to visit their families and remain a part of the community. This type of program helped form the basis for halfway houses and other community interventions. Chapter 10 will address such actions in more detail.

One of the best known of the experimental interventions of this time period was the Chicago Area Project (CAP). Based on the ecological analysis of crime and delinquency (see Chapter 4), the CAP viewed deviance as a result of the community environment. The project had three distinct aspects: recreation programs for youths, vigilance and community self-renewal, and mediation. Work with juveniles primarily fell under the first and third of these ideas. The basic intent of the CAP was to involve youths in nondeviant activities; provide outlets for youthful exuberance; guide youths to finding proper, acceptable solutions for problems; assist youths with school and jobs; and work with youths who had been released back into the community after institutional stays. While the impact of the program on delinquency has never been clearly demonstrated, recent analyses (Schlossman and Sedlak, 1983; Schlossman, Zellman, and Shavelson, 1984) have indicated some success with individual problems. The scope of the CAP prompted the adoption of various parts of its program in other cities.

CHANGES SINCE THE 1970s

Challenges to the *parens patriae* doctrine through a growing number of court cases in the late 1960s and early 1970s were early signals of major changes in society's approach to both juvenile misbehavior and adult criminality. The strong reliance on and belief in rehabilitation and treatment that dominated throughout the twentieth century has given way to more punitive responses (Garland, 2001). Retribution, just deserts, and deterrence have emerged as the watchwords for both the juvenile and criminal justice systems. Rather than look for the causes of deviant behavior in the inequities of society or the surroundings of the offender, there is a stronger belief that individuals of all ages choose to commit offenses and need to be held responsible for their actions.

Garland (2001) views these changes in social control as a result of numerous changes and forces over the past 30 years. Among those influences have been rising crime rates, changing economic conditions that marginalize greater number of individuals, challenges to the welfare state, growing concern for victims, the diversification of the population, the perceived inability of the state to control the citizenry, and the perception that families and other institutions have lost their ability to control the behavior of their members. Passing new laws, increasing the use of punishment, and similar responses have emerged as responses to these and other perceived problems. Changes in the juvenile justice system and society's response to youths is a clear reflection of these broad social changes.

SUMMARY

The growth of juvenile justice from the 1920s to the early 1960s followed a pattern of new programs, all within the original mandate and scope of the early reformers. The issues that fueled debate in the early years have returned to be debated in recent years. While there has been an increased emphasis on punishment and due process in the system, many of the rehabilitation and treatment ideas are still being tried and adapted in an attempt to live up to the *parens patriae* ideals that still underlie the juvenile justice system. The remainder of the text will look at the varied issues and the operation of the juvenile system, primarily since the early 1960s. Questions of theory, implementation, practice, and evaluation form the core of the discussion.

Discussion Questions

1. Concern over child abuse has greatly increased over the past two decades. Many people argue that society's young are treated worse today than at any time in history. Based on your knowledge, place this view within a historical framework. That is, outline the historical view of children and some of the major practices for handling kids.

2. You are an administrator of an early house of refuge and are asked to give a dispassionate view of your institution. What are the strengths and weaknesses of this type of institution? What problems do you face and how can you correct them?

3. The legislature is proposing to abolish the juvenile court. Argue in favor of the legal philosophy that is the basis for the court. What is the philosophy, why has it been legally upheld throughout the years, and why should it be maintained?

Chapter 3

Explaining Delinquency—
Biological and Psychological
Approaches

INTRODUCTION

Throughout the history of juvenile justice, criminologists and others interested in deviant behavior have sought to explain why certain individuals act in certain ways at certain times. The number of theories for deviant behavior has grown considerably over the past 100 years as the field of criminology has progressed and the level of research has improved. A **theory** can be described as an attempt to answer the question "Why?" Why does an individual violate the norms of society? Why do certain conditions seem to accompany deviant behavior? Why does deviance occur when it does? These and other "why" questions form the basis for the theories that have been proposed for explaining delinquent behavior.

The types of factors that have been used to explain delinquency take a wide variety of forms. Early **spiritualistic** or **demonologic** explanations reflected the belief that deviant acts were the result of the battle between good and evil—God and the devil. Individuals who committed crimes were possessed by the devil. Consequently, the solution to deviance

KEY TERMS

atavistic

biosociology

Classicism

concordance

demonologic

determinism

dizygotic

free will

hedonistic calculus

hypoglycemia

id-ego-superego

Interpersonal Maturity Levels

IQ

medical model/analogy

mesomorphic characteristics

Minnesota Multi-phasic Personality Inventory (MMPI)

modeling

monozygotic

involved exorcising the devil and delivering the individual back to God. Often times, this could be accomplished only through the death of the devil's vessel: the individual. The soul would then be freed to join God.

These nonscientific explanations gave way in the 1700s with the advent of classicism and the movement into positivistic approaches in the later 1800s. Classicism and positivism are "schools of thought" rather than specific theories of behavior. These schools lay out general beliefs about people and the world, which shape the form that individual theories will take.

THEORETICAL SCHOOLS OF THOUGHT

Every explanation of behavior, whether it be conventional or deviant behavior, rests on a number of implicit assumptions about individuals and the world within which they operate. These beliefs form the core of many arguments about the causes of crime and how to deal with offenders. For example, differences in opinions about the death penalty often boil down to different beliefs about whether punishment can deter people. Every science has schools of thought that organize its ideas. In criminology the two schools are classicism and positivism.

The Classical School

Classicism finds its roots in the writings of Cesare Bonesana Marchese de Beccaria (1738-1794) and Jeremy Bentham (1748-1832). Beccaria was an Italian aristocrat who broke with the ruling classes to condemn the methods of dealing with crime and morals in society. In outlining a new set of criminal and penal practices, he set forth a number of beliefs about humankind and the function of society in dealing with deviance.

Under classicism, humans are viewed as having **free will**. That is, individuals choose to act the way that they do after calculating the pros and cons of an activity. Coupled with the idea of free will is the belief that humans are hedonistic. Under the "**hedonistic calculus**," individuals seek to maximize

KEY TERMS
—continued

moral development
multiple causation
nature–nurture controversy
Neoclassicism
neurotransmitters
operant conditioning
orthomolecular factors
phrenology
physiognomy
Positivism
premenstrual syndrome
psychoanalysis
reactive hypoglycemia
soft determinism
somatotypes
spiritualistic
testosterone
theory

pleasure and minimize pain (Bentham, 1948). Individuals, therefore, choose activities and behaviors based on their calculation of the amount of pleasure and pain that will result. Pleasurable behaviors will be undertaken and repeated, while painful activities will cease. Under classicism, individuals make a conscious, rational decision to commit crime based on the expectation of a pleasurable outcome.

These beliefs about free will and hedonism suggest that the solution to crime requires altering the outcome of the hedonistic calculation. That is, increasing pain and reducing pleasure can reduce, and possibly eliminate, deviant behavior. Beccaria and other classicists, therefore, focused their efforts on making laws and setting punishments that would alter the choices of individuals. Beccaria felt that individuals could not make an informed decision to avoid crime unless they were presented with

Cesare de Beccaria (1738-1794)—Italian economist and jurist. The publication of his *Essay on Crimes and Punishments* in 1766 marked the beginning of the science of penology.

a clear set of laws and punishments. The emphasis must be on the offense and the legal system, not the offender. There must be a set punishment for each crime, and the level of punishment must be sufficient to offset any pleasurable consequence of an individual's behavior.

Classicism seeks to prevent and deter crime by punishing the offender for the offense. Ideally, individuals should be deterred from crime by knowing the pain that would come from being caught and punished. Punishment is not meant to be a form of retribution or retaliation by society. Instead, punishment is solely for the purpose of altering the outcome of the "hedonistic calculus."

Classicism dominated discussions of crime, deviance, and the law in the 1800s. Indeed, changes in laws reflected the general belief in free will and attempts to deter individuals from becoming involved in crime. However, crime did not disappear and new ideas about behavior began to emerge in the late 1800s. Much of this movement toward a new "school of thought" grew out of the developing medical sciences.

Table 3.1   Major Elements of Classicism and Positivism

Classicism	Positivism
Free will	Determinism
Hedonism	Multiple causation
Rational offender	Emphasize offender/
Emphasis on offense	situation differences
Legal responses—	Medical model—
Clear laws and procedures	Crime as "symptom"
Punishment for prevention	Individualized response
and deterrence	Rehabilitation and treatment

Neoclassicism

Soft determinism
Free will with limited choices
Punishment or treatment

The Positivistic School

The basic tenets of positivism are diametrically opposed to those of classicism. Rather than hold the individual responsible for his or her actions, positivists absolve the doer of guilt and claim that both deviant and conventional behavior is determined (caused) by factors beyond the control of the individual. That is, the behavior of the individual is determined for the person. Altering behavior, therefore, cannot be brought about through simply raising the amount of pain a person will receive if caught and punished. Rather, changing behavior can be accomplished only by identifying and eliminating the factors that are causing the individual to act in a certain way.

Positivism typically recognizes that there are multiple causes of behavior. Deviance may be the result of many different things. It could be a single factor, multiple causes, or a series of events or situations occurring over a period of time. The same deviant act committed by different people may be the outcome of totally different causes. The fact that there is no single cause of crime requires looking at each individual case for reasons behind behavior. The approach used by positivists to identify causes is typically referred to as a **medical model** or **medical analogy**.

Using a medical model, the scientist approaches deviance the same way that a doctor approaches a sickness. Just as a doctor considers coughs and fevers to be symptoms of other problems, the positivist views deviant acts, like burglary and rape, as symptoms of other underlying causes or conditions. Doctors do not simply seek to eliminate the cough or fever. Instead, they work to identify and eliminate the cause of those symptoms. Similarly, the positivist attempts to identify why an individual commits a deviant act and to prescribe a tailored response to the person and circumstances. For example, two burglars may have committed their acts for different reasons, thus necessitating totally different interventions. The positivist, like a doctor, seeks to diagnose the underlying cause and prescribe an appropriate treatment. The emphasis in positivism, therefore, is not on the offense. Rather, the emphasis is on the offender, the unique situation, and the various factors causing the individual to be an offender.

The logical extension of the focus on **determinism** and **multiple causation** is the belief in rehabilitation and treatment. Instead of punishing an individual for his or her actions, positivism seeks to remove the root causes of the deviant behavior. The proper rehabilitation or treatment strategies may be as diverse as the number of clients. For example, one burglar may need financial assistance for his or her family because the offense served to provide food for the family, while another burglar may need group counseling to address the specific animosity toward the victim he or she had that caused the action. Treatment and rehabilitation need to be tailored to the circumstances of the individual. This does not mean that similar responses cannot be used for similar offenders. Rather, positivism argues that uniqueness must be recognized and addressed in all responses to deviance.

Positivism emerged from the 1800s as the dominant school of thought. Advances in the medical fields and the development of psychology and sociology presaged a more scientific approach to explaining and understanding deviance. The emerging juvenile justice system focused on identifying the causes of delinquency and sought ways to correct the inadequacies that led to delinquency. While the criminal justice system retained vestiges of classicism and deterrence, the juvenile justice system and the emerging field of criminology embraced the ideas of positivism.

Neoclassicism and a Summary

In recent years, the juvenile justice system has shifted back to a more classical viewpoint, with mandatory punishments, deterrence, and the waiver of youths to the adult system displacing the traditional treatment emphasis. While positivism has not totally disappeared, the dominant approach better fits a label of neoclassicism. **Neoclassicism** takes the position that an individual exercises some degree of free will. The choices, however, are limited by factors both within and outside of the individual. Sometimes referred to as **soft determinism**, under this thinking, an individual can make decisions only based on the available choices. The available options determine the extent to which the person can exercise his or her free will. This compromise gives both the classicist and positivist a stake in the criminal and juvenile justice system.

The balance of this chapter and the entire following chapter discuss a wide range of theories. The biological and psychological theories appearing in this chapter are primarily positivistic in orientation. For the most part, they approach deviance as the outcome of forces beyond the control of the individual. The sociological theories appearing in Chapter 4, however, more often incorporate elements of free will in their arguments.

BIOLOGICAL AND SOCIOBIOLOGICAL THEORIES

Explanations of deviance based on biological factors are among the earliest and the most recent theories in criminology. Medical advances, particularly in the 1800s, led to explanations of behavior that focused on the biological makeup of the individual. The underlying assumption made by the early biological theorists was that if the biological makeup of the individual dictated his or her physical capabilities, these characteristics could also contribute to the type of behavior exhibited by the person.

Physical Appearance

Early biological explanations focused almost exclusively on observable physical features of offenders. One approach, **physiognomy**, suggested that facial features were related to behavior. Typical features associated with criminals included shifty and beady eyes, a weak chin, and facial hair that is characteristic of the opposite sex. Interest in physical appearance and the lack of any scientific basis for physiognomy led to the introduction of **phrenology**, which concerned itself with both the shape of the skull and facial features. The phrenologists' true interest, however, was in the brain, which was housed in the skull. The absence of the ability to examine and study the brain directly simply led them to find a proxy for the brain. Phrenologists believed that any abnormalities (e.g., bumps or crevices) in the skull would be repeated in the shape of the brain. Assuming that different areas of the brain handled different dispositions (i.e., aggressiveness, friendliness), it would be possible to identify those persons who would be more aggressive by inspecting the shape of their skulls. While phrenology had a more scientific argument than physiognomy, it too suffered from the lack of scientific proof.

Lombroso's Atavism

Physical appearance theories received their greatest support from the work of Lombroso, who is considered the father of modern criminology. Lombroso, basing his ideas on Charles Darwin's theory of the survival of the species, viewed criminals as throwbacks to an earlier state of human existence. These individuals were not as physically or mentally advanced as the rest of society. Lombroso (1876) identified a number of **atavistic**, or ape-like, qualities that generally reflected the physical features of the apes from whom humankind was descendant (see Table 3.2). In a study of incarcerated offenders, Lombroso (1876) noted that more than 40 percent of the criminals had five or more atavistic traits. These "born criminals" were a direct result of the lack of evolutionary progression found in the person. The remaining criminals fell into categories of "criminaloids," "insane" criminals, and criminals of "passion." Criminaloids were composed of individuals who entered criminal activity due to a variety of factors including mental, physical, and social conditions that, when occurring at the same time, would trigger deviant behavior (Vold and Bernard, 1986). "Insane" criminals included idiots and mentally deranged individuals, while criminals of "passion" acted out of anger, hate, love, or other—generally spontaneous—emotions.

Table 3.2   Lombrosian Atavistic Characteristics

Physical Characteristics	Nonphysical characteristics
Protruding jaw	Sensitivity to temperature changes
High forehead	Agility
Asymmetrical face	Lacking a sense of right or wrong
Bad teeth	Fondness for animals
Deep, close-set eyes	Tolerance of pain
Excessively long arms or legs	
Abnormal nasal features	
Exaggerated sex organs	

Much of Lombroso's research looked only at incarcerated criminals. His failure to include a control group of noncriminals (or even nonincarcerated criminals) meant that he was unable to state whether the results would be different if he studied people in the general public. Indeed, subsequent research by Lombroso, which added control groups, pointed out this weakness and led him to consider a second set of nonphysical atavistic qualities, as well as environmental and social factors, for explaining deviance.

Lombroso's work led to a great deal of controversy. In an early critique of Lombroso's ideas, Goring (1913) found only minor differences in the physical makeup of convicts and a control group of noncriminal citizens. Conversely, Hooton (1931) claimed to find a great deal of physical difference between 14,000 convicts and 3,000 noncriminal subjects. Hooton also claimed that various physical features could be used to identify persons participating in different types of offenses. A number of criticisms, however, have been leveled at Hooton's work (Vold and Bernard, 1986). Foremost among these are the facts that Hooton did not consider the past offense history of his subjects and he ignored information that clearly contradicted his conclusions.

Somatotypes

Despite the criticisms of Lombroso and his contemporaries, the relation between physical appearance and deviance has appeared in research into **somatotypes**, or body types. Perhaps the best known of these studies was that by Sheldon (1949). Building on the work of Kretschmer (1925), Sheldon identified three basic somatotypes. He then extended the argument by outlining a specific temperament corresponding to each type (see Table 3.3). Sheldon (1949) used his somatotypes to classify delinquents being treated in a residential facility. He found that **mesomorphic characteristics** were most prevalent and ectomorphic features were the least common. Based on his observations of these delinquent boys, he concluded that mesomorphic individuals were more likely to commit delinquent acts than were other youths. Support for the relationship between mesomorphy and delinquency was presented in the studies of Sheldon Glueck and Eleanor Glueck (1956) and Cortes (1972).

Table 3.3   Sheldon's Physiques and Temperaments

Physique	Temperament
Endomorph: short, fat, round, soft	**Viscerotonic:** soft, easygoing, extrovert
Mesomorph: muscular, large, barrel chested, thick, hard	**Somotonic:** dynamic, active, athletic, aggressive, talkative
Ectomorph: bony, thin, skinny, small, delicate	**Cerebrotonic:** nervous, complainer, introvert

Source: Constructed from W.H. Sheldon (1949). *Varieties of Delinquent Youth: An Introduction to Correctional Psychiatry.* New York: Harper and Brothers.

All of these somatotype studies shared similar methodological problems. First, much of the research was based on subjective determinations of body type, often by simply looking at photographs of the youths. Second, the researchers did not consider changes in body type as the youths grew older. Third, the researchers ignored the possibility that mesomorphic youths were more often recruited into delinquency because of their physical build, rather than having a natural propensity to commit delinquent acts. Fourth, defining delinquents as incarcerated youths may bias the results if mesomorphic delinquents are institutionalized more frequently because they are perceived as greater threats than are smaller youths. Finally, the determination of mesomorphs as being somotonic (aggressive, active, etc.) often rested on the finding that many delinquents were mesomorphs and delinquent behavior, by its nature, is considered aggressive. Based on these problems, physical type theories have fallen out of favor and are rarely addressed in contemporary juvenile justice.

Genetic-Inheritance Studies

The possibility that criminality may be inherited can be found in many of the early writings of those interested in physical appearance (see Goring, 1913). Physical features are clearly passed on from generation to generation. A logical extension is that nonphysical factors, such as behavioral tendencies, are also passed on from parents to offspring. Two basic methods for studying this question are the comparison of the behavior of twins and comparing the behavior of offspring to their biological parents.

Table 3.4   Traditional Genetic Explanations

Twin Studies	Assume greater similarity in behavior for monozygotic twins (identical) than for dizygotic twins (fraternal) or normal siblings
Adoption Studies	Assume similar behavior between offspring and biological parents even when reared in another environment

Twin Studies

Studying twins for the genetic propensity to be deviant requires knowing whether the siblings are monozygotic (MZ)(identical) or dizygotic (DZ)(fraternal) twins. **Monozygotic** (MZ) twins are the product of a single fertilized egg that separates into two individuals with an identical genetic makeup. **Dizygotic** (DZ) twins are the result of two separate eggs fertilized by separate sperm. While genetically similar, the two offspring will not be genetically identical and are no more genetically similar than any two siblings born at different points in time. An examination of the genetic propensity for deviant behavior rests on finding greater **concordance**, or similarity, in behavior for MZ twins than for DZ twins or common siblings.

Several studies of twins claim to find a genetic component to behavior. Newman and associates (1937), for example, found that in 93 percent of the cases in which one MZ twin was delinquent, the other twin was also delinquent. The corresponding results for DZ twins was only 20 percent. The higher concordance in behavior for the MZ twins was interpreted as evidence of a genetic factor in delinquency. Similarly, using a registry of 6,000 pairs of twins in Denmark, Christiansen (1974) found that, for MZ twins, 36 percent of those who had a criminal record also had a brother with a criminal record. Criminal DZ twins only had a criminal brother 12 percent of the time.

More recently, Lyons (1996), reporting on the Harvard Twin Study, a large-scale analysis of subjects from a registry of Vietnam-era veterans born between 1939 and 1957, found higher concordance for MZ twins than DZ twins, especially in adult criminality. Each of these studies concluded that genetic factors have an influence on the actions of individuals.

While other reviews find support for a genetic component to behavior (see, for example, Ellis, 1982; Wilson and Herrnstein, 1985), a number of problems plague the studies. First, most of the observed relationships are small and insignificant (Reiss and Roth, 1993). Second, several studies show that DZ twins are more concordant than normal siblings, which would not be expected from a genetic argument (Rutter, 1996). Third, most studies lack control over any environmental influences impacting on the individuals (Katz and Chamblis, 1995; Reiss and Roth, 1993). The levels of concordance may be due to similarity in rearing practices or imitation between siblings. Identical twins may be expected to act more similarly by family and friends as a result of the "identical" label. Fraternal twins may be expected to be more individual and not so similar. Finally, distinguishing between MZ and DZ twins can be done only using laboratory tests. In most studies, the determination is based on how similar the siblings look, what they have been told throughout their lives, or the visual determination of a doctor (often at the time of birth). The failure to adequately distinguish the two types of twins could greatly affect the study results.

Adoption Studies

A second method of investigating the genetic contribution to deviance is through the comparison of the behavior of adopted offspring and their biological parents. Adoption studies assume that any similarity between the adopted offspring and the biological parent must be due to the genetic similarity between the subjects because the child has been raised in a different environment from the parent.

Various adoption studies provide support similar to that found in twins studies. Schulsinger (1972) finds a greater number of psychopathic biological relatives for psychopathic subjects than for nonpsychopaths. The difference, however, is not great (7%) and is based on a total of only 114 observations. Crowe (1972), analyzing 104 females and their offspring, reports a 13 percent difference in the arrests of offspring of offending and nonoffending mothers. The results, however, reflect a total difference of only six fewer offenders in the nonoffending mother group. While the results tend to support a genetic argument, they are, at best, weak. Hutchings and Mednick (1977), using a much larger sample, report that 49 percent of criminal boys have criminal biological fathers, while only 31 percent of noncriminal boys have criminal biological fathers. Whether the adoptive father is criminal or not does not eliminate this relationship, although it does temper the results.

One important qualifier that must be considered in adoption studies involves the separation of the genetic and environmental influences on the individuals. The assumption throughout the research is that the simple fact of adoption is enough to guarantee that the environment of the biological parents is being controlled. Ellis (1982) points out, however, that one overwhelming consideration in many adoptions is the matching of the adopting environment to that from which the individual is being taken. This would seriously impair a study's ability to distinguish the effects of genetics and environment. A related factor deals with the point of the adoption. Few studies can substantiate when the adoptions actually took place. Adoptions close to birth would have the best chance of eliminating the environmental influence of the biological parents. Adoptions after that point in time could carry a good deal of environmental impact to the new environment. Additionally, some authors (Kopp and Parmelee, 1979; Sameroff and Chandler, 1975) argue that the environment can play a significant part even when the child is still in the womb. This could be accomplished through trauma to the mother, nutrition, or other environmental factors. While each of these qualify and temper the results of adoption studies, they do not negate the fact that most such studies show a tendency toward a genetic component in behavior.

In an attempt to clarify the varied findings from twin and adoption studies, Walters (1992) undertook a meta-analysis of 38 projects dating from 1930 to 1989. In a meta-analysis, the researcher uses the reported data from past studies and computes a common statistic for all studies, thereby allowing a direct comparison of the different results. Walters (1992) reports that there is a "low-moderate" correlation between heredity and crime. The significance of this finding, however, is problematic because the stronger methodological studies provided less support for the relationship. This was especially true for the adoption studies, which have the best chance of separating genetics from the environment (Walters, 1992).

To date, theorists have not provided strong support for their genetic arguments. This is not to say that genetics hold no influence on behavior. Genetic research is still in its infancy, and future advances may reveal contributors to a wide range of behaviors. Nevertheless, the problem of separating the environmental influences from a genetic component will remain a serious concern.

Biosocial Factors

The recent trend in seeking biological explanations of behavior involves what is known as biosocial approaches. **Biosociology,** or sociobiology, refers to the idea that the biological makeup of the organism and the surrounding environment are intimately related. The environment plays a part in shaping the organism, and the organism, through its daily activity and interpretation of the world, shapes the environment. In terms of deviant behavior, the old belief that deviance is a direct result of a biological condition is no longer tenable. Instead, biosociology sees deviance occurring when specific biological conditions coincide with appropriate sociological or environmental factors. For example, an individual with a congenital hormonal defect may be overly aggressive in situations that force him or her into a choice between fight and flight. This individual, however, does not seek out such situations or become aggressive without the external stimulus. The more modern biological explanations of behavior, therefore, accommodate both biological and sociological factors.

Table 3.5   Biosocial Influences

Endocrine/hormonal factors—natural bodily chemicals; Key targets in past research: testosterone, menstruation

Orthomolecular/chemical factors—substances introduced to the body that may alter behavior; Key targets: sugar, alcohol, drugs

Central nervous system—examines the makeup and functioning of the brain and its relation to behavior; different areas of the brain involved in different behaviors; Key targets: brain abnormalities, neurotransmitters that transmit information in the brain (e.g., dopamine)

Endocrine/Hormone Influences

Among the normal functions of the body is the production and secretion of various hormones. These natural chemicals control many of the basic bodily functions, including growth, reproduction, and functioning of the central nervous system. In terms of deviant behavior, most attention has focused on reproductive hormones (Shah and Roth, 1974). Androgen, the male sex hormone present in **testosterone**, has been found to be related to aggressive behavior, particularly in animal studies. Studies on human subjects, typically of incarcerated offenders, have found higher testosterone levels among more aggressive and more serious offenders (Booth and Osgood, 1993; Ehrenkrantz, Bliss, and Sheard, 1974; Kreuz and Rose, 1972; Rada, Laws, and Kellner, 1976). While such studies suggest that testosterone leads to greater levels of aggression, the evidence is not totally convincing. Among the problems are conflicting findings in the research (Shah and Roth, 1974), the fact that testosterone levels vary over even short time periods and testosterone is affected by diet, stress, exercise, and social factors (Booth and Osgood, 1993; Katz and Chamblis, 1995; Nassi and Abramowitz, 1976; Reiss and Roth, 1993), and aggressive behavior may cause testosterone levels to increase, rather than the other way around (Harris, 1999).

A second examination of hormonal influences on behavior involves the female menstrual cycle. Changes and hormonal imbalances during premenstrual and menstrual days may alter a woman's mood and behavior. In an early study, Morton and associates (1953) reported that more than three-quarters of the violent female offenders committed their crimes during the menstrual and premenstrual days. Based on prisoner self-reports concerning their menstrual cycles, Dalton (1964) claimed that 49 percent of the women committed their offenses during the premenstrual or menstrual days. Despite these results, there are a number of problems in the analyses.

First, menstrual cycles exhibit a great deal of variability over time and age, which makes the determination of past cycles based solely on recall almost impossible (Horney, 1978). Second, other factors, such as psychological and emotional factors, can influence menstruation and account for the relationship. The evidence, therefore, suggests a weak relationship between **premenstrual syndrome** and crime.

Orthomolecular/Chemical Imbalances

While endocrine factors deal with naturally produced bodily chemicals, **orthomolecular factors** refer to chemicals that are introduced to the body or altered through diet or other influences. One commonly discussed potential problem is the influence of sugar on behavior. Hypoglycemia is the term most often used in these discussions. However, hypoglycemia, a condition of low blood sugar, manifests itself in a lack of energy, lethargy, nervousness, and, in the extreme, a coma. It is difficult to imagine these individuals taking aggressive deviant actions against anyone or anything. The proper term for the relationship between blood sugar levels and criminal activity is **reactive hypoglycemia**, which refers to changes in the blood sugar level, both higher and lower, as a result of dietary intake.

While various researchers claim to have found support for a relationship between hypoglycemia and crime (Bonnett and Pfeiffer, 1978; Geary, 1983; Hippchen, 1978, 1981; Podolsky, 1964; Schauss, 1980), their conclusions rest upon suspect research methodology (Gray and Gray, 1983). Much of the support comes from anecdotal accounts of physicians and psychologists who simply compare a person's diet to his or her behavior without establishing the different bodily needs or processes of the different individuals. What constitutes an overconsumption of sugar by one individual may be minor for another individual. In addition, the commonly used oral glucose tolerance test is not a definitive measure of blood sugar (Gray and Gray, 1983). When more accurate measures are used, the studies fail to support reactive hypoglycemia as an explanation for deviance. Most studies also fail to note that nutrition and diet are highly related to social class, which may be the operant factor in the relationship with deviance (Katz and Chamblis, 1995). Given the state of the evidence, reactive hypoglycemia is considered a minor cause of deviance (American Dietetics Association, 1984; Gray and Gray, 1983; National Dairy Council, 1985).

Alcohol and other drugs are also linked to deviant behavior. That alcohol correlates with delinquency and criminality is indisputable. What is questionable is the mechanism at work. Many would argue that alcohol is a disinhibitor, thus allowing for normally avoided behavior to become manifest. Reiss and Roth (1993) suggest a more biological connection in which alcohol alters the processing of information and, depending on the dosage, may prompt aggression and irritability, or more passivity and sluggishness. The use of licit and illicit drugs may also lead to criminal behavior. The mechanism underlying the correlation between drugs and deviance, however, is not clear. From a psychopharmacological perspective, drugs have a direct causal impact on crime by inducing the user to act out in a certain way (Goldstein, 1989). At the same time, drug use may be related to deviance as a result of crime and violence related to the need to purchase drugs in uncontrolled settings. Such systemic crime is the result of competition between drug dealers or the need to commit property crimes in order to obtain money for drug purchases (Goldstein, 1989). Whether the drugs–crime relationship is psychopharmacological or systemic may be a function of the type of drug and related factors (its addictive properties, its cost, etc.).

The Central Nervous System

A wide range of factors related to the brain and central nervous system have received attention in studies of deviant behavior in recent years. Recognition that different parts of the brain are related to different behaviors has led some researchers to look at brain abnormalities and functioning and deviance. Various methods are available for such analyses, including magnetic resonance imaging (MRI), positron emission tomography (PET) scans, and electronencephalography (EEG). An MRI can show the physical makeup of the brain and reveal any physical problems (Rowe, 2002). A PET scan reveals differing levels of brain activity when faced with varying stimuli (Rowe, 2002). Similarly, an EEG measures a person's electrical brain waves, which can be compared to those of other individuals (Rowe, 2002). Based on these new technologies, Raine and colleagues have concluded that there is clear evidence relating brain functioning, especially frontal and temporal lobe problems, to deviant activity (Raine, Venables, and Williams, 1995). The impact of these factors relative to other variables, such as the environment, however, is not clear.

A related topic deals with whether different **neurotransmitters** (chemicals involved in the transmission of electrical impulses through the nervous system) are capable of altering an individual's behavior. Among the neurotransmitters that have been investigated are dopamine, norepinephrine, and serotonin. Goldman, Lappalainen, and Ozaki (1996) report that dopamine is directly related to aggressive behavior. Similarly, Virkkunen, Goldman, and Linnoila (1996) note that serotonin levels influence impulse control, hyperactivity, and other behaviors related to deviance. Research has shown that it is possible to alter various neurotransmitters, both purposefully with drugs and inadvertently through the use of alcohol and other substances. Such changes can alter social behavior (Brunner, 1996). While still in its early stages, this research suggests that there is a relationship between different neurotransmitters and deviance (Brennan, Mednick, and Volavka, 1995; Reiss and Roth, 1993). Most of the research is based on small samples, and the degree of the relationship remains questionable.

Most of the recent biosocial approaches suffer from similar problems. First, the identification of correlations is often touted as clear evidence of a causal relationship. Second, there may be reversed time order in many of the relationships (Reiss and Roth, 1993). For example, aggressive behavior may lead to physical confrontations that involve head injuries and alterations in the functioning of the brain. Third, the ability to generalize results of studies based on animals to human beings is questionable. Finally, the studies typically fail to consider other spurious factors, such as social status, diet, and the environment, in the consideration of biosocial influences. It is possible that these other factors are influencing both deviance and neurological functioning.

Implications for Juvenile Justice

At the present time, there is still relatively little known about the relationships between biological influences and deviant behavior. Despite methodological problems, studies have provided qualified support for biosocial explanations. At the same time, they raise many more questions.

Early biological explanations of delinquency had only minor impact on juvenile justice due to the great shift toward psychological and sociological explanations in the early 1900s. The new biosocial approaches, however, have engendered renewed interest in biological influences on behavior. Conditions that have a genetic component, such as schizophrenia, can be modified or controlled by drugs. Behaviors related to hormonal or orthomolecular problems can also be altered through changes in diet or drug therapy. Depoprovera, for example, is a drug that inhibits the production of testosterone and has been used with sex offenders. As biosocial research progresses, additional practical uses for curbing deviance will emerge.

While biological explanations have yet to gain prominence in juvenile justice, there is reason to believe that they will continue to draw increased attention in the future. As Brennan and associates note:

> Understanding of the interaction of genetic and environmental factors in the causes of crime may lead to the improvement of treatment and prevention. Partial genetic etiology does not in the least imply pessimism regarding treatment or prevention. Quite the contrary! Several genetically based conditions are treated very successfully by environmental intervention (Brennan, Mednick, and Volavka, 1995:90).

At the same time, caution must be taken when implementing programs based on biosocial research. These activities may also bring about more harm than good. For example, altering a diet to do away with "problem" foods may inadvertently damage an otherwise good diet. The most prudent direction for biosocial advocates to pursue at the present time would be expanded research.

PSYCHOLOGICAL EXPLANATIONS

A second general area of explanations for delinquency entails psychological theories. As with other types of theories, psychological explanations take a variety of forms and include a wide range of factors. Early psychological theories were based on biological/physical factors. Indeed, psychiatry, which is usually seen as a part of the general psychological field, is distinguished by its strong commitment to finding physiological bases for aberrant behavior. Psychiatrists are medical doctors who have specialized in the general area of mental disorders.

Many psychological explanations, however, do not look for a physical explanation. Instead, the psychological orientation can be seen as having a few distinctive characteristics. First, and foremost, these approaches generally view problems as arising out of early life experiences. Deviance is seen as a result of problems and flaws that were not recognized and corrected during the adolescent years. Second, psychological explanations are highly individualistic. While many individuals may display the same or similar behavior, different explanations or factors (such as incomplete socialization or poor personality development) may be at work for each person. Finally, because of the individualistic orientation, psychological explanations lend themselves to a treatment orientation. Rather than focus on who will become deviant, the emphasis is on working with individuals who are already having problems and assisting them to overcome the problem.

Psychoanalytic Explanations

Perhaps one of the most widely recognized names in psychology is Sigmund Freud (1856-1939). Freud pioneered the psychoanalytic approach to understanding human behavior. The major premise of **psychoanalysis** is that unconscious, and perhaps instinctual, factors account for much of the behavior displayed by individuals. In particular, deviance is seen as the outward manifestation of the unconscious desires and drives of the individual. Problems arise from the individual's inability to exert personal control over his or her desires due to faulty or incomplete training during the early years of life. The goal of psychoanalysis is the identification of unconscious, precipitating factors and the development of conscious methods for dealing with them.

Table 3.6	The Freudian Personality
Id	unconscious desires, drives, instincts
Superego	learned values, behaviors; moral character of the individual; outlines the acceptable and unacceptable; may be conscious or unconscious
Ego	social identity of individual; actual behavior; conscious activity

Freudian psychoanalysis outlines three distinct parts to the personality that are involved in behavior. The **id** reflects the unconscious desires, drives, and instincts within the individual. In simple terms, the id can be seen as the selfish, "I want" part of the individual. The **superego** entails values that the individual learns from those around him or her. These values form the moral character of the individual and help dictate what the person considers acceptable or unacceptable behavior. The superego is where self-criticism and positive self-image reside. The superego is a result of early moral training and provides the rationale for refraining from various types of behavior. Where the id looks for satisfaction of desires, the superego responds with either a "can't have" orientation or a "must do" response. That is, the superego helps orient the individual's behavior away from simple desires and toward the value system that the person has incorporated. The actions of the superego may be both conscious and unconscious depending on the type of behavior in question and the degree of moral training involved. The final part of the personality, the **ego**, is the social identity that is exhibited through behavior. It is often the manifestation of the conflict between the id and the superego. The ego is the conscious attempt to satisfy the needs of the id while continuing to abide by the mandates of the superego. This aspect is always conscious because it is the solution to the question of whether the individual follows his or her drives or the morally correct line of activity.

Psychoanalysis seeks to uncover the causes of behavior by bringing the unconscious conflict between the id and the superego to consciousness. Often, psychoanalysis is undertaken only when an individual develops criminally deviant behavior. The conflict between the id and the superego, however, will not always appear as deviance. Instead, the internal conflict can be manifested in various ways. Table 3.7 outlines eight possible "defense mechanisms." Deviance may appear in some mechanisms (such as repression, rationalization, or displacement), while other mechanisms may lead to socially acceptable behaviors.

Where Freud did not specifically address criminality, other researchers have tried to apply it to delinquent behavior. Erikson (1968) suggests that some youths fail to develop an identity (or ego) of their own. Instead, they gather much of their self-image from the peers with whom they associate. Delinquent peers, therefore, would lead the individual to delinquency. Where Erikson (1968) focuses on the failure to develop an ego, Abrahamson (1944) and Aichorn (1963) target the poor development of a superego. The absence of an adequate superego leaves the id unchecked, which results in behavior reflective of the individual's uncontrolled instincts, drives, and desires.

Table 3.7   Psychoanalytic Defense Mechanisms

REPRESSION	An active attempt to push desires and thoughts out of one's consciousness or to keep material from reaching consciousness. Example: You forget that you owned a pet that was run over by a car when you were a child.
DISPLACEMENT	A change in the primary object of a feeling or desire to a secondary one that is less threatening. Example: You are angry at your boss but you yell at your husband or wife instead.
SUBLIMATION	Here the displacement is more long-term and the object chosen is socially acceptable. Example: You want to hit and hurt your father, but you become a professional boxer or football player.
DENIAL	The truth of certain facts or experiences is denied, rather than forgotten as in repression. Example: Your daughter dies but you act as if she is alive, keeping a bed made up for her.
REACTION FORMATION	A desire is changed or transformed into the opposite feeling or desire. Example: You hate or deeply resent your father, but you tell everyone how much you love him and act toward him in a loving manner.
PROJECTION	You have an unconscious desire or thought, but you attribute it to someone else instead of acknowledging it in yourself. Example: You no longer love someone but accuse him or her of no longer loving you instead.
RATIONALIZATION	The process of finding an acceptable reason for doing something unacceptable. Example: You punish your child harshly, but say "I'm doing this for your own good."
REGRESSION	You replace your desires or thoughts with those from an earlier stage of your development. Example: You are under stress and get angry at someone who works for you, so you throw a temper tantrum.

Source: P. Van Voorhis, M. Braswell, and D. Lester (2004). *Correctional Counseling and Rehabilitation*, 5th ed. Cincinnati: Anderson, p. 44.

Despite the development of a large body of literature, the psychoanalytic approach has been subjected to strong criticism. One of the most problematic concerns is the lack of empirical referents for the theory. Psychoanalysis relies on vaguely defined terms and constructs to represent its key concepts. Consequently, it is difficult to undertake empirical tests of the theory. There is no clear method for measuring the id, ego, or superego. A second major criticism involves the fact that psychoanalysis is totally retrospective. That is, it is useful only for looking at what has already happened. It is geared toward uncovering the reasons why something happened and working to correct those reasons. A third area deals with the emphasis on early childhood. With few exceptions (such as Erickson), it is assumed that little change occurs after adolescence. Adult behavior is viewed as a result of poor childhood socialization and not from factors appearing in adult life. Finally, psychoanalysis is criticized for ignoring social-structural factors in the determination of behavior. Indeed, with the heavy emphasis on the unconscious, psychoanalysis examines the social setting of the individual only to the extent that it failed to provide the necessary moral atmosphere during early adolescence.

Developmental Approaches

A number of writers identify the source of deviance in interrupted or arrested developmental patterns during childhood. The basic assumption behind these explanations is that all individuals develop through a number of stages. Each stage provides an integral part of the total knowledge and understanding that a person needs to operate in society. The failure of an individual to complete any one of these stages or steps successfully may lead to some form of socially unacceptable behavior. This basic argument can be seen in Freud's psychoanalytic explanation in which the failure to develop appropriate superego and ego responses to the id takes place in early childhood. The child is born with the id but must learn and internalize the moral dictates of society as he or she grows.

Interpersonal Maturity

Perhaps one of the most well-known developmental approaches in delinquency research is the **Interpersonal Maturity Levels** (I-levels). The various I-levels reflect the progressive development of social and interpersonal skills. The I-levels represent a continuum from the most basic stage of development through the most advanced stage (see Table 3.8). The interruption of any stage makes the attainment of later stages difficult, if not impossible.

Table 3.8   **Interpersonal Maturity Levels**

Level 1:	The individual learns to discriminate between themselves and others.
Level 2:	The individual starts to separate things into persons and objects, partly on the basis of their own needs and what they can control.
Level 3:	At this level the individual begins to learn rules and can start to manipulate the environment for their own benefit.
Level 4:	The individual begins to perceive things from the standpoint of others. He/she sees conflicts between expectations of others and their own needs.
Level 5:	Here the individual becomes aware of patterns of behavior and relationships. There becomes an awareness of distinctions made between events, objects, and roles in society.
Level 6:	The individual is able to distinguish between himself/herself and the roles they play. These are not one and the same and can accomodate one another.
Level 7:	At this level, the individual begins to perceive a variety of methods for dealing with the world and makes choices based on his/her and other's past experiences and for the benefit of everyone.

Source: Compiled from C. Sullivan, M.Q. Grant, and J.D. Grant (1957). "The Development of Interpersonal Maturity: Applications to Delinquency." *Psychiatry* 20:373-385.

Most delinquency and deviance occurs in Levels 2, 3, and 4. Level 2 individuals operate primarily on the basis of their own need and use others only as a source of enjoyment or fulfillment. While Level 3 individuals begin to integrate rules, they are still oriented toward their own needs. As a result, they may realize that what they are doing is wrong but cannot justify the rules with their desires. Finally, persons in Level 4 may resort to delinquent behavior as a means of striking out against what they perceive as contradictory demands. The inability to cope with competing demands may result in choosing delinquent activity. Individuals at any level try to balance their own needs against the expectations and needs of others. Operating at the lower maturity levels, however, leads to behavior that is counter to societal demands, with or without the cognizant understanding of those demands.

Moral Development

A second well-known developmental approach is Kohlberg's (1981) model of **moral development**. Kohlberg's model notes that individuals progress through six stages of moral development that are arranged into three levels (see Table 3.9). The preconventional level is characteristic of young children, while most adults fall into the conventional level. Only a small proportion of adults reach the postconventional or principled level. Deviant individuals typically fail to display the same level of moral development as noncriminals with the same or similar characteristics. As in the I-level classification scheme, Kohlberg views deviance as a result of interrupted or incomplete development. For example, an individual at Stage 2 sees his or her own needs and feels that he or she does not get enough. As a result, that person may turn to deviance to "balance" the exchange.

Both the I-level and moral development perspectives, as well as others, are limited primarily to treatment. As with psychoanalysis, the identification of developmental stages and problems typically occurs *after* a problem has become manifest. The individual then undergoes a one-on-one evaluation in which the potential for subjective evaluation becomes a problem. In instances in which developmental typologies have been used for prediction (such as with I-levels), the predictive capacity of the tools has been found to be weak. Further, developmental approaches have been criticized as imprecise, contradictory, and not necessarily sequential (see, for example, Rich and DeVitis, 1985; Simpson, 1974; Williams and Williams, 1970). In general, developmental arguments have proved much more useful in the treatment of deviant individuals.

Table 3.9   Kohlberg's Moral Development

Level I.   Preconventional Level

Stage 1   Right is obedience to authority and rules, and avoiding punishment. There is clear concern for one's own physical well-being.

Stage 2   Right corresponds to seeing one's own needs, taking responsibility for one's self, and allowing others to do the same. At issue is a fair exchange with others.

Level II.   Conventional Level

Stage 3   Right is avoiding the disapproval of others, having good intentions and motives, and being concerned for others. Individuals are aware of others and their needs.

Stage 4   Right is doing one's duty to society and others, and upholding the social order. The individual is capable of looking at things from society's viewpoint.

Level III.   Postconventional or Principled Level

Stage 5   Right is based on upholding the rules and values agreed upon by society. The individual feels obligated to society. There is a recognized social contract between the individual and society that outlines acceptable behavior.

Stage 6   Right is a reflection of universal ethical principles. The individual recognizes the moral rightness of behavior and acts accordingly.

Source: Compiled from L. Kohlberg (1981). *The Philosophy of Moral Development.* San Francisco: Harper and Row.

Learning Theories

Implicit in developmental discussions is the idea that people learn right from wrong, and learning takes place over a long period of time. There is a cumulative nature to learning. In learning theories, the emphasis is on how an individual learns and what factors are effective in promoting learning. The failure of an individual to complete a developmental stage successfully, therefore, may be due to a problem in the learning process.

Modeling is perhaps the simplest form of learning. According to Bandura and Walters (1963), children learn by copying the behavior of others. Most modeling follows the behavior of significant others, particularly parents, siblings, peers, and other individuals close to the child. Modeling, however, is not limited to the people around the youth. Children also can learn from characters, both real and fictional. If the child continuously sees deviance, either real or fictional, the child may begin to copy that behavior. The child may not know whether it is right or wrong. He or she only knows that this is how people act. (Further discussion of modeling and identification will be taken up in Chapter 4.)

A more classical psychological learning theory is that of **operant conditioning**. Operant conditioning deals with the reinforcement of behavior through a complex system of rewards. Skinner (1953) and others view subsequent behavior as a consequence of past responses to behavior. Specifically, an individual repeats (or does not repeat) a behavior based on what happened when the behavior in question appeared in the past. For example, a child who does as he or she is told by his or her parents is given a treat for being good. The treat becomes a reinforcer for future good behavior. In operant conditioning, the reinforcement comes after the behavior or action of the individual. Actions that result in a pleasurable response (positive reinforcer) or that eliminate painful or unpleasant situations (negative reinforcer) will be repeated. Learning, therefore, becomes an ongoing process, with every choice made by the individual resulting in some form of response. Future actions are based on the reinforcement, or lack thereof, of past behavior.

Bandura and Walters (1963) combined conditioning and modeling in a general discussion of learning. They noted that the degree to which a child models his or her behavior is mitigated by the level of reward or punishment that the model receives. For example, a child observing an act of aggression by another person or a fictional character is more likely to copy that act if the aggressive person is rewarded or not punished. Therefore, the process of learning through operant conditioning can take a vicarious route through observation of the experiences of others.

Two key concerns have been raised in relation to psychological learning theories. First, while modeling and operant conditioning make intuitive sense and receive support from anecdotal and case studies, most of the supportive studies rely on correlational analyses and contain serious methodological flaws. A second problem is that modeling and operant conditioning approaches ignore the contribution of the individual to behavior. The basic assumption is that the individual is a product of the environment and has little influence on his or her choice of activity.

Personality and Delinquency

Various researchers have proposed that deviants display certain personality characteristics that can be used to explain deviant and criminal behavior. Psychologists have developed a wide array of personality classifications and measures for uncovering personality traits. Indeed, the *Diagnostic and Statistical Manual of Mental Disorders*, Fourth Edition (DSM-IV) of the American Psychiatric Association includes the classification of "antisocial personality disorder," which refers to individuals who show a continuing pattern of behavior that is harmful to others.

One of the early attempts to distinguish delinquents from nondelinquents using personality factors was conducted by Sheldon Glueck and Eleanor Glueck (1950). Glueck and Glueck compared 500 delinquents to 500 nondelinquents along a wide range of factors. The two groups were matched on age, ethnicity, residence, and intelligence. Examining the entire range of personality features, Glueck and Glueck claimed that

> delinquents are more extroverted, vivacious, impulsive, . . . less self-controlled . . . are more hostile, resentful, defiant, suspicious, . . . destructive . . . and are less fearful of failure or defeat than the nondelinquents. They are less concerned about meeting conventional expectations and are more ambivalent toward or far less submissive to authority. They are, as a group, more socially assertive (Glueck and Glueck, 1950:275).

This picture of the delinquent was meant to summarize the delinquent's overall personality pattern and indicate differences from conventional youths.

While the work of Glueck and Glueck still draws attention today, several concerns have been raised about the findings. First, not all the traits associated with the delinquents are undesirable. For example, being extroverted, assertive, less fearful of failure, and less submissive are traits that many individuals would find valuable. Second, the authors assume that the individuals had these traits before they exhibited delinquent behavior. It could be argued, however, that the delinquents were hostile, resentful, defiant, and ambivalent to authority due to their contact with the justice system. These feelings may come after contact with the system, rather than before the delinquent act. Thus, they cannot be a cause of the antisocial behavior. Finally, the individuals who evaluated the youths were aware of which youths were delinquent and which were not delinquent. It is possible that knowing that an individual is delinquent and in an institution may prompt an evaluator to expect the subject to be more assertive, more hostile, or have less self-control. Despite these concerns, interest in personality types continues.

A major change in personality research has been to try to develop standardized measures of personality. Such an effort would avoid some of the pitfalls seen in the Glueck and Glueck study. The **Minnesota Multi-phasic Personality Inventory (MMPI)** is one standardized method for uncovering personality traits in individuals. The MMPI is an inventory of 556 true-false questions that are designed to tap 10 personality dimensions identified in past clinical analyses (Megargee and Bohn, 1979) without the need for extended clinical observation. The MMPI assumes that everyone answers some questions in a deviant manner. Therefore, no single scale question is associated with deviant behavior. Instead, deviance is considered more likely as the individual answers in a deviant fashion on a number of questions. The key, therefore, is the overall tendency in the scales.

While the MMPI has been used extensively, it has been challenged on a number of grounds. First, to the extent that the prior clinical evaluations are in error, poorly conceived, or invalid, the MMPI results also are questionable. The results are only as good and useful as the underlying clinical factors. Second, the MMPI is useful primarily in the treatment of offenders, and not for predicting or explaining deviance prior to its occurrence. Finally, because the MMPI has been refined using institutionalized subjects, it is possible that it reflects factors related to institutional life and experiences, rather than a deviant personality. The inventory has been subjected to relatively few tests outside of the institutional setting.

Waldo and Dinitz (1967) and Tennenbaum (1977) present a number of problems with the studies of personality. Perhaps the most damaging problem is that many studies fail to probe whether personality leads to delinquency or whether delinquency and system processing produce the observed personalities. A second problem is the fact that personality scores and studies often rely on subjective evaluations by clinical workers. Knowledge that the incarcerated subjects have committed certain types of actions may lead to identifying personality traits that fit that behavior. A final concern reflects the poor research methodology used in many analyses. Typical problems are the failure to draw adequate (or random) samples, the lack of control groups for comparison, and the failure to consider other (spurious) variables that may be more important in explaining the phenomenon under question. While these criticisms make the results problematic for the identification and prediction of behavior, they do not negate the potential usefulness of the techniques in the rehabilitative setting.

Mental Deficiency and Delinquency

Since the late 1800s, low intelligence has been offered as a prime cause of deviant behavior. The scientific interest in the relation between intelligence and deviance can be traced to the development of IQ testing. The **IQ**, or intelligence quotient, was developed by Alfred Binet in the early 1900s as a numerical representation of the mental ability of the individual. The formula for IQ is simple:

$$IQ = (mental\ age/chronological\ age) \times 100$$

The mental age of an individual is determined by performance on a standardized test. The test consists of questions geared toward individuals of different ages. Persons of the age of 10 are expected to be able to answer a certain level of questioning as well as all those from the easier levels. More difficult questions are assumed to be beyond the ability of the average 10-year-old. Once an individual's mental age is determined, the researcher simply divides that figure by the respondent's actual age and multiplies by the base of 100.

Since the development of the IQ test, many researchers have attempted to show that delinquency and deviance are related to low intelligence. The assumption that IQ is related to crime is not a surprising one given the knowledge that most incarcerated offenders tend to be less educated and display below-average scores on academic achievement tests. The major source of debate concerning IQ revolves around the question of whether IQ is due to nature or nurture.

The **nature–nurture controversy** refers to the question of whether intelligence is inherited and therefore determined at conception (nature), or whether intelligence is an outcome of growth in the environment (nurture). The nature argument views IQ as set at birth and not subject to outside influences. The social and physical environment, including education, has little or no influence on a person's IQ. Conversely, the nurture side of the debate proposes that an individual's IQ is the outcome of complex interactions between the genetic makeup of the person and the environment to which the individual is exposed. This view suggests that IQ can be altered through education and other environmental interventions. It is this latter argument—that IQ is impacted by the environment—that was held by Binet and many of his contemporaries.

The view that intelligence is genetically determined received a great deal of support in the United States, where low IQ scores were used as a means of denying immigrants entry to the country. This position rested on the work of Goddard (1920), who found that most criminals were "feeble-minded" (IQ of less than 75). The government's position was that excluding such individuals was in the best interests of the country. However, Goddard (1920) examined only incarcerated "criminals" and did not use a comparison group in the analysis. Consequently, he had no way of knowing whether they were more or less "intelligent" than anyone else. More recently, Wilson and Herrnstein (1985) and Herrnstein and Murray (1994) have argued that IQ is substantially due to genetics and that IQ is a strong predictor of criminal activity. Wilson and Herrnstein (1985) claim that IQ is a stronger predictor of deviance than is social class. The authors also assert that minorities, particularly blacks, score lower on IQ tests. Tied to the genetic argument, this opens the door for claims of racism and obscures the rest of their argument.

Hirschi and Hindelang (1977) provide the most widely cited argument in the IQ-delinquency literature. The authors argue that IQ is at least as important in predicting delinquency as social class or race, and is related to delinquency regardless of the race or social class of the individual. Their opinion is that IQ is an indirect cause of delinquency. Low IQ, through genetics and/or environment, leads to poor school performance, which prompts a lack of concern for education, a rebellious attitude toward the school and societal demands, and eventually a heightened chance of deviant behavior. To the extent that there is an environmental factor, individuals with a low IQ who can be encouraged to stay in school, receive special help, or otherwise enhance their abilities may not experience the problems and frustrations that precipitate deviant activity.

Implications for Juvenile Justice

Before addressing the impact of psychological theories, it is important to point out some of the criticisms leveled at these explanations. As has been noted throughout the above discussions, psychologically oriented explanations are not particularly good for the prediction of behavior. Many are formulated after the fact and seek primarily to explain the observed behavior retrospectively. The emphasis is on why something happened and not predicting what will happen in the future. A second concern with psychological studies is the reliance on subjective interpretations. Most psychological endeavors rest on the opinion of individuals who have been trained in the field of psychology. There is no single orientation or perspective that drives the entire field, or even subfields, of psychology. The subjective nature of psychology, therefore, often leads to conflicting opinions, even when individuals are looking at the exact same information.

Some commentators criticize what they see as the individualistic nature of psychological explanations. Indeed, many psychological endeavors examine individual subjects, and the precise explanation for deviance could vary from subject to subject. This criticism may be shortsighted, however, given the fact that these individualistic approaches form the basis of other, more general theories. For example, operant conditioning is a key component of differential association–reinforcement theory, and hedonism is at the heart of Gottfredson and Hirschi's general theory of crime (see Chapter 4 for discussions of both of these theories).

Psychological explanations have their greatest impact on the correctional end of the juvenile justice system. Psychology's emphasis on identifying the cause of an individual's behavior fits the general treatment orientation of juvenile justice. As a result, juvenile corrections places heavy emphasis on counseling, education, and other rehabilitative methods. Techniques such as I-level classifications and the MMPI are used to gain insight into a juvenile's problems and subsequently design a response to those problems. Additionally, behavior modification techniques are used to set up token economies in detention centers and training schools. Psychology will more than likely remain primarily a correctional tool in juvenile justice until such time that more precise methods of evaluation are generated or the predictive ability of psychological findings are enhanced.

SUMMARY

The biological and psychological explanations discussed in this chapter represent theories and perspectives developed over many decades. While some have been discounted because of their lack of rigor and relevance, they still have engendered discussions that may lead to more applicable and useful theories. Psychological explanations have found a clear place in the juvenile justice system. This is particularly true in the juvenile court and in the correctional phase of processing. Biological explanations have not fared so well. This is due mainly to the poor quality of the early explanations and the current lack of expertise in the physical sciences held by criminologists and criminal justicians. The next chapter turns to a discussion of sociological explanations that hold the dominant position in modern discussions of delinquency and criminality.

Discussion Questions

1. Compare and contrast the classical and positivist schools of thought. What are the basic assumptions each hold about the individual and behavior? What implications do each have for the juvenile justice system?

2. There is a movement to shift the emphasis in the juvenile justice system from the sociological theories and explanations for delinquency to the biosocial perspective. Point out and explain what you see as the more promising biosocial approaches. Also, predict the problems or shortcomings that will result if the emphasis is shifted. (That is, what are the problems with the biosocial approach?)

3. Identifying a "criminal or delinquent personality" has proven to be quite difficult. Outline some of the more well-known methods for isolating this personality and what problems exist in these approaches. Which method would you use if you had to pick one, and why?

4. Psychological theories are common in correctional practice. Pick specific psychological approaches and illustrate their usefulness and shortcomings for use in correcting juvenile delinquents (i.e., critique the approaches).

Chapter 4

Sociological Explanations of Delinquency

INTRODUCTION

The most prevalent explanations of delinquent behavior are sociologically oriented theories. Indeed, criminology, criminal justice, and juvenile justice in the twentieth century have grown around sociological perspectives. The reasons for this are understandable. First, the great changes in society during and after the industrial revolution were accompanied by increased levels of deviant behavior. This behavior, however, was more prevalent in the cities. This led to a view that deviant behavior was an outgrowth of social relationships, especially those in urban areas. Second, sociological theories hold a great deal of intuitive appeal. Many of the ideas, as will be seen, are based on common sense and do not require a great deal of education or training for simple understanding. A third reason behind the dominance of sociological explanations entails the ability to test such theories. While tests of biologically oriented theories fail to provide empirical support, and psychological theories often defy empirical testing or are restricted to only individuals, most sociological explanations are accompanied by attempts at empirical research and often find some degree of support.

KEY TERMS

anomie

bond to society

Chicago School

concentric zone theory

containment theory

culture conflict

developmental theories

differential association

differential identification

differential reinforcement

division of labor

dramatization of evil

drift

ecological fallacy

ecological perspective

elaboration model

focal concerns

gemeinschaft society

general strain theory

generic control theory

gesselschaft society

inner containment

invasion, domination,
  succession

labeling

75

Sociological theories and perspectives reflect elements of both classicism and positivism. From the positivistic view, sociological theories consider a wide array of social and environmental factors as explanations of deviant behavior. Delinquency is a response to the setting in which the individual finds himself or herself. The neighborhood in which an individual grows up, one's peers, the views of others, social and moral training, the organization of society, economic conditions, and the effect of being processed in the criminal justice system are among the many factors considered in sociological theories. Classical elements appear in discussions of deterrence, control, and routine activity theories, in which the individual is presumed to have some degree of choice in his or her behavior. This chapter attempts to outline the major points of each theory or view and draw out similarities and differences in the sociological explanations for deviance.

THE ECOLOGICAL PERSPECTIVE

Perhaps the earliest sociological explanation to gain importance in criminology, the **ecological perspective** (or "**Chicago School**," so named because of the research done using the city of Chicago as a focus) sought to explain deviance as a natural outgrowth of the location in which it occurs, particularly large cities and areas within large cities. Research in the early twentieth century recognized the great growth in the number and size of large cities. European immigrants and southern blacks were flocking to the industrial cities of the north and northeast. These new urban areas were densely populated, and many of the new residents were uneducated, unemployed, and could not speak English. Along with this great influx of people came increases in various social problems— including criminal activity.

KEY TERMS
—continued
life-course theories
looking-glass self
modes of adaptation
natural areas
outer containment
primary deviance
private, parochial, and public (control)
rational choice
reintegrative shaming
role-taking
routine activities
secondary deviance
self-control
social area analysis
social control
social disorganization
strain theory
subculture
successful status degradation ceremony
symbolic interactionism
tautological
techniques of neutralization
transfer of evil
vertical integration

Table 4.1   The Ecology of Crime

Concentric Zones	"Natural areas"; city growth as expanding circles from the city center; central business district and zone in transition are key for deviance; Key author: Burgess
Social Disorganization	The idea that an area is unable to come together and exert control over the behavior of individuals in the area; Key authors: Shaw and McKay
Social Areas	Focus on similarities in social characteristics rather than geographical location; social disorganization argument; "vertical integration"; private, parochial, and public control; Key authors: Lander, Bordua, Chilton, Bursik and Grasmick

Concentric Zones

Ernest Burgess (1925) and his colleagues at the Univeristy of Chicago studied the growth of the emerging cities and their accompanying social problems. In general, they saw cities expanding in increasingly larger circles around the original city center. This **concentric zone theory** borrowed ideas from plant ecology, where the proliferation of plant life follows a natural progression. Just as plants take root and prosper in areas that provide the needed requirements for growth, the city grows in terms of logical movement from the existing structure. While there are various **natural areas** for different plants, such as ferns and moss growing in areas where there is shade and moisture, cities promote natural growth, such as having new businesses locating near established businesses where their needed resources already exist.

Burgess (1925) presented a simple graphic display of the various zones or concentric circles that made up an emerging large city (see Figure 4.1). Zone 1, the "Central Business District" (CBD), was the original core of the city. Using the ecological or natural area analogy, the city was originally established in a certain spot because of the features of the location. Crossroads of major trade routes, locations providing water transportation or water power, and the availability of natural resources would all be factors making the establishment of a city in that place a "natural" choice. Zone 1, therefore, represented the earliest settlement of business in the city. Zone 2 was considered the "zone in transition." This area had traditionally been residential but was becoming more industrialized. As new industry was established and moved to the city, it was only natural for business leaders to seek locations that provided same advantages that prompted the original establishment of the city. These businesses wished to settle in and around the CBD. In turn, the residents living around the CBD desired to move away from the new industrial factories. Those individuals who could not afford to move were forced to stay in Zone 2. The homes in this zone were mostly rental property and were left in disrepair. It was not a desirable area in which to live.

Figure 4.1   **Concentric View of the City**

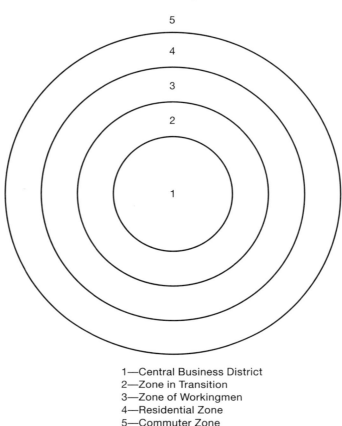

1—Central Business District
2—Zone in Transition
3—Zone of Workingmen
4—Residential Zone
5—Commuter Zone

The remaining zones represented areas of generally increasing affluence. The "zone of working men," Zone 3, was populated by lower-class and lower-middle-class factory workers. These families had the resources to move out of Zone 2 but had to remain within close proximity to the employment and retail establishments of the inner zones. During the early years of the twentieth century, there was little or no public transportation, and most people moved around the city on foot. In addition, many individuals worked long hours throughout the day and night, making close living accommodations to work a necessity. Zones 4 and 5, the residential and commuter zones, were populated by more wealthy middle- and upper-class families.

Shaw and McKay: Social Disorganization

Using the concentric zone theory, Clifford Shaw and Henry McKay (1942) analyzed the occurrence of delinquency in Chicago. After plotting concentric circles on a map of Chicago, the researchers identified the location of every recorded delinquent act in the city. Based on where it occurred, Shaw and McKay (1942) reported that crime and delinquency was highest:

1) in and around the Central Business District,

2) in poor areas of the city, and

3) in areas dominated by immigrants and African-Americans.

All three conclusions pointed to the same physical location in the city, specifically the city center where economic conditions were poorest and new arrivals were able to find affordable housing.

The stability of the delinquency levels in the same areas over time led Shaw and McKay (1942) to examine what it was about these areas that could explain the findings. What they uncovered was a continuing process of **invasion, domination, and succession** taking place. That is, these areas were undergoing constant change. They saw that, over a period of time, poor, for- eign-born, and southern immigrants would invade the central city areas due to their economic situation and the availability of cheap living condi- tions in the areas. Over time, one group would gain some degree of domi- nance in the area. As the residents gained employment and were assimilated into American society, however, they would leave these inner-city areas for the more desirable outer zones. Meanwhile, new groups of poor people would take their place in Zones 1 and 2.

The delinquency problem was a result not of specific people, but of the constant turnover of people in the area. This turnover caused a problem referred to as **social disorganization** (Shaw and McKay, 1942). The people in these core areas were unable to exert any control over the behavior of those living there. The major concern for the people was to better themselves and move on to other areas. Life in Zones 1 and 2 was seen as a temporary state. As a result, people did not concern themselves with improving the area, get- ting to known one another, or taking control of conditions. There was a lack of social organization that could bring about improvements.

Social Areas

Research since Shaw and McKay's has shown that many cities do not fol- low the concentric zone form of growth. As a consequence, ecological the- orists have shifted to **social area analysis**. Where natural area analysis emphasized a strict ecological analogy and physical geographic approach, social area analysis identifies areas in terms of their social characteristics. Where common distance from the CBD defined a natural area in the con- centric zonal approach, similarities in average income, education, popula- tion density, and other variables are used to identify areas in social area analysis. A single social area may consist of two geographically separate land areas. They are considered the same social area due to their similar makeup in terms of the social factors under observation. This move to social area analysis has held more intuitive appeal for social scientists.

Analyses since the 1950s have consistently uncovered concentrations of crime in certain residential areas. Analyses of Baltimore, Indianapolis, and Detroit all found that poor economic conditions, social heterogeneity, and an inability of residents to exert control and conformity among area residents were related to higher levels of delinquency in neighborhoods (Bordua, 1958; Chilton, 1964; Lander, 1954). Bursik and Grasmick (1993) claim that neighborhood control requires input from **private, parochial, and public** sources (see Table 4.2). Unfortunately, lower-class, transient, high-crime neighborhoods have trouble developing these sources of control. Areas undergoing a great deal of change will have an unstable base for private and parochial control mechanisms, while even in stable neighborhoods with strong private and parochial networks the residents may not be able to marshal the public support needed for effective delinquency control (Bursik and Grasmick, 1993). Hope (1997) refers to this as a problem of **vertical integration**. That is, some neighborhoods are left out when it comes to working with those in power.

Table 4.2   **Sources of Neighborhood Control**

Private	interpersonal relationships: family, friends, and close associates
Parochial	neighborhood networks and institutions: schools, churches, businesses, social organizations/groups
Public	agencies and institutions of the city, state, or other governmental unit

Source: See A. Hunter (1985) "Private, Parochial and Public School Orders: The Problem of Crime and Incivility in Urban Communities." In G.D. Suttles and M.N. Zald (eds.), *The Challenge of Social Control: Citizenship and Institution Building in a Modern Society* (pp. 230-242). Norwood, NJ: Ablex; and R.J. Bursik and H.G. Grasmick (1993). *Neighborhoods and Crime: The Dimensions of Effective Community Control.* New York: Lexington.

Critique of the Ecological Approach

While the ecological approach and the Chicago School shifted attention away from the biological views of Lombroso to a more sociological orientation, these new ideas also suffered from various problems. First, despite the frequent use of social disorganization as a theoretical base, the ecological perspective borrowed various theories and themes (such as anomie) when the occasion arose. This lack of a single coherent theory hampered the growth and use of the ecological approach. Second, many researchers fell into the trap of invoking the **ecological fallacy**. The ecological fallacy refers to attributing to an individual results that are based on grouped data. For example, suppose a researcher finds that delinquency was highest in areas of low income, low average education, and high density. If the researcher then states that an uneducated individual from a poor family living in a two-bedroom home with nine people would be delinquent, the researcher commits an ecological fallacy. The fact that an area with certain characteristics has a high rate of delinquency does not mean that an individual exhibiting similar personal characteristics will be delinquent. In fact, many of the delinquents in the identified area may exhibit the exact opposite traits. Knowledge about an area would not tell anything about a specific individual.

A third area of concern dealt with the heavy reliance on official records of delinquency. The finding that delinquency was highest in low socioeconomic areas found a great deal of support in official records. Various examinations using self-report studies (Short and Nye, 1958; Dentler and Monroe, 1961; Hindelang, Hirschi, and Weis, 1981; Tittle, Villemez, and Smith, 1978), however, found little difference in delinquency between the social classes. The findings of many ecological studies, therefore, could have been attributable to biased official records.

Despite problems with the ecological approach, this early work brought crime and delinquency theory squarely into the sociological tradition. For the most part, these early sociological explanations provided a clean break from the biological work of Lombroso and his followers. The ecological studies also provided much of the framework for subsequent theoretical advances.

LEARNING THEORY

Just as under the psychological banner, many sociological theorists see deviance as a result of learning. A variety of factors contribute to the learning process, including with whom an individual has contact, what the individual observes, and the consequences of one's behavior. The most prominent of the social learning theories is differential association, which forms the basis for other learning theories.

Sutherland: Differential Association

Sutherland's (1939) **differential association** views learning as the culmination of various social inputs faced by individuals throughout their lives. Sutherland observed, as did Shaw and McKay, that delinquency was concentrated in the inner-city areas. Instead of attributing this to the area and the problem of social disorganization, Sutherland proposed that deviance was more easily learned in these areas. The disorganization of the area provided a degree of instability that led to the growth of deviant lifestyles and points of view. Juveniles came into daily contact with both deviant and conventional ideas. As a result, children could just as easily learn to accept deviance as they could conventional behavior.

In explaining his views, Sutherland proposed nine specific points to differential association (see Table 4.3). Underlying these nine points is the idea that deviance is learned in the same fashion as conforming behavior. The major sources of that learning are the people with whom an individual comes in contact, particularly the family, peers, and religious institutions. Explicit in the theory is the idea that everyone is exposed to both deviant and conforming information. The choice of activity depends on the relative amount of influence favoring either deviant or conventional behavior.

Table 4.3	Sutherland's Differential Association Theory

1. Criminal behavior is learned.
2. Criminal behavior is learned in interaction with other persons in a process of communication.
3. The principal part of the learning of criminal behavior occurs within intimate personal groups.
4. When criminal behavior is learned, the learning includes (a) techniques of the crime, which are sometimes very complicated, sometimes very simple; (b) the specification of motives, drives, rationalizations, and attitudes.
5. The specific direction of motives and drives is learned from definitions of the legal codes as favorable or unfavorable.
6. A person becomes delinquent because of an excess of definitions favorable to violation of law over definitions unfavorable to violation of law.
7. Differential associations may vary in frequency, duration, priority, and intensity.
8. The process of learning criminal behavior by association with criminal and anti-criminal patterns involves all of the mechanisms that are involved in any other learning.
9. While criminal behavior is an expression of general needs and values, it is not explained by those general needs and values, because noncriminal behavior is an expression of the same needs and values.

Source: Compiled from E.H. Sutherland and D.R. Cressey (1974). *Criminology*, 9th ed. Philadelphia: Lippincott, pp. 75-76.

The basic formula for differential association has been criticized from a variety of perspectives. One of the criticisms revolves around Sutherland's failure to define or operationalize his terms. For example, he failed to define frequency, duration, priority, and intensity of associations. The common definitions of frequency (number of contacts), duration (length of a contact), priority (temporal order of the contacts), and intensity (significance of the contact) have been supplied by other researchers. Sutherland also failed to explicitly define "an excess of definitions." A second problem, stemming from the first, entails the lack of convincing empirical support for the theory. Although there have been a large number of studies focusing on differential association (for example, Adams, 1974; DeFleur and Quinney, 1966; Reiss and Rhodes, 1964; Short, 1960), most of the empirical support is indirect and highly qualified. The fact that Sutherland assumes that deviance is a rational decision is a further possible problem. Many researchers and theorists would argue that choosing deviant behavior is irrational. A final problem deals with the fact that Sutherland explicitly discounted the influence of factors other than social, face-to-face contacts. While reasonable for the early 1900s, changes in the modern world have prompted researchers to modify and extend the original ideas of differential association.

Modifications in Differential Association

One of the most logical modifications to make in differential association is the inclusion of the mass media and non-face-to-face communication in the theory. Glaser's (1956) **differential identification** proposes that personal association is not always necessary for the transmission of behavioral guidelines. Glaser sees real and fictional presentations on television and other forms of the

Indiana University Archives

Edwin Sutherland (1883-1950) proposed the theory of differential association, a learning theory of delinquency. Sutherland's theory can be considered the first truly sociological effort to explain crime.

mass media as providing information concerning acceptable behavior, especially to children. The basic idea is one of imitation or modeling. An individual observes the activity of a character and begins to copy that character. Another term for this is **role-taking**. The child assumes the role that is portrayed. This is especially problematic because children fail to realize that the media portrayals are in themselves roles and not the actual behavior of the actor playing the role. Youthful observers see the behavior as life-like and may not realize the fictional nature of the material. A youth might observe a glorified version of crime from a desirable fictional character and, thus, act in accordance with that portrayal.

A second set of modifications of differential association revolves around the ideas of operant conditioning. **Differential reinforcement** (Jeffery, 1965) and differential association–reinforcement (Burgess and Akers, 1968) theories propose that an individual can learn from a variety of sources, both social and nonsocial. Social factors include the ideas of both differential association and differential identification. Nonsocial factors, on the other hand, can refer to the outcome of the behavior. If the behavior results in a pleasurable payoff (e.g., useful stolen goods), the behavior will be repeated. The absence of an acceptable return on the behavior or the receipt of an adverse stimuli (an undesirable outcome such as being caught and imprisoned) would prompt avoidance of the activity in the future. Burgess and Akers (1968) rewrote differential association using operant conditioning terminology.

Subcultural Theories

Subcultural explanations owe a great deal to the same research that prompted the early ecological and social learning theories. A key to the discussions of Shaw and McKay (1942), Sutherland (1939), and others was the diversity of people in the cities. It was this cultural diversity that prompted the idea of social disorganization and that provided different inputs to the learning process. Subcultural theorists took these ideas and focused directly on the fact of diversity in the population.

Defining **subculture** is not an easy task. In the simplest sense, a subculture is a smaller part of a larger culture. While it must vary to some degree from the larger culture, it is not totally different. The subculture exists within and is part of the larger culture. More detailed definitions typically refer to a set of values, beliefs, ideas, views, and/or meanings which a group of individuals hold and which are to some degree different from those of the larger culture.

From a subcultural perspective, delinquency and criminality are the result of individuals attempting to act in accordance with subcultural norms. This can occur in two ways. First, an individual acts according to subcultural mandates, which may be considered deviant by the larger cultural mandates of society. This problem could be common for new immigrants who have traditionally acted according to one set of cultural mores and are now faced with a different set of expectations in a new cultural setting. Second, deviance may result from the inability to join or be assimilated into a new culture. Consequently, the individual may strike out against society because of the frustration faced in attempting to live according to the new cultural expectations.

The Work of Cohen and Miller

Albert Cohen (1955), recognizing the concentration of delinquency among lower-class boys, proposed that these youths feel ill-equipped to compete in and deal with a middle-class society. The middle-class orientation of society is set up in such a fashion that lower-class youths cannot succeed. This is compounded by the fact that they are expected to follow the goals and aspirations of the middle class. All youths are measured against a middle-class measuring rod. A key component to this problem is the failure of lower-class families to assimilate their young into the middle-class value system.

The failure to succeed in terms of middle-class values leads to feelings of failure and diminished self-worth among the lower-class youths. As a result, these boys join together in groups and act in concert with the group (subcultural) norms instead of with the mandates of the larger culture. While this provides the youths with some degree of self-worth, status, and success, it also leads to **culture conflict**. That is, by following one set of cultural (or subcultural) practices, the individual is violating the proscriptions of another culture. In Cohen's study, adherence to the subcultural group's mandates means violating the laws of middle-class society.

Cohen (1955) identifies three aspects of the emergent "lower-class gang delinquency." He claims that the subculture is malicious, negativistic, and nonutilitarian. In support of this contention, Cohen points out that the youths often steal items, with the intent of causing trouble and harm for another person, not because they want the item. He sees much of the deviant activity as a means of tormenting others. The behavior brings about an immediate "hedonistic" pleasure instead of supplying any long-term need or solution to a problem. In general, there appears to be little point in the behavior besides causing trouble for the larger middle-class culture.

Walter Miller's (1958) subcultural explanation goes beyond the behavior of juveniles to include lower-class males of all ages. Miller views the lower class as operating under a distinct set of cultural values, or **focal concerns** (see Table 4.4). These are: trouble, toughness, smartness, excitement, fate, and autonomy. Adherence to these lower-class focal concerns or values provides status, acceptance, and feelings of belonging for the lower-class individual (Miller, 1958).

Table 4.4   Miller's Lower-Class Focal Concerns

Trouble	Refers to the fact that lower-class males spend a large amount of time preoccupied with getting into and out of trouble. Trouble may bring about desired outcomes such as attention and prestige.
Toughness	Emphasis on physical prowess, athletic skill, masculinity, and bravery. Partly a response of lower-class males raised in female headed households.
Smartness	Basically the idea of being "streetwise." The concern is on how to manipulate the environment and others to your own benefit without being subjected to sanctions of any kind.
Excitement	Refers to the idea that lower-class individuals are oriented around short-term hedonistic desires. Activities, such as gambling and drug use, are undertaken for the immediate excitement or gratification that is generated.
Fate	The belief that, in the long run, individuals have little control over their lives. Luck and fortune dictate the outcome of behavior. Whatever is supposed to happen will happen regardless of the individual's wishes. This allows for a wide latitude in behavior.
Autonomy	While the individual believes in fate, there is a strong desire to resist outside control imposed by other persons. Individuals want total control over themselves until fate intervenes.

At the same time that these values provide positive reinforcement in the lower-class world, they bring about a natural conflict with middle-class values. The goal of the lower-class individual is not to violate the law or the middle-class norms. Instead, the goal is to follow the focal concerns of their class and peers. Deviant behavior, therefore, is a by-product of following the subcultural focal concerns (Miller, 1958). This is different from the view of Cohen (1955), in which deviance is a conscious method of striking out against the middle-class society and value system. Whereas Cohen (1955) sees the origins of the subcultural behaviors in the reaction of lower-class individuals faced with a middle-class world, Miller (1958) views the focal concerns as an integral part of the lower class.

Similar criticisms have been leveled against both Cohen's and Miller's subcultural theories. First, they fail to provide any empirical support for their assertions. Indeed, self-report studies show a more even distribution of offending in society than assumed by Cohen or Miller. Second, both explanations are **tautological**, or circular. That is, the key factors define the subculture (such as being malicious, negativistic, and nonutilitarian). In turn, the subculture causes these features. The authors are unable to identify explicitly the elements that make up the lower-class subculture, except for those features caused by the subculture. Third, there is a possible middle-class bias on the part of the authors. They develop their arguments by observing the behavior of lower-class individuals. Then, these middle-class researchers impute values and beliefs (the core ideas for a subculture) to those behaviors. From their point of view, the behaviors appear to be malicious, negativistic, and nonutilitarian, or indicators of trouble, toughness, or similar traits. The lower-class individuals, however, may be acting as they do for entirely different reasons from those assumed by Cohen or Miller.

Sykes and Matza: Techniques of Neutralization

Throughout the discussion of subcultural explanations there is a subtle failure to address the fact that no individual operates in just the subculture. Rather, every individual must deal with both subcultural as well as the larger cultural expectations. Indeed, many individuals attempt to abide by both sets of values—those of the subculture and those of the larger culture. Juveniles, in particular, often act in accordance with one set of values or rules and still maintain a self-image that places them in the realm of acceptable behavior of the larger culture.

Matza (1964) attempts to explain how this can happen by discussing the amount of **drift** that occurs throughout an individual's life. He states that individuals are pushed and pulled at different times in their lives into various modes of activity. A deviant at one point in time may be a model citizen at another. People drift between different modes of behavior throughout their lives and are never completely deviant or completely conforming. Behavior depends on the different circumstances confronting the person.

Accommodating the different lifestyles and behaviors, however, requires individuals to find justifications for the discrepancies. For example, juveniles who commit delinquent acts often see themselves as no better and no worse than anyone else, despite recognizing their deviant activity. Sykes and Matza (1957) outline five **techniques of neutralization** that allow the juvenile to accommodate the deviant behavior while maintaining a self-image as a conformist (see Table 4.5). Each technique requires the individual to admit to the behavior under question. The youth invokes one of the techniques in order to justify his or her behavior in light of confrontation with conventional cultural values. These techniques allow the individual to accommodate both subcultural and cultural values at the same time. While an exact understanding of how, when, and by whom neutralization techniques are used is not known, evidence does show that such techniques are used in various settings (Agnew, 1994; Agnew and Peters, 1986; Minor, 1981; Thurman, 1984).

Table 4.5	Sykes and Matza'a Techniques of Neutralization
Denial of Responsibility	The youth may claim that the action was an accident or, more likely, assert that he or she was forced into the action by circumstances beyond his or her control.
Denial of Injury	Focuses on the amount of harm caused regardless of violating the law. The absence of harm to an individual may involve pointing to a lack of physical injury, the action was a prank, or the person or business could afford the loss.
Denial of the Victim	The juvenile can deny the existence of a victim by claiming self-defense or retaliation, the absence of a victim (such as involving a business and not a person), and/or that characteristics of the victim brought the harm on himself or herself (such as hazing a homosexual).
Condemnation of the Condemnors	The youth turns the tables on those individuals who condemn his or her behavior by pointing out that the condemnors are no better than he or she. In essence, the condemnors are also deviant.
Appeal to Higher Loyalties	Conflict between the dictates of two groups will be resolved through adherence to the ideas of one group. The juvenile may see greater reward and more loyalty to the subcultural group on some issues which, in turn, lead to deviant behavior.

Source: Constructed from G.M. Sykes and D. Matza (1957). "Techniques of Neutralization: A Theory of Delinquency." *American Sociological Review* 22:664-670.

Critique of the Subcultural Approach

The attempt to explain deviance through the use of subcultures faces a number of problems. The greatest problem entails identifying a subculture. As noted earlier, the typical process of identifying subcultures through the behavior of the individuals leads to a good deal of circular reasoning—the behavior indicates that a subculture exists, and the subculture is used to explain why the behavior occurs. The use of behaviors for identifying subcultures also faces the problem of substituting behaviors for values. A subculture entails a difference in values, beliefs, and norms from those held by the larger culture. It is questionable to what extent you can impute values from behaviors. Two separate forms of activity may reflect the same basic value. For example, in order to feed their families (basic value), one individual takes a low-paying job while another robs the local grocery store (different behaviors).

A second problem entails finding ways of identifying which set of values (subcultural or cultural) is being followed at which times. This becomes especially problematic when the values are similar to one another. Assuming that there is variability in values and beliefs from group to group, how many values and how great a difference must exist in order to consider the group a subculture? Additionally, not all values can have the same degree of importance. Further, to what extent can an individual be deviant without belonging to a subculture? There is ample evidence that middle- and upper-class individuals also partake in deviance. Subcultural theorists have spent little, if any, time addressing the behavior of these individuals. Clearly, subcultural explanations require a good deal of additional research before they can be accepted or rejected.

ROUTINE ACTIVITIES AND RATIONAL CHOICE

Yet another theoretical area with ties to the ecological school is one dealing with routine activities and rational choice. While the two areas have developed out of different backgrounds, they both accept the basic premise that the movement of offenders and victims over space and time places them in varying situations in which criminal activity will be more or less possible. Within these different situations, individuals will make choices about what to do and what not to do (see Clarke and Felson, 1993). Routine activities and rational choice arguments, therefore, rest in the arena of neoclassicism, in which there is an element of choice.

The **routine activities** perspective assumes that the normal behavior of individuals contributes to deviant events. Cohen and Felson (1979) outline three criteria necessary for the commission of a crime: (1) the presence of a suitable target, (2) a motivated offender, and (3) an absence of guardians. The possibility for deviance is enhanced when these three elements coincide. Changes in family life over the past several decades offer one example of how routine activities may impact delinquency. The increase in two-earner households means that many youths are unsupervised after school and at other times. This results in a lack of guardianship, while also offering suitable targets (such as other unsupervised youths or unoccupied homes) for potential offenders. Another example appears in schools, particularly large secondary schools, where motivated offenders and suitable targets (both students) are required to be in close proximity with relatively few teachers or staff (guardians) available to oversee what takes place. Research has shown that the routine activities of individuals are related to a wide array of both personal and property offenses (Belknap, 1987; Kennedy and Forde, 1990; Miethe, Stafford, and Long, 1987; Roncek and Maier, 1991).

Closely tied to routine activities theory is rational choice theory. **Rational choice** theory assumes that potential offenders make choices based on various factors in the physical and social environments. Among the factors influencing choices are the payoff, effort, support, and risks involved in the potential behavior (Cornish and Clarke, 1986). In essence, the individual chooses if, when, and where to commit a crime based on the opportunities that are presented to him or her. There is ample evidence that offenders do make choices. Studies of burglars demonstrate that these offenders consider an array of factors when deciding to commit a crime, including the financial or emotional need, the availability of concealment, the effort needed to gain entry, the presence of potential observers, the anticipated payoff, and familiarity with the area (Bennett, 1986; Bennett and Wright, 1984; Cromwell, Olson, and Avery, 1991; Decker, Wright, and Logie, 1993; Rengert and Wasilchick, 1985; Reppetto, 1974; Taylor and Nee, 1988; Wright and Decker, 1994). This does not mean that offenders plan their behavior in detail. Rather, unplanned, spontaneous behavior may rest on past observations and experiences that lay the foundation for unconscious decisionmaking.

The support for rational choice, however, is not without qualification. The factors identified as important in decisionmaking can vary greatly from situation to situation. Rational choice theory is criticized for its inability to explain impulsive acts and actions that clearly take place in high-risk settings. This may reflect the fact that individuals can make choices only from available alternatives. It is possible that some individuals will make what appears to be an irrational choice because of limited choices or an inability to identify other options. The neoclassical nature of the theory does not assume total volition by the individual. Finally, Akers (1990) argues that rational choice is little more than an extension of learning theory in which individuals respond to rewards and punishments. Rather than argue its uniqueness, most researchers see rational choice as an extension of and complement to various ideas, including learning theories (see, for example, Fattah, 1993; Harding, 1993; Trasler, 1993).

Rational choice theory poses an interesting conundrum for juvenile justice. If one assumes that youths do not have the capacity to make truly informed decisions, to what extent can it be claimed that they are making rational choices? The traditional view of the juvenile justice system is that the youths cannot form the requisite intent to be held accountable for their actions. Thus, they are not rational. Instead, their behavior is determined by other factors. At the same time, it is naive to assume no rationality by youths. Coupled with routine activities, rational choice may be helpful for explaining increased delinquency during after-school hours (when there are fewer targets but less supervision) or why theft is more common than robbery.

ANOMIE AND STRAIN

Strain theory views deviance as a direct result of a social structure that stresses achievement but fails to provide adequate legitimate means of succeeding. Unlike many other theories, strain theory moves the onus for deviance away from the individual, placing it on society. Unacceptable behavior by an individual is seen as a natural (and expected) response to the problems posed by the social structure.

The Form of Society and Anomie

An understanding of strain theory begins with an examination of changes in the form of society. Toennies (1957) points out that (Western) society has largely changed from a gemeinschaft society to a gesselschaft society (see Table 4.6). A **gemeinschaft society** was one characterized by small, rural, agrarian cities and towns. People in these homogenous communities knew each other very well and, in some respects, the entire community formed a large extended family. Everyone in the community led a simple, hard-working existence. There was little to differentiate the individuals in terms of status or wealth. On average, no one person or group was significantly more wealthy or well-to-do than anyone else. In gemeinschaft society, individuals expected very little from their labors except daily subsistence. Acquiring wealth to provide for a good retirement, buy comforts, or go on a vacation were luxuries alien to most people. As a result, most people did not look upon one another as competitors.

Table 4.6   The Changing Society

Gemeinschaft Society	Gesselschaft Society
rural, agrarian	urban, technocratic
small, homogeneous communities	large, heterogeneous communities
primary relationships	secondary relationships
mechanical solidarity—	organic solidarity—
functional independence	functional interdependence
	division of labor

Today, we have evolved into a **gesselschaft society**, which is more urbanized, technocratic, and diverse (Toennies, 1957). The growth of large cities has prompted more impersonal, secondary relationships in which an individual may have many acquaintances but few truly close relationships (such as their immediate family and close friends). As society has become more technologically oriented, jobs have become specialized and complex (Durkheim, 1933). Every person supplies something different to the production of goods and to societal needs. In essence, there is a **division of labor** by which everyone has a specific job with different expectations and different rewards. The gesselschaft society led to competition for better jobs and increased wealth.

The problem with the gesselschaft form of society is the fact that humans are inherently egoistic (Durkheim, 1933). Everybody aspires to the top and desires the best. Happiness is the result of realizing one's expectations. The specialized jobs of modern society mean that one person runs the company while another sweeps the floor. Each job is important to the whole, but the compensation for different jobs is not the same. As a result, some individuals receive more than others while everyone aspires to reach the top. The inability of individuals to recognize the necessity of different jobs and payoffs and the inability to control one's egoistic urges made up what Durkheim called **anomie**. Loosely translated, anomie refers to a state of normlessness or inadequate regulation. More specifically, it is the inability of the individual to regulate his or her expectations in accordance with the societal structure. Anomie may result in various forms of deviant behavior, including crime.

Merton: Modes of Adaptation

In 1938, Robert Merton took the basic ideas of anomie and the changes in society and expanded the discussion to what is known as **strain theory**. Merton (1938) saw anomie as the lack of correspondence between culturally accepted goals and socially institutionalized means to achieve those goals. According to Merton, the problem is that American society presents everyone with the goals of achieving material success and reaching the top, while at the same time limiting access to the means for achieving those goals. For example, higher education is a necessary prerequisite for entrance into many professions. Not all individuals, however, have the money or opportunity to obtain this needed schooling. Thus, the means to succeed have been blocked for some societal members. The disjuncture between goals and means is a property of the social structure. Merton argues that what is needed is equal access to the means of achieving the goals.

Merton (1938) outlines five **modes of adaptation**, or ways an individual may respond, to the strain between goals and means (see Table 4.7). Each mode of adaptation reflects an individual's acceptance or rejection of culturally prescribed goals and socially institutionalized means of achieving those goals. *Conformity* represents the acceptance of both the goals and means, regardless of whether he or she succeeds. *Innovation* reflects acceptance of the prescribed goals but, when faced with an inability to succeed via acceptable means, the individual resorts to unacceptable or illegitimate methods of achieving success. In *ritualism*, the exact opposite occurs. While the individual gives up on achieving the goals, he or she continues to act in a socially acceptable fashion. A *retreatist* rejects both the goals and the means. This individual retreats from society through such means as alcohol or other drug use, vagrancy, or psychological withdrawal. The final mode of adaptation, *rebellion*, reflects an attempt to replace the existing societal goals and means with a new set that provides more opportunity for everyone in society.

The choice of adaptation varies from one individual to the next. The most common response, according to Merton (1938), is conformity. This line of action presents the individual with the least amount of resistance and does not add the problems of deviance to the problem of not succeeding. In the remaining modes, individuals can be considered deviant either in their outlook or in their actions. Delinquency appears in innovation, retreatism, and rebellion, in which accepted modes of behavior (means) are replaced by unacceptable actions. While the root problem of anomie is structurally determined, the choice of adaptation can be understood only in light of individual circumstances.

Table 4.7   Merton's Modes of Adaptation

Mode of Adaptation	Cultural Goals	Institutionalized Means
Conformity	+	+
Innovation	+	–
Ritualism	–	+
Retreatism	–	–
Rebellion	±	±

+ means acceptance, – means rejection, ± means rejection and substitution

Source: R.K. Merton (1938). "Social Structure and Anomie." *American Sociological Review* 3:672-682.

General Strain Theory

Critics of strain theory have argued that not everyone aspires to the societally proscribed goals underlying Merton's discussion. Rather than focus only on the inability to achieve the societally proscribed goals, Agnew (1992) has proposed a **general strain theory** that suggests that strain can arise from two other sources. The first entails the removal of desired or valued stimuli. Examples may include restricting a youth's normal activities, moving to another city and away from friends, canceling a long-planned trip, or being forced to quit a sports team. A second source of strain may be the presentation of negative stimuli that may cause an individual to become angry or frustrated. Having to walk to school through a dangerous neighborhood, being bused to a distant school, living in an abusive household, or being harassed by other youths are all potential forms of negative stimuli. These two sources of strain may prompt individuals to respond with delinquent or criminal behavior (Agnew, 1992). There are also many nondeviant coping mechanisms that an individual can utilize (Agnew, 1997). Agnew and White (1992) provide empirical support for general strain theory. They report finding a positive relationship between measures of generalized strain and delinquent behavior.

Assessing Strain Theory

The practical implication of traditional strain theory (Merton's view) would appear to be changing the structural barriers to success that underlie deviant activity. Problems with strain theory, however, suggest that such activity would be premature. One major issue is the problem of operationalizing the key concepts, such as anomie, aspirations, opportunity, and perceptions. Differing definitions of these terms leads to conflicting empirical support for the theory.

Studies by Kornhauser (1978), Quicker (1974), Agnew (1984), and others have noted that the assumed relationship between strain and deviant behavior is not clear. Kornhauser's (1978) review of the literature found that, in some instances, deviance appears to be related to low aspirations, while in others deviance may actually cause changes in aspirations instead of the reverse. For example, some individuals may substitute immediate gratification and goals in place of the long-term, societal goals. This may be a direct result of the recognized inability to achieve the societal goal.

A second problem stems from the fact that many studies focus on middle- and upper-class youths, while the Mertonian strain theory appears more applicable to lower-class and gang activity. Third, strain theory fails to present any explanation for the choice of adaptation. Little attention is directed to why one person chooses deviance and another does not. Finally, Mertonian strain assumes that all deviance is a result of unfulfilled aspirations. Agnew's (1992) theory addresses some of these issues. It appears that future research should take the broader approach offered by Agnew.

SOCIAL CONTROL THEORY

Where most theories look to identify factors that lead or push a juvenile into delinquency, **social control** theories seek to find factors that keep an individual from becoming deviant. Control theorists ask why many people refrain from violating the law even though they are presented with ample opportunity to commit crimes. Reckless (1967) views the main issue as explaining why one individual becomes deviant and another does not when both are faced with the same situations. The explanation they offer deals with the degree of control exerted on the individual.

Hirschi: Control Theory

Hirschi's (1969) theory states that "delinquent acts result when an individual's bond to society is weak or broken" (Hirschi, 1969:16). The underlying assumption is that the individual's behavior is controlled by the connections the person has to conventional social order. Deviance shows up when a person's **bond to society** is weak or broken. According to Hirschi (1969), bond is developed through socialization during early childhood and consists of four elements: attachment, commitment, involvement, and belief (see Table 4.8). The failure of an individual to care about what others think about his or her behavior and views (attachment), to work toward acceptable goals (commitment), to use one's energies and time in socially acceptable behaviors (involvement), and/or to accept the common value system in society (belief) opens the door for deviant and delinquent behavior. Weak or broken bond does not *cause* deviance. Rather, it *allows for* deviance. In other words, weak or broken bond could be viewed as necessary for deviance but not sufficient. An individual with weak bond may or may not choose to commit deviant acts.

Table 4.8   **Elements of Hirschi's Bond**

Attachment	"sensitivity to the opinion of others" (p. 16)
	The more an individual cares about what others think of himself/herself, the less likely he/she will choose behavior that brings about negative input.
Commitment	a "person invests time, energy, himself, in a certain line of activity" (p. 20)
	As a person builds an investment in conventional endeavors, any choice of deviant behavior will place that investment at risk.
Involvement	"engrossment in conventional activities" (p. 22)
	Because time and energy are limited, once they are used in the pursuit of conventional activities, there is no time or energy left for deviant behavior.
Belief	"the existence of a common value system within the society or group" (p. 23)
	As a person is socialized into and accepts the common belief system, he/she will be less likely to violate those beliefs through deviant activity.

Source: Constructed by authors from T. Hirschi (1969). *Causes of Delinquency*. Berkeley: University of California Press.

Numerous tests of Hirschi's social control theory have been undertaken. Hirschi's (1969) own analysis involved surveying more than 4,000 high school boys about their delinquent activity and elements of bond. He found that delinquency was related to weaker attachment to parents, education, and school; lower aspirations (i.e., lacking commitment); more time spent "joy riding" in cars or being bored (involvement); and less respect for the police and the law (belief). These findings are consistent with Hirschi's theory. Other studies (Hindelang, 1973; Krohn and Massey, 1980; Poole and Regoli, 1979; Wiatrowski, Griswold, and Roberts, 1981) report similar supportive findings.

Despite support for the theory, a number of problematic issues remain. First, the theory does not adequately explain how bond becomes weak or broken. The theory tries to explain why an individual is deviant and not how they became that way. While poor socialization is the easiest explanation, the theory fails to demonstrate how this occurs. Second, the issue of relative impact of the four elements of bond is left unresolved. For example, if attachment is strong and commitment is moderate but involvement and belief are weak, will this permit deviance or not? As a result of this problem, the theory cannot directly offer suggestions on how to avoid the weakening of bond or how to repair bond.

Another area of concern deals with episodic deviance. Many youths vacillate between delinquent and conventional behavior. This "drift" cannot be explained using control theory. While an individual chooses to commit deviance, the theory does not explain the vacillation in choices over time and place. Such drift can be adequately explained only by proposing that the bond is strengthened and weakened both easily and often. Finally, the theory assumes that all bonding is to conventional, nondeviant lifestyles. It may be possible that a juvenile is raised in a household where the parents are deviant and espouse nontraditional behaviors. A juvenile in these circumstances should be bonded to deviance. Indeed, Jensen and Brownfield (1983) reported that juveniles will follow the deviant behaviors of their parents as well as the nondeviant themes.

Reckless: Containment Theory

Reckless's (1962) **containment theory** differs from Hirschi's bond argument in two fundamental ways. First, containment theory proposes that the individual may have some control over his or her own behavior, rather than having controls imposed by others. Second, while there are factors that promote conformity, there are also forces that promote deviance.

Reckless (1962) outlines two types of containment: outer containment and inner containment (Table 4.9). **Outer containment** offers direct control over the individual from outside sources. These include family members, friends, teachers, and others who provide supervision, training, and pressure to conform. Conversely, **inner containment** is necessary due to the fact that an individual is not always under the direct control of outer containment. Thus, internalized moral codes, tolerance of frustration, and other factors help the individual refrain from deviance. The combination of these two factors should provide an effective means of avoiding deviant behavior. The factors that promote deviant behavior include internal pushes, external pressures, and external pulls (Reckless, 1962). Each of these influence an individual's activity. Poverty, unemployment, discontent, anxiety, deviant peers, and other factors may lead or push people into deviant activity as a viable form of behavioral response. These three factors make deviance an acceptable alternative, while inner and outer containment work to offset their influence.

Table 4.9   Elements of Reckless's Containment Theory

Forces promoting conformity:

Outer Containment	The influence of family, peers, and environment on behavior; social pressure, supervision, training, and group membership
Inner Containment	Individual factors such as self-concept, tolerance of frustration, goal-directedness, internalized moral codes

Forces promoting deviance:

Internal Pushes	Restlessness, discontent, anxiety, hostility
External Pressures	Poverty, unemployment, minority status, social inequality
External Pulls	Deviant peers, subcultures, media presentations

Source: Compiled from W.C. Reckless (1962). "A Noncausal Explanation: Containment Theory." *Excerpta Criminologica* 1:131-134.

Containment theory has received both support and criticism. Much of the support revolves around the fact that the theory includes factors related to both society and the individual. Additional support comes from Reckless's theory explaining conforming behavior as occurring amidst great amounts of deviance. The major argument against containment theory has come in the form of methodological critiques centering on the ability to operationalize the key ideas. For example, peers work as both constraining forces in outer containment and deviant-producing features of external pulls. Such inconsistency makes the theory hard to test empirically. This may be one cause of the lack of empirical support uncovered by other researchers (Schwartz and Tangri, 1965; Tangri and Schwartz, 1967). Another criticism of containment theory centers around the idea of positive self-concept as an "insulator" against deviance. Indeed, research has failed to empirically find a self-concept/deviance connection.

Self-Control Theory

Control theory has undergone its greatest change with the introduction of **self-control**. Rather than assume that behavior is controlled by outside forces throughout an individual's life, Gottfredson and Hirschi (1990) argue that self-control, internalized early in life, can serve to keep a person from involvement in deviant behavior. Self-control serves as a restraint from choosing the short-term gratification endemic to most criminal behavior. Gottfredson and Hirschi (1990:90) claim that

> people who lack self-control will tend to be impulsive, insensitive, physical (as opposed to mental), risk-taking, short-sighted, and nonverbal, and they will tend therefore to engage in criminal and analogous acts.

Self-control theory assumes that humans are hedonistic and make choices emphasizing immediate, short-term pleasure.

According to Gottfredson and Hirschi (1990), the primary source of self-control is good parenting. Poor self-control is the result of ineffective child-rearing practices by the parents. Good parenting requires exhibiting concern for the child, consistent monitoring of the child's behavior, the ability to identify problematic behaviors, appropriate reactions to inappropriate behavior, and the time and energy to carry through with parental responsibilities. Should the parents fail to build self-control, other social institutions, such as schools, may influence its formation but are typically poor substitutes for the family (Gottfredson and Hirschi, 1990). Once self-control is internalized, it serves to modify an individual's behavior throughout his or her life.

Self-control theory has received both support and criticism. A number of studies have found evidence that a lack of self-control is related to deviant behavior (Grasmick et al., 1993; Piquero, MacIntosh, and Hickman, 2000; Wood, Pfefferbaum, and Arneklev, 1993). Indeed, both a global measure of self-control as well as individual components (such as risk-taking, self-centeredness, and immediate gratification) exert strong influence on various forms of deviance, with the more global measure having the greatest consistency and impact (Wood, Pfefferbaum, and Arneklev, 1993). At the same time, the theory has been criticized for its inability to explain significant changes in behavior later in life and to consider the basic social structure as a contributor to parenting and self-control (Lilly, Cullen, and Ball, 1995). In addition, Akers (1991) argues that the theory is tautological. That is, low self-control is determined by the commission of deviant acts, and the deviant acts are the result of low self-control.

THE LABELING PERSPECTIVE

Another approach that places the blame for much deviance on society is the **labeling** perspective. The basic assumption of labeling is that being labeled as deviant by social control agents forces the person to act according to the label. Further deviance is a result of being contacted and sanctioned by the system. Consequently, continued deviance is a response to the actions of society. For example, being labeled a "delinquent" may lead to exclusion from participation in extracurricular school activities. This inability to participate in conforming activities may prompt further deviant behavior.

The Construction of Self-Image

The labeling perspective owes much to the ideas of **symbolic interactionism**. Symbolic interaction proposes that every individual develops his or her self-image through a process of interaction with the surrounding world

(Mead, 1934). How an individual sees himself or herself is determined by how that person thinks others see him or her. That is, a person's self-concept comes out of interaction with other people and the environment. Interaction with other people provides an individual with input about his or her own self. If an individual perceives a positive image of himself or herself from others, the person will hold a positive self-image. A simple way of viewing this process is through what Cooley (1902) calls the **looking-glass self**. The idea is that the individual views himself or herself the way that other people look at him or her. The individual attempts to see what other people see and acts accordingly.

Labeling takes these ideas and proposes that individuals mold their behavior in accordance with the perception of others. Tannenbaum (1938) saw the sanctioning of deviant behavior as a step in altering a juvenile's self-image from that of a normal, conventional youth to that of being a delinquent. System processing identifies a youth as delinquent, emphasizes the label, and ultimately segregates the youth from normal juvenile behavior. Juveniles begin to view themselves as deviant, which leads to actions consistent with the self-image. Basically, the process of labeling entails a **transfer of evil** from the act to the actor (Tannenbaum, 1938). Instead of viewing the act as deviant and bad, the actor becomes bad and the focus for social action. No longer is the individual someone who committed a crime, the individual is a criminal.

Lemert: Primary and Secondary Deviance

Edwin Lemert (1951) distinguishes between two types of deviance: primary and secondary. **Primary deviance** comprises those actions that "are rationalized or otherwise dealt with as functions of a socially acceptable role" (Lemert, 1951). These deviant acts are common and garner minimal attention and mild sanctions. As a result, the individual is not labeled and his or her self-image is not altered. **Secondary deviance**, however, occurs when an individual "begins to employ his deviant behavior or a role based upon it as a means of defense, attack, or adjustment to the overt and covert problems created by the consequent societal reaction to him" (Lemert, 1951). This means that society has successfully labeled the individual. The individual now views himself or herself as different and/or deviant, and will act accordingly.

It is important to note that primary and secondary deviant acts entail the same types of behavior. What distinguishes secondary from primary deviance is the reason behind the action. The behavior is secondary if the act cannot be rationalized as the outcome of a nondeviant social role and is committed as an attack or defense against societal reaction. Secondary deviance, therefore, is a *mentalistic construct*. That is, it relies on the mind-set and attitude of the individual involved.

Table 4.10   **Lemert's Labeling Perspective**

Primary Deviance	Actions that are rationalized as a result of socially acceptable roles; deviance is considered an aberration and results in only minor sanctions; the offender continues to see self as a normal member of society.
Secondary Deviance	Actions that are taken by an individual as a result of accepting the label, i.e., fulfilling the role proscribed by the label; individual commits deviance as a defense against the negative connotation of being seen as a "deviant."

The reasons for conforming to the label are simple. First, a deviant label makes participation in conventional activity difficult. Societal members expect deviance and react to the individual as a deviant, regardless of whether specific behavior is deviant or conforming. Second, by accepting the label, the individual blunts the impact of any negative feedback provided by society. For example, young children cry when told they are bad because the information is counter to their beliefs. Children would not be affected, however, if they saw themselves as bad. Negative input would simply point out what they already knew and accepted. Finally, individuals conform to labels as a means of striking out against those who are condemning them. Using a kind of "if that is what you think" attitude, individuals decide to show society just how bad they can really be if that is what society wants.

The process by which an individual assumes a negative label is not simple. A single deviant act generally will not lead to the successful application of a label. Lemert (1951) proposes an outline of the process that culminates in secondary deviance:

> (1) primary deviation; (2) social penalties; (3) further primary deviation; (4) stronger penalties and rejections; (5) further deviation, perhaps with hostilities and resentment beginning to focus upon those doing the penalizing; (6) crisis reached in the tolerance quotient . . .; (7) strengthening of the deviant conduct as a reaction to the stigmatizing and penalties; (8) ultimate acceptance of deviant social status and efforts at adjustment on the basis of the associated role (p. 77).

Lemert notes that this process is not set with any definite number of steps or particular sequence of events. Rather, the process is an illustration of the types of factors that occur.

Status Degradation

Garfinkel (1956) expands on the "process" of labeling in his discussion of successful status degradation ceremonies. A **successful status degradation ceremony** is one that moves a person to a lower social status (for example, from "conforming individual" to "deviant"). Table 4.11 outlines the requirements for a successful degradation ceremony. The eight requirements can be classified into three types of factors. First, the individual and his or her behavior must be seen as different and unacceptable compared to what is socially approved. Second, the individual or agency that is doing the denouncing must be given the power to denounce on behalf of society. Finally, there must be some sort of ritualistic separation of the denounced individual from the rest of society. This could take the form of actual physical separation (incarceration) or proclamation to society (court proceedings). The successful application of a label requires that all three of these factors take place. An individual who is not labeled after multiple acts of primary deviance has not been subjected to a "successful" degradation ceremony.

Table 4.11   Garfinkel's Successful Status Degradation Ceremonies

1.	"Both event and perpetrators must be . . . made to stand out as 'out of the ordinary.'"
2.	"Both event and perpetrator must be placed within a scheme of preferences that show" that the behavior is ordinary for the individual and is in opposition to the desired behavior.
3.	"The denouncer must so identify himself to the witnesses that during the denunciation they regard him not as a private person but as a publically known person."
4.	The denouncer must make the denunciation in the name of the larger group.
5.	"The denouncer must arrange to be vested with the right to speak in the name of [the group's] ultimate values."
6.	"The denouncer must get himself so defined by the witnesses that they locate him as a supporter of these values."
7.	Both the denouncer and witnesses "must be made to experience their distance from" the denounced.
8.	"The denounced person must be ritually separated from a place in the legitimate order."

Source: Compiled from H. Garfinkel (1956). "Conditions of Successful Status Degradation Ceremonies." *American Journal of Sociology* 651:420-424.

The Impact of the Labeling Perspective

The assumptions of labeling suggest that youths who have contact with the juvenile justice system are successfully labeled and act accordingly. This view led to major changes in the juvenile justice system in the 1970s. Most of the changes involved diverting youths away from system processing and attempting to find alternatives to incarcerating youths, particularly minor and status offenders. Empirical research presents conflicting evidence on whether a label leads to more delinquency.

Most support for labeling comes from studies that report higher recidivism for youths with prior system contact. The assumption is that the later deviance is due to successful labeling. What is interesting is that there is no measure of the individual's self-concept in these studies. It is impossible, therefore, to identify the recidivistic behavior as secondary deviance (the result of labeling) or further primary deviance.

Studies that directly examine changes in self-concept after system intervention present conflicting results. Various studies (Foster, Dinitz, and Reckless, 1972; Lipsett, 1968; Snyder, 1971) report little or no effect of system contact on self-image, while others uncover lower self-concept (Ageton and Elliott, 1973; Jensen, 1972; Street, Vinter, and Perrow, 1966). Any inability to find changes in a person's self-image would interrupt the proposed causal chain and raise doubt about labeling's impact.

Part of the failure of the labeling perspective may be due to the lack of attention paid to the impact of family, friends, and peer groups. For example, a youth may report no change in self-concept after contact with the formal justice system because he or she actually aspires to gain the label of "gang member." The youth pursues system contact in order to legitimize his or her gang affiliation. Formal system labeling also may fail if the individual receives accolades from family and friends. Conversely, a youth may be labeled by peers even if the system decides not to act. Each of these cases demonstrates that system intervention may not be the necessary nor sufficient for imposing a label. Most evaluations of labeling ignore the many potential confounding factors that may be at work (see Palamara, Cullen, and Gersten, 1986).

THE INTEGRATION AND ELABORATION OF THEORIES

One trend in criminological theorizing is the attempt to integrate various theories into more unified, coherent explanations of deviance. Many writers feel that, rather than attempt to show that any single theory is appropriate in all situations, each theory should be viewed as applicable to different domains of behavior. A number of authors have experimented with linking different explanations into an integrated theory of deviance. This process, also referred to as an **elaboration model**, attempts to take components of various theories and construct a single explanation that incorporates the best parts of the individual theories. Delbert Elliott and his colleagues (Elliott, 1985; Elliott, Ageton, and Canter, 1979; Elliott, Huizinga, and Ageton, 1985), working with extensive longitudinal data, have constructed and tested a model that includes elements of social control, strain, and differential association theories. In their studies, the authors provide a rough sequential process leading to deviance. Strain is seen as leading to a weakened bond to conventional society, which in turn leads to increased bonding with deviants and subsequent deviant behavior. Mediating this entire process is the influence of learning.

Other authors also report on attempts at linking social control (bond) and differential association theories (see Marcos, Bahr, and Johnson, 1986; Massey and Krohn, 1986; Thornberry, 1987; Thornberry et al., 1994) and control and subcultural theories (Giordano, Cernkovich, and Pugh, 1986). In general, these investigations uncover a dynamic process in which different effects influence deviance at various points in the process. These attempts at building more elaborate explanations have not gone unchallenged (see, for example, Hirschi, 1987). The challenges, however, are not widespread and often appear to reflect rhetorical positions based on defense of favored theories that may not fare well in the new models.

Recent interest in **developmental theories**, or **life-course theories**, generally reflect efforts that incorporate ideas from several theories and perspectives. Conger and Simmons (1997), for example, point out that biological factors play a role in cognitive ability, which impacts on how family, friends, and schools may treat the person, which may then impact on an individual's success in school or in making choices. Throughout this process, the individual faces different demands and opportunities for which he or she may or may not be adequately prepared. Similarly, Moffitt (1997) posits a sequence in which neuropsychological deficits alter an individual's temperament, speech, learning ability, and other factors, which may cause withdrawal, rejection by others, poor self-concept, failure at school, and a host of other problems. Each of these problems appear as an important factor in several theories. The key for Moffitt (1997) is the sequential and cumulative nature of the various factors.

LeBlanc (1997) offers a **generic control theory**, which draws on ideas from a variety of perspectives. He proposes that control can come from several sources that vary over time and situation. He offers four primary categories of control mechanisms. The first, "bonding," deals with how individuals are integrated to and act as part of the community. A second source is "unfolding." This control reflects growth and development of individuals, especially in terms of internalizing values. "Modeling," the third type, incorporates patterns that the person can emulate in order to conform. Finally, "constraining" refers to regulation imposed by others. Each of these interact to enhance the level of control. In support of his propositions, LeBlanc (1997) offers a multi-layered model that simultaneously discusses criminal acts, the criminal, and criminality. LeBlanc notes, however, that the model requires more work before it can be operationalized for testing. For our purposes, the value of the theory is in its use of concepts and ideas from a wide range of individual theories.

A final example of the integration/elaboration approach involves the idea of **reintegrative shaming**. Braithwaite (1989) offers shaming as a key mechanism for showing societal disapproval. The shaming, however, needs to be imposed in such a fashion as to draw the offending party into conforming society. Elements of several theories are incorporated in this argument. Labeling and symbolic interaction are important for understanding the risk in shaming someone without concern for reintegration. Social control elements appear in the need to bond the person to society. Additionally, the family is a key actor in teaching proper behavior (learning theory). Braithwaite (1989) also argues that a great deal of shaming takes place vicariously through stories and examples (modeling and imitation ideas).

Many of these newer theories have yet to undergo rigorous testing. This is partly due to the complexity of the proposed theoretical models and the lack of appropriate data for testing the full explanation. The advantage of the elaboration/integration approach lies in the attempt to draw together long theoretical traditions, each of which has demonstrated some empirical support. The fact that no single theory has adequately explained deviance suggests that this new direction should be continued.

THE IMPACT OF THEORIES ON JUVENILE JUSTICE

While a good deal of theorizing has been devoted to the causes of delinquent activity, the extent to which these explanations have an impact on the daily operations of the juvenile justice system is highly variable. Court dispositions and correctional treatments display the closest relationships between the theories and justice system action. As noted in Chapter 2, the rhetoric of the juvenile court has consistently emphasized the importance of learning and benevolent care of youths. Social learning theory provides support for interventions that focus on providing proper role models and environments conducive to conforming behavior. Trends toward deinstitutionalization rely on the arguments of labeling theory as well as learning principles. Thus, the past 20 years have experienced movements to community corrections and less restrictive interventions (see Chapter 12). Recent movements toward incarceration and deterrence of juveniles clearly rely on classical and neoclassical assumptions of free will and hedonistic choice.

On a larger scale, various theoretical perspectives have helped influence general social movements. The Great Society reforms that began in the mid-1960s attempted to address the social inequities that lead to deviance. Educational programs, economic assistance, vocational training, physical improvement of inner cities, and other efforts can be traced to strain, subcultural, learning, and ecological explanations of social ills. In many of these social actions, delinquency and criminality were only two of many social problems being addressed. The impact of these specific programs is a matter of debate. The consistency in crime, delinquency, and recidivism rates suggests that there has been little impact on these problems. Why there was no impact is not clear. Some authors argue that the interventions were too short-lived to alter longstanding social problems. Others claim that the implementation of the programs was incomplete or inappropriate. Still others deny the adequacy of the theoretical explanation being utilized. Regardless of past failures, the various theories continue to find their way into the policies and procedures of the juvenile justice system.

SUMMARY

Explanations of delinquent and criminal behavior, whether biological, psychological, or sociological in nature, provide some insight into the reasons for deviance. The diversity in perspectives, however, illustrates the lack of understanding that still exists. Indeed, the search for a single theory that explains all, or almost all, deviance appears to be an effort in futility. The most reasonable consideration is to view deviance as multifaceted. The explanation, therefore, must consider a wide range of variables and influences. Juvenile justice must not ignore theory simply because until this point it has failed to arrive at a totally adequate explanation. Rather, the system must take care to select, implement, and evaluate ideas in light of expanding knowledge and research. While the remainder of the text deals with various interventions and system actions, theory forms an implicit base for all discussions.

Discussion Questions

1. Sociological explanations for deviance are currently the most well known. Pick any sociological theory, outline the argument, and translate those ideas into practical applications for dealing with juveniles.

2. The President has called for a study that will set the tone for future directions in juvenile justice. As a member of that commission, you have the opportunity to advocate an underlying theory. Which sociological theory will you fight for? And why is it the best possible approach for guiding the juvenile justice system? Present the strengths and weaknesses of your choice.

3. A recent trend in delinquency explanations is the integration or elaboration model. Discuss how subculture, learning, and control theories can be integrated. How are they related, and what will the new explanation provide that any single theory cannot?

Chapter 5

Gang Delinquency

INTRODUCTION

For many individuals, agencies, and communities, the problem of youthful misbehavior is most notably gang delinquency. Indeed, a great deal of early research shows that juveniles commit more deviant acts while in the company of other youths than when they are alone (see, for example, Erickson, 1971; Hindelang, 1971). Research on group delinquency dates back to the early twentieth century and the work of Thrasher (1936), Sutherland (1939), and Shaw and associates (1929).

Early delinquency research often focused on the idea that youthful misconduct was a result of peer influences. Differential association theory (Sutherland, 1939) proposed that much delinquent activity was the result of learning that took place in interactions between youths. Shaw and associates (Shaw et al., 1929; Shaw and McKay, 1942) focused heavily on the idea that juvenile misbehavior took place in groups. This theme of group behavior has persisted throughout the study of delinquency.

While studies claim a propensity for juveniles to act in groups, it is possible that much of the group dimension in offending is due to differential responses by society (Erickson, 1973; Feyerherm, 1980). The **group hazard hypothesis** proposes that delinquency committed in groups has a greater chance of being detected and acted upon by the juvenile and criminal justice systems (Erickson,

KEY TERMS

Boston Gun Project

Community-Wide Approach to Gang Prevention, Intervention, and Suppression Program

detached worker programs

foray

gang

ganging

Gang Resistance Education and Training (G.R.E.A.T.) Program

group hazard hypothesis

hybrid gangs

interstitial areas

National Youth Gang Survey (NYGS)

near group

pulling levers

rumble

STEP Act

wilding gangs

1973). In a study of 336 youths, Erickson (1973) reports that the group hazard hypothesis holds for select types of delinquent acts, especially more serious offenses. Group behavior simply may make recognition of a problem easier, thus more youths involved in group delinquency become involved with the juvenile justice system. The finding of high levels of group behavior in self-report surveys, however, suggests that the group hazard hypothesis is not a complete explanation of the group nature of delinquent activity.

Much of the interest in group delinquency revolves around the idea of juvenile gangs. Popular concern about gangs can be attributed to the finding that many youthful offenses are committed in concert with other juveniles. Another source for the public's concern may be the portrayal of gang behavior in the mass media. Movies and plays such as *The Blackboard Jungle*, *West Side Story*, and *Colors* dramatize the lure of gangs for youths and the aggressive nature of these groups of youths.

Interest in gangs has waxed and waned over the years. From the 1950s to the early 1960s there was a great deal of attention paid to gang delinquency. This interest subsided in the late 1960s, possibly due to the shift in attention to broader concerns over the social order, such as the Vietnam War, the economy, and racial unrest (Bookin-Weiner and Horowitz, 1983). New theoretical orientations also shifted interest from the offenders to the structure of society and its systems of social control. As a result, gang problems did not retain their priority as research issues. Not until the late 1980s did we see a renewed interest in gangs and gang behavior. Gang researchers attribute the renewed interest to the escalation of gang violence and the belief that gangs are the driving force behind growing drug problems, particularly crack cocaine.

GANGS DEFINED

While there has been a great deal of interest and research in gang activity, no single definition of a gang has developed. In general, the term **gang** has referred to groups that exhibit characteristics setting them apart from other affiliations of juveniles. Various researchers have proposed different definitions of a gang.

In one of the earliest gang definitions, Thrasher (1936) defined a gang as:

> an interstitial group originally formed spontaneously, and then integrated through conflict. It is characterized by the following types of behavior: meeting face to face, milling, movement through space as a unit, conflict, and planning. The result of this collective behavior is the development of tradition, unreflective internal structure, *esprit de corps*, solidarity, morale, group awareness, and attachment to a local territory (p. 57).

This definition introduced a number of key ideas. First, a gang was a specific form of a group. Second, what made these groups different from others was a system of activity and behavior that included conflict and mutual support of members. Finally, gangs were found in those areas of a city that were deteriorating and in a state of disorganization (**interstitial areas**). Gangs, therefore, were seen by Thrasher as a unique phenomenon of the poor, inner-city, immigrant areas of the early twentieth century.

Today, most definitions include the need for society to recognize the group as a threat and for the group to be involved in some degree of criminal/delinquent activity. The need for official recognition as a threat is evident in the definition used by the **National Youth Gang Survey (NYGS)** (2000), which defines a youth gang as:

> a group of youths or young adults in [the] jurisdiction that you or other responsible persons in your agency or community are willing to identify or classify as a "gang."

The NYGS specifically excludes motorcycle gangs, hate groups, prison gangs, or gangs composed exclusively of adults from it work.

Klein (1971) offers perhaps the most widely accepted definition. He claims that a gang refers to:

> any denotable adolescent group of youngsters who (a) are generally perceived as a distinct aggregation by others in their neighborhood, (b) recognize themselves as a denotable group (almost invariably with a group name) and (c) have been involved in a sufficient number of delinquent incidents to call forth a consistent negative response from neighborhood residents and/or enforcement agencies (p. 13).

The degree to which a group must be deviant before being considered a gang, however, is not clear-cut. Where Klein requires "a sufficient number of delinquent incidents," Huff (1993) needs "frequent and deliberate" illegal activities. A more extreme view posits that "violence" is the key element denoting a gang (Yablonsky, 1962). Violence, however, is not universally accepted as critical to defining a gang.

Curry and Decker (1998) identify six elements typical in most gang definitions: group, symbols, communication, permanence, turf, and crime (see Table 5.1). Being a group is perhaps the easiest of the elements to understand, although most definitions require a minimum number of members. Symbols serve to provide the group with an identity. These elements often are developed for internal use and may not convey meaning outside the group. The symbols also may be used in communication between and among gangs, their members, and others. The development of symbols and unique forms of communication can contribute to the longevity or permanence of the gang. As groups gain permanence they become harder to combat and dismantle. The element of turf, while common, is not as universal as the other elements because there are many examples of gangs that do not claim a physical territory. The final element, crime, is the most important, because group involvement in criminal activities is key to distinguishing a gang from other groups of people who may use the other elements, such as college fraternities and the Boy Scouts (Curry and Decker, 1998).

Table 5.1   Typical Elements of a "Gang" Definition

GROUP	usually a specified minimum number of members, certainly more than two
SYMBOLS	clothes, hand signs, colors, etc. which serve to indicate membership
COMMUNICATION	verbal and nonverbal forms, such as made up words, graffiti, hand signals, etc.
PERMANENCE	gangs must persist over time, generally at least one year or more
TURF	territory claimed and/or controlled by the gang (not as common in many definitions)
CRIME	involvement in criminal behavior

Source: Compiled from G.D. Curry and S.H. Decker (1998). *Confronting Gangs: Crime and Community*. Los Angeles: Roxbury.

That a single definition of a gang has not been agreed upon should be clear to the reader. The term *gang* has different meanings to different individuals, in different locations, at different times. What is common about gangs is the perception that they pose some form of threat to the safety of others.

EARLY GANG RESEARCH

Interest in gangs formed a good portion of the empirical and theoretical research prior to the mid-1960s. Much of the early research on gangs focused on describing the gangs and examining the daily workings of these groups. The research relied to a great extent on participant observation techniques. This research approach involved going out and observing the gangs on a daily basis. Such analysis provided a first-hand look at the structure and behavior of the gangs under study.

Thrasher's Gangs

Perhaps the most noted of the early studies of gangs was that of Frederick Thrasher. Thrasher (1936) studied 1,313 gangs with roughly 25,000 members in Chicago. He noted that the beginnings of gangs were found in spontaneous play groups within the interstitial areas of town that were characterized by a large amount of transiency, great numbers of immigrant youths, poor living conditions, and a state of social disorganization. These ideas were simple extensions of the early work of Shaw et al. (1929), Shaw and McKay (1942), and the Chicago School. The gangs supplied needed inter-action and social contact for the youths, which were not supplied by fami-lies or other social institutions.

Thrasher also viewed gangs as an outgrowth of innocent, everyday behavior among adolescents. Spontaneous play groups provided the basis and possibility for conflict. The groups provided a feeling of belonging and togetherness for the participants. The development of leadership, cohe-sion, and conflict served to strengthen the spontaneous groups and the establishment of a gang.

Thrasher (1936) did not see gangs as a stable or permanent entity. The development of gangs, or **ganging**, was a continuous process. Gangs were comprised mostly of juveniles between the ages of 11 and 17, and few members remained in gangs past young adulthood due to the movement into marriage and legitimate employment. Change in gangs was due to the maturing of individual members, the movement of members out of the immediate community, and the ability of the gang to provide meaningful activity for its members. While the specific make-up of the gang changed, many gangs would survive by replacing old members with new recruits. The recruits would come from those youths residing in the territory controlled by the gang.

Gang activity very often centered on conflict within the individual gang and between different gangs. According to Thrasher (1936), conflict helped build *"esprit de corps"* and unity among the gang's members. Within group disputes settled through conflict provided a basis for common values, loyalty, and cohesion among the membership. Successful conflict also pro-vided the individual group member with prestige and status. Conflict with other gangs brought about increased cohesion among group members and helped to draw the gang into a more formal, organized, and long-term sys-tem of interaction.

The gang was a means for youths in disorganized, inner-city areas to gain acceptance and exert some power over their situation. Gangs were not a planned response to problems in the neighborhoods by the youths. Instead, gangs were formed from the spontaneous play groups in which the youths found themselves.

Bloch and Neiderhoffer: Gangs as a Natural Response

Twenty years after Thrasher's (1936) monumental work, Bloch and Nei-derhoffer (1958) expanded on many of his ideas. Where Thrasher viewed gangs as primarily a lower-class juvenile phenomenon, Bloch and Neider-hoffer proposed that gangs were different from other juvenile groups sim-ply by a matter of degree. The gang provided its members with status, success, and feelings of belonging that they were not being provided by the larger society (Bloch and Neiderhoffer, 1958). Lower-class youths, who made up most gangs, were simply striving to succeed in the same sense as middle- and upper-class youths. Their social position, however, led them into situations that made gang behavior an acceptable alternative.

The organization of the gang was not greatly different from that portrayed by Thrasher (1939). Gangs developed leadership, cohesion, loyalty, and support through their daily activities. Bloch and Neiderhoffer (1958), however, saw gangs as somewhat more fragile in terms of their longevity. The loss of a leader was seen as bringing about the dissolution of the gang. The gang was viewed as having less permanence than those studied by Thrasher. Despite this departure in views, both studies saw the gang as providing needed social support and status for participating youths.

Yablonsky: Near Groups

A different view of gangs is found in Yablonsky's (1962) explanation of gang formation and participation. First, he concentrates mainly on violent gangs whose activity focuses on violence and aggression. The violent gang strives for emotional gratification through hostile actions toward gang members and nonmembers. It also provides a sense of power for the participating individuals. Second, Yablonsky repudiates the idea that a gang is a well-organized group. Instead, he sees the violent gang as a **near group**, characterized by a relatively short lifetime, little formal organization, a lack of consensus between members, a small core of continuous participants, self-appointed leadership (as opposed to group-approved), and limited cohesion. Most "members" of the gang participate on the fringe and become involved only when individual or group violence is indicated. Self-aggrandizement, not group issues, is the major concern for gang members. This near group view is restricted only to the violent gangs in Yablonsky's (1962) discussion. Other gangs may reflect the more classic portrayal found in other writings, although Yablonsky would argue that the violent "near group" is the dominant form of gang in society.

THE EXTENT OF GANG MEMBERSHIP

Measuring gang delinquency and/or gang involvement is not an easy task. A number of problems arise when attempting to assess the extent of gang membership. First, there is no single, accepted definition of what constitutes a gang. Any attempt to measure gang membership across jurisdictions, therefore, runs the risk of collecting data that reflect different problems or groups. This problem persists even when a survey provides a definition for agencies to use (such as the NYGS), because the agency records typically reflect a local definition and the information is not reclassified to correspond to the desired definition before it is submitted. Second, many agencies classify individuals as gang members only if the individual self-identifies as such (Egley et al., 2004). Many youths may not claim gang membership, even if they fit a legal or other definition of a gang member.

Third, many jurisdictions may actively deny the existence of gangs and not collect any data on gangs, thus any count would be an undercount. Similarly, jurisdictions may fail to respond to surveys because they do not collect data (even if they recognize they have a problem) or do not keep special enumerations of "gang crime" separate from general crime. Despite these, and other, problems/issues, many attempts have been made to assess the extent of gangs and gang membership.

Table 5.2 offers a number of estimates on the extent of gangs and gang membership. The first of these estimates by Miller (1975) is considered the modern benchmark for assessing the extent of gang membership. Miller (1975) surveyed 159 professionals from 81 agencies in 12 major U.S. cities (New York, Chicago, Los Angeles, Philadelphia, Houston, Detroit, Baltimore, Washington, Cleveland, San Francisco, St. Louis, and New Orleans). Using a very strict definition of gangs, Miller (1975) reported an estimated 760 gangs with more than 28,000 members in six of the cities. Using a more liberal definition of gangs that included simple group behavior, the estimates jumped to 2,700 gangs with 81,500 members. Miller notes that his figures probably underrepresent the actual number of gangs in the target cities and do not include the number of gangs and members found in other American cities.

Table 5.2   **Estimates of the Number of Gangs and Gang Members**

	# of Gangs	# of Members
Miller (1975)—6 cities		
low estimates	700	28,450
high estimates	2,700	81,500
Spergel et al. (1999)—45 cities	1,400	121,000
Curry et al. (1993)—79 cities	4,881	≈250,000
OJJDP (1997)—3,440 jurisdictions	23,388	≈665,000
Egley and Arjunan (2002)—2,542 jurisdictions	24,500	>772,000
Egley and Major (2004)—2,182 jurisdictions	21,500	731,500

The last three sets of figures in Table 5.2 are from successive versions of the NYGS. Since 1995, the National Youth Gang Center (NYGC) has conducted annual surveys to gauge the extent of gang behavior and responses to that activity. The NYGC surveys the police departments of all cities with a population greater than 25,000, sheriff and police departments of all suburban counties in the United States, and randomly selected police and sheriff's departments serving small towns (between 2,500 and 24,999 population) and rural counties. More than 2,000 law enforcement agencies are surveyed each year. As can be seen in the figures, the number of gangs and gang members reported in the NYGS is substantial. Data from the 2000 NYGS reveal an estimated 24,500 gangs with almost three-quarters of a million members (Egley and Arjunan, 2002). Results from 2002 (Egley and Major, 2004) show a slight reduction in both the number of gangs and gang members, but the figures are still substantial.

Gangs appear in virtually all areas of the country, and in both big and small cities and counties (see Table 5.3). The data show that all cities of 250,000 population and greater report having gangs, with the percent of cities reporting gangs decreasing with the size of the population. Similarly, the number of gangs and gang members is greatest in the larger cities and decreases with the population size and the move to more rural locations.

Table 5.3   Percent of Agencies Reporting Gang Activity by City/County Categories

	Cities				Counties	
	250,000+	100,000-249,999	50,000-99,999	2,500-49,999	Suburban	Rural
Reporting Gangs	100.0%	92.0%	74.8%	33.5%	44.2%	15.2%
# Gangs:						
<4	4.5%	8.7%	23.2%	57.8%	27.1%	53.5%
4-6	1.5%	17.4%	27.9%	20.2%	18.3%	29.6%
7-15	10.4%	30.2%	30.4%	9.8%	21.9%	9.9%
16-30	16.4%	21.5%	8.3%	2.9%	10.1%	2.8%
>30	61.2%	14.8%	2.9%	0.0%	9.8%	0.0%
# Members:						
<51	1.5%	12.1%	26.4%	55.5%	27.5%	59.2%
51-200	6.0%	20.8%	29.3%	12.7%	19.0%	21.1%
201-500	9.0%	20.1%	13.0%	5.8%	7.8%	1.4%
501-1000	9.0%	14.8%	8.3%	0.0%	2.9%	0.0%
>1000	61.2%	16.8%	4.3%	0.0%	8.8%	0.0%

Source: Constructed by authors from data reported in A. Egley (2005). *Highlights of the 2002-2003 National Youth Gang Surveys.* Washington, DC: Office of Juvenile Justice and Delinquency Prevention.

Despite the development of standardized surveys and growing interest in documenting gang membership, the figures are suspect. Many of the concerns and issues noted earlier have the potential of biasing any results. Spokespersons for the Gang Investigators Network suggest that nonresponse by many police agencies may be reducing the reported number of gang members by 200,000 or more (Johnson, 2005).

The annual nature of the NYGS also allows an inspection of trends in gang activity. Where comparison across studies, such as those in Table 5.2, can be made, they reflect different methodologies and definitions. At least with the NYGS, the methods and definitions remain stable over time. The trend data (see Figure 5.1) reveal that while the presence of gang problems has remained at 100 percent for the largest cities, these has been a general decrease in the percent of jurisdictions reporting gang problems for all other community sizes. The greatest reductions appear in the smallest cities and suburban and rural counties.

Where national surveys provide global estimates, they typically fail to put the problem into any context. That is, what proportion of the juvenile population participate in gangs? More localized examinations of the gang problem

A group of youths demonstrate some signs that are generally used by gang members. While the proportion of youths claiming membership to gangs varies from place to place, it is clear that a small but significant portion of youths are involved in gangs.

provide some insight to this question. Mays, Fuller, and Winfree (1994), surveying junior and senior high school students in southeast New Mexico, report that 20 percent claim gang membership, and an additional 25 percent indicate a desire to be in a gang. Thornberry and Burch (1997) find that 30 percent of the youths in the Rochester (NY) Youth Development Study claim gang membership at some point prior to high school graduation. Many studies, however, report smaller proportions of youths claiming gang membership. Based on a study of Denver youths over a five-year period of time, Esbensen and Huizinga (1993) report that less than 7 percent of the respondents in any given year could be classified as gang members. Similarly, Esbensen and his colleagues (2001) note that only 16.8 percent of the eighth grade respondents in the G.R.E.A.T. evaluation (discussed later) claimed past membership in gangs. Finally, slightly more than 10 percent of the junior and senior high students in one midwestern urban area claim to be gang members (Lab and Clark, 1994).

Three clear results emerge from attempts to measure gang participation. First, gangs are found throughout the United States, in both large and small cities, and both urban and rural areas. Second, the scope of the gang problem is large. Finally, the majority of youths do not belong to gangs and probably never will. While the proportion claiming membership varies from one site to another, a small but significant percent of youths do claim gang membership.

Figure 5.1   Trend in Gang Problems (percent jurisdictions)

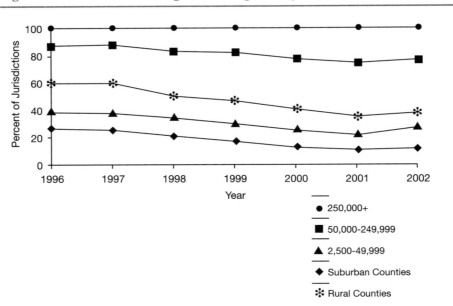

Source: Computed by authors from A. Egley and A.K. Major (2004). "Highlights of the 2002 National Youth Gang Survey." *OJJDP Fact Sheet*. Washington, DC: Office of Juvenile Justice and Delinquency Prevention; and A. Egley, J.C. Howell, and A.K. Major (2004). "Recent Patterns of Gang Problems in the United States: Results from the 1996-2002 National Youth Gang Survey." In F. Esbensen, S.G. Tibbetts, and L. Gaines (eds.), *American Youth Gangs at the Millennium*. Long Grove, IL: Waveland.

CHARACTERISTICS OF GANGS

Research over the past 30 years has provided a great deal of information on gangs. Unfortunately, there is as much disagreement as agreement on many issues. As with the definition of a gang, questions still exist concerning characteristics of gang membership, gang organizational structure, and gang migration. The following pages attempt to synthesize the diverse literature and provide a general view of gangs in today's society.

Age

Most early research portrayed the typical gang member as a teenage adolescent (Cooper, 1967; Kanter and Bennett; 1968; Klein, 1971; Miller, 1975; Robin, 1967; Short and Strodbeck, 1965). Miller's (1975) national survey showed that the peak age years tend to fall in the mid-teen age group. The fact that gangs often used schools as recruiting grounds (Hutchinson and Kyle, 1993) added to the youthful dominance in most gangs. This does not mean, however, that younger or older individuals have been excluded from gang membership.

Research since the mid-1980s (see, for example, Hagedorn, 1988; Horowitz, 1983; Howell, 1997; Klein and Maxson, 1989; Moore, 1993; Spergel et al., 1990; Toy, 1992) shows that the age range of gang members has expanded, particularly at the older end. NYGS data show that individuals age 18 or older make up 50-60 percent or more of all gang members. This suggests that gangs are retaining their members into young adulthood. The lack of meaningful employment opportunities, coupled with potentially lucrative gang behavior, is one reason for individuals to retain their gang membership into their twenties and thirties (Moore, 1991).

Social Class

Most studies find that the vast majority of gangs are found in lower-class areas and are comprised of lower-class juveniles. The lower-class nature of gangs finds a great deal of support in the early examinations and explanations of ganging behavior. Thrasher's (1936) definition of gangs relies heavily on the physical location of the groups in the lower-class, deteriorating areas of the city. Subsequent analyses paint a similar picture of gang behavior through explanations of deviance heavily reliant on the conflict between lower-class individuals and dominant middle-class society (Cloward and Ohlin, 1960; Cohen, 1955; Miller, 1958). More recent studies suggest that gang delinquency is no longer restricted to the inner city (Johnstone, 1981; Spergel, 1984). The growth of gangs in suburban and rural areas provides further evidence that gang behavior is not restricted to lower-class, inner-city areas.

A separate phenomenon appearing in the literature involves middle-class gangs. Such gangs are in opposition to the usual view of gang membership and causes of ganging. Middle-class youths are not faced with the same degree of blocked success as lower-class juveniles. Lowney (1984) views the middle-class gang more as a "near group" along the lines of Yablonsky (1958). **Wilding gangs** fit this "near group" image and, while not as disadvantaged as other youths, these groups strike out at what they perceive as inequalities and infringements on their rights by other ethnic groups (Cummings, 1993). Such middle-class gangs typically do not have well-defined roles, they lack cohesion, and much of the group activity revolves around casual interaction. While many middle-class groups do not fit the traditional image of a gang, the similarity between members and the participation in group-organized behavior leads some to conclude that the youths are a gang (Lowney, 1984). These gangs tend to be less numerous and typically are centered around less violent behavior than their lower-class counterparts.

Race and Ethnicity

Gangs do not appear to be reserved for any particular ethnic or racial groups. Virtually all races and ethnic groups have provided gang delinquents over the years, although different racial/ethnic groups have dominated at different points in time. Thrasher's (1936) gangs consisted mainly of white youths of European descent. Evaluations in the 1950s and 1960s tended to report greater numbers of black gangs. Most recent studies (e.g., National Alliance of Gang Investigators Associations, 2005; National Youth Gang Center, 2000) have found a predominance of Hispanic gang members. Today, whites and other ethnic groups are in the clear minority.

The prevalence of Hispanic and black gangs is clearly indicated in reports of gang investigators from across the United States. In a recent report, the National Alliance of Gang Investigators Associations (NAGIA) (2005) lists gang presence by region. Table 5.4 presents the percent of jurisdictions that report high or moderate presence of various gangs in their areas. The bulk of the listed gangs are of Hispanic make-up, with black gangs making up most of the remaining gangs.

Table 5.4   **Percent of Jurisdictions Reporting High or Moderate Gang Presence by Region**

Gang	Northeast	South	Midwest	West
Bloods	54.9%	23.7%	12.5%	24.5%
Latin Kings	37.2%	12.1%	33.0%	
United Blood Nation	25.5%			
Crips	37.3%	30.1%	12.5%	36.4%
MS-13	11.7%	19.1%	9.1%	
Asian Gangs	11.8%	12.7%	30.8%	
Sur-13	24.9%	30.6%	72.0%	
Gangster Disciples	15.6%	39.8%		
Vice Lords	25.0%			
Black Gangster Disciples	18.2%			
Nortenos	35.0%			
18th St.	26.6%			
Skinheads	26.6%			
Mexican Mafia	24.5%			
La Nuestra Familia	12.6%			

Source: Compiled by authors from National Alliance of Gang Investigators Associations (2005). *National Gang Threat Assessment.* Washington, DC: Bureau of Justice Assistance.

Traditionally, gangs tended to be homogeneous in terms of race and ethnicity (Klein, 1971; Short and Strodbeck, 1965; Spergel, 1966; Thrasher, 1936). That is, there were relatively few gangs that had white, black, Hispanic, and Asian members all in the same gang. Part of the reason for this was the similarity between the youths that prompted them to come together as a group. If, as some theorists suggested, gangs are an outgrowth of spontaneous play groups, it would be natural for like individuals to join together and participate in joint activities. Gang delinquency can be seen as a simple extension of other daily activities.

Today, there is a developing trend toward hybrid gangs. The term **hybrid gangs** generally refers to gangs that are mixed racially or ethnically, but these gangs also can be characterized in other ways. For example, members may belong to more than one gang, or different gangs may cooperate with one another in some endeavor (Starbuck, Howell, and Lindquist, 2001). These gangs also may not fit the traditional definition of a gang and may not claim turf or utilize colors, signs, or other symbols typically considered important in recognizing gang behavior. While most gangs remain racially and ethnically homogeneous, Starbuck, Howell, and Lindquist (2001) note that roughly one-third of the gangs identified in the 1998 NYGS fit the definition of a hybrid gang.

Females and Gangs

Traditional research on gangs has been devoted almost exclusively to the role of males. This is due primarily to the failure of females to contribute to any large extent to gang membership or activity. Thrasher's (1936) path-breaking study of 1,313 gangs found only five or six female gangs over the course of his study. Most other research or theories on gangs (e.g., Bloch and Neiderhoffer, 1958; Cohen, 1955; Miller, 1958; Yablonsky, 1962) ignored the participation of females. Recent NYGS reports reveal that roughly 10 percent of all gang members are female. Similarly, the number of female gangs is also very small, Only 2 percent of all gangs in the United States are female-dominated (i.e., 50% or more of the members are female) (National Youth Gang Center, 2000). While the number of female-dominated gangs is greater in more populated areas, the prevalence of such gangs remains about the same.

Table 5.5   **Female-Dominated Youth Gangs, 1998**

Population Size	Number	Percent
250,000 and over	120	2
100,000-249,000	46	2
50,000-99,999	29	1
25,000-49,999	34	2
10,000-24,999	13	2
Less than 10,000	3	1
Overall	245	2

Source: National Youth Gang Center (2000). *1998 National Youth Gang Survey: Summary*. Washington, DC: Office of Juvenile Justice and Delinquency Prevention.

The overwhelming dominance of male gangs found in law enforcement data (such as the NYGS) is not mirrored in other sources of information. Other research shows that while there are still more male gangs and gang members, there is a greater presence of females in gangs. Esbensen and Huizinga (1993) report that at least 20 percent of the gang membership in Denver is female. Data from the Rochester Youth Development Study show a higher prevalence of gang membership among females than males (Bjerregaard and Smith, 1993). Fagan (1990), Campbell (1990), and Esbensen and Osgood (1997) claim that females comprise roughly one-third of gang members. Curry et al. (1993) uncovered more than 7,000 female gang members in 27 cities. In many cases the females are still part of auxiliary groups (Monti, 1993) and respond to the mandates and activities of their male counterparts (Campbell, 1984, 1990; Miller 1995). This auxiliary status of female gangs is most clearly seen in the adoption of similar names to the dominant male gangs (i.e., Disciples and Lady Disciples).

There are indications of growing numbers of autonomous female gangs with their own leadership and separate meetings, which operate independently from the male gang in many instances (Campbell, 1984; Fishman, 1988; Moore, 1991). Female gang members are known to act as lookouts and to carry weapons for male members, as well as participate in their own deviant activities (Fishman, 1988). Indeed, female gang members tend to participate in many of the same forms of deviance as males, including drug use and violence (Bjerregaard and Smith, 1993; Campbell, 1990; Decker and Van Winkle, 1996; Fishman, 1988).

Organization and Size

Gangs tend to have some type of internal organization that affects the activities of its members, the status of those members, and the decision-making processes of the group (Bloch and Neiderhoffer, 1958; Curry and Decker, 1998; Thrasher, 1936; Yablonsky, 1962). The degree of formality and control exercised by the gang varies greatly from gang to gang. Gangs that are more entrepreneurial tend to have a more formal hierarchical structure. Territorial gangs are more loosely organized and have an informal structure (see, for example, Sanders, 1994). Knox (1991) offers a typology of gangs that reflects diversity in organization (see Table 5.6) from loosely knit groups with no clear structure or leadership to large "formalized gangs" that have stable leadership and formal rules and regulations.

Table 5.6   Knox's Gang Typology

Pre-Gang	small, loose knit, lacks label, no criminal activity, unstable leadership
Emergent Gang	informal organization, small group, recognized as gang, developing leadership, minor offending
Crystallized Gang	larger group, formal leadership and rules, community recognition as gang, active criminal involvement, gun use
Formalized Gang	large, interstate, use of automatic weapons, stable leadership, organized crime, formal rules and regulations

Source: Constructed by authors from G.W. Knox (1991). *An Introduction to Gangs*. Berrien Springs, MI: Vande Vere.

At the heart of most gangs is a single core of devoted members. This core may vary in size but is always much smaller than the purported size of the entire gang. The majority of the gang usually reflects a large body of fringe members who rarely take part in decisionmaking and participate in gang activities only at selected times. Gangs that claim memberships of 100 and greater are probably counting a large number of fringe members.

The core of the gang provides the leadership and decision-making body of the group. Not all gangs, however, have the same leadership structure (Kelling, 1975). In some groups, leadership is provided by a single individual determined according to the talents of the core members. Physical prowess usually determines who becomes the leader of the gang, but this is only a general statement. Other gangs have highly differentiated leadership roles in which different talents call for varied leadership according to the present needs of the group. Fights and violence will call on the best fighter. Criminal activity for profit may require the efforts of another youth who knows more about committing the crime and fencing the goods. Internal conflict may necessitate the efforts of someone who can negotiate and come up with alternative solutions. The extent of such specialization is determined by the abilities of the core members and the needs of the group. Still other gangs may vest leadership in different individuals for each subgroup of the gang or may have a very informal leadership structure in which no clear leaders can be identified (Sanders, 1994).

Besides the core group, many gangs include a range of different subgroups (Miller, Geertz, and Cutter, 1961). This is especially true in recent years as we see gang members from different age groups, as well as more intergenerational gangs (Hutchinson and Kyle, 1993; Moore, 1991, 1993). Often, the subgroups are based on the age of the gang members. A simple form of organization may have only three membership groups—young "wannabes," the core of the gang, and "old guard" members. The different subgroups of a gang may be identified by various names or labels such as PeeWees, Juniors, Seniors, or Old Heads. It is important to note that this tripartite view of a gang is only a simple presentation. Various gangs may have a more complicated system of subgroups, including female auxiliaries or affiliations with gang chapters in other areas of a city. The actual organization varies greatly from gang to gang and place to place. ·

Gang Migration

One of the oft-mentioned "facts" about recent gang behavior is that of gangs migrating from place to place. Typically, this discussion centers around the idea that gangs are deliberately moving and setting up chapters in other places for the purpose of selling drugs. Support for this assertion is most often anecdotal and relies on the simple observation of the same or similar gang names, colors, graffiti, or behavior from place to place. Solid proof of gang migration, however, is not available.

For the most part, the apparent migration is more accidental than planned. Skolnick, Bluthenthal, and Correl (1993) note that most gang travel and migration begins with non-gang, non-crime-related activities. Visits to family members in other places or the relocation of a family are typical means by which gang members find themselves in a new environment. In essence, the gang migration is an unintended consequence of normal family behavior. The connection between gangs in different cities, usually considered a result of planned migration, is also more illusory than real (Huff, 1993; Spergel et al., 1990; Valdez, 2000). Survey respondents note that most cities experience gang problems before any significant level of migration is apparent (Maxson, Woods, and Klein, 1996). While gangs in different cities may have the same name, colors, and symbols, these are borrowed from other places. The appearance of established gangs, such as the Crips and Bloods, in cities with no history of gang problems can often be attributed to the arrival of a single gang member who is displaced through family migration.

That there may be gang "chapters" in different cities cannot be totally discounted. Indeed, as competition for drug territory has increased, some gangs have attempted to move operations into smaller cities. This movement, however, is typically limited and does not indicate state-wide or country-wide organizations of juvenile gangs. One possible, and plausible, explanation for the apparent "franchising" of gangs in different cities is that more sophisticated drug dealers and organizations recruit youths and emerging gangs as local "employees" in the drug trade. Migration for drug selling, therefore, is more an illusion than a reality. Indeed, low migration levels result in relatively small impacts on a city's existing drug problems (Maxson, Woods, and Klein, 1996). For the most part, juvenile gangs are not as entrepreneurial as the public likes to think.

Summary

Attempts to delineate what a gang looks like are doomed to failure. We must recognize that gangs, like any other collective of individuals, will take on different characteristics based on the desires of the members and the underlying goal of the group. Some gangs may be highly structured with many members, clear leadership, and set agendas. Other gangs may be loose confederations of a few individuals who interact on a sporadic basis. Names, colors, territory, leadership, and other components of gangs are in themselves only potential indicators of ganging. Just as the general characteristics of gangs vary, so do the behavioral tendencies of these groups.

WHY DO YOUTHS JOIN GANGS?

Gang members come together and associate with one another for a wide array of reasons. The early work of Thrasher (1936) suggests that the gang provides inner-city youths with a sense of belonging and acceptance. Several early writers (Bloch and Neiderhoffer, 1958; Cohen, 1955; Miller, 1958) argue that the relative disadvantages of being a lower-class youth faced with middle-class goals leads youths to joining gangs as a response to their inability to succeed through normal channels. The lower-class youths find support and unity with others facing similar problems, and gang activity can offer status and a sense of success not available elsewhere. The extent to which the gang is entrepreneurial may provide the members with an income (possibly significant) that is otherwise not available.

Table 5.7	Reasons for Gang Membership
	A Sense of Belonging
	Financial Gain/Rewards
	Status
	Social Support
	Improved Self-esteem
	Feelings of Family
	Group Cohesion
	Acceptance
	Social Activities

More recent research on gangs, particularly that dealing with different racial and ethnic gangs (Horowitz, 1983; Moore, 1991, 1993; Sanders, 1994; Vigil, 1993, 1997; Zatz, 1985) and Asian (Chin, 1990; Chin, Fagan, and Kelly, 1992; Huff, 1993; Joe and Robinson, 1980; Sanders, 1994; Toy, 1992), also portray gang membership and activity as a result of life in lower-class communities. Many gang members are recent immigrants or are first-generation Americans. The youths often face problems with success in schools and other social situations. Gang behavior is seen as an alternative to the lack of success and status faced by youths. Lower-class youths, regardless of ethnic or racial background, spend a good deal of time on the streets where they meet and interact with other youths. Education is provided through daily street activity.

The gang provides marginal ethnic youths with many of the same things desired by other youths. The gang offers its members a sense of belonging, self-esteem, and status, which may not be forthcoming at home (Moore, 1991; Vigil, 1993, 1997). Brown (1978) portrays the gangs as a form of extended family. This view of gangs is not unlike the explanations for gang behavior set forth in earlier analyses.

Similarly, explanations for female ganging have been rare but generally follow the same pattern of logic found for male gangs. Brown (1978), Short and Strodbeck (1965), and others have pointed to many of the same social factors associated with male gangs. Blocked opportunity, lack of success at school and home, lack of status, desire for belonging, abuse and family problems at home, and community disorganization were among the cited reasons for female gang participation (Bowker and Klein, 1983; Campbell, 1990; Miller, 2000; Moore, 1988). Welfare reform in the mid-1990s has been particularly problematic for females who are already marginalized in the work force and also have to care for children (Moore and Hagedorn, 2001). Gang membership and participation is one possible response to these increased pressures.

Clearly, juveniles who find themselves faced with poor opportunities for advancement, poverty, poor school performance, lack of familial support, or other factors may find support and acceptance in the gang. The increased intergenerational nature of gang membership also contributes to the growth and construction of gangs. Younger members are often siblings or offspring of current or past gang members. "Apprenticeship" periods for "wannabes" and initiation rituals help build the sense of belonging. The gang provides its members with things they do not get at home, school, or elsewhere.

The importance of a gang to its members can be seen in the level of group cohesion often found among the group. Many of the early writers view cohesion as an essential element of gangs (e.g., Bloch and Neiderhoffer, 1958; Thrasher, 1936; Vigil, 1993; Zevitz, 1993). Cohesion may arise out of different factors that lead to gang membership and activities of the gangs. Gang behavior, particularly conflict activity, is considered essential to building cohesion. Fights in defense of territory, a gang's honor, or an individual member can all strengthen a gang's organization and cohesion.

The extent of gang cohesion can be found in the names, territory, and other identifiers associated with different gangs. Many gangs choose identifying names for themselves that reflect their ethnic or racial backgrounds. Examples of such names include the Black Assassins and the Latin Kings. Names can also reflect the territory claimed by different gangs. Many gangs award the right to wear distinctive clothing to their members. This clothing typically includes the wearing of "colors" or jackets emblazoned with the group name or symbol. Graffiti is used for a variety of reasons, ranging from promoting an individual gang member's reputation to demarcating the territory controlled by a gang. It must be recognized, however, that these outward symbols do not in themselves guarantee cohesion. Indeed, use of names, colors, or graffiti only provide an indicator of cohesion. These features of a gang, however, demonstrate that the gang provides something of value to its members—a sense of belonging, status, feelings of success, financial gain, or something else.

GANG BEHAVIOR

The typical view of gang activity, especially as it has been portrayed in the media, has not changed much over the years. Gangs are portrayed as in constant violent confrontation with one another and with the general public. Contrary to this media portrayal, gangs participate in a variety of different behaviors. This does not mean that the gang fights and drive-by shootings are fictional. Such confrontations have taken place in the past and continue to occur today. The image, however, is distorted. Past and present research suggests that such violent confrontations are rare relative to other gang behavior. Indeed, gangs are involved in many nonviolent activities. Thrasher (1936) noted that many gangs supplied leisure activities, a forum for talk and play, and even gambling. Jankowski (1990) points out that gangs provide a forum for recreation, partying, and companionship.

When gang aggression does occur, it is not necessarily physical in nature. Miller, Gertz, and Cutter (1961) note that less than 7 percent of one gang's aggressive acts involved physical attacks, and none of those actions involved a weapon. Almost 94 percent of the aggression was verbal, and most did not contain anger (Miller, Gertz, and Cutter, 1961). Miller (1966) reported that gang sentiments in favor of violence are rarely manifested in actual physical expression.

While physical aggression may not dominate gang behavior, gangs are involved in significant numbers of crimes. One source of information involves surveys of law enforcement agencies. Estimates from law enforcement data reveal that almost 17,000 gangs were responsible for more than 580,000 offenses in 122 cities and eight counties in 1992 (Curry, Ball, and Decker, 1996).

That gangs are involved in criminal activity is an indisputable fact. Indeed, except for robbery, more than 50 percent of the law enforcement respondents in the 1998 NYGS claimed that some, most, or all of the gang members in their jurisdictions are involved in aggravated assaults, burglaries, motor vehicle thefts, larcenies, and drug sales (National Youth Gang Center, 2000). Similarly, the NAGIA survey (2005) notes high or moderate gang involvement in a significant percent of crimes in all regions of the United States (see Table 5.8). Clearly, criminal behavior by gangs and gang members is evident in data supplied by law enforcement agencies.

The extent of criminal behavior by gang members also can be addressed through self-report surveys. According to the Rochester Youth Development Survey, the 30 percent of respondents who claim gang membership also report committing 65 percent of the delinquent acts (Thornberry and Burch, 1997). More specifically, they report 69 percent of the violent acts and 68 percent of the property offenses. This criminal activity, therefore, more than doubles their representation in the survey (Thornberry and Burch, 1997). Finally, Spergel and colleagues (1990) point out that gang members are more criminally active than nonmembers, and commit three times the level of violence.

Table 5.8   **Percent of Jurisdictions Reporting High or Moderate Gang Involvement in Crime by Region**

Crime	Northeast	South	Midwest	West
Street Drug Sales	60.8%	53.2%	52.0%	73.5%
Firearms Possession	37.2%	35.3%	41.0%	
Vandalism/Graffiti	53.0%	44.5%	54.5%	82.5%
Felony Assault	43.2%	34.1%	43.2%	71.4%
Homicide	27.5%	20.2%	26.2%	44.1%
Burglary	31.4%	33.0%	37.5%	60.9%
Firearms Trafficking	29.4%	22.0%	30.7%	37.5%
Auto Theft	31.3%	33.5%	30.7%	67.9%
Intimidation/Extortion	21.6%	24.3%	30.7%	48.3%

Source: Compiled by authors from National Alliance of Gang Investigators Associations (2005). *National Gang Threat Assessment*. Washington, DC: Bureau of Justice Assistance.

Do Gangs Cause Delinquency?

Based on the level of gang-member delinquency, one could argue that the elimination of gangs would significantly reduce the level of youthful deviance. An alternative possibility, however, is that gangs simply attract already delinquent youths, rather than causing increased deviance. The delinquency, therefore, is independent of gang membership. Following this argument, Thornberry and colleagues (1993) identify three possible models of the delinquency–gang relationship—selection, social facilitation, and enhancement. The selection model maintains that gangs recruit or attract already delinquent youths. In this model the level of delinquency would be independent of gang status. Under the social facilitation model, belonging to a gang is the cause of increased deviance. Periods of gang membership, therefore, will result in delinquent activity not found during non-membership. Finally, the enhancement model strikes a middle ground in which gangs recruit delinquency-prone youths and enhance their deviance.

Two studies have sought to test these models of gang influence directly. Using panel data from the Denver Youth Survey, Esbensen and Huizinga (1993) report that gang members are indeed more delinquent while they are actively involved in the gang. At the same time, however, these youths also report higher levels of offending both before and after active gang participation. Thornberry and colleagues (1993) find that the gang–delinquency relationship varies according to the type of offense and the level of commitment to the gang. The social facilitation model fits for personal and drug-related offenses, while property offenses do not fit any of the models very well. In addition, youths who remain in the gangs for a longer period of time tend to increase their offending (the enhancement model) more than do transient gang members (Thornberry et al., 1993). What these two studies suggest is that the gang is not necessarily the cause of delinquent behavior. Rather, gang membership appears to add to an already established level of deviance by participating youths.

Gang Behavior and Types of Gangs

Not all gangs participate in the same types of deviant behavior as other gangs. Indeed, recent research shows that some gangs tend to specialize in some form of criminal activity. That same research even suggests that a few gangs exist primarily as a forum for criminal behavior, as opposed to a forum for more generalized group behavior. The identification of specific types of offending by gangs, however, is as elusive as identifying a single gang definition. Each gang may do something slightly different from every other gang.

Asian gangs, for instance, often appear to serve a definitive purpose for their members, and do so through a more narrow selection of criminal acts. A number of studies (Chin, Fagan, and Kelly, 1992; Huff, 1993; Toy, 1992) report that Asian gangs appear to be very profit-oriented and tend to restrict their deviant activities to those that bring a monetary return. Chin, Fagan, and Kelly (1992) show how extortion, primarily from Asian businesses, is a central focus of Asian youth gangs. Violence for these gangs is used only as a means to maintain financial control over an area and is not an end in itself (Chin, Fagan, and Kelly, 1992; Toy, 1992). Both Huff (1993) and Chin, Fagan, and Kelly (1992) claim that these gangs often have strong ties to organized crime, which directs both the financial dealings and the use of violence in the Asian communities.

Analyses of Chicano gangs portray a somewhat different picture. While these gangs are strongly territorial-based (Moore, 1991; Sanders, 1994; Vigil, 1993, 1997), there does not appear to be a strong entrepreneurial reason for control of the territory. Rather, control over territory or turf provides the youths with a sense of control. The territory also provides the gang with a delineated area from which it has almost exclusive rights to gang recruitment. Besides the territorial nature of Chicano gangs, these groups tend to be more heavily involved in drug use (Moore, 1991, 1993) and general deviance (Vigil, 1993).

In recent years, more atypical gangs have appeared in the literature. Two of these are skinhead gangs and tagger gangs. Skinheads advocate white supremacy and are portrayed as very violent and racist, although this is not true of all skinheads. They also often take an anti-government stance and advocate withdrawal from the dictates of the government, including taxes and all regulatory laws. Skinheads use violence primarily against those who are perceived as a threat to white supremacy (Wooden and Blazak, 2001). At the other extreme are tagger gangs, whose members often view themselves as urban artists. These youths try to have their art seen by as many people as possible, and do not view the graffiti as vandalism, denoting ownership of turf, or harmful to others. It is solely an expression of individuality and a means of gaining status (Wooden and Blazak, 2001).

Of the various types of deviance in which gang members participate, two claim the greatest amount of attention. These are drug violations and violence. This is true in the academic literature, among common citizens, and in societal responses to gang behavior.

Drug Activity

Drug activity is a major topic of discussion in relation to gang behavior. The NAGIA (2005:1) notes that "gangs . . . are the primary distributor of drugs throughout the United States." There is no doubt that many gang members use and sell drugs, and that drug sales are an integral part of some organized gangs. The degree to which gangs are involved in drugs, however, is highly variable. For example, drug sales in one gang may involve sales only among its own members, while another gang may be deeply involved in the drug trade throughout the community. Fagan (1990), in a survey of Los Angeles, San Diego, and Chicago gang members, finds that roughly 28 percent are rarely involved in drug use, while 35 percent are seriously involved in both use and sales. Much of the distribution of drugs may be tied to more organized, older gangs. Two examples of this would be outlaw motorcycle gangs (National Alliance of Gang Investigators Associations, 2005) and Jamaican posses (Gay and Marquart, 1993), which have emerged as organized forces for the distribution and sale of marijuana, cocaine, and other drugs in the United States. Research also shows that, while there is a great deal of drug use among youth gangs, the sale of drugs for profit by local gangs is highly variable (Decker and Van Winkle, 1994; Hagedorn, 1994; Mays, Fuller, and Winfree, 1994; Padilla, 1993).

Gang Violence

One clear trend in gang behavior has been an increase in the level of violence and physical aggression in recent years. Where much of the early research attempted to dispel the dominant myth of the centrality of violence in the gangs, more recent studies note that violence is on the rise. Miller (1975, 1982) notes that as early as the late 1970s there was a clear increase in the use of weapons and participation in physical confrontation. While confrontations appeared in the past, they were not a dominant activity and often occurred within the confines of the gang. Miller and associates (1961) noted that 70 percent of all aggressive gang activity was against members of the same gang. While recent research suggests that violence is now a more open activity directed at a greater array of targets, both inside and outside the immediate gang, the bulk of violence is still aimed at other gang members. Both Cohen (1969) and Miller (1975) find that roughly 60 percent of gang victims are themselves members of gangs. An additional 12 percent of the victims are non-gang peers.

The seriousness of the violence is also high as demonstrated by the number of gang-related killings. According to Miller (1975), Chicago and Los Angeles had a combined average of 81 gang-related killings in the early 1970s. By the late 1980s this average climbed to 187 (Block and Block, 1992; Meehan and O'Carroll, 1992), and in 1994, these cities combined for a total of more than 1,000 gang-related homicides (Howell, 1997). Data from the FBI Supplemental Homicide Reports show that more than 5 percent of all homicides from 1993-2003 were gang-related, and that between 7.1 and 9.9 percent of homicides committed with firearms were gang-related (Harrell, 2005). These figures are probably low estimates due to the lack of adequate data collection methods used by law enforcement in relation to gang problems (National Youth Gang Center, 2005).

Gang violence no longer conforms to the typical image of a **rumble** or gang fight. Rather, most violence appears as forays. A **foray** typically entails an attack by two or three youths upon a single member (or possibly a few members) of a rival gang. A typical form of attack is a "drive-by" shooting. For example, three members of the Bloods drive around a corner where a member of the Crips lives, they shoot from the car, and then speed away from the scene. A similar retaliatory foray by the Crips is the consequence of the Bloods' action. The foray becomes a self-perpetuating activity.

Modern gang violence differs from earlier portrayals in a number of ways. First, the violence appears to be more random, partly due to the use of automobiles and the willingness to attack when innocent bystanders are present. Second, the violence occurs more frequently through constant small forays rather than in the occasional large rumble. Third, the hit-and-run tactics of the foray make the violence appear more impersonal. Non-gang peers and other individuals who become victims may often be injured as a result of a foray that occurs on the street. Finally, gangs use lethal weapons, particularly firearms, more often.

Firearms and Gang/Delinquent Behavior

The role of firearms in increased levels of violence, whether by gang members or individual youths, is very clear. Sheppard and colleagues (2000) note that the great increases in juvenile homicides in the mid- to late-1980s and early-1990s was due to the increased availability and use of firearms by youths. From 1984 to 1993, there was a 158 percent increase in the age 15-24 homicide rate involving handguns (Sheppard et al., 2000). According to UCR data, almost nine out of 10 murder victims are age 18 or younger, and 65 percent of the murder victims are killed with a firearm (Snyder, 2000).

Besides looking at data on gun use in crime, it is possible to examine the extent to which juveniles carry or own weapons. According to a Centers for Disease Control and Prevention survey, 14 percent of all male youths claim to have carried a gun outside their home in the prior month (Office of Juvenile Justice and Delinquency Prevention, 1999). Several studies report that significant numbers of youths are threatened with a weapon at school or carry weapons to school for protection (see Kaufman et al., 1998; Lab and Clark, 1996; Sheley and Wright, 1993). Most studies place the level firearms in schools at better than 10 percent of the student body. Given the above, it is not surprising that there are a large number of juvenile offenses that involve firearms.

Firearms use by gang members is an even greater problem. According to the 1998 NYGS, more than one-half of the law enforcement respondents claim that gang members use firearms often (21%) or sometimes (32%) in assault crimes (National Youth Gang Center, 2000). Gang members are the most likely to own guns (Decker, Pennel, and Caldwell, 1997), and recruit youths who already own guns, and they are more likely to carry guns than are non-gang youths (Bjerregaard and Lizotte, 1995). As noted earlier, access to firearms has altered the confrontational approach of gangs from more face-to-face personal interaction to more impersonal drive-by shootings. The result of this use of lethal weapons by gangs is a much higher mortality rate among gang members when compared to the general population (Decker and Van Winkle, 1996; Morales, 1992).

Explaining Gang Behavior

The reasons behind gang behavior and violence are varied. An examination of different research studies provides different insights. The most prevalent reasons appear to be status, control of turf or territory, and financial gain. Each of these factors are interrelated. As noted earlier, most gang members are from the lower classes. Opportunities for legitimate success and for gaining status in the community are limited by the realities of the world—jobs are few, education seems irrelevant, many must quit school before graduation to help support the family, and male role models are missing due to the absence of fathers in the home, among other factors. The gang serves to provide a means of gaining status. Gang members can prove themselves on the street and are accepted for their contributions to the gang. They can gain honor through their allegiance to other gang members. They are provided with a sense of family and belonging that does not come from the broken, female-headed household. The need for belonging and status also appears in "wilding" gang activity, in which youths randomly attack individuals from a different ethnic background as a form of retaliation for reduced opportunities and perceived injustice (Cummings, 1993; Pinderhughes, 1993). Often, wilding gangs are composed of nonminority youths striking out at minorities.

Turf or territory, a second reason for violence, provides a sense of ownership and control, which often is denied the gang youth (Vigil, 1993). Overcrowded living conditions, frequent movement from place to place, lack of finances to purchase personal property, and other factors lead youths

to feel a lack of control. The turf is a means of exerting control and ownership. While it is not ownership in the legal sense of the term, such control helps
provide the feelings of status desired by the gang youth. Attacks on the turf
are seen as an attack on the property, honor, and status of the individual gang
members, and violence is used to protect the turf (Hutchinson and Kyle, 1993).

Financial gain is a third major reason for gang membership and activity. The lower-class gang youth is faced with a lack of legitimate job opportunities. The gang can provide training in criminal activity (such as robbery
and burglary), the opportunity for such criminal actions, and support for this
behavior. Trafficking in illegal drugs is a lucrative activity for the gangs. It
also brings about contact and opportunities with organized crime and a
means of increasing status in the gang and community. At the same time that
the drug trade has opened new doors for the gang members, it has also added
to the stakes in control of turf and the level of violence between gangs.

Drugs and gang violence are typically portrayed as going hand in hand.
Whether drug involvement is a driving force behind gang violence, however,
is not clear. Klein, Maxson, and Cunningham (1991) report little evidence that
drugs are more prevalent in gang homicides than non-gang homicides, and
violence is rare in both gang and non-gang drug arrests. Similarly, Maxson
(1995) notes that violence in drug sales is rare, occurring in roughly 5 percent of the cases. A recent review of studies also finds little support for a
drug–homicide connection in gang behavior (Howell, 1997b). Despite these
findings, there is no doubt that conflicts over drugs and sales territories do
escalate to violence. It is the extent to which such instances occur that needs
further exploration.

While the outward appearance of gang behavior is different from socially
acceptable activity, the reasons for the behavior are not much different
from those of most other persons. The gang youth values status, belonging,
ownership, control, and financial gain. These are major reasons behind the
behavior of nondeviant youths and adults. The gang has simply supplied alternative methods for achieving its ends.

Intervention with Gangs

Responding to gangs and gang problems is an area in which much work
remains to be done. Unfortunately, the first response by many cities to an
emerging gang problem is one of denial (Hagedorn, 1988). Cities often do
not want to admit that they have gangs. The outcome of such denial is the
emergence of a full-blown problem before the authorities are prepared to deal
with it. Once the problem is identified, a number of different responses have
been used to address the problem.

Spergel and Curry (1993), in the National Youth Gang Survey (NYGS),
identified five common intervention strategies (see Table 5.9). The approach
listed by 44 percent of the respondents as their primary form of response is

suppression, or the use of arrest, prosecution, incarceration, and other criminal justice system procedures. The intervention ranked second in primacy is social interventions (31.5%), followed by organizational change and development (10.9%) and community organization (8.9%). The approach listed as having the lowest ranking is opportunities provision. These results indicate that traditional criminal justice system responses are the most common responses to gang problems, while efforts to alter the social conditions that cause ganging are addressed the least. Interestingly, in an analysis of the perceived effectiveness of the five types of intervention strategies, Spergel and Curry (1993) report that opportunities provision is viewed as the most effective/promising approach, while suppression is seen as the least effective.

Table 5.9   **Gang Intervention Strategies**

Suppression	Includes any form of social control in which the criminal justice system (police, courts, or corrections) or society attempt to impose formal or informal limits on behavior
Social Intervention	Basically a social work approach to working with gangs in the neighborhoods (such as detached worker programs)
Organizational Change and Development	Deals with altering the organization(s) that respond(s) to gang problems, such as through the establishment of gang units or specialized training of its personnel
Community Organization	Efforts aimed at mobilizing the community toward self improvement and change, including both physical and social alterations
Opportunities Provision	Recognizing the lack of meaningful jobs and the training needed to succeed, and taking steps to change the problems; education, vocational training, and job placement are elements

Source: I.A. Spergel and G.D. Curry (1993). "The National Youth Gang Survey: A Research and Development Process." In Goldstein, A.P., and C.R. Huff (eds.), *The Gang Intervention Handbook* (pp. 359-400). Champaign, IL: Research Press.

Historically, criminal and juvenile justice system personnel have had the primary responsibility for addressing gang behavior. At one extreme this has been done through the simple application of the criminal code against offending youths. At the other end of the spectrum, law enforcement agencies have involved themselves in more social work functions, such as midnight basketball leagues and youth clubs. In between these extremes fall specialized gang units, conflict resolution/response teams, and similar activities. The following pages will address four approaches to gang problems, including detached worker programs, legal/law enforcement avenues, the G.R.E.A.T. program, and recent comprehensive initiatives.

Detached Worker Programs

Detached workers have been an integral part of many programs dealing with youths over the years. **Detached worker programs** place gang workers into the community and free the workers from heavy paperwork and administrative requirements (Klein, 1969). The workers are expected to spend considerable time in the neighborhoods, maintain more consistent contact with the gangs, and provide immediate assistance and input to the youths. Many programs rely on past gang members for workers. Klein (1971) notes that the strength of the program includes the ability to reach youths who normally are not contacted, the flexibility of workers to handle situations in unique ways, and the ability to establish confidential relationships with youths.

Unfortunately, many of these strengths also provide the basic weaknesses of the program (Klein, 1969). First, the flexibility of the workers may result in inconsistency among workers and a lack of clear focus. A more important problem is that close work with the groups may lead to increased gang cohesion through the provision of directed group activities and interaction. Third, the use of former gang members as workers provides mixed messages. While these individuals should have a good rapport and have intimate knowledge of gangs, contact with former rival gangs and gang members could cause friction and pose a danger to the worker. Finally, intensive contact with gangs often results in high turnover among the workers.

The impact of detached workers on gangs has been mixed. Klein (1969), in perhaps the most noted evaluation of such programs, noted that the detached workers in Los Angeles organized 113 sporting events, 90 outings, 16 service projects, and 14 self-help programs. However, in assisting the groups to find alternative behaviors, the project inadvertently caused greater cohesiveness and, indirectly, delinquent behavior (Klein, 1969). Greater contact between the gangs and a worker led to gangs becoming closer and more unified, and the gangs were more successful at recruiting new members. Additionally, these groups participated in greater numbers of delinquent acts after the intervention of the detached workers. Lundman's (1993) review of detached worker programs in various locations also pointed out the failure of this approach to reduce delinquency.

Recent proposals for intervention with gangs typically include a heavy detached worker component, although they may not use that terminology. Spergel's (1984, 1986) and Fox's (1985) discussions of gang interventions reveal a striking similarity with detached worker programs. Emphasis is placed on intimate contact with gang members, providing alternative lines of behavior, and serving as a resource for gangs. Based on Klein's earlier work, it could be argued that this approach is ill-fated.

Legal/Law Enforcement Changes

Increased concern about gangs has prompted the development of new organizational structures and the passage of new legislation as means of combating gang problems. Many police departments, particularly in large cities, have established specialized gang crime units (Curry et al., 1992). In support of such efforts, many states have passed legislation making gang affiliation a crime, or increasing penalties for gang-related criminal behavior. California's **STEP Act** (Street Terrorism Enforcement and Prevention) of 1988 effectively criminalizes membership in a street gang. Under STEP, the police can invoke civil penalties against gang members for associating with one another in public, promoting their gang, displaying gang symbols, and being involved in other similar gang behavior. Many states have enhanced the penalties for crimes committed as a result of or in connection to gang membership. Statutes such as those in Florida (Florida Statutes 874.01) and Georgia (Georgia Code 16-16-3) require harsher penalties for gang-related crimes. Despite such efforts, ganging has not abated.

Two recent evaluations look at the operations and effectiveness of specialized gang units. Katz and Webb (2003) report on units in Albuquerque, Las Vegas, Phoenix, and Inglewood (CA). Weisel and Shelly (2004) consider units in San Diego and Indianapolis. In all locations the formation of the units was in response to political pressure, and the operations of the units were generally separate from the rest of the police activities. Katz and Webb (2003) find the units rely mostly on routine police responses and receive little training specific to gangs and gang problems. In both analyses, activities to prevent the formation of gangs is lacking. Rather, most attention seems to be directed at intelligence gathering and investigations aimed at crimes committed by gangs. In general, in neither analysis is there evidence of the units having any significant impact on gangs, gang formation, or gang crime.

One approach that has received a great deal of attention in recent years is to have the police strictly enforce any and all codes and regulations (basically a suppression approach) in an attempt to change the behavior of a target group. This approach, referred to as **pulling levers**, is most notable in the **Boston Gun Project**, which targeted firearms use by gangs. Pulling levers simply seeks to deter behavior by taking a zero-tolerance stance with any transgressions (Cook, Moore, and Braga, 2002). For example, if a single gang member commits an offense with a firearm, the police inform the entire gang that they are subject to increased attention from police and the criminal justice system. Officers and other system personnel will enforce trespassing laws and curfews, frequently stop and question gang members, enforce vagrancy and loitering ordinances, check on and enforce probation and parole rules, seize illegal goods obtained through illegal activities, restrict plea bargaining, and impose the highest penalties possible for even the most minor transgressions (Kennedy, 1998). All of this represents a form of "legal harassment" that is meant to influence gangs and gang members to avoid the use of firearms. An evaluation of the Boston Gun Project reveals significant decreases in several offenses, including homicides, assaults with firearms, and other weapons offenses (Braga et al., 2001). The success of this approach has prompted several other jurisdictions to adopt similar programs (such as Project Excite in Richmond, Virginia).

The G.R.E.A.T. Program

The **Gang Resistance Education and Training (G.R.E.A.T.) Program** is the most recognizable prevention program targeting gangs. The program began in 1991 under a grant from the Bureau of Alcohol, Tobacco, and Firearms (ATF) (now called the Bureau of Alcohol, Tobacco, Firearms, and Explosives) to the Phoenix, Arizona, Police Department. Not unlike the Drug Abuse Resistance Education (D.A.R.E.) program, G.R.E.A.T. is taught by local police officers in middle schools. The original curriculum consisting of nine lessons was expanded to 13 one-hour lessons and is presented in middle schools. The goal of the program is to:

> Prevent youth crime, violence, and gang involvement while developing a positive relationship among law enforcement, families, and our young people to create safer communities (Bureau of Justice Assistance, 2005).

The thrust of the program is to provide youths with the necessary skills for identifying high-risk situations and resisting the pressure/allure of taking part in gangs and gang activity. Beyond targeting just ganging, program curricula are geared toward increasing self-esteem, changing attitudes, and eliminating participation in violent behavior. A key component of G.R.E.A.T. is to teach nonviolent conflict resolution techniques to the youths. The program has been adopted by schools throughout the United States. There is also a six-week program for fourth and fifth grades, a six-session family program, and a summer component that reinforces the materials learned in school and provides alternative activities to gang participants.

The original nine-week middle-school program underwent an extensive evaluation from 1995 to 2000. Esbensen and his colleagues utilized both cross-sectional and longitudinal data to check on program effectiveness. Esbensen and Osgood (1999) reported promising findings from the initial cross-sectional survey. Based on survey results from 5,935 eighth-grade students in 11 school districts, students who completed the G.R.E.A.T. curriculum report lower delinquency rates, more prosocial attitudes about the police and schools, and higher self-esteem (Esbensen and Osgood, 1999). While only a one-year follow-up, the results suggest that the program has an impact on ganging activity.

Figure 5.2   G.R.E.A.T. Middle School Curriculum

1. Welcome to G.R.E.A.T.
   - Program Introduction
   - Relationship Between Gangs, Violence, Drugs, and Crime

2. What's the Real Deal?
   - Message Analysis
   - Facts and Fiction About Gangs and Violence

3. It's About Us
   - Community
   - Roles and Responsibilities
   - What You Can Do About Gangs

4. Where Do We Go From Here?
   - Setting Realistic and Achievable Goals

5. Decisions, Decisions, Decisions
   - G.R.E.A.T. Decision-Making Model
   - Impact of Decisions on Goals
   - Decision-Making Practice

6. Do You Hear What I Am Saying?
   - Effective Communication
   - Verbal vs. Nonverbal

7. Walk In Someone Else's Shoes
   - Active Listening
   - Identification of Different Emotions
   - Empathy for Others

8. Say It Like You Mean It
   - Body Language
   - Tone of Voice
   - Refusal-Skills Practice

9. Getting Along Without Going Along
   - Influences and Peer Pressure
   - Refusal-Skills Practice

10. Keeping Your Cool
    - G.R.E.A.T. Anger Management Tips
    - Practice Cooling Off

11. Keeping It Together
    - Recognizing Anger in Others
    - Tips for Calming Others

12. Working It Out
    - Consequences for Fighting
    - G.R.E.A.T. Tips for Conflict Resolution
    - Conflict Resolution Practice
    - Where to Go for Help

13. Looking Back
    - Program Review
    - "Making My School a G.R.E.A.T. Place" Project Review

Source: Bureau of Justice Assistance (2005). *Gang Resistance Education and Training*. Available at: http://great-online.org

The longitudinal evaluation also shows positive outcomes of G.R.E.A.T. participation. Esbensen and colleagues (2004) evaluated the program using more than 1,750 students in schools from six different cities. Using data for the four years following program participation, the authors report finding less victimization, less risk-taking behavior, improved attitudes toward the police, increased numbers of prosocial peers, and more negative views about gangs among those youths receiving the G.R.E.A.T. lessons (Esbensen et al., 2004). Unfortunately, the evaluation failed to find any impact on the more important target of the project—reduced gang participation. While this is disappointing, the promising results led the sponsors of the G.R.E.A.T. program to undertake a revision of the curriculum, which resulted in the current 13-lesson scheme. No evaluations of the new curriculum are available.

A Planned Comprehensive Response to Gangs

In the mid-1990s, the Office of Juvenile Justice and Delinquency Prevention (OJJDP) initiated the **Community-Wide Approach to Gang Prevention, Intervention, and Suppression Program**. In essence, the program aimed to initiate a comprehensive set of strategies mirroring the five strategies outlined by Spergel and Curry (1993) (see Table 5.9). OJJDP funded program implementation and evaluation in five cities (Bloomington-Normal, Illinois; Mesa, Arizona; Riverside, California; Tucson, Arizona; and San Antonio, Texas).

Several factors emerge across the evaluations. First, in San Antonio, the program was never fully implemented (Spergel, Wa, and Sosa, 2004a). Second, suppression remains the primary response in at least three cities (Spergel, Wa, and Sosa, 2001, 2002, 2003, 2004b). Third, several cities struggled with building programs that included grass-roots community organizations. Most of the participants remained official criminal justice agencies and other social service providers (Spergel, Wa, and Sosa,, 2001, 2002, 2004a, 2004b). Finally, the more successful programs offered a wider array of activities that could be considered opportunities provision and social interventions, such as counseling, referrals, and job training.

The program's impact on gang membership and crime is also mixed. The evaluations of the Bloomington-Normal, Mesa, and Riverside programs report reduced offending and reduced arrests among youths in the experimental neighborhoods (Spergel, Wa, and Sosa, 2001, 2002, 2003). While the Bloomington-Normal program appears to have reduced the level of gang participation (Spergel, Wa, and Sosa, 2001), there was no apparent impact in Riverside, Tucson, or San Antonio (Spergel, Wa, and Sosa, 2003, 2004a, 2004b). Despite the mixed results of the programs, the evidence suggests that a successfully implemented program that targets a wider array of interventions than just suppression activities has the ability to impact positively on the level of gang crime and gang membership.

Overview of Interventions

Evidence concerning the effectiveness of dealing with gangs mirrors the research concerning interventions with individual offenders. The basic conclusion is that many methods of intervention have had little impact on deviant activity. Indeed, some evaluations suggest that intervention exacerbates the problem. A large part of past failures may be due to what Klein (1995) refers to as "conceptually misguided, poorly implemented, half-heartedly pursued" responses and programs.

We must recognize that most programs do not address the major underlying cause of ganging and gang behavior—the lack of social opportunities. Despite the recognition that opportunity provision has the most promise, there are few programs that target this area. The more recent OJJDP community-wide approach is an exception to this problem. The lack of education, training, and jobs receives little attention in most gang interventions. Rather, arrest, prosecution, and incarceration remain the mainstay of society's response. Many authors (see, for example, Cummings and Monti, 1993; Goldstein, 1993; Hagedorn, 1988; Huff, 1990, 1993; Moore, 1991) claim that until major changes are made in the basic social structure, gangs will persist and thrive.

There is room for some hope in dealing with gangs, largely due to recent initiatives that transcend typical narrowly focused local programs. The establishment in 1994 of the National Youth Gang Center has helped coordinate research and knowledge about gangs. Similarly, programs such as the Chicago Gang Violence Reduction Project and the OJJDP Comprehensive Community-Wide Approach to Gang Prevention are relying on multiple interventions to address gangs and ganging. These programs incorporate elements of suppression, community organization, social interventions, and others into a unified approach to the problems (Thornberry and Burch, 1997). Finally, programs such as G.R.E.A.T., as well as appropriately implemented detached workers, are receiving attention and being evaluated for their effectiveness.

SUMMARY

Interest in gang activity has a long history in juvenile justice and appears to have engendered renewed interest in the last few years. The research efforts to date provide striking similarities to one another. The form and explanations for ganging have changed little since Thrasher's (1936) early work. The most clear difference in recent work has been the finding of more serious violence directed against a wider range of victims. Despite the persistent and increasingly dangerous problem, there do not appear to be any clearly successful methods for dealing with gangs.

Discussion Questions

1. Gang delinquency is apparently on the rise and you are called on to explain to the public about gangs and gang behavior. How would you define a gang? What is the typical gang like? How much danger to gangs pose to the average citizen?

2. Gangs are typically accused of dominating violence and drug use/sales. What can you tell about gang involvement in these actions? How does this compare to the general impression about gangs? What is the G.R.E.A.T. program and how does it relate to these problems?

3. Due to the apparent increase in gang violence, the police are called on to do something about the problem. As a member of the police department, what programs, interventions, or actions would you suggest for dealing with gangs and/or the public's perception? Be as specific as possible. If past programs form the basis of your suggestions, provide information on the strengths and weaknesses of those programs and how you would improve on them.

Chapter 6

Drugs and Delinquency

INTRODUCTION

Youthful drug use continues to be a societal concern. Beyond the fact that drug use itself is a crime, such behavior is often associated with other criminal actions, including violence and property crime. As noted in the last chapter, drug use and distribution is related to ganging and gang behavior. There is a continuing perception that drug use is epidemic in the United States, especially among youths. A team of drug use experts contends that our high school students report "a level of involvement in illicit drugs which is greater than has been documented in any other industrialized nation in the world" (Johnston, O'Malley, and Bachman, 1996).

Beyond the fact that drug use (from alcohol and tobacco to heroin and cocaine) is illegal for juveniles, there is evidence that many youths are under the influence of alcohol or other drugs at the time they commit delinquent acts (Beck, Kline, and Greenfeld, 1988). While the causal relationship between drugs and delinquency is the matter of some debate, the indisputable correlation between the two (Huizinga, Loeber, and Thornberry, 1995) raises a variety of issues for the juvenile justice system. This chapter will examine the various issues involved in the drugs–delinquency connection—the extent of drug use, the evidence on the causal relationship, and ways to combat the problem. Before examining these topics, however, it is necessary to define some key terms involved in drug research.

Three common terms used in any discussion of the drug problem are **use, abuse,** and **addiction**. While definitions for these ideas vary from source to source, we can identify some uniform components in most definitions. Use and abuse are considered to be synonymous by most authors when juveniles are considered. This is due to the fact that juveniles are legally barred from the use of any drug, including alcohol. Indeed, even medically prescribed drugs are supposed to be administered by an adult following strict guidelines. Abuse generally refers to the use of any drug beyond that legally prescribed for a medical condition. For juveniles, therefore, any use constitutes abuse. Addiction refers to chronic use of a drug to the point at which the individual develops a need to continue use of the drug, increases the amount used over time, and develops a psychological or physical dependence on the drug (World Health Organization, 1964).

> KEY TERMS
> *—continued*
> psychopharmacological explanations
> reciprocal relationship
> spurious relationship
> systemic violence
> therapeutic communities
> use, abuse, addiction

GAUGING THE EXTENT OF DRUG USE

Measuring the extent of drug use is somewhat difficult due to the private nature of the behavior. The only individual involved is the user. There is no victim who calls the police and files a complaint. In essence, the victim and offender are the same person. Consequently, the primary source of information on drug use (the extent of it and changes in it) is individual self-reports of behavior. Such self-report surveys have been conducted on both the general population and groups of known offenders. Data from both sources are considered below.

Drug Use Among Adolescents

Drug use by juveniles has been measured on a yearly basis since the 1970s by the Monitoring the Future (MTF) Project carried out by Johnston and associates at the University of Michigan. The MTF Project surveys eighth-, tenth-, and twelfth-grade students every spring (as well as college students and young adults) (Johnston et al., 1996). The project gathers information on a wide variety of behaviors, including levels and types of drug use. In addition, MTF presents drug use information for different time frames, ranging from "ever" using a drug to "daily use" in the past 30 days.

Table 6.1 presents information on the lifetime, annual, past month, and daily prevalence of drug use for high school seniors graduating in 2004. **Prevalence** indicates how many respondents used the drug during the year, as opposed to how many times (**incidence**) that the drug was used. A number of key observations can be made from this information. First, drug use varies greatly by type of drug. Second, only a small fraction of respondents uses any drug other than alcohol or tobacco on a regular basis. This table clearly supports arguments that much drug use—other than marijuana, alcohol, or cigarettes—is experimental.

Table 6.1   Lifetime, Annual, Past Month and Daily Drug Use by 12th Graders, 2004

Drug	Lifetime	Annual	Past Month	Daily Use
Any Illicit Drug	51.1	38.8	23.4	—
Marijuana	45.7	34.3	19.9	5.6
Cocaine	8.1	5.3	2.3	0.2
Crack	3.9	2.3	1.0	0.1
Heroin	1.5	0.9	0.5	0.1
Hallucinogens	9.7	6.2	1.9	0.2
Amphetamines	15.0	10.0	4.6	0.3
Methamphetamine	6.2	3.4	1.4	0.2
Barbiturates	9.9	6.5	2.9	0.1
Alcohol	76.8	70.6	48.0	2.8
Cigarettes	52.8	—	25.0	15.6
Smokeless Tobacco	16.7	—	6.7	2.8

Source: Compiled by authors from L.D. Johnston, P.M. O'Malley, and J.G. Bachman (2004). *Monitoring the Future 2004*. Washington, DC: National Institute on Drug Abuse.

The most striking finding from the data on daily use is that very few youths use any drug (except cigarettes). Less than 6 percent claim daily use of marijuana, and roughly 3 percent claim daily alcohol use. Overall, the data suggest that drug use is not the rampant problem portrayed by the media or assumed by the public. Roughly 3 percent or less of the high school seniors used any one drug other than marijuana, alcohol, tobacco, or amphetamines at least once in the last 30 days in 2004, and daily use was below 1 percent for all categories except marijuana, alcohol, and tobacco products. It is only when annual or lifetime figures are considered that drug use begins to appear to be a serious problem, with several categories of drugs being used by 5 percent or more of the high school senior respondents.

These self-report figures, however, must be considered cautiously due to the question of respondent representativeness in the MTF. Specifically, MTF data represent the responses from individuals who were attending school at the time of the survey. This ignores the fact that many youths drop out of school. Dropping out is especially great in the inner city, where the drug trade appears to be most concentrated. Johnston, O'Malley, and Bachman (1987) point out that roughly 15 to 20 percent of students drop out and are not included in the senior survey each year; moreover, they contend that dropouts tend to use drugs more often than those who remain in school. This suggests that the data underreports the level of drug use in the population. Given this caveat, the MTF data are useful from the point of view that the survey is conducted annually and provides a standardized set of data that can be compared over time.

Another source of self-report data on youthful drug use is the **National Survey on Drug Use and Health** (formerly referred to as the National Household Survey). The figures from the survey reflect drug use among a sample of youths ages 12 to 17 years, as compared to the data on students in individual grades in the MTF project. The National Survey, therefore, includes a larger number of younger respondents. Table 6.2 presents lifetime, annual, and past month use data for the 2004 household survey. The pattern in the results is similar to the MTF data in terms of both use in different time frames and drug categories. Alcohol is the most commonly used substance, followed by tobacco and marijuana. In addition, use is greater when longer time frames are considered. The figures are smaller in most categories compared to the MTF data for high school seniors, primarily due to the inclusion of a wider range of younger respondents.

Table 6.2   Drug Use by 12-17 Year Olds, 2004

Drug	Ever Used	Past Year	Past Month
Any Illicit Drug	30.0	21.0	10.6
Marijuana/Hashish	19.0	14.5	7.6
Cocaine	2.4	1.6	0.5
Crack	0.5	0.3	0.1
Inhalants	11.0	4.6	1.2
Heroin	0.3	0.2	0.1
Stimulants	3.4	2.0	0.7
Meth	1.2	0.6	0.2
Hallucinogens	4.6	3.0	0.8
Cigarettes	29.2	18.4	11.9
Smokeless Tobacco	7.1	4.3	2.3
Alcohol	42.0	33.9	17.6

Source: SAMHSA (2004). *National Survey on Drug Use and Health.* Appendix H: Selected Prevalance Tables. Washington, DC: SAMSHA. Available at: http//oas.samsha.gov/nsduh/2k4nsduh/2k4results/apph.html

The data in these tables, particularly those reflecting lifetime or annual use (and to some extent monthly use), often form the basis for claims of a drug problem or epidemic in the country. Use in the past year should not be used as an indicator of a drug "problem" because such use may simply reflect simple experimentation. Stephens (1987) argues that much drug use is "experimental or occasional recreational use" and that "[o]ther than alcohol and cigarettes, marijuana is clearly the most abused . . . psychoactive drug in American society" (p. 50; see also Glassner and Loughlin, 1987, and Macdonald, 1984). In other words, when attention is focused on a more accurate indicator of serious abuse (such as daily use within the last 30 days, instead of on *any* use within the last year or even 30 days), the percentages of adolescents reporting frequent use are much lower and much less alarming.

Trend data for monthly drug use (see Table 6.3) suggest similar conclusions from the preceding discussion. First, use of more serous drugs has been relatively rare and has remained low throughout the years. Only minor fluctuations in use appear in the data over time. Second, alcohol, tobacco, and marijuana have traditionally dominated the drug use data. Of particular note is that the most prevalently used substance (alcohol) has seen a significant decrease in use of the past 30 years (from a high of 72% in 1980 to a low of 48% in 2004). On the other hand, marijuana/hashish, the second most commonly used substance, has exhibited wide fluctuations in use.

Table 6.3   Trends in Past Month Prevalence of Use of Various Drugs for Twelfth Graders, 1975-2004

	Year						
	1975	1980	1985	1990	1995	2000	2004
Any Illicit Drug	30.7	37.2	29.7	17.2	23.8	24.9	23.4
Marijuana/Hashish	27.1	33.7	25.7	14.0	21.2	21.6	34.3
Inhalants	—	1.4	2.2	2.7	3.2	2.2	1.5
Hallucinogens	4.7	3.7	2.5	2.2	4.4	2.6	1.9
LSD	2.3	2.3	1.6	1.9	4.0	1.6	0.7
PCP	—	1.4	1.6	0.4	0.6	0.9	0.4
Cocaine	1.9	5.2	6.7	1.9	1.8	2.1	2.3
Crack	—	—	—	0.7	1.0	1.0	1.0
Heroin	0.4	0.2	0.3	0.2	0.6	0.7	0.5
Other Narcotics	2.1	2.4	2.3	1.5	1.8	2.9	4.3
Amphetamines	8.5	12.1	6.8	3.7	4.0	5.0	4.6
Barbiturates	4.7	2.9	2.0	1.3	2.2	3.0	2.9
Tranquilizers	4.1	3.1	2.1	1.2	1.8	2.6	3.1
Alcohol	68.2	72.0	65.9	57.1	51.3	50.0	48.0
Cigarettes	36.7	30.5	30.1	29.4	33.5	31.4	25.0

Source: Compiled and computed by authors from L.D. Johnston, P.M. O'Malley, and J.G. Bachman (2002). *Monitoring the Future: National Results on Adolescent Drug Use.* Washington, DC: National Institutes of Health; and L.D. Johnston, P.M. O'Malley, and J.G. Bachman (2004). *Monitoring the Future 2004.* Washington, DC: National Institute on Drug Abuse.

One major concern with the use of the MTF or the National Household Survey data is over the representativeness of the results. Various researchers argue that the level of drug use is much greater than appears in these sources. They claim that if more representative samples of youths and samples of inner-city residents were used, the figures would be substantially higher. Fagan and Pabon (1990), for example, note that while 30 percent of school students report drug use in the past year, 54 percent of high school dropouts report drug use over the same time period. Similarly, Altschuler and Brounstein (1991) note that while 6 percent of Washington, DC, in-school respondents claim drug use in the past year, 31 percent of the out-of-school respondents make the same claim. Studies such as these illustrate the biased nature of surveys that exclude dropouts or otherwise fail to sample more at-risk populations. At the same time, however, dropout samples are similarly biased toward portraying drug use in its most negative light.

Self-report figures, even those based on samples from high-crime areas, suggest that the drug problem has been blown out of proportion. The data show that the use of illicit drugs is not rampant in society. Relatively few individuals use illicit drugs with even a gross measure of regularity (within 30 days). Figures for daily use fall to almost zero for most illicit drugs. This does not mean that adolescent drug use is not a problem. Indeed, any use of an illicit drug by juveniles is a problem.

Concern over drugs is also justified in light of the availability of illicit substances. Besides asking about drug use, the MTF project also asks students about the ease of availability of different drugs (see Table 6.4). While the figures are lowest for eighth-grade respondents, even among that group drugs appear relatively easy to obtain. This is true not only for alcohol (65% report very easy or fairly easy to obtain), cigarettes (60% very or fairly easy), and marijuana (41% very or fairly easy), but also for serious illicit drugs such as powder cocaine, crack cocaine, and amphetamines. The results for twelfth-grade respondents are even more significant when one-quarter of all respondents claim that every substance is either very easy or fairly easy to obtain.

Table 6.4   Percent Reporting Drugs Very Easy or Fairly Easy to Obtain, 2004

	8th Graders	10th Graders	12th Graders
Marijuana	41.0	73.3	85.8
LSD	12.3	21.6	33.1
PCP	11.4	18.0	24.2
Cocaine	19.4	31.2	47.8
Crack	20.6	30.6	39.2
Heroin	14.1	18.7	29.6
Other Narcotics	12.4	23.1	40.2
Amphetamines	21.9	35.7	55.4
Barbiturates	18.0	30.0	46.3
Tranquilizers	15.8	25.6	30.1
Alcohol	64.9	84.3	94.2
Cigarettes	60.3	81.4	—

Source: Compiled and computed by authors from L.D. Johnston, P.M. O'Malley, and J.G. Bachman (2004). *Monitoring the Future 2004*. Washington, DC: National Institute on Drug Abuse.

Self-report data provide several insights. First, the drug problem has been exaggerated. Relatively few youths use drugs on a regular basis, although many may experiment at some point in their lives. Second, drug use is a greater problem among those youths who have dropped out of school or are otherwise considered at-risk. Third, drugs are widely available to youths, meaning that the potential for greater use is present. Perhaps of greater interest is to what extent drug use causes further deviance. Alternative sources of data are needed to shed light on this issue.

The Extent of Drug Use Among Offenders

While information on the general population suggests that drug use is not a major problem and that relatively few youths use drugs on a regular basis, data based on offenders presents a different picture. Various data sources suggest that drug use is a critical problem for offenders, including adolescents. One source for information on drug use among offenders has been the **Arrestee Drug Abuse Monitoring (ADAM) program.**

The ADAM program (formerly the Drug Use Forecasting program) collected drug use data through a combination of self-reports and urinalyses from arrested subjects. The program began in New York City in 1987, and there were 35 cities participating in the program as of 2000. Arrestees voluntarily agreed to be interviewed and give a urine sample for testing. The urinalysis tested for 10 different drugs (cocaine, opiates, marijuana, PCP, methadone, benzodiazepine [Valium], methaqualone, propoxyphene [Darvon], barbiturates, and amphetamines). All interviews and tests were anonymous. While the ADAM program did not originally target youths, nine sites collected information on youthful offenders in 2000. Table 6.5 presents 2000 data for male and female arrestees ages nine to 18 in the juvenile ADAM sites.

Table 6.5   **Drug Use among Male/Female Juvenile Arrestees in 9 Sites, 2000 (Percentages)**

Site	Any Drug	Cocaine	Marijuana	Opiates	Methamphetamine
Birmingham	41.5/16.7	0.0/0.0	41.5/16.7	1.9/5.6	0.0/0.0
Cleveland	56.7/—	7.6/—	54.7/—	0.0/—	0.0/—
Denver	66.5/65.4	11.2/11.5	64.5/57.7	1.5/0.0	1.0/0.0
Los Angeles	62.1/38.3	8.5/2.1	56.7/25.5	0.7/2.1	3.8/8.5
Phoenix	59.6/45.6	12.8/10.5	54.9/38.6	1.0/0.9	5.7/9.6
Portland	51.0/44.7	3.4/2.1	46.1/36.2	2.4/12.1	5.8/10.6
San Antonio	53.5/25.8	4.5/4.7	53.5/22.9	3.0/0.0	0.0/0.0
San Diego	47.3/43.1	3.1/3.4	44.1/32.8	1.2/1.7	7.8/22.4
Tucson	53.6/44.4	11.3/18.5	51.8/33.3	0.6/3.7	0.0/3.7

Source: Arrestee Drug Abuse Monitoring (2003). *Annual Report, 2000: Arrestee Drug Abuse Monitoring.* Washington, DC: National Institute of Justice.

The ADAM results show that drug use is very common among youthful arrestees. Urinalysis reveals that more than one-half of all male juvenile arrestees in seven of the nine sites tested positive for recent use of any drug (24-48 hours for all drugs except marijuana, which has a 30-day test period), and more than 40 percent did so in the other two sites. Positive tests ranged (for any drug) from 41.5 percent in Birmingham to 66.5 percent in Denver. For cocaine, positive tests for males ranged from zero in Birmingham to roughly 13 percent in Denver. For marijuana, positive tests for males ranged from 41.5 percent in Birmingham to 64.5 percent in Denver. Marijuana was the most prevalent individual drug in every city for both males and females. While male test results reveal higher use than for females, the data reveal significant drug use by female arrestees (Arrestee Drug Abuse Monitoring, 2003).

Besides information from the ADAM program, drug use among adolescent offenders can also be gauged through other official data. In 2003, more than 246,000 juveniles were arrested for drug abuse, liquor law, or drunkenness violations in the United States (Federal Bureau of Investigation, 2003). Roughly 14 percent of these violations were committed by juveniles age 15 or younger (FBI, 2003). From 1994 to 2003, drug law violations among youths increased by roughly 20 percent. Almost 40,000 youths coming to the juvenile court for drug violations were detained in 2000 (an increase of roughly 100% from 1985) and 800 were waived to the adult court (Puzzanchera et al., 2004).

Data on incarcerated youths also can provide information on the use of illicit drugs. Almost 10,000 youths were placed in residential facilities as a result of a drug law violation in 1999 (Sickmund, 2002). Based on a national one-day count of juvenile facilities in 1999, 9 percent of the youths in public facilities and 10 percent of those in private facilities were there due to drug-related offenses (Sickmund, 2004). State by state data reveal wide variation in the percentage of youths who are held for drug offenses. In two jurisdictions (Maryland and the District of Columbia), roughly one-quarter of all youths being held in custody are there for drug offenses, and more than 10 percent of those being held are there for drug offenses in 16 states (Sickmund, 2004). Court and correctional data provide support to the argument that youthful drug use is highly related to contact with the juvenile justice system.

It must be remembered that statistics on youths involved in the juvenile court and institutions represent a worst case scenario. These youths are not indicative of the majority of juveniles in the population and, therefore, the drug use figures are not applicable to youths not involved in the juvenile justice system. Indeed, this information reflects only those individuals who are caught by the system. It is possible that the use of drugs increases the risk of apprehension. To put offender drug use statistics in perspective, it is helpful to compare offender and nonoffender use. Using the most recent available data on use in the past month (month prior to commitment offense for incarcerated juveniles), 11 percent of youths ages 12 to 17, and 23.4 percent of high school seniors report use of any illicit drug. Roughly 50 percent of male

A 17-year-old former heroin addict listens during a biology class for participants in the Hartford Youthful Offender Program in Hartford, Connecticut. She claims that without the program, which gives her a chance to earn her General Equivalency Diploma, she would have been back on the street or ended up in jail for life.

AP Photo/Bob Child

arrestees use drugs, and approximately 40 percent of female arrestees use drugs. The rate of offender usage is much higher than the usage rate of nonoffenders. While the drug problem is not limited to offenders, it is clearly greater for those individuals.

A Summary of Youthful Drug Use

The fact that relatively few youths use drugs, particularly on a regular basis, does not mean that adolescent drug use is not a problem. At the same time, high levels of drug use by offending youths do not mean that use is a rampant problem in society. Rather, these figures point out that drugs are used by a small but significant number of youths, particularly by offenders, and that the problem needs to be addressed. Use becomes a greater issue if it engenders further delinquent behavior. The degree to which drug use causes delinquency, however, has been the subject of much debate.

THE DRUGS–DELINQUENCY CONNECTION

Statistics showing drug use among delinquent youths (particularly incarcerated individuals) are often pointed to as proof that drug use causes delinquency. The evidence on the drugs–delinquency connection, however, is unclear. A variety of studies note that there is a high degree of correspondence between drug use and delinquent/criminal behavior (Anglin and Speckart, 1986; Ball, Shaffer, and Nurco, 1983; Bennett and Wright, 1984; Fagan, Weis, and Cheng, 1990; Greenbaum, 1994; Huizinga, Menard, and Elliott, 1989; Inciardi, Horowitz, and Pottieger, 1993; Johnson et al., 1991; McBride, 1981; Newcomb and Bentler, 1988). What is not clear is which one causes which, or whether they are both the result of something else.

Possible Relationships

The actual relationship between drug use and delinquency can take a variety of forms. White (1990) outlines four possible relationships. First, *drug use may cause delinquent activity*. This argument typically focuses on the high cost of drugs and the need for youths to commit property crimes in order to secure the funds needed to buy drugs. Indeed, various authors point out that drug users often are involved in property offenses (Anglin and Speckart, 1988; Chaiken and Chaiken, 1982; Collins, Hubbard, and Rachal, 1985; Johnson et al., 1985; National Institute of Justice, 1990). Such an "economic need" argument, however, is only one reason that drug use would cause other forms of deviance. Goldstein (1989) suggests that drugs also may cause crime through their psychopharmacological effects and through systemic violence inherent in the drug market. **Psychopharmacological explanations** suggest that drugs have a direct effect on the user, either physically or psychologically, that impel him or her to act in a certain way. **Systemic violence** refers to violence due to factors such as competition between dealers, retaliation for the sale of bad drugs, the simple need to obtain a drug, or other factors related to the sale and marketing of drugs.

Figure 6.1   Possible Relationships Between Drug Use and Delinquency

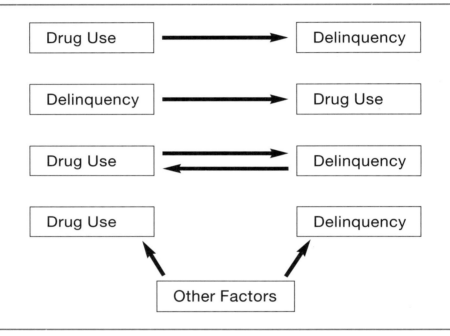

A second approach to the drugs–delinquency relationship is the view that *delinquent activity causes drug use* (White, 1990). This line of reasoning argues that delinquency leads to association with deviant peers and that it is within these peer groups that drug use appears (Akers et al., 1979; Elliott, Huizinga, and Ageton, 1985; Johnston, O'Malley, and Eveland, 1978; Kandel, 1973). This explanation views drug use as a form of deviance just like other delinquent acts. As youths associate with others who are involved in deviant behavior, they will participate in the same activities as the other youths. If the group is using drugs, the individual will be more prone to use drugs.

A third possible relationship views drug use and delinquency as feeding one another in a **reciprocal relationship**. This approach is a combination of the first two. The final possibility is that *the relationship between drug use and delinquency may be spurious*. Under this assumption there would be other factors that cause both drug use and delinquency. In essence, the theoretical explanations for why a youth becomes involved in delinquency would also apply to the reasons for drug use. Drug use and delinquency are simply two manifestations of the same basic problems. Identifying which of the four possible relationships between drug use and delinquency is correct is not an easy task. Most attempts have focused on uncovering the time order between the two variables. That is, which came first, drug use or delinquency?

Research on the Drugs–Delinquency Relationship

Delinquency Causes Drug Use

Research on the temporal (time) order of drug use and delinquency reveals a complex relationship. A variety of studies suggest that the dominant direction in the relationship is from delinquent activity to drug use. In a study using longitudinal data on almost 2,000 high school graduates, Johnston and associates (1978) claim that general delinquency predates most drug use. They argue that youthful drug use is an extension of other deviant behavior. This same pattern of drug use following delinquency is uncovered by Inciardi, Horowitz, and Pottieger (1993) in a study of the behavior of serious inner-city delinquents. They claim that drug use most often appears after youths have become involved in minor delinquency. Other authors (Huba and Bentler, 1983; Johnston, O'Malley, and Eveland, 1986; Kandel, Simcha-Fagan, and Davies, 1986; Speckart and Anglin, 1985) also note that delinquent behavior predates actual drug use. That is, the youths commit delinquent acts, join up with other delinquent peers, and enter into drug use along with their peers.

Data from the **National Youth Survey (NYS)** support this basic argument. The NYS collected data on delinquency, drug use, and demographic factors on a yearly basis from a representative sample of youths. The use of a panel design allows for the inspection of changes in behavior over time and the identification of the temporal order in the data. Elliott, Huizinga, and Ageton (1985) note that minor delinquency and tobacco use typically precede the use of alcohol and other drugs. Similarly, Huizinga, Menard, and Elliott (1989) show a general progression from minor delinquency to alcohol use, Index offending, marijuana use, and polydrug use, in that order. With the exception of alcohol, the data show that drug use temporally follows more general delinquent behavior. From these studies, drug use is a product and not a cause of deviant behavior.

Drug Use Causes Delinquency

Other studies indicate the opposite direction in the relationship—that drug use precedes and causes delinquency or crime. Ball and associates (1983) report that heroin addicts commit four to six times as many offenses when they are actively using drugs than when not using drugs. Based on subjects in public drug treatment programs, Collins, Hubbard, and Rachal (1985) point out that daily heroin/cocaine users tend to commit substantially more property offenses than nonusers or weekly users. Anglin and Hser (1987) and Anglin and Speckart (1988) note that both official and self-reported criminal activity, particularly property offenses and drug possession/sales, increase with narcotics use. Other studies report a similar trend of elevated criminality during periods of heavy drug use (Nurco et al., 1988).

Two recent analyses also provide support for the argument that drug use precedes delinquency. Huizinga, Loeber, and Thornberry (1994), in a summary of the Denver, Pittsburgh, and Rochester youth studies, note that changes in the type and level of substance abuse typically precede significant changes in the level of other delinquent activity. This relationship was found for males and females as well as for different age and ethnic groups. This analysis is especially important because of the longitudinal nature of the data and the use of more than a single research site. Inciardi and associates (1993) arrive at similar conclusions in their study of serious delinquents in Miami, Florida. They point out that regular drug use (and often drug sales) precedes other forms of delinquent behavior. Further, they note that the mean age of onset for drug use is younger than the mean age of onset for offending. The early onset of drug use also predicts early participation in serious delinquency (Inciardi, Horowitz, and Pottieger, 1993).

Reciprocity and Spuriousness

The fact that no consensus has emerged on the correct causal direction between drug use and delinquency suggests that the more plausible explanation is that the relationship is reciprocal. That is, criminal activity leads to drug use *and* drug use leads to criminal activity. Support for a reciprocal relationship can be found in many of the same studies presented above. A number of authors note that increased drug use by already delinquent or criminal individuals leads to higher delinquency levels or more serious offending, not to a first offense (Anglin and Hser, 1987; Anglin and Speckart, 1988; Collins, Hubbard, and Rachal, 1985; Huizinga, Loeber, and Thornberry, 1994; Inciardi, Horowitz, and Pottieger, 1993; Nurco et al., 1988). Similarly, Elliott, Huizinga, and Menard (1989) point out that while delinquency precedes drug use, polydrug use is a typical precursor of serious persistent delinquency. Van Kammen and Loeber's (1994) analysis of the Pittsburgh youth study data reports that property offending predicted the onset of drug use. At the same time, however, the initiation of drug use was related to escalating participation in personal offenses. From these studies, it would appear that, regardless of which came first, drug use and delinquency contribute to each other. It appears that drug use leads to crime and crime leads to drug use.

Similar to the argument for a reciprocal relationship is the view that posits a **spurious relationship** between drug use and delinquency. This simply means that drug use and crime are contemporaneous—they exist at the same time and vary in a similar fashion, and neither is the ultimate cause of the other. Rather, they are caused by either the same common factors or by different factors. Various authors (Huba and Bentler, 1983; Kandel, Simcha-Fagan, and Davies, 1986; White, Pandina, and LaGrange, 1987) argue that there are common causal factors, such as peer and school influences, that underlie both delinquency and drug use. Carpenter and associates (1988) claim that the spurious nature of the drugs–delinquency relationship is evident in the fact that few youths routinely use drugs and commit delinquent acts. They further note that the majority of drug use and delinquent actions occur in the absence of the other behavior. The more plausible argument, therefore, is for a spurious relationship. Similarly, the same analysis of the NYS data that points out a sequence of behavior beginning with minor offending and ending with polydrug use (Huizinga, Menard, and Elliott, 1989) concludes that the actual cause of the behaviors probably lies with a common set of spurious influences. Other research leads to the same conclusion (Collins, 1989; Elliott, Huizinga, and Ageton, 1985; Fagan and Weis, 1990; Fagan, Weis, and Cheng, 1990; Loeber, 1988; White, 1990).

Summarizing the Relationship

The fact that drug use is related to delinquency cannot be disputed. While the causal relationship is unclear, a strong correlation between the two behaviors means that drug use can be used as a predictor of other delinquent behavior (Elliott and Huizinga, 1984; Kandel, Simcha-Fagan, and Davies, 1986; Newcomb and Bentler, 1988). The research also suggests that each behavior contributes to the other, thereby providing insight for intervention and treatment. It may be possible to attack delinquency by attacking drug use. Drug use in itself is a delinquent act that can bring about action by the juvenile justice system. By acting on it the system is intervening in the lives of youths who are at a higher risk of participating in other delinquent activities.

INTERVENTIONS

Interventions aimed at drug use and abuse can take a variety of forms and fall under the general categories of treatment and prevention. Treatment programs typically are aimed at those individuals who already have established a pattern of continued drug use. In essence, treatment programs are geared toward addicted individuals and can take a variety of forms, including maintenance programs, detoxification programs, therapeutic/residential communities, and outpatient programs. Prevention programs are geared more at keeping individuals from initial involvement with drugs or, at the least, keeping casual users from more frequent and varied drug use. Drug prevention programs for juveniles often include a variety of approaches, such as information dissemination, affective education, and resistance and social skills training. Each of the various treatment and prevention approaches will be examined below.

Treatment Approaches

What is known about the impact of drug treatment programs comes mainly from the study of programs focusing primarily on adults. This is because there have been relatively few studies of treatment programs for youths and because most juvenile interventions take a more preventive approach. The increased concern over drug use and related problem behavior (such as violence) has resulted in greater attention to treatment programs for juveniles. While programs may have a different emphasis, many similarities and common features appear across programs. For example, counseling and therapy of one sort or another appear in virtually all of the programs. The following discussion offers examples of the more well-known or effective treatment approaches. Other programs appear elsewhere in this book.

Research on treatment programs has led the **National Institute on Drug Abuse (NIDA)** to list 13 principles of effective treatment (see Box 6.1). Rather than attempt to offer a prescriptive set of activities for an "ideal" program, NIDA's principles address more generalized issues that can be implemented in different ways. Indeed, the very first principle notes that no one program is effective for all individuals or situations. In general terms, the principles argue that treatment must be responsive to the multiple needs of each individual.

Maintenance and Detoxification Programs

Maintenance programs, a common intervention for addicted individuals, seek to establish a steady state in which the individual does not experience withdrawal symptoms when the drug begins to wear off. Consequently, the user will be able to function more normally and participate in everyday activities without the constant need for the drug (Stephens, 1987). The most common maintenance program involves the use of methadone, an oral substitute for heroin. Besides periodic checks (usually urinalysis) to

Box 6.1 NIDA's 13 Principles of Effective Treatment for Drug Abuse

1. No single program is appropriate for all individuals

2. Treatment needs to be readily available

3. Effective treatment attends to multiple needs of the individual

4. Treatment and service plans must be assessed continuously and modified as necessary

5. Remaining in treatment for an adequate period of time is critical for effectiveness

6. Counseling (individual and/or group) and other behavioral therapies are critical components

7. Medications are an important element of treatment for many patients

8. Addicted or drug-abusing individuals with coexisting mental disorders should have both disorders treated in an integrated way

9. Medical detoxification is merely the first stage of addiction treatment and by itself does little to change long-term use

10. Treatment does not need to be voluntary to be effective

11. Possible drug use during treatment must be monitored continuously

12. Treatment programs should provide assessment of HIV/AIDS and other infectious diseases, and counseling to help patients modify or change behaviors

13. Recovery from drug addition is a long-term process and frequently requires multiple episodes of treatment

Source: National Institute on Drug Abuse (1999). *Principles of Drug Addiction Treatment: A Research-Based Guide*. Washington, DC: National Institute on Drug Abuse.

establish abstinence from other drugs, maintenance programs rely heavily on individual and group counseling and the establishment of behavioral guidelines (Anglin and Hser, 1990). Some programs also include incentives/rewards given to clients who test negative for drug use (NIDA, 1999). Evaluations of maintenance programs generally report reduced drug usage and the commission of fewer crimes by patients when they are in the program (Anglin and McGlothlin, 1985; Ball et al., 1987; Hser, Anglin, and Chou, 1988). Unfortunately, the impact of these programs tends to disappear after program participation, and patients return to preprogram levels of drug use and criminal activity when they leave the program (Anglin et al., 1989; McGlothlin and Anglin, 1981).

Often closely aligned with maintenance programs are programs that emphasize **detoxification**. This approach attempts to remove an individual from an addiction by weaning him or her off drugs. Drugs are used over the short term to minimize the pain and discomfort of withdrawal. Detoxification programs target a wide range of drugs, from alcohol to heroin, and can be found in many hospitals and facilities throughout the country. Anglin and Hser (1990) point out that while short-term follow-ups show that detoxification is successful at eliminating drug use, detoxification has not been adequately evaluated over the long term. Unfortunately, some drug users rely on detoxification to reduce the need for massive amounts of drugs to get high. They then return to more normal drug use until they again reach a point at which small amounts are no longer sufficient to serve their needs (Bellis, 1981).

Evaluations of both maintenance and detoxification programs are somewhat mixed. Sells and Simpson (1979) note that they are effective at lowering arrests and illegal activities among juvenile drug abusers. Other positive support is found in the fact that criminal activity is lower among drug users in treatment than among those receiving no intervention (Kaplan 1983; Wish, Toborg, and Bellassai, 1988). NIDA (1999), in its list of effective principles for treatment, notes that the use of medications are an important part of treatment for some individuals. Critics, however, allege that they are crutches that do not solve the problem, but instead lead to a nonproductive lifestyle of methadone, alcohol, other drugs, and petty crime (Stephens, 1987). An additional problem is that many maintenance drugs become simple substitutes for the original drug. A prime example of this is the fact that heroin was developed to solve morphine addiction. Today, instead of curing heroin addiction, methadone addiction has itself become an issue.

Therapeutic/Residential Communities and Outpatient Programs

Another major form of treatment, **therapeutic communities**, emphasizes the provision of a supportive, highly structured, family-like atmosphere within which individuals can be helped to alter their personality and develop social relationships conducive to conforming behavior (Anglin and Hser, 1990). Group sessions, called "games," often involve attention on one member because he or she is a new member of the therapeutic community, is suspected of violating a house rule, or is suspected of using drugs. Pressure is exerted to induce the person to admit the particular problem and the need for support from the group (Stephens, 1987). Group counseling is used to explore the reasons for drug use and to suggest alternative methods for dealing with the factors that lead to substance abuse. Therapeutic communities, such as Synanon, Daytop Village, and Phoenix House, boast positive results—including lower levels of drug use and criminal activity (Anglin and Hser, 1990; Coombs, 1981; DeLeon, 1984; DeLeon and Rosenthal, 1989).

The KEY/CREST program combines a residential therapeutic community with post-release assistance in the community. Along with the therapeutic community, clients participate in educational activities, HIV education, a 12-step alcohol program, and other activities aimed at preparing the clients for success outside the institution. The New Vision Therapeutic Community program rests primarily on services while the clients are in prison, with an initial aftercare period upon release. Like the KEY/CREST program, clients undergo individual and group counseling, as well as educational activities.

Evaluations of therapeutic communities and residential treatment programs have revealed success in reducing recidivism and drug use. An evaluation of the KEY/CREST program showed the greatest success for those completing both the residential and aftercare components of the program, when compared to those completing part of the program, dropping out, or not participating at all (Office of Justice Programs, 2000). An evaluation of the New Vision program found similar results, with participants doing significantly better, especially for those with some serious criminal and drug use in their background (Office of Justice Programs, 2000). Lipton (1995) concludes that prison-based therapeutic communities "can produce significant reductions in recidivism rates . . . and . . . show consistency of such results over time" (p. 51). It is important to note, however, that even successful programs do not prevent all crime, eliminate all drugs, or graduate all of their initial clients. In a California program, only 28 percent of the offenders completed the program *and* aftercare, and 22 percent dropped out prior to completing the program (Lipton, 1995).

The final treatment modality, **outpatient drug-free programs**, often follows similar approaches to those in therapeutic communities or residential settings. The greatest difference is the lack of a residential component. Individual and group counseling form the cornerstone of these programs. Programs such as Alcoholics Anonymous bring together current and former addicts to help one another stay off drugs. At meetings, members recount their drug histories and how the group is supporting them in their efforts to abstain from drug use. Other components of outpatient programs may include social skills training, vocational programming, social interaction, referral to other sources of assistance, and possibly short-term drug maintenance (Anglin and Hser, 1990).

Several outpatient drug-free programs exist for youthful offenders. The Bridge program targets youths either being released from custody or in danger of being institutionalized (Office of Justice Programs, 2000). **Multidimensional Family Therapy (MDFT)** is centered on the family, peers, and community influences around the youths. Similarly, multi-systemic therapy addresses the multiple sources of inputs to youthful behavior, including the family, schools, peers, and neighborhoods (National Institute on Drug Abuse, 1999). The programs assess the needs of the youths and the youths' families, and provide intensive services to the youths within the different social contexts in which they operate. The intent of the programs is to ensure that youths and their needs do not go unaddressed. Each of these programs have been successful at reducing recidivism and drug use (National Institute on Drug Abuse, 1999; Office of Justice Programs, 2000).

Treatment Summary

There are several problems with the various treatment approaches. First, it is often difficult to motivate addicts and abusers to enter a treatment program. Convincing addicts that they have a problem is often half the battle against the problem. Besides getting drug users into programs, it is also difficult to retain them. Studies of therapeutic communities, for example, have indicated that up to 70 percent of those entering such communities drop out before completing the program (Stephens, 1987; see also Lipton, 1995). One solution to the participation problem may entail mandatory participation as an outcome of either criminal or civil litigation. While research suggests that coerced treatment is less effective than voluntary participation (Anglin, 1988; DeLong, 1972; Maddux, 1988), there is evidence that mandatory treatment does lead to reduced drug use (Anglin and McGlothlin, 1984; Hubbard et al., 1989; Leukefeld and Tims, 1988; National Institute on Drug Abuse, 1999; Visher, 1990). This may be due to the fact that such clients receive more extensive treatment.

Despite various qualifications, treatment appears to be effective at reducing the use of and need for drugs (Visher, 1990). In one summary evaluation of drug treatment, Simpson and Sells (1981) report lower drug use, lower criminal behavior, and improved employment status for clients as long as six years after the end of treatment. Non-treatment control clients fared significantly worse. A National Institute on Drug Abuse (1999) review of treatment programs offers numerous examples of successful programs, although mostly in relation to adult offenders. Conversely, Stephens (1987) suggests that maturing out of the addiction cycle may be the most frequent way out of the drug problem. As addicts age, it is simply harder physically to be a drug addict. As a result, some addicts find it easier to give up drugs than to continue addiction. Walker is also cautious about the ability of treatment to have much impact on the drug problem. He concludes that treatment is quite effective for those individuals who have decided to quit drugs, but treatment, "as a primary strategy, will not reduce the national drug problem" (Walker, 1998:261).

Prevention Approaches

The National Institute on Drug Abuse (2004) offers 16 principles of effective drug prevention (see Box 6.2). These include a focus on protective factors; reducing risk factors; including families, peers, and communities in the interventions; dealing with social competence; coupling multiple approaches; and recognizing the long-term needs of the clients (National Institute on Drug Abuse, 2004). Many prevention programs incorporate more than one approach and rely on input from a variety of sources, such as the schools, families, and the community. These approaches can be seen in several of the prevention programs discussed below.

Box 6.2 NIDA's 16 Principles of Effective Prevention for Drug Abuse

1. Prevention programs should enhance protective factors and reverse or reduce risk factors.

2. Prevention programs should address all forms of drug abuse, alone or in combination, including underage use of legal drugs; the use of illegal drugs; and the inappropriate use of legally obtained substances, prescription medications, or over-the-counter drugs.

3. Prevention programs should address the type of drug abuse problem in the local community, target modifiable risk factors, and strengthen identified protective factors.

4. Prevention programs should be tailored to address risks specific to population or audience characteristics, such as age, gender, and ethnicity.

5. Family-based prevention programs should enhance family bonding and relationships and include parenting skills; practice in developing, discussing and enforcing family policies on substance abuse; and training in drug education and information.

6. Prevention programs can be designed to intervene as early as preschool to address risk factors for drug abuse, such as aggressive behavior, poor social skills, and academic difficulties.

7. Prevention programs for elementary school children should target improving academic and social-emotional learning to address risk factors for drug abuse.

8. Prevention programs for middle or junior high and high school students should increase academic and social competence.

9. Prevention programs aimed at general populations at key transition points, such as the transition to middle school, can produce beneficial effects even among high-risk families and children.

10. Community prevention programs that combine two or more effective programs can be more effective than a single program alone.

11. Community prevention programs reaching populations in multiple settings are most effective when they present consistent, community-wide messages in each setting.

Box 6.2, *continued*

12. When communities adapt programs to match their needs, community norms, or differing cultural requirements, they should retain core elements of the original research-based intervention.

13. Prevention programs should be long-term with repeated interventions to reinforce the original prevention goals.

14. Prevention programs should include teacher training on good classroom management practices such as rewarding appropriate student behavior.

15. Prevention programs are most effective when they employ interactive techniques, such as peer discussion and parent role-playing, that allow for active involvement in learning about drug abuse and reinforcing skills.

16. Research-based prevention programs can be cost-effective.

Source: National Institute on Drug Abuse (2004). *Lessons from Prevention Research. Info Facts*. Washington, DC: National Institute on Drug Abuse.

The "Just Say No" Campaign and Similar Programs

Perhaps the most direct and simplest prevention programs are those that encourage youths to simply say "no" and resist drug use. During the 1980s, the federal government pushed **"Just Say No"** as the cornerstone of its prevention activities. These programs promote the belief that drugs are inherently evil and must be avoided at all costs. Thus, the key is convincing youths of the harmful effects of drugs and the need to abstain from them. These programs emphasize dealing with peer relationships and interpersonal involvement. Indeed, many authors refer to these approaches as "peer programs."

The "Just Say No" and peer campaigns assume that juvenile drug use develops out of peer interaction, and that use occurs mainly in group situations. Children, therefore, are encouraged to make a personal decision in the face of peer influences to refuse any offer to use illicit drugs. Included in this approach is the basic message that drugs are harmful. Many of the media and school efforts convey this message without relying on specific information about the physical, psychological, and legal aspects of drug use (Tobler, 1986), but some programs couple this approach with basic information about drugs. The emphasis in the "Just Say No" campaign, however, is on total avoidance of drugs.

The total avoidance of illegal drugs in light of peer pressure through a simple "no" response is somewhat shortsighted. Trebach (1987) compares such a prevention approach to related efforts to tell kids to abstain from any premarital sexual activity. As some children are going to use drugs or engage in sex no matter what adult society says, there is an unrealistic naïveté involved in "Just Say No" and similar campaigns. In addition, there may be a certain amount of hypocrisy associated with a total-abstinence crusade because youths recognize drug use by adults and are influenced by advertising aimed at adults. Some "Just Say No" advocates recognize that kids will use drugs anyway, but justify the approach as a way to convey a message against drugs.

Knowledge/Education Programs

A related approach to "Just Say No" programs is the provision of factual knowledge about drugs and their effects. The **knowledge approach** entails providing youths with information on different types of drugs, such as the physical and psychological effects of the drugs, as well as the extent, impact, and possible legal consequences of drug use. In many instances these programs are offered as a part of the normal school curriculum. The basic assumption is that such knowledge will allow the individual to make an informed choice about drug use. It is further assumed that informed youths will opt against using drugs.

Interestingly, evaluations of knowledge/education approaches often suggest that the programs *increase* drug use by participants. What appears to be happening is that the increased knowledge leads to enhanced curiosity and experimentation by youths in a kind of "I want to find out for myself" attitude (Abadinsky, 1989; Botvin, 1990; Botvin and Dusenbury, 1989; Eiser and Eiser, 1988; Hanson, 1980; Kinder, Pape, and Walfish, 1980; Swadi and Zeitlin, 1987; Weisheit, 1983). Based on information from 143 prevention programs, Tobler (1986) concluded that knowledge programs fail to show any reductions in drug use behavior. The single point on which these programs can demonstrate success is in their ability to increase subject's knowledge about drugs (Botvin, 1990).

Affective Approaches

Rather than provide information about different substances and issues related directly to drug use, **affective interventions** focus attention on the individual. The assumption is that by building self-esteem, self-awareness, and feelings of self-worth, the youth will be able to make wise choices and resist pressures to use drugs. Few programs, however, rely solely on affective education elements. Programs such as Here's Looking at You 2000 (HLAY 2000), which purports to use an affective approach, typically also include drug information and social skills training. Consequently, it becomes difficult to isolate the impact of affective elements such as self-esteem on subsequent drug involvement.

One well-known program that incorporates a heavy affective component is the Big Brothers/Big Sisters program. This program matches adult mentors with at-risk children in the community. The goal of the program is to provide positive role models to the youths, help build self-esteem, promote healthy attitudes and behaviors, and prepare the youths for daily living. A key component is helping youths feel good about themselves. The Big Brothers/Big Sisters program can be found in more than 500 communities. Evaluations of the initiative show success at reducing drug use, reducing arrests, increasing educational success, and improving the overall quality of life for youths (Office of Justice Programs, 2000). These results are in contrast to other evaluations of affective programs where the interventions have failed to find any significant impact on substance use (Hansen et al., 1988; Kim, 1988; Kim, McLeod, and Shantzis, 1993; Newcomb and Bentler, 1988; Tobler, 1986). It is possible that this failure is due to attempts to look at affective interventions separated from other preventive elements, such as those found in Big Brothers/Big Sisters and similar programs.

Life Skills Training Approaches

Perhaps the failure of affective approaches to have an impact on drug use is the failure to include other elements along with building self-esteem. **Life skills training** often includes affective interventions along with a variety of elements, ranging from basic personal and social skills development (which deal with general life situations and how to deal with them) to the provision of specific resistance skills aimed directly at substance abuse issues. This approach assumes that individuals who use drugs are poorly prepared to address the issues and pressures involved in daily decisionmaking. For example, individuals who find themselves left out of the societal mainstream due to the lack of education and/or job training need to be taught the skills necessary to obtain a job and succeed in an acceptable manner. Individuals who get into trouble because they simply follow the group need to be taught how to be independent, make decisions for themselves, and resist following others into unwise situations. The key resistance skills taught include how to recognize a problematic situation and what alternatives are available to the individual, how to resist outside pressures (such as peers or advertising), how to identify help, how to cope with stress, and how to make wise choices.

Research on life skills or resistance skills training has shown positive results. Perhaps the best example of this impact comes from a series of studies dealing with tobacco, alcohol, and marijuana use by Botvin and associates (see, for example, Botvin and Dusenbury, 1989; Botvin, Renick, and Baker, 1983; Botvin et al., 1984, 1995, 1997, 2003). In these studies, "life skills training" was successful at reducing the number of youths using drugs. Positive results also appear in evaluations of other programs that focus on life skills, social competence, and related topics (see, for example, Eisen et al., 2002; Greenberg and Kusche, 1998; Hawkins et al., 1999). While most of the analyses focus on relatively short-term effects, positive outcomes do appear in longer follow-up assessments.

The D.A.R.E. Program

Perhaps the best-known drug prevention program in existence today is the **Drug Abuse Resistance Education (D.A.R.E.)** program, which incorporates elements of all the previously discussed approaches to prevention. D.A.R.E. is a police-taught, school-based program that began in the Los Angeles United School District in 1983. The program is aimed at elementary students in fifth or sixth grade, although there are companion programs for younger and older youths as well as for the parents of participating students. The D.A.R.E. curriculum is taught by police officers who have been trained by the program, and it is offered as part of the normal school experience. The topics covered in the program have recently been revised; the current curriculum (see Box 6.3) reflects aspects of affective training, "Just Say No" approaches, peer resistance, and social skills training. The primary focus of the program is on enhancing the social skills of the individual.

The D.A.R.E. program is probably the best-known drug prevention program for youths. Despite the program's popularity, the majority of methodologically rigorous studies have found that the police-taught, school-based program has little or no impact on subsequent drug use.

Mark C. Ide

Based on its widespread adoption by schools in every state, one would assume that the program has proved successful at combating youthful substance use. Interestingly, however, this is not the case. Indeed, D.A.R.E. is not even mentioned in NIDA's (2003) guide to proven strategies for preventing drug use. The discussion that follows is based on evaluations of D.A.R.E. prior to its recent reconfiguration. No evaluations have yet to be completed on the new curriculum.

One of the early evaluations of D.A.R.E. indicated that participation in the program was related to lower levels of subsequent drug use (DeJong, 1987). However, there was no evidence of changes in knowledge, attitudes, or expectations about future use. This evaluation suffered from serious methodological problems, including the lack of randomized assignment of subjects to treatment and control groups, the absence of a pretest, and the fact that the posttest was conducted immediately after completion of the program.

Box 6.3 Elements of the New D.A.R.E. Curriculum

Elementary School Lessons

Purposes and Overview of D.A.R.E.—introduce D.A.R.E. decision-making model

Tobacco and You—focus on facts and beliefs about tobacco

Smoke Screen—use of decision-making model; discussion of media advertising

Alcohol and You—focus on facts and beliefs about alcohol

The Real Truth—examine alcohol advertisements; discuss inhalants

Friendship Foundations—examine peer pressure and decision making

Putting It Together—application of assertiveness skills

Personal Action—practice decision-making skills in light of peer pressure

Practice! Practice! Practice!—apply assertive refusal skills; affirm healthy choices

Culmination—make public statements about choices to resist drugs and violence

Middle and High School Lesson Topics

Overview and purpose of D.A.R.E.

Respect of self and others

Teach effects of drugs, alcohol, and other substances on body and brain

Discuss normative beliefs

Discuss media advertising and how to critically analyze ads

Develop communication skills, decision-making skills, and assertiveness

Discuss personal anger, frustration, conflicts, and violence; consequences of these

Teach skills to handle anger, frustration, and conflicts

Develop students' ability to assess the social and legal implications of behavior

Share insights and observations about their behavior and changes in their beliefs

Parent Program

Effective Communication

Drug Abuse Prevention—Birth Through Eight Years

Drug Abuse Prevention and Intervention—Ages Nine Through Adolescence

Youth Pressures/Resistance Skills

Prevention Strategies and Conflict Resolution

Panel Discussion

Source: Compiled from D.A.R.E. web site. Available at: http://www.dare.com

More methodologically rigorous studies have failed to find any significant changes in drug use behavior after participation in D.A.R.E. Ringwalt, Ennett, and Holt (1991), in a randomized experiment in 20 North Carolina schools, reported finding no impact on drug use or the intent to use drugs. Clayton, Catterello, and Walden (1991), using data from schools in Lexington, Kentucky, also failed to uncover any impact on participant drug use. Perhaps the one promising outcome of these projects is that both evaluations uncover changes in attitudes toward drug use and peers that corresponded with the intent of the program. In another evaluation, Rosenbaum and associates (1994) examined data from 36 schools in Illinois that were randomly assigned either to receive the D.A.R.E. program or to serve as a control. The outcome of their tests showed no significant difference in substance use between the experimental and control groups after a one-year follow-up. There was also no change in attitudes or beliefs as a result of program participation (Rosenbaum et al., 1994).

Based on these analyses, it appears that D.A.R.E. has little or no impact on subsequent drug use. Why then does D.A.R.E. enjoy such a good reputation, and why should it continue on our schools? The first part of the question can be answered by pointing out that D.A.R.E. is a relatively nonintrusive intervention that has good intentions and has shown no negative impacts. By using the schools, no specific individuals are singled out or identified. Everyone participates in the program. As part of the educational curriculum, it also gains an immediate legitimacy among students, parents, and the public. Perhaps the best reason why D.A.R.E. should continue in schools deals with the potential it has for engendering positive changes among youths in attitudes and beliefs toward the school, the police, and societal rules. The presence of a police officer in the school for a nonarrest situation opens the door for greater familiarity and understanding between juveniles and the police. It may also produce positive changes in the school environment by promoting other appropriate activities. While the program may not, in itself, bring major change in drug use, D.A.R.E. can contribute to a more general positive school environment that may engender more broad-based changes in attitudes and actions.

The recent incarnation of D.A.R.E. complies with suggestions for change, such as Tobler's (1997) observation that interactive programs are more effective at reducing substance use and abuse than noninteractive programs, which usually use a lecture approach. The new D.A.R.E. curriculum includes a great deal of interactive work with students. It also includes a parent component and emphasizes follow-up activities both within the schools and outside the educational setting throughout the year. Police officers involved in D.A.R.E. receive training in how to use a more participatory style of presentation and how to engender student participation.

The most recent version of D.A.R.E. (summarized in Box 6.3) is in the early stages of implementation and testing. The program has been undergoing review in six cities using a randomized experimental design. Students in the study were to be followed from 2001-2005 (D.A.R.E., 2005). The results of the project should be available in the near future.

Prevention Summary

The evidence on prevention programs suggests that drug use can be impacted by certain types of programs. Resistance/life skills training appears to be the most promising at reducing the level of drug use, although more rigorous and extensive testing needs to be completed. On the other hand, programs based on knowledge provision may result in increased curiosity and experimentation with illicit drugs. Programs that stress self-esteem, self-awareness, and interpersonal growth in the absence of other strategies for dealing with life situations, including drugs (typically referred to as affective education programs), also fail to exhibit any strong influence on drug use (Botvin, 1990; Schaps et al., 1986; Tobler, 1986). Interactive programs are more effective than noninteractive programs (Tobler, 1997). In general, while many prevention programs exist and show promise, most still need to be evaluated with longer follow-up periods and better research designs (particularly using adequate comparison groups).

Alternative Responses to Drug Use

Responses to drug use do not always reflect pure treatment or prevention. The persistence of drug use in society over time, particularly coupled with the failure or modest impact of most prevention and treatment approaches, has prompted various alternate responses. Among the responses are increased enforcement of drug laws, the development of comprehensive programs that combine legal responses with treatment and prevention, and controversial responses, such as the legalization or decriminalization of drugs.

Increased Enforcement

The typical response in the United States is to invoke the legal process. Aggressive police tactics, strict prosecution, and mandatory sentencing are the norm in most communities. Examples of this include police crackdowns on drug markets, drug interdiction at borders, civil abatement procedures in court, and mandatory prison terms for drug possession or sale. This kind of "get tough" orientation permeates the national drug policy, as evidenced in the 2005 National Drug Control Strategy (see Box 6.4) and the funding that accompanies the strategy. While the strategy appears to be heavily oriented toward prevention and treatment, the reality is that enforcement and interdiction are the primary efforts. The total fiscal year budget for Drug Control in 2005 was more than $12.1 billion. Of that amount, $3.5 billion (roughly 29%) is clearly for treatment or prevention. The balance is mainly for arrest, interdiction, prosecution, and punishment.

Box 6.4 2005 National Drug Control Strategy

I.   Stopping Use Before it Starts: Education and Community Action

II.   Healing America's Drug Users: Getting Treatment Resources Where They are Needed

III. Disrupting the Market: Attacking the Economic Basis of the Drug Trade

---

Source: The White House (2005). *National Drug Control Strategy*. Washington, DC: The White House.

Enforcement Coupled with Treatment

The fact that many offenders use drugs and come to the juvenile justice system with an established pattern of substance use/abuse places the system in the position of needing to respond to the individual as both an offender and someone who needs help. As a result, both the adult and juvenile justice systems have developed processes that couple enforcement with treatment. Two examples of this are drug courts and the Breaking the Cycle program.

Drug Courts. The drug court movement began in 1989, with the first juvenile drug court appearing in 1995. Based on the most recent national statistics, there are 285 drug courts in operation (Office of Justice Programs, 2003). At that time, there were another 110 in the planning stages, and it is reasonable to assume that most of those are now operating. As of 2003, juvenile drug courts had already handled more than 12,000 youths (Office of Justice Programs, 2003).

The underlying philosophy for **drug courts** is to use the court's authority to prompt participation in and successful completion of treatment aimed at reducing drug use and related criminal behavior. The courts represent a coalition of prosecutors, police, probation, judges, treatment professionals, social service agencies, and other community groups working together to get the offenders off drugs and keep them off drugs (Drug Courts Program Office, 2000). While the drug court process varies from location to location, there is a set of common core strategies that are found throughout most programs (see Box 6.5). Among the common elements are frequent appearances before the court, regular drug testing, treatment assessment, participation in treatment programs, focusing on families, working with schools, aftercare, and providing interventions that are tailored to the individual.

Box 6.5 Juvenile Drug Court Strategies

1. Collaborative Planning—Engage all stakeholders in creating an inter-disciplinary, coordinated, and systemic approach to working with youth and their families.

2. Teamwork—Develop and maintain an interdisciplinary, nonadver-sarial work team.

3. Clearly Defined Target Population and Eligibility Criteria—Define a target population and eligibility criteria that are aligned with the program's goals and objectives.

4. Judicial Involvement and Supervision—Schedule frequent judicial reviews and be sensitive to the effect that court proceedings can have on youth and their families.

5. Monitoring and Evaluation—Establish a system for program monitoring and evaluation to maintain quality of service, assess program impact, and contribute to knowledge in the field.

6. Community Partnerships—Build partnerships with community organizations to expand the range of opportunities available to youth and their families.

7. Comprehensive Treatment Planning—Tailor interventions to the complex and varied needs of youth and their families.

8. Developmentally Appropriate Services—Tailor treatment to the developmental needs of adolescents.

9. Gender-Appropriate Services—Design treatment to address the unique needs of each gender.

10. Cultural Competence—Create policies and procedures that are responsive to cultural differences and train personnel to be culturally competent.

11. Focus on Strengths—Maintain a focus on the strengths of youth and their families during program planning and in every interaction between the court and those it serves.

12. Family Engagement—Recognize and engage the family as a valued partner in all components of the program.

13. Educational Linkages—Coordinate with the school system to ensure that each participant enrolls in and attends an educational program that is appropriate to his or her needs.

14. Drug Testing—Design drug testing to be frequent, random, and observed. Document testing policies and procedures in writing.

15. Goal-Oriented Incentives and Sanctions—Respond to compliance and noncompliance with incentives and sanctions that are designed to reinforce or modify the behavior of youth and their families.

16. Confidentiality—Establish a confidentiality policy and procedures that guard the privacy of the youth while allowing the drug court team to access key information.

Source: Bureau of Justice Assistance (2003). *Juvenile Drug Courts: Strategies in Practice*. Washington, DC: Bureau of Justice Assistance.

Advocates of drug courts point to a number of potential advantages resulting from the programs. One key advantage is providing treatment to offenders. While most correctional intervention programs, whether residential or nonresidential, offer the opportunity for some types of treatment component, their primary concern with suppression and control often means that treatment is not always available or appropriate. Drug courts, however, are premised upon the need to match offenders with appropriate treatments. The offenders who are admitted to the drug court program are guaranteed to receive some type of treatment. A second advantage is keeping the offender in the community and using community resources to address the offender's needs. The youths are not cut off from their family and community support groups, which are crucial for long-term success.

The literature on the effectiveness of drug court programs presents a mixed picture. Various analyses report that drug court participants recidivate at a significantly lower level than comparison groups (Brewster, 2001; Goldkamp and Wieland, 1993; Gottfredson, Najaka, and Kearley, 2003; Harrell, 1998; Listwan et al., 2003; Spohn et al., 2001). Other analyses, though, find no difference between treatment and comparison groups or higher recidivism for drug court clients (Belenko, Fagan, and Dumanovsky, 1994; Granfield, Eby, and Brewster, 1998; Miethe, Hong, and Reese, 2000).

Despite the fact that evaluations have not been able to declare drug courts an unqualified success, this approach continues to grow and attract attention. The number of drug courts is growing, particularly in terms of juvenile and family drug courts. One driving force behind the movement is the attraction of combining legal sanctions with treatment into a coordinated response. What is still needed is extensive evaluation of the juvenile drug courts in terms of the impact on general delinquent behavior and the use of drugs in particular.

Breaking the Cycle. The **Breaking the Cycle (BTC) program** takes a similar approach to that found in drug courts. The program seeks to identify offenders with substance abuse problems early in their system processing, assess the appropriate treatment needs of the offender, and establish an integrated set of interventions (sanction, treatment, and rewards) for the individual. The key to the BTC program is coordinating services offered by law enforcement, the courts, corrections, families, schools, social service agencies, communities, and substance abuse treatment providers. The court is a pivotal participant because it can provide sanctions if youths fail to comply with the program. The BTC program has been used in several sites with adult offenders.

Lattimore and colleagues (2005) report on an evaluation of a juvenile BTC program in Lane County, Oregon. The evaluation of the juvenile BTC program provides mixed results (see Lattimore et al., 2005). Comparing program youths to a nonequivalent comparison group, the researchers report greater access to and use of drug treatment interventions by experimental subjects. Participants also report reductions in marijuana use, although there were no reductions in any other drug use, including alcohol use. In addition, while there was little impact on subsequent arrest immediately after program participation, there were clear reductions between six and 12 months after participation (Lattimore et al., 2005).

Evidence from both juvenile drug courts and the juvenile BTC project show that comprehensive interventions in which the juvenile justice system is heavily involved have the potential to reduce drug use and offending. The impact, however, is not uniformly positive. Further study is need to identify the keys to success. More consistent positive results are required before either approach receives uncritical acceptance.

Ready Availability of Drugs

A proposal at the other end of the political spectrum from those discussed elsewhere in this chapter is the call for the free (or inexpensive) availability of psychoactive drugs. This is a call to legalize or to decriminalize at least the possession of drugs such as heroin and marijuana. Nadelman (1997), for example, argues that drugs should be available on a mail-order basis.

Proponents argue that such action would have several benefits. First, drug addicts would be less likely to suffer adverse health consequences from adulterated drugs or contaminated needles. Second, it could reduce street crime because addicts would not have to steal to obtain the funds to purchase drugs (Goldstein, 1989). Third, it would reduce the possibility of society alienating adolescents. "Youth may generally lose respect for a society that defines them as criminal because they use marijuana" (Stephens, 1987:119). Fourth, legalization would reduce our law enforcement war on drugs, including the disturbing rates of arrest and incarceration of African Americans.

A major concern with the proposal to legalize drugs is that drug use might escalate at an alarming rate. Nadelman argues that this is not a problem because most Americans already resist drugs for reasons other than their status as illegal substances. He notes that 70 percent of Americans resist cigarettes, and 90 percent either do not use drugs at all or use them in moderation. Nadelman concludes that these percentages suggest that Americans "do not really need drug laws to prevent them from entering into destructive relationships with drugs" (Nadelman, 1997:287).

Although legalization may be practical for marijuana, it does not seem to be a realistic possibility for many other psychoactive substances. Current attitudes simply do not favor such a liberal approach. For example, even among high school seniors, 72 percent favor current laws against taking heroin in private, and 44 percent think that smoking marijuana in private should be prohibited (Johnston, O'Malley, and Bachman, 1996). Thus "our value system, rooted in the Protestant ethic, simply will not permit lawmakers to make freely available such powerful mind-altering and euphoria-producing drugs" (Stephens, 1987:120).

SUMMARY: THE RESPONSE OF THE JUVENILE JUSTICE SYSTEM

The juvenile justice system must face several issues concerning drugs and juvenile offenders. First, many of the delinquents committing the worst crimes and the most frequent crimes have drug problems. Statistics clearly demonstrate that offenders tend to have drug problems. It is unclear whether drug use leads to delinquency, delinquency causes drug use, or something else causes both drug use and delinquency. What is clear is that something needs to be done.

The literature on drug treatment and prevention does offer some suggestions for action. As noted earlier, interactive prevention programs fare better than noninteractive programs. Therapeutic communities have had some success in prison settings, especially when followed by aftercare. Multidimensional, comprehensive initiatives appear to hold more promise than single-modality programs, and interventions that include the juvenile justice system (such as drug courts) show that coercive programs can have a positive impact.

The juvenile justice system often attempts to deal with less serious drug users by diverting those youths to other programs. The problem with diverting users of alcohol and other drugs to voluntary programs is that such actions may lead to net-widening. That is, more youths are sent to private programs than really need to be sent. In reaction to this problem, some states, such as Washington, simply opt to divest the juvenile court of its jurisdiction over users of alcohol and other drugs. Unfortunately, such a decision can result in complaints "from disgruntled parents who believed that social control—mandated by the court—was essential for straightening out their children" (Schneider 1988:123-124).

Beyond the problems directly faced by the juvenile justice system, there is the fact that society has failed to take a consistent approach toward drug use. For example, while many drugs are illegal, they are still favored by both youths and adults. This puts parents and drug counselors in a bind. Warnings to avoid drugs completely may fall on unreceptive ears. On the other hand, if a parent or counselor condones some sort of "reasonable" drug use,

> this position pits him or her against the prevailing laws and drug policies of the community, even though this option might be the preferred treatment strategy for some youths (Mandel and Feldman, 1986:39).

There is also a long-standing effort in American society to label some drugs as dangerous and criminal and others as socially acceptable. Heroin, marijuana, cocaine, and other drugs fit the first category. Alcohol, tobacco, and some prescription drugs represent the latter. Thus, adults can buy and use alcohol and tobacco with little or no restraint but have to break the law to obtain even extremely small amounts of controlled substances. This societal "schizophrenia" (Hills, 1980) leads to conflicts in attitudes and hypocrisy in enforcement. Many interventions focus on certain drugs (such as heroin, cocaine, and marijuana) and ignore the serious problems of alcohol and tobacco abuse. Such slighting occurs even though alcohol and tobacco cause harm to more people than any of the so-called "dangerous" drugs.

In summary, there are no easy answers to the question of how the juvenile justice system should deal with drug offenders. Clear, Clear, and Braga (1993) argue that the criminal and juvenile justice systems must be realistic in their efforts. They take the position that any search for a drug-free society is unrealistic. A more realistic vision is the following:

> The purpose of correctional intervention is to prevent crimes where possible, reduce harms to families and communities where feasible, and take reasonable steps to encourage and assist offenders to forgo drug use and related criminal activity. The aim is to reduce, in small measures, the pain experienced by all citizens, offenders and others alike, resulting from drugs in America (Clear, Clear, and Braga, 1993:196).

Discussion Questions

1. You are asked whether drug use causes delinquency. Discuss the possible relationships between drug use and delinquency and take a position on which one is correct. Justify your position.

2. The state legislature has just appointed you to oversee all treatment and prevention programs dealing with drug use. What programs will you keep or institute to fight the drug problem? Why have you selected these programs?

3. Legislation has been proposed to decriminalize drug use in your state. Assuming that this legislation passes, what would you expect to happen to drug use and delinquency? What impact would this have on the juvenile justice system? What other impacts will this have in the state? Provide support for your position.

4. The local police department seeks to continue its D.A.R.E. program. Having just completed a degree in criminal justice, you are called upon for advice. What advice would you offer about this issue?

Chapter 7

Policing and Juveniles

INTRODUCTION

Policing brings to mind images of arresting suspects, shooting at criminals, writing traffic tickets, testifying in court, driving on patrol, and interrogating murder suspects in the detective bureau. Police still do these things, but they also engage in activities that many people are not aware of. For instance, today police also lead community meetings to discuss the extent and causes of neighborhood crime and disorder. Together with community members they are searching for solutions to urban problems. Police go to homes of juveniles who are on probation to assist probation officers in making curfew checks and try to determine what can be done to help juvenile probationers stay out of trouble and adjust. Police also facilitate **restorative justice conferences**, in which, perhaps, a burglary victim meets a juvenile burglar and explains precisely how the burglary impacted the victim. Supporters for both sides are present and, with the help of the police officer leader, they work out an agreement on how the youth can make amends for what he or she did.

So policing today means much more than it did 25 years ago. Twenty years ago police were wondering how they could adjust car patrol to reduce crime. They were wondering if more cars would reduce crime or if faster response time would reduce crime. Today police are raising questions about the definition of policing. What is policing? What role do the police have in a democratic society? These questions and the solutions raised so far are having important effects on how police interact with juveniles.

KEY TERMS
"broken windows" policing
citizen attitudes toward the police
community policing
CompStat
deadly force
decline of social capital
juvenile curfew laws
police attitudes toward citizens
police effectiveness
police use of excessive force
professional policing
racial profiling
restorative justice conferences

In this chapter we will look at police and juveniles. We will discuss the police role, including such new developments as community policing and CompStat. We will also look at attitudes and the police, including both **citizen attitudes toward the police** and **police attitudes toward citizens**, some recent developments in policing, the effectiveness of policing, and improper use of police force.

STATISTICS ON POLICE WORK WITH JUVENILES

A highlight of recent arrest statistics on juveniles is that in 2003 there were an estimated 2.2 million arrests of persons under age 18. There were 1,130 arrests of juveniles for murder, down from the 3,790 arrests in the peak year of 1993. The juvenile violent crime rate was at its lowest point since 1980. The juvenile arrest rate for property crime Index offenses was at its lowest level since the 1970s (Snyder, 2005).

The FBI Uniform Crime Reports show that the majority of juveniles taken into custody (71%) were referred to juvenile court jurisdiction. Twenty percent were handled within the police department and released. Seven percent were referred to criminal or adult court, less than 1 percent were referred to a welfare agency, and 1 percent were referred to another police agency (Federal Bureau of Investigation, 2004).

Two points are noteworthy. The percentage of offenders that police refer to criminal or adult court (7%) is up from 1996 when police referred only 6 percent to criminal court. This parallels recent changes in state laws allowing greater processing of juveniles in adult court. Second, the fact that 20 percent of juveniles taken into custody are simply handled and released shows the discretion that police have with juveniles. Such discretion can have critical consequences for youths. Youths released in this manner do not have to worry that if they commit a new delinquent act a year later the first one will be held against them and they will be treated as having a prior record. Instead, these youths may be treated as not having any record. If police impose any racial or other biases into their decisions to handle and release, those racial biases can have serious effects in later decisions by police, prosecutors, and judges. Much of this discretion is hidden and thus difficult to discover.

THE POLICE ROLE

For much of the twentieth century police tried to be professional crime fighters. This often translated into police driving in one- or two-officer patrol cars until they saw something suspicious or received a radio call to respond to a crime or a call for service. The rationale was that quick response to calls would enable the police to apprehend suspects or deal quickly with problems that citizens reported to central dispatch. Many called this the **professional policing** model. Others have called it "911 policing" because 911 is the emergency phone number used to contact police.

There were several problems with this professional or 911 policing model. One was that increased professionalism did not reduce crime. Studies showed, for example, that simply increasing the extent of patrol in a given sector did not reduce crime. In addition, research showed that quicker response time did not have dramatic effects on crime (Walker, 1998), and that much of a police officer's shift did not even involve crime. Citizens often call the police for all types of problems that are not directly crime-related. Some of the actions prompting those calls could escalate into crime, but many of the calls occur because people regard the police as government workers who are available seven days a week, 24 hours a day, and thus should be able to deal with their problems.

Another problem with the professional model is that it built barriers between the police and citizens. When officers sit in one- or two-person cars, they do not have the opportunity to interact with citizens. Interaction can have positive consequences. It can alert police to problems in the neighborhood, or it can produce tips about who might be engaged in either criminal activity or disorder. The old-fashioned foot patrol officer could get to know both neighborhood problems and tips about who might be causing the problems by having opportunities to meet with shopkeepers, pedestrians, and people sitting or standing near corners or other gathering places. Professional policing decreased the number of foot patrol officers and put the police car as a barrier between the officer and citizens.

Community or Problem-Solving Policing

One response to the shortcomings of the professional policing model is **community policing**, which is also called problem-solving or problem-oriented policing. Community policing does not necessarily mean exactly the same thing to everyone who subscribes to it. Some key features do emerge, however, as critical common elements.

One critical factor is problem solving. As Herman Goldstein (1990) has noted, police can and should be problem solvers in the community. Racing at 60 miles per hour in patrol cars to crime scenes is often a case of too little and too late. Even if the police are quick enough to get there and apprehend a suspect still on the scene or catch him or her fleeing the scene, they are too late—a crime has already occurred.

Problem solving, on the other hand, involves an effort to deal with conditions or factors that lead to crime or disorder. If the police can solve the problem, then they prevent crime from happening. A simple example with juveniles is police in one community leading the community to transform a vacant lot into a skateboard park. This solved the disorder problem of kids skating in the street and on sidewalks (Chaiken, 2004).

Another critical element of community policing is community building (Novak et al., 2002). Because the community shares responsibility for policing the community, an important part of community policing is to strengthen the community and its ability to solve problems and prevent and minimize crime, disorder, and other difficulties.

Such problem solving and community building can take numerous forms. One attempt at problem solving and community building is through holding community or neighborhood meetings. Here police meet with community members to identify problems. Citizens might note that an abandoned house or a house in violation of the housing code is a crack house where dealers are conducting business. Alternatively, citizens might complain that a particular street corner or bus stop is a center for gang-related activity. After problem identification, police and citizens together explore possible solutions. In Chicago, citizens decided to conduct marches in gang-related areas to discourage gang activity there. Together with police, Chicago citizens also worked with the bus company to relocate a particular bus stop where school children were being harassed. Citizens and police also sought the help of city housing inspectors and housing courts to close down buildings ("crack houses") where drug dealers were conducting business.

In another Chicago neighborhood, citizens found that the local juvenile court was so busy that it was ignoring minor offenders. In response to this problem, the community started an alternative-consequence program. This was a program that gave out community service orders for juveniles accused of misdemeanors such as drinking, graffiti, vandalism, shoplifting, and bicycle theft. Youthful offenders usually performed between eight and 100 hours of community service, usually in beautification projects (Skogan and Hartnett, 1997).

In still another Chicago neighborhood, citizens thought that panhandlers, loiterers, and gang members were taking over an important commercial strip. So citizens decided to start Operation Beat Feet, a program in which citizens walked the strip for one to three hours every night. In six months, police reported a 33 percent decrease in five key crimes compared to the previous year (Skogan and Hartnett, 1997).

In San Diego, California, youths involved in defacing public property with graffiti were directed into voluntary focus groups. These groups helped the youths understand why they had gotten involved in graffiti and taught the kids positive ways to contribute to their communities, such as painting murals at locations frequently targeted with graffiti (Carroll, 2001).

In Indianapolis, police act as facilitators at restorative justice conferences. (For a complete discussion of restorative justice, see Chapter 12.) This program is intended for first-time offenders, age 14 and younger, charged with battery, trespass, mischief, conversion, or felony D theft. If the youth is willing to participate, supporters from both sides (offender and victim) meet in a conference. The coordinator tries to get the group to understand what happened. For example, the coordinator asks the youth about the effects of his or her behavior on the victim and asks the victim how the crime affected him or her. After a thorough exploration of the event, the group tries to work out an agreement to repair the harm that was done. Restitution and community service are key elements of agreements. In Indianapolis, police and others (neighborhood prosecutors, civilian volunteers) have coordinated restorative justice conferences, which have taken place in police stations, schools, libraries, and community centers (McGarrell et al., 2000).

More than 90 percent of victims in conference cases report being satisfied with the way the case was handled. Ninety-eight percent said they would recommend the conference approach. At six months after the initial incident, only 20 percent of the youths who went through restorative justice conferences recidivated, compared to 34 percent in the control group. One year after the initial incident, 31 percent of the restorative justice conference youths had been arrested, compared to 41 percent of the control group. Both differences were statistically significant (McGarrell et al., 2000).

In Houston, Texas, community police officers provide a "Knock and Talk" service for truants; they visit truants and talk to them about their truancy problems. In Tacoma, Washington, community police officers deliver truants to a community truancy center (Baker, Sigmon, and Nugent, 2001). In Cleveland, Ohio, police converted houses used as crack houses into police substations. In these so-called "RAPP houses" (named for the Residential Area Policing Program) youths could come in and talk to police officers who were there around the clock (Dunworth, 2000). All of these examples are efforts to both solve problems related to crime and disorder and to enhance the ability of the community to participate in policing itself.

Boston police have taken an approach considerably different from the restorative justice approach used in Indianapolis, but it is still considered to be a problem-solving approach. The problem targeted was violence, specifically homicide. In the Boston Gun Project's Operation Ceasefire, police targeted gangs engaged in violent behavior and used a strategy called "pulling levers," which entailed delivering a message to violent gangs that violence will not be tolerated. In Operation Ceasefire, police hold forums with gang members to announce their intent to apply whatever sanctions they can. Police then arrest gang members for trespassing, public drinking, overt drug use, disorder offenses, probation violations, and outstanding warrants. Evaluators report that Operation Ceasefire "was associated with a 63 percent decrease in youth homicides per month, a 32 percent decrease in shots-fired calls for service per month, a 25 percent decrease in gun assaults per month, and a 44 percent decrease in the number of youth gun assaults per month in the highest risk district" (Braga et al., 2001:3). It should be noted, however, that other research indicates that youth gun homicides had begun to decline in 1995 and that they declined 75 percent in other Massachusetts cities during this period (Fagan, 2002).

In Baton Rouge, Louisiana, police assist probation officers in supervising juveniles and young adults placed on probation for a gun-related offense. Police-probation teams make unscheduled evening visits to probationers about six times per month to check for compliance with probation conditions and to assess needs. In addition to such surveillance, police, probation, and other program participants offer services to address substance abuse, anger management, educational and employment needs, and parental skills (Lizotte and Sheppard, 2001).

Similar to Baton Rouge, St. Louis has a Nightwatch Program in which deputy juvenile probation officers and police officers make random home visits to verify curfew compliance for juvenile probationers. Sanctions such as community service, increased reporting to probation officers, home detention, and regular detention are applied to curfew violators. Rewards such as small gift certificates for products or services are used with compliant youths (Urban, St. Cyr, and Decker, 2003).

The Office of Juvenile Justice and Delinquency Prevention has supported the development of comprehensive, community-wide approaches to gang prevention. These programs involve both suppression and services. Suppression means that police—and often probation—work together in surveillance and information sharing. Service means efforts to provide academic, economic, and social opportunities for gang members. One program targeted older members (17 to 24) of two of the most violent gangs in the Little Village neighborhood of Chicago. Results were favorable, including reduced serious gang violence among the targeted gang members, compared to gang members in a comparison group. Specifically, the program resulted in reduced arrests for serious gang crimes (especially aggravated batteries and assaults) among the targeted youths (Howell, 2000).

Riverside, California, has a gang program that appears to be more comprehensive than the Boston program. Gang youths are supported in attending school and receive job training and opportunities for employment. There is even a stipend for job training. Both probation officers and police make home visits and engage in surveillance efforts that do result in arrests (Howell, 2000). Thus, it appears that suppression and services together are helpful in combating gang delinquency.

Allender (2001) suggests that sometimes the police role in dealing with juvenile gangs may be relatively simple. He suggests that one important thing police can do is simply to notify prosecutors that an arrested juvenile is a gang member. Then the prosecutor can recommend to the judge that sentencing include orders forbidding association with gang members and counseling to discourage gang participation.

Concerns about Community or Problem-Solving Policing

There are some concerns about community or problem-solving policing. One issue is that many practices are labeled community policing that are not actually related to either problem solving or community building. Many police chiefs have claimed that they were practicing community policing simply in order to receive grant money set aside for community policing initiatives or to appear progressive. A second issue is that while the creators of problem-solving policing intended that the police get involved with their community and come up with innovative solutions to crime and disorder problems, many police efforts labeled as problem-solving have been traditional police strategies. A recent study of problem solving in San Diego distinguished between problem solving by police and problem-oriented policing. Many officers do engage in problem solving; they "take a thoughtful approach, try to gather some information before proceeding, and often implement a multipronged response to problems" (Cordner and Biebel, 2005:177). The solution, however, may often be either targeted enforcement or saturation patrol or targeted investigation. In other words, the police put additional attention and presence on the problem, but it appears that not many police are engaging in problem-oriented policing in the sense that they are trying to devise tailor-made nontraditional responses and trying to assess impact (Cordner and Biebel, 2005). In other words, police who claim to be practicing problem-solving policing often are not going beyond traditional police tactics to work with communities to come up with innovative solutions to such problems as crime, drug abuse, and disorder.

"Broken Windows" Policing

In **"broken windows" policing**, the police also broaden their concerns and actions, compared to in traditional 911 policing. Instead of focusing only on crime, the police pay attention to both crime and disorder. Based on the "broken windows" hypothesis, police consider disorder—that is rowdy teens hanging out on street corners, "squeegee men" offering to wash car windows for cash "contributions," prostitutes plying their trade, youths or adults trying to jump turnstiles to avoid paying subway fare, "winos" urinating on the street or sleeping in public places like subway stations, and so on—as a serious problem that leads to street crime.

> Disorder demoralizes communities, undermines commerce, leads to the abandonment of public spaces, and undermines public confidence in the ability of government to solve problems; fear drives citizens further from each other and paralyzes their normal, order-sustaining responses, compounding the impact of disorder (Kelling and Coles, 1996:242).

"Broken windows" theory holds that disorder creates fear in citizens, causing them to stay off the streets. The more citizens avoid streets, the more deserted the steets get and the more citizens avoid them. This affects urban trafficking, both auto and pedestrian, hurts business, and can contribute to crime. Some of the strategies used as part of "broken windows" policing are opportunity reduction, problem solving, and crime prevention through environmental design. (Kelling and Coles, 1996). Some cities (e.g., Indianapolis) have focused on the "broken windows" model of community policing, while other cities (e.g., St. Petersburg) have focused more on police-community cooperation and problem-solving (Paoline, Myers, and Worden, 2000).

More controversial has been the use of zero-tolerance policing. In New York City, Commissioner William Bratton decided to arrest the aforementioned "squeegee men," subway fare beaters, and panhandlers. Bratton decided on a policy of no—"zero"—tolerance for disorder and minor crimes. It has been found that many of the persons stopped by police for disorder or minor crimes (such as subway fare evasion) are wanted on warrants for more serious crimes. So campaigns against disorder have the advantage of catching a considerable number of street criminals who normally escape apprehension.

We have distinguished community policing from "broken windows" policing, but this distinction is not always clear-cut. In New York City, for example, the get-tough approach to petty offenders was considered to be problem solving. We prefer to consider it distinct from community policing efforts such as those in Chicago where the police attended and promoted community meetings and community problem solving. In New York, the police resorted to what we consider a rather traditional approach—making arrests, with minimal community participation. In Chicago, the police tried to maximize community involvement, and that community participation led to such innovative solutions as citizen marches, alternative dispute resolution, and even getting the bus company to relocate a bus stop.

Questions about "Broken Windows" Theory and Policing

"Broken windows" theory and policing rests on a fundamental assumption: disorder causes crime. The thinking is that if a community allows vagrants to panhandle, prostitutes to cruise streets for customers, and teenagers to congregate on street corners, then law-abiding citizens will retreat, the streets will become even more disorderly, and crime will follow.

There is some support for the hypothesis. For example, the Jersey City POP at Violent Places Project used aggressive disorder enforcement tactics at 24 places noted for violent crime. Results showed significant decreases in total calls for service and total crime incidents (Braga, 2001).

However, there are problems with the "broken windows" hypothesis. The first and most important is that it has not been proven conclusively that disorder causes crime. After a thorough review of the research, Harcourt concludes that "[t]here is little evidence that Mayor Guiliani's quality of life initiative in New York City significantly contributed to the concurrent sharp decline in crime" (Harcourt, 2001:124). Harcourt thinks that the addition of more police officers and consequent enhanced surveillance contributed to the decline in crime in New York City, but fighting disorder had no impact.

Second, sophisticated research shows that common factors cause both disorder and crime. Sampson and Raudenbush (1999), for example, have found that concentrated disadvantage (such factors as poverty, unemployment, and single-female-headed households) and collective efficacy are the real causes.

Another problem with the hypothesis that disorder causes crime is that "broken windows" policing actually involves a great deal of disorder: disorder by the police in their enforcement tactics. Wilson and Kelling (1982) freely admit that "broken windows"–style police officers "kick ass" and "knock them [gang members] on their ass" (Harcourt, 2001:127). Police are justified in doing just about anything if their suspicions are aroused. This can lead to rampant discrimination and excessive force. For example, allegations of police misconduct increased 68 percent in New York City from 1993 to 1996 (Harcourt, 2001).

Still another problem with the "broken windows" theory of policing is that it makes a simplistic dichotomy between law-abiding and disorderly citizens. It implies that citizens hanging out on the streets and tossing ice cream wrappers on the street are disorderly. The theory makes no allowance for other interpretations of what perhaps appears to be disorder—interpretations such as "artistic ferment, a youth hangout, rebellion, or an alternative lifestyle" (Harcourt, 2001:132). In addition, it focuses on lower-class disorder and ignores upper- or middle-class disorder. It ignores the disorder of paying a housekeeper under the table, tax evasion, insider trading, and noncompliance with environmental regulations. In summary, "broken windows" theory and policing "embraces an unmediated aesthetic of order, cleanliness, and sobriety" (Harcourt, 2001:134).

A final problem with the theory is that it is contrary to a general finding that coercive crime measures do not seem to work but social support is effective in preventing crime (Colvin, Cullen, and Vander Ven, 2002). (For further discussion of the importance of social support, see Chapter 14.) More specifically, the disintegrative shaming practices used in this strategy "stigmatize individuals and push them away from the law-abiding community" (Colvin, Cullen, and Vander Ven, 2002:32).

For still another perpsective on community policing, see Box 7.1.

Box 7.1 Questioning Community Policing

Most of the experts who write about community policing consider it a positive innovation, but David Garland raises some interesting questions about the focus on quality of life and disorder. Whereas writers such as George Kelling subscribe to the "broken windows" hypothesis that disorder leads to crime, Garland notes that behaviors used to be interpreted quite differently. Now, however, "[p]ublic drinking, soft drug use, graffiti, loitering, vagrancy, begging, sleeping rough, being 'uncivil': these cease to be tolerable nuisances or pricks to the middle-class conscience and become the disorderly stuff upon which serious crime feeds. . . . Every minor offence, every act of disorderly conduct—particularly if committed by poor people in public spaces—is now regarded as detrimental to the quality of life" (Garland, 2001:181). What he means is that the presence of vagrants and street people used to make some people think about the less fortunate and the need for shelters for the homeless and what might be done to address urban poverty. Now the focus is to arrest vagrants and simply get them off the street.

So who is right? Are acts of disorder really precursors to serious crime? Or are such acts "trivia" (Garland, 2001) that used to "prick . . . conscience"? Does the sight of a beggar cause us to think "worthless panhandler trying to con me out of my hard-earned dollars"? Or does it make us think about the reality of poverty in a consumer society where many can satisfy every whim including cars that cost up to $100,000?

CompStat Policing

Several years ago, New York City started using **CompStat**, a strategic-management process in which police managers are held responsible for the control of crime and the enhancement of the quality of life in New York City. CompStat involves the collection of data on the incidence and location of crimes and other problems. This information is shared and police managers are held responsible for reducing crime and taking care of quality-of-life problems (e.g., the presence of alcoholics and vagrants) in their precincts. The process is now being copied in such cities as Indianapolis, Louisville, and Boston.

The process consists of several steps. First, police must gather accurate and timely information. Crime statistics and information about quality-of-life issues are collected and shared. A second component is rapid deployment: police commanders need to send officers out to address the problem. A third component is effective tactics: police need to focus specific resources on the problem. A fourth component is relentless follow-up and assessment. Police must check to see that crime and other problems are decreasing (Walsh and Vito, 2004).

Box 7.2 Community Policing in an Age of the Disappearing Community

Community policing advocates insist that communities are responsible for policing themselves, that they must join efforts with police to make the community safe. Citizens need to participate in community meetings, Neighborhood Watch programs, citizen patrols, and simply the basic task of informing police about neighborhood problems. The police cannot do it alone. Crime and disorder prevention and control should be a joint responsibility. Together the police and the community can and should work together to define problems, explore possible solutions, and implement actions to address those problems.

A difficulty with this emphasis on the joint responsibility of police and community to define and solve community problems is that the sense of community appears to be disappearing.

In Robert Putnam's metaphor, whereas we used to bowl together in leagues, we are now "bowling alone": "We have been pulled apart from one another and from our communities over the last third of the century" (Putnam, 2000:27). Participation in politics and public affairs, clubs and community associations, churches, unions, and professional societies has been decreasing. To give just one example, in 1975-76 approximately two-thirds of all Americans attended club meetings such as Kiwannis or Rotary, but by 1999 two-thirds of Americans were never attending such meetings (Putnam, 2000).

This **decline of social capital** (community support) suggests a logical question: Is it reasonable to believe that Americans will participate in community policing efforts in an era of "bowling alone"? If Americans don't even want to bowl together, join clubs together, go to church together, how can police expect them to participate in community meetings or to participate in programs such as Neighborhood Watch to deal with crime, disorder, and other community problems? If, as Putnam suggests, we are watching more television and spending more time on the Internet, then how can police get citizens to turn off their TVs and computers and participate in community policing efforts?

Related to Putnam's concerns, an evaluation of community policing in Houston, Texas, found that the program seemed to favor the interests of homeowners. There was less information about community policing and less participation by less affluent residents. So community policing "can be difficult in places where the community is fragmented by race, class, and lifestyle" (Skogan and Hartnett, 1997:234). In Chicago, however, community policing seemed to enjoy "fairly inclusive recognition, and fairly widespread benefits" (Skogan and Hartnett, 1997).

So policing experts are calling for greater civic involvement while sociologists such as Putnam are noting the decline of social capital. Should community policing enthusiasts give up or continue their efforts to return policing to its more community-oriented roots?

Although, in New York City, crime and disorder did decrease with CompStat, some questions have been raised about the practice. Some question whether it was CompStat that was responsible for the decrease. Noting that crime went down in other cities at the time that CompStat was being practiced, Moore (2003) argues that other factors were therefore responsible for the decrease. Moore and others also question the aggressive tactics used in New York City, such as rounding up derelicts and so-called "squeegee men." Related to this criticism, Moore also argues that CompStat focuses on arrest and ignores efforts at prevention that could both reduce crime and achieve more overall justice

Box 7.3 Community Policing: A Conflicting Opinion

Most police and most commentators speak of community policing in glowing terms. The reason for such praise is that it is difficult to criticize efforts to involve the community, especially if such involvement means asking community members to define police priorities and to help come up with solutions for crime and disorder problems.

One dissident voice is Neil Websdale, who did a participant observation study of community policing in Nashville, Tennessee. Websdale contends that community policing is actually a subterfuge to cover up societal neglect of inner cities. Globalization of the economy has resulted in the "economic devastation" of inner-city communities, which contributes to drug use and dealing. Community policing is merely a veneer to cover saturation policing in urban areas. Such policing does nothing to deal with the roots of urban problems and urban crime. Moreover, the residents of inner-city Nashville do not consent to saturation policing but report feeling "under siege" (Websdale, 2001:200). Thus,

> The ideology of community policing fits sweetly with the spread of global capitalism and the joblessness, anomie, and despair left in its chaotic wake. Community policing and global capitalism pose as the forces of democratic progress without ever really asking subject populations what they want (Websdale, 2001:218).

Websdale argues that what residents of inner cities really want is not saturation policing that arrests and incarcerates more and more African Americans. What they want is "gainful employment and the creation of safe, wholesome living conditions where their families can flourish" (Websdale, 2001:219).

What do you think? Do inner-city communities want community policing? Or do they want basic changes in the economy so that more jobs are available?

A recent review of what CompStat and non-CompStat police departments were actually practicing showed that both types of departments were pursuing "traditional, police-enforcement strategies" (Weisburd et al., 2003:444). Specifically, both CompStat and non-CompStat departments were emphasizing the following tactics against crime and disorder: increasing arrests for targeted offenders, using check points, targeting repeat offenders, making gun seizures, and improving victim services (Weisburd et al., 2003). CompStat, then, has not been innovative in terms of forcing the police to do new things. The innovation has been directed more at holding upper-level and middle managers accountable for crime and disorder.

Defenders of CompStat argue that the basic ingredients of CompStat policing are its focus on strategic analysis and accountability. In other words, the basics of CompStat are analysis of problems such as crime and disorder, devising strategies to reduce crime and disorder, and measurement to determine if the strategies work. Managers (police chiefs and commanders) are held accountable for results; if they do not reduce crime and disorder, they can and will be replaced (Walsh and Vito, 2004).

One additional note is that similarities can be seen between CompStat policing and the emphasis on accountability currently going on in probation (see Chapter 11). Both of these developments reflect more general trends in both government agencies and business to emphasize strategic management, performance-based objectives, and accountability. Both the public and the private sector see the necessity for government agencies to state their mission and objectives and the need to monitor their activities to see if they are indeed achieving what they set out to achieve. The public demands demonstration that government and business are effective and efficient.

CITIZEN ATTITUDES TOWARD POLICE

Contrary to what many police believe, citizens actually hold rather positive attitudes toward the police. For example, a 2003 Gallup Poll reported that 59 percent of those polled rated the honesty and ethical standards of police either very high or high. Respondents rated police below nurses, clergy, druggists, veterinarians, and doctors, but above college teachers, engineers, dentists, psychiatrists, bankers, chiropractors, journalists, lawyers, and others (Maguire and Pastore, 2004). In November of 2001, in the aftermath of the September 11th terrorist attacks, the rating of police jumped; 68 percent of respondents rated police honesty and ethical standards as very high or high (Gallup Organization, 2001). Another survey in 2002 showed that high percentages of the respondents rated the police "excellent" or "pretty good" at solving crime, preventing crime, and being helpful and friendly (Maguire and Pastore, 2004). Almost 60 percent (57%) of the respondents said that they had a "great deal of confidence" or "quite a lot of confidence" in the police as one of the institutions in American society (Maguire and Pastore, 2001).

Citizens vary considerably, however, in their approval of the police. For example, 62 percent of whites but only 32 percent of blacks rated the honesty and ethical standards of police as high or very high. Similarly, 61 percent of whites but only 43 percent of blacks and 41 percent of Hispanics think that the police treat all races fairly. Less than one-half of young respondents (age 18 to 24 years) think that the police treat all races fairly, compared to more than 50 percent for all other age groups, including 71 percent of senior citizens (age 65 and up). Only 16 percent of whites but 42 percent of blacks and 39 percent of Hispanics fear that the police may stop and arrest them when they are completely innocent (Maguire and Pastore, 2004). In a recent survey in New York City, "blacks were three times more likely than non-blacks to perceive that racially biased policing was widespread, that it was unjustified, and that it had been experienced personally" (Rice and Piquero, 2003:111). Thus, citizen attitudes toward the police are not uniform. Some citizens are more positive, while others are more negative.

Of great relevance to the police and juvenile justice is the fact that lower-class youths comprise one group holding negative attitudes toward the police. Anderson (1994) argues that lower-class youths have little faith in the police and subscribe to a street code whereby the "police are most often seen as representing the dominant white society and not caring to protect inner-city residents" (Anderson, 1994:82). As a result of the perception and/or the reality that police do not respond when called, the inner-city youth often relies on self-protection: "taking care of himself" (Anderson, 1994:82) is a critical part of this street code.

A study of more than 5,000 eighth-grade students found that youths were "indifferent" toward the police, that they were neither positive nor negative (Taylor et al., 2001). Part of the reason for youths' indifference or negative attitudes toward the police is that youths often have negative experiences with the police. A recent study in Hartford, Connecticut, for example, found that the 132 youths interviewed reported approximately 400 negative experiences. Thirty-nine percent involved physical encounters (force, hitting, injury), 24 percent involved verbal harassment, and 34 percent were categorized as "other." For example, a 15-year-old Hispanic female reported being thrown against the ground and then against a wall when she was hanging out on the street with friends. A black youth suspected of dealing drugs when he was talking to a friend on the street was grabbed, thrown up against the car, and hit with billy clubs. (He admitted possessing but not dealing drugs.) Another youth was driving and was signaled to pull over. The officer smashed his car window and several officers grabbed, beat, and injured the youth (Borrero, 2001).

It is interesting to speculate about how changes in the nature of policing might affect attitudes toward the police. Recall that Chicago made a major effort to implement community policing. In response, in four of the five experimental districts, residents reported improved police responsiveness to neighborhood concerns, and African-American residents had improved perceptions about police misconduct (Skogan and Hartnett, 1997). In Boston, where Operation Ceasefire meant a tough, deterrent message and approach to violent gang members, interviews with community members indicated that they felt the deterrence strategy was effective but worried about the long-term effects. They were concerned that simply sending troubled youths to prison was not the complete answer and might just increase youths' hostility and hopelessness (Stoutland, 2001).

These variations in attitudes toward the police helps to explain the paradox that police often hold negative or cynical views of citizens while citizen attitudes toward the police are actually rather positive. Part of the explanation for this apparent contradiction is that the police are much more likely to come in contact with citizens with less positive views—minority and younger citizens—than with older citizens who hold more positive views. A second explanation for the paradox is that the police often come into contact with citizens at inopportune times—in instances in which citizens have broken the law (even if only a traffic law), been victimized, or witnessed a crime. At such times, citizens are likely to be under stress. They may react with frustration at receiving a speeding ticket or at hearing an officer say that there is little hope of recovering their $400 video recorder that has just been stolen. Citizens may lash out at the available target (i.e., the police officer) much like a frustrated customer reacts to

Mark C. Ide

Police need to be especially careful in their dealings with those citizens who hold less positive attitudes toward police. In many cities, young blacks have experienced negative encounters with police and expressed fears about their future.

a customer service representative who is not responsible for the problem but has the unpleasant job of trying to rectify it. Repeated contacts with citizens in times of crisis can also lead the police to job burnout (Maslach and Jackson, 1979), cynicism (Niederhoffer, 1967), suspicion (Skolnick, 1966), and/or stress (Crank and Caldero, 1991; Kroes, Hurrell, and Margolis, 1974). In addition, dissatisfaction with a specific police contact leads to lower evaluations of police services in general (Huebner, Schafer, and Bynum, 2004).

One final observation on this matter concerns the fact that any victim of crime views his or her situation as unique while the police view the same situation as routine. The victim often is a first-time victim who is frightened, stunned, and excited about something that is entirely new to him or her.

The officer is simply experiencing the third burglary report that night, the twentieth that week, or the one-thousandth in his or her career. Additionally, the officer's realistic judgment that little or nothing can be done to "solve" the crime leads him or her to rush through the encounter with the citizen in order to write up a report so that the victim can file an insurance claim. Based on television or movie stereotypes, the naïve citizen may expect the officer to drop everything, spend as much time as possible on the victim's case, and solve it. Realizing that the officer has a very different definition of the situation, the citizen becomes upset and reacts accordingly—possibly accusing the officer of incompetence or laziness. Such negative encounters reinforce officer perceptions of citizens as being negative toward the police, even while the public opinion poll research shows the contrary.

Implications of the Attitudinal Research

Several conclusions can be drawn from this discussion of police attitudes toward citizens and citizen attitudes toward the police. First, both sides could benefit from clarification. The police might benefit from becoming aware that citizens generally are positive about the police. Citizens, on the other hand, need to know why police may be somewhat cynical toward them. Citizens should be aware that police officers have likely seen their problem before and have had contact with some victims who precipitated the crime or were otherwise tainted. More importantly, citizens must be realistic in their expectations of what the police can do. For example, the police often can do little or nothing to recover a stolen television or car. Second, police need to be careful in their dealings with citizens who hold less positive attitudes—namely, youths and minorities. Because these groups may be less favorable in their attitudes toward the police, the police need to target them for more positive treatment. Otherwise, these groups may interpret police indifference and cynicism as evidence of prejudicial attitudes and discriminatory behavior. Furthermore, police sensitivity to the attitudes of youthful and minority citizens can lead to improved police–community relations.

As noted, there has been recent emphasis on the police as problem solvers. Some police experts think that traditional policing can do little more than take reports for many problems. If policing were restructured, however, perhaps more could be done about many of the concerns that citizens have. If police spent less time running from call to call and more time exploring the causes and solutions of various problems, then the police could be more effective and have greater impact (see, e.g., Trojanowicz et al., 1998).

THREE RECENT ISSUES IN POLICING CONCERNING JUVENILES

In addition to the major issue of community policing, a number of issues have arisen in the last few years specifically concerning juveniles. Here we will discuss three of these issues: racial profiling, curfew laws, and intensive supervision.

Racial Profiling

One recent issue affecting attitudes toward the police is racial profiling. **Racial profiling** is defined "as the police use of race as the *sole* basis for initiating law enforcement activity (e.g., stopping, searching, and detaining a person)" (Meehan and Ponder, 2002:403). One form of alleged racial profiling was the practice of stopping African-American drivers for "driving while black" on the New Jersey Turnpike. Police were targeting black drivers for about two-thirds of all traffic stops based on claims that blacks were more likely to be carrying drugs. However, searches of white drivers were in fact producing more contraband than searches of black drivers (Roane, 2001). Similarly, a recent study of profiling in a medium-sized suburban police department found that profiling increased "as African Americans travel farther from 'black' communities and into whiter neighborhoods" (Meehan and Ponder, 2002).

It should be noted that charges of racial profiling need thorough investigation. A scientific study of New Jersey State Trooper stops of motorists showed that the troopers were stopping black drivers "in approximate proportion to their representation among speeders" (Lange, Johnson, and Voas, 2005:216). Although this does not automatically rule out profiling, it shows that there is a need to have an accurate measure of the composition of violators and not just a measure of the composition of the population in the jurisdiction (Lange, Johnson, and Voas, 2005). Similarly, an observational study in Savannah, Georgia, showed that race affected whether police viewed blacks as suspicious, but such nonbehavioral suspicion did not influence the officer's decision to stop and question (Alpert, MacDonald, and Dunham, 2005).

Writing in *Time*, Jack White noted that as an African-American parent he was also a racial profiler. By this he meant that he and other African-American parents teach their sons survival tactics that are the flip side of police racial profiling, that is, profile all white police as racist and expect the worst. White taught his sons: "No back talk if a cop pulls you over. Looking straight ahead and keeping your hands on the steering wheel where the officer can see them. Asking permission before you reach for your driver's license. And never, ever running away" (White, 2001:45).

Some conservatives argue that racial profiling is somewhat justified because blacks seem to commit a disproportionate share of street crime. John Derbyshire, for example, cited statistics showing that victims report that 60 percent of robberies are committed by blacks (Derbyshire, 2001). Similarly, columnist Woody West noted that "[i]f tiny green men were sticking up convenience stores late at night in Elk's Breath, Wyoming, police would be derelict if they did not look suspiciously on tiny green men loitering near convenience stores late at night" (West, 2001:48).

What supporters of profiling forget is that profiling can contribute to such statistics and can produce very negative consequences. Profiling can lower deterrence by lowering trust in the police and willingness to report crime. "Further, hostility between minorities and the police creates an unwillingness to testify at trials, and, when serving on juries, an unwillingness to convict defendants" (Leitzel, 2001).

What is the solution? Leitzel suggests that the police ask themselves the following when considering stopping or searching a minority member: "Would I stop or search this person if he or she were white? If the answer is no, then the minority individual should not be stopped or searched either, even if, for instance, the neighborhood is predominantly white and blacks stopped in the area have been associated with crime in the past (Leitzel, 2001). A problem with this is that racial stereotyping can be unconscious; the officer may not be aware that he or she is employing a racial stereotype (Graham and Lowery, 2004). Another suggested solution is for the police to record information on stops. Some think that such forced record keeping will decrease profiling. A problem with this suggestion is that police can avoid recording stops and still continue to profile (Meehan and Ponder, 2002).

A caution is that focusing on police profiling can be misguided if the profiling is a reflection of prejudice and discrimination in the community. "If racial profiling reflects society-wide patterns of segregation and a generalized attitude about who belongs where, focusing on police 'attitudes' or 'cultural sensitivity' will not solve the problem" (Meehan and Ponder, 2002:423). What is needed is attention to the broader problem of racial inequality in that community.

A recent study addressed the related and important question of possible racial bias in arrest practices. Using data from the National Incident-Based Reporting System (NIBRS), Pope and Snyder found that in the 17 jurisdictions analyzed there was "no evidence to support the hypothesis that police are more likely to arrest nonwhite juvenile offenders than white juvenile offenders, once other incident attributes are taken into consideration" (Pope and Snyder, 2003:6). Overall, victims identified 69.2 percent of offenders to be white, and 72.7 percent of juvenile offenders arrested were white. The only indication of bias was indirect: "nonwhite juveniles . . . are more likely to be arrested when the victim is white than when the victim is nonwhite" (Pople and Snyder, 2003:6).

Juvenile Curfew Laws

Juvenile curfew laws have been enacted in numerous cities across the country in an effort to reduce victimization of and by juveniles. Charlotte's curfew law included such objectives and also strove to "reinforce and promote the role of parents in raising and guiding children" (City of Charlotte Code, cited in Hirschel, Dean, and Dumond, 2001). To accomplish these goals, children under 16 years of age were prohibited from being on the streets from 11:00 PM to 6:00 AM during the week and from midnight to 6:00 AM on Friday and Saturday nights. Other cities with curfews may have different age or time stipulations. Vernon, Connecticut, for example, enacted a curfew for juveniles under 18 and prohibited them being on the streets from 11:00 PM to 6:00 AM every night of the week (Males, 2000). In one California city, the curfew applied from 11:00 PM to 5:00 AM on week nights and from 1:00 AM to 5:00 AM on weekends. Exceptions involved standing in front of their own homes, returning home within one hour of attending certain activities, working, or being in the company of a parent (Stuphen and Ford, 2001).

Research on the effectiveness of curfews indicates that curfew laws do not reduce crime or victimization. For example, after the implementation of the curfew law in Vernon, Connecticut, Part I crimes did decrease, but the decrease "was similar to or less than the crime declines experienced in similar cities and the state as a whole" (Males, 2000:259). A time-series analysis of victimizations in New Orleans showed that the law was "ineffective for reducing victimizations, victimizations of juveniles, and juvenile arrests (Reynolds, Seydlitz, and Jenkins, 2000:219). In addition, the laws do not appear to reduce subsequent offending by juveniles who are cited for curfew violations. In Charlotte, for example, 40 percent of the youths cited for curfew violations were arrested for an offense following their first curfew violation (Hirschel, Dean, and Dumond, 2001). A national evaluation of 52 counties showed that curfew laws only affected significant decreases in three of 12 crimes (burglaries, larcenies, and simple assaults). The authors concluded that their research "provides, at best extremely weak support for the hypothesis that curfews reduce juvenile crime rates" and that the "results do not encourage the idea that curfews help prevent juvenile crime" (McDowall, Loftin, and Wiersema, 2000:88).

Similarly, in a recent review of studies of teen curfews, Adams (2003) identified 10 empirical studies of juvenile curfews. Adams concluded that the weight of the evidence from these 10 studies overall "fails to support the argument that curfews reduce crime and victimization" (p. 155). Generally, any arrests that are made are for curfew-related offenses such as lying about one's age. Adams does not totally reject the use of teen curfews. He notes that they might be useful on a temporary basis in hot spots or that they can be helpful in identifying teens with problems. There is evidence that up to one-third of the children picked up for curfew violations have to be taken to shelters because there is no parent or guardian to care for them.

One reason for the ineffectiveness of curfews is that the hours covered by the laws may not be times evidencing high victimization. In Vernon, Connecticut, for example, it was found that juvenile crime was much more likely to occur in the afternoon (Males, 2000). Nationally, it appears that violent offenses and gang crimes peak at approximately 3:00 PM (Sickmund, Snyder, and Poe-Yamagata, 1997). One response to this issue is to have daytime curfews for those youths who are not under the jurisdiction of truancy laws. A recent survey found that 10 percent of the responding jurisdictions had daytime curfews. In fact, some were so restrictive that even a youngster cutting class and not being in the place he was supposed to be in was technically in violation of that city's daytime curfew law (Bannister, Carter, and Schafer, 2001)

Another problem is that curfew enforcement may only ensnare youths who are "already embedded in a criminal lifestyle at an early age" (Hirschel, Dean, and Dumond, 2001:210). As suggested by research in New Orleans, another problem is that juveniles do not necessarily comply with curfew laws. In New Orleans during the first year of the law, more than 3,500 youths were taken into custody just for curfew violations (Reynolds, Seydlitz, and Jenkins, 2000). Most importantly, curfew laws do nothing to improve juveniles' relationships with peers, schools, and family, all of which are important correlates of delinquency. As shown in earlier chapters, parental supervision and attachment to parents are critical factors in preventing delinquency. Curfew laws do nothing to strengthen such supervision or bonding.

One suggestion to salvage some good out of the curfew laws is to use them to identify youths with problems, particularly with regard to problems relating to inadequate parental supervision. This could be done by having a youth service worker screen youths who appear to be experiencing such lack of supervision and refer the youths to appropriate community services (Hirschel, Dean, and Dumond, 2001).

It is interesting that police think curfew laws are effective even though they do not have concrete evidence that the curfews are effective in reducing crime (Bannister, Carter, and Schafer, 2001). Perhaps police enthusiasm for curfews would decrease if they became more familiar with the literature showing that curfews are not effective.

Part of the reality of curfew laws is the panacea phenomenon. As will be noted in Chapter 11 in the discussion of Scared Straight programs, we are often guilty of expecting quick and inexpensive fixes for complicated problems such as delinquency. Unrealistically, we hope that a simple measure such as a curfew law will cure the delinquency problem in our local community. So we pass curfew laws and expect police enforcement of such laws to magically wipe out juvenile crime.

Another reason for the popularity of curfew laws is the "broken windows" theory. The evidence that curfew laws do not decrease crime is further evidence that combating disorder does not always reduce crime (Harcourt, 2001). For a note on curfews and high school proms, see Box 7.4.

Box 7.4 Curfews and Proms

In 2001 the Georgia legislature enacted a year-round curfew forbidding anyone under 18 from driving after midnight. So, like Cinderella, prom-goers need to be off the road by the stroke of 12 midnight. Breaking this curfew law can mean a penalty of up to one year in jail or a fine of up to $1,000.

Legislators created this law in response to some highly publicized auto deaths of teenagers in the Atlanta area. Unlike the curfew laws discussed in this chapter, this is a safety curfew more than a crime prevention curfew.

In response, schools are planning to end their proms some time before midnight so that students can get home by 12:00. One school will end its prom at 11:30 PM to allow for plenty of time to beat the curfew. Police say that they are not making any exceptions for prom night.

What do you think? Should there be an exception for prom night?

Source: M. Scott (2002). "Georgia Prom-goers to Face Curfew Thanks to Recent Legislation." *Johnson City Press* (May 1, 2002):6.

Assistance with Intensive Supervision of Probationers

Anchorage, Alaska, tried using police officers to enhance probation officer supervision of juvenile offenders. Anchorage used police officers to turn regular supervision into intensive supervision. This means that the juvenile probationers received additional contacts, contacts with their probation officers, and contacts with police officers. Like many previous intensive supervision programs, there was no reduction in criminal recidivism; there was no significant difference in the percentage of offenders under intensive supervision who committed any new offense or the percentage of offenders under regular supervision who committed any new offense. However, about 30 percent of the intensive supervision offenders had a probation violation, compared to 17 percent of the regular offenders. Thus, increased supervision translates into increased monitoring and detection of technical violations.

It is interesting that Anchorage tried an intensive supervision effort using police when so much prior research on intensive supervision has not been promising. What is promising is a program such as Operation Eiger in Baton Rouge, Louisiana. Here police also help probation officers conduct unscheduled evening visits six times per month, but the program involves addressing needs as well as enforcing probation conditions. Services are provided to deal with substance abuse, anger management, academic difficulties, and employment needs (Lizotte and Sheppard, 2001). Hopefully, this combination of intensive supervision and treatment will have greater success than the intensive supervision alone program in Alaska. For a little known program in policing, the Police Corps, see Box 7.5.

Box 7.5 Police Corps: Is It for You?

Not many people are aware that the federal government funds the Police Corps, a program modeled after the Peace Corps. In the Police Corps, college students receive scholarships to go to college and to receive police training. After college they must serve four years as police officers in return for the scholarship assistance.

The program started as part of President Clinton's Crime Bill. It has never been formally evaluated. Recently, however, the Maryland Police Corps class finished its four years of mandatory service. Twenty-four of the 28 graduates have remained with the Baltimore Police Department.

The International Association of Chiefs of Police opposes the program. The Association favors providing scholarships for persons who are already police officers and want to get a college degree (Klein, 2002).

What do you think? Is it a beneficial idea to offer scholarships in return for a four-year commitment to policing? What are the benefits? What are the problems with such a program? Would you commit to four years of police service in return for a college scholarship?

Source: J. Klein (2002). "The Supercop Scenario." *The New Yorker* (March 18):72-78.

POLICE EFFECTIVENESS

It is clear that the police are making a variety of efforts to combat juvenile crime. As noted earlier, police are staffing RAPP houses in Cleveland, facilitating restorative justice conferences in Indianapolis, going to community meetings in Chicago, enforcing curfews all over the country, and participating in demonstration projects such as Operation Ceasefire in Boston.

Overall, how effective are the police in their new efforts against crime and delinquency? For many of these programs, we have already noted specific outcome results. Here a summary is in order.

First, some things simply do not work. Juvenile curfew laws, for example, have been tried in numerous cities. Most evaluations indicate that they are not very effective in the fight against juvenile crime.

Second, a very possible reason that some interventions do not work is that they are simplistic and contrary to what we know. Both the juvenile curfew laws and the Anchorage intensive supervision program, for example, stem from a Scared Straight panacea phenomenon that looks for simple answers: pass a law to keep juveniles off the street or ask a police officer to stop in at a juvenile's house. Human behavior is more complicated that this.

Third, it is critical to avoid unrealistic expectations. In their study of community policing in Chicago, for example, Skogan and Hartnett (1997) found that some neighborhood conditions improved. Every neighborhood had at least one improvement. Victimization declined in two areas, street crime dropped in two others, drug and gang problems declined in two, and graffiti declined in another. Overall, compared to comparison areas, there were positive changes in 27 of the 51 outcomes that the evaluation measured, an overall success rate of 53 percent (Skogan and Hartnett, 1997:244). Skogan and Hartnett emphasize that communities should have realistic expectations from community policing. A success rate of 50 percent appears to be realistic. Expectations of 95 percent or even 75 percent success rates are fanciful.

Fourth, the police are only part of the picture. Eck and Maguire (2000), for example, contend that the decrease in crime in the last 10 years is the result of communities and the nation mobilizing to fight crime. Such mobilization involves police initiatives such as community policing, increased use of prison, demographic trends (the aging of the population and the decrease in the proportion of young males), and the decline of retail drug markets. A realistic perspective on the police impact on crime can be summarized as follows:

> There is one thing that is a myth: The police have a substantial, broad, and *independent* impact on the nation's crime rate. Rather than think of the police as an isolated institution that has a distinctive impact on crime, perhaps we should think of the police as part of a network of institutions, some of them formal (e.g., courts and schools) and some of them informal (e.g., families and churches), that respond to crime. . . .

> When considered in isolation, the effectiveness of any one element of this diverse array of people and organizations may be slight. But collectively, the response might be more dramatic (Eck and Maguire, 2000:247-248).

POLICE USE OF EXCESSIVE FORCE (BRUTALITY)

Police use of excessive force is a sensitive topic and thus it is difficult to gain accurate information about its extent. Like any profession, police will not just open up and reveal professional secrets. They will not readily disclose how frequently and under what circumstances they may use excessive force. So researchers often survey citizens to derive estimates of police use of force.

Based on an observational study of police-citizen encounters about 25 years ago, Albert Reiss reported that teens were the most likely targets of the least damaging type of police brutality, namely, abusive language and commands to "move on." Such commands were particularly frequent in the summer when youths living in the ghetto were likely to spend more time on the streets. Police told both black youths and white youths to leave or go home (Reiss, 1980). Recent research shows that such problems continue, especially for African-American youths. A 1991 survey of more than 300 Cincinnati youths revealed that almost one-half (46.6%) of the black youths reported having been personally hassled by police, compared to only about 10 percent of white youths. In addition, approximately two-thirds of the blacks said that they knew someone who had been hassled (Browning et al., 1994).

As noted previously in the section on attitudes, a recent study in Hartford, Connecticut, found that the 132 youths interviewed reported approximately 400 negative experiences. Thirty-nine percent involved physical encounters (force, hitting, injury), 24 percent involved verbal harassment, and 34 percent were categorized as "other."

Geller and Toch (1996) argue that the process of stereotyping can be an important factor leading to the use of force against juveniles. A police officer can stereotype a youth as a "typical gang member," and a youth can stereotype a police officer as a "typical white cop." This stereotyping very easily leads to a process of arrest, resistance or actions interpreted as resistance, and excessive force or actions so interpreted so that a series of self-fulfilling prophecies are set in motion. The problem is to stop the start of such self-fulfilling prophecies.

A hopeful note is that a recent review concluded that "physical force is infrequently used by the police and that improper force is used even less" (Worden, 1996:46). One problem with this research conclusion is that it may not be in sync with perceptions on the street, especially perceptions in some of the trouble spots of inner-city areas of cities such as New York and Los Angeles. In such locations, contrary perceptions help to trigger the stereotyping process just noted and lead to tragic results.

A national survey on this topic, the Police Public Contact Survey, showed that in 1999 an estimated 43.8 million Americans, 16 or older, had at least one face-to-face contact with a police officer (Langan et al., 2001). More than 400,000 persons (less than 1 percent of those reporting contact) reported that the police used force or threatened the use of force against them. Most of this was pushing or grabbing. Most of those who experienced force (76%) said the force was excessive. Most persons (85%) involved in force incidents said the officer was white. More than one-half of those who experienced police force said that they had argued with, disobeyed, or resisted the police or used alcohol or other drugs. It should be noted that respondents ages 16 through 19 reported the most frequent experience of force or threat of force by police. About 3 percent of 16-19-year-olds reported force or threat of force, compared to 1.4 percent of 20-29-year-old respondents and less than 1 percent of all age categories 30 or older (Langan et al., 2001). (For a discussion of possible use of force in schools, see Box 7.6.)

An observational study of subjects in Indianapolis and St. Petersburg showed that in many instances police could have used more force on resistant suspects but did not do so. On the other hand, in encounters in which the suspect did not resist, officers engaged in behavior that could be perceived as an attempt to increase the level of police response, such as resorting to a threat or low-level physical force (Terrill, 2005).

Box 7.6   Police Use of Tasers in Schools

An estimated 1,700 police officers assigned to U.S. schools carry tasers (stun guns) to use against unruly students. Reports indicate that about 24 students in central Florida were shocked, and at least four students have been shocked in the Charlotte, North Carolina, area. One proposal is to ban the use of such stun guns in elementary schools but allow them, but only as a last resort, in middle schools and high schools.

What do you think? Is there a need for such devices in schools? Are they also necessary in elementary schools?

Source: D. Leiwand (2005). "Schools Restrict Use of Tasers." *USA Today* (June 3, 2005):1A.

A study of police use of force in Arizona found that race did not affect use of force overall but was a significant factor in treatment of males in custody. Force was significantly more likely against black and Hispanic males who were not in custody (Schuck, 2004). Race was not a factor, however, in a study of cases of use of force investigated by an internal affairs unit in California. The typical officer investigated was a young male officer with less than a decade of experience who had been investigated before (McElvain and Kposowa, 2004).

Thus, we have conflicting estimates of force and other negative behaviors by police against youths. The national survey indicates about 3 percent of youths experience police force in a typical year. Surveys of youths in two separate cities, Cincinnati and Hartford, report as many as almost 50 percent of certain groups of youths (e.g., blacks) reporting force.

Worden thinks the use of improper force is infrequent, a conclusion supported by the national survey. The hopeful conclusion is that Worden and the national survey are correct. A more pessimistic conclusion is that force is more frequent, especially against minority youths, and that efforts are required to reduce any use of force as much as possible.

A related study sheds some additional light on the issue of police transgressions. Gould and Mastrofski (2004) conducted observation of police behavior in "Middleberg," a medium-sized city in the middle of illicit drug shipment routes. They found that 30 percent of the observed searches (115 over three months) conducted by police were illegal or unconstitutional. This would extrapolate to about 12,000-14,000 unconstitutional searches per year in Middleberg. Thus, a major finding of the research in Middleberg was that "those sworn to uphold the law regularly and repeatedly transgressed constitutional boundaries" (Gould and Mastrofski, 2004:331). One police expert concludes: "The "dirty secret" of contemporary American criminal justice is that prosecutors and judges know full well the corners that police cut and often turn a blind eye. The success of the entire system depends on convicting the guilty as quickly as possible, even if that means taking liberties with strict due process" (Bayley, 2002:137-138).

Thus, there is police misconduct, ranging from improper searches to improper use of force, and progressing all the way up to the improper use of deadly force. Police administrators must forever be vigilant to reduce such misconduct as much as possible.

Deadly Force

In a review of the literature on **deadly force**, William Geller (1983) describes the typical victim of police shooting as between 17 and 30. This means that not many juveniles—only the 17-year-olds—are likely to be shot by police officers. All police shootings, however, are not typical; some do involve younger victims. In fact, a test case on the use of deadly force involved the shooting of a 15-year-old youth in Memphis, Tennessee. A Memphis police officer shot and killed Edward Garner, a 15-year-old eighth-grade student, under that state's common law "fleeing felon" rule, which authorized police to shoot any fleeing felon—even nondangerous ones. Garner had been prowling inside an empty house and refused to halt in the yard when the police officer warned him to stop. Consequently, the officer shot the youth as he tried to climb a fence to escape. After this incident, the United States Supreme Court ruled that police may not institute a policy to shoot any and all fleeing suspects; rather, they may shoot only those escaping felons who pose a threat to the officer or to others. Box 7.7 presents excerpts from the decision. This critical case (*Tennessee v. Garner et al.*) ordered police to be much more selective in using deadly force. Research has shown that as a result of the case there has been a decrease both in shooting overall and in the appearance of discrimination in deadly force (Sparger and Giacopassi, 1992). What has happened is that police departments have been forced to devise guidelines for the use of deadly force, and the enforcement of those guidelines has been successful in decreasing police shootings (Locke, 1996).

AP Photo/Cincinnati Enquirer/
Steven M. Herppich, Pool

Mourners view the casket of Timothy Thomas during funeral services at the New Prospect Baptist Church Saturday in Cincinnati, Ohio. The shooting of the fleeing Thomas, who was wanted on 14 warrants for misdemeanors and traffic violations, led to three days of rioting in the city.

Box 7.7 The U.S. Supreme Court on Deadly Force

In *Tennessee v. Garner et al.*, the U.S. Supreme Court set down guidelines for the constitutional use of deadly force by police officers. Here are some excerpts from the majority opinion by Justice White:

The use of deadly force to prevent the escape of all felony suspects, whatever the circumstances, is constitutionally unreasonable. It is not better that all felony suspects die than that they escape. Where the suspect poses no immediate threat to the officer and no threat to others, the harm resulting from failing to apprehend him does not justify the use of deadly force to do so. It is no doubt unfortunate when a suspect who is in sight escapes, but the fact that the police arrive a little late or are a little slower afoot does not always justify killing the suspect. A police officer may not seize an unarmed, nondangerous suspect by shooting him dead. . . .

. . . Where the officer has probable cause to believe that the suspect poses a threat of seriosu physical harm, either to the officer or to others, it is not constitutionally unreasonable to prevent escape by using deadly force. Thus, if the suspect threatents the officer with a weapon or there is probable cause to believe that he has committed a crime involving the infliction or threatened infliction of serious physical harm, deadly force may be used if necessary to prevent escape, and if, where feasible, some warning has been given (*Tennessee v. Garner et al.*, 1985).

SUMMARY

It is an intriguing time for policing. Both police themselves and outsiders are debating the meaning of policing. Some, like former New York City police commissioner William Bratton, argue that police should take a tough approach (zero tolerance) and arrest even "squeegee men" who harass motorists by foisting unwanted window washing on them. In Boston, this tough approach, called "pulling levers," takes the form of arresting suspected violent gang members for disorder offenses, criminal acts, and outstanding warrants. Other developments in policing, however, take a completely different approach. In Indianapolis, for example, police are coordinating restorative justice conferences in which youths, victims, and supporters on both sides sit down and try to repair the harm done by victimizations. Here offenders learn how they harmed their victims and what they can do to repair that harm.

In other places, such as Chicago, police are attending neighborhood meetings and trying to learn what the community considers to be problems and how those problems should be solved. Problems vary from crack houses operating in residential neighborhoods to gangs harassing youths at bus stops after school.

Whatever specific approaches police are taking, many are also following the lead of CompStat in attempting to specify their mission and objectives more explicitly and trying to measure how closely they are actually achieving their goals. Accountability is a current emphasis in both business and government.

Many cities continue to use juvenile curfew laws in an attempt to reduce juvenile crime. The goal is to reduce both offending and victimization. Apparently these curfew laws and their enforcement continue despite a lack of supporting research evidence.

Perhaps the answer is to combine both approaches. Perhaps violent gang members need the tough (pulling levers) approach while first offenders charged with certain offenses can benefit from a restorative justice conferencing approach. What is clear, however, is that policing is changing and will continue to change. Many police officers undoubtedly continue to drive patrol cars and respond to 911 calls. In many communities, however, more innovative efforts are underway. Hopefully, such innovation will continue to change our ideas and expectations of what the police can and should do to prevent and control delinquency, disorder, and crime.

An important point to remember in any consideration of the police is that policing is only part of the effort to prevent, reduce, or control crime. When crime increases, much of society reacts, and many institutions and actors try to mobilize against crime. It is erroneous to think that the police alone can reduce crime. So instead of focusing only on the police,

> we should think of the police as part of a network of institutions, some of them formal (e.g., courts and schools) and some of them informal (e.g., families and churches), that respond to crime. When violent crime grows into a serious social concern, it is not just the police that focus more attention on the problem. Schools, community groups, businesses, health officials, and many other organizations and individuals also respond to crime . . . In summary, as the police mobilize to address crime more effectively, so do many other institutions (Eck and Maguire, 2000:249-250).

So we will repeat our citation of Eck and Maguire at the end of the section on **police effectiveness**: it is a myth that the "police have a substantial, broad, and *independent* impact on the nation's crime rate" (Eck and Maguire, 2000:249), but a realistic review of the research shows evidence "for focused policing strategies contributing to the drop in violent crime" (p. 245). It is also important to note that "[s]ome of the policing strategies that have received the most attention (for example, CompStat and zero-tolerance policing in New York City) are the least plausible candidates for contributing to the reduction in violent crime" (Eck and Maguire, 2000:245).

We need to be realistic in our expectations of the police. Surely the police play a role in combating delinquency, but to expect the police to be the only factor—or even the most important factor—is unrealistic. Many factors contribute to delinquency and crime. All the institutions of society must play a part.

Discussion Questions

1. Community policing is based on the assumption that the job of the police is to solve the problems that lead to crime. Do you agree or disagree with this assumption? To what extent can society hold the police responsible for the problems that cause crime?

2. Police are trying new types of policing such as community or problem-solving policing, "broken windows" policing, and CompStat. Which approach do you favor? Discuss. Note any possible problems with the various approaches.

3. What do we know about police attitudes toward citizens? About citizen attitudes toward the police? What can be done to improve attitudes on both sides?

4. What do curfew laws seek to accomplish? Are they effective?

5. What do we know about police use of force with juveniles? What can be done to minimize any improper use of force by police?

6. Policing is changing. Would you want to be a police officer in light of all the change that is taking place in policing?

Chapter 8

The Juvenile Court Process

INTRODUCTION

Once a police officer takes a youth into custody, it is likely that the police will refer that youth to juvenile court. As noted in the police chapter, other than traffic and neglect cases, in 2003 police referred the majority (in fact, 71%) of the juveniles they took into custody to juvenile court jurisdiction. Twenty percent were handled within the police department and released. Seven percent were referred to criminal or adult court, less than 1 percent were referred to a welfare agency, and 1 percent were referred to another police agency (Federal Bureau of Investigation, 2004).

When police refer a youth to juvenile court, the court personnel must then make one or more critical decisions: whether to detain (jail) the youth, whether to actually file a **petition** (charges) against the youth, whether to find (adjudicate) the youth a delinquent, and how to dispose of the petition. These decisions correspond to the adult court decisions of bail versus jail, formal charge versus dismissal, determination of guilt by plea or by trial, and sentencing. An additional decision is the decision to prosecute the youth as an adult in criminal court or retain jurisdiction in juvenile court. Several juvenile court actors—probation officers, defense attorneys, prosecutors, and judges—are involved in these important decisions. While the judge is often the primary decisionmaker, other court personnel play important roles in deciding the fate of juvenile suspects.

KEY TERMS

adjudication

blended sentencing

concerned adult role

day-evening centers

detention

   home detention

   secure/nonsecure detention

disposition

drug courts

informal adjustment

intake decision

legislative waiver (statutory exclusion)

"once an adult, always an adult" provisions

petition

plea bargaining

prosecutorial waiver

reverse waiver

teen courts

token economy program

transfer (waiver)

zealous advocate role

This chapter will examine the critical decision points in the juvenile court process: detention, intake, file, transfer (waiver), adjudication, and disposition. We will look at the roles the various court personnel play and should play in the court process. We will describe what happens when a juvenile suspect goes through the juvenile court process and will compare the ideal with the reality. Finally, we will examine some of the controversial issues facing juvenile court today, such as the question of the impact of race on decisionmaking and whether juveniles should have the right to a jury trial.

In 2000 (the latest year for which complete figures were available), juvenile courts processed more than 1.6 million delinquency cases (see Figure 8.1). More than one-half (58%) of the delinquency cases were petitioned, and approximately 5,600 cases were transferred to adult court via judicial waiver. More than 600,000 youths (624,400) were adjudicated delinquent in juvenile court, and 82,800 were adjudicated as status offenders (Puzzanchero et al., 2004). Finally, several thousand youths were processed in adult court as a result of direct file by prosecutors or by statutory exclusion (see below for additional details).

Due to the smaller number of cases processed, not as much information is available about the processing of status offense cases. Figure 8.2, however, shows processing for typical runaway, truancy, ungovernability, and liquor law violation cases based on information from 1985 to 2000 (Puzzanchero et al., 2004).

Figure 8.1   Juvenile Court Processing of Delinquency Cases, 2000

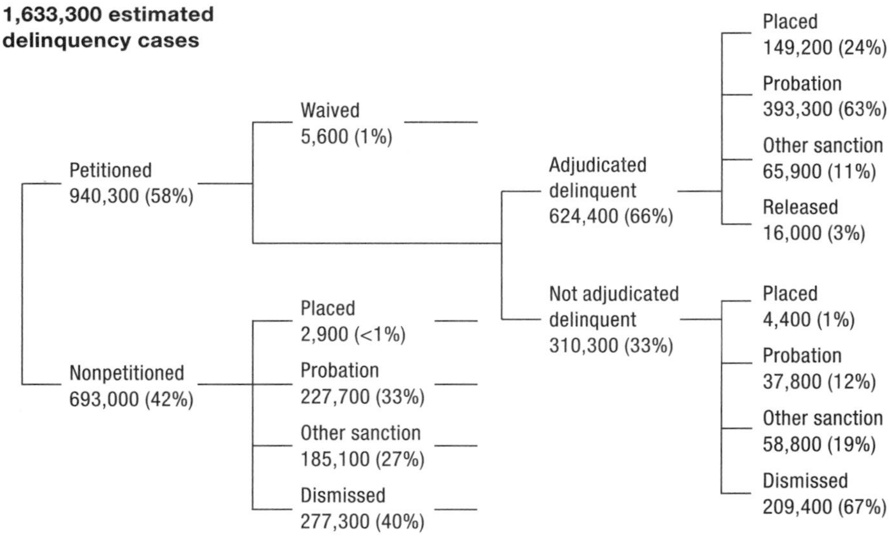

1,633,300 estimated delinquency cases

Petitioned 940,300 (58%)
- Waived 5,600 (1%)
- Adjudicated delinquent 624,400 (66%)
  - Placed 149,200 (24%)
  - Probation 393,300 (63%)
  - Other sanction 65,900 (11%)
  - Released 16,000 (3%)
- Not adjudicated delinquent 310,300 (33%)
  - Placed 4,400 (1%)
  - Probation 37,800 (12%)
  - Other sanction 58,800 (19%)
  - Dismissed 209,400 (67%)

Nonpetitioned 693,000 (42%)
- Placed 2,900 (<1%)
- Probation 227,700 (33%)
- Other sanction 185,100 (27%)
- Dismissed 277,300 (40%)

Notes: Cases are categorized by their most severe or restrictive sanction. Detail may not add to totals because of rounding. Annual case processing flow diagrams for 1985 through 2000 are available online at http://ojjdp.ncjrs.org/ojstatbb/court/faqs.asp.

Source: C. Puzzanchera, A.L. Stahl, T.A. Finnegan, N. Tierney, and H.N. Snyder (2004). *Juvenile Court Statistics 2000*. Pittsburgh: National Center for Juvenile Justice. Reprinted with permission.

Figure 8.2   **Juvenile Court Processing of Petitioned Status Offense Cases, 1985-2000**

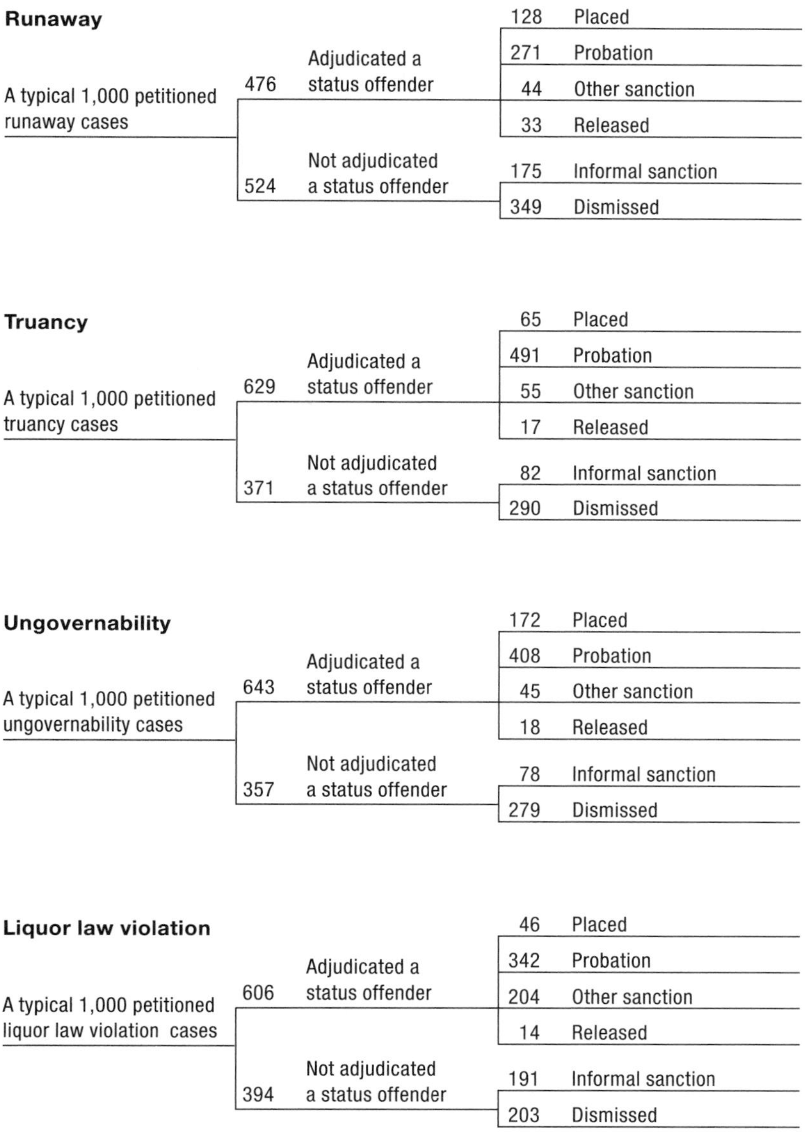

Runaway

A typical 1,000 petitioned runaway cases

476 — Adjudicated a status offender
- 128 Placed
- 271 Probation
- 44   Other sanction
- 33   Released

524 — Not adjudicated a status offender
- 175 Informal sanction
- 349 Dismissed

Truancy

A typical 1,000 petitioned truancy cases

629 — Adjudicated a status offender
- 65   Placed
- 491 Probation
- 55   Other sanction
- 17   Released

371 — Not adjudicated a status offender
- 82   Informal sanction
- 290 Dismissed

Ungovernability

A typical 1,000 petitioned ungovernability cases

643 — Adjudicated a status offender
- 172 Placed
- 408 Probation
- 45   Other sanction
- 18   Released

357 — Not adjudicated a status offender
- 78   Informal sanction
- 279 Dismissed

Liquor law violation

A typical 1,000 petitioned liquor law violation cases

606 — Adjudicated a status offender
- 46   Placed
- 342 Probation
- 204 Other sanction
- 14   Released

394 — Not adjudicated a status offender
- 191 Informal sanction
- 203 Dismissed

Note: Cases are categorized by their most severe or restrictive sanction. Detail may not add to totals because of rounding.

Source: C. Puzzanchera, A.L. Stahl, T.A. Finnegan, N. Tierney, and H.N. Snyder (2004). *Juvenile Court Statistics 2000*. Pittsburgh: National Center for Juvenile Justice. Reprinted with permission.

DETENTION

The first decision that juvenile court personnel must make is the detention decision. It must be decided whether to keep a juvenile in custody or to allow the youth to go home with his or her parents while awaiting further court action. The **detention** decision is the juvenile court counterpart of the bail decision in adult court. It is very important because it concerns the freedom of the child and, therefore, resembles the disposition decision. In fact, children sent to detention may stay there for an extensive period of time—perhaps even for a longer time than children sent to state training schools (i.e., youth prisons for juveniles determined to be delinquent).

In 2000, approximately 329,800 youths in delinquency cases were detained. This number represents approximately 20 percent of delinquency cases, about the same proportion detained in 1985 (detention in 21% of delinquency cases). Detention was used in 28 percent of person offense cases, one-third of property cases, 11 percent of drug cases, and 28 percent of public order cases (Puzzanchero et al., 2004). It should be noted that detention can be also used in some states as a disposition for a brief period of incarceration and as a sanction for violations of probation conditions (Griffin and King, 2004).

For status offenders, between 1985 and 2000, detention was used in 17 percent of runaway cases, 3 percent of truancy cases, 10 percent of ungovernability cases, and 7 percent of liquor law violation cases. The proportion of white youths in detained status offense cases was approximately 70 percent; black youths accounted for approximately 25 percent of detained cases (Puzzanchero et al., 2004).

In 2000, detention was used in 18 percent of delinquency cases involving white youths, 25 percent involving black youths, and 24 percent involving youths of other races (Puzzanchero et al., 2004). In one study the average IQ score of detainees was 82.6, well below average (Viljoen, Klaver, and Roesch, 2005).

A recent estimate was that it cost about $85 to keep one child in detention for one day (Tyler, Darville, and Stalnaker, 2001). Recent figures also indicate that crowding is a problem. One study found that the population was exceeding capacity by approximately 1,000 youths (Wordes and Jones, 1998). In response, California planned to add 3,150 new detention beds in 2001 (Wordes, Krisberg, and Berry, 2001).

Detention workers or probation officers usually make the initial detention decision. State law may stipulate that a detention hearing be held within a specified period of time so that a judge can rule on the continued need for detention. The Model Juvenile Delinquency Act, a guideline for state codes, stipulates that the detention hearing be held with 36 hours and that certain criteria be used to decide whether to detain a particular youngster (Rossum, Koller, and Manfredi, 1987:34; see Box 8.1 for the relevant section of the Model Juvenile Delinquency Act).

Box 8.1. Model Juvenile Delinquency Act

Section 26.   [Grounds for Pre-Hearing Detention] A youth taken into custody may be detained if there is probable cause to believe that
    (A) The juvenile is a fugitive from justice;
    (B) The juvenile has committed a felony while another case was pending;
    (C) The juvenile has committed a delinquent act and
        (1) The juvenile will likely fail to appear for further proceedings,
        (2) Detention is required to protect the juvenile from himself or herself,
        (3) The juvenile is a threat to the person or property of others,
        (4) The juvenile will intimidate witnesses or otherwise unlawfully interfere with the administration of justice, or
        (5) There is no person available or capable of caring for the juvenile.

Source: R.A. Rossum, B.J. Koller, and C.P. Manfredi (1987). *Juvenile Justice Reform: A Model for the States* (p. 33). Clairmont, CA: Rose Institute of State and Local Government and the American Legislative Exchange, p. 33.

Detention Options

Court personnel have several options at the detention decision point. Releasing a child to his or her parents is the most frequently used option; this is the preferred decision in most states (e.g., Alabama Code 12-15-59). **Secure detention**—placing a child in the juvenile equivalent of a local jail—is another alternative. It involves placement in a locked facility of 10, 20, or more youths who are awaiting further court action or are awaiting transfer to a state correctional facility. In some places, **nonsecure detention** is another option for youths involved in less serious crimes and for those who do not pose much threat to the community or themselves. Such youngsters may be placed in small group homes that are not locked or not locked as comprehensively as a secure detention facility—hence the term "nonsecure." Youngsters housed in nonsecure detention centers might even go to regular public school classes during the day. Alternatives to detention, such as home detention, will be discussed later in this chapter.

Detention Decisionmaking

Some research on detention decisionmaking has indicated that while race is not a significant factor influencing the detention decision, gender is important (see McCarthy, 1987, for a review of the research). As noted above, in 2000, nonwhite youths were placed in detention more often than white youths (Puzzanchero et al., 2004).

Raising further disturbing questions, one of the most comprehensive studies on factors affecting the detention decision used a sample of 55,000 cases from one state and found that neither relevant legal variables (offense severity and prior record) nor sociodemographic characteristics had much impact on detention decisions. One possible conclusion of this research is that the decision "process is idiosyncratic, causing some juveniles to suffer significant deprivations of liberty based on considerations that are irrelevant to the approved purposes of detention" (Frazier and Bishop, 1985:1151). Another study that reviewed the literature, however, concluded that race *is* a factor in the detention decision (Wordes, Bynum, and Corley, 1994).

A troubling feature of detention hearings is that often they are the first opportunity for the juvenile to meet with an attorney. In one study, more than one-half of the public defenders did not meet their clients prior to the detention hearing. In one site, an unsupervised law student with no background investigations on the youths represented youths at detention hearings (Puritz et al., 1995). In Pennsylvania, a study found that at detention hearings attorneys did not have much opportunity to confer with their juvenile clients and were not familiar with alternatives to detention (Miller-Wilson and Puritz, 2003).

Detention Programming

Detention programs can range from very inadequate to rather complex programs. About 25 years ago, Charles Silberman (1978) toured several detention centers across the country in preparation for writing a book on criminal violence and criminal justice. He found that "boob tube" therapy was often the normal programming. By this he meant that staff often allowed the children to watch television for hours on end. As many parents at home have found, parking children in front of the television set serves to occupy the children as well as to free the supervising adults (detention houseparents or workers) from the challenging task of finding more constructive activities for the detainees.

Ironically, a new "boob tube" therapy is emerging in today's detention centers. A detention center in Kansas was investing considerable funds in a television distribution center that included local cable, satellite, VCR, and even locally generated programming. One possibility was for video case conferencing. So detention officials in that state were envisioning video technology, in addition to computers in the classrooms and a separate computer lab, as central components in modern programming (Karst and Frazier, 2000).

Programming should include attention to alcohol, drug, and mental disorders. A preliminary investigation of detainees in Chicago found that two-thirds of the youths have one or more of these disorders (Teplin, 2001). Actual drug testing in three detention centers showed that approximately 20 to 25 percent of the youths tested positive for marijuana (Crowe, 1998). If drug testing is desired, the costs would be about $6 per test (Crowe and Sydney, 2000). Actual therapy would cost considerably more than this.

Besides "boob tube" therapy, the psychological technique of behavior modification has inspired many detention centers to use **token economy programs**. With this approach, staff members use points or dollar values to reward detained youths for appropriate behavior and withhold or subtract points for inappropriate behavior. Youths earn credits when they follow the rules, and they lose credits when they disobey the rules. If they have more credits than losses, they can "purchase" rewards such as snacks, table games, and room privacy at the end of the day and/or on the weekend. (See Boxes 8.2 and 8.3 for examples of rewards, punishments, and costs.) This type of program is based on psychological principles of conditioning that contend that human behavior is learned through reinforcements.

Box 8.2. Detention Rewards and Fines

How Dollars May Be Earned

1.	School attendance	$10
2.	YMCA activities	$10
3.	Cleaning room (make beds, sweep, mop, etc.)	$5
4.	Extra work (per hour)	$5
5.	Good hygiene	$5
6.	Attending church, etc.	$5
7.	Cleaning unit	$10
8.	Good behavior	$5

Fines for Inapproprate Behaviors

1.	Body Contact (slapping, etc.)	$20
2.	Disrespect (sarcastic or abusive speech, not following rules)	$30.
3.	Profanity	$10
4.	Instigating (influencing others to break rules)	$30
5.	Arguing (other youth or staff)	$30
6.	Lying	$40
7.	Complaining (irritating staff with complaints about program, food, other staff, dollars, etc.)	$25
12.	Contraband	$50
18.	Fighting (another resident)	$100
20.	Attempted Escape	$150

Source: Handbook of Procedures, Rules, and Regulations (Jefferson County Detention Center, Birmingham, Alabama).

Figure 8.3   Detention Dollar Price List

Item	Price
Soft Drinks	$10
Envelopes and 2 Sheets of Paper	$5
Chips	$5
Popcorn	$10
Second Comb	$15
Second Toothbrush	$15
Extra Shampoo	$5
Hair Cuts	$10
Alcohol	$5
Vaseline	$5
Coffee	$10
Pencils	$5

Source: Handbook of Procedures, Rules, and Regulations (Jefferson County Detention Center, Birmingham, Alabama).

Given the unique needs of girls in detention, it is critical that detention centers develop gender-specific programs for girls. One issue is that about 70 percent of girls in the juvenile justice system have histories of physical abuse, compared to only about 20 percent of the boys (Lederman and Brown, 2000). (For a description of the poor conditions in one girls' detention center, see Box 8.4.)

Positive Programs

While some detention centers use either "boob tube" therapy or behavior modification–inspired token economies (or both), at least some detention facilities are trying to implement meaningful detention programming, especially educational programming. Several states have implemented literacy programs using intensive systematic phonics. In Mississippi, students improved their reading comprehension scores by approximately one grade level. In a detention center in the state of Washington, the average gain in reading was two grade levels. In a phonics program in Ohio, the average gain in reading was 1.5 grade levels one year and 2.5 grade levels the next year (Hodges, Giulotti, and Porpotage, 1994). These results show that well-designed educational programs can have a postive impact in detention centers.

Research has found that education should be the cornerstone of detention programming. It is important for detention centers to teach basic academic skills, general education development (GED) test preparation, and also special education, employment readiness training, and programs about

Box 8.4 One Girls' Detention Center

The Miami-Dade County Juvenile Detention Center has a therapeutic module for the most troublesome boys but not one for the most troublesome girls. As a result, there is sufficient staff for boys to go outdoors for recreation but girls can go up to two weeks without outdoor recreation. In fact, due to staff shortages, on some days girls cannot even attend school (Lederman and Brown, 2000).

A description of the physical conditions of the girls' facility is depressing:

The girls sleep on concrete slabs with thin mats on top. They are issued thin blankets even though the temperature of the modules is very cold. There is no vacuum cleaner. The staff only has a broom to move around the dust. The walls are bare and depressing. One small window fights to illuminate each cell—which is tinted so little light comes in. When the modules are over-crowded, two girls share a cell meant for one (Lederman and Brown, 2000:920).

Clearly, this is another example where the rhetoric of juvenile justice as a benevolent parent comes crashing down into the harsh reality of undesirable conditions.

social, cognitive, and life skills such as problem solving and moral reasoning (Stephens and Arnette, 2000). For example, in Jackson, Mississippi, the detention center is actually an extension of the district public school alternative school. In addition to academic programming, the school also offers vocational training and parent training (an "effective parenting" course) (Stephens and Arnette, 2000).

Positive progamming can have several benefits. In response to a lawsuit, the Broward Detention Center in Florida cut its population from 166 in 1988-89 to 53 in 1992 and added educational programs, a new exercise area, and refurbished sleeping areas. Detainee uniforms were relaxed (changed to a "golf style" shirt), and additional child care and specialized staff (recreation, nursing, and mental health workers) were hired. Such changes were associated with fewer behavioral incidents; both disciplinary confinements (isolation) and room confinement decreased. Such changes were also associated with less punitive attitudes among the staff (Bazemore, Dicker, and Nyhan, 1994).

Often the best programming is to find an alternative to detention. The Maryland Detention Response Unit uses social workers to try to find appropriate community and residential alternatives to detention and to determine the need for mental or educational evaluations. Attorneys also investigate how court-ordered detention can be modified or amended to permit community-based alternatives (National Juvenile Defender Center, 2004).

Detention Workers

A study of workers in two detention centers in Florida found that the workers strongly supported a treatment or rehabilitation orientation. More than 80 percent reported that they took their job "to help and rehabilitate youth" and "to provide care and services for youth" and that detained youths "should receive treatment and rehabilitative services" (Bazemore and Dicker, 1994:304). On the other hand, a punishment or control orientation was also prevalent. Sixty-nine percent of the workers overall agreed that "youth in detention primarily need firm discipline," and 41 percent agreed that "most youth in detention only respond to physical intervention or the threat of physical intervention" (Bazemore and Dicker, 1994:304). Younger employees and males were more likely to agree with such punitive statements, suggesting that maturity may produce greater tolerance (Bazemore and Dicker, 1994). As noted above, the center that had adopted a number of program improvements—the Broward Detention Center—had staff with less punitive attitudes than the other center. Still, significant percentages of staff at Broward professed punitive attitudes. This research suggests that detention workers do favor rehabilitation but that a considerable percentage report punitive attitudes, including attitudes that are contrary to detention policy. This suggests that detention administrators need to monitor detention policies and also attempt to improve detention workers' salary and occupational prestige, which are low compared to other juvenile justice and human service occupations (Bazemore, Dicker, and Nyhan, 1994).

A survey of youths in secure custody (some were in training schools and some were in detention) showed some problem areas. One-quarter (26%) of the youths reported staff use of excessive force, one-half reported seeing staff use excessive force on other inmates, 45 percent said that staff ignored possible trouble, and almost one-half said that staff said or did something to put an inmate at risk. So it appears that staff often allow or induce juveniles to use force on other juveniles in custody. On the positive side, however, two-thirds of the youths surveyed agreed that they had received help from staff and felt protected by staff (Peterson-Badali and Koegl, 2002).

DETENTION ALTERNATIVES

Because of criticisms of detention programming and because of the high costs of detaining youngsters in secure detention facilities, many jurisdictions have sought alternatives to traditional detention facilities. For example, a few years ago, New York City found that secure detention cost about $58,000 per year per child and that nonsecure detention (foster care and boarding homes) cost about $20,000 per year. Hence, they began using converted stores or lofts as **day-evening centers**. In such centers, mornings involved formal educational programs, early afternoons were devoted to remedial and tutorial work, and late afternoons were reserved for recreational programs (e.g., weekly swimming at YMCA facilities). Two of the four New York City centers also offered evening hours twice a week for children considered to need extra supervision and for those on a waiting list for admission into the day program (Lindner, 1981).

Home Detention

Another popular alternative to traditional detention is **home detention**. This is the juvenile court counterpart of supervised pretrial release for adult criminal defendants. In home detention, the youth awaiting further juvenile court action is allowed to live at home but is also under the supervision of a detention worker who ensures that the youth is attending school (or working on a job) and maintaining a curfew. The detention worker, often a paraprofessional, may check on the home detention youngster up to four times a day if the worker suspects

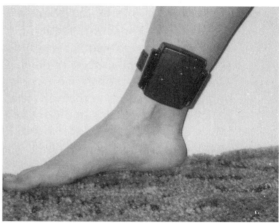

Many home detention programs use electronic monitoring. With this technology, an electronic anklet functions as a transmitter and is tracked by a receiver installed in the detainee's home. A central monitoring unit is then able to determine the whereabouts of the youth wearing the device.

that the child is getting into new trouble (delinquency). Studies show that 70 to 90 percent of home detention youths do not reoffend and appear in court (Austin, Johnson, and Weitzer, 2005).

Bail

Bail is not universally available in juvenile court (Rossum, Koller, and Manfredi, 1987:109), but bail for juveniles appears to be an option that is receiving greater attention. New Mexico, for example, recently authorized bail for serious youthful offenders detained before trial in an adult facility (National Conference of State Legislatures, 1993). This is a reflection of the changing philosophy of juvenile court, from *parens patriae* to punishment. Bail is considered inappropriate in the traditional juvenile court, in which the judge acts like a concerned parent in deciding to detain or release juveniles awaiting further court action. With the changing views of juvenile crime and juvenile court, however, states are beginning to see bail as a reasonable option. The current view that the juvenile is a responsible criminal rather than an immature youth in need of help is consistent with the use of bail as a means to guarantee continued appearance for court hearings.

THE INTAKE DECISION

The second major decision point in juvenile court is the **intake decision**, analogous to the filing decision in adult court. At intake, a court official—either a probation officer or a prosecutor (or both)—decides whether to file a court petition of delinquency, status offense, neglect, abuse, or dependency in a particular case. Traditionally, a probation officer has made the intake decision. The *parens patriae* philosophy of the court dictated this approach because its treatment orientation indicated that the probation officer (ideally a trained social worker) should consider the best interests of the child as well as the legal aspects of the case (as an adult court prosecutor might). That is, an intake probation officer is supposed to resolve every case in light of the considerations of the welfare of the child and the legal demands of the police and victim. This tradition is changing; a number of states even allow prosecutors to make the decision to file certain cases directly in adult criminal court and thereby completely bypass the juvenile court.

Informal Adjustment

One frequent decision of the intake officer is not to file a petition alleging delinquency or a status offense, but instead to try to resolve the matter without resorting to a formal petition against the child. As noted above, almost one-half (42%) of the 1.6 million delinquency cases coming to juvenile court in 2000 were not petitioned (Puzzanchero et al., 2004). (Statistics on the number of status offense cases not petitioned are not available.) Many (four out of 10) of the nonpetitioned cases were dismissed; others were handled informally. Informal handling is usually called adjustment at intake or **informal adjustment**. Examples would include requiring a first-time shoplifter to pay restitution to the store or ordering a vandal to paint the public building he or she has defaced. Similarly, intake probation officers often try to counsel troubled family members on a short-term basis or to refer them to counseling services in the community. As a result, a youth involved in runaway behavior, chronic disobedience ("incorrigibility"), or repeated truancy will not be immediately petitioned to court as a status offender. Instead, the youth receives help in dealing with the problem that brought him or her to the attention of court officials.

It is important to note that such informal adjustment practices occur as frequently as 25 percent of the time (Butts, 1994; McCarthy, 1987) and have been part of juvenile court since its inception. With the emphasis on diversion in the 1970s, informal adjustment practices by intake officers took on added dimensions.

Teen Courts

One diversion option to the traditional juvenile court is the use of **teen courts** (sometimes called youth courts). Here the philosophy is based on restorative justice, and youths act as judge, attorney (prosecutor and defense attorney), and jury in cases involving status offenses, misdemeanors, and occasionally a low-level felony. (About one-half of teen courts use adult judges.) The most common penalty is community service. Other sentences include teen court jury duty, writing essays about offending, writing apologies to victims, community service, and monetary restitution. As of 2002, it was estimated that there were more than 800 teen court programs in operation handling more than 100,000 cases per year, making them a primary diversion option (Butts, Buck, and Coggenshall, 2002).

Two studies of the effectiveness of teen courts found no difference between teen courts and comparisons, but three studies found lower recidivism rates in teen court cases than for comparison youths. A recent study of an Illinois teen court found that most of the offenses handled were low-level infractions such as shoplifting (43% of the cases processed), curfew violation, possession of marijuana, disorderly conduct, and so on. Recidivism was only 12 percent after one year and 19 percent after two years (Rasmussen, 2004).

A multi-site study of teen courts in Alaska, Arizona, Maryland, and Missouri found statistically less recidivism for teen court youths in two of the four sites. In Alaska, 6 percent of teen court youths recidivated, compared to 23 percent of non–teen court youths; in Missouri, 9 percent of teen court youths recidivated, compared to 28 percent of non–teen court youths. The authors of the study concluded that "teen courts represent a promising alternative for the juvenile justice system" (Butts, Buck, and Coggenshall, 2002:34). It is also noteworthy that volunteer staff and low budgets mean that teen courts are inexpensive.

Teen court is not intended to deal with serious delinquency, but it appears to be an alternative method for dealing with status offenses, minor delinquent acts such as shoplifting, or problems with alcohol or marijuana. As one author put it, teen court may be a "partial solution to the juvenile justice system's failure to give anything more than a 'slap on the wrist' to first-time offenders" (Rasmussen, 2004:615).

Drug Courts

Another diversion option is juvenile **drug courts** in which the judge, prosecutor, and defense attorney collaborate as a team with drug treatment specialists. Like adult drug courts, juvenile drug courts attempt to intervene in both the criminal activity and the drug usage of clients. The courts use treatment, coordination, and extensive monitoring. The youths must appear in court frequently so that judges can monitor progress and offer encouragement and admonishment to the juveniles. There is frequent drug testing, and there are penalties for failing to test negative. Sanctions for youths that are not following the rules can range from a warning, an order to write a book report or paper or to do household chores, to fines, community service hours, or even detention. There also incentives such as the dismissal of charges and termination of probation requirements upon graduation. Other rewards include verbal praise and such incentives as gift certificates and tickets to local events. Drug courts usually celebrate completion with a graduation ceremony in court that may include additional features, such as a gift of athletic shoes (Rossman et al., 2004).

There is some indication that drug court supervision in addition to probation or in place of probation may produce better results. The evaluation of a drug court in Phoenix, Arizona, showed that juvenile drug court participants had lower recidivism than the comparison group of regular probationers. On the other hand, only 30 percent of the drug court participants successfully completed the program; 62 percent were put on probation or sent to a state correctional facility (Rodriguez and Webb, 2004).

One problem with drug courts is that they may be reaching the wrong population. If drug courts are actually intended for drug-dependent or addicted youths, they are not capturing many such youths with severe drug problems. "If, on the other hand, juvenile drug courts are designed to deliver prevention services for a broad cross-section of youth involved with alcohol and other drugs, then their current mode of operating may be appropriate, but such a broad mission would raise other questions about the risks of labeling, net-widening, and iatrogenic effects (i.e., the cure may be worse than the disease)" (Butts, Zweig, and Mamalian, 2004:142). Much like the "war" on drugs in general, drug courts often paint a wide stroke that takes in more than is necessary. We worry so much about adolescent drug use that we overreact and do too much.

The question of whether drug courts have positive effects such as reducing recidivism and drug usage is still unanswered. Although there are studies that have had positive results, the findings are not yet settled. Thus, one recent review of research on drug courts concluded that "[r]esearch on drug courts has so far produced only limited evidence of drug court impact" (Roman and DeStefano, 2004:133).

Other Programs

A victim–offender mediation program in Texas emphasizing the offender's accountability has been successful. The mediator is often a trained volunteer. An early evaluation found that 29 percent of referrals ended in successful mediation. A few years later the successful mediation rate was 77 percent (Kurlychek, Torbet, and Bozynski, 1999). For a critical perspective on victim–offender mediation, see Box 8.5.

Box 8.5 A Critical Perspective on Victim-Offender Mediation

Not everyone is completely positive about victim–offender mediation. One criticism is that it can be quite coercive. The offender might well perceive that the victim and the mediator as a representative of the state are lined up together against the offender. In this atmosphere of coercion, the offender might simply perceive the admonitions of the mediator as "paternalistic reprimands" (Arrigo and Schehr, 1998). Still another criticism is that by focusing on the persons of the offender and the victim, the process ignores larger forces—social, economic, and political—that may have contributed to the victimization. This "personalizing . . . of crime and criminal behavior, however, makes it unlikely that cultural, political, and economic transformations will follow" (Arrigo and Schehr, 1998:640). In other words, if poverty and social inequality contributed to the juvenile resorting to burglary or theft, victim–offender mediation ignores that context and simply treats all victimizations as personal encounters between actors assumed to be responsible.

What do you think? Does victim–offender mediation paint an unrealistic picture that ignores larger social forces at work? Is it just to treat victimizations as only personal events? Is this just a paternalistic ploy that allows society to ignore its role in creating and maintaining delinquency?

Still another new diversion program is the ACT Now Truancy Program in Pima County, Arizona. This truancy-reduction program combines services to get at the root causes of truancy and even misdemeanors with criminal fines and penalties for parents who do not do enough to get their children to attend school. In those cases in which parents were prosecuted, the usual sanction was community service or a $200 fine (Baker, Sigmon, and Nugent, 2001).

These newer programs share several features. Contrasted with diversion programs of 25 years ago, these programs place more emphasis on the accountability of the offender and concern for the victim. Older diversion programs focused on treating the offender without parallel concern for victims. There is also a tendency to involve community members (either teenage, adult, or both) in the process, whereas older diversion programs relied more on expert staff. In general, these programs emphasize both accountability and concern for victims, whereas older programs emphasized treatment for the offender.

The Prosecutor's Role

If an intake probation officer decides to file a petition against a child, often that decision requires the approval of an attorney, normally the prosecutor. The prosecutor's approval of the probation officer's decision to file a petition ensures that a legally trained official has reviewed the legal criteria for a properly authorized petition. The prosecutor checks the legal wording of the petition, determines that enough evidence is available for establishing the petition (finding the delinquent or status offender "guilty"), and makes sure that the offense occured in the court's jurisdiction and that the child was of proper age at the time of the offense.

Because of the importance of such legal criteria, and because of the growing emphasis on more punitive juvenile models, some jurisdictions have turned away from the traditional probation-officer model of intake toward models in which the prosecutor is either the first or the sole intake decision-maker. Such models are more consistent with more legalistic views of juvenile court in which the state has abandoned the traditional *parens patriae* philosophy. For example, the state of Washington has switched responsibility for the intake decision to the prosecutor for all felony charges and most misdemeanors. There prosecutors make such decisions on the basis of explicit criteria: offense seriousness, prior record, and the age of the youth. Furthermore, informal adjustments are no longer permitted at intake, although police agencies can still "exercise their traditional discretion regarding whether to refer or adjust incidents involving juveniles" (Schneider and Schram, 1986:214). In place of informal adjustments at intake, minor offenses are supposed to be diverted to restitution programs. This action by Washington represents a radical break with traditional juvenile court thinking and practice and is a close approximation of adult processing with its retributive emphasis. (For a diagrammatic comparison of traditional intake and the Washington state practice, see Box 8.6.) Like the legislation in the state of Washington, the Model Juvenile Delinquency Act also stipulates that the prosecutor shall "[d]irectly supervise all matters relating to intake," although the probation officer may continue to make the file-divert decision in misdemeanor cases if the prosecutor so delegates (Rossum, Koller, and Manfredi, 1987:40). Similarly, the National District Attorneys' Association stipulates a very active role for the prosecutor (Shine and Price, 1992), and Louisiana has given the prosecutor greater authority over the intake process (National Conference of State Legislatures, 1993).

A further development is that the prosecutor is now taking on increased responsibility in juvenile cases as increasingly more states are allowing prosecutors to file cases directly in adult criminal court. In addition to traditional waiver (transfer), several mechanisms allow prosecutors to proceed against juveniles in criminal court: concurrent jurisdiction, statutory exclusion, presumptive waiver, reverse waiver, and "once adult/always an adult" statutes. Bishop (2000) estimates that approximately one-quarter million youths under 18 were prosecuted as adults in 1996. (These prosecutor options will be discussed in greater depth later in this chapter.)

Box 8.6   The Intake Process

Traditional Intake:

Police, parents, school officials, or victims bring youths to attention of Intake	Intake officer files petition	Juvenile Court Hearing
	OR makes an informal adjustment	
	OR diverts to a treatment program	

Prosecutorial Model (e.g., Washington State)

Police, parents, school officials, or victims bring youths to attention of Intake	Prosecutor files a petition	Juvenile Court Hearing
	OR declines to file a petition	
	OR diverts to a restitution program	

Many prosecutors are now pursuing a two-pronged or bifurcated approach with juveniles. The first prong is aggressive prosecution of violent repeat offenders; the second prong is early intervention to prevent further delinquency. One example is Duval County, Florida, where prosecution in one year resulted in more than 750 juveniles being incarcerated as adults in the county jail and another 155 juveniles sentenced to the Florida State Prison. At the same time, minor offenders were sentenced to community service or handled in diversion programs. Prosecutors are now collaborating extensively with other agencies such as schools (Coles and Kelling, 2002).

A number of jurisdictions are pursuing community prosecution. Like some versions of community policing, community prosecution's "overarching goal is to improve the quality of life in a community" (Harp et al., 2004:3). There are three key elements to community prosecution. First, the prosecutor attempts to involve the community in defining and solving problems. Second, problem solving goes beyond traditional enforcement strategies. Third, the prosecutor forms partnerships with law enforcement, probation, schools, and community groups. All this is done in clearly defined target areas, and there is an emphasis on quality-of-life issues, not just serious felonies. Part of the reason for the emphasis on quality-of-life issues is the "broken windows" theory that helped spur the development of community policing efforts (Coles and Kelling, 2002).

An example of community prosecution in action is the Multnomah County (Portland), Oregon, District Attorney's Office. In the mid-1990s, teens had created an unofficial skateboard park in an industrial section of Portland. Business owners complained about litter and about the teen skateboarders grabbing onto trucks for rides on their skateboards. Rather than simply close down the park and prosecute the teens for littering and disorderly conduct, the prosecutor's office met with both sides and an agreement was reached. The teens agreed to stay within a defined area and not litter; the business owners paid for the signs placed around the park and also provided a portable toilet. So the prosecutor's office helped create an innovative solution to a quality-of-life issue that previously would have resulted in prosecution and conviction (Harp et al., 2004).

Research on Intake Decisionmaking

As was the case with police discretion (see Chapter 7), many researchers and analysts have been concerned about the discretion of intake decisionmakers either to file or not file petitions. Of particular concern has been the question of whether race is an important factor in the intake decision and whether racial discrimination occurs at intake. Several conclusions can be drawn from the studies that have been conducted on intake decisionmaking. First, seriousness of the alleged offense clearly influences the decision to file a petition, though it is not necessarily the prime factor. Thus, youths accused of more serious offenses are more likely to be petitioned to court than youths accused of less serious offenses (Bell and Lang, 1985; Cohen and Kluegel, 1978; Fenwick, 1982; McCarthy and Smith, 1986; Minor, Hartmann, and Terry, 1997; Thornberry, 1973). Second, prior record is a factor. Youths with prior records are more likely to be referred (Cohen and Kluegel, 1978; Fenwick, 1982; McCarthy and Smith, 1986; Thornberry, 1973). Third, demeanor often has an effect; uncooperative youths are more likely to be petitioned than cooperative youths (Bell and Lang, 1985; Fenwick, 1982). However, demeanor often is not measured in studies because many researchers rely on official records that do not include any record of the attitude of the child when he or she is interviewed by the court official making the intake decision. Finally, variables such as age, race, class, and gender have produced mixed results. As a result, there is considerable controversy surrounding the impact of each of these variables on the intake decision (Bell and Lang, 1985; Cohen and Kluegel, 1978; McCarthy and Smith, 1986; Pope and Feyerherm, 1993; Thornberry, 1973).

The methodology used in many previous studies was deficient. Specifically, many early studies looked at small, nonrepresentative samples that made it impossible to generalize to courts nationwide. Other studies used only bivariate rather than multivariate statistical analyses of their data. This means that they examined the independent effects of individual variables (such as race) on intake decisions but did not consider the effects on decisions of several variables at once. In addition, many of the studies were conducted years ago, prior to the introduction of due process guarantees in juvenile court and to the relatively recent civil rights movement focusing on eliminating various forms of discrimination.

Furthermore, at least some researchers (e.g., McCarthy and Smith, 1986; Sampson and Laub, 1993) contend that it is misleading to isolate the intake decision apart from the detention, adjudication, and dispositional decisions. They argue that those decisions are basically parts of one complex whole that must be studied together to avoid possible distortions. An analogy would be studying decisions of college football coaches about what play to call on first down but ignoring strategy decisions on the second, third, and fourth downs. Research on first-down strategy is interesting but incomplete. First-down decisions make the most sense when understood in the context of the other downs.

Going even further, Conley (1994) argues that too many studies have been quantitative rather than qualitative and have thus neglected critical factors. Conley argues that observational studies of both court decision-making processes and of police decisions are needed.

In summary, race appears to have some effect on the intake decision. The research of McCarthy and Smith (1986) indicated some disadvantage for blacks (e.g., greater chance of being petitioned), but Bell and Lang (1985) found a more complex situation. Rodriguez (2005) found that race even affected the selection process for a restorative justice program, with both black and Hispanic/Latino juveniles less likely to be selected.

Sampson and Laub (1993) have placed the discussion of the impact of race on juvenile court decisionmaking in a theoretical context. They see race as linked to structural changes in American society, such as the deindustrialization of central cities and the concomitant rise of the underclass. Their research found that "structural contexts of 'underclass' poverty and racial inequality are significantly related to increased juvenile justice processing" (Sampson and Laub, 1993:305). In simple terms, counties with greater poverty and racial inequality showed higher rates of detention and out-of-home placement of juveniles. Their findings are consistent with the notion that "underclass black males are viewed as a threatening group to middle-class populations and thus will be subjected to increased formal social control by the juvenile justice system" (Sampson and Laub, 1993:306).

Pope (1995) concludes that race is a factor, and he suggests that some changes need to be added to the traditional intake process to ensure that race is not a consideration. One suggestion is training. A second suggestion to have two intake officers decide each case. A third suggestion is to have a review board examine all the decisions to look for any impact of race. If attention is given to such suggestions to improve court processing and if attention is also given to social and economic factors associated with race problems in the United States, race could cease to be a factor in juvenile court decisionmaking.

PROCESSING JUVENILES IN ADULT CRIMINAL COURT

Many juvenile offenders are now being handled in adult criminal court rather than juvenile court. This is a crucial decision because processing a youth in adult court makes the juvenile subject to adult penalties such as lengthy incarceration in an adult prison as opposed to a relatively short period of incarceration in a juvenile training school. Such a decision also results in the creation of an adult criminal record, which is public and may hinder future opportunities for employment in certain occupations. A juvenile court record, on the other hand, is usually confidential, and, therefore, should not harm the child in any way.

There are several methods that states use to place juveniles into adult court jurisdiction: transfer or waiver, statutory exclusion, prosecutorial waiver, and lowering the age of juvenile court jurisdiction. Traditionally, **waiver** or **transfer** was the primary method of placing juveniles into adult criminal court. In 2004, 46 states and the District of Columbia had statutes allowing judicial waiver (Griffin, 2005).

In 2000, approximately 5,600 juveniles were waived to adult criminal court. This was considerably below the peak number of 12,100 cases waived in 1994. Forty percent of waived cases in 2000 involved a person case and 36 percent involved a property offense (Puzzanchera et al., 2004). One reason for the low number of waivers in 2000 is that states are using other methods (direct file and statutory exclusion) to prosecute juveniles in adult criminal courts. For example, a survey of 40 of the nation's largest urban counties showed that of 7,100 juveniles charged with felonies in adult criminal court in 1998, three-quarters of them got to criminal court by direct file or statutory exclusion. Approximately one-quarter (24%) were waived to adult court, about 35 percent resulted from prosecutor direct file, and 42 percent were the result of statutory exclusion (Rainville and Smith, 2003). If these proportions are accurate for the entire nation, then the 2000 juvenile court number of 5,600 juveniles waived would suggest a significantly higher total number of youths overall being tried in adult court.

Statutory exclusion, also called **legislative waiver**, means that state legislatures rule that certain offenses, such as murder, automatically go to adult court. In 2004, 29 states had exclusion laws (Griffin, 2005). In Illinois, the list of offenses excluded from juvenile court jurisdiction includes murder, aggravated sexual assault, robbery with a firearm, drug and weapons offenses committed on or near public housing, and gang-related felonies. The law applies to most juveniles 15 and older but includes 13- and 14-year-olds for murder and sexual assault (Bishop, 2000).

Prosecutorial waiver (direct file/concurrent jurisdiction) is another method for placing juveniles into adult criminal court. State law gives juvenile and adult court concurrent jurisdiction over certain cases. Depending on the offense, the age of the offender, and/or the youth's prior record, the prosecutor decides whether to file the case in juvenile or adult court. In 2004, prosecutorial waiver (concurrent jurisdiction) was available in 15 states and the District of Columbia (Griffin, 2005). For example, in Florida, prosecutors can waive 16- and 17-year-olds charged with any felony, 16- and 17-year-olds charged with a misdemeanor if they have one prior felony and at least one prior misdemeanor, and even 14- and 15-year-olds charged with certain offenses (Bishop, 2000).

Another way to direct juveniles to adult court is for state legislatures to lower the maximum age of juvenile court jurisdiction. As of 2002, three states defined age 16 as the beginning age for criminal court jurisdiction and 10 states set age 17 as the age for adult court jurisdiction (Bozynski and Szymanski, 2004).

It should be noted that 23 states allow for **reverse waiver**. This means that the criminal courts can return certain cases that they received due to mandatory judicial waiver, legislative exclusion, or prosecutorial waiver back to juvenile court. It is also important to note that 34 states have **"once an adult, always an adult" provisions** (Griffin, 2005). This means that all or certain categories of youths placed in criminal courts must automatically be processed in adult court for any subsequent offenses (Bishop, 2000).

The waiver decision is made at a hearing that is analogous to the preliminary hearing in adult court. At a waiver hearing, the prosecutor must only show probable cause that an offense occurred and that the juvenile committed the offense. The prosecutor does not have to prove guilt beyond a reasonable doubt. Proof of guilt is reserved for the trial in adult court (if waiver is successful) or for the adjudication stage in juvenile court (if the waiver motion fails). The juvenile transfer hearing differs from an adult court preliminary hearing in that the prosecutor must go further and establish that the juvenile is not amenable to juvenile court intervention or that the juvenile is a threat to public safety. An example of nonamenability would be the case of a youth who is already on parole from a state training school for an earlier delinquent act who then commits another serious offense (e.g., armed robbery). If probable cause were established that the youth committed the robbery, then the judge would have to find that the juvenile court had a history of contacts with the boy dating back several years and that one more juvenile court effort to deal with the boy's problems—either through probation or a training school placement—would be futile. An example of a case involving a threat to public safety would be a murder case or an offender with a history of violent offenses.

The Effectiveness of Transfer and Other Methods of Adult Court Processing

Research on transfer and other methods of placing youths into adult court has produced mixed results. Donna Bishop and her colleagues have done extensive research on transfer in the state of Florida. They constructed a matched sample of 2,738 youths transferred in 1987 and nontransfer matches. On the one hand, the transferred youths were more likely to receive longer sentences in the adult system than their juvenile system matches. They were also more likely to be incarcerated for longer periods (they actually served longer sentences) than nontransferred youths. Their recidivism, however, was higher than the nontransferred youths, which cancelled out any deterrent or incapacitative effects of transfer (Bishop et al., 1996).

When Bishop and colleagues used a longer follow-up period, however, the nontransferred youths had a similar prevalence of recidivism. In other words, similar percentages of both transferred and nontransferred youths committed new crimes. There were still disadvantages to transfer, however, because the transferred youths who committed new crimes were arrested more frequently and more quickly than nontransferred youths (Winner et al., 1997).

Fagan examined robbery and burglary cases handled in New York criminal court and New Jersey juvenile court for identical offenders in matched communities. In New York, 16-year-olds are under the jurisdiction of adult court, whereas New Jersey uses the traditional cut-off point of 18. Incarceration rates were considerably higher in the adult court than in juvenile court. Approximately six out of 10 juvenile robbers and burglars received probation but in criminal court 46 percent of both types of offenders were incarcerated. Fagan also found that rearrest rates were higher for the robbery offenders processed in criminal court and that there were no differences in recidivism for the burglary offenders. Robbery offenders processed in criminal court offended more often and more quickly than their juvenile court counterparts. Fagan concluded that "public safety was, in fact, compromised by adjudication in the criminal court" (Fagan, 1995).

A study of waiver in Texas found that sentences handed down in adult court were longer than those in juvenile court but that the waived youths were often released before the length of time they could have been kept in the juvenile system. That is, the average sentence handed out in adult court was 12.8 years but the average time served until parole was 3.5 years. So the actual sentence (time served) could have been carried out in the juvenile justice system (Fritsch, Caeti, and Hemmens, 1996).

A study of 22 girls who had been tried as adults in Ohio and who were sentenced to an adult prison showed that five had no prior record, 10 had never been placed in residential treatment, and most had histories of sexual and physical abuse, neglect, school difficulties, and chemical dependency. Although the sample was small, it suggested that many of the decisions to transfer these girls to adult court had been "questionable decisions" (Gaarder and Belknap, 2002:509).

A study of 1,042 juveniles prosecuted and sentenced in Pennsylvania adult criminal court between 1997 and 1999 showed that juveniles received harsher sentences in adult court than did young adults, even controlling for legal factors such as offense seriousness and prior record. Specifically, the juveniles were 10 percent more likely to be incarcerated and received a 29 percent increase in sentence length (average sentence length of 2.18 months per juvenile compared to 1.69 months per adult). These "findings suggest that judges may assign greater levels of culpability and dangerousness to transferred juveniles than to young adult offenders" (Kurlychek and Johnson, 2004).

The research suggests that transfer and other means of putting juveniles into adult court are not magic solutions to some of the perceived problems in the juvenile court. There is conflicting evidence about whether youths put into adult court are more likely to be sentenced to incarceration or are more likely to serve a longer time incarcerated. Recidivism statistics do not indicate any advantage for transferred youths. In several instances the transferred youths do worse than the nontransferred youths. Nevertheless, the current climate favoring punishment suggests that transfer and other mechanisms to get juveniles into adult court will continue. This probably will occur even though some research evidence questions whether this trend is actually protecting the public more than juvenile court processing could. (For a contrasting view on what the public wants, see Box 8.7.)

Box 8.7 Attitudes Toward Early Intervention Programs

Although the "get tough" movement seems to be based on what the public wants, there is impressive evidence that the public still wants help for troubled youths. In a recent survey of residents of a southern state (Tennessee), on average, 86 percent of the respondents endorsed providing human services to at-risk children. Specifically, respondents endorsed preschool programs, treatment for troubled children in neglecting or abusing households, parent education programs, psychological services for identified youths, after-school programs, drug education, and rehabilitation programs for first offender youths. Even among a subsample of conservative men, two-thirds favored early intervention rather than incarceration (Cullen et al., 1998).

Youth and Worker Attitudes

Research on both youth and worker attitudes toward adult court processing indicates that there are some problems with moving juveniles to adult court jurisdiction.

In interviews with 95 serious and chronic adolescent male offenders in Florida (49 of whom had been transferred to criminal court), Bishop and her colleagues found that almost all described juvenile courts favorably but had criticisms of adult court. Most transferred youths believed that criminal court judges did not show interest in them, saw the proceedings as rushed, and, most importantly, had difficulty understanding everything that took place in criminal court. The transferred youths also perceived the criminal courts to be involved in game playing and felt that the public defenders were more interested in talking the youths into accepting pleas. The youths also perceived the courts to be clearly focused on punishment based not so much on what they had done but on judgments that "they were depraved or irredeemable" (Bishop, 2000:137).

A survey of court worker attitudes on transfer produced some interesting results. Workers did not see transfer as necessary for protecting society from extremely dangerous or violent youthful predators. Instead, juvenile court staff claimed that transfer

> prevented juvenile courts having to address youths who had problems that were beyond the rehabilitative capacities of the system and who threatened to contaminate others' chances of rehabilitation. The workers considered transfer as simply the inability of juvenile court to service all youths, rather than as acting like a safety valve or a form of societal retribution. Most respondents rejected numerous opportunities to adopt get tough measures in certification policies; even prosecutors advised against expanding their waiver powers (Sanborn, 1994a:275).

In another study of 100 juvenile court personnel in three courts, workers, especially defense attorneys and probation officers, expressed prime concern for rehabilitation. Forty-seven percent of judges, 65 percent of public defenders, 80 percent of private attorneys, and 70 percent of probation officers said that rehabilitation was the paramount concern of judges. However, 40 percent of judges and 64 percent of prosecutors rated balancing the interests of child and society as the paramount concern (Sanborn, 2001).

In other words, although the public and politicians may favor transfer as a way to "get tough" on juvenile crime, not all youths and workers agree that this is the best course of action.

ADJUDICATION AND DISPOSITION

For children not sent to adult criminal court, the next steps after the filing of a petition are **adjudication** and **disposition**. In these decisions, a judge determines whether there is enough evidence to establish the petition and then decides what to do if there is enough evidence. These decisions are comparable to the plea, trial, and sentencing decisions in adult court.

Ideally, the determination of the truth of the petition occurs in a rational fashion, with the prosecutor, defense attorney, and judge using their abilities and training to seek justice. In reality, juvenile court sessions often are hectic and hurried, and may reflect the self-interests of the parties involved rather than justice or the best interests of the child. For example, Peter Prescott has described one day in the operations of the Bronx (NY) Family Court as a

> flow of incompetence and indifference. One court officer perpetually frowns, shaking his head in mute consternation at so much exposure to human fallibility. The court clerk, arrogant and disdainful, speaks as little as possible as if in fear of contamination. When he must speak, his tone is dry and contemptuous, his words chopped short: the burden of dealing with these people and their problems! "I've been here two years," a court officer remarks. "Two years too long. But once you're assigned to Family Court, you're stuck because no one wants to come here" (Prescott, 1981:85-86).

An account of the Los Angeles juvenile court system (Humes, 1996) indicates that numerous problems continue to plague juvenile court, an institution marked by both frustration and heroism.

Attorneys in Juvenile Court

There are several problems concerning attorneys in juvenile court. First, many juveniles do not have attorneys. Many juveniles waive their right to an attorney, often because they do not fully understand their rights, especially the importance of the right to an attorney (see, e.g., Brooks and Kamine, 2003). A second critical problem is the burden of high caseloads for public defenders in juvenile court. Depending on the state, the caseload for the average public defender can range from 360 to 1,000 cases per defender (Jones, 2004). With attorneys being so overworked, many juvenile defendants got the clear impression that "their attorneys do not care about them" (Puritz et al., 1995:47).

Additional problems with public defender systems may include insufficient funding, lack of training, high turnover, low prestige, and low salaries (Feld, 1999). Starting salaries

Attorneys and other court personnel gather in a courtroom to complete paperwork prior to the presiding of the judge. In the juvenile court setting, many attorneys are reluctant to use the zealous advocate approach that is the norm in U.S. adult courts.

for public defenders in Ohio, for example, were as low as $35,000, and hourly rates for appointed counsel in several counties paid only $50 an hour for in-court work and $40 an hour for out-of-court work (Brooks and Kamine, 2003). Similarly, Georgia only pays appointed attorneys $60 per hour for in-court work, and one county has a cap of $300. Maine pays $50 per hour with a cap of $315. In Louisiana, the state only pays public defenders from $22,000 to $30,000 per year (Jones, 2004). Such low rates do not help to attract or retain competent attorneys.

Many attorneys in juvenile court, both public defenders and private attorneys, are reluctant to utilize the **zealous advocate role** that is (at least theoretically) the norm in adult criminal court. Attorneys in adult criminal courts justify such zealous advocacy (where the attorney fights as hard as possible for all defendants, even defendants who have admitted that they are factually guilty) on the grounds that the system is adversarial and that the adversarial process is best for bringing out the truth. In juvenile court, some attorneys, parents, and judges feel that the adult criminal court norm of zealous advocacy is inappropriate. They may worry that strong advocacy can result in an outcome by which a child who "needs help" will not get it because failure to establish the petition leaves the court with no jurisdiction over the child. As a result, at least some attorneys assume a **concerned adult role** rather than a zealous advocate role, encouraging youths to admit to petitions in cases in which an adversarial approach may have resulted in a dismissal of the petition. Additional problems are that juvenile court is not considered prestigious (it is called "kiddie court") and that judges may pressure attorneys into cooperating rather than being adversarial (Feld, 1999). (For a look at one attorney's thoughts on juvenile court, see Box 8.8.)

In a survey of 100 court workers in three juvenile courts, Sanborn (1994b) found that 79 percent of the workers thought that attorneys gave inadequate representation; one-third were of the opinion that attorneys engaged in behaviors that undermined a fair trial for their juvenile defendants. In addition, about 25 percent of the respondents thought that defense attorneys would not vigorously represent their youthful clients, and 29 percent claimed that attorneys acted like guardians rather than zealous advocates. Because of this, Sanborn (1994b) suggests that juveniles be given the right to trial by jury to counteract "judicial contamination by learning the defendant's record from countless sources and sloppy performances by judges and defense attorneys perpetrated within a private, laissez-faire atmosphere" (Sanborn, 1994b:613).

A recent qualitative study indicated that attorneys expressed considerable concern for their youthful clients but that the attorneys were not always sure of the correct course of action. Specifically, interviews with 10 attorneys and 10 clients showed that many of the juveniles did not always understand what was going on either during police interrogation or in court—often they "just didn't get it" (Tobey, Grisso, and Schwartz, 2000:230). For example, one youth waived his *Miranda* rights and talked to the police because he did not understand his right to remain silent. Many of the youths just wanted to "get it over with" (p. 234). Attorneys, in turn, felt that their youthful clients were often passive about decisions such as pleading guilty and thus attorneys "spoke of walking an ethical tightrope regarding who, in fact, was making the decision about such matters . . . (Tobey, Grisso, and Schwartz, 2000:237).

Box 8.8 One Lawyer's Observations about Juvenile Court

Thomas Geraghty has defended children in Cook County, Illinois (Chicago), for 28 years. He believes in juvenile court; he thinks it is preferable to an adult criminal court that has "no special focus on the unique problems associated with the adjudication, support, and treatment of children" (Geraghty, 1998:206). He notes that representing children allows lawyers to get to know children and the external forces such as poverty and child abuse that brought them to juvenile court. Geraghty notes that many of these external factors "are factors that our clients did not create and for which they are in no way responsible" (Geraghty, 1998:236).

He notes the important background details that need to be considered before calls are made for the transfer of youths to adult court or for the elimination of juvenile court. For example, consider a 12-year-old who allegedly shot and killed two teenagers. Investigation showed that this youth was trying to impress two older gang members. More importantly,

> What came out of this investigation was the story of a child's life. It turned out to be a story of a broken home, a child lost to gang culture despite the efforts of his family and school teachers, and access to a snub-nosed .38 caliber gun. The story of this child's life . . . is the product of all of its parts. Unless we focus our efforts on understanding these stories, in a setting supportive of understanding, we are unlikely to provide justice for children (Geraghty, 1998:241).

Buss (2000) agrees that many juveniles do not understand the role of the attorney as zealous advocate. Youths usually see adults as in control, not as advocates willing to listen to their wishes. Lawyers, in turn, may reinforce inaccurate images. Large caseloads prevent lawyers from devoting sufficient attention to juveniles. In addition, attorney hesitation to embrace the role of zealous advocate instead of concerned parent can influence attorneys to be paternalistic toward youthful clients. The result of any misunderstanding of the lawyer's role is that juveniles often are not fully honest with their attorneys. One way to help juvenile defendants to see their attorneys as zealous advocates is to honor confidentiality, especially by respecting confidentiality in relation to parents. If the attorney shows the youth that he or she will not divulge confidences to the youth's parents, that will demonstrate the attorney's undivided loyalty to the youthful defendant. Another important matter is to simply spend more time with youthful clients to counteract any impression that the youth does not matter (Buss, 2000).

Plea Bargaining

As in adult criminal court, the vast majority of cases in juvenile court are resolved by plea bargains (Puritz et al., 1995). Because of the pressure on youths to plead guilty (admit the allegations in the petition) and because of the problems with **plea bargaining** (see, e.g., Newman, 1986), the American Bar Association has recommended that plea bargaining either be made visible or eliminated entirely (Institute of Judicial Administration–American Bar Association, 1980). The Bar Association maintains that if plea bargaining is retained, the judge should not participate in the process. However, the judge "should require disclosure of the agreement reached and explicitly indicate the conditions under which he or she is willing to honor it" (Institute of Judicial Administration–American Bar Association, 1980:39). If the judge will not accept the plea agreement, he or she should give the juvenile a chance to withdraw his or her plea. Finally, the judge should consult with the juvenile's parents before accepting a plea (Institute of Judicial Administration–American Bar Association, 1980:47). These regulations (or alternatively, the abolition of plea bargaining) would eliminate many of the traditional abuses of the practice.

The issue of plea bargaining may take on increasing importance. Texas, for example, recently revised its laws to allow more determinate sentencing in juvenile court as an alternative to waiving some youths to adult court. Youths subject to this provision can get longer prison sentences and may complete their sentences, when they turn 21, in the adult system. Mears (2000) found that such increased sentencing options gave prosecutors greater leverage in pressuring juveniles to accept plea bargains.

Attorney Effectiveness

Research has shown some interesting results concerning the effectiveness of defense attorneys in juvenile court. First, Michael Fabricant's (1983) study of juvenile court public defenders in Brooklyn and the Bronx (NY) found that, contrary to stereotypes, public defenders were more effective (or at least as effective) as private attorneys in defending their juvenile clients. Specifically, the public defenders were very effective in obtaining adjournments, avoiding detention, and gaining dismissals. Such indicators of adversarial effectiveness led Fabricant (1983) to conclude that New York City public defenders were not inadequate. This is an impressive finding because they were representing roughly 75 percent of the delinquency and status offense cases in New York City at the time of the study.

Stevens Clarke and Gary Koch (1980), however, found conflicting evidence. Specifically, data from two North Carolina juvenile courts in the mid-1970s indicated that "the assistance of an attorney was on the whole not helpful—and may have actually been detrimental—with respect to reducing the child's chance of being adjudicated delinquent and committed" (Clarke and Koch, 1980:307). The attorneys may have been more concerned with "helping" the youths receive treatment than in simply "beating the rap." It should be noted that an alternative interpretation of the findings from North Carolina is that the attorneys studied were receiving the toughest cases, cases that judges had essentially decided were going to wind up in youth prisons anyway. Finally, it is important to remember that juvenile court is often a low-prestige assignment for both new public defenders and new prosecutors. Many of these attorneys "try to stay as briefly as possible" (Mahoney, 1987:10) in these jobs. The resultant lack of experience may influence the effectiveness of both prosecutors and public defenders in juvenile court.

In an analysis of six states, Feld (1988) found results very similar to those in North Carolina. In three states many children did not have attorneys. In all six states, however, "unrepresented juveniles seem to fare better than those with lawyers" (Feld, 1988:418). Juveniles with attorneys were more likely to receive placement outside the home or secure confinement than juveniles without attorneys.

In a study of more than 500 juvenile felony court cases in Missouri, Burruss and Kempf-Leonard (2002) also found an adverse effect of attorneys. In other words, "out-of-home placement was more likely to occur if a youth had an attorney, even when other relevant legal and individual factors were the same" (Burruss and Kempf-Leonard, 2002:60). To be more specific, concerning youths charged with felonies in three Missouri courts (one urban, one suburban, and one rural), suburban youths with counsel were almost three times more likely to be removed from home, and rural youths were two and a half times more likely to get out-of-home placement than youths without attorneys. All the urban youths had counsel (Burruss and Kempf-Leonard, 2002). This negative effect of attorney representation raises an interesting point: Would kids be better off without attorneys? Burruss and Kempf-Leonard think not. They think that the negative impact of attorneys in juvenile court may be due to high caseloads, retaining counsel too late in the process, or other court personnel co-opting the attorneys out of an adversarial role.

Similarly, in a study of two midwestern courts, Guevara, Spohn, and Herz (2004) found that "the presence of an attorney (especially a private attorney) was an aggravating factor. Specifically, youths who appeared with a private attorney were the least likely to have the charges dismissed and the most likely to be securely confined" (p. 366). Most importantly, these findings about the negative impact of private attorneys call "into question the basic and fundamental right to counsel in juvenile court" (Guevara, Spohn, and Herz, 2004:366).

A recent American Bar Association investigation of Ohio juvenile courts produced several disturbing findings. First, "large numbers of poor youth throughout Ohio go unrepresented, even during some of the most critical proceedings that affect their liberty interest" (Brooks and Kamine, 2003:25). In many counties investigators noted that waiver of counsel was common, with as many as 80 percent of juveniles going without counsel. Second, many attorneys (slightly over 40%) saw their role as representing the "best interest" of the youth rather than being the youth's advocate. In some counties this view of the attorney role was so strong that it did not seem important to have an attorney represent the youth. Third, for many youths who did have attorney representation, the quality of that representation was questionable. The report found that many Ohio youths "receive ineffective assistance of counsel from attorneys who are ill-prepared, insufficiently trained, and/or overwhelmed by high caseloads, insufficient resources and low pay" (Brooks and Kamine, 2003:29). Thus, most cases are handled informally or by plea bargaining, and attorneys had little impact at disposition. One specific problem was low compensation. Starting annual salaries for public defenders were as low as $35,000, and hourly rates for appointed counsel in several counties paid only $50 an hour for in-court work and $40 an hour for out-of-court work. Such low rates do not help to attract or retain competent attorneys (Brooks and Kamine, 2003).

An American Bar Association study in Pennsylvania showed similar problems. Significant numbers of youths did not have representation, and many others had ineffective counsel due to lack of preparation or training. At detention hearings attorneys often had little chance to confer with their juvenile clients and were not familiar with alternatives to detention. Most cases were resolved by pleas, and attorneys saw many courts simply interested in dispensing treatment or punishment. Probation officers made disposition recommendations with little challenge from attorneys. At disposition, many attorneys simply were not acting as advocates for their juvenile clients. The investigators found that probation officers were very influential in the juvenile justice system, to the extent that "the system's over-dependence on [probation's] role has tipped the scales toward a 'best interest' system in delinquency cases in lieu of a system that demands the Commonwealth [of Pennsylvania] prove its case" (Miller-Wilson and Puritz, 2003:59).

Thus, the situation in America's juvenile courts appears to be such that some attorneys are adversarial, some are still traditional and act as concerned adults, and some are in between the two extremes. Furthermore, in some states, many juveniles are not represented by attorneys (Brooks and Kamine, 2003; Feld, 1993; Miller-Wilson and Puritz, 2003). One frequent problem is simply that many juveniles waive their right to an attorney (Jones, 2004). This state of affairs raises the issue of which is the best approach: zealous advocate, concerned adult, or some compromise between the two alternatives? The chief advantage of the zealous advocate model is that it is probably the best insurance that only truly guilty youths will come under court jurisdiction. Because the attorney does not pressure the child to admit to the petition (plead guilty), there is less danger that the court will attempt some type of intervention program with youths who are not really guilty. An added advantage is that this approach may well generate the most respect from juveniles for the court system. Fewer youths will feel that they have been betrayed or tricked into something that some adult thought was best for them, despite their own wishes.

The biggest danger of the zealous advocate approach is that it may contribute to what Fabricant (1983) calls the contemporary version of benign neglect. That is, because many youths appearing in juvenile court come from families racked with problems, such as low income, public assistance, and/or broken homes, they do need assistance. An adversarial approach may prevent these children from being railroaded into juvenile prisons or other types of intervention due to insufficient legal defense. That adversarial approach, however, does nothing about the real problems faced by these children in their homes and their neighborhoods:

> It must be presumed that these youngsters' fundamental problems will neither be addressed nor resolved through a faithful adherence to process. Just as important, their troubles are likely to be compounded by social indifference. Therefore, a policy of calculated nonintervention may, over time, cause severer and/or increased antisocial behavior from troubled youths who initially are ignored by the court or state (Fabricant, 1983:140).

The advantage of the concerned adult model is that it seeks to address the problems of the child that presumably led the child into delinquency. The problem is that this helping philosophy has been the rationale of the juvenile court since 1899, and, as David Rothman has so aptly phrased it, the rhetoric of individualized attention has always far outstripped the reality of ineffective if not abusive programs (Rothman, 1980).

Jury Trials for Juveniles

Because the U.S. Supreme Court has not mandated the right to a jury trial for all juveniles (see Chapter 9), only 10 states generally allow jury trials as a right for juveniles, and another 11 states allow jury trials in special circumstances (Szymanski, 2002). Some contend that it is critical for juveniles to have the right to a jury trial. For example, Barry Feld (1987b) has argued that judges require less proof than juries and, therefore, it is easier to convict a youth in front of a judge than in front of a jury. The American Bar Association agrees that judges may be biased and further states:

> A jury trial gives enhanced visibility to the adjudicative process.
> A jury trial requires the trial court judge to articulate his or her
> views of the applicable law in the case through jury instructions,
> thereby facilitating appellate court review of the legal issues
> involved. Without the focus on legal issues that such an exercise
> entails, the danger is great that the applicable law may be mis-
> perceived or misapplied and that the error will go uncorrected on
> appeal (Institute of Judicial Administration–American Bar Asso-
> ciation, 1980:53).

Having the right to a jury trial, however, may not make that much difference in juvenile court. In her study of a suburban juvenile court, Mahoney
(1985) found that only seven cases out of the 650 actually went to trial. For
those seven youths, and for 87 other youths who initially requested a jury trial
but later settled without a jury trial, there was no impact of setting (scheduling) a case for trial on outcomes. Thus, "in a handful of serious cases in
which a child denies charges, it [a jury trial] may be essential to the cause
of justice, but it is unclear how much a jury trial benefits a youth or the community in the great majority of cases (Mahoney, 1985:564). Similarly,
recent research in Ohio showed that most attorneys reported that 10 percent
or less of cases went to trial; trials were almost nonexistent in some counties (Brooks and Kamine, 2003).

The Recent Emphasis on Punitiveness

Traditionally, the disposition stage of juvenile court has been the epit-
ome of the *parens patriae* philosophy. With the advice of probation officers,
social workers, psychologists, and psychiatrists, the judge has tried to act in
the best interests of the child. Recently, however, disposition (sentencing)
in juvenile justice has taken on an increasingly punitive character.

One indicator of this increasingly explicit focus on punishment is the revision of the purpose clauses of state juvenile codes. In the past, states emphasized prevention, diversion, and treatment. As of 2005, at least six states
emphasized "community protection, offender accountability, crime reduction through deterrence, or outright punishment, either predominantly or
exclusively," and only four states had traditional child welfare emphases (Griffin, Szymanski, and King, 2005). Sixteen states used the language of balanced and restorative justice, emphasizing public safety, individual
accountability to both victims and the community, and offender skill development. Nine states modeled their statutes on the Standard Juvenile Court
Act, and six states had a multi-part purpose clause based on the Legislative
Guide for Drafting Family and Juvenile Court Acts (Griffin, Szymanski, and
King, 2005).

Parallel to the amendment of the purpose clauses, the states have taken more concrete measures to emphasize punishment. Three additional states (Washington, New Jersey, and Texas) have adopted determinate sentencing statutes with an emphasis on proportionality. The law in such states limits the discretion of judges at disposition and attempts to set penalties that are proportionate to the seriousness of the offense. Some states have enacted mandatory minimum provisions. This means that if the judge commits a child to the state youth authority, the law dictates that the youth must serve a certain minimum amount of time. Some states have adopted dispositional guidelines or suggested sentences for most adjudicated delinquents. Unless a case has some unusual factors, judges are supposed to sentence within the ranges stipulated in the guidelines. Finally, there is the fear that the conditions of confinement have become more negative or soon will become so. This fear is based on the experience of the adult prison system, where determinate sentencing has led to overcrowding and other negative consequences in the institutions (Feld, 1987a).

A prime indicator of the trend toward punitiveness is the move by many states to expand provisions for processing juveniles in adult criminal court rather than juvenile court. Between 1998 and 2002, 31 states changed their laws governing the prosecution and sentencing of juveniles in adult criminal courts. For example, 18 states expanded their transfer laws, including the addition of new offenses eligible for transfer. Three states (Illinois, Maryland, and North Carolina) legislated "once an adult, always an adult" laws in which processing in criminal court automatically excludes the juvenile from any juvenile court jurisdiction after that (Griffin, 2005). The overall result is that it is easier to process juveniles as adults in criminal court.

Still another development in this direction is **blended sentencing**. In blended sentencing, either the juvenile court or the adult court imposes a sentence that can involve either the juvenile or the adult correctional system or both systems. The adult sentence may be suspended pending either a violation or the commission of a new crime. Fifteen states have juvenile blended sentencing schemes (the juvenile court imposes sentence), and 17 states have criminal blended sentencing laws (the criminal court imposes sentence) (Griffin, 2005).

One example of a jurisdiction with blended sentencing is New Mexico. That state's "exclusive blend" of sentencing applies to 15-year-olds charged with first-degree murder, 15–17-year-olds charged with serious offenses, or 15–17-year-olds charged with a felony and three prior separate felony adjudications in a two-year period. The juvenile court has jurisdiction and can sentence the youth to a juvenile *or* an adult sentence. In *juvenile-inclusive* blended sentencing, the juvenile court has jurisdiction and can sentence to a sanction including both the juvenile correctional system *and* the adult correctional system. Usually, the adult sanction is suspended unless the youth violates the juvenile sanction (examples of jurisdictions with this are Connecticut, Minnesota, and Montana). Two other options are *criminal-exclusive* (e.g., California and Florida) and *criminal-inclusive* blended sentencing (e.g., Arkansas and Missouri), by which the criminal court tries and sentences the youth. In criminal-exclusive systems the sentence can be to juvenile *or* adult corrections; in criminal-inclusive states the sentence can be to both systems. The other type of blended sentencing is *juvenile-contiguous*, by which the juvenile court has authority to impose a sanction that goes beyond the age of its jurisdiction. Then differing procedures are used to decide whether the remainder of the sentence is imposed in the adult corrections system (Torbet et al., 1996).

Still another sign of increasing punitiveness is the passing of statutes concerning the confidentiality of juvenile court records and proceedings. Traditionally, such records and court proceedings were closed to the public. The *parens patriae* rationale dictated that this would protect the juvenile from publicity so that a delinquent act would not stigmatize him or her permanently. In the last few years, however, critics have called for publicity to assure community protection, and legislatures have responded. Between 1992 and 1997, 47 states modified or eliminated traditional juvenile court confidentiality provisions; they made records and proceedings more open (Office of Juvenile Justice and Delinquency Prevention, 1999).

A possible consequence of these punitive developments is that the involved states create two ways of processing juveniles. If a youth is older, commits a serious offense, and/or has a prior record, he will be treated as an adult or similar to an adult. If a younger youth commits a less serious offense and lacks a prior record, he will be handled in a traditional juvenile court. Much of the rationale behind this division of juveniles into quasi-adults and children is the belief that youths have changed. Youths who commit what appear to be willful violent crimes are considered mature and responsible adults who should be held accountable for their actions. Younger youths who commit less serious offenses are still looked on as wayward youths who can be salvaged by the traditional *parens patriae* juvenile court.

Dispositional Decisionmaking

A major issue in juvenile justice is the question of which factors influence judges in their dispositional (sentencing) decisions. Research indicates several general conclusions. Legal variables such as seriousness of the offense and prior record have a strong influence on dispositions (e.g., Clarke and Koch, 1980; Cohen and Kluegel, 1978; Dannefer and Schutt, 1982; McCarthy and Smith, 1986; Staples, 1987; Thornberry, 1973; Thomas and Cage, 1977). The impact of prior record on dispositions, however, may reflect bias amplification (Dannefer and Schutt, 1982; Sampson, 1986). In other words, prior record may mask the influence of race or social class in police decisionmaking. The impact of offender characteristics such as age, race, social class, and gender has mixed results (for reviews of prior research in this area, especially prior research on the impact of race, see Bishop and Frazier, 1996; Feld, 1999; Guevara, Spohn, and Herz, 2004; Krisberg and

Austin, 1993; Leiber and Mack, 2003; McCarthy and Smith, 1986; Pope, 1994). Usually, the impact of these variables is weaker than the impact of legal variables. One study, however, indicated that "measures of social class and race become increasingly important as direct influences on the final disposition as youths are selected into the system for further processing" (McCarthy and Smith, 1986:58). Another way to put this is that racial bias at early decision points such as detention hearings can have a cumulative effect at disposition such as being sentenced to residential placement (Guevara, Spohn, and Herz, 2004). Leiber and Mack argue that more recent research does suggest a race effect due to decisionmakers perceiving minorities, "especially African-Americans, as either dangerous, delinquent, and/or sexually promiscuous, which in turn had an effect on the case processing of these youth" (Leiber and Mack, 2003:37).

A number of studies report that females receive more severe dispositions than males for minor offenses, especially status offenses, stemming from traditional sex-role expectations. Other studies find leniency for females following the chivalry hypothesis, a paternalistic attitude toward female misbehavior compared to an excusing of boys "sowing their wild oats" (Chesney-Lind, 1977; Chesney-Lind and Shelden, 1992; Cohen and Kluegel, 1979). On the other hand, some studies show no gender bias after controlling for offense type or severity (see Leiber and Mack, 2003).

Prior case processing decisions exert some influence on dispositions. For example, detained youths receive harsher dispositions (Bailey and Peterson, 1981; Chused, 1973; Clarke and Koch, 1980) or are more likely to be formally processed (Frazier and Bishop, 1985; McCarthy, 1987) than youths who are not detained. Moreover, prior case dispositions can affect subsequent dispositions (Henretta, Frazier, and Bishop, 1985, 1986; Thornberry and Christenson, 1984). Finally, some authors report that dispositions vary from one jurisdiction to the next (e.g., Belknap, 1984; Dannefer and Schutt, 1982), while others fail to find such differences (e.g., Staples, 1987).

Recent research has shed additional light on this issue. Feld's (1993) research on dispositional decisions in Minnesota is pessimistic. He argues that one interpretation of his findings is that

> there is no rationale to dispositional decision making; it consists of little more than hunch, guesswork, and hopes, constrained marginally by the youth's present offense, prior record, and previous dispositions (Feld, 1993:232).

A statewide study of youths in Florida found:

> a consistent pattern of unequal treatment. Nonwhite youths referred for delinquent acts are more likely than comparable white youths to be recommended for petition to court, to be held in pre-adjudicatory detention, to be formally processed in juvenile court, and to receive the most formal or the most restrictive judicial dispositions (Bishop and Frazier, 1996:405-406).

A statewide study of all youths petitioned to juvenile court in Nebraska from 1988 to 1993 (from 5,000 to about 7,000 youths per year) found the disposition decision to be "relatively race-neutral" (Secret and Johnson, 1997:468), but race was related to the detention decision in three years and the detention decision "consistently relates to harsher treatment at the adjudication and disposition stages of juvenile processing" (Secret and Johnson, 1997:474).

A study of almost 5,000 cases in Pennsylvania found that race did not have a direct effect on the decision to place a juvenile in a secure facility. However, black youths charged with drug offenses had more severe dispositions than black youths charged with other offenses. In addition, black youths in rural courts were more likely to be placed than black youths in urban courts. This led the authors to conclude that "the problem of disparity in sentencing is subtle, and is embedded in multiple variable relationships" (DeJong and Jackson, 1998:503).

A study of judges' responses to hypothetical vignettes instead of actual cases found that aspects of the offense (e.g., presence of a weapon, violent offense) and prior record had the largest effects on probability of a decision to incarcerate. The judges also considered age and the willingness of the family to cooperate with the court (Applegate et al., 2000).

A study of commitment decisions for almost 2,000 first-time offenders in Pennsylvania found an "apparent lack of any direct racial effect" (Fader et al., 2001). It is interesting to note that decisionmakers were looking at the needs of the youth and his or her family and thus showing "the retention of *parens patriae* principles in the face of mandates to treat juveniles more like their adult counterparts" (Fader et al., 2001:339). *Parens patriae* was not the only consideration, however, as drug history offenders were just as likely to be sent to disciplinary programs (i.e., boot camps) as to programs with drug treatment.

A recent study of juvenile case processing in Texas found "an absence of strong and consistent race and ethnic differentials in juvenile processing in Texas" (Tracy, 2002:175). Based on his research findings, Tracy contends that there is in fact differential involvement of minority youths in delinquency—minorities do commit a disproportionate share of delinquency. So attention needs to be directed to factors that cause such involvement in delinquency rather than squandered on the false issue of disproportionate treatment in juvenile court.

After examining the research on disposition decisions in juvenile court, it appears that the research findings are mixed; some studies find little or no impact of race while other studies reveal a race effect. The race effect may be indirect but nevertheless very real. For example, race may affect the detention decision, which then affects the disposition. Because the research is often limited to one jurisdiction or state, this may mean that sentencing varies from place to place. Apparently, some jurisdictions have achieved better success than others in making the disposition stage race-neutral. Hopefully, juvenile courts everywhere will make further progress in eliminating race as a factor in juvenile court dispositions.

Where race is still a factor in juvenile court dispositions, it may be that more is needed than simply addressing the problems of juvenile court. Krisberg and Austin (1993), for example, argue that problems in juvenile court dispositions, especially any findings of possible racial disproportionality, cannot be resolved in isolation but are "tied inextricably to the pursuit of social justice. Reforms will continue to fail, as they have in the past, if they do not address the maldistribution of wealth, power, and resources throughout society" (Krisberg and Austin, 1993:110). (For a discussion of other changes intended to improve juvenile court dispositions, see Boxes 8.9, 8.10, and 8.11.)

Box 8.9 A Critique of Processing Juveniles in Adult Criminal Court

Donna Bishop argues against overuse of adult court for juvenile offenders. First, she argues that psychological research shows that juveniles are less mature, more likely to take risks, and more vulnerable to peer pressure. Second, the recent trend to let prosecutors make the decision rather than juvenile court judges puts the decision in the hands of young and inexperienced actors who may not be fully aware of all the options in the juvenile justice system. Similarly, prosecutor decisions mean that youths do not get the protections of a waiver hearing, as envisioned by the Supreme Court in the *Kent* decision (see Chapter 9 for a full explanation of *Kent*). Fourth, the research shows that adult court processing often translates into higher recidivism compared to juvenile system processing. Bishop sees the need for some juveniles to be processed in adult criminal court but advocates for most "the protections from harsh criminal sanctions that they deserve and the opportunities for growth and change that they need" (Bishop, 2004:641).

Box 8.10 The Silverton, Oregon, Reform of Juvenile Court

Silverton, Oregon, passed a law in 1995 making parents liable for juvenile status offenses such as truancy and delinquency. Parents may be fined up to a $1,000, ordered to pay damages, and/or ordered to attend parenting classes.

One school official claimed that the new law has been quite effective in combating truancy. After passage of the law, parents are now calling the principal to check that their children are in school, whereas prior to the law the principal had to call parents of truant children.

Box 8.10, *continued*

Critics of the law say that it punishes parents when children break the law despite honest efforts of parents to instill good discipline. Another criticism is that the law does not send the message that children are responsible for their own conduct ("ABC Good Morning America," June 1, 1995).

What do you think? To what extent should parents be held accountable for their children's misdeeds? Are critics right that this law might send a message that children themselves are not responsible for their actions?

Box 8.11 Suggestions for Reducing the Effect of Race on Court Dispositions

Frazier and Bishop (1995) studied 137,028 cases referred to juvenile justice intake units in Florida between 1985 and 1987. They found significant race effects in dispositions even after controlling for the possible effects of other variables such as seriousness of the offense.

They offer several suggestions to reduce the impact of race in juvenile court. First, states should establish policies for reporting, investigating, and responding to individual instances of suspected racial bias. A second suggestion is diversity training for employees. Third, lack of parental cooperation should not be a ban for admission to more informal juvenile justice system options. Fourth, if persons with economic resources can utilize private care instead of harsher system dispositions, then "precisely the same treatment services should be made available at state expense to serve the poor—whether minority or majority race youths" (Frazier and Bishop, 1995:45).

SUMMARY

This chapter has examined the critical decision points in juvenile court: intake, detention, waiver and other means of getting youths to adult court, adjudication, and disposition. This review has shown that the ideal of a beneficent court system has not always been reached. Sometimes, for example, detention facilities have been deteriorating physical facilities concealing punitive practices. Even though 40 years have elapsed since the *In re Gault* decision established due process protections for juveniles, attorneys in juvenile court may be confused about their role and often have high caseloads that prevent them from effective representation of juveniles. Many juveniles do not even have attorney representation. Despite the history of civil rights legislation and concern, sometimes race appears to be a factor in juvenile court decisionmaking. Most recently, critics have become concerned about juvenile crime and the adequacy of the juvenile justice system to handle the serious offender. Thus, increased use of waiver, legislative exclusion, and prosecutorial waiver and of other more punitive measures such as blended sentencing have begun to characterize many juvenile court systems. This trend will probably continue.

In light of the ferment in juvenile court and the growing emphasis on harsher measures, concern for the due process rights of juvenile offenders is more critical than ever. In the next chapter, we will discuss due process issues and the rights of juveniles in general.

Discussion Questions

1. H. Ted Rubin argues that token economies and other detention programs are violations of juvenile detainees' rights because most of the youths have not been adjudicated delinquent. Do you agree or do you feel that such programs can be justified because they establish order and thereby protect the detainees? Are such practices similar to what "free" youngsters experience everyday in a typical school setting?

2. Much of the research described in this chapter concerns the decisions to detain, petition, and dispose of alleged delinquents. One of the basic issues in all of these decisions is whether the decisionmakers should or should not consider social factors in their decisionmaking. For example, should the attitude of the youth or the quality of parental care influence whether he or she is formally processed or allowed to go home with a warning or a much less severe consequence? Do such social factors have a place in these decisions, or are such social factors so liable to ethnic bias that the decisions should be based *solely* on legal factors?

3. Do you favor the use of bail in juvenile court? If so, for what sorts of offenders and under what circumstances?

4. Would you consider a career in juvenile detention as an administrator, counselor, teacher, or attendant (guard)?

5. Consider the following: A juvenile is accused of raping a 24-year-old high school teacher. You are a defense attorney and the defendant has asked you to represent him. You are convinced that you could "get the juvenile off" on a technicality. However, several members of your extended family are teachers and feel very strongly about this case. Would you accept the case? Would you pursue the technical defense that would exonerate the defendant, or would you encourage the youth to plead guilty and accept the psychiatric help that an expert feels is needed for the young man?

Discussion Questions, *continued*

6. What do you think about the trend toward increased punitiveness (increased criminal court processing of youths, blended sentences, changes in purpose clauses to include punishment and incapacitation as juvenile court objectives, and changes in confidentiality)? Do you favor this trend, or does it represent an abandoning of the ideals of juvenile court?

7. Suppose that a 13-year-old youth became extremely agitated and angry. He went to his parents' bedroom and got a pistol that was kept there in case an intruder broke in. He then murdered a family member. If this youth had no prior record but also no evidence of psychiatric disturbance, would you favor or oppose processing this youth as an adult in criminal court? How would the factor of a prior record influence your decision? What details of a prior record would most affect your decision? What are your reasons for your position?

8. The use of blended sentences and the increased processing of juveniles in adult court will probably result in an increase in the number of youths being incarcerated in adult prisons or in new youthful offender prisons instead of traditional training schools. What might be some positive and negative consequences of this?

Chapter 9

Due Process and Juveniles

INTRODUCTION

Juveniles share some—but not all—of the same constitutional rights as adults. While a comprehensive analysis of juvenile rights would require an entire book and is, therefore, beyond the scope of this text, it is important to examine some of the rights pertaining to juveniles. This chapter will first examine the landmark juvenile Supreme Court cases of the 1960s and 1970s (such as *In re Gault*) because those cases fundamentally altered the contours of the juvenile justice system. Then we will examine the Fourth Amendment rights of juveniles in terms of search and seizure by the police. Finally, we will analyze some other important rights of juveniles such as rights in school and rights at home.

THE LANDMARK SUPREME COURT CASES

Between the founding of the juvenile court in 1899 and the *Kent v. United States* case in 1966, the United States Supreme Court basically left the juvenile court alone. In other words, the Supreme Court respected the intentions of juvenile court officials to seek the best interests of the child by allowing juvenile court judges and related personnel a great deal of discretion in attempting to achieve those objectives. In the mid-1960s, however, the Supreme Court was confronted with several cases that indicated that such a hands-off approach was no longer appropriate.

KEY TERMS

Breed v. Jones

consent search

corporal punishment

curfew laws

Fare v. Michael C.

freedom of speech

graduated licensing

In re Gault

In re Winship

Kent v. United States

legal drinking age

McKeiver v. Pennsylvania

New Jersey v. T.L.O.

preventive detention

Schall v. Martin

school prayer

school suspensions

search and seizure

student search

Kent v. United States

In *Kent v. United States* (1966), the Supreme Court was faced with a waiver case appeal wherein a 16-year-old, Morris Kent, had been waived (transferred) to adult criminal court without a hearing, without the assistance of counsel, and without any statement of the reasons for the judge's decision to transfer the matter to the adult court. A judge had decided to transfer Kent, who had been charged with rape, simply on the basis of a review of the youth's social service and probation files. The judge did not allow Kent's privately retained attorney to review any of the files, nor did the judge conduct any hearing on the matter or state the reasons that convinced him to transfer the case. Thus, the waiver decision, a very critical decision that results in the possibility of an adult criminal record and adult penalties, had been made by the judge acting alone, without any concern for Morris Kent's rights.

The Supreme Court justices decided that due process of law entitles a defendant like Morris Kent to certain minimum safeguards, including a hearing, the right to the assistance of an attorney, and a statement of the reasons for transfer if the judge decides to transfer the case to adult court. The Supreme Court reasoned that the juvenile court judge denied Kent his right to the assistance of an attorney. Without a hearing, Kent's attorney had no opportunity to represent the youth. The denial of the assistance of counsel, a Sixth Amendment right, was compounded by the judge's denial of access to the case files. That denial prevented the attorney from raising any challenges to possible errors in social service or probation staff reports about the defendant.

The *Kent* case is important not so much because it corrected the wrongs done to one individual or because it put some order into the waiver (transfer) procedure, but because it marks the Supreme Court's first major examination of juvenile court processing. This examination found serious shortcomings in both the particular juvenile court that had handled Morris Kent and juvenile courts in general:

> While there can be no doubt of the original laudable purpose of juvenile courts, studies and critiques in recent years raise serious questions as to whether actual performance measures well enough against theoretical purpose to make tolerable the immunity of the process from the reach of constitutional guaranties applicable to adults. There is much evidence that some juvenile courts, including that of the District of Columbia, lack the personnel, facilities and techniques to perform adequately as representatives of the State in a *parens patriae* capacity, at least with respect to children charged with law violation. There is evidence, in fact, that there may be grounds for concern that the child receives the worst of both worlds: that he gets neither the protections accorded to adults nor the solicitous care and regenerative treatment postulated for children (*Kent v. United States*, 1966).

A final comment on the *Kent* case is that many states are now resorting to prosecutor direct file and statutory exclusion (see Chapter 8 for more details) instead of transfer or waiver to prosecute juveniles as adults in criminal courts. Reliance on these other methods means that the affected juveniles do not get the waiver hearing and protections that *Kent* was intended to guarantee.

In re Gault

The case of ***In re Gault*** was even more significant. Gerald Gault was a 15-year-old Arizona youth who was arrested for allegedly making obscene phone calls to an adult woman. He was adjudicated a delinquent in a court proceeding that resembled a kangaroo court or a dictatorial tribunal rather than a court of law and was sentenced to the state training school for a possible six-year sentence. The maximum penalty for an adult committing the exact same offense was a $50 fine and two months in jail.

Gault, after being accused, was taken into police custody and detained. Within about a week, Gerald was adjudicated a delinquent and committed to the state training school until he was discharged or turned 21 years of age, whichever came first. All of this occurred without the complainant (the target of the obscene phone calls) ever appearing in court to testify, without any detailed and specific charges being filed (Gerald was simply *accused* of being a "delinquent"), without the assistance of an attorney for Gerald (his probation officer "represented" him), and without any transcript of the proceedings. The end result was the possibility of a six-year sentence for what was at worst a nuisance offense.

In reviewing the case, Supreme Court Justice Abe Fortas traced the history of the juvenile court and of the *parens patriae* philosophy and found some fundamental problems. Supposedly, due process guarantees such as the assistance of an attorney were to be relaxed in juvenile court so that youths would receive the treatment benefits promised by both the founders and current advocates of the juvenile court. Instead, as the Court observed in the *Kent* case, the child often received the worst of both worlds: lack of procedural fairness and substandard treatment.

Interestingly, the Supreme Court did not go on to discard the juvenile court philosophy of *parens patriae*. Instead, Justice Fortas observed that due process rights would not hinder juvenile court judges from seeking the best interests of the child but actually would assist them in that effort:

> But recent studies . . . suggest that the appearance as well as the actuality of fairness, impartiality and orderliness—in short, the essentials of due process—may be a more impressive and more therapeutic attitude so far as the juvenile is concerned (*In re Gault*, 1967).

Judge Fortas went on to rule that juveniles do have certain due process rights in delinquency proceedings in which there is the possibility of confinement in a locked facility. Specifically, such juveniles have the Fifth Amendment privilege against self-incrimination (the right to remain silent) and Sixth Amendment rights to adequate notice of the charges against them, to confront and cross-examine their accusers, and to the assistance of counsel.

In re Winship

In 1970, the Supreme Court went a step further. In the case of *In re Winship*, an appeal of a New York case involving a 12-year-old boy who had stolen $112 from a woman's purse from a locker, the Supreme Court turned its attention to the issue of the standard of proof (how strong a case must be to prove delinquency) in juvenile court. The Court made two rulings. First, the Court ruled that the U.S. Constitution requires that adult criminals be convicted only by the standard of "guilty beyond a reasonable doubt" (the reasonable doubt standard of proof). This had been standard practice in adult courts; the Court simply stated that the Constitution mandated what the states had been doing all along. Second, the Court extended the reasonable doubt standard of proof to juvenile delinquency proceedings in which there was the possibility of commitment to a locked facility. As was the case in *In re Gault*, the Court reasoned that this safeguard of the reasonable doubt standard would not detract in any way from the noble intentions of the *parens patriae* philosophy. It also suggested that, rhetoric aside, juvenile training schools were the functional equivalents of adult prisons because both resulted in deprivation of liberty—and any such deprivation of liberty requires due process protections. Finally, the Supreme Court noted that New York State's standard of proof in juvenile proceedings (i.e., guilty by a preponderance of the evidence) was open to inaccurate findings. There was a real possibility that youths could be found delinquent when in fact there was insufficient evidence for such findings.

McKeiver v. Pensylvania

A year later, in 1971, the Supreme Court took up the issue of a juvenile's right to a jury trial in the case of *McKeiver v. Pennsylvania*. In *McKeiver,* the Supreme Court declined to go so far in extending adult rights as to grant juveniles the right to trial by jury. The Supreme Court decided not to grant juveniles the right to jury trials for several reasons. First, the Court did not want to turn the juvenile court process into a fully adversarial process and end "the idealistic prospect of an intimate, informal protective proceeding" (*McKeiver v. Pennsylvania*, 1971). Second, the Court noted that because bench trials (trials decided by a judge rather than by a jury) for adults often result in accurate determinations of guilt, jury trials are not an absolute necessity for accurate determinations of delinquency. The Court also indicated that it was reluctant to impose a federal requirement of a jury trial because such a mandate could prevent individual states from experimenting with different methods. Finally, the Court noted that it had not reached such total disillusionment with the juvenile justice system that it sought to abandon it.

Barry Feld (1987b) contends that the denial of the right of a jury trial to juveniles was an important decision because judges and juries view cases differently. The result of the denial of the right to a jury trial is that it is "easier to convict a youth appearing before a judge in juvenile court than to convict a youth, on the basis of the same evidence, before a jury of detached citizens in a criminal proceeding" (Feld, 1987:530). In other words, Feld believes that judges need less evidence to convict than do juries and that delinquents would fare better before juries.

These cases of *Kent*, *Gault*, *Winship,* and *McKeiver* constituted a philosophical revolution in juvenile court. Together, they forced juvenile courts to at least pay lip service to the notion that juveniles deserve many of the due process safeguards available to adults. Although the *McKeiver* case ruled against extending the right of trial by jury to juveniles, even this case indicated that the Supreme Court would not tolerate the wholesale denial of rights to juveniles. The *McKeiver* case implied that if accurate fact-finding were not available to juveniles, then the Supreme Court might have to impose additional limits on juvenile court discretion.

Still, it must be remembered that a philosophical revolution is not always a revolution in practice. Just because the Supreme Court has ruled that juveniles should be entitled to certain rights, such a pronouncement alone does not guarantee the actual provision of those rights. There is evidence that many children waive their right to counsel and that high caseloads prevent many lawyers representing juveniles from being effective (Miller-Wilson and Puritz, 2003; see also Feld, 1999). Thus, court practices and lack of resources can prevent juveniles from actually benefiting from Supreme Court rulings.

ADDITIONAL SUPREME COURT RULINGS

Since the landmark cases just discussed, the U.S. Supreme Court has decided several cases concerning delinquency proceedings in juvenile court.

Roper v. Simmons: A Ruling on the Death Penalty

In 2005, in *Roper v. Simmons*, the Supreme Court ruled that the death penalty is unconstitutional for juveniles. This case is discussed in detail in Chapter 14.

Breed v. Jones: **A Ruling on Waiver**

In *Breed v. Jones* (1975), the Court made the waiver process more explicit by ruling that states cannot first adjudicate a juvenile a delinquent and then waive or transfer the youth to adult court. The Court ruled that by doing this in a particular case, the state of California violated the youth's Sixth Amendment protection against double jeopardy (being tried twice for the same crime). The state of California had claimed that double jeopardy was not at issue because the juvenile was only punished once, but the Supreme Court ruled that being tried both in juvenile court and then again in adult court did indeed constitute a violation of the double jeopardy provision.

In a sense, the case of *Breed v. Jones* was not much of a victory for juvenile rights. Prior to the case, juveniles were tried in juvenile court, adjudicated delinquent, and then transferred to adult criminal court where they were tried as adults and sentenced. All that the U.S. Supreme Court ruling accomplished was a procedural change by which the juvenile court would now conduct a waiver or transfer hearing to determine if there was probable cause to believe that the juvenile committed the delinquent act. If the juvenile court finds probable cause and also determines that the juvenile is not amenable to juvenile system intervention (for example, the youth is getting too old for juvenile programs or has been in juvenile programs previously without much success), the juvenile court simply transfers the juvenile to the adult system without any final determination of the charge. A few years ago, one of the authors of this text observed such a waiver hearing, which equaled a full trial on the delinquency petition in every respect except that the judge declared a finding of "probable cause" rather than "delinquent" at the end of the hearing. The practical result of such waivers (transfers) to adult criminal court is the same as if the child had been adjudicated a delinquent. *Breed v. Jones* may be more a case of window dressing rather than an influential juvenile justice case.

AP Photo/Pablo Martinez Monsivais

Seventeen-year-old sniper suspect John Lee Malvo is escorted from court after his preliminary hearing in Fairfax, Virginia. The hearing determined that Malvo would be waived to adult court in Fairfax County and possibly face the death sentence. Malvo and an adult accomplice were arrested for the shooting of 18 people, killing 13, and wounding five.

Fare v. Michael C.: A Ruling on Interrogation

As noted above, two of the provisions of the *Gault* case were its explicit endorsements of the Fifth Amendment privilege against self-incrimination and the Sixth Amendment right to the assistance of counsel for juveniles. *Gault* applied to juvenile delinquency suspects the *Miranda* rights granted to adult criminal suspects. Like adults, juveniles may waive these two rights and consent to police interrogation without any attorney being present. A voluntary confession can then be used against the juvenile in court.

Gault left it unclear whether a juvenile could waive these so-called *Miranda* rights without first speaking with at least one parent or an attorney. The American Bar Association has gone so far as to recommend mandatory consultation with an attorney prior to any confession to the police (Institute of Judicial Administration–American Bar Association, 1982). Most states, however, simply stipulate that the police give *Miranda* warnings in language that is understandable to juveniles (see Holtz, 1987).

The Supreme Court clarified this issue in the case of ***Fare v. Michael C.*** (1979). In this case a juvenile murder suspect consented to an interrogation after he was denied the opportunity to consult with his probation officer. The Court ruled that there is no constitutional mandate to allow a suspect to speak with his or her probation officer. The rationale of the Court was that the Sixth Amendment specifies the right to the assistance of counsel, while a probation officer is basically on the side of the police in seeking to prosecute any juvenile who has violated his probation. More importantly, the Court ruled that the child can voluntarily waive his or her privilege against self-incrimination without first speaking to his or her parents and without first consulting an attorney. In such a situation the trial court judge must evaluate the voluntariness of any confession based on the totality of the circumstances rather than on any ironclad rule (called a *per se* rule) mandating the police to bring in at least one parent or an attorney to advise the child about the wisdom of waiving his or her rights. In evaluating the totality of the circumstances of the waiver, the trial court must consider such factors as the age, maturity, experience, and intelligence of the youth. Thus, judges might allow as admissible the waiver of rights by a 17-year-old high school student with a prior record but probably not the waiver of rights by a 13-year-old first offender of below-average intelligence.

It is important to note that there is some controversy about the Supreme Court's wisdom in not requiring more explicit or extensive warnings for juvenile suspects prior to interrogation. First, some research indicates that not all juveniles clearly understand their rights when arrested (Huang, 2001). In one study, about one-third of a sample of institutionalized delinquents thought (erroneously) that they were required to talk to the police (Robin, 1982). Other research has indicated that more than one-half of the youths tested lacked full understanding of all the *Miranda* warnings, and only about one-fifth adequately understood all of the warnings (Holtz, 1987:550;

see also Grisso and Schwartz, 2000). Recent neurobiological research confirms difficulties for minors in understanding and asserting their *Miranda* rights (Juvenile Law Center, 2004). Second, parents tend not to be the best protectors of juvenile rights. One study showed that about one-third of the parents would advise their own children to confess criminal involvement to the police (Robin, 1982). Due to considerations such as these, some model juvenile law codes stipulate that police must have juvenile suspects consult with an attorney prior to police interrogation (Institute of Judicial Administration–American Bar Association, 1982).

Most states follow the "totality of the circumstances" approach outlined in the *Fare* case. A few states put in so-called *per se* rules requiring that juveniles have the opportunity to confer with a parent, guardian, attorney, or other interested adult. Unfortunately, a number of states (Georgia, Louisiana, and Pennsylvania) overturned their *per se* rules as part of the "get tough" movement (Huang, 2001). However, appellate courts in three states—Alaska, Minnesota, and Wisconsin—have ordered that police electronically record all juvenile interrogations in order to assure the voluntariness of confessions and prevent police coercion (Ziemer, 2005). The Pennsylvania Supreme Court ruled that a juvenile can waive his or her right to counsel only after a judge questions the juvenile to determine if the juvenile understands the allegations and that a lawyer can be helpful (Burke, 2005).

In *Yarborough, Warden v. Alvarado* (2004), the U.S. Supreme Court ruled that age was not a factor in determining that a juvenile was not in custody for purposes of police questioning. The case involved a two-hour police interview of a 17-year-old murder suspect in a police station without giving the *Miranda* warnings or allowing the boy's parents to be present in the interview room. Based on his statements to the police, the youth was convicted of murder. The court ruled that the lower court made a correct ruling on the noncustodial status of Alvarado based on objective factors such as: (1) the police did not transport the juvenile to the station; (2) his parents were in the lobby, and (3) at the end of the interview the youth went home. The dissent argued, among other factors, that age is an objective factor that the police and courts should consider in determining custody status.

Schall v. Martin: A Ruling on Preventive Detention

In *Schall v. Martin* (1984), the U.S. Supreme Court ruled that a juvenile who is awaiting court action can be held in **preventive detention** if there is adequate concern that the juvenile would commit additional crimes while the primary case is pending further court action. The juvenile, however, does have the right to a hearing on the preventive detention decision and a statement of the reasons for which he or she is being detained. The Court justified its decision on the basis that every state permits such preventive detention for juveniles and on the rationale that such detention protects "both the juvenile and society from the hazards of pretrial crime" (*Schall v. Martin*, 1984). Furthermore, the Court majority reasoned that "juveniles, unlike adults, are always in some form of custody" (*Schall v. Martin*, 1984). The three dissenting justices, on the other hand, noted the impossibility of predicting which juveniles will engage in future crime (this is often labeled the false positive issue) and considered the punitive nature of many detention facilities.

SEARCH AND SEIZURE

Consideration of these landmark U.S. Supreme Court cases demonstrates that juveniles do indeed have basic rights at important stages of the juvenile justice process, especially the waiver (transfer) hearing and the adjudication (trial) stage. Very important are the Fourth Amendment rights of juveniles during investigation or arrest.

The issue of **search and seizure** is a complex one involving a myriad of U.S. Supreme Court interpretations of the Fourth Amendment. This amendment reads:

> The right of the people to be secure in their persons, houses, papers, and effects, against unreasonable searches and seizures, shall not be violated, and no Warrants shall issue, but upon probable cause, supported by Oath or affirmation, and particularly describing the place to be searched, and the persons or things to be seized.

The Fourth Amendment indicates a preference for warrants before the police can search or arrest suspects, but this preference for warrants is riddled with numerous exceptions. This is not the place to describe those exceptions (but see, for example, O'Brien, 1997). Here it is important to examine one question that does affect juveniles: the **consent search** in which a defendant voluntarily allows the police to search someone or one's effects without a search warrant. Since *Schneckloth v. Bustamonte* (1973), the U.S. Supreme Court's ruling on adult consent searches has been that the police may simply ask a person for consent to search the person or his or her house, car, or effects. Unlike the *Miranda* situation, in which the police must advise a person of the right to refuse interrogation, the police do not have to specifically advise an adult suspect that he or she has the right to refuse a search. The police may simply ask an adult, "Do you mind if we take a look around your house?" If the person agrees, then—aware of it or not—the individual has agreed to a consent search. This would be a reasonable search in terms of Fourth Amendment guarantees.

In the case of juveniles, the issue arises whether a juvenile is mature enough to withstand police pressure and intelligent enough to understand his or her rights. The American Bar Association has recommended that juveniles be advised of their right to refuse a consent search and that they also be advised of the opportunity to consult an attorney (Institute of Judicial Administration–American Bar Association, 1982). The Bar Association felt that these two safeguards would compensate for any youthful susceptibility to police coercion and any lack of sophistication needed to understand fully one's rights. Another set of standards, the American Law Institute Model Code of Pre-arraignment Procedure, stipulates that if a person about to be asked to consent to a search is under 16 years of age, then a parent should be the one who gives consent. The Model Code further advocates that in *any* consent search situation involving juveniles or adults, the police should advise the individual that he or she "is under no obligation to give such consent and that anything found may be taken and used in evidence" (Wadlington, Whitebread, and Davis, 1983:301). In other words, the Model Code drafters advocated warnings for consent searches that were similar to the *Miranda* warnings used in interrogation situations. They felt that it should not be assumed that juvenile offenders are aware of their right to refuse a consent search without a clear warning of their right to do so.

A recent Supreme Court case suggests that today's courts are probably inclined to rule on the side of law enforcement rather than to extend offender rights. In *United States v. Mark James Knights* (2002), the Court ruled that a warrantless search of a probationer, supported by reasonable suspicion and authorized by a probation condition, satisfied the Fourth Amendment. This follows *In re Tyrell* (1994), in which a California court ruled that a search of a juvenile on probation (which found marijuana in his pants) did not violate the Fourth Amendment. Police made a pat-down search of the youth when they saw a knife on one of two other youths with him. Even though the police did not have probable cause to conduct the search and even though the youth did not consent to the search, the Court felt the police did not violate the juvenile's expectation of privacy because the boy had been placed on probation, which stipulated the condition that he submit to searches by police, probation officers, or school officials. This probation condition erased any reasonable expectation of privacy (*Juvenile Justice Update*, 1995).

RIGHTS IN SCHOOL

Because juveniles spend much of their time in school, many questions about juvenile rights have arisen within the context of school policies and procedures.

Corporal Punishment

In *Ingraham v. Wright,* the U.S. Supreme Court ruled that **corporal punishment** (e.g., paddling) of students is permissible so long as it is reasonable. The reasonableness decision depends on

> the seriousness of the offense, the attitude and past behavior of the child, the nature and severity of the punishment, the age and strength of the child, and the availability of less severe but equally effective means of discipline (*Ingraham v. Wright*, 1977).

The Court noted that corporal punishment could be abused, but observed that common law remedies were effective deterrents to any such abuse of the practice. The Court reasoned that students and their parents could sue school officials or charge them with criminal assault if they went too far in paddling any particular student.

As is often the case, dissenting opinions in Supreme Court cases raise very interesting issues. In fact, dissents sometimes are more noteworthy than the majority or plurality opinions of the Justices. Box 9.1 presents excerpts from the dissenting opinion of Justice White in the case of *Ingraham v. Wright*. These show that there are other sides to the issue of the constitutionality of **corporal punishment** in schools. The American Bar Association has followed Justice White's dissent and has recommended that "[c]orporal punishment should not be inflicted upon a student. . . ." (Institute for Judicial Administration–American Bar Association, 1982:136). Finally, a review of the research on corporal punishment concluded that it should be banned because children who receive corporal punishment are more prone as adults to various deviant acts. Among the later problems are depression, suicide, physical abuse of children and spouses, commission of violent crime, drinking problems, attraction to masochistic sex, and problems attaining a prestigious occupation (Straus, 1994).

Box 9.1. Excerpts from Justice White's Dissent in *Ingraham v. Wright*

If there are some punishments that are so barbaric that they may not be imposed for the commission of crimes, designated by our social system as the most thoroughly reprehensible acts an individual can commit, then, *a fortiori*, similar punishments may not be imposed on persons for less culpable acts, such as breaches of school discipline. Thus, if it is constitutionally impermissible to cut off someone's ear for the commission of murder, it must be unconstitutional to cut off a child's ear for being late to class. Although there were no ears cut off in this case, the record reveals beatings so severe that if they were inflicted on a hardend criminal for the commission of a serious crime, they might not pass constitutional muster.

. . .

The essence of the majority's argument is that school children do not need Eighth Amendment protection because corporal punishment is less subject to abuse in the public schools than it is in the prison system. However, it cannot be reasonably suggested that just because cruel and

Box 9.1, *continued*

unusual punishments may occur less frequently under public scrutiny, they will not occur at all. The mere fact that a public flogging or a public execution would be available for all to see would not render the punishment constitutional if it were otherwise impermissible. Similarly, the majority would not suggest that a prisoner who is placed in a minimum-security prison and permitted to go home to his family on the weekends should be any less entitled to Eighth Amendment protections than his counterpart in a maximum-security prison. In short, if a punishment is so barbaric and inhumane that it goes beyond the tolerance of a civilized society, its openness to public scrutiny should have nothing to do with its constitutionality.

. . .

By holding that the Eighth Amendment protects only criminals, the majority adopts the view that one is entitled to the protections afforded by the Eighth Amendment only if he is punished for acts that are sufficiently opprobrious for society to make them "criminal." This is a curious holding in view of the fact that the more culpable the offender the more likely it is that the punishment will not be disproportionate to the offense, consequently, the less likely it is that the punishment will be cruel and unusual. Conversely, a public school student who is spanked for a mere breach of discipline may sometimes have a strong argument that the punishment does not fit the offense, depending upon the severity of the beating, and therefore that it is cruel and unusual. Yet the majority would afford the student no protection no matter how inhumane and barbaric the punishment inflicted on him might be.

. . .

This tort action [student lawsuits against teachers who abuse corporal punishment] is utterly inadequate to protect against erroneous infliction of punishment for two reasons. First, under Florida law, a student punished for an act he did not commit cannot recover damages from a teacher "proceeding in utmost good faith . . . on the reports and advice of others,"; the student has no remedy at all for punishment imposed on the basis of mistaken facts, at least as long as the punishment was reasonable from the point of view of the disciplinarian, uninformed by any prior hearing. The "traditional common-law remedies" on which the majority relies, thus do nothing to protect the student from the danger that concerned the Court in Goss [v. Lopez]—the risk of reasonable, good-faith mistakes in the school disciplinary process (*Ingraham v. Wright*, 1977).

In a recent Ninth Circuit case, the judges ruled that "no reasonable principal could think it constitutional to intentionally punch, slap, grab, and slam students into lockers" (*P.B. v Koch*, 1996). (For a note on excessive discipline in schools, see Box 9.2.)

Box 9.2 Excessive Discipline/Cruel and Unusual Punishment

Cruel and unusual punishment is an issue in prisons. The parallel issue in schools is excessive discipline. For example, recently a teacher ordered a 10-year-old student to clean a toilet. She had mistakenly concluded that the student intentionally put too much toilet paper in the toilet in order to clog the toilet. She made the boy put his hands in the toilet and pull out the paper. He washed his hands and returned to class.

The case made it to the Tenth Circuit. Judges used the "shock the conscience" test. The judges concluded that the teacher had not acted with malice and so her actions were not deliberate, conscience-shocking actions.

The general lesson from cases such as this is that appeals courts use the standard of shock the conscience. But they interpret

a very high threshold, and that school personnel's conduct must truly be outrageous. Finally, it is of considerable import that both courts focused primarily on the intent of the school personnel to do harm. Therefore, it is important to ask the question: What inspired the school personnel's action? Unless it was malice or sadism or the injury is substantially severe, there is a strong likelihood the school and its personnel will prevail (Colwell, 2002:3).

What do you think? Did this teacher's actions "shock the conscience"? If not, what would she have to do to shock the conscience?

Source: B. Colwell (2002). "Shocking the Conscience: Excessive Discipline of Elementary and Secondary Students." *School Law Reporter* 44(1):1-3.

Freedom of Speech for Students

Another school rights issue is the First Amendment right to **freedom of speech**. Here the U.S. Supreme Court has upheld the basic principle that students have at least some degree of constitutional protection in that they do not "shed their constitutional rights to freedom of speech or expression at the schoolhouse gate" (*Tinker v. Des Moines Independent Community School District*, 1969). This does not mean that students can say or express anything they wish in whatever manner they wish. What it means is that the right of free speech is to be balanced with the school's interest in education and discipline. Students are entitled to express themselves as long as their expression does not materially and substantially interfere with school discipline or the educational process.

In the *Tinker* case, for example, at issue was the wearing of black armbands by students to protest United States involvement in the Vietnam conflict. The students doing so were suspended and sent home. When the case reached the U.S. Supreme Court, the majority of the justices ruled that the students' First Amendment rights had been violated, noting that the students had expressed themselves without creating any disturbance or interfering with school discipline. Furthermore, the school system had been inconsistent in that it had allowed some students to wear political campaign buttons and others to wear the traditional symbol of Nazism (the swastika). Writing for the majority, Justice Fortas took serious issue with school system prohibition of student expression of only one particular type:

> In our system, state-operated schools may not be enclaves of totalitarianism. School officials do not possess absolute authority over their students. Students in school as well as out of school are "persons" under our Constitution. They are possessed of fundamental rights which the State must respect, just as they themselves must respect their obligations to the State. In our system, students may not be regarded as closed-circuit recipients of only that which the State chooses to communicate. They may not be confined to the expression of those sentiments that are officially approved. In the absence of a specific showing of constitutionally valid reasons to regulate their speech, students are entitled to freedom of expression of their views. . . . (*Tinker v. Des Moines Independent Community School District*, 1969).

This case can be misinterpreted as an outstanding victory for children's rights if some cautions are not noted. First, the Court was probably more concerned with the issue of free speech in general rather than with free speech for children. That is, the ruling in favor of the pupils can probably be traced to the Supreme Court's "long tradition of zealous protection of first amendment rights" (Davis and Schwartz, 1987:58). Second, the case may be interpreted not so much as a children's rights case as a parents' rights case, because the children in this case shared the same views as their parents on governmental involvement in Vietnam (Davis and Schwartz, 1987). If the views of the students and their parents had not been the same, the ruling may have been otherwise. Finally, the case distinguished between passive expression and disruptive expression of views. Passive speech (for example, wearing armbands) is less disruptive than disturbances or other types of expression. The Court is more likely to uphold such passive speech rather than more rowdy forms of speech. (For a case about free speech by students on the World Wide Web, see Box 9.3.)

In other First Amendment cases, the Supreme Court has addressed the issue of whether school officials can discipline a student for giving a lascivious speech and who holds editorial control over student publications. In *Bethel School District Number 403 v. Fraser* (1986), the Court addressed the issue of "whether the First Amendment prevents a school district from disciplining a high school student for giving a lewd speech at a school assembly." Matthew Fraser nominated a fellow student for a student office by using

Box 9.3 Free Speech in Schools: Posting a Web Site

A Pennsylvania middle school student created a web site that had negative comments and pictures about his algebra teacher and school principal. Pictures on the site showed the teacher's head dripping with blood and her face changing into Adolf Hitler. The site also offered money for a hit man to kill the teacher.

In a unanimous decision, the Pennsylvania Supreme Court ruled that school officials could punish the student because the web site created a substantial disruption of school activities. The Court reasoned that there was a nexus between the web site and the school so that the speech could be considered as occurring on-campus. Following the *Fraser* and *Tinker* cases (see text), the Court concluded that "the web site created disorder and significantly and adversely impacted the delivery of instruction" (see http://www.firstamendmentschools.org).

What do you think? Does the school have the legal authority to punish a student for the contents of a web site that the student creates in his or her own home? Should a student be able to create a web site and put highly negative content about teachers on that web site? Should a student be able to devise a web site that criticizes the teaching ability of his or her teachers but does not go so far as to compare the teachers to Hitler or mention anything such as hiring a hit man? What are the limits of free speech for students on web sites?

"an elaborate, graphic, and sexual metaphor." His obscene language violated a school rule, so he was suspended from school for two days. Both the District Court and the Court of Appeals ruled that the school had violated Fraser's First Amendment right to free speech. They reasoned that the speech was basically the same sort of action as the wearing of the protest armbands in the *Tinker* case. The U.S. Supreme Court, however, reversed the lower courts' decision and determined that the school does have a right to ban sexually explicit language, even if it is couched within a political speech, because it is counter to the basic educational mission of the school (see Box 9.4). The Court also limited the degree of freedom students have in expressing themselves in student publications, again pointing out the educational mission of the schools for justification (see Box 9.5).

In November of 1995, the U.S. Supreme Court declined to hear a case (denied *certiorari*) involving the right of a Tennessee junior high school teacher to refuse a research paper on the life of Jesus. In 1991, Britanny Settle, a junior high school student in Dickson County, submitted an outline on the life of Jesus for her research paper assignment. The original assignment noted that the topic must be "interesting, researchable, and decent." The teacher rejected Brittany's outline because, among other factors, she failed

Box 9.4 Lewd Speeches in School

In the *Bethel School District Number 403 v. Fraser* (1986) case, the U.S. Supreme Court argued that students do not have an absolute right to free speech under the First Amendment. They refused to equate lewd language given as part of a political statement with the wearing of protest armbands in the *Tinker* case. The justices distinguished the *Fraser* case from *Tinker* in that in the *Tinker* case the speech involved political expression and therefore it merited greater protection whereas

> the penalties imposed in this case were unrelated to any political viewpoint. The First Amendment does not prevent the school officials from determining that to permit a vulgar and lewd speech such as respondent's would undermine the school's basic educational mission. A high school assembly or classroom is no place for a sexually explicit monologue directed towards an unsuspecting audience of teenage students. Accordingly, it was perfectly appropriate for the school to disassociate itself to make the point to the pupils that vulgar speech and lewd conduct is wholly inconsistent with the "fundamental values" of public education (*Bethel School District Number 403 v. Fraser*, 1986).

Further, the Court noted that schools play an important role in preparing students for adult citizenship:

> The process of educating our youth for citizenship in public schools is not confined to books, the curriculum, and the civics class; schools must teach by example the shared values of a civilized social order. Consciously or otherwise, teachers—and indeed the older students—demonstrate the appropriate form of civil discourse and political expression by their conduct and deportment in and out of class. Inescapably, like parents, they are role models. The schools, as instruments of the state, may determine that the essential lessons of civil, mature conduct cannot be conveyed in a school that tolerates lewd, indecent, or offensive speech and conduct such as that indulged in by this confused boy.

> The pervasive sexual innuendo in Fraser's speech was plainly offensive to both teachers and students—indeed to any mature person. By glorifying male sexuality, and in its verbal content, the speech was acutely insulting to teenage girl students. The speech could well be seriously damaging to its less mature audience, many of whom were only 14 years old and on the threshold of awareness of human sexuality. Some students were reported as bewildered by the speech and the reaction of mimicry it provoked (*Bethel School District Number 403 v. Fraser*, 1986).

to get permission for the topic, the teacher thought that Brittany's strong belief would interfere with objectivity in a research assignment, and the assignment required four sources but Brittany used only one source: the Bible. In the U.S. District Court case, Brittany relied on *Tinker* for the right of free speech. The Court, however, relied on *Hazelwood School District v. Kuhlmeier*:

> The free speech rights of students in the classroom must be limited because effective education depends not only on controlling boisterous conduct, but also on maintaining the focus of the class on the assignment in question . . . Teachers therefore must be given broad discretion to give grades and conduct class discussion based on the content of speech. . . . *Settle v. Dickson County Sch. Bd.*, 53 F.3d 152 [100 Educ. L. Rep. 32] (6th Cir. 1995) at 155.

Box 9.5 Censorship of Student Publications

In an important First Amendment school case, the Supreme Court ruled that school officials can exercise broad editorial control over student publications:

> Instead, we hold that educators do not offend the First Amendment by exercising editorial control over the style and content of student speech in school-sponsored expressive activities so long as their actions are reasonably related to legitimate pedagogical concerns (*Hazelwood School District v. Kuhlmeier*, 1988).

The case involved a principal's censorship of a high school newspaper. The principal prevented publication of an article describing three students' experiences during pregnancy and of another article describing student reactions to parental divorce. Writing for the majority, Justice White distinguished the *Tinker* case type of speech as "a student's personal expression that happens to occur on the school premises" from "school-sponsored publications, theatrical productions, and other expressive activities" that are "part of the school curriculum" and "are supervised by faculty members and designed to impart particular knowledge or skills" (*Hazelwood School District v. Kuhlmeier*, 1988). For educational reasons, schools have "greater control" over the latter type of speech.

In his dissent Justice Brennan castigated the majority viewpoint as approving "thought police" and the violation of "the First Amendment's prohibitions against censorship of any student expression that neither disrupts classwork nor invades the rights of others, and against any censorship that is not narrowly tailored to serve its purpose" (*Hazelwood School District v. Kuhlmeier*, 1988). Justice Brennan concluded that "[t]he mere fact of school sponsorship does not . . . license such thought control in the high school, whether through school suppression of disfavored viewpoints or through official assessment of topic sensitivity. . . ." (*Hazelwood School District v. Kuhlmeier*, 1988).

Two additional areas in which freedom of speech in schools has been questioned involve compulsory community service and school prayer. At first glance, the issue of compulsory community service would not appear to be a First Amendment issue. With the advent of programs that require service for high school graduation in several places (such as Dodge City, Kansas; Boston; and the state of Maryland), opponents have argued that such service forces a student to engage in "expressive conduct." That is, the activity serves as an expression of support for the agency receiving the service. For example, a student might object that doing community service at the Girl Scouts sends the message that the student believes in what the Girl Scouts organization represents. This issue was argued in *Steirer v. Bethlehem Area School District*. On appeal the Supreme Court denied *certiorari* (i.e., the Court declined to consider the case, letting the lower court ruling stand). The Court stated that there was no First Amendment free speech issue because expressive conduct was not clearly at stake. The Court noted that engaging in community service is not the same thing as wearing a black armband or burning a draft card, acts that clearly do express a viewpoint. Despite this ruling, Charters (1994) argues that community service can be seen as fostering an ideological viewpoint and that "students have no civic duty to perform acts of altruism and self-sacrifice the omission of which would justify a school district's withholding a student's diploma" (Charters, 1994:613).

School prayer has become a topic of much debate in recent years. The key to the debate is the issue of whether school prayer represents the promotion of religion by the school. The Supreme Court, in *Lee v. Weisman* (1992), ruled that school officials erred in providing guidelines and permitting prayer at a high school graduation ceremony. However, the U.S. Fifth Circuit Court upheld the right of students to plan and lead prayer at school functions (*Jones v. Clear Creek Independent School District*, 1992). The degree to which prayer in school will be permitted has yet to be determined. Box 9.6 provides some insight into this issue.

In May of 1997, the United States Court of Appeals for the Eleventh Circuit affirmed the decision of a federal district court that upheld a 1994 Georgia statute authorizing a "moment of quiet reflection" to begin the school day. The statute noted that this moment of quiet reflection "shall not be conducted as a religious service or exercise but shall be considered as an opportunity for a moment of silent reflection on the anticipated activities of the day" (O.C.G.A 20-2-1050 (1996). The judges noted that there was no coercion in the statute:

> All that students must do under this Act is remain silent for 60 seconds; they are not encouraged to pray or forced to remain silent while listening to others' prayers (*Bown v. Gwinnett County Sch. Dist.* 112 F.3d 1464 ([11th Cir. 1997] at 1473).

The court also noted that there was no endorsement of religion in the law and no authorization of any prayer. (For a recent Supreme Court ruling on permitting a religious club to conduct meetings on school premises after school hours, see Box 9.7.)

Box 9.6 Prayer at Graduation and at Football Games

"God of the Free, Hope of the Brave:

For the legacy of America where diversity is celebrated and the rights of minorities are protected, we thank You. May these young men and women grow up to enrich it.

For the liberty of America, we thank You. May these new graduates grow up to guard it.

For the political process of America in which all its citizens may participate, for its court system where all may seek justice we thank You. May those we honor this morning always turn to it in trust.

For the destiny of America we thank You. May the graduates of Nathan Bishop Middle School so live that they might help to share it.

May our aspirations for our country and for these young people, who are our hope for the future, be richly fulfilled.

Lee v. Weisman 112 S.Ct. 2649 (1992) at 2652-2653.

A rabbi gave this invocation at graduation for a middle school and a high school in Providence (RI) in June of 1989. The middle school principal had given the rabbi a guideline for nonsectarian prayers at civic ceremonies and recommended that the invocation and benediction be nonsectarian. One of the students' fathers unsuccessfully attempted to get a restraining order prohibiting any invocation or benediction. The District Court held that the actions of the school violated the Establishment Clause of the First Amendment banning governmental advancement of religion. The United States Court of Appeals for the First Circuit affirmed the judgment of the District Court. The case was then appealed to the Supreme Court.

Judge Kennedy's opinion for the court affirmed the lower court decision against the school's actions. Justice Kennedy was concerned about the principal's participation in the composition of the prayer: ". . . our precedents do not permit school officials to assist in composing prayers as an incident to a formal exercise for their students" (at 2657). He was also concerned "with protecting freedom of conscience from subtle coercive pressure in the elementary and secondary public schools" (at 2658). He distinguished a graduation ceremony from prayer at the opening of a legislative session "where adults are free to enter and leave with little comment" (at 2660). He concluded that "the prayer exercises in this case are especially improper because the State has in every practical sense compelled attendance and participation in an explicit religious exercise at an event of singular importance to every student, one the objecting student had no real alternative to avoid" (at 2661). Thus, "the State, in a school setting, in effect required participation in a religious exercise" (at 2659).

Writing for the dissent, Justice Scalia argued that standing silently during a prayer does not automatically imply that the person is joining in the prayer but may simply signify "respect for the prayers of others" (at

Box 9.6, *continued*

2682). Justice Scalia ridiculed the argument of subtle coercion, noting that the opinion treats students "as though they were first-graders" instead of individuals "old enough to vote" (at 2682). Theoretically, Justice Scalia lambasted the decision as "the bulldozer of its social engineering" for ignoring historical precedent and laying "waste a tradition that is as old as public-school graduation ceremonies themselves, and that is a component of an even more longstanding American tradition of nonsectarian prayer to God at public celebrations generally" (at 2679). Justice Scalia's reading of history showed that the "history and tradition of our Nation are replete with public ceremonies featuring prayers of thansgiving and petition" (at 2679).

Shortly after the Supreme Court decision, the Fifth Circuit Court ruled that a graduation prayer did not violate the First Amendment because students voted on the prayer, participation was voluntary, and students themselves, rather than a religious official, led the prayer (*Jones v. Clear Creek Independent School District*, 977 F.2d 963 [5th Cir. 1992]). Shortly thereafter, several state legislatures introduced bills authorizing student-initiated prayer in the schools (Rossow and Parkinson, 1994). In the spring of 1994 Congress passed an education act that would prevent funds from going to schools adopting "policies designed to prevent students from engaging in constitutionally protected prayer or silent reflection" (cited in Underwood, 1994:1040).

Similarly, the Santa Fe School District allowed a student to deliver a "nonsectarian, nonproselytizing" prayer over the public address system before each football game.

Writing for the majority in *Santa Fe Independent School District v. Doe* (2000), Justice Stevens noted that the invocations were authorized by a government policy and took place on government property at a government-sponsored event. In addition, the process of selecting the student to deliver the invocation focused on the majority and denied voicing of minority voices. Justice Stevens ruled that the invocation policy and practice was unconstitutional because

> the realities of the situation plainly reveal that its policy involves both perceived and actual endorsement of religion. In this case, as we found in Lee, the "degree of school involvement" makes it clear that the pregame prayers bear "the imprint of the Sate" and thus put school-age children who objected in an untenable position (at 590).

What do you think? Should prayers such as the one above be permitted at graduation ceremonies? Is such a prayer at graduation improper governmental intrusion into religion? If you were an atheist or a member of a nonmainstream religion, how would you feel during a nonsectarian invocation before a football game? Would it make a difference if each week different students—atheists, Buddhists, Hindus, and so forth—got up to deliver these invocations?

Box 9.7 Is the Good News Club Good for School?

The Milford Central School allowed the Good News Club, a private Christian organization for children ages six to 12, to hold weekly meetings in the school cafeteria after school. The club sang songs, heard Bible lessons, memorized scripture, and prayed.

Proponents claimed the First Amendment right of free speech. Opponents were concerned about a violation of the Establishment Clause versus the separation of church and state.

The majority concluded that in denying the club the right to meet, the school board denied the Good News Club its right to free speech. Justice Thomas saw this as viewpoint discrimination and argued that no Establishment Clause interpretation justified that restriction. Justice Thomas wrote that there was no indication that the school board was endorsing religion or creed. Justice Thomas saw the club as similar to organizations like the Boys Scouts that rely on "the invocation of teamwork, loyalty, or patriotism . . . to provide a foundation for their lessons" (*Good News Club v. Milford Central School*, 533 U.S. 98 [2001]).

In their dissent Justices Souter and Ginsberg cited a sample lesson about how "the Bible tells us how we can have our sins forgiven by receiving the Lord Jesus Christ" and "to trust the Lord Jesus to be your savior from sin." Such content led the dissenting Justices to conclude that:

> It is beyond question that Good News intends to use the public school premises not for the mere discussion of subjects from a particular, Christian point of view, but for an evangelical service of worship calling children to commit themselves in an act of Christian conversion.

What do you think? Should religious clubs be allowed to meet on school premises after school hours? Is a club that invites children "to trust the Lord Jesus to be your savior from sin" simply another club that fosters "teamwork" and "loyalty" (in Justice Thomas' terminology)? Or, in the words of the dissent, does opening the school for the Good News Club in effect open the school "for use as a church, synagogue, or mosque"?

According to the Gallup Poll, 72 percent of Americans favor allowing the use of school facilities for religious groups, 66 percent favor daily prayer in the classroom, and 80 percent favor graduation speech prayers (Saad, 2001).

Should students be allowed to hold religious group meetings on school premises?

In 2003 the Secretary of Education issued a directive about constitutionally protected prayer in public elementary and secondary schools (available at http://www.ed.gov/policy/gen/guid/religionandschools/ prayer_guidance.html). The guidelines address such issues as prayer during noninstructional time, moments of silence, graduation ceremonies, and organized prayer groups. For example, the directive noted that if a school has a "minute of silence" or other quiet times during the school day, then "[t]eachers and other school employees may neither encourage nor discourage students from praying during such time periods" (p. 4 of Directive). Education law attorneys warn that schools should not follow the guidelines blindly because the guidelines are not necessarily an accurate rendering of case law (Colwell, 2003). Opinion poll research, however, shows that the overwhelming majority of students favor at least some form of prayer being allowed in schools, especially a moment of silence but not necessarily a prayer that mentions Jesus Christ (Ott, 2005).

Student Searches

Another issue involving students is the right of school officials to conduct searches of students versus the students' right of privacy. This issue was highlighted in the Supreme Court case of *New Jersey v. T.L.O.* (1985), which involved the search of a student's purse by an assistant vice principal based on a teacher's suspicion that the student had been smoking in the lavatory in violation of school rules. The Court ruled that such a **student search** was legitimate if it was reasonable in its justification and its extent. By this, the Court meant that:

> Under ordinary circumstances, a search of a student by a teacher or other school official will be "justified at its inception" when there are reasonable grounds for suspecting that the search will turn up evidence that the student has violated or is violating either the law or the rules of the school. Such a search will be permissible in its scope when the measures adopted are reasonably related to the objectives of the search and not excessively intrusive in light of the age and sex of the student and the nature of the infraction (*New Jersey v. T.L.O.*, 1985).

It is important to realize that the Supreme Court explicitly noted that it was not ruling about a student's right to privacy in lockers or desks, about whether it would make a difference if the school was acting in cooperation with or at the suggestion of a police department, or about whether "individualized suspicion" is such an essential element of the reasonableness standard for school searches so as to preclude general searches of students or lockers (*New Jersey v. T.L.O.*, 1985). Thus, the U.S. Supreme Court left open many of the troubling issues surrounding searches on school premises, but it did grant school officials considerable latitude to conduct warrantless searches of students. It gave school officials greater authority to search students than other governmental officials have to search adults. In the case of *New Jersey v. T.L.O.*, Justices Brennan and Marshall concurred in part but also dissented in part. Box 9.8 indicates some of their concerns about the majority opinion.

Box 9.8 Excerpts from the Brennan-Marshall Partial Concurrence–Partial Dissent in *New Jersey v. T.L.O.*

In this case, Mr. Choplick [the assistant vice-principal who conducted the search] overreacted to what appeared to be nothing more than a minor infraction—a rule prohibiting smoking in the bathroom of the freshmen's and sophomores' building. It is, of course, true that he actually found evidence of serious wrongdoing by T.L.O., but no one claims that the prior search may be justified by his unexpected discovery. As far as the smoking infraction is concerned, the search for cigarettes merely tended to corroborate a teacher's eyewitness account of T.L.O.'s violation of a minor regulation designed to channel student smoking behavior into designated locations. Because this conduct was neither unlawful nor significantly disruptive of school order or the educational process, the invasion of privacy associated with the forcible opening of the T.L.O.'s purse was entirely unjustified at its inception.

. . .

The schoolroom is the first opportunity most citizens have to experience the power of government. Through it passes every citizen and public official, from schoolteachers to policemen and prison guards. The values they learn there, they take with them in life. One of our most cherished ideals is the one contained in the Fourth Amendment: that the Government may not intrude on the personal privacy of its citizens without a warrant or compelling circumstance. The Court's decision today is a curious moral for the Nation's youth. Although the search of T.L.O.'s purse does not trouble today's majority, I submit that we are not dealing with "matters relatively trivial to the welfare of the Nation. There are village tyrants as well as village Hampdens, but none who acts under color of law is beyond the reach of the Constitution. . . ." (*New Jersey v. T.L.O.*, 1985).

A 1981 action of the Supreme Court sheds additional light on the Court's attitude toward student searches. Specifically, the Court (*Doe v. Renfrow*, 1981) that year refused to consider an Indiana case in which school officials and police used dogs to sniff students and their possessions for marijuana, searched pockets and purses, and even went so far as to conduct nude body searches of a few students. By refusing to hear the case, the

Supreme Court let stand the lower court ruling that the school could use a canine team to conduct a general search of classrooms and could legally search pockets and purses, but went too far in requiring nude body searches (*Doe v. Renfrow*, 1979).

Since the Supreme Court ruling in *New Jersey v. TLO*, two Circuit Court decisions have ruled that strip searches are constitutional. In one of those cases, a 16-year-old student was strip-searched for drugs suspected to be hidden in his crotch area (none were found). The Seventh Circuit Court found no violation of *TLO* (*Cornfield by Lewis v. Consolidated High School District No. 230*, 1993). Two observers conclude that the courts are trying to assist schools in combating drugs and violence in our country's schools by authorizing strip searches. These commentators are fearful that the courts may be taking the wrong approach: "unfortunately, students appear to be paying the price with the loss of their privacy and, apparently now, their clothes (Rossow and Parkinson, 1994:1).

The stretching of the right to search students has continued to advance. In 1995 the Supreme Court ruled that public schools could make student athletes undergo random drug testing as a condition for playing on school sports teams (*Vernonia School District v. Acton*, 1995). In *Todd v. Rush County Schools* (1998), the Seventh Circuit relied on *Vernonia* to uphold the actions of an Indiana school district that required students to undergo random, unannounced drug tests (urinalysis) before participating in *any* extracurricular programs or being able to drive to and from school. In a November 1997 case, the U.S. Court of Appeals for the Seventh Circuit upheld a "medical assessment" of a high school student suspected of having smoked marijuana. The "assessment" involved a school nurse taking the student's blood pressure and pulse. In 1996, the Eighth Circuit upheld a search of all male sixth through twelfth graders. The students had to remove their jackets, shoes, and socks; empty their pockets; and be given a metal detector test after a school bus driver informed the principal that there were fresh cuts on the seats of her bus (*Thompson v. Carthage School District*, 87 F. 3d 979 [110 Educ. L. Rep. 602] (8th Cir. 1996). Rossow and Parkinson (1994b) argued that this decision would be welcomed by schools using metal detectors at school entrances.

In *Board of Education of Independent School District No. 92 of Pottawatomie County, et al. v. Lindsay Earls et al.* (2002), the Supreme Court ruled that random drug tests of students participating in extracurricular activities such as band or Future Farmers of America are not a violation of the Fourth Amendment. The court noted that schools were concerned about the health risks to students from drug use and made note of the voluntary character of participation in such extracurricular activities. Dissenting Justice Ginsburg, however, argued that such drug testing violates the reasonable subjective expectation of privacy that students have about being forced to submit to urine tests. Justice Ginsburg also noted that participation in extracurricular activities is not completely voluntary but rather "a key component of school life, essential in reality for students applying to college, and, for all participants, a significant contributor to the breadth and quality of the educational experience" (*Board of Education of Independent School District No. 92 of Pottawatomie County v. Lindsay Earls et al.*, 2002).

RIGHTS AT HOME AND IN THE COMMUNITY

Not all questions of juvenile rights have emerged in the context of school. Several issues and cases arise in the home and community.

The Constitutionality of Curfews

Curfew laws have mushroomed in the United States. Cities have enacted curfews to decrease juvenile crime and to protect juveniles from victimization (Davis et al., 1997). Courts have upheld some curfew laws and struck down others. The recent trend seems to be to uphold the laws if they are narrowly drawn and if they provide exceptions for reasonable activities.

A recent case involving a curfew law that was challenged and ruled to be constitutional is *Qutb v. Strauss*. This was a 1993 case that concerned the Dallas, Texas, curfew law. That ordinance prohibited juveniles under age 17 from being on the streets from 11:00 P.M. until 6:00 A.M. on week nights and from midnight until 6:00 A.M. on weekends. Exceptions included being accompanied by a parent, doing an errand for a parent, or attending school, religious, or civic activities. The ordinance also allowed interstate travel or playing on one's own or a neighbor's sidewalk.

The United States Court of Appeals ruled that the law did not violate either equal protection or free association grounds and therefore was not unconstitutional. The Court ruled that the law did serve a compelling state interest, namely, "to reduce juvenile crime and victimization, while promoting juvenile safety and well-being" (*Qutb v. Strauss*, 1993). Here the Court noted that the City of Dallas presented statistics on juvenile crime and victimization during the hours covered by the curfew to substantiate the argument of reducing crime and victimization. Concerning a juvenile's right to free association (a First Amendment right), the Court noted that the law had sufficient exceptions in it so that impositions on association were minor. For example, contrary to arguments that the law prohibited playing midnight basketball, the Court noted that the juvenile could play in such a game as long as it was sponsored by some organization or as long as a parent accompanied the youth to the game.

Similarly drawn curfew laws have stood appeals court challenges, while overly broad laws without exceptions have been struck down. For example, a 1981 case, *Johnson v. City of Opelousas*, was struck down because its only exception was for "emergency errands." Here the judges noted that there was no exception for such associational activities "as religious or school meetings, organized dances, and theater and sporting events, when reasonable and direct travel to or from these activities has to be made during the curfew period" (*Johnson v. City of Opelousas*, 1981).

Thus, clearly drawn curfew laws are withstanding constitutional challenge as long as they allow reasonable exceptions. One author, however, thinks that the constitutional issues merit further review by the Supreme Court in order to clarify some conflicting rulings (*Harvard Law Review*, 2005). In a related matter, the Supreme Court recently struck down Chicago's anti-loitering ordinance as vague. The law prohibited two or more people from loitering for "no apparent purpose." The Court said that the law was too vague to give the public adequate notice of the conduct that is prohibited (*Chicago v. Morales*, 1999).

The Legal Drinking Age

An important children's rights issue is the question of the appropriate age for adolescents to drink alcoholic beverages. In fact, because of the actions of groups such as Mothers against Drunk Driving (MADD) and because of the threat of reduced federal highway funds, all states prohibit the purchase of alcohol by persons under 21 years of age.

Interestingly, raising the **legal drinking age** to 21 is the flip side of the previous historical trend to *lower* the drinking age. Not too many years ago, lowering the drinking age was very much the norm, and it was part of a more general trend in both the United States and Canada of lowering the age of privilege-responsibility, including lowering the voting age to 18. In Canada the rationale behind this movement was that because "youths paid taxes, could quit school and work, join the military, vote federally, and drive cars, it was felt that they should be allowed to drink" (Vingilis and DeGenova, 1984:163). In the United States, the military draft provided the added argument that if "boys were old enough to be sent to Viet Nam, . . . they were old enough to drink" (Vingilis and DeGenova, 1984:163). Finally, there was some feeling that if "youth had to use substances, alcohol was society's preferred drug" (Vingilis and DeGenova, 1984:163).

Proponents of a high minimum drinking age argue that it reduces automobile accidents and fatalities, especially for adolescents themselves. They reason that teens need to be protected from their immaturity and impulsiveness because they are both inexperienced at both driving and drinking alcohol.

It appears that these arguments make good sense because the research suggests that lowering the drinking age is indeed associated with increases in alcohol-related collisions and with higher fatality rates for nighttime and single-vehicle crashes involving young drivers. Conversely, raising the drinking age is associated with a reduced number of collisions (Vingilis and

DeGenova, 1984:166-169). Specifically, the Department of Transportation estimates that raising the legal age for drinking to 21 saved more than 16,000 lives between 1975 and 1996 (Walker, 2001). In related research, it appears that states with the most restrictive graduated driver licensing laws have lower rates of heavy drinking among drivers ages 15 to 17 than states with the least restrictive laws but that there is no comparable difference in binge drinking (SAMHSA, 2004).

The issue, however, is not simple. Some "research indicates that the minimum legal drinking age laws do not deter the majority of teenagers from drinking" (Vingilis and DeGenova, 1984:170). Thus, a reasonable inference from this research on the impact of lowering and raising the drinking age seems to be that it would have some impact but it would not eliminate the problem.

A second problem with raising the drinking age is the question of fairness. That is, the specific issue of raising the drinking age raises the more general issue of the fairness of prohibiting 18-, 19-, and 20-year-olds from drinking, thereby, in effect, treating them as children when the law treats them as adults for other purposes. We have seen, for example, that all states consider 18-year-olds as adults in terms of their responsibility for criminal actions. In fact, one trend in juvenile justice is toward more liberal waiver and related provisions that allow younger and younger juveniles to be tried as adult criminal suspects (subjecting them to the possibility of imprisonment in adult facilities and even capital punishment). The question arises whether it is fair to subject teens to adult criminal court sanctions while at the same time treating them as immature children in terms of their legal ability to drink alcohol. Additional arguments against a high minimum drinking age include the "forbidden fruit" argument, which maintains that it increases the attraction of alcohol, and the "teach-them-to-do-it-right" argument, which contends that parents can use a lower minimum age as an educational device (*USA Today*, 1997:9a)

Franklin Zimring (1982) argues that it is fair to prohibit 18-year-olds from drinking, but he does not necessarily agree that it is fair to submit adolescents to criminal court sanctions, especially the death penalty. He states several reasons for his view that age 21 is a fair minimum drinking age. First, he believes that 18-year-olds are not mature but that they are in the process of becoming mature adults. Second, he is opposed to a low minimum drinking age because of the leakage problem. Leakage means, for example, that if 18-year-olds can legally purchase alcoholic beverages, then their 16-year-old dates may also drink and be subject to auto accidents and fatalities. Finally, he argues that there are three different aspects to adulthood: liberty, entitlement, and responsibility. Liberty refers to the freedom of choice that adults possess in matters such as making decisions about medical care. An entitlement is a benefit or program offered by government such as the Job Corps, which provides free job training for young persons. Responsbility means "paying the full price for misdeeds and being responsible, as are adults, for self support" (Zimring, 1982:111). It is Zimring's position that it is better to keep the ages for these three aspects of adulthood separate rather than to lump them together. Thus, he sees no inconsistency in permitting adolescents to drive at 16, vote and be drafted at 18, and be able to purchase alcoholic beverages at 21.

Zimring also raises the intriguing issue of raising the drinking age to 25. Based on evidence that single male drivers under 25—not just under 21—are a serious driving risk, he contends that these actuarial facts and logic would argue for an even higher drinking age than 21 to prevent many accidents and fatalities. He notes that there is some precedent for this in that the Constitution does require Senators and the President to be older than 21 years of age. However, Zimring rejects raising the minimum drinking age to 25 because:

> That kind of law is not merely politically implausible and socially divisive, it is also unjust. I have argued elsewhere that our current deferral of liberties can be justified because adolescence merely *seems* like forever. But using age-grading to defer common liberty into the mid-20's is exploitation in almost every case. Adding four or seven years onto an already long wait is simply too much of a burden. The twenty-first birthday has a long history of serving as the outer boundary for legal disability based on age. There is no good reason to risk the legal incoherence and social division that pushing beyond this limit impose (Zimring, 1982:124).

Zimring was writing just before the recent push to waive increasingly younger juveniles to adult court, so he did not explictly address the issues of the age of criminal responsibility and the appropriate age for capital punishment. There are strong indications, however, that he would not favor such actions. For example, he clearly believes that even 19- and 20-year-olds are not fully mature and may need some protection from their youthful mistakes. Thus, Zimring is convinced that our legal policy should be one that "preserves the life chances for those who make serious mistakes, as well as preserving choices for their more fortunate (and more virtuous) contemporaries" (Zimring, 1982:91-92).

Zimring's position is worth considering. Contrary to many contemporary voices, he does not advocate a policy that on the one hand would prohibit drinking until 21, but on the other hand would allow waiver to criminal court at 14. Instead, he takes the more consistent view that persons under 21 are not fully mature and responsible, but that certain aspects of adulthood may be more appropriately begun at 18.

In connection with this issue, Barnum (1987) argues that it is false to justify the existence of a separate juvenile court system on the claim that children are less mature and less responsible for their behavior than adults. Rather, "normal intrinsic cognitive development is sufficient for this capacity [to appreciate what they are doing or what effect it will have] by age two or three" (Barnum, 1987:72). Nevertheless, many think there are developmental differences between children and adults that do justify a separate court for juveniles:

. . . children are less able to be responsible for themselves, . . . adolescents normally experience transient irresponsibility, and . . . even poorly socialized children may have a better prognosis for rehabilitation than do poorly socialized adults" (Barnum, 1987:78).

In other words, most children do know right from wrong, just as do most adults. However, there are other differences between children and adults that may justify a separate juvenile court system. (For discussion of the related issue of the appropriate age to allow driving, see Box 9.9. For a discussion of the privacy rights of teen drivers versus parental efforts to track teen driving habits, see Box 9.10.)

Box 9.9 Drivers Licensing

Graduated drivers licensing laws are new licensing laws under which teens gradually earn the privilege to drive. For example, they may have to drive with adults for at least six months and cannot drive after dark until they learn advanced skills. In Michigan, parents have to certify that they have provided 50 hours of supervised driving for their child, including 10 at night. A Level II license in Michigan allows unsupervised driving for 16-year-olds but no driving between midnight and 5:00 A.M. Level III requires drivers to be age 17 plus six months at Level II. In addition, teen drivers must be accident- and violation-free for 12 consecutive months to earn a Level III license.

What do you think? Is graduated licensing a necessary reform, or does it represent a needless incursion into the lives of adolescents?

Source: T. Curley (1997). "Easing Teens into the Driver's Seat. *USA Today* (April 21, 1997):3A.

Perhaps a fitting conclusion to this discussion is Davis and Schwartz's observation that there is a fundamental tension in the law between paternalism (protecting children) and autonomy (granting them responsibility) that will not disappear:

> The law is protective of children, for example, in the areas of contracts, employment, and to a great extent, medical decision making in life-threatening cases. The law grants a measure of autonomy to children or their parents in other areas—for example, abortion decision making (but only to a limited extent), torts (but more as a result of a policy favoring compensation of victims than of a desire to grant children greater responsibility), non-life threatening medical decision making, and emancipation decision making. These disparate results stem from an inherent conflict in the law—a kind of schizophrenia—between the desire to accord chil-

dren a greater degree of control over their lives and freedom of choice, and the need, on the other hand, to protect them from others, their surroundings, and, sometimes, from their own folly (Davis and Schwartz, 1987:201).

It is interesting that at present society is lowering the age of criminal responsibility but at the same time insists on making 21 the age of eligibility to purchase alcohol and is pushing for **graduated licensing**. Davis and Schwartz's description of this as "a kind of schizophrenia" seems most fitting.

Box 9.10   Parental Tracking of Teen Driving

Some parents are installing black boxes in cars that monitor the driving habits of their teenage sons and daughters. The devices record such behaviors as seat-belt use and speed of the car. The devices also make a noise when the driver exceeds safety thresholds while driving.

One teen rights advocate argued that these boxes are an "invasion of privacy" (Davis and O'Donnell, 2005). What do you think? Are automobile black boxes an invasion of privacy or is this simply a reasonable attempt by parents to monitor the driving behavior of teens? Is it legitimate for 16- and 17-year-olds but not for youths 18 or older?

Source: R. Davis and J. O'Donnell (2005). "Some Teenagers Call Tracking Driving an Invasion of Privacy," *USA Today*, 1B.

SUMMARY

This chapter has examined the landmark U.S. Supreme Court cases involving juveniles. The Fourth Amendment rights of juveniles and some of the controversial rights issues in school and in the home were examined. There is no perfectly consistent treatment of juveniles and their rights. Sometimes the law treats them as children, and sometimes it treats them as adults. As Zimring (1982) has pointed out, however, because the issue of juveniles' rights is so complex, perhaps a refusal to come up with one magical age for all children's rights issues is the best solution. Finally, as was noted in the discussion of the landmark Supreme Court cases, the mere stipulation of a right by the Court does not guarantee that police or courts will actually or fully protect that right. Practice is not always the same as philosophy.

Discussion Questions

1. Has the Supreme Court gone too far or not far enough in protecting the rights of juvenile delinquency suspects? If you were on the Supreme Court, what would you seek to change concerning those rights?

2. Your 15-year-old brother has been arrested for the robbery of a movie video rental store. He is of average intelligence but is immature and impulsive. This is his first arrest. Do you think that he should be allowed to waive his privilege against self-incrimination and his right to confer with an attorney, or do you feel that state law should mandate that an attorney be brought in before the police can conduct any interrogation?

3. Assume that you are the editor of the high school newspaper and that one of your best reporters has just completed a lengthy article on drug use in your school. No names are mentioned in the article; in fact, your reporter has gone to great lengths to protect confidentiality. The principal has read the article and has said that she does not want it published in the school paper. What would you do?

4. Do you agree with the Supreme Court's position that corporal punishment is permissible as a school discipline technique? If you became a teacher or principle, would you use corporal punishment? If so, when and under what circumstances? More generally, how would you feel about your children being subjected to corporal punishment?

5. If you were a high school principal, what would your policy on student searches be? The Supreme Court has recently ruled that drug testing of students in band and clubs is permissible. Would you follow the direction of the Supreme Court and initiate testing of band members and the Future Farmers of America?

6. What is your opinion about compulsory community service? Do you think high schools should be allowed to force students to perform community service as a condition for graduation? Why or why not?

7. What is your opinion about school prayer? Should a school be allowed to invite a priest, minister, rabbi, or other religious leader to graduation to offer a nonsectarian invocation? Should the students be allowed to compose and lead their own invocation at graduation? What do you think about a moment of silence to begin (or end) the school day? Should prayer be permissible at athletic events?

8. What age do you favor as the minimum legal drinking age? How would you feel about the age being set at 25? What do you think about graduated licensing laws? Do you favor or oppose them?

Chapter 10

Institutional/Residential Interventions

INTRODUCTION

This chapter will examine juvenile institutional correctional interventions, both public and private. Although more youths are in community correctional programs, residential programs are a critical component of juvenile corrections.

INSTITUTIONAL CORRECTIONS FOR JUVENILES

On the latest one-day count of juveniles in residential placement in 2001, 104,413 youths were in detention, correctional, or shelter facilities. Most (99,297) of these were delinquency offenders. More than 73,000 of the youths were in public facilities, and approximately 31,000 (30,891) were in private facilities. Seventy-three percent of these youths were committed (after being tried in court) and a little over one-fourth (26%) were being detained prior to adjudication. More than 5,000 of the youths in custody were status offenders—approximately 2,000 in public facilities and just over 3,000 in private facilities (Sickmund, Sladky, and Kang, 2004). The latest information available indicates that the average length of stay was approximately four months and that the average yearly cost of custody in a public institution was $32,488 (Smith, 1998). Many juvenile facilities are outdated, built in the 1970s at best (Roush and McMillen, 2000).

KEY TERMS

behavior modification

blended sentencing

boot camps

common sense corrections

deinstitutionalization

inmate code

institutional life

program effectiveness

racial tension

shock incarceration

state training schools

victimization

wilderness programs

Although probation handles many more youths, institutions involve a significant minority of the offenders who go through the juvenile justice system. They are the costliest part of the system. One public facility in New York was reported to cost more than $80,000 a year (Singer, 1996).

In 2004, the residential population was 85 percent male and 15 percent female. The racial composition of all 104,413 youths in 2001 was 39.6 percent white, 39 percent black, and 17.3 percent Hispanic (the rest were "other") (Sickmund, Sladky, and Kang, 2004). Thus, blacks are overrepresented in juvenile institutions, but there is no clear explanation for the overrepresentation (Sickmund, 2004).

Because more juveniles are now being tried in adult criminal courts, it is important to note statistics about juveniles in adult prisons. Based on the best estimates available, approximately 5,600 new court commitments to state adult prisons in 1999 were juveniles (youths under 18 at time of admission to prison). Most, 75 percent, were age 17 at time of admission (Sickmund, 2004).

Correctional managers contend that juvenile correctional facilities seek to serve the "best interests of the child," which means that they attempt to provide educational, therapeutic, and recreational programs staffed by concerned caregivers. Critics argue that, at best, the facilities are warehouses or holding tanks where little, if any, positive change takes place. Past critics have contended that juvenile facilities harbor as many horror stories as they do children: tales of neglect, abuse, and even death (Wooden, 1976).

This chapter examines various types of institutional and residential interventions with juveniles, including state training schools, youth camps, private placements, and group homes. After describing these various placements, we will examine some of the current issues about their operation, such as the determination of appropriate targets for intervention, effectiveness in reducing recidivism, and client and worker adaptations to the pressures of institutional life. The chapter concludes with information on innovative trends in this area such as deinstitutionalization and wilderness programs.

STATE TRAINING SCHOOLS

Description

State training schools are the juvenile justice system's equivalent of the adult prison; they house those delinquents whom juvenile court judges consider unfit for probation or some other lesser punishment. Some training schools actually resemble adult prisons in terms of their architecture: high walls or fences, locked cell blocks, self-sufficiency (they have their own laundry, hospital, and maintenance facility), and solitary confinement for persistent rule breakers. Other training schools have the so-called cottage system of architectural design. Unfortunately, the cottage system is often a far cry from the homelike atmosphere intended by its founders. Cottages are often deteriorating dormitories with decrepit plumbing, heating, and lighting, and an accompanying host of social-cultural problems as well.

Training School Programs for Residents

The programming at state training schools is often a combination of academic and vocational education and **behavior modification**. Residents attend school much of the day just like their noninstitutionalized counterparts, but the school run by the prison teaches youths who are usually two to three years below their appropriate grade level in both reading and mathematics. (For a list of the school rules in one training school, see Box 10.1; for a typical daily schedule, see Box 10.2.)

Box 10.1   Sample of One Training School's Rules

Below is an actual set of rules and a list of minor rule violations from a southeastern training school:

Rules:
1. There will be no misuse of any property.
2. There is to be no use of vulgar or profane language.
3. There will be no gambling.
4. There will be no tampering with fire and safety equipment.
5. Students will remain in their assigned areas.
6. Students may not borrow, sell, lend, or trade their property.
7. Students are expected to always be courteous.
8. Students are expected to respect privacy and property of others.
9. Students are expected to follow all dress codes.
10. Students are expected to follow instructions of staff.

Minor Rule Violations:
1. Disruptive behavior
2. Failure to follow institutional rules
3. Horseplay
4. Out of assigned area
5. Racial slurs
6. Refusal of a direct order
7. Self-mutilation
8. Sexual slurs
9. Use of obscene language

Source: Student Handbook from a southeastern state.

Box 10.2   Typical Weekday Daily Schedule at a Residential Placement for Delinquents

6:30AM	Wake Up: dress and clean room
7:00AM	Calisthenics
7:30AM	Hygience (showers, etc.)
8:00AM	Clean dormitories
8:30AM	Breakfast
9:00AM	Start school
10:30AM	"Rap" half-hour
11:00AM	Return to school
12:00AM	Lunch
12:30PM	"Rap" half-hour
1:00PM	School
3:30PM	Group therapy
5:00PM	Dinner
5:30PM	Work details (kitchen clean-up and dormitory clean-up)
6:00-7:00PM	TV news
7:00-9:00PM	Activities (vary by day: Example: Values Clarification; Occupational Therapy; Recreational Therapy, etc.)
9:00PM	Bedtime for Phase 1 (9:30PM in the summertime)
10:00PM	Bedtime for Phase 2 and above.

Source: Manual from a midwestern residential facility. Note: In this context, to "rap" is to talk freely and frankly.

In addition to standard academic subjects, educational programs may include life skills development, remedial reading and writing, conflict resolutions skills development, computer literacy, and learning skills assessment. Additional programming may include groups on anger management and substance abuse resistance and recreation such as sports, crafts, board games, reading, and computer games (Roush and McMillen, 2000).

The behavior modification system usually involves the grading of children at one of several levels. The system includes the daily awarding of points for almost every possible action of the child's day, from getting up on time to getting to bed quietly and on time. The points earned each day can be spent on various privileges, ranging from games, television time, and telephone calls home to off-campus group outings and visits home. The higher the child's level, the more extensive the privileges available. (Box 10.3 gives an actual list of opportunities for earning and spending points at a southeastern training school.) In addition to qualifying for daily privileges, such as television, the points earned also count toward movement from one level to another with additional privilege possibilities. One training school employee characterized the point system as working both as a behavioral control device and as a device to monitor progress within the institution.

Box 10.3 Typical Institutional Point System

Responsibilities	Points	
1. Get self up on time (6:00 a.m.)	+25	−50
2. Locker neat, orderly, clean room or area with bed made	+50	−100
3. Appropriately dressed	+25	−50
4. Brush teeth and comb hair	+25	−50
5. Daily bath and use deodorant	+25	−100
6. Exercise	+25	−50
7. Acts appropriately: a: Breakfast	+10	−20
b: Lunch	+10	−20
c. Dinner	+10	−20
8. School	+40 per hour	
9. Study hour or watching news	+25 per hour	
10. Daily chores	+50	−100
11. Volunteer work	+60 per hour (120 maximum per day)	
13. See counselor	+25 per hour	
14. Attend group	+50	−100 per hour
15. Attend church or Sunday school services	+25	
16. Bonus points	+100 maximum per day	

Note: A +25 indicates that a resident can earn up to 25 points for performing the specified behavior. A −100 indicates that a resident can have as many as 100 points deducted if the behavior is not performed or not performed properly.

Spending Opportunities

1. Swimming	25 points
2. Recreation room	25 points
3. Parlor games (checkers, cards, etc.)	25 points
4. Telephone calls	20 points
5. Use of television room	25 points
6. Play outside	25 points
7. Group outing off campus	300 points
8. Group outing on campus	200 points
9. Living room	25 points
10. Movies in dorm	100 points
11. Home pass	350 points

Source: Student manual from a southeastern training school.

Concern for the victim and for crime control has translated into some new programs in juvenile institutions. In California, for example, the Impact of Crime on Victims program combines an educational curriculum with presentations by victims and victims' advocates. In Texas, juvenile murderers receive group psychotherapy and role-playing sessions to help them learn responsibility for their crimes and to imagine what they put their victims through (Bilchik, 1999).

Other Placements

Traditional training schools are not the only means that states use for housing delinquents. In some years, almost 10,000 youths are held in long-term open facilities that allow greater freedom for residents within the facilities and more contacts with the community. The open facilities category of placements includes shelters, halfway houses, group homes, and a few ranches. Group homes are residential facilities for relatively small numbers of youths (perhaps one or two dozen youngsters). The residents often attend regular public schools but participate in group counseling sessions and recreational activities at the group home.

Juvenile court judges also have been known to commit juvenile delinquents to detention centers for a short period of time. Youths are placed on probation, and one condition of probation is a short stay in the local detention facility.

States also utilize private residential placements to house delinquents and some status offenders. In 2001, private facilities held almost 28,000 delinquent youths and slightly more than 3,000 status offenders (Sickmund, Sladky, and Kang, 2004). Private facilities, like state facilities, range from relatively large institutions to small group homes and even wilderness programs where juveniles camp out. Many were originally started by churches as charitable institutions but have evolved into nonsectarian operations that charge the state thousands of dollars each year for each child they handle.

Boot Camps

A continuing trend is the use of **boot camps** (also called **shock incarceration**). Boot camps are short-term facilities (90-day/120-day/six-month) that are intended to resemble basic training facilities for the military. There is considerable emphasis on discipline and physical training such as marching, running, calisthenics, and other types of conditioning. Usually a "drill instructor" is assigned to each group of offenders. Many boot camp programs also involve aftercare supervision for program graduates. Box 10.4 shows the daily schedule at one boot camp.

Box 10.4   Daily Schedule for Offenders in a New York Boot Camp

A.M.

5:30	Wake up and standing count
5:45-6:30	Calisthenics and drill
6:30-7:00	Run
7:00-8:00	Mandatory breakfast/cleanup
8:15	Standing count and company formation
8:30-11:55	Work/school schedules

P.M.

12:00-12:30	Mandatory lunch and standing count
12:30-3:30	Afternoon work/school schedule
3:30-4:00	Shower
4:00-4:45	Network community meeting
4:45-5:45	Mandatory dinner, prepare for evening
6:00-9:00	School, group counseling, drug counseling, prerelease counseling, decision-making classes
8:00	Count while in programs
9:15-9:30	Squad bay, prepare for bed
9:30	Standing count, lights out

Source: C.L. Clark, D.W. Aziz, and D.L. MacKenzie (1994). *Shock Incarceration in New York: Focus on Treatment*. Washington, DC: U.S. Department of Justice.

The rationale behind boot camps is multifaceted. It is claimed that boot camps can protect the public, reduce prison crowding, reduce costs, punish offenders, hold offenders accountable, deter additional crime, and rehabilitate (counseling and education) (Cronin, 1994).

The effectiveness of boot camps for both adult and juvenile offenders is mixed. There is some indication that boot camps can reduce state correctional costs and that participants rate their experience in camp as positive, but the evidence shows that boot camps have little or no effect on recidivism (Cronin, 1994; Parent, 2003). It does appear clear, however, that "the military atmosphere alone does not reduce recidivism and increase positive activities during community supervision" (MacKenzie, 1994:66). Ironically, even though many politicians like boot camps because they appear to be "tough," it appears that the educational and rehabilitative programming is what helps the offenders.

An evaluation of three boot camps in Cleveland, Mobile, and Denver offers insights about their advantages and disadvantages. Eligible youths for these camps were youths ages 13 to 17 who had been adjudicated by the juvenile court and were awaiting disposition. Youths considered eligible could not have any history of mental illness or involvement in violent crime but were rated at "high risk" of chronic delinquency and minimal risk of escape.

The graduation rates were positive, ranging from a low of 65 percent at Denver to 87 percent at Mobile and 93 percent at Cleveland. There was significant academic progress at Cleveland and Mobile: from half to two-thirds of the youths at Cleveland improved at least one grade level in various academic skills. In Mobile about 80 percent of the youths improved at least one grade level (Peters, Thomas, and Zamberlan, 1997)

The findings on recidivism, however, were discouraging. There were no significant differences in recidivism between boot camp offenders and the control group offenders at Denver or Mobile. In Cleveland, the experimental youths did worse than the controls. Moreover, at all three sites, survival times—time to the commission of a new offense—were shorter for the youths who went through the boot camps than for control cases (Peters, Thomas, and Zamberlan, 1997).

AP Photo/Kelley McCall

Cadets from the Missouri National Guard's juvenile boot camp program at Camp Clark practice a drill routine in front of the armory in Poplar Bluff, Missouri. The popularity of boot camps may be seen as part of a broader trend in criminal justice focusing on retribution, deterrence, and incapacitation.

Concerning cost-effectiveness, the costs per day of the boot camps were similar to one day of institutionalization but more expensive than a day of probation. Costs per offender were lower than controls because boot camp offenders spent less time in the boot camps. The data on annual costs per offender were: Cleveland: $14,021, compared to $25,549 for the Ohio Department of Youth Services; Denver: $8,141, versus $23,425 for a state facility; Mobile; $6,241, versus $11,616 for a state facility (Peters, Thomas, and Zamberlan, 1997:24-25).

Peters and his colleagues conclude that boot camps are not a panacea but they do offer some advantages:

> As an intermediate sanction, boot camps are a useful alternative for offenders for whom probation would be insufficiently punitive, yet for whom long-term incarceration would be excessive. As such, under certain conditions, boot camps can free bed space for more hardened offenders, thereby reducing the financial burden on correctional budgets (Peters, Thomas, and Zamberlan, 1997).

Boot camps are part of a more general trend in society to "get tough" on crime. One author (Clear, 1994) calls this trend the "penal harm movement"; another team of authors calls it "the punishment paradigm" (Cullen and Wright, 1995). These authors contend that since 1980 the United States has operated on the premise that more punishment is needed to deter crime and incapacitate offenders. Boot camps are one component of the movement, which includes increased use of prisons and jails, lengthier sentences, determinate sentences, career criminal sentencing provisions, increased use of capital punishment, and harsher community sanctions (intensive supervision, house arrest, and electronic monitoring). For juveniles the punishment paradigm has translated into greater prosecution of juveniles in adult court and blended sentences involving the adult correctional system. Thus, boot camps are not an isolated phenomenon but are part of a broader trend in criminal justice focusing on retribution, deterrence, and incapacitation.

A final word on boot camps comes from Cullen and his colleagues (2005), who see the boot camp phenomenon as a clearcut example of the dangers of "common-sense thinking" in corrections and criminal justice. What they mean is that based on the common-sense thinking that military boot camps made men out of boys for the army, many individuals were convinced that correctional boot camps would do the same for juvenile offenders. The research on the lack of success of boot camps, however, shows the dangers of relying on such common-sense thinking: "It is dangerous precisely because it seems so correct, leaves our biases unchallenged, and requires virtually no effort to activate" (Cullen et al., 2005:66).

PROGRAM EFFECTIVENESS

One of the most critical issues facing residential interventions is the *effectiveness* issue: Do the interventions have any impact on the criminal behavior of their charges? Although much of what follows pertains most directly to publicly run placements (especially state training schools), the problems also affect private placements.

Reviews of Multiple Studies

While much of the **program effectiveness** research has focused on specific programs, some researchers have tried to summarize individual program research into a global conclusion on effectiveness. Most of these studies have used the technique of meta-analysis. Meta-analysis is a technique that allows researchers to re-analyze individual studies and arrive at a summary statistic of effectiveness for each individual study that can then be compared to the summary statistics from the other studies.

A meta-analysis of 443 studies published between 1970 and 1987 focused on formal contact with the juvenile justice system as an outcome measure and reported that approximately two-thirds of the study outcomes favored the treatment group over the control group. Behavioral, skill, and multimodal treatment programs resulted in greater effects than other approaches. Deterrence-based programs were not effective (Lipsey, 1992).

Lipsey and Wilson (1998) conducted a meta-analysis of 83 studies of institutional programs for serious offenders and found that there were many instances of programs that had positive effects. The most effective treatment types had an impact on recidivism that was equivalent to reducing a control group baseline recidivism rate of 50 percent to around 30 or 35 percent. If the recidivism rate for these juveniles would have been 50 percent without treatment, the most effective programs reduced it to 30-35 percent. They concluded that this represents a "considerable decrease, especially in light of the fact that it applies to institutionalized offenders, who can be assumed to be relatively serious delinquents" (Lipsey and Wilson, 1998:336). Successful interventions included aggression replacement training, behavior modification, and a stress inoculation program that helped youths define anger, analyze recent anger episodes, review self-monitoring data, and construct an individualized six-item anger hierarchy.

Conclusions about Program Effectiveness

Several cautious conclusions about the effectiveness of institutional programs for delinquents are in order. First, some research, such as an evaluation of the Provo program, indicate that community programs are at least as effective as traditional training schools (Lundman, 1993). The Provo program was a community program that was an alternative to sending youths to the Utah training school. Second, research, such as the evaluation of the Silverlake Project in California, suggests that an innovative and less repressive residential program can be at least as effective as a traditional training school (Gottfredson, 1987; Lundman, 1993). Third, even training schools may have an effect in suppressing the average number of crimes youths commit after release, but such institutions may not be able to deter their charges from committing *any* crimes after release. Fourth, this alleged suppression effect may be the result of such factors as regression toward the mean, simple maturation, or the rehabilitation programs in the training schools instead of the deterrent effect of a punitive regime in the training school (Lundman, 1993). Finally, the effectiveness literature suggests that certain interventions can be effective in reducing recidivism from about 50 percent to 30 or 35 percent. It is imperative, however, that these interventions follow the principles that research has identified as effective (Lipsey and Wilson, 1998). [We review those principles in Chapter 11 on community corrections.] Examples of successful strategies that follow effective principles are *multisystemic therapy* (MST) and *functional family therapy*. Multisystemic Therapy, for example, has been shown to reduce days in treatment by about half at a cost of approximately $6,000 per youth, less than one-fourth of an eight-month stay in a juvenile facility. One MST program alone, Youth Villages, served 1,600 Tennessee youth in the year 2000 (Mendel, 2001).

Before proceeding to discuss other current issues in juvenile institutions, it is important to note that the measurement of the effectiveness of treatment programs in such settings assumes that the programs are in fact carried out as originally intended. Unfortunately, that is not always true. Although Wooden did his research years ago, his observations on this matter apply today. Specifically, Wooden contended that institutions were using behavior modification techniques "to manipulate and control the child for the convenience of the custodians" (Wooden, 1976:101). In a New York facility "education" actually meant watching movies on the VCR, especially on Friday (Singer, 1996). In what was intended to be a new model facility in Arizona, treatment quickly deteriorated. Staff appeared inconsistent and capricious in such matters as scoring youths' behaviors, staff were disrespectful and interrupted youths in group meetings, a few staff made racially insensitive remarks, and youths were shackled when transported to medical treatment. A key educational program did not accomplish its objectives, and substance abuse treatment was not provided. In short, there was a "repeated and systematic violation of the program's fundamental principles and spirit" (Bortner and Williams, 1997:112). Therefore, impressive terms such as "behavior modification," "model program," and "education" do not necessarily translate into humane and progressive interventions. If such interventions are implemented in such negative ways, it is hardly possible to know what results an evaluation study will find or what sort of confidence can be placed in the results.

INSTITUTIONAL LIFE

An important concern in juvenile justice is the effect of **institutional life** on youths. The theory of institutional placements is that they will provide a caring and nurturing environment that will allow the delinquents to change to prosocial behavior in the institution. This will then carry over into future behavior after release. As we shall see, however, the practice often falls far short of the theoretical ideal.

Victimization

As is true of adult prisons, probably the most dramatic example of a negative effect of the institution on incarcerated youths is the problem of **victimization**, which ranges from the relatively insignificant act of taking a boy's dessert to forcing a boy to take the "female" role in oral sodomy. Such victimization knows no geographic boundaries. In one northern training school, 53 percent of the boys exploited others, and 65 percent were exploited at least on occasion (Bowker, 1980). In a study of six southeastern training schools, more than one-third of the whites, but less than 25 percent of the blacks, reported frequent victimization. In addition, 61 percent of the whites, but less than 50 percent of the blacks, reported that other residents "took advantage of them" in the institution (Bartollas and Sieverdes, 1981:538). It appears that institutionalized girls are less subject to forceful sexual attacks but that "attacks sometimes occur, usually involving adolescent inmates who have expressed an unwillingness to participate in homosexuality and who are zealous in ridiculing inmates who engage in this behavior" (Giallombardo, 1974:160). In one New York facility, some guards formed a "wake-up club," which administered regular beatings to misbehaving or disrespectful youths (Singer, 1996). Although it is difficult to obtain an accurate and up-to-date picture of what victimization takes place across the country, it is safe to say that the institutionalized youngster is deprived of the security that teenagers in positive home environments take for granted.

Table 10.1   Incident Rates per 100 Juveniles and Annualized Estimates of Incidents in Juvenile Facilities

Type of Incident	Rate per 100 juveniles (last 30 days)	Estimated incidents (per year)
Injuries		
Juvenile-on-juvenile	3.1	24,200
Juvenile-on-staff	1.7	6,900
Staff-on-juvenile	0.2	106
Escapes		
Completed	1.2	9,700
Unsuccessful attempts	1.2	9,800
Acts of suicidal behavior	2.4	17,600
Incident requiring emergency health care	3.0	18,600
Isolation incidents		
Short-term (1-24 hrs.)	57.0	435,800
Longer-term (more than 24 hours)	11.0	88,900

Source: Abt Associates (1994). *Conditions of Confinement: Juvenile Detention and Corrections Facilities: Research Report*, E-7. Washington, DC: U.S. Department of Justice.

Statistics on incident rates in juvenile facilities from one report are summarized in Table 10.1. As the table shows, it is estimated that about 24,200 juvenile-on-juvenile injuries and approximately 7,000 juvenile-on-staff injuries take place every year. Every year there are about 17,600 acts of suicidal behavior and more than 18,000 incidents requiring emergency health care. Subjectively, approximately 20 percent of confined youths report not feeling safe when in custody (Abt Associates, 1994). This may be a conservative estimate, however, because youths compare their safety in an institution with their safety on the outside. For some youths, life in the institution may be perceived as safer than life on the streets. For example, one institutionalized youth reported that he only had to fear a punch or being hit with furniture in the institution. On the outside he had to fear being shot. Thus, in the institution "he felt perfectly safe" (Abt Associates, 1994:111). (For further discussion of living conditions in juvenile prison, see Boxes 10.5 and 10.6.)

Box 10.5   Making Juvenile Prisons Spartan

Many state legislatures have passed laws to make adult prisons as Spartan as possible. Responding to alleged citizen displeasure with "soft" prisons, politicians have passed laws forbidding cable television and physical training equipment (weight-lifting and other body building equipment) in adult prisons.

To date this movement has only affected institutions for juveniles placed in adult facilities via transfer, direct file, or blended sentencing. But the call for amenity-free prisons raises the issue of what level of "comfort" is appropriate for offenders—adult or juvenile? Is broadcast television all right but premium cable services such as Home Box Office (HBO) inappropriate? Is weight-lifting equipment inappropriate because inmates can use the equipment to get in better shape and assault other inmates or staff?

Years before this controversy erupted, prison authority John Conrad (1982) addressed this question of "What do the undeserving deserve?" His answer was that there are four essentials needed in prison: safety, lawfulness, industriousness, and hope (Conrad, 1982).

What do you think? Can prisons be too soft? Can they be too tough? Are Conrad's four essential ingredients a good guideline? Why? Why not? What are your suggestions for juvenile prisons? For adult prisons?

Despite apparent increases in staff victimization, a study of correctional officers in two juvenile detention facilities in Virginia showed low levels of fear of victimization and perceived risk of victimization. In addition, it did not matter whether the guard was working in a therapeutically oriented detention center or a more traditional detention center (Gordon, Moriarty, and Grant, 2003).

A recent study of 500 juveniles in institutions (about half were in traditional institutions such as training schools and the other half in boot camps) focused on the psychological states and perceived environments of the residents. First, juveniles perceived their institutional environments to have high levels of both activity and justice. So the juveniles felt that they had things to do and were being treated fairly. However, they also perceived the environments to be restrictive and controlled. Levels of anxiety and depression both decreased over time. Childhood maltreatment (e.g., coming from an abusive home) increased the levels of depression and anxiety. It appears that institutional staffs should target therapeutic programming for youths with histories of child maltreatment (Gover and MacKenzie, 2003).

Box 10.6 Abuses in One Juvenile Facility

In 2000, the U.S. Justice Department won a lawsuit to gain custody of juvenile inmates at the Jena Juvenile Justice Center in Jena, Louisiana, from a private corrections company, the Wackenhut Corrections Corporation. The following are some of the allegations that led to the lawsuit:

- Staff used force against a youth with a colostomy, which caused his intestines to go out of the colostomy hole.

- One nurse accused another nurse of forcing youths against the wall, tossing water on them, and refusing them medication if they were not obedient.

- One youth attempted suicide twice (tied a sock tightly around his neck) to avoid sexual victimization and racial tension.

- Nine juveniles accused a guard of taking food off their trays and snacks.

- One youth damaged his testicles and inflicted other injuries to get to the medical treatment ward to avoid victimization by peers.

- One youth wrote his mother that a female guard forced him to take off his shirt and move like a snake.

Source: "I Know Why the Cajun Bird Sings." *Harper's Magazine* (July 2000), 301:29.

Girls may face special problems. For example, girls have undergone strip searches and cavity searches in the presence of male guards. This tends to reinforce the belief that they do not have control over their own bodies. Some facilities have not given girls clean clothes or clean towels and washcloths, and some have provided limited hygiene supplies. These abuses and deprivations can be especially important to adolescent girls as they make the transition to womanhood (Acoca, 1998).

A recent study of 22 girls in a large women's prison in the midwest indicated several problem areas for juvenile girls who had been sentenced to adult women's prisons. One problem was lack of recreation time and equipment. Recreation equipment had been ordered for the under-21 unit but had not arrived by the time of the research. No girl reported having been "raped" by an older woman, but some had experienced either name-calling or more serious sexual comments. Four girls indicated that they were in a sexual relationship with an older woman prisoner but that it was consensual. GED education and even college education (an associate degree program in Social Services) were available. Most programs were designed for adult women, but anger management, a Girl Scouts program, and a gang awareness program were specifically targeted at the young prisoners. The authors concluded that their research "raises critical questions about the quality of care given to girls in adult prisons, particularly in programming areas such as education, life skills, recreation, and work training" (Gaardner and Belknap, 2004:75). The authors call for improvements in all these areas but add the cautionary note that their ideal solution is to not put any girls or women in women's prisons because "[w]omen's prisons mirror the regulatory mechanisms and treatment of women in society at large, and we seek to dismantle both" (Gaarder and Belknap, 2004:77).

Racial Tension

The statistics on victimization also suggest that **racial tension** is a problem in juvenile institutions. For example, Bartollas and Sieverdes found African-American youths to be both more dominant and more aggressive than white inmates: "Twice as many black as white residents were classified by staff members as highly aggressive toward others; over 40 percent of whites were defined by staff as passive" (Bartollas and Sieverdes, 1981:538). Bartollas and Sieverdes attributed this situation to role reversal in the institution, where white Southern youths found themselves in the novel position of being in the minority. White inmates were outnumbered by black inmates (about 60% of the inmates were black), and about half of the staff members were black. The white youths felt threatened because they were in an environment very different from "the southern culture, [where] whites are used to a position of greater superiority in the free society relative to minority groups than are youth elsewhere in the United States" (Bartollas and Severiedes, 1981:541). Even a model youth prison in Arizona experienced some racial tensions. It was reported that one staff member called a youth a "taco bender" and another staff member called an African-American youth "colored" (Bortner and Williams, 1997).

The fact that training schools continue to be places with significant proportions of several ethnic groups suggests that racial/ethnic tensions will continue into the foreseeable future. As noted at the beginning of this chapter, in 2001, minorities constituted 60 percent of the juveniles in residential placement. Blacks made up 39 percent of those in placement; Hispanics accounted for 17 percent (Sickmund, Sladky, and Kang, 2004).

The federal government, through legislation, research, training, and technical assistance, has been attempting to reduce disproportionate minority confinement. One strategy to reduce such disproportionate confinement is using standardized risk assessments at decision points in the juvenile justice system. Such risk assessment structures decisionmaking and thus has the potential to reduce racial bias by court officials (Hsia, Bridges, and McHale, 2004).

The Inmate Code

Another negative effect of institutions is that youths may develop or maintain allegiance to peer norms that run counter to staff efforts to rehabilitate the youngsters. This is the problem of the **inmate code**, which can stress such maxims as "exploit whomever you can," "don't play up to staff," "don't rat on your peers," and "be cool"(Sieverdes and Bartollas, 1986:137). In other words, juvenile inmates develop feelings of distrust and resentment toward staff. These feelings operate in opposition to staff efforts to build trust and openness. There has been some indication that the inmate code is moving away from minding one's own business ("do your own time") to greater exploitation of others:

> In other words, the "old con" who did his/her own time has disappeared from the juvenile correctional system and from most adult correctional systems. Inmates are now more likely to show certain allegiances to other prisoners, especially those in the same racial group or social organization. But, at the same time, this inmate is scheming to manipulate staff and to take advantage of weaker peers (Sieverdes and Bartollas, 1986:143).

As might be expected, research indicates that organizational structure affects the norms and behavior of youthful prisoners. In other words, "[t]he more custodial and punitive settings had inmate cultures that were more violent, more hostile, and more oppositional than those in the treatment-oriented settings (Feld, 1981:336). This finding on the impact of organizational structure on inmate culture suggests that it is possible for administrators to reduce the negative environments in juvenile prisons by opting for an organizational structure that emphasizes treatment over custody. One specific option that administrators can take is to limit the size of juvenile residential placements. Larger populations are more susceptible to custodial climates than smaller populations. Another option is to facilitate communication between treatment staff and custodial staff so that staff members do not exacerbate potential treatment-custody conflicts.

Deprivation of Heterosexual Contact

Another negative effect of institutions is that incarcerated youths are deprived of heterosexual relationships at a time when such relationships are critical in helping the teenager to define himself or herself as a mature sexual adult. Although written about incarcerated girls, Giallombardo's comments on this matter apply equally well (with the appropriate adjustments) to imprisoned boys:

> They are developing images of themselves as adult women, and they are beset with many anxieties concerning their sexuality and acceptance by males. The exclusion of males in their own age group is a source of confusion for adolescent girls. . . . Their confusion is compounded by virtue of the fact that during incarceration they are socialized to view other women as legitimate sex objects (Giallombardo, 1974:244).

In response to this deprivation, many of the girls adjust by participating in kinship role systems and/or homosexual alliances. In the training schools Giallombardo (1974) studied, for example, the girls had affectionate nicknames for one another, wrote love letters to other girls, picked their own special songs, "went steady," and even got married in formal ceremonies (out of staff view). Another study reported that only about 17 percent of the institutionalized girls reported at least one homosexual experience (ranging from kissing to intimate sexual contact) but about half of the girls reported taking a "make-believe family" role (Propper, 1982). Such behavior was clearly not intended by the authorities and has been labeled a "secondary adjustment" (Goffman, 1961:199). The problem with secondary adjustments is that they divert the youths' attention away from the main aspects of the supposedly rehabilitative programs, such as education and counseling, and direct that attention to making life within the training school as pleasant as possible.

Other problems faced by incarcerated youths include loss of liberty, deprivation of personal possessions, and boredom. Particularly important in terms of possessions is the loss of clothing articles. This is important because it entails a loss of the opportunity to explore various clothing styles. According to Giallombardo (1974), such exploratory behavior is very directly related to a girl's sense of identity as well as her popularity.

An important national study on living conditions in juvenile facilities found "substantial and widespread deficiencies" in four matters: living space, security, control of suicidal behavior, and health care (Abt Associates, 1994). Many institutions experience problems concerning crowding, safety and prevention of escapes, suicidal behavior, and health screening. That same report also felt that there was a need to collect systematic data on confined youths' educational and treatment needs. Further evidence that problems continue to exist in juvenile institutions is the publication of a recent American Bar Association manual that offers suggestions for litigation strategies to contest problematic conditions (Puritz and Scali, 1998). It is unfortunate but true that often a lawsuit is the only way that problems in youth prisons become known. For example, it took a lawsuit in Arizona to make it known that one of the state youth prisons maintained "harsh conditions, arbitrary and capricious decision making, and an unduly punitive, unrehabilitative environment" (Bortner and Williams, 1997:3).

NEW DIRECTIONS IN INSTITUTIONAL INTERVENTIONS

Deinstitutionalization of Status Offenders

Since the mid-1970s there has been a movement away from placing status offenders and delinquents in the same state-operated institutions. It is felt that any mixing of status offenders and delinquents can have harmful consequences on the status offenders. In fact, much of this movement has been one of **deinstitutionalization**: trying to avoid any involuntary placements of status offenders (the practice of some states to deinstitutionalize delinquents as well as status offenders will be discussed in the next section). The strength of this movement is indicated by the fact that 97 percent of the juveniles in public custody in 2001 were delinquents, and only 2.7 percent were status offenders. This is a considerable decrease from the 7 percent figure in 1985 (Sickmund and Baunach, 1986; Sickmund, Sladky, and Kang, 2004).

Deinstitutionalization (Closing Training Schools)

Several states, including Massachusetts, Maryland, Pennsylvania, and Utah, have decreased dramatically their use of training schools by closing some of these facilities. In Massachusetts, for example, only about 15 percent of the approximately 800 youths committed to the State Department of Youth services each year are first placed in a locked treatment program. The other 85 percent of the committed youths are placed in community-based programs such as group homes, forestry camps, day treatment programs, outreach-tracking programs, or foster care. Most of the programs have been privatized; private agencies run the programs on a contract basis with the state. In addition, the residential programs are small in size, with no more than 30 youths housed in a facility (Krisberg and Austin, 1993). What this means for most youths is that they spend only about four weeks in secure placement and then are placed in nonsecure treatment programs. In states with heavy reliance on traditional training schools, most youths spend several months in secure confinement and then are placed on aftercare (parole).

The National Council on Crime and Delinquency evaluated the Massachusetts reform and found it to be successful. Compared to other states still relying on traditional training schools, Massachusetts had similar recidivism results, and the effort was cost-effective. More specifically, depending on how long Massachusetts would incarcerate youths in traditional training schools, it would have to spend $10 to $16.8 million more per year than it was spending in its deinstitutionalization mode (Krisberg and Austin, 1989).

An evaluation of the closing of one institution in Maryland, however, found contrary results. Almost three-quarters (72%) of the youths committed to the State Department of Juvenile Services after the institution's closing were rearrested during the one-year follow-up period, whereas only about 45 percent of the youths who had been institutionalized at the training school prior to its closing were rearrested. In a two-and-one-half year follow-up period, 83 percent of the post-closing group were rearrested, compared to 66 percent and 69 percent of the two groups that had been incarcerated at the training school under study. The authors concluded that "the alternatives available when Montrose [the state training school] was closed were less effective in reducing crime than institutionalization would have been" (Gottfredson and Barton, 1993:604). The authors suggest that their findings support the conclusion that "neither institutional nor community-based programs are uniformly effective or ineffective. The *design* [emphasis in original] of the intervention rather than its location appears important" (Gottfredson and Barton, 1993:605). In other words, simply closing traditional training schools is only half of a strategy. The other half is to devise effective programs for the youths that would have been committed to the training schools. It appears that Massachusetts was able to devise such effective alternative programming for its delinquent commitments. Maryland apparently did not come up with effective alternative programming, so the recidivism rates for the group not sent to the training school were disappointing.

Another state that has tried to reduce its institutional population is Missouri. It closed its only training school in 1983 and has tried to keep newer institutions at 33 beds or fewer. To accomplish the goal of reduced placements, Missouri uses such strategies as day treatment programs and trackers. Day treatment is intended for youths released from residential confinement; it involves education, counseling, tutoring, and/or community service. Trackers are personnel, often college students completing a degree in social work or a related field, who monitor and support about 800 youths in community supervision. Trackers offer support, mentoring, and assistance. Missouri also uses nonsecure group homes. One benefit has been cost saving. In 2000, Missouri spent about $94 per every youth ages 10 to 17 in the state, compared to $140 per youth in surrounding states. The state also reports that only about 11 percent of youths released from custody were rearrested or returned to juvenile custody within one year (Mendel, 2001). Mendel (2001) argues that much of the reason for the apparent success of Missouri's emphasis on community programming is the hiring of high-quality staff. At all times youth are overseen by at least two educated and highly trained staff members, compared to other states in which less skilled officers supervise youths.

Blended Sentencing

The creation of **blended sentencing** allows either the juvenile court or the adult court to impose a sentence that can involve either the juvenile or the adult correctional system or both (see Chapter 8 for further discussion of blended sentencing). The adult sentence may be suspended pending either a violation or the commission of a new crime. Texas, for example, allows juveniles convicted of certain violent crimes or of habitual offender status to be sentenced to terms of up to 20 years for a second-degree felony and up to 10 years for a third-degree felony (Feld, 1998). One result of blended sentencing will be a growing number of youthful offenders in adult prisons. Note that juvenile offenders in adult prisons may still be considered "minors" for other purposes. In Wisconsin, for example, 17-year-olds in adult prisons are still subject to mandatory education and require parental consent for medical treatment (Torbet et al., 2000).

A study on victimization among youthful inmates in adult prisons is important in light of the development of blended sentencing. Maitland and Sluder interviewed 111 inmates ages 17 to 25. They found that less than 1 percent reported that they had been forced to engage in sexual activity, 3 percent had been forced to give up their money, and 5.5 percent had had a weapon used on them. Less serious victimization experiences, however, were much more frequent. Fifty-nine percent had been verbally harassed, approximately 50 percent had had their property stolen, and 38 percent had been hit, kicked, punched, or slapped. The authors concluded that "young, medium-security prison inmates are most likely to be subjected to less serious forms of victimization by peers during their terms of incarceration" (Maitland and Sluder, 1998:68). Thus, any trend toward putting delinquents in adult prisons when they are 17 or 18 can be expected to produce such victimization results for the youthful offenders so incarcerated.

Another negative aspect of blended sentencing and putting juveniles into criminal court and adult institutions is that the youths may have negative perceptions of how they were processed. In research on criminal court processing of youths in Florida, it was found that the court message to the youths was that their behavior was bad and they were bad. Prison staff also communicated a similar negative message; the youthful prisoners heard that "they were lost causes who could never redeem themselves or return to normal personhood" (Bishop, 2000:153).

Wilderness Programs

Another example of what Cullen and his colleagues (Cullen et al., 2005:66) call "**common-sense corrections**" is the use of various types of wilderness experiences, ranging from relatively short stays in outdoor settings to rather long wagon train or ocean ship trips. Both private operators and some states have used this type of programming, which places delinquents in settings where they learn survival skills, limits, and self-esteem. The youths are put in natural settings where they must learn to cook, obtain shelter from the elements, tell directions (read a compass), start fires, and so forth. In the process of accomplishing such tasks, the youths learn to depend on both others and themselves. The thinking is that a successful survival experience in a natural setting will then transfer to the youth's normal environment and he or she will turn to more constructive activities than delinquency. The program, then, is based on common-sense notions (perhaps stemming from experience or familiarity with Boy Scouts and Girl Scouts) that outdoors know-how is beneficial.

A wilderness program in Georgia recently received attention when a 13-year-old boy died. Authorities fired several staff members due to the incident. It is alleged that camp counselors restrained the boy face down and denied him his inhaler (he was asthmatic) (Miller, 2005).

Some studies have shown **wilderness programs** to be effective in reducing recidivism, but the overall research has not been encouraging. In their meta-analysis of effective treatments, Lipsey and Wilson (1998) conclude that wilderness programs generally have shown to have weak effects or no effects on the recidivism rates of the youths who have gone through the programs, compared to control groups. So although the contestants who went through a "Survivor" experi-

Adequate basics, such as food, clothing, and shelter, are some of the required criteria for wilderness treatment programs such as RedCliff Ascent's outing in the Wah Wah Mountains of Southwestern Utah. Troubled youths from around the world are sent to such programs in hope that they will straighten out their lives.

ence on television may claim it made them better persons, there is no consensus that wilderness programs reduce delinquency. Once again, common sense is not always accurate (Cullen et al., 2005:66).

SUMMARY

This chapter has examined state and private residential placements, ranging from training schools to wilderness experience programs. An examination of the effectiveness of institutional placements indicates that many children do not really need to be in training schools. Instead, they can be handled in less restrictive settings without any increase in recidivism. This part of the chapter also examined several problematic factors in residential placements, such as victimization, racial tension, and homosexual behavior. Unfortunately, residential placements often translate into horror stories for the children rather than therapeutic havens. Sexual assaults and racial tension have been well-documented components of placements in the past, and they are unlikely to disappear completely. Because of these and related problems, states such as Massachusetts, Maryland, Pennsylvania, and Utah turned to noninstitutional approaches to delinquency, in which fewer youngsters are placed in state training schools. Blended sentencing and increased processing of juvenile offenders in adult court, however, may translate into significant numbers of youthful offenders being incarcerated in adult prisons and to youths serving longer sentences than in the past. The most extreme possibility is that states will abolish juvenile court. If that happens, probably more juveniles will go to adult prisons but some youths will continue to be housed in institutions reserved for offenders under 18.

The only safe prediction is that juvenile corrections will not be the same as it was 25 years ago. It is likely that changes will continue to multiply as society attempts to minimize youth crime.

Discussion Questions

1. Many are calling for harsher punishment for juvenile offenders, especially violent juvenile offenders. Do you think that persons holding that position are aware of the information on victimization in juvenile training schools (prisons)? Would knowledge of victimization risks in juvenile prisons affect calls for tougher measures for juveniles?

2. Do juveniles deserve prisons that are quite different from adult offenders? Should we continue to model juvenile prisons after schools? Should we drop any pretense of lesser punishment for juveniles and make juvenile facilities very similar to adult prisons?

3. Would you consider a career in juvenile corrections, in either public or private facilities?

4. Should corrections for juveniles go back to its roots and try to emphasize rehabilitation, or should it attempt to incorporate more punitive dimensions? What would the ideal residential program for juveniles look like?

6. Common sense has led to correctional efforts such as boot camps and wilderness experience programs. Evaluation research often indicates that these common-sense solutions are not all that effective. Why is common sense often a poor guide to public policy?

7. How do you envision juvenile corrections in 10 years? What will juvenile prisons look like a decade from now?

Chapter 11

Juvenile Probation and Community Corrections

INTRODUCTION

Even before the founding of the first juvenile court in Illinois in 1899, community interventions had been a central weapon of those seeking to fight delinquency. This chapter will examine both traditional and nontraditional community interventions and focus on some of the problems with these approaches to the delinquency problem. The chapter will first describe probation and aftercare for juveniles, highlight some of the current trends in community interventions, and then look at some of the concerns in the field. One of the key issues examined in this chapter is the **effectiveness** issue: Do community interventions have any impact on recidivism? In other words, do community interventions help to reduce the number of offenses committed by the juveniles exposed to the programs, or are the programs ineffective in reducing delinquent activity?

KEY TERMS

aftercare

balanced approach

community justice

community service

effectiveness

emphasis on status
  offenses

goal confusion

peacemaking

probation

punitive model

restitution

restorative justice

social history investigation
  (predisposition report)

PROBATION

Statistics demonstrate that **probation** continues to be a critical part of the juvenile justice system. In 2000 (the most recent year for which data are available), an estimated 393,300 youths were adjudicated delinquent in juvenile court and placed on probation. This represents well over half (63%) of the 624,400 youths who were adjudicated delinquent. Another 37,800 youths who were not adjudicated delinquent agreed to some form of probation. Another 227,700 youths who were not petitioned agreed to some form of voluntary probation. So probation handled more than 650,000 delinquents altogether in 2000. Approximately 60 to 75 percent of status offenders, varying with type of status offense, were placed on probation. So probation was the most common disposition for adjudicated status offenders (Puzzanchera et al., 2004). (Box 11.1 shows the offenses for which delinquents were placed on probation.) Thus, probation continues to be the workhorse of the juvenile court (Torbet, 1996).

Box 11.1 Adjudication Offenses for Juvenile Probationers

Delinquency Probationers:

Adjudicated Delinquent Offender Profiles

Most Serious Offense	1985	2000
Person	16%	23%
Property	61	40
Drugs	7	13
Public Order	16	24
Total	100%	100%

Source: C. Puzzanchera, A.L. Stahl, T.A. Finnegan, N. Tierney, and H.N. Snyder (2004). *Juvenile Court Statistics 2000.* Pittsburgh: National Center for Juvenile Justice.

Social History (Predisposition) Investigations

When a child has been adjudicated as either a delinquent or a status offender, usually a probation officer conducts a **social history investigation (predisposition report)** of the youngster and his or her family. Similar to the so-called presentence investigation in adult courts, social history reports offer judges legal and social information. Legal information includes descriptive material about the delinquency or status offense, including the child's, the victim's, and the police officer's (if a delinquent act) version of the offense, and verified data on the child's prior contacts, if any, with the juvenile court and with the police department's juvenile bureau. Social history information includes verification of the child's age (a critical legal condition for court action) and information on the child's development, family, education, and possible problems such as alcohol or other drug abuse.

Probation officers gather such information by interviewing the youth; the youth's family, teachers, and other school personnel; the victim; and the police; and by checking various police, court, and school records. They usually collect information on previous arrests from police and court files. Likewise, they may obtain a copy of the child's cumulative school record, which contains information on the child's grades, attendance, disciplinary history, and intelligence testing. If necessary, in probation departments that have the resources, the officer may also see to it that a psychologist and/or a psychiatrist examine the child for any suspected emotional problems and to determine the child's intelligence quotient (IQ) more accurately (by an individual IQ test rather than a group test). The probation officer then summarizes all of this information in a report that provides the judge with a more informed basis for the disposition decision.

Some adult courts are now omitting all the social history information. Determinate sentencing in many jurisdictions means that only information about the current charges and the prior record of the accused pertains to sentencing.

Racial disparity can enter into probation reports. A recent examination of more than 200 narrative reports in a western state indicated that probation officers were more likely to note negative personality factors in reports about blacks but were more likely to note negative environmental factors in reports about white youths. Officers were also more likely to assign a higher risk of reoffending to black youths than white youths. There were no racial differences in sentencing recommendations (Bridges and Steen, 1998).

Probation Supervision

Youths who are placed on formal probation supervision in court must follow various conditions, such as reporting regularly to a probation officer, obeying the law, attending school, and remaining within the geographical jurisdiction of the court. Judges may also order specific conditions, such as restitution to the victim(s) of the delinquent act or community service restitution (e.g., performing cleanup work at the local park or playground). Another special condition might be to attend counseling sessions with a social worker, psychologist, or psychiatrist, or require the parents to attend the counseling sessions. A judge might also order a short stay (about one month) in detention as a condition of probation (Schwartz et al., 1987).

If a juvenile follows the conditions of the probation disposition and is adjusting favorably at home, in school, and in the community, then the probation officer can request an early discharge from supervision. If a youngster is not abiding by the conditions and is not adjusting well, then the probation officer may request that the judge order that the youth is in violation of the probation agreement. In that case, the judge can either order the probation to continue (perhaps with additional conditions such as more frequent reporting to the probation officer) or can terminate the probation and place the youth under the supervision of the state youth correctional authority for placement in a public facility or place the youth in a private residential setting.

AFTERCARE

Many states also have **aftercare** or parole programs for youths released from state training schools, group homes, or forestry camp placements. Aftercare supervision is very similar to probation supervision. In fact, in some states, probation officers also perform aftercare supervision duties. Just as with probation, youths on aftercare status must follow specific conditions and report on a regular basis to a parole officer. If they do not, parole can be revoked and they can be sent back to an institutional placement.

A recent national evaluation of intensive juvenile aftercare proved disappointing. Approximately one-half the youths were arrested for one or more new felonies, and if technical violations (breaking the rules of probation) were included, about 80 percent were arrested for something. The most disturbing conclusion was that "no statistically significant or substantive differences were seen between IAP [intensive aftercare] and control youth on almost all the recidivism measures" (Wiebush et al., 2005:80). Recidivism measures included percent arrested, number of offenses, severity and frequency of offenses, and time to first arrest. There was some minor evidence that more treatment was associated with less recidivism, but this finding was significant in only one of the study sites. (For an evaluation of one aftercare program in California, see Box 11.2.)

SUPERVISION AND COUNSELING

Probation and aftercare (parole) officers working with juveniles use various combinations of assistance and control (Glaser, 1964) to help youthful offenders avoid further trouble. Some officers act like social workers or counselors as they try to understand the youth and his or her problems and assist the youngster in gaining greater self-insight and self-esteem. Such officers also might attempt some family therapy to help parents better understand the family interaction patterns that have contributed to the child's misbehavior. Other officers assume a tougher role: a quasi-police officer who first threatens the youth with punishment and then monitors the compliance of the child to the court conditions. This "surveillance"(Studt, 1973) type of officer typically believes that deterrence and incapacitation are more important goals than rehabilitation.

Box 11.2   The Lifeskills '95 Program

The Lifeskills'95 program is a 13-week reintegration treatment program based on reality therapy. It is intended to help chronic, high-risk juvenile offenders in their re-entry phase upon release from secure confinement. Participants receive exposure to lifestyle choices and counseling about substance abuse awareness. The program attempts to reinforce small increments in such routine matters as getting up and getting to work on time. One module is titled "Dealing with Your Emotions" and includes sections on anger, hate, guilt, anxiety, despair, isolation, and death. Another module focuses on family dynamics and family conflicts.

An evaluation of California Youth Authority parolees who went through the Lifeskills'95 program compared to a group of parolees who had regular parole without the program components showed some success. At three months, only 14 percent of the treatment group parolees had been arrested, compared to 25.5 percent of the control group. At the end of the study, 32 percent of the experimental group had been arrested, compared to 54 percent of the control group. Both of these differences were statistically significant. However, some of the subjects in both groups had only been under supervision for three months.

The research concluded that this program appears to have been helpful in the early phase of the re-entry process following release from prison. They argue that what the community offers to parolees is critical:

In the long run, the postrelease adjustments made will depend fundamentally on the opportunities available to parolees. A program such as "Lifeskills '95" can lead parolees to opportunities, but those opportunities must be available and meaningful (Josi and Sechrest, 1999:77).

Whether oriented toward assistance or control, probation and parole officers tend to use one of several counseling techniques—including reality therapy, client-centered (nondirective) therapy, rational emotive therapy, or behaviorism. Assistance-oriented officers utilize these counseling techniques to a greater extent than control-oriented officers, but even the latter use some of the basic principles of these approaches to interview probationers and to establish some rapport (for more information on counseling techniques, see Van Voorhis, Braswell, and Lester, 2004). Both cognitive techniques (Chavaria, 1997) and behavior modification have proven effective in community interventions with juveniles (Gendreau, Cullen, and Bonta, 1994).

CURRENT TRENDS IN COMMUNITY SUPERVISION

Several developments are taking place in community corrections. Many are calling for tougher community corrections with greater attention to punishment and controlling offender risk. Other voices, however, continue to insist that probation and other community interventions need to be more than just strict punishment for crime.

The Balanced Approach

One current approach in juvenile corrections is the **balanced approach**. "This philosophy requires the system to provide balanced attention to the need for competency development, accountability, and community safety and requires efforts to restore, to the greatest extent possible, the victim and community to their precrime status"(Kurlychek, Torbet, and Bozynski, 1999:3). It is thought that restitution and community service send out a message that the offender is responsible for his or her crime and is being held accountable for it. It is considered important that the offender come to realize the harm he or she has caused the victim(s). As of 2004, at least 16 states had juvenile court laws with purpose clauses focusing on the balanced approach (Griffin, Szymanski, and King, 2005).

As you might guess, the balanced approach is actually a combination of traditional rehabilitation, restorative justice, and classical criminology. One example of the balanced approach is Utah's juvenile restitution program, which includes a restitution workfund. Juveniles without jobs or money can perform community service tasks and thereby earn money for their restitution orders. In Boston, Operation Night Light has police and probation officers together on street patrol checking to ensure that probationers are complying with their probation conditions. St. Louis uses deputy juvenile officers and police to make random home visits to check compliance with court-ordered curfews (Urban, St. Cyr, and Decker, 2003). A similar program in Maryland has the probation officers and police targeting selected crime "hot spots" (Kurlychek, Torbet, and Bozynski, 1999).

Another example is the Gang Violence Reduction Program in Chicago, which combines surveillance of violent or potentially violent gang members and the provision of services. Police and probation officers increase their supervision of target youths and provide education, employment, employment training, and some counseling. Evaluation has found decreased serious gang violence and improved perceptions among residents concerning gang crime and police effectiveness in targeting such crime (Howell and Hawkins, 1998).

Pennsylvania has attempted to implement the balanced approach. In fact, the state legislature amended the juvenile law purpose clause in 1995 to include balanced and restorative justice principles. A recent report on outcome measures in 12 Pennsylvania counties for calendar year 2003 provides a snapshot of what the departments have been attempting to do and what they have achieved. Related to the objective of community protection, the counties report that 87 percent of probation cases had no new offenses, and 87 percent also had no serious probation violations. Under the objective of accountability, more than 100,000 hours of community service were completed, with 92 percent of probationers ordered to perform community service actually completing such orders. Almost one-half million dollars of restitution was paid ($479,587), 47 percent of the amount ordered. Eighty-four percent of the probationers ordered to pay restitution paid it in full. In summary, more than 75 percent of the juveniles on probation were attending school or GED classes or were working at case closing. Almost 80 percent were closed as "successful," and only 3 percent were closed as unsuccessful (Griffin and Thomas, 2004).

This report on juvenile probation in Pennsylvania contrasts very favorably with a federal (GAO) report on adult probation some 20 years ago. That report noted the woeful lack of case plans and treatment objectives and unenforced probation conditions for the adult probationers under study. It was a picture of much not even being attempted. Here there is an accountant-like depiction of activity and outcomes. Reports like this can be used to show both legislators and taxpayers that probation is working—that it is accomplishing something. As a recent report on probation noted, "The bottom line is results" (Griffin and Torbet, 2002:134).

On the other hand, it is necessary to keep a certain caution about glowing outcome reports. A focus on outcome reporting can lead to attempts to make the statistics as positive as possible, even if those statistics hide deficiencies. Officers can be tempted to close cases as "successful" even where there is less than complete or desired success. The perfect evaluation would be a controlled or quasi-experiment in which probation is compared to a control group that gets supervision from a nonofficial agency or perhaps no supervision at all. This is especially important in analyzing juvenile probation because many of the youths are first offenders or less serious offenders, and a good scare in court might well deter them from future delinquency.

A specific example of the need for caution is the information on community service. The report notes that in Allegheny County alone (Pittsburgh, PA), probationers completed almost 69,000 hours of community service in 2002, the equivalent of more than $350,000 in labor if the youths had been paid the minimum wage for all those hours. (They simply multiply the number of hours worked times the minimum wage to get this estimate of value.)

This estimate of value makes several critical assumptions. One is that the youths actually worked all those hours and worked them fully—not wasting time. A recent report suggests that even regular, paid workers waste about two hours a day at work (drinking coffee, gossiping with coworkers, surfing the Internet, etc.). A second assumption is that those hours and the work were truly necessary, not "make-work" projects that somebody devised to fill the time that the youths were supposed to serve. Did the walls the youths painted really need a fresh coat of paint, or was painting those walls a way to "keep those kids from probation busy"? Finally, the estimate of $350,000 in "free" labor does not include any accounting of how much it cost to supervise the youths; a probation officer or someone else had to make sure the kids got to the work sites and actually did some work. So while reports such as the one from Pennsylvania are encouraging, the actual benefits may not be quite as rosy as depicted.

The Punitive Model: Attack (Tough) Probation

One concern about the balanced approach is whether it in fact "balances" the concerns for competency development, accountability, and community safety, or simply places emphasis on accountability. If the balanced approach is not actually balanced, then it might be considered a **punitive model**. This philosophy is quite direct; the offender, even if a juvenile, deserves to be punished.

Miller (1996), for one, argues that the toughening of probation has gone too far. He contends that probation has lost much of its original mission of helping the offender. He argues that probation officers have abandoned any pretense at a social work role and have become "ersatz" (imitation) cops. He says that in this new "attack probation" style (a term developed by British criminologist Andrew Rutherford) officers see "their role as one in which to search out any means possible to get the probationer into prison. The motto of this practice was mounted on the office wall of one of California's chief probation officers: 'Trail 'em, Surveil 'em, Nail 'em, and Jail 'em.'" (Miller, 1996:131). In other words, if probation officers are out on the streets at night in "hot spots" (areas with high rates of crime), they are there as quasi-police officers looking for trouble and not as friendly social workers.

A critical question about getting tough is whether such tactics are effective in reducing recidivism. That issue is discussed in the next major section of this chapter. Another interesting question posed by this get-tough movement is whether it is appropriate to use shame tactics in probation. For a discussion of this issue, see Box 11.3.

Box 11.3 Shame Tactics in Probation and Community Corrections

Shame strategies take several forms. One form of shame penalty is apology. For example, one school vandalizer was forced to apologize in front of the student bodies at the 13 schools he vandalized. Some shame penalties, however, are much more negative, and objections arise that they are stigmatizing rather than reintegrative. For example, some offenders have been required to wear t-shirts or display signs on their car or residence proclaiming their offense ("I am a convicted shoplifter" or "convicted drunk

Box 11.3, *continued*

driver"). Karp (1998) contends that such dramatic strategies are ineffective or worse: "Shame penalties that emphasize humiliation are likely to be counterproductive as they drive a wedge between offenders and conventional society" (p. 291). Thus, shame penalties can isolate the offender rather than assist him or her to rejoin the community. He also questions whether shame penalties are effective in modern society, which has an anonymous aspect compared to the potentially more effective informal small group setting (Karp, 1998). In other words, modern America is so big that we do not know our neighbors and thus we do not really experience shame when others (who are strangers) learn that we have done wrong. Shame only has meaning in a small community where people know one another.

Andrew von Hirsch argues against shaming tactics based on an ethical position that such tactics violate the respect that the offender as a human deserves. Von Hirsch argues that punishments should not demean the dignity of the offender. If they destroy the dignity of the offender, they are unacceptable:

> Acceptable penal content, then, is the idea that a sanction should be devised so that its intended penal deprivations are those that can be administered in a manner that is clearly consistent with the offender's dignity. If the penal deprivation includes a given imposition, X, then one must ask whether that can be undergone by offenders in a reasonably self-possessed fashion. Unless one is confident that it can, it should not be a part of the sanction (von Hirsch, 1990:167).

Thus, von Hirsch is opposed to t-shirts for offenders or bumper stickers that make drunk drivers advertise their offense because there "is no way a person can, with dignity, go about in public with a sign admitting himself or herself to be a moral pariah" (1990:168).

Proponents of identifying labels for offenders would argue that they enhance the punishment value of community corrections. Such marks make probation or parole tougher rather than a lenient "slap on the wrist." Supporters would also argue that there may be deterrent value in the measures. It is embarrassing to wear such markings, and this could serve to deter others from drunk driving or whatever offense results in the added penalty.

What do you think? What kinds of shaming might be effective for juvenile offenders? What are the limits of acceptable strategies?

Renewed Emphasis on Status Offenses

An **emphasis on status offenses** such as truancy is making a comeback in some circles. Kern County, California, for example, has instituted a truancy program that uses two deputy probation officers to work with students and families. If initial efforts to resolve truancy fail, the truant youth is referred to one of the deputy probation officers, who then meets with the family at least four times. The officer also makes unannounced home visits, monitors attendance, counsels the youth and his or her parents, and refers the family to appropriate service providers. Tracking continues for one year. If unsuccessful, the case is referred back to the school for possible referral to the district attorney for court action (Garry, 1996). What makes this emphasis on status offenses like truancy new is that status offenses are receiving increased attention due to research that indicates

AP Photo/Post & Courier, Bill Jordan

Tonya Kline, age 15, is led by her mother to family court in Monks Corner, South Carolina. A family court judge allowed Kline to remain tethered to her mother instead of going to a state detention facility. She is required to be tethered to one of her parents until she is sentenced on truancy and other charges.

that they are risk factors for serious and violent delinquency. So there is a fear that if these troublesome behaviors are not dealt with, then there is a definite possibility of much worse behavior in the future.

Restorative Justice

Bazemore and Maloney argue that **restorative justice** should be the theme in a new paradigm for criminal justice, juvenile justice in general, and probation in particular. In contrast to retributive justice, which focuses on vengeance, deterrence, and punishment, restorative justice "is concerned with repairing the damage or harm done to victims and the community through a process of negotiation, mediation, victim empowerment, and reparation" (Bazemore and Maloney, 1994:28). As another commentator puts it, "restorative justice is about relationships—how relationships are harmed by crime and how they can be rebuilt to promote recovery and healing for people affected by crime" (Kurki, 2000:266).

As Chapter 12 discusses restorative justice in full, we will end the discussion of restorative justice in probation at this point.

Peacemaking

Like restorative justice, **peacemaking** is a positive philosophy that seeks to go beyond simply criticizing the status quo and beyond a simple focus on recidivism reduction. Peacemaking is a perspective that supports efforts of corrections workers, whether prison counselors or probation officers, to help offenders find greater meaning in their lives. Two proponents, Bo Lozoff and Michael Braswell, contend that all great religions teach four classic virtues: honesty, courage, kindness, and a sense of humor. In this perspective, reductions in recidivism and programs like counseling or vocational training are still important but they are more external. The deeper goal is internal personal change: "The primary goal is to help build a happier, peaceful person right there in the prison [if working with prisoners], a person whose newfound self-honesty and courage can steer him or her to adjust to the biases and shortcomings of a society which does not feel comfortable with ex-offenders" (Lozoff and Braswell, 1989:2).

In a peacemaking perspective, both personal transformation and institutional change are critical, but personal change is seen as the basis of social change. It is critical to begin with yourself. It is also a lifetime task that needs constant work (Braswell, Fuller, and Lozoff, 2001).

Community Justice

Another recent development in community corrections is **community justice**. The mission of community justice is to help community residents "to manage their own affairs, solve their own problems, and live together effectively and safely. This goal is best achieved by giving everyone a stake in the quality of community life" (Clear and Karp, 1998:55). To achieve this mission, community justice involves risk assessment and control of offenders, victim restoration, community contracting, and cost sharing.

Like community policing, community justice is based on the principle that the community has a responsibility to deal with offenders. The community cannot simply assume that probation officers will by themselves take care of offenders and offender problems. The community must allow the offender to make reparation to the victim and also enable the offender "to obtain the assistance, supervision, and supports (including treatment intervention programs) necessary to live in the community crime-free" (Clear and Karp, 1998:54).

Community justice is an ideal that sounds plausible and desirable. One question about community justice is just how open communities are to such an ideal. When talk radio and television commentators focus on prosecutors, judges, and even governors that they consider too soft on crime, one has to ask how much room there is for community justice programs? If a sufficient number of observers think such programs are too lenient, will the programs be given a chance to operate? Programs such as community justice inevitably have failures. Whenever you allow offenders to remain in the community, whether on probation, parole, or some new community justice initiative, a percentage will commit new crimes. If community programs are criticized for such recidivism, public outrage may well force the programs to close or to become much more restrictive in the numbers and types of offenders they serve. Public receptivity to such programs is an important issue.

Another question about community justice is a question raised in the chapter on policing, namely, whether contemporary communities are cohesive enough and have enough resources to support efforts such as community policing or community justice. In other words, are communities willing to do the work required to make community justice succeed? Are people willing to get involved in programs that help victims and help offenders? Or are most people spending so much time on jobs and family that they simply do not have the time or the willingness to help make something like community justice work? As discussed earlier, Putnam (2000) noted that people are having less and less time to give to voluntary organizations such as Kiwannis and Rotary. And even if people are willing to devote time to community justice, do impoverished communities have sufficient resources to assist juvenile offenders in their midst? On the other hand, Vermont has had considerable success in attracting volunteers to serve on reparative boards in that state (Karp, Bazemore, and Chesire, 2004).

Another concern about community justice is that many of the communities with the worst crime problems are problematic communities in other ways as well. Communities with high crime rates also have low employment rates, lower rates of intact families, more problem schools, and fewer support networks. A community justice center may have many caring judges, prosecutors, and defense attorneys, but if the community does not have resources, these caring justice center personnel may not be able to truly assist community residents. Clear and Karp (1998) suggest that cost savings generated by community justice programs be directed to the programs to pay their way. They contend that every person diverted from a prison sentence saves the state about $45,000 a year; such savings could be used to fund community justice. The problem is that such apparent savings are not necessarily real; one less prisoner does not mean that the prison system can fire a guard making $45,000 a year, for example. Even if such savings did result, the state prison system does not have the legal authority to send $45,000 directly to the community justice center.

A recent PBS documentary on Independent Lens inadvertently brought home the problem of lack of community resources. A male youth was back in court on a progress check. The judge asked him where he had looked for a summer job. The youth mentioned some fast food places he had applied to but had not heard back from. The judge then asked the youth if he had applied at Company X because X did a lot of hiring. The youth said that X went out of business some months earlier. Apart from the slight embarrassment on the judge's part for mentioning a company that was out of business, this exchange in court shows that well-intentioned judges and probation officers face a structural battle. Many jobs for teens and young adults now exist in suburban sprawl areas far removed from city districts that are the sites of community justice centers.

Based on restorative justice principles and on concepts about corrections of place (see work by Todd Clear), one California jurisdiction started an intensive probation program aimed at providing a wide range of services to both probationers and their families. The study design involved random assignment to either the experimental probation program or a control group that received regular probation (one office visit to the probation officer per month and a home visit by the officer every three months).

Evaluation results showed that program youths received significantly more services than control youths. The program youths experienced an average of 14 contacts per month, whereas regular probation officers saw their clients once a month. Despite the dramatic differences in services, there were no significant differences in any of the recidivism measures, including arrest measures and incarceration (Lane et al., 2005).

It should be noted that although this project was supposed to be an implementation of some of Clear's ideas of "corrections of place," the evaluation did not measure efforts to affect the community such as community development and community service (Clear and Karp, 1998). It appears that what was measured was the services provided to each probationer and the recidivism of the probationers. Therefore, the final word is not yet in about the effectiveness of community justice efforts.

Current Trends: What Does the Future Hold?

It is difficult to predict where community corrections will go from here. One possible path is to continue down the "get tough" road. A grim reality is that further financial cutbacks will force probation to do less and less. Another path is to attempt to return probation to a more traditional focus on trying to rehabilitate offenders. Other departments may seek to implement the balanced approach, restorative justice, or community justice (or some combination of such programs). An important issue in deciding on which direction to take is the effectiveness of community corrections. The next two sections will discuss some important findings from the effectiveness literature. The first section will review major findings on the effectiveness of community sanctions such as probation. The second section will review the research on effective treatments. Together these findings give some assistance in thinking about the most appropriate direction for community corrections to take.

EFFECTIVENESS OF JUVENILE PROBATION AND RELATED SANCTIONS

Although national recidivism statistics on juvenile probationers are not readily available and although the research on juvenile probation has not been as extensive as the research on adult probation, there are considerable research findings available to illuminate the effectiveness issue for juvenile probation. Based on research on both juveniles and adults, several conclusions about the effectiveness of community correctional interventions for juveniles seem sound.

One implication of the research is that simply making probation tougher does not work (Cullen, Wright, and Applegate, 1996). The cumulative research on such get-tough measures as Scared Straight programs, boot camps, and intensive supervision has demonstrated that harsher measures, without more, do not reduce recidivism. Experimental evaluations of such programs have shown that these tough measures do not reduce recidivism (new arrests or convictions).

Related to this is the finding that often community supervision may be no worse than incarceration—that is, at least as effective as incarceration (see Krisberg and Howell, 1998). In fact, Lipsey and Wilson (1998) found that among programs that produced consistent evidence of positive effects for serious offenders, noninstitutional programs showed greater reductions in recidivism than institutional programs. This is important. Although offenders released to community supervision commit some new crimes, the fact that they do no worse (and may do better) than offenders sentenced to training schools and then released on traditional aftercare suggests that society can use community supervision knowing that it is not more harmful than incarceration.

Another clear lesson is that the effectiveness of probation varies from place to place. An initial report on the effectiveness of adult felony probation found that the failure rate (new arrests) was 65 percent (Petersilia et al., 1985). Subsequent studies found some rates as low as 22 percent and others in between those two rates (Whitehead, 1991). There are several explanations for such variation. Some locations may be under budgetary pressures and may not have the financial resources to provide much treatment or surveillance of offenders. In adult corrections, for example, an effort to implement results-oriented strategic planning in the Alabama prison system failed because the program did not deal with the central problem: lack of resources. Alabama was only spending about $9,000 per prisoner, compared to a national average of about $27,000 (Moynihan, 2005). Some locations, on the other hand, may be implementing treatment programs that have proven to be effective (for a discussion of such principles, see the next section below). Thus, juvenile probation may be quite effective in some locations but experience serious problems in other locations.

Still another lesson is that intensive supervision can lead to easier detection of technical violations (Petersilia, 1997). In other words, officers are more likely to detect intensive supervision offenders violating the rules of probation such as not reporting to the probation officer, leaving the jurisdiction without permission, breaking curfew, testing positive on a urine drug test, and skipping school. This explains why intensive supervision can be ineffective if the goal is to reduce prison or training school populations. Detection of technical violations often results in revocation of probation. Then the offender is incarcerated as punishment for breaking the conditions of probation. So a sanction (intensive supervision) intended to reduce the number of persons being institutionalized can in fact increase the number being institutionalized. This problem can be avoided, however, if a court and correctional agency put in place a system of graduated penalties for technical violations (Altschuler, 1998). A discouraging finding is that some studies have shown that simply being on probation supervision without any officer contacts sometimes is just as effective as being on probation and being seen by an officer (National Council on Crime and Delinquency, 1987). This finding questions whether probation officers have much impact on their clients. One explanation is that perhaps officers are not doing much for their clients. Another explanation is that some offenders do not need much supervision. Perhaps being caught and being placed on probation sent a clear message to these probationers and they have learned their lesson and will not re-offend.

Perhaps the most encouraging finding in recent research is that intensive supervision that includes treatment components can reduce recidivism (Petersilia, 1997). This suggests that although being tough is not enough, addressing offender needs can make a difference. Recall also that a national evaluation of intensive juvenile aftercare did not show effectiveness but that in one of the study sites treatment was associated with less recidivism (Wiebush et al., 2005 [see discussion earlier in this chapter]). (Contrary to this claim, a recent study of aftercare with treatment did not show any effectiveness. The study, however, involved a sample of all substance-abusing offenders (Sealock, Gottfredson, and Gallagher, 1997). Because research indicates that treatment is critical, the next section will review the treatment research to show which types of treatment appear to offer promise and which seem to be ineffective.

EFFECTIVE AND INEFFECTIVE TREATMENT INTERVENTIONS WITH OFFENDERS

Although several well-publicized reports claimed that little seemed to be effective in changing offenders and reducing recidivism, there now appears to be considerable consensus that there is knowledge about effective interventions and ineffective interventions. This section will discuss both types of interventions.

Gendreau and his colleagues have spearheaded much of the treatment research. They have concluded that there are several principles of effective interventions. First, interventions need to be intensive and behavioral. Intensive means that the intervention takes up at least 40 percent of the offender's time and goes on for three to nine months. Behavioral interventions are based on the principles of operant conditioning, especially reinforcement. Simply, there must be rewards for desirable behaviors. Some examples are token economies, modeling, and cognitive behavioral interventions, such as problem solving, reasoning, self-control, and self-instructional training. Successful programs target criminogenic needs such as antisocial attitudes, peer associations, substance-abuse problems, and self-control issues rather than noncriminogenic needs such as low self-esteem, anxiety, or depression. The responsivity principle means that attention needs to be paid to matching offenders, therapists, and programs. For example, offenders who prefer structure do better in a more structured program such as a token economy. More anxious offenders do better with therapists who show more interpersonal sensitivity. Programs need to enforce their rules in a firm but fair manner, and positive reinforcers should outnumber punishers by a ratio of at least 4:1. Therapists need to be sensitive and adequately trained and supervised. Relapse prevention and advocacy and brokerage with other community agencies are also necessary (Gendreau, 1996).

Lipsey (1999) has done extensive meta-analysis research on effective programming for juvenile offenders. Recall that meta-analysis is a research technique that studies the overall effects of interventions based on grouping together individual studies. If five studies have looked at the impact of individual counseling programs, for example, meta-analysis would convert the individual findings of each study into an overall effect size for all the studies combined. Using this technique, Lipsey concluded that for noninstitutionalized offenders (e.g., offenders on probation or in other community programs) the interventions of individual counseling, interpersonal skills development, and behavioral programs all had consistent positive effects in reducing recidivism, compared to their respective control groups. In fact, these interventions reduced recidivism of 50 percent in the control groups to 30 percent or lower in the treatment groups (Lipsey, 1999). Such reductions are both significant and important. (For details on the recidivism reductions of various interventions for noninstitutionalized offenders, see Table 11.1. For a summary of the research findings on successful intervention principles, see Box 11.5.) This is only a brief summary of the effectiveness literature but it gives an outline of effective intervention principles.

It is also important to note what has been found to be ineffective. For example, Freudian psychodynamic therapy is ineffective with offenders, as is Rogerian nondirective (person-centered) therapy (Gendreau, 1996). Freudian therapy seeks to uncover and resolve unconscious conflicts stemming from the failure to adequately resolve critical developmental crises in childhood. It is probably something of a blessing that it is not appropriate for offenders because it is both expensive and time-consuming. Nondirective counseling assumes that clients have the potential to change and can do so if the therapist offers unconditional positive regard and a listening forum so that the client can explore options and achieve his or her full potential. It is probably more appropriate for other populations, such as college student populations, in which the clients are more mature and independent. It should be noted, however, that certain principles of nondirective therapy—such as positive regard and empathy—still apply in other counseling strategies.

Table 11.1   Most and Least Effective Types of Intervention with Noninstitutionalized Offenders and Estimated Effects on Recidivism

Intervention Type (N)	Estimated Effect Size	Treatment/Control Recidivism Contrast*
Positive Effects, consistent evidence		
Individual counseling (8)	.46	.28/.50
Interpersonal skills (3)	.44	.29/.50
Behavioral problems (7)	.42	.30/.50
Positive Effects, less consistent evidence		
Multiple services (17)	.29	.36/.50
Restitution, Probation/parole (10)	.15	.43/.50
Mixed, but generally positive effects, inconsistent evidence		
Employment-related (4)	.22	.39/.50
Academic programs (2)	.20	.40/.50
Advocacy or casework (6)	.19	.41/.50
Family counseling (8)	.19	.41/.50
Group counseling (9)	.10	.45/.50
Weak or no effects, inconsistent evidence		
Reduced caseload probation/parole (12)	−.04	.52/.50
Weak or no effects, consistent evidence		
Wilderness or challenge (4)	.12	.44/.50
Early release, probation/parole (2)	.03	.48/.50
Deterrence programs (6)	−.06	.53/.50
Vocational programs (4)	−.18	.59/.50

*Recidivism of intervention group in comparison to assumed control group recidivism of .50. For example, Individual counseling would produce a recidivism rate of 28 percent compared to the control group without counseling having a recidivism rate of 50 percent.

Numbers in parentheses represent number of studies in that category

Source: M.W. Lipsey (1999). "Can Intervention Rehabilitate Serious Delinquents?" *Annals of the American Academy of Political and Social Science* 564:1421-166.

Box 11.5   Summary of Research Findings About Successful Correctional Interventions

Research indicates that correctional interventions should:

1. Concentrate on changing negative behaviors by requiring juveniles to recognize and understand thought processes that rationalize negative behaviors.

2. Promote healthy bonds with, and respect for, prosocial members within the juvenile's family, peer, school, and community network.

3. Have a comprehensible and predictable path for client progression and movement. Each program level should be directed toward and directly related to the next step.

4. Have consistent, clear, and graduated consequences for misbehavior and recognition for positive behavior.

5. Recognize that a reasonable degree of attrition must be expected with a delinquent population.

6. Provide an assortment of highly structured programming activities, including education and/or hands-on vocational training and skill development.

7. Facilitate discussions that promote family problem solving.

8. Integrate delinquent and at-risk youths into generally prosocial groups to prevent the development of delinquent peer groups.

Source: M. Kurlychek, P.M. Torbet, and M. Bozynski (1999). *Focus on Accountability: Best Practices for Juvenile Court and Probation*. Washington, DC: U.S. Department of Justice and Delinquency Prevention.

Additional Factors Related to Effectiveness

The effectiveness research is critical. It is imperative to know what works and what does not work. It is also important, however, to recall some additional factors about successful intervention with offenders. One point to note is that often programs are simply not available for offenders. For example, in 1990, the estimate was that 26 percent of all probationers needed drug abuse treatment. At the same time, the average wait for entry into outpatient programs was 22 days (Duffee and Carlson, 1996). So although research indicates that resolving criminogenic needs such as substance-abuse problems is critical in changing offenders and reducing recidivism, the programs to change such offenders are not always readily available. Another problem is that the public and politicians are reluctant to increase government spending even for worthy projects.

A second factor that probation officers need to consider is that youths on probation may have more serious or more prevalent problems than official records indicate. In a study of juvenile probationers in Southern Illinois, official records indicated that only 20 percent of the youths were truant and only 6 percent were involved in drug usage, whereas almost one-half of the youths themselves admitted to truancy and 43 percent admitted to drug usage (Cashel, 2004). This reflects the strong possibility that juvenile probationers have problems that are more extensive than officers know.

Another factor to consider is that interventions that would appear to offer benefits for offenders do not always do so. For example, many people assume that part-time employment for teens reduces their chances of committing delinquent acts. These people assume that having a job teaches important life lessons in responsibility. Some recent research, however, shows that employment is not always beneficial. Wright and his colleagues found that the "number of hours employed had an indirect effect in increasing delinquency across the sample" (Wright, Cullen, and Williams, 1997:215). In fact, much of the delinquency of working teens is occupationally related (Wright and Cullen, 2000). So it may not always be productive for probation officers to help teenage probationers get part-time jobs. Instead it may be productive to provide teens with "modest" cash incentives to graduate. In one study such incentives prevented approximately the same amount of crime as a three-strikes law at one-tenth the cost (Wright, Cullen, and Williams, 1997).

This issue is complex, however. Several programs for older adolescents that included an emphasis on employment or advanced skills training had very positive effects. Thus, Krisberg and colleagues (1995) argue that such programs are effective for older teens.

A recent study confirmed the oft-repeated observation that workers perceive working with delinquent girls to be more difficult than working with delinquent boys. Baines and Alder interviewed youth workers in Victoria, Australia, and found that perceptions of girls were that they were "more 'devious,' 'full of bullshit,' and 'dramatic' contrasted with their understanding of young men as 'open' and 'honest' and therefore easier to engage" (Baines and Alder, 1996:481). A distressing implication of this study is that workers dislike working with girls. Thus, female offenders, who have very real and serious needs, are not getting the attention and treatment that they need. This is especially distressing given that this "may be a last chance opportunity for many of the young women who are clients of these services" (Baines and Alder, 1996:483).

Another study of officer attitudes toward girls found that many probation officers see girls as manipulative yet the officers do not take the next step. They do not try to understand if such manipulative behaviors may be a reasonable response to real problems and then seek out appropriate programs to address the girls' problems. Instead, they just write off the girls (Gaarder, Rodriguez, and Zatz, 2004).

Many also thought that alternative education programs that have distinct school schedules intended for students not doing well in traditional classrooms would be beneficial for delinquents. A recent meta-analysis of alternative schools found that they could have positive effects on school performance and attitude but they did not reduce delinquent behavior (Cox, Davidson, and Bynum, 1995).

Perhaps the most important cautionary note in any discussion of effectiveness is that financial cutbacks often make any debate about effectiveness moot. When state legislators reduce probation budgets, it is simply impossible for probation officers to implement lessons from research findings on effective interventions. In California, for example, a recent report indicated that cutbacks caused caseloads to mushroom to 200 probationers per officer. In response, some offices resorted to computer monitoring of probationers. As a result, the probationers were not receiving any personal contacts or supervision. When there are no funds for probation supervision, all the research on effective interventions becomes meaningless. As one youth told Humes, "Probation isn't worth shit!" (Humes, 1996:360). As noted above, a recent national survey of probation agencies confirmed that declining budgets are a reality for many agencies (Lindner and Bonn, 1996). On the positive side, the state of Ohio has had success in using financial incentives to encourage counties to send only the most serious offenders to state training schools and to treat less serious youths without committing them to state training schools (Moon, Applegate, and Latessa, 1997).

CONTINUING CONCERNS IN COMMUNITY CORRECTIONS

As juvenile court and probation enter into their second century of formal existence since the historic founding of the Illinois juvenile court in 1899, several concerns continue. This section will discuss the concerns of goal confusion, the no-fault society, restitution, and community service.

Goal Confusion

Goal confusion means that judges, probation and aftercare officers, probation directors, state legislators, and juvenile justice experts disagree about the purposes and objectives of juvenile court and community supervision. Part of the reason for such goal confusion is that we have conflicting images of juvenile offenders. At times we see them as "kids gone wrong"—as victims who are not completely evil. At other times we see them as "hostile predators" and "full-fledged" criminals (Morse, 1999). These conflicting images influence how we treat juveniles. Thus, what was once a rather clear institution for supplementing parental concern by means of adult advice and psychological/social work skill has become a matter of controversy. Some courts, officers, and experts still advocate a *parens patriae* and rehabilitation philosophy. In Glaser's (1964) terminology, the emphasis is on assistance to the probationer rather than on controlling the offender. As noted above, however, developments such as "attack" probation see the juveniles as hostile predator. They indicate that many no longer adhere to a pure assistance model. Moreover, advocates of restorative justice argue that it is time to go beyond the stale debates of the past and place new attention on the concerns of the victim. Proponents of the balanced approach would second that suggestion and add that community safety should also be a prime concern.

Restitution

Restitution occurs when juvenile offenders pay for all or part of the damage inflicted on crime victims or property. Restitution can take the form of either the payment of money or the performance of work (chores) for the victim. Restitution may be part of victim–offender reconciliation in which the offender and victim meet to express their concerns and feelings. In some cases probation officers or restitution officers help juveniles find jobs so they can afford to make restitution payments.

The costs of victimization show the importance of restitution to victims. For 2003, the FBI reports that the average dollar value loss per robbery was $1,778; per burglary, $1,626; and per larceny-theft (e.g., shoplifting), $698. Even thefts of bicycles and coin-operated machines and purse snatching resulted in average losses of $247, $262, and $367, respectively (Federal Bureau of Investigation, 2004).

Although restitution has many positive features, especially concern for the victim, there are some problems. Some critics think that it is unfair to law-abiding juveniles to help law-breaking youths find jobs. From this viewpoint, job assistance seems like a reward for delinquency. Second, the claims made about the amounts of money paid back to victims are often exaggerated. Victims may be told that all of their losses will be recouped, but actual restitution often falls short. One study, for example, found that the percentage of youths paying all of the restitution ordered by the judge varied from 40 percent to 88 percent and that judges did not always order full restitution (Schneider and Schneider, 1984). Another study (of adults) found that 48 percent of the offenders ordered to pay restitution paid it in full, 35 percent paid some, and 17 percent paid none. More negatively, 41 percent paid either nothing or less than half of the restitution ordered in their case (Outlaw and Ruback, 1999). Third, restitution advocates often neglect to consider all of the costs involved in administering a restitution program, such as the salaries of those who oversee the program.

Some evaluation research on restitution has been promising. In one study, in two of four sites, about 10 percent fewer offenders sentenced to restitution recidivated than offenders not ordered to pay restitution (Schneider, 1986). Restitution also resulted in clear suppression effects. Those juveniles ordered to pay restitution had lower arrest rates in the year after their sentences compared to the year prior to their sentences (Schneider, 1990). A study of more than 7,000 cases handled informally and more than 6,000 cases placed on formal probation in Utah showed that "the use of restitution is associated with significant reductions in recidivism among certain juvenile offenders" (Butts and Snyder, 1992:4). In a New Hampshire program cited as a model program by the Office of Juvenile Justice and Delinquency Prevention, more than 80 percent of the offenders completed their community service and restitution obligations. The recidivism rate was below 30 percent (Allen, 1994). Restorative justice programs in general, however, do not appear to have recidivism rates significantly better or worse than traditional criminal justice programs (Kurki, 2000).

Some juveniles have been unable to pay restitution because they could not find jobs or because of family circumstances. To deal with such problems, Utah established a restitution workfund that allows juveniles to work in community service projects. Victims receive restitution from the state fund. Youths have cleaned buses, removed graffiti, cleaned up parks, and worked in public libraries (Kurlychek, Torbet, and Bozynski, 1999).

Community Service

Community service is similar to restitution. It means that offenders perform unpaid work for government or private agencies as payment for crimes without personal victims (e.g., vandalism of public property). Community service could include cutting grass at local parks, doing volunteer work in hospitals, or painting the clubhouse of a Boys Club. Advocates argue that community service helps delinquents realize the extent of the damage they have done and feel they have paid their debt to society. Proponents also argue that cost benefits result from the "free" labor of the youths. Critics argue that extensive use of community service could take away jobs from law-abiding citizens and that the actual cost benefits of community service are not as impressive as claimed. More specifically, critics contend that the work done is not always necessary (e.g., the clubhouse did not really need a new coat of paint) and that many of the hours of community service labor included such nonproductive activities as learning the job, work breaks and dawdling if an adult supervisor is not in constant watch over the work. These criticisms do not mean that restitution or community service is worthless but that claims about their worth should be realistic rather than exaggerated.

As noted in the earlier discussion of restorative justice, an important question is whether the community service is simply busy work or has some relationship to the delinquent's offense. If a delinquent can see the connection between his or her community service order and the harm he or she has done, or can see that the community service is a meaningful contribution to the community, he or she is then more likely to see the importance of such service. The offender is then more likely to learn something positive from the community service assignment rather than merely see it as a boring burden to finish as quickly as possible. Community service needs to be taken seriously by both the juvenile justice system and the juvenile so that it is a teaching tool and not just something to keep a youth busy for a few hours a week.

SUMMARY

Probation is under scrutiny. One author has gone so far as to state that in the 1990s probation faced a "crisis of legitimacy" (Corbett, 2002:175). By this Corbett meant that in light of the alarming statistics on juvenile violence at that time, many were questioning whether probation could do anything to stem the tide. Like all government programs, probation is under pressure to show results. Two well-researched studies, one on intensive probation and one on aftercare, showed no differences in recidivism, despite hopes that increased services in both programs would produce such differences. On the other hand, the research on Pennsylvania probation demonstrates that probation agencies can show that they are producing outcomes such as hours of community service, restitution dollars, and probationers being engaged in meaningful activities such as education. In addition, programs such as Boston's Operation Night Light offer statistics on homicide reduction that are at least compelling in a public relations sense, if not scientifically.

The future of probation will probably include stating desired outcomes, working on achieving those outcomes, and reporting statistics to demonstrate success for those outcomes. (See Box 11.6 for a contemporary mission statement for probation.) It is clear that probation and other community corrections efforts can state and produce a number of desirable outcomes and thus address demands that probation be accountable for demonstrating clear actions that have some levels of success. It will be interesting to see to what extent probation can blend its traditional emphasis on rehabilitation with current demands to show effective outcomes and to be "tough" on crime and delinquency.

The only safe prediction is that juvenile corrections will not be the same as it was 25 years ago. It is likely that changes will continue to multiply as society attempts to minimize youth crime.

Box 11.6   A Contemporary Vision Statement for Juvenile Probation

We envision the role of juvenile probation as that of a catalyst for developing safe communities and healthy youth and families. We believe we can fulfill this role by:

–holding offenders accountable,

–building and maintaining community-based partnerships,

–implementing result-based and outcome-driven services and practices,

–advocating for and addressing the needs of victims, offenders, families, and communities,

–obtaining and sustaining sufficient resources, and

–promoting growth and development of all juvenile probation professionals.

Source: P. Griffin and P. Torbet (2002). *Desktop Guide to Good Juvenile Probation Practice*. Pittsburgh: National Center for Juvenile Justice.

Discussion Questions

1. Many are calling for harsher punishment for juvenile offenders, especially violent juvenile offenders. Do you think that community corrections can supervise such offenders and protect the public? Will the public support community corrections for violent juvenile offenders?

2. Would you consider a career in juvenile corrections, either prisons or community corrections?

3. What measures should community corrections take to best serve juveniles? Give specific suggestions.

4. Should community corrections for juveniles go back to its roots and try to emphasize rehabilitation, or should it attempt to incorporate more punitive dimensions? Do advocates of restorative justice or the balanced approach have the answer to the question of how can we make juvenile probation better? What would the ideal probation program for juveniles look like?

5. Probation is placing increasingly more emphasis on outcomes and outcomes assessment. What are the positive implications of this emphasis? Are there any possible problems with greater attention to outcomes and outcomes assessment?

6. Where do you envision juvenile community corrections in 10 years? What will juvenile probation and aftercare look like a decade from now?

Chapter 12

Restorative Justice

INTRODUCTION

Bazemore and Maloney (1994) argue that restorative justice should be the theme in a new paradigm for criminal and juvenile justice in general and probation in particular. In contrast to the dominant theme of retributive justice, which focuses on vengeance, deterrence, and punishment, restorative justice "is concerned with repairing the damage or harm done to victims and the community through a process of negotiation, mediation, victim empowerment, and reparation" (Bazemore and Maloney, 1994:28). As one commentator puts it, "restorative justice is about relationships—how relationships are harmed by crime and how they can be rebuilt to promote recovery and healing for people affected by crime" (Kurki, 2000:266).

This chapter examines the idea of restorative justice as a means of addressing the needs of youthful offenders, victims, and the community. Restorative justice is a major shift from existing practices. Consequently, it is important to define and discuss the philosophical and practical differences between restorative justice and most juvenile justice system activity. This chapter also examines precursors to restorative justice that attempt to shift some problems out of the formal justice system as well as historical practices used by different cultural groups to handle

KEY TERMS

collective efficacy

community group conferencing (CGC)

conflict resolution

dispute resolution

exchange theory

family group conferencing (FGC)

neighborhood reparative boards (NRBs)

net-widening

peacemaking circles

peer mediation

reintegrative shaming

Reintegrative Shaming Experiments (RISE)

reparative justice

restorative justice

retributive justice

sentencing circles

social disorganization

victim–offender mediation (VOM)

social problems. These various efforts include victim–offender mediation, family-group conferencing, and circle sentencing. This chapter examines the emergence of these and other restorative justice alternatives for addressing the needs of offenders, victims, and the community.

BACKGROUND OF RESTORATIVE JUSTICE

Over the past 30 years there has been an increasing call for programs that pay more attention to the combined needs of victims, offenders, and the community. There is a recognition that juvenile justice processing of offenders is not effective at deterring crime and reducing victimization (McLaughlin et al., 2003). Consequently, there has been a growing demand for new methods of working with offenders. These apparent competing concerns (i.e., finding an alternative to the system for some offenses, assisting the victim, intervening with offenders, and addressing community needs) suggest that any new intervention needs to serve a broader audience. The concept of restorative or **reparative justice** seeks to use interventions that return the victim and offender to their pre-offense states. For offenders, it means assuring that the action will not be repeated. For victims, this means repairing the harm done. For the community, it means returning things to their state prior to the offensive behavior.

Discussions of restorative justice often begin with a comparison between this new idea and that of retributive justice. **Retributive justice** generally focuses on the lawbreaker and the imposition of sanctions for the purposes of deterrence, vengeance, and/or punishment. The formal criminal justice system operates primarily from a retributive justice approach. **Restorative justice** seeks to repair the harm that was done to both the victim and the community, while simultaneously changing the behavior of the offender. Figure 12.1 contrasts some of the basic assumptions underlying both retributive and restorative justice.

A major difference between retributive and restorative justice is the role of victims and the community in addressing the harm caused by the criminal/delinquent act. Under retributive justice, a criminal act is viewed as an offense against society or the state, and the victim is nothing more than a witness for the state. Zehr and Mika (2003:41) note that "crime is fundamentally a violation of people and interpersonal relationships." Restorative justice sees crime as an act against the victim and community, and the focus shifts from what is best for the state to repairing the harm that has been committed against the victim and community.

This shift in focus to the victim, community, and harm done means that the typical retributive response to crime of punishment and deterrence is no longer appropriate. Instead, restorative approaches seek to repair the harm done to the victim and community (Zehr and Mika, 2003). This requires a focus on the type of harm done and the desire of the victim and community for actions such as restitution and conciliation. The victim and community must be involved in the process in order to identify the harm and the appropriate responses desired by those victimized.

Figure 12.1   Assumptions of Retributive and Restorative Justice

Retributive Justice	Restorative Justice
Crime is an act against the State, a violation of a law, an abstract idea.	Crime is an act against another person or the community.
The criminal justice system controls crime.	Crime control lies primarily in the community.
Offender accountability defined as taking punishment.	Accountability defined as assuming responsibility and taking action to repair harm.
Crime is an individual act with individual responsibility.	Crime has both individual and social dimensions of responsibility.
Punishment is effective. a. Threat of punishment deters crime. b. Punishment changes behavior.	Punishment alone is not effective in changing behavior and is disruptive to community harmony and good relationships.
Victims are peripheral to the process.	Victims are central to the process of resolving crime.
The offender is defined by deficits.	The offender is defined by capacity to make reparations
Focus on establishing blame, on guilt, on past (did he/she do it?).	Focus on problem solving, on liabilities/obligations, on future (what should be done?).
Emphasis on adversarial relationship.	Emphasis on dialog and negotiation.
Imposition of pain to punish and deter/prevent.	Restitution as a means of restoring both parties; goal of reconciliation/restoration.
Community on sideline, represented abstractly by State.	Community as facilitator in restorative process.
Response focused on offenders's past behavior.	Response focused on harmful consequences of offender's behavior; emphasis on the future.
Dependence upon proxy professionals.	Direct involvement by participants.

Source: Adapted from G. Bazemore and M. Umbreit (1994), *Balanced and Restorative Justice: Program Models*. Washington, DC: Office of Juvenile Justice and Delinquency; and H. Zehr (1990), *Changing Lives: A New Focus for Crime and Justice*. Scottdale, PA: Herald Press.

The entire focus of restorative justice, however, is not on the victim and the community. There is also a belief that the offender is in need of assistance in recognizing the impact of his or her actions and identifying what needs to change in order to avoid such behavior in the future. Rather than focusing on punishment and deterrence as the major approach to dealing with the offender, restorative interventions seek to understand the causes of the behavior and eliminate those factors.

A quick review of the assumptions in Figure 12.1 demonstrates the centrality of the harm done to the victim and community and the need for the entire community, including the offender and victim, to participate in repairing the harm. The community, rather than the juvenile justice system alone, should shoulder the burden of dealing with crime (Nicholl, 1999). Braithwaite (2003) points out that restorative justice seeks to restore the victims, restore harmony in society, restore social support for all parties, and restore the offenders.

This is accomplished by bringing together a range of interested parties in a nonconfrontational setting, including the victim and the offender as well as family members or friends, criminal justice system personnel, and members of the general community. The participants, as a group, seek to understand the actions that led to the criminal or antisocial behavior, reveal the feelings and concerns of all parties, negotiate or mediate a solution agreeable to everyone, and assist in implementing that solution (Bazemore and Maloney, 1994). Kurki (2000:266) notes that "restorative justice is about relationships—how relationships are harmed by crime and how they can be rebuilt to promote recovery and healing for people affected by crime."

Precursors to Restorative Justice

The basic elements of restorative justice can be found throughout history. Braithwaite (1999:2) argues that: "Restorative justice has been the dominant model of criminal justice throughout most of human history for all the world's peoples." There was no formal criminal or juvenile justice system as we know it today throughout most of history. There were no authorities to turn to for help if an individual was victimized. Victims and their families were expected to take action themselves to address the problems and repair the harm from the offense. The earliest codified laws, such as the Law of Moses, the Code of Hammurabi, and Roman laws, all outlined the responsibility of individuals to deal with criminal acts committed against them. The development of formal justice systems, particularly the police and criminal courts, shifted the emphasis for taking redress from the victim to the state. It was at this point that the victim became little more than a witness for the state, and the response to crime and delinquency became punishment rather than addressing the harm that was inflicted.

Many restorative justice practices being used today, however, can be traced directly to historical traditions that have survived in indigenous cultures (Weitekamp, 1999). Of particular note are the practices of the Maori in New Zealand, the Aboriginal tribes in Australia, the Inuits in Alaska, and the First Nations tribes in Canada (Crawford and Newburn, 2003). While there is some debate over the degree to which restorative justice comes directly from the traditions of these groups (see Daly, 2002), there is little doubt that the ideas underlying restorative justice are not new in the last quarter century.

In many respects, it could be argued that the very bases for the development of a juvenile court and juvenile justice system are found in restorative justice principles. The *parens patriae* philosophy of the juvenile court focuses not on the offense but the offender and the actions needed to help the youth. The emphasis was not on punishment. Rather, the emphasis was on correcting the deficiencies in the family and community in order that the youth could lead a productive life, while at the same time making society safer. As seen in earlier chapters in this book, the juvenile justice system (at least according to its rhetoric) focuses on fixing problems for the offender and society.

Dispute Resolution

An immediate precursor to restorative justice, particularly in the United States, is dispute resolution or dispute mediation. One can trace modern dispute resolution back to the early 1970s. During this time, a number of jurisdictions started programs to divert minor disputes out of the formal court system. While many programs were adjuncts to prosecutor's offices and the judiciary, others were sponsored by outside groups or organizations. These initial programs provided an arena in which victims and offenders could meet and work out mutually agreeable solutions. The goal, of course, was to avoid going to court.

Dispute resolution is a mechanism for achieving a number of goals simultaneously. First, the parties involved in the situation work together to resolve the problem rather than having some outside authority impose a solution. Second, any dispute that reaches a settlement is one less case with which the formal justice system must contend. This alternative alleviates some congestion in the court system. Third, this informal approach empowers victims by giving them a direct voice in their own matters. Victims retain complete veto power over the final outcome. Finally, dispute resolution provides the victim with a face-to-face encounter with the offender. This meeting enables the victim to vent anger and seek understanding—something that many victims deeply desire.

The basic idea behind dispute resolution is to bring opposing parties together in an attempt to work out a mutually agreeable solution. While dispute resolution programs can vary in terms of the cases they handle or the procedures they use, they typically share five traits in common (Garofalo and Connelly, 1980):

1.   A third-party mediator is involved.

2.   Disputants usually know each other.

3.   Participation must be voluntary.

4. Processes are informal.

5. Disputants are usually referred to the process by someone in the criminal justice system.

First, these programs involve a third-party mediator who monitors participant interaction. This arbitrator keeps the discussion focused and makes suggestions whenever the need arises. Most mediators are volunteers who are not affiliated with the formal justice system. Because of this independence, some people refer to these programs as "neighborhood dispute resolution."

A second characteristic is that many disputants have known each other over a period of time. Often, they are neighbors, friends, or family members (although store owners and customers can utilize such a program). This familiarity can be helpful when trying to forge a compromise. It can also be a challenge because the dispute may be the result of a long-term issue or problem that may not be amenable to a short-term intervention.

Third, most programs insist that participation be completely voluntary. Both disputants must agree to handle the problem through the program. If either party declines to take part, the dispute moves back to the realm of more formal legal action.

Fourth, the actual resolution of a dispute follows a very informal process. Rules of evidence are not enforced, and attorneys are not allowed to attend these sessions. Instead, the process calls for discussion rather than rigid fact-finding. As one might expect, the mediator has a free hand to conduct each meeting as he or she sees fit.

The fifth and final common aspect is that most disputants enroll in the program after being referred to it by a member of the criminal justice system. Most often, the prosecutor has reviewed the case and decided that the interests of justice can be better served in a nontraditional manner.

The approach of dispute resolution programs appeals to a diverse audience. Consequently, they garner support from many corners and have spread rapidly. Prosecutors and judges welcome the chance to reduce overcrowded dockets, and victim advocates see a tremendous potential to help their clients. More than 80 United States cities had dispute resolution programs in place in 1980, with roughly 4,000 trained mediators (Ray, Kestner, and Freedman, 1986). Six years later, that number swelled to 350 programs with 20,000 mediators (Ray, Kestner, and Freedman, 1986). Its popularity is evident in the proliferation of similar arrangements now operating in Canada, Great Britain, Australia, Denmark, Finland, Germany, and many other countries (Umbreit, 1997).

The types of cases found in dispute resolution take a variety of forms. Interpersonal disputes between family members and friends comprise a large portion of the cases brought to mediation. Domestic disputes, harassment, neighborhood nuisances, and landlord/tenant problems make up the bulk of the disputes. Merchant/customer disputes are more evident in programs that rely heavily on prosecutor's offices for referral. Mediation with juveniles is an attempt to keep the youth out of the formal system and eliminate the negative consequences of formal processing (Veevers, 1989).

Dispute resolution and similar programs also appear in a variety of forms in school settings. **Peer mediation** programs bring together disputing parties with a peer mediator to discuss the situation and attempt to resolve the dispute to the satisfaction of both parties. In many cases, there is no clear victim and offender. Instead, the two parties are involved in an argument or disagreement that, left unchecked, could escalate into a physical confrontation. The goal of the mediation is to defuse the situation before it reaches that stage and to keep it from occurring again in the future. Many schools have instituted **conflict resolution** programs and training. While peer mediation may be included in these programs, the most important element of conflict resolution in schools is teaching youths alternative methods for resolving conflicts before they occur. These programs are addressed in more detail in Chapter 13.

The Theoretical Basis of Restorative Practices

The basic argument underlying restorative justice is that reactions to crime and harmful behavior should seek to repair the harm done to the individual and society while simultaneously reintegrating and addressing the needs of the offender. Van Ness and Strong (2002) propose three basic principles inherent in restorative justice:

- Repairing harm (to victim and community)

- Engendering stakeholder involvement (victims, offenders, families, and community)

- Transforming the role of community and government

Within these principles are a variety of more specific goals or dimensions, such as making amends, building relationships, exchanging ideas, and taking ownership of community problems (Bazemore and Schiff, 2005). A number of different theories may be used to underscore the tenets of restorative justice.

The explanation most often proffered is Braithwaite's (1989) reintegrative shaming. **Reintegrative shaming** rests on the assumption that typical processing of offenders through the criminal justice system serves to isolate the offender and stigmatize him or her. This action marginalizes the offender (even more than he or she may already be in society). In addition, it does nothing to correct the behavior or repair the harm done to the victim. Basically, typical system processing serves only to exact a punishment (retribution) for the criminal act.

The underlying premise of Braithwaite's (1989) theory is that shame can be used in a positive fashion to bring the offender back into society. Under reintegrative shaming, the system needs to express its disapproval of the criminal activity while simultaneously forgiving the offender for the action if the offender is willing to learn from the event and make reparations to the victim and society. The key is "reintegration," rather than "stigmatization" (Braithwaite, 1989). The ability to employ reintegrative shaming effectively rests on shifting the sole focus of societal response from the offender to a shared focus on the offending behavior, social disapproval (often by family, friends, and significant others), the needs of the victim and community, and a shared response to make things better (Harris, 2003).

A second theoretical explanation involves exchange theory. **Exchange theory** proceeds from the assumption that equal reciprocity is a cornerstone of social interaction. Parties to a confrontation (such as an offense and subsequent restorative justice program) are looking to establish a balance in the relationship. The offender is expected to make amends for the harm caused, in exchange for reintegration back into society (Bazemore and Schiff, 2005). Under the retributive system of justice, the offender is punished and, while this may be accepted by the victim and community as payment, the punishment can be seen as harmful in itself and not appropriate for truly repairing the harm and ensuring that the problem does not occur again. Bazemore and Schiff (2005) argue that the offender needs to actually make amends in order to be accepted back into society by the victim and the community.

A third theoretical perspective in restorative justice involves the need to develop community resources to address social problems. Many communities display a level of **social disorganization** that mitigates the ability of residents to effect change and control in the area. Restorative justice offers a mechanism to build the social capital necessary to address youthful offenders and the causes of misbehavior (Bazemore and Schiff, 2005). Bazemore and Schiff suggest the need to transform communities into active participants in controlling problem youths and socialize them into proper societal roles. Community members need to feel empowered to do something about problems, that is, they need **collective efficacy**.

It should be apparent that principles of restorative justice rest on a wide array of theories and theoretical perspectives. This is attributable to the fact that restorative justice seeks to do more than just punish offenders, assist victims, or control the community. Instead, it offers opportunities to do all of these things simultaneously, as well as accomplish other related tasks.

TYPES OF RESTORATIVE JUSTICE

Restorative justice takes a variety of different forms, although they all attend to the same basic tenets. Indeed, "restorative justice" is often referred to as "transformative justice," "social justice," "balanced and restorative justice," "peacemaking," or other terms. Braithwaite (2002) notes that many of these terms and programs have been incorporated into the more general idea of restorative justice.

Harris (2003) proposes a model by which to evaluate restorative justice practices (see Figure 12.2). Beyond its use for evaluation, the model contains six aims for any restorative justice program. The four primary aims are:

- Empowerment
- Restoration
- Reintegration
- Emotional and social healing

Empowerment reflects the need for all interested parties to be involved in the process. This provides a sense of legitimacy for both the victim and the offender. *Restoration* simply refers to repairing the harm done to all participants. At the same time, retribution is disavowed as a legitimate response to the behavior. Restorative justice also seeks to *reintegrate* both the offender and the victim into the community, without the stigma of being an offender or being different from the other community members. Finally, there is a clear need to address the *emotional harm* that accompanies the behavior.

Figure 12.2   A Model for Evaluating Restorative Practices

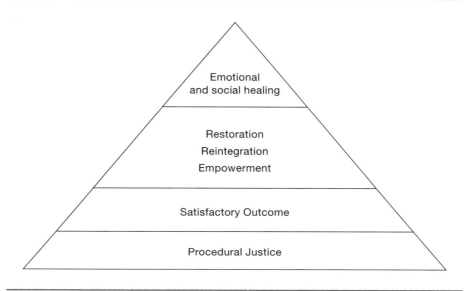

Source: N. Harris (2003). "Evaluating the Practice of Restorative Justice: The Case of Family Group Conferencing." In L. Walgrave (ed.), *Repositioning Restorative Justice*. Portland, OR: Willan.

Achieving these primary aims requires that the restorative approach be grounded on two additional factors:

- Procedural fairness
- Satisfactory outcome

Procedural fairness refers to the fact that the process must respect all the parties involved. The rights (both legal and human) and wishes of all participants must be recognized as legitimate by the participants. There must also be a *satisfactory outcome* reached. This means that all parties agree with the proposed resolution and are willing to follow through with the plan of action. The failure to achieve procedural fairness and a satisfactory outcome from the process itself will make it impossible to fully realize the major aims of restorative justice (Harris, 2003).

Bazemore and Schiff (2005) outline a variety of objectives/foci addressed by different restorative justice processes. As can be seen in Table 12.1, restorative justice seeks to achieve multiple aims, ranging from preventing offending to repairing harm to providing a voice for victims in the formal justice system to rehabilitating the offender. These goals can be realized through various practices and programs located throughout the community and the formal justice system.

Table 12.1   Restorative Justice Objectives, Practice, and Typical Location

Objective/Focus	Practice	Typical Location/Use
Prevention, peace-making, youth development, community building, family and school discipline	School and neighborhood conferencing, youth development circles, victim awareness education, restorative discipline family support and discussion groups	Schools, neighborhoods, churches, civic groups
Provide decision-making alternative to formal court or other adversarial process for determining obligations for repairing harm	Victim-offender dialogue, family group conferencing, circles, neighborhood accountability boards, other restorative conferencing approaches	Police and community diversion, court diversion, dispositional/sentencing alternatives, post-dispositional planning, residential alternative discipline, conflict resolution, post-residential reentry
Victim and community input to court or formal decision-making	Written or oral impact statement to court or other entity	Court, probation, residential facilities
Provide reparative sanctions or obligation in response to crime or harmful behavior	Restitution, restorative community service, service to victims, service for surrogate victims, payment to victim service funds	Diversion, court sanction, probation condition, residential program, reentry
Offender treatment/rehabilitation/education	Victim impact panels, victim awareness education, drunk driving panels, community service learning projects	Probation, residential facilities, diversion program, jails
Victim services and support groups	Volunteer support groups, faith community groups, counseling	Multiple settings
Reentry	Reentry conferences, support circles, restorative community service	Neighborhood and community

Source: G. Bazemore and M. Schiff (2005). *Juvenile Justice Reform and Restorative Justice: Building Theory and Policy from Practice.* Portland, OR: Willan, p. 31. Reprinted with permission.

The degree to which restorative justice programs achieve the results outlined above can vary greatly. Indeed, the diversity in restorative programs can be seen in the extent to which they address the different goals for the varied participants in the restorative process. Figure 12.3 presents a graphic depiction of the types of restorative justice programs and the degree to which they can be considered fully restorative.

Figure 12.3   Types and Degrees of Restorative Justice Practice

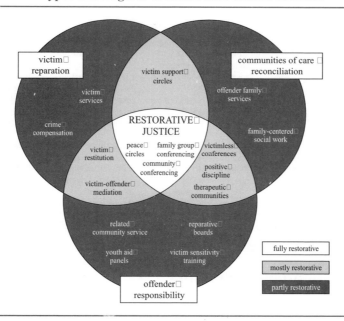

Source: P. McCold and T. Wachtel (2002). "Restorative Justice Theory Validation." In E.M. Weitekamp and H. Kerner (eds.), *Restorative Justice: Theoretical Foundations*. Portland, OR: Willan. Reprinted with permission.

The restorative practices typology represents an intersection of three different dimensions—a victim reparation orientation, an offender responsibility focus, and a communities of care domain—all indicated by a separate circle. Each of these dimensions contributes something to address crime and victimization, although each dimension alone offers only limited restoration. Victim reparation, for example, focuses exclusively on the needs of the immediate crime victim through things like victim compensation and victim services, and excludes concerns for the community or the offender. Similarly, the offender responsibility dimension relates to activities that help the offender understand his or her actions and take responsibility. The intersection of different dimensions brings about greater restoration, with the greatest level of restoration occurring where all three dimensions overlap.

Four broad types of restorative conferencing are victim–offender mediation, family group conferencing, neighborhood reparative boards, and peacemaking/sentencing circles. Each of these approach restorative justice in slightly different ways using the involvement of different individuals and groups (see Table 12.2).

Table 12.2   **Restorative Conferencing Models Administration and Process**

	Victim–offender mediation	Family group conferencing	Neighborhood board	Peacemaking circles
Who normally participates	Mediator, victim, offender (family)	Facilitator, offender family (victim)	Board chair, volunteers, offender, family (victim)	Keeper, offender, volunteers, family, victim and offender supporters
Common permanent structure/staffing	Program coordinator, volunteer mediators (some paid mediators)	Program coordinator, facilitator (volunteers)	Coordinator, volunteer board chair, volunteer board members	Coordinator, volunteer circle members
Facilitation and dominant process	Victims option to speak first; mediator facilitates open-ended dialogue with minimal interference	In most programs facilitator follows script or outline in which offender speaks first, followed by victim and other participants; seeks to move process through phases	Board chair initiates member deliberation after questioning offender and parents, though some variation emerging toward circle or family group conferencing process	Keeper opens session and closes session, person allowed to speak when talking piece is passed to them. Shared leadership and consensus decision-making
Dominant philosophy	Meeting victim and offender needs, healing dialogue as transformative	Family group as essential problem-solver. Respectful, normative, disapproval with support; offender empathy and emotion key	Neighborhood social support and community norm affirmation; neighborhood problem-solving focus	Collective healing; community focus; broad problem-solving, community building focus beyond individual offense

Source: G. Bazemore and M. Schiff (2005). *Juvenile Justice Reform and Restorative Justice: Building Theory and Policy from Practice*. Portland, OR: Willan, p. 38. Reprinted with permission.

Victim–Offender Mediation

Victim–offender mediation (VOM), also referred to as victim-offender reconciliation programs (VORP), is a direct outgrowth of the early dispute resolution/dispute mediation programs of the early 1970s and is considered the oldest form of restorative justice (Umbreit, 1999). The first documented VOM program was one run by the Mennonites in Kitchener, Ontario, Canada, in 1973. VOM is typically a post-conviction process (although pre-conviction programs exist) in which the victim and the offender are brought together to discuss a wide range of issues. A trained mediator attends these meetings.

The basic premise of VOM is that the criminal incident and its consequences are complex and beyond the ability of the criminal code to address on its own (Nichol, 1999). Where the formal criminal justice response to crime is to simply impose the sanction outlined in the statutes, VOM seeks to deal with the needs of both the victim and the offender. Perhaps the most important concern addressed in the VOM meetings is to identify for the offender the types and level of harm suffered by the victim as a result of the crime. The victim is given the opportunity to express his or her concerns about the crime and his or her loss. At the same time, the offender is given the chance to explain why he or she committed the act and the circumstances that may underlie the behavior.

The aim of this discussion is for the two parties to gain an understanding of the other person as a starting point for identifying a response to the event. The focus of the meetings is on repairing the harm done to the victim, helping the victim heal (both physically and emotionally), restoring the community to the pre-crime state, and reintegrating the offender into society (Umbreit et al., 2003). Among the potential tangible outcomes for the victim may be the offender making monetary restitution or providing service to repair the harm done. Perhaps of equal importance are changes in behavior and attitude on the part of the offender.

Participation in VOM is voluntary for the victim, but the offender may be required by the court to participate as a part of the court process (Umbreit, 1999). Some programs allow for mediation to occur without the need for a face-to-face meeting between the victim and offender. This typically takes place only when the victim desires to participate in mediation but is reluctant to have any further direct contact with the offender.

Victim–offender mediation programs may be a part of the formal criminal justice system or may be run by other agencies that are not directly connected to the system. In some jurisdictions, mediation may be ordered by the judge in lieu of formal sentencing. A successful mediation may mean that the original conviction is vacated or expunged. On the other hand, the failure of an offender to participate in mediation or the failure of the mediation to reach an agreeable resolution may result in the offender being returned to the court for formal sentencing.

Family Group Conferencing

Family group conferencing (FGC) finds its roots in indigenous practices of the Maori in New Zealand. Family group conferencing came to prominence in 1989 when New Zealand, responding to the increasing number of Maori youths being handled in the formal justice system, passed the Children, Young Persons and Their Families Act (Crawford and Newburn, 2003). This Act removed all youths, ages 14-17 (with only a few exceptions for very serious offenders) from formal court processing and mandated that they be diverted to family group conferencing (Kurki, 2000). Since its inception in 1989, FGC has spread to Australia, the United States, Europe, and other countries.

The greatest difference between FGC and VOM is the inclusion of family members, close friends, and other support groups of the victim and offender in the conferences. There is also the possibility of including criminal justice system personnel, including social workers, police officers, and an offender's attorney (Van Ness and Strong, 2002). The basic ideas of FGC were adapted by the police in Wagga-Wagga, Australia, in 1991 into a process known as **community group conferencing (CGC)** (McCold, 2003). One main difference between FGC and CGC is the possible inclusion of a broader set of support groups and community members to the conference (McCold, 2003). Figure 12.4 graphically depicts the potential involvement of different individuals and support groups in FGC and CGC. The expansion of participants from the victim, offender, and mediator in VOM to support persons and community representatives is very important in a variety of ways.

Figure 12.4   Parties Involved in Conferencing

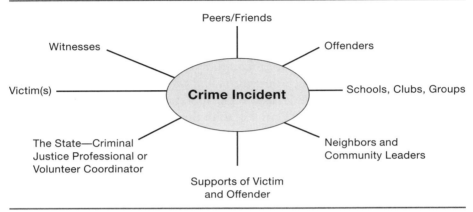

Source: C.G. Nichol (1999). *Community Policing, Community Justice, and Restorative Justice: Exploring the Links for the Delivery of a Balanced Approach to Public Safety.* Washington, DC: Office of Community Oriented Policing Services.

Another difference between FGC and VOM is the absence of a mediator who participates in constructing a resolution to the issues. Instead, FGCs are led by a trained facilitator who serves in various roles. Most often the facilitator will make contact with all participants prior to the conference. At that time he or she will explain the process and the role of each individual. The facilitator will also emphasize the fact that the conference should conclude with a resolution to which all parties are in agreement.

Once the conference begins, the facilitator leads the participants through a discussion of the facts of the case, the impact of the victimization on the parties, the feelings of all participants toward the action and the offender, and the development of a mutually agreed-upon resolution (Nicholl, 1999). The families and support persons are very important to this process. They are expected to voice their feelings about the harm that was committed, their concern for the victim of the crime, their disappointment about the offender's behavior, and their suggestions for how to resolve the problem. Of great importance is that the support groups are expected to take some responsibility in monitoring the offender and making certain that any agreements are carried out after the conference (Kurki, 2000). Conferences can be held either pretrial or post-trial, and have become a part of police and pretrial diversion programs in many countries (McGarrell et al., 2000; Moore and O'Connell, 1994).

Neighborhood Reparative Boards

Neighborhood reparative boards (NRBs), or neighborhood account-ability boards, have existed since the mid-1990s and typically deal with non-violent youthful offenders. Not unlike other restorative practices, NRBs seek to restore the victims and community to pre-offense states, require the offender to make amends, and aid the offender in understanding the impact of his or her actions on the victim and community. Cases are referred to the boards by the court, most often prior to formal adjudication.

Despite the philosophical similarities between NRBs and other types of restorative conferencing, there are several key differences in how this approach operates. First, victims are not required to participate. Indeed, many early boards frowned on victim participation (Strickland, 2004), although vic-tim participation is becoming more common. Second, while the confer-ences are often open to the public, actual participation is limited by the board and who they wish to interview. The board questions the offenders and examines statements made by members of the offender's family and others knowledgeable about the event (Bazemore and Umbreit, 2001). Third, the boards are composed of a small group of citizens who have been specially trained in conducting hearings and constructing appropriate sanctions.

At the conclusion of the hearing, the board undertakes private deliber-ations and outlines a suggested set of actions to be followed by the offender. If the offender agrees with the plan, the board oversees the offender's com-pliance with the terms and reports to the court about the success or failure of the offender (Bazemore and Umbreit, 2001). Typical conditions of agree-ments include restitution, apologies, and community service (Karp, 2001).

Peacemaking and Sentencing Circles

The final type of restorative justice program to be discussed is peace-making and sentencing circles. **Peacemaking circles** are based on Canadian First Nation practices and began formal operation in the early 1990s. Cir-cles invite members from across the community to participate in deter-mining the appropriate sanctions for offenders (Van Ness and Strong, 2002). As a sentencing procedure, this process typically occurs after a case is concluded and the offender is found guilty in court. Participants in circles typically include all of the parties found in FGCs, as well as general com-munity members who wish to be included.

Sentencing circles may function as either a part of the court or separate from the court. In many jurisdictions, this sentencing alternative is used at the discretion of the trial judge and is not provided for under any statutory authority (Crawford and Newburn, 2003). Most cases handled by sentenc-ing circles involve minor offenses, although some programs will consider more serious crimes (Stuart, 1996). Because of the fact that this process takes place post-conviction and can include a wide array of participants, circles normally require a great deal of preparation before they actually convene (Kurki, 2000).

A facilitator is responsible for meeting with all participating parties prior to the actual circle. These meetings are used to explain the process, outline the facts of the case for those who have more limited knowledge, answer any questions the parties may have, and make plans for the actual meeting. In many cases the offender will work on an initial plan to address the harms he or she committed, which will be presented when the circle meets (Nicholl, 1999). This extensive preparation may mean that the circle takes place months after the crime occurred and the court case concluded.

Every participant in the sentencing circle is given the opportunity to speak, express his or her feelings about the crime, and offer opinions and rationales about the outcome of the discussion. The intended outcome of the circle is consensus on a plan of action that may include a wide array of activities. Plans of action may include further meetings between the victim and offender, apologies by the offender, restitution, community service, treatment/rehabilitation programs (such as counseling or drug/alcohol treatment), and/or explicit sentencing recommendations to the trial judge (Nicholl, 1999; Van Ness and Strong, 2002), including possible jail or prison time (Stuart, 1996). The decision of the circles is often binding on the offender (and may be specifically incorporated into the official court record), and a failure to adhere to the decision may result in further criminal justice system processing or being returned to the circle (Van Ness and Strong, 2002).

Beyond the reparative plan for the offender, sentencing circles are meant to bring about action by all parties to the crime. The victim is supposed to receive support and be an active participant in healing himself or herself. The community's role is to identify the factors that lead to the offending behavior and seek ways to eliminate those problems. These causal factors may be specific to the individual offender (such as lack of parental supervision or underage alcohol use) or may be larger social-structural issues (such as unemployment or the presence of gangs in the community).

Summary

While each of the forms of restorative justice take a slightly different approach to repairing the harm done by the criminal act, all are considered restorative because they seek to address the needs of the victim, the offender, and the community. The various approaches (outlined in Figure 12.2) bring about restoration by attempting to build understanding between the parties, identifying the factors at work in the behavior, and arriving at a plan of action that is agreed to by all parties. The extent to which these restorative justice programs are successful is addressed next.

The Impact of Restorative Justice

Restorative justice programs are intended to have a number of different possible outcomes, including rehabilitating the offender and repairing the harm done to the victim. Assessing the impact of the interventions, however, is more difficult to do. Many evaluations focus on victim and offender satisfaction with the process and the level of compliance or completion of the agreed-upon settlement. Less common are analyses of the impact of the programs on subsequent offending by the offender.

Satisfaction, Fairness, and Compliance

Assessments of the impact of restorative justice have most often relied on outcomes such as victim satisfaction, feelings of fairness by victims, and compliance with the agreements. With very few exceptions, participants express satisfaction with the restorative process in which they have participated (Braithwaite, 1999). This is true of VOM, FGC, and circle sentencing. Evaluations of VOM typically reveal that between 75 and 100 percent of the participants express satisfaction with the mediation (Kurki, 2000). Similarly high levels of satisfaction arise from FGCs (Bazemore and Umbreit, 2001; Moore and O'Connell, 1994; Umbreit et al., 2003). The level of satisfaction is also reflected in feelings by participants that the process is fair (McCold, 2003; McGarrell et al., 2000; Umbreit, 1999; Umbreit and Coates, 1992; Umbreit et al., 2003). These results contrast greatly with those found in analyses of formal criminal justice system processing, in which victims and offenders report lower satisfaction and feelings of fairness.

An important caveat when considering whether a type of program is effective is that not all projects are implemented with the same degree of success. Some attempts to establish a restorative justice program may be more successful than others. Given this fact, outcomes may also vary from one evaluation to another. Attempting to address this problem, McCold and Wachtel (2002) rated restorative justice programs according to the degree to which they were fully restorative, mostly restorative, or not restorative. They then looked at reports of satisfaction and fairness by victims and offenders. Their results are very illuminating. In general, participants in fully restorative programs report higher levels of satisfaction and perceived fairness, followed by those in mostly restorative programs. Individuals from programs rated as not restorative report the lowest levels of satisfaction and fairness (McCold and Wachtel, 2002).

The success of restorative justice programs is also measured in terms of the ability of the meetings to achieve consensus on a solution and whether the parties carry through with the agreement. Again, there is evidence that most meetings culminate in an agreement and most parties comply with the settlement (Braithwaite, 1999; Kurki, 2000; Schiff, 1999; Umbreit and

Coates, 1993). Restitution is a common component of many agreements, and evaluations reveal that 90 percent or more of the offenders in FGC comply with the ordered restitution (Wachtel, 1995). McGarrell and colleagues (2000) note that participants in a conferencing program completed the program at a significantly higher rate than normal diversion clients.

This information on satisfaction and compliance must be tempered somewhat by the fact that participation in the programs is voluntary. The fact that a program is voluntary may mean that only those individuals who are more amenable to the process to begin with are included in the programs. There may be a built-in bias in favor of positive results. Umbreit and colleagues (2003), for example, point out that only 40 to 60 percent of the victims and offenders who are asked to participate in VOM agree to do so. McCold and Wachtel (1998) report that almost 60 percent of the cases never materialize due to a refusal to participate. Similarly, an analysis of youth conferencing panels in England and Wales finds that only 20 percent of the victims participate (Crawford and Newburn, 2003). There is no way of knowing if positive results are actually a function of the willingness to participate and effect change, rather than of the program itself.

Recidivism

Reducing reoffending is an important restorative goal, particularly in a discussion of juvenile justice. Unfortunately, there is relatively little research on offender recidivism found in the restorative justice literature. There is some evidence, however, that restorative justice programs are able to reduce the level of subsequent offending. In addition, there is a greater emphasis being placed on assessing the impact of restorative justice programming on recidivism.

Most evaluations of recidivism have appeared in relation to VOM programs. Umbreit and Coates (1993), comparing youths who participated in VOM to those undergoing typical juvenile justice processing in three states, report significantly less recidivism on behalf of the VOM sample. In their analysis of restorative justice conferences for youths in Indianapolis, McGarrell and associates (2000) report a 40 percent reduction in recidivism for the program youths, compared to those undergoing normal system processing. Umbreit and colleagues (2001) provide evidence that youths completing VOM projects in two Oregon counties reduced their offending by at least 68 percent in the year after program participation compared to the year before the intervention. Finally, Nugent and associates (1999) note that both the level of reoffending and the seriousness of subsequent offenses is lower for youths who enter and complete VOM programs.

Examinations of recidivism from conferencing are less common, although those that do exist provide some positive assessments. Daly (2003), examining juvenile conferencing in South Australia, finds significantly less recidivism by participants in the conferences. This is particularly true for conferences that are rated as highly restorative. Similarly, Hayes and Daly (2004) uncover reduced recidivism levels after conferencing. The results are strongest for first-time offenders who are participating in the programs. The results also vary by other characteristics of the offenders, suggesting that conferencing is not equally effective with all individuals and cases (Hayes and Daly, 2004). Hayes and Daly (2003) note that reductions in recidivism are strongly related to the ability of a conference to achieve a genuine consensus on a plan of action. Finally, Rodriguez (2005) reports reduced recidivism from FGC, particularly for older offenders and cases involving property crimes.

Discrepant recidivism results appeared in the **Reintegrative Shaming Experiments (RISE)** conducted in Australia. Sherman and Strang (2003) examined the impact of RISE on victims and offenders involved in drunk driving, juvenile property offenses, juvenile shoplifting, and violent youth-

ful offenses. The authors found that conferences reduced recidivism among violent youths by 38 percent. Conversely, there was no impact on either shoplifting or property offenses. Analysis of drunk driving reveals some promising results, but the low number of crimes makes it difficult to evaluate any changes adequately (Sherman and Strang, 2000). Finally, the authors report that the impact of RISE varies across facilitators, suggesting that the training and preparation of these individuals is key to successful conferencing (Sherman and Strang, 2003).

While positive results on recidivism appear in several analyses, a great deal of additional research is needed on the impact of restorative justice programs. This is especially true for FGC and peacemaking circle programs, which have not undergone as extensive evaluations as VOM. There remains a need to identify and understand the conditions under which different restorative justice programs work and do not work (Braithwaite, 2002).

A detainee in the Florida Parishes Juvenile Detention Center works in the center's garden in Goodbee, Louisiana. Detainees are giving back to the community by harvesting the produce and donating it to a local food pantry. Juvenile detainees are experiencing restorative justice with programs that teach new skills and encourage them to give back to the community.

AP Photo/Daily Star, Kari Wheeler

Problems and Issues with Restorative Justice

Despite the growing popularity of restorative justice approaches, there are a number of problems and concerns that remain unanswered. Figure 12.5 presents a number of concerns with restorative justice. Because a full discussion of critical issues is available elsewhere (see Ashworth, 2003; Feld, 1999; Kurki, 2000), only a few of the major concerns are presented here.

One problem is that restorative justice programs may be too ambitious in their attempt to solve very complex societal problems (Kurki, 2000). Simply gathering common citizens together to talk about a problem and brainstorm possible solutions is only the beginning of a much more complex process to address major social forces that may cause crime. Many problems involve long-standing interpersonal disputes that may not be amenable to simple mediation or conferencing.

Figure 12.5   Key Concerns with Restorative Justice

Lack of Victim Participation
Emphasis on Shaming and Not Enough on Reintegration/Reconciliation
Inadequate Preparation
Inability to Engender Participation
Problems with Identifying Appropriate Participants
Problems Recruiting Representative Panels
Coercive Participation (particularly coercion of offenders)
Net-Widening
Inadequate Screening of Cases
Inability of Participants (e.g. Families, Communities) to Meaningfully Contribute
Lack of Neutrality by Participants and/or Facilitator
Inability to Address Serious Violent Crimes
Inability to Address Long-Standing Interpersonal Disputes
Too Victim-Oriented
Inability to Protect Constitutional Rights of Offenders

A second concern, related to the first, is that restorative justice has been used primarily with less serious and property crimes. There is a great deal of debate over whether this approach can be used successfully with serious violent offenses (see Bannenberg and Rössner, 2003). This is especially true when offenses such as spouse abuse, sexual assault, aggravated assault, murder, and others are considered. While few programs have directly assessed this question, there is some evidence that restorative justice can be used in more serious personal crime cases. For example, Umbreit and colleagues (2003) report success using VOM with murderers and the families of their victims. Corrado, Cohen, and Odgers (2003) also find positive results (mostly in terms of satisfaction) for a VOM program dealing with serious and violent offenses in British Columbia, Canada. The strongest finding in these studies is the need for very lengthy and extensive preparation prior to the intervention. Despite the fact that most cases involve more minor offenses, Bazemore and Schiff's (2005) survey of juvenile conferencing programs in the United States reveals that a significant percent of programs accept serious personal crimes for settlement (see Table 12.3).

Third, there exists a concern that, while voluntary, there is an underlying level of coercion in most programs. What makes this truly problematic is that many programs do not allow (or at least frown upon) the presence of defense attorneys, thus raising the issue of an accused's constitutional rights and procedural safeguards (Feld, 1999; Levrant et al., 1999). In some

Table 12.3   **Charges Accepted by Type of Restorative Conferencing Program (percentages)**

Charges	VOM/D	Multiple Practice	Circle	FGC	Board	Total
Minor assault	79.3	81.8	100.0	67.6	91.7	78.8
Property damage	76.9	77.3	83.3	70.3	61.5	74.5
Personal theft	70.4	81.8	50.0	73.0	92.3	73.1
Business theft	51.9	59.1	33.3	73.0	76.9	59.5
Breaking and entering	41.8	86.4	66.7	45.9	61.5	51.9
Vandalism	50.0	59.1	33.3	48.6	61.5	51.6
Serious assault	40.7	45.5	66.7	29.7	23.1	38.8
Minor drug	14.6	18.2	33.3	32.4	52.8	23.6
Domestic violence	23.1	21.7	33.3	12.8	21.4	21.3
Serious drug	4.9	4.5	16.7	13.5	7.7	8.1
Other*	44.4	36.4	33.3	64.9	23.1	45.6

*Other charges include arson, harassment, loitering, alcohol, behavior issues, auto theft, bomb threat, disorderly conduct, DUI, forgery, weapons, menacing, trespass, possession of stolen property, and various other charges and combination of charges.

Source: G. Bazemore and M. Schiff (2005). *Juvenile Justice Reform and Restorative Justice: Building Theory and Policy from Practice*. Portland, OR: Willan, p. 112. Reprinted with permission.

instances, the participation of the offender is actually coerced by the fact that he or she is required to participate under threat of being processed in court. Compounding this problem is the need for the offender to admit to the act during the process. This is especially problematic if the intervention is taking place pre-adjudication.

A fourth concern with restorative justice is over how the "community" is defined and who is allowed to represent the community (Kurki, 2000). This can be a very important concern because the participants help mold the outcome and the expectations for the solution. The participants can bring a wide array of differing expectations. This may not be a problem in smaller, more homogeneous communities, such as Maori or Native American communities, but it can certainly be problematic in large, diverse cities.

Fifth, Feld (1999) notes that there is a distinct imbalance of power in most restorative justice programs. This is especially problematic when juvenile offenders must face not only the victim but also the victim's support groups, members of the criminal justice system, and strangers from the general community. The power differential must be a prime consideration in meetings.

A sixth area of concern deals with the issue of net-widening. **Net-widening** refers to the situation in which the introduction of a new program or intervention serves to bring more people under the umbrella of social control. This is especially problematic when the new programs are intended to take people currently being served in the formal justice system in order to divert them to the new program. The expectation is that the new programs will relieve some of the burden from the formal system while simultaneously offering a better response to the problems. It is not clear the extent to which restorative justice has resulted in net-widening, but there is a legitimate concern that this has occurred.

Despite these and other concerns, restorative justice is receiving a great deal of increased attention. Within a relatively short time frame, restorative programming has spread to countries around the world and is being used with a wide array of problems and events. While used most commonly with youthful offenders and property or minor offenses, advocates are working to include serious and violent acts under the umbrella of restorative justice programming. The increased interest in restorative justice is evident in the proposal made by the Commission on Crime Prevention and Criminal Justice of the United Nation's Economic and Social Council in 2002. This proposal recommends that restorative justice practices be used whenever feasible and sets forth guidelines on that use.

Summary

Restorative justice programs offer another method for handling youths after an offense has occurred. The intent of these programs is multifaceted. The programs attempt to repair the more general harm that has been done to both the victim and the larger community. Equally important is rehabilitating the offender so that he or she does not commit future offenses. There is also a desire to build the community's capacity to address social issues before or as they emerge.

Restorative justice involves various constituencies (Bazemore and Umbreit, 2001; Umbreit, 1997; Van Ness, 1990; Van Ness and Strong, 2002). Under this approach, victims are compensated through restitution, are given a voice in the case handling, and become an integral part of the treatment or intervention provided to the offender. The offender is held accountable for his or her transgressions and may be subjected to a wide array of possible interventions.

The restorative justice model is also very attractive for juvenile justice because it offers a plausible alternative to the get-tough paranoia that is currently popular. It focuses on the victim as well as the offender and the community. It seeks to make the offender more competent and productive in an effort to bond the offender more closely to the community. Finally, the public has a more favorable attitude about such programs with juvenile rather than adult offenders (see Chapter 14 for more details).

Discussion Questions

1. Restorative justice programs are appearing throughout the United States. Do you think this approach is the most appropriate direction for the juvenile justice system to pursue? If so, what form of restorative justice practice should be emphasized (VOM, FGC, NRB, or peacemaking/sentencing cirles)? If not, what should be done instead of restorative justice?

2. Advocates of restorative justice point to an array of potential advantages. What features or advantages are there in the restorative justice approach, and which of these should be considered as most important from a juvenile justice perspective?

3. To what extent do you see restorative justice practices meeting the philosophical goals of juvenile justice? Discuss specific features of restorative justice that do and do not correspond to the philosophy of the juvenile justice system.

4. Compare and contrast the different types of restorative justice (i.e., VOM, FGC, NRB, peacemaking/sentencing circles). Which appear to be best suited for use in the juvenile justice system?

Chapter 13

The Victimization of Juveniles

INTRODUCTION

The juvenile justice system does not deal exclusively with delinquent youths. As has already been seen, the juvenile court is tasked with handling noncriminal misbehavior by juveniles, typically considered as status offenders or unruly/ungovernable. In many jurisdictions, it also has the responsibility of handling youths who are the victims of maltreatment. Beyond the fact that the juvenile justice system must deal with more than just juvenile offenders is the reality that most victims of juvenile offenders are themselves juveniles, and these youths are also in need of assistance.

The present chapter turns the orientation of the book on its head and focuses on youths as victims rather than offenders. Several topics are explored. First, the chapter presents evidence on the extent of juvenile victimization as depicted in both victimization survey data and data on child abuse and neglect. The chapter also discusses explanations for the different forms of victimization. What will become apparent is that there is no single explanation for victimization, just as there is no single explanation for delinquency. Individuals also respond to victimization in different ways, and these methods are explored. Finally, the chapter addresses the role of the juvenile and criminal justice systems in dealing with youthful victims.

THE EXTENT OF VICTIMIZATION

Gauging the extent of victimization can be accomplished through the use of various data collection techniques. Official records, such as the Uniform Crime Reports, provide some indication of the overall extent of victimization in society through counts of offenses brought to the attention of social control agencies. In discussions of victimization, however, most attention turns to surveys that ask respondents about their experiences as a victim of crime. Victim surveys are only about 40 years old and were developed in response to criticisms that official measures underreport the level of crime in society. Consequently, most victim surveys tend to address offenses similar to those found in the Uniform Crime Reports. Victim surveys, however, have been used to address crimes occurring in specific locations, such as in schools and at work, as well as other types of activities, such as abuse and neglect. Beyond victim surveys, organizations such as the American Humane Association and various medical groups also collect information on specific types of victimization.

General Victimization

The most well-known source of victimization data is the **National Crime Victimization Survey (NCVS)**. The current version of the NCVS is the direct descendant of early work in the 1960s and 1970s that explored both the extent of self-reported victimization and the best ways to survey the public. Among the earliest victimization surveys were those commissioned by the 1967 President's Commission on Law Enforcement and Administration of Justice. Those early surveys indicated that, on the average, there was twice as much crime occurring as reflected in police records. The NCVS (originally called the National Crime Survey and begun in 1972) provides a great deal of information about the extent of victimization; characteristics of the victim; known information about the offender; data on the time, place, and circumstances of the offense; the economic and physical impact of the crimes; responses by victims; and contact with the criminal justice system.

One important piece of information provided by the NCVS is the breakdown of crimes by victim age and demographic characteristics. Table 13.1 presents estimated 2002 victimization rates for youths ages 12 to 15 and 16 to 19. For these age groups, the estimated rate of all personal crime victimizations is approximately 45 per 1,000 youths ages 12-15 and 59 per 1,000 youths ages 16-19. This means that almost 5 percent of all youths ages 12-15 and 6 percent of youths ages 16-19 are victims of a personal crime in a single year. Note that almost all of these offenses entail physical confrontations with an assailant.

Table 13.1   Estimated Victimization Rates for Youthful Age Groups (per 1,000), 2002

Age	Total 12-15	Total 16-19	White 12-15	White 16-19	Black 12-15	Black 16-19	Male 12-15	Male 16-19	Female 12-15	Female 16-19
All personal crimes	45.3	58.8								
Crimes of violence	44.4	58.2	47.5	56.6	39.6	73.9	46.1	58.4	42.6	58.1
Rape/sexual assault	2.1	5.5	2.0	3.4	3.0	18.1	0.0	0.8	4.3	10.4
Robbery	3.0	4.0	2.6	4.2	4.5	4.3	4.9	4.9	0.9	3.2
Aggravated assault	5.0	11.9	5.3	10.9	4.7	21.1	5.4	16.3	4.5	7.4
Simple assault	34.3	36.7	37.6	38.1	27.4	30.4	35.8	36.3	32.8	37.1
Purse snatching/ Pocket picking	0.9	0.6	1.2	0.8	0.0	0.0	1.8	1.2	0.0	0.0

Source: Bureau of Justice Statistics (2003). *Criminal Victimization in the United States, 2002—Statistical Tables.* Washington, DC: Bureau of Justice Statistics.

An important note is that victimization rates have been decreasing. The rates in Table 13.1 are down considerably from those for 1994. In 1994, for example, the personal victimization rates were 117.4 for youths ages 12-15 and 125.9 for youths ages 16-19. In other words, the 2002 rates are less than half of what the rates were in 1994.

Despite this decrease, compared to victimization figures for persons age 25 and older, youths are victimized at much higher rates. Personal crime victimization rates are 26.8 per 1,000 for persons 25-34, 18.8 for person 35-49 years of age, 11.0 for 50-64 years of age, and only 4.0 for those 65 and over (Bureau of Justice Statistics, 2003). What these data show is that youths contribute disproportionately to the ranks of crime victims.

Breakdowns by race and sex (see Table 13.1) reveal some interesting results. In terms of race, black youths and white youths age 12-15 are victimized at similar levels, with slightly higher victimization of younger white youths in crimes of violence and simple assault. Older black youths, however, are more often victims of violent crimes, rape/sexual assault, and aggravated assault than are older white youths. Comparisons of males and females show only small differences for youths ages 12-15. For older youths, males are more likely to be victims of aggravated assault and less likely to be victims of rape/sexual assault.

The NCVS figures demonstrate that a significant number of youths are victims of crimes ranging from simple larceny to aggravated assault and robbery. A number of other facts are also apparent from the NCVS. First, youths are more likely to be victimized by offenders of the same age, race, and sex as the victim. Second, youths also know the offender more often than do adults. Third, juveniles are less likely to report their victimization experience to the police. Many youths report the offense to someone other than the police.

Whitaker and Bastian (1991) note that many youths are victimized at school. Because youths spend more than one-third of their waking hours at school, it should not be surprising that they experience victimization at school. Unfortunately, victimization at school has only recently become a major concern, mostly due to media portrayals of violence and weapon use on school grounds. According to the NCVS, 13 percent of all crimes of violence occur in school or on school grounds (U.S. Department of Justice, 1997).

The United States Departments of Education and Justice issue an annual report on school crime and safety based on multiple indicators. Some of the indicators are from the NCVS, and some are from other sources. Students 12 through 18 reported more than 1,750,000 victimizations (thefts and violent crimes) at school in 2002 and more than 1.5 million victimizations away from school in 2002 (see Table 13.2). These figures translate into rates of 64 victimizations per 1,000 youths at school and 55 per 1,000 away from school. The rate for theft (both at and away from school) far exceeds the rates for violent and serious violent crimes. The fact that both the raw numbers and the rates are higher at school should not be surprising. Youths spend a majority of their waking hours at school during the school year. In addition, schools bring together potential victims with potential offenders, thus enhancing the possibility for victimizations.

Table 13.2   Number and Rate of Crimes Against Students At and Away From School, 2002

Type of Crime	At School		Away from School	
	Number	Rate*	Number	Rate*
Theft	1,095,000	40	790,100	29
Violent Crime	658,600	24	720,300	26
Serious Violence	88,100	3	309,200	11
Total	1,753,600	64	1,510,400	55

* rate per 1,000

Source: J.F. DeVoe, K. Peter, P. Kaufman, A. Miller, M. Noonan, T.D. Snyder, and K. Baum (2004). *Indicators of School Crime and Safety: 2004*. Washington, DC: Bureau of Justice Statistics.

The trends in victimization rates, both at school and away from school, are illustrated in Figures 13.1 and 13.2. In every case, victimization rates have declined from 1992 to 2002. At school, the decline in serious violent victimizations has been modest. This should be expected given the fact that such offenses are relatively rare with the more controlled environment of the school. Away from school, while the magnitude of rates differ, the relative decreases are strikingly similar.

Data on victimization of youths at school also provide the ability to inspect differences across demographic dimensions. Table 13.3 shows the percent of students who report being the victims of different types of crimes,

Figure 13.1   Trends in At-School Victimization Rates

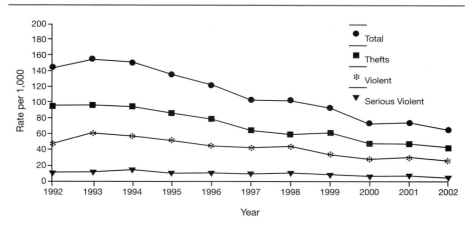

Source: Constructed by authors from J.F. DeVoe, K. Peter, P. Kaufman, A. Miller, M. Noonan, T.D. Snyder, and K. Baum (2004). *Indicators of School Crime and Safety: 2004*. Washington, DC: Bureau of Justice Statistics.

Figure 13.2   Trends in Away-from-School Victimization Rates

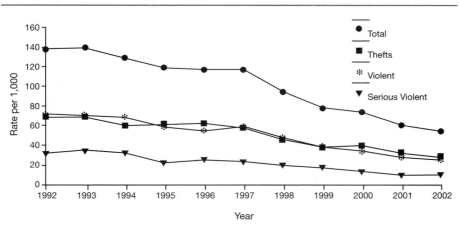

Source: Constructed by authors from J.F. DeVoe, K. Peter, P. Kaufman, A. Miller, M. Noonan, T.D. Snyder, and K. Baum (2004). *Indicators of School Crime and Safety: 2004*. Washington, DC: Bureau of Justice Statistics.

as well as breakdowns by gender, race/ethnicity, and grade level. The most striking thing about the data is the relative uniformity in the results across almost every student characteristic. The level of victimization reported by males and females is almost identical for all types of offenses. The same is true for different racial/ethnic groups. In terms of grade level (a good proxy for age), the results are very similar for all categories except being bullied, where those in lower grades are more victimized.

Table 13.3   **Percent Students Reporting Victimization at School by Selected Characteristics, 2003[a]**

Student Characteristics	Total	Theft	Violent[b]	Serious Violent[c]	Being Bullied
Total	5.1%	4.0%	1.3%	.2%	7.3%
Gender					
Male	5.4	4.0	1.8	.3	7.8
Female	4.5	4.1	.9	.1	6.5
Race/Ethnicity					
White	5.4	4.3	1.4	.2	7.8
Black	5.3	4.0	1.6	.1	6.4
Hispanic	3.9	3.0	1.1	.4	5.7
Other	5.0	4.4	.6	.2	6.8
Grade					
6th	3.8	2.2	1.9	—	13.9
7th	6.3	4.4	1.7	.3	12.7
8th	5.2	4.1	1.5	.3	8.8
9th	6.3	5.3	1.5	.6	6.7
10th	4.8	3.7	1.4	—	3.5
11th	5.1	4.1	1.0	.1	3.5
12th	3.6	3.1	.5	—	2.2

[a] Data for students aged 12 to 18.
[b] Violent crimes include rape, sexual assault, robbery, aggravated assault, and simple assault.
[c] Serious violent crimes include the violent crimes except for simple assault.

Source: J.F. DeVoe, K. Peter, P. Kaufman, A. Miller, M. Noonan, T.D. Snyder, and K. Baum (2004). *Indicators of School Crime and Safety: 2004*. Washington, DC: Bureau of Justice Statistics.

One attention-grabbing form of victimization at school has been killings of students by other students. The killings in Jonesboro, Arkansas, and at Columbine High School, as well as others, attracted a great deal of media attention and claims of "crises" facing schools. The reality, however, is that such actions are rare and have been declining. The data in Table 13.4 show that the number of homicides at school is very low, both in terms of absolute levels and relative to the numbers occurring away from school. It is also important to note that the figures in Table 13.4 subsume the multiple homicides that occur in many cases (such as at Columbine). The data clearly demonstrate that youths are safer at school than in the community.

Beyond being directly victimized, youths may also experience **vicarious victimization**; that is, they may recognize and respond to the victimizations of others. In a survey of 11,000 junior and senior high school students in one midwestern county, Lab and Clark (1994) asked respondents how often other students were victims of assault, robbery, and theft over a six-month period of time. Roughly 50 percent of the respondents report both assaults and thefts occurring against others at least one or two times per month at school. Additionally, more than 30 percent report robberies against others at least one or two times per month (Lab and Clark, 1994). What these figures show is that students perceive a large problem with victimization against others at school.

Table 13.4   Homicides of Youths At and Away from School

School Year	At School	Away from School
1992-1993	34	3,583
1993-1994	29	3,806
1994-1995	28	3,546
1995-1996	32	3,303
1996-1997	28	2,950
1997-1998	34	2,728
1998-1999	33	2,366
1999-2000	16	2,124
2000-2001	10	2,045

Source: J.F. DeVoe, K. Peter, P. Kaufman, A. Miller, M. Noonan, T.D. Snyder, and K. Baum (2004). *Indicators of School Crime and Safety: 2004*. Washington, DC: Bureau of Justice Statistics.

Victimization at school raises a number of perplexing problems. The most direct concern is the victimization itself. These youths are suffering losses and injuries. A second concern is that when the victimization takes place at school, the schools are failing to protect the youths under their care. This raises potential issues of liability. Third, the level of victimization at school may have a direct impact on the quality of education received by the students. This may result from students missing days of school because of the offense or fear of being victimized. It also may occur because school officials must spend time trying to establish discipline and control, or because the level of crime makes the staff feel that the students are not interested in receiving an education. Crime and victimization, therefore, may replace educating as the primary concern of the school. Consequently, victimization has both immediate and long-term impacts on students.

Child Abuse and Neglect

Victimization surveys and most official sources of crime data generally miss a major form of victimization against youths, namely **child abuse and neglect**. What makes this type of victimization especially noteworthy is the fact that the offender is typically a parent or other relative. Abuse and neglect can take a variety of forms, ranging from sexual assaults and physical beatings to the denial of food and daily necessities to simply ignoring the child. While not a new phenomenon, it is only since the 1960s that child abuse and neglect have been seen as a social problem. Prior to that time, these types of actions were primarily considered private problems that were best dealt with by the family.

Measuring child abuse and neglect is difficult due to the nature of the actions and the victim-offender relationship. First, abuse and neglect typically do not take place in public. Instead, they occur at home where there are no witnesses besides the victim, offender, and other family members. Second, in many cases, the victim may not recognize the action by the parent as wrong. The child is either too immature to understand the nature of what is happening, cannot adequately verbalize the events, or does not know who to tell about the abuse or neglect. Third, despite the abuse, children often still express love and affection for the parent/relative and may not want to do something that will get the offender into trouble. As a result, the child will not report, and may even deny, the existence of maltreatment.

Due to these problems, no firm figures on abuse and neglect are available. What is known is that the problem of child maltreatment is widespread. One source of data on child abuse and neglect is child protective services (CPS) agencies in each state. Data from these agencies is collected and compiled by the **National Child Abuse and Neglect Data System (NCANDS)**. In 2003, there were almost 900,000 documented cases of child abuse or neglect in the United States (see Table 13.5) out of almost three million referrals to CPS agencies (Administration on Children, Youth, and Families, 2005). More than one-half of the maltreated children (55%) experienced some form of neglect. Less than 20 percent experienced physical abuse, while almost 9 percent experienced sexual abuse and 4 percent psychological maltreatment (Administration on Children, Youth, and Families, 2005). Victimization rates were similar for males and females. In terms of race/ethnicity, the rate of victimization for African Americans and other minority youths was roughly twice that of white youths (Administration on Children, Youth, and Families, 2005).

Table 13.5   Number and Rate of Child Maltreatment, 2003

Type	Number	Rate
Physical Abuse	148,877	2.3
Neglect	479,567	7.5
Medical Neglect	17,945	.3
Sex Abuse	78,188	1.2
Psychological Maltreatment	38,603	.6
Other Abuse	132,993	3.7
Unknown	1,792	.3

Source: Administration on Children, Youth, and Families (2005). *Child Maltreatment, 2003.* Washington, DC: U.S. Department of Health and Human Services.

Unfortunately, child maltreatment often leads to the death of the victim. According to the Uniform Crime Reports, 225 infants were killed in 2003, 307 murder victims were ages one to four, and an additional 82 murder victims were between the ages of five and eight. A total of 1,333 juveniles under age 18 were murdered in 2003 (Federal Bureau of Investigation, 2004). Two cautions concerning these figures are in order. First, not all juvenile homicides are committed by parents or other family members. Forty percent of juvenile murder victims, however, were killed by family members, and it is reasonable to assume that this percentage increases as the age of the victim decreases. Second, it must be kept in mind that these figures reflect only those cases in which the death of a child has been determined to be due to criminal homicide. It is possible that many more children die due to neglect or abuse but the cases are not officially classified as homicides. Indeed, according to the NCANDS, approximately 1,500 children died as a result of child abuse or neglect in 2003 (Administration on Children, Youth, and Families, 2005). Almost 80 percent of these victims were under four years of age, males were more likely to be victims, and more than one-third of the cases were due to some form of neglect (Administration on Children, Youth, and Families, 2005).

The figures for the extent of abuse and neglect are only estimates. There is no accurate count for this type of victimization. The fact that most such acts occur behind closed doors between relatives means that we may never have a complete picture of the problem. What can be concluded is that these are baseline figures and that the real extent of abuse and neglect is probably much higher.

EXPLAINING JUVENILE VICTIMIZATION

Attempts to explain why an individual is a victim can take a variety of forms. Certainly, one way to explain victimization is to turn the equation over and focus on the offender. The various theories addressed earlier in this text (Chapters 3 and 4) follow this more traditional approach to understanding unacceptable behavior. Because the perpetrator is the one who has violated the law, it is natural to focus attention on that individual, rather than the victim. There must be something about the offender that led to the victimization. The realm of victimology, however, does not rely exclusively on the theories already presented in this text. Rather, attempts to explain juvenile victimization range from those that attempt to blame the victim for the action to others targeted at specific forms of victimization.

From Victim-Blaming to Lifestyle

Early research on victims paid considerable attention to who the victims were and the circumstances surrounding the events. Throughout these works was an underlying theme that individuals became victims because of something they did, did not do, or could not do. For example, von Hentig (1941) outlined 13 categories of victims, including the young, females, the elderly, minorities, and mentally defective individuals. What made these people victims was the fact that they were somehow vulnerable. Some people cannot physically ward off an attack, others do not recognize they are being victimized, and others see themselves outside the societal mainstream and accept the victimization. Mendelsohn (1956) takes this argument one step further in a classification relying on the culpability of the victim. "Victims with minor guilt" place themselves into a position in which victimization is possible. The "victim more guilty than the offender" actively initiates the event that causes the victimization. Similarly, the "most guilty victim" starts out as an offender and ends up the victim.

This line of reasoning reached its apex with the work of Wolfgang (1958) and Amir (1971). Both of these authors argued that substantial numbers of offenses are victim-precipitated. **Victim precipitation** posits that the victim is actively involved in the offense. Wolfgang (1958) stated that

> victim-precipitated [homicide] cases are those in which the victim was the first to show and use a deadly weapon, to strike a blow in an altercation— in short, the first to commence the interplay of resort to physical violence (p. 252).

The victim, therefore, holds some responsibility for his or her own status due to his or her actions or inactions. Amir (1971) extended this argument to rape offenses by claiming that how the victim acted, where she was, how she dressed, and similar factors placed the victim in the role of contributing to her own victimization. While these early ideas of victim culpability have been referred to as **victim-blaming** and subjected to much criticism (see Curtis, 1974; Franklin and Franklin, 1976; Weis and Borges, 1973), the idea that the actions of individuals may contribute to their victimization has not been completely discounted.

Today, consideration is given to **lifestyle** as an explanation of how victims contribute to their situation. Hindelang, Gottfredson, and Garofalo (1978) argue that the choices individuals make about what to do, where to go, who to go with, and when to go all define their lifestyle and their chances of victimization. This is directly analogous to **routine activities theory** (see Chapter 4), in which the convergence of motivated offenders, suitable targets, and an absence of guardians allows for the commission of crime (Cohen and Felson, 1979). If one's lifestyle places him or her in an area where crime is common, at a time when there is no one to provide protection, then the chances for victimization are enhanced. That person's lifestyle, therefore, contributes to becoming a victim.

Examples and support for a lifestyle explanation of juvenile victimization are plentiful. The fact that juveniles are disproportionately represented among offenders would suggest that juveniles would also be the victims for a variety of reasons. First, other youths are available to victimize—at school, out-of-doors in the neighborhood, in play groups, and as acquaintances. Second, juvenile offenders will view other youths as more physically vulnerable than most adults. Third, interaction with other youths provides knowledge and opportunities for offending. Fourth, individuals who engage in deviant behavior are themselves at higher risk of being a victim. In essence, the juvenile lifestyle includes more youths to victimize than adults.

Recent research uncovers a strong relationship between offending and victimization. Using data from the National Youth Survey, Lauritsen and associates (1991) note that delinquents are four times as likely to be victims of assault, robbery, and vandalism than are nondelinquents. The most consistent predictor of victimization for most youths is their delinquent lifestyle. Similarly, Esbensen and Huizinga (1991) report that victimization is strongly related to both the commission and frequency of delinquent behavior. This relationship between delinquent/criminal lifestyle and victimization has been found in numerous other studies of both juveniles and adults (Clark and Lab, 1995; Jensen and Brownfield, 1986; Sampson and Lauritsen, 1990; Shaffer, 2004). Clearly, as youths either find themselves or place themselves in situations in which delinquency is more likely, they will invariably be victimized.

Explanations of Child Abuse and Neglect

Where the lifestyle approach emphasizes the behavior and choices of the victim as contributors to victimization, explanations of child maltreatment focus exclusively on the offender and society. The victim is not considered culpable. In general, explanations for child maltreatment can be divided into three categories: intraindividual theories, sociocultural explanations, and social learning theories (Doerner and Lab, 2005). **Intraindividual theories** view child maltreatment as an internal flaw or defect of the abuser. The key is to identify the flaw and intervene to avoid future abusive behavior (Belsky, 1978). Abusers are considered to exhibit some form of psychopathological condition (Steele and Pollock, 1974), such as role reversal. Under role reversal, the abuser/parent expects the child to provide nurturance and love to the parent, rather than having to supply those things to the victim/child. Intraindividual theories have been used to absolve society of any responsibility for child abuse and lay the blame on a few "sick" individuals.

Sociocultural explanations shifts the emphasis from the individual to society and the environment. The abuser may be stressed by any number of factors, such as unemployment, conflicts at work or home, family size, social isolation, and economic problems (Belsky, 1978; Garbarino and Gilliam, 1980; Gelles, 1980; Gil, 1971). This stress leads the individual to strike out against someone or something that cannot retaliate. Where a spouse, other adults, or an employer will not tolerate inappropriate action, a child has neither the physical stature nor the social standing to resist maltreatment. A child, therefore, becomes the recipient of abuse as a proxy outlet for stress.

Social learning approaches to child maltreatment rest on the assumption that an individual has learned to be abusive by observing past abusive behavior. This observation includes the possibility that the abuser was himself or herself abused as a child. The idea that a child who is abused or who

AP Photo/South Bend Tribune, Jim Rider

Guarded by police, Madelyne Gorman Toogood is escorted to her car after a hearing in South Bend, Indiana. Toogood, caught on videotape beating her 4-year-old daughter in a department store parking lot, was arraigned on a felony charge of battery to a child. Explanations for child maltreatment are still in their infancy. To date, there is no concurrence on just why an adult abuses or neglects a child.

witnesses abuse will grow up to be an abuser is often referred to as the **cycle of violence** (Schwartz, 1989; Straus, 1983). Following basic social learning tenets, a child who observes abusive behavior that is not sanctioned, particularly if it is perpetrated by a respected significant adult, is more likely to model his or her future behavior accordingly. This same argument has been used as an explanation of spousal abuse (U.S. Attorney General's Task Force on Family Violence, 1984). Widom (1989, 1995), following abused/neglected youths and a control group into adulthood, reports a significant relationship between abuse/neglect as a child and deviant behavior of various types later in life. Researchers of the cycle of violence theory point out a variety of methodological problems and issues and call for further research before the theory is accepted as a causal factor in abuse and deviant behavior (see Gelles and Cornell, 1990; Pagelow, 1984; Simons et al., 1995).

Explanations for child abuse and neglect are still in their infancy. Indeed, scholarly interest in this form of victimization is relatively new, with most work dating since the 1960s. Consequently, little consensus exists on the scope of the problem, explanations for maltreatment, or how to best attack the problem. This state of affairs will persist until further research is completed.

RESPONSES TO VICTIMIZATION

Victimization, whether direct or vicarious, has the potential of eliciting a number of responses from the victim. While victims may view the responses as beneficial, they are often debilitating and may lead the victims into criminal or delinquent behavior. Responses can range from taking direct action at the time of an offense to raised levels of fear of crime to various actions aimed at reducing the risk of initial or further victimization. Responses chosen by youthful victims include the carrying of weapons for protection or joining gangs. In both cases, however, the response may be illegal and/or lead to more victimization.

Immediate Responses

One response to victimization is for the victim to take action at the time of the offense. According to the National Crime Victimization Survey (NCVS), almost 70 percent of youthful victims invoke some self-protective action (Bureau of Justice Statistics, 2004). Where the NCVS breaks down self-protective action by age group, it does not do so for individual forms of response. Using information for all respondents on type of self-protective behavior (see Table 13.6), it is apparent that most measures are not confrontational in nature. The most common responses to violent crimes are to resist or capture the offender (24.5%), run away or hide from the offender (14.1%), get help/give alarm (12.0%), or try to persuade or appease the offender (11.0%). Less than 10 percent of victims directly attack or threaten an offender (Bureau of Justice Statistics, 2003).

Table 13.6   **Percent of Victims Taking Self-Protective Measures in Violent Victimizations and Type of Measures Taken**

Measure	Percent
Attacked offender with weapon	.8
Attacked offender without weapon	9.4
Threatened offender with weapon	.8
Threatened offender without weapon	1.9
Resisted or captured offender	24.5
Scared or warned offender	9.3
Persuaded or appeased offender	11.0
Ran away or hid	14.1
Got help or gave alarm	12.0
Screamed from pain or fear	2.7
Took another method	13.5

Source: Bureau of Justice Statistics (2003). *Criminal Victimization in the United States, 2002*. Statistical Tables. Washington, DC: Bureau of Justice Statistics.

Fear of Crime as a Response

Whether or not a victim takes an action at the time of an offense, there will probably be some changes in beliefs or behavior subsequent to the victimization experience. Many people believe that fear of crime is directly related to victimization. While most studies show that roughly 40 to 50 percent of the population are fearful of crime (Hindelang, 1975; Skogan and Maxfield, 1981; Toseland, 1982), there is evidence that fear far exceeds the actual level of victimization (Flanagan and Maguire, 1990; Skogan and Maxfield, 1981). Further, there is some debate to what extent fear is influenced by victimization, whether direct or indirect (see Ferraro and LaGrange, 1987; Gomme, 1988; Lab, 1992).

Interestingly, despite the fact that youths are among the most victimized, they are the least fearful of all age groups (Maguire and Pastore, 1994; Skogan and Maxfield, 1981). Not all research, however, is in agreement on this finding. Ferraro (1995) has found that fear is greater among the young and suggests that the discrepancy in the research is a result of different definitions of fear, methods of data collection, and a focus on individual crimes. There is also a tendency for greater fear among youths in more recent analyses, perhaps indicating a change over time. One drawback to most studies is the fact that they compare older youths (e.g., ages 18-20) to adults and omit any discussion of younger individuals.

When research looks exclusively at youths, fear does not appear to be minor. For example, Lab and Clark (1994), in their study of junior and senior high school students, found that 30 percent of the students claim to fear being attacked at school, independent of whether they had ever been victimized in the past. Interestingly, fear was higher for younger respondents. Similarly, the 1989 NCVS School Crime Supplement found that 22 percent of youths were fearful of being attacked at school, and 53 percent of those who had been victimized feared further attacks (Bastian and Taylor, 1991).

Fear can be debilitating, regardless of whether it is a result of past victimization. Fear leads some people to avoid other persons and places. It makes others decide to carry a weapon for protection. Still others may join groups to fight crime. The very fact that fear can cause people to change their normal routine is evidence that it is something to be addressed. This is not to suggest that fear is always a bad thing. Indeed, to the extent that fear alters a person's behavior and chances of being victimized, fear is a useful tool.

Avoidance

One common reaction to actual or potential victimization and fear is **avoidance** of certain places or people. Avoidance is possibly the leading response to fear of victimization (Gates and Rohe, 1987; Skogan, 1981). Two analyses designed to identify citizen responses to fear and victimization (Lab, 1990; Lavrakas and Lewis, 1981) found that avoidance behavior is common. Reasonable avoidance behavior for a youth may include staying away from a playground where gang members are known to hang out or refraining from walking alone at night in an area with a high crime rate.

Unfortunately, there are some instances in which avoidance is not a viable alternative. For youths, victimization at school raises the option of staying home from school or avoiding certain places at school. Avoidance at school, however, means that school work is missed, the student is distracted from work while at school, and/or there is discomfort and inconvenience involved in avoiding important parts of the school (such as a restroom or the cafeteria). In their study of in-school victimization, Lab and Clark (1994) report that 9 percent of the students stayed home at least once over a six-month time period due to fear of being assaulted at school, and 5 percent avoided school for fear of having something stolen. While the majority of students do not avoid school or places at school, there is a small but significant percent of students who feel they must stay away from important parts of the school. Using the NCVS School Crime Supplement data to identify the predictors of avoidance behavior by students, Lab and Whitehead (1994) reported that fear is by far the most important consideration, even surpassing actual victimization experiences.

Resorting to Weapons

An inescapable fact about youths in recent years is their ability to obtain and use weapons. Nationally, one-fifth of the population reports having bought a gun for their own protection or to protect their homes. Eleven percent (11%) report actually carrying (or having carried) a weapon for protection (Saad, 2001). Surveys of students show that weapons are an everyday occurrence in and around many schools. One national survey reveals that 17 percent of youths carried weapons at least once in the past month, with 6 percent claiming to have carried them at school (DeVoe et al., 2004). Similarly, a survey of New York City high school students reveals that, in schools without metal detectors, almost 14 percent of the students carried a weapon inside school at least once within a 30-day period ("Violence-Related Attitudes," 1993). Finally, Lab and Clark (1994) report that 24 percent of their respondents carried a weapon for protection at school at least once during the preceding six months. The most frequent weapon being carried according to most studies is a knife or razor. Guns are not the most prevalent weapon.

The carrying of weapons for self-protection is problematic for a number of reasons. First, most of these items are illegal for youths to possess. Second, possession of weapons by any individual on school grounds is illegal in most jurisdictions. Third, the presence of a weapon has the potential of escalating any confrontation to much higher levels and mitigates the possibility of defusing a situation. Fourth, a weapon may result in the victim being hurt more than if

A police officer monitors the hall of United South High School in Laredo, Texas. More than a dozen students were expelled from the school in the 2003-2004 school year for possession of drugs or weapons, a number so high that the state named it one of Texas's first "persistently dangerous schools."

no weapon was available. Finally, accepting the premise that you meet force with force portends a mindset wherein force becomes the solution of choice, rather than a solution of last resorts.

Grouping Together to Respond

In times of crisis or turmoil, it is natural for people to seek out support from those around them. Most victims will turn to family members for such assistance. Another source of support is close friends and peers. Yet another alternative may be to join an organized group, such as a Neighborhood Watch organization or a victim's of crime group. Not all of these options, however, are equally available or feasible for everyone. Some victims may not have any family members nearby or may have family members who are not supportive. Others may not be aware of support organizations, or none may be available. Consequently, an individual may see little choice in support groups.

For youths, particularly those in large inner cities, the available peer support groups may consist of juvenile gangs. The response to victimization, therefore, may entail joining a gang for protection. This possibility is extremely salient given the reasons why youths join gangs. As noted in Chapter 5, gangs provide a sense of belonging, status, support, and control. All of these things are missing in a victimization experience. Some youths may see joining a gang as a means of restoring a feeling of security. If a youth is victimized by gang members, either directly or by mistake, joining a gang further becomes a self-defense mechanism.

Joining gangs as a response to victimization, however, is a double-edged sword. While the gang may supply some sense of protection, it typically demands participation in illegal behavior and conflict with other gangs and individuals. These demands often result in further victimization of the individual, rather than protection from victimization. At the same time that gang membership may alleviate victimization, joining a gang can also contribute to ongoing victimization, albeit as a member of a group and not just as an individual.

Peer Mediation and Other Responses to Victimization

In recent years there has been increased attention paid to the youthful victim. Most of this interest is a simple extension of more general efforts to improve the standing of victims in the criminal justice system. **Peer mediation** programs represent one area in which juvenile victims have been provided a means of responding to the offense and offender. Under peer mediation, the disputants in a matter are brought together with a third-party peer mediator in an effort to resolve the dispute to the satisfaction of both parties. Not all disputes in mediation have a clear victim and offender. Rather, each party may have a grievance with the other. The goal is to defuse the situation and keep it from recurring. Under these programs, the victim has the possibility of correcting the harm done.

Peer mediation takes a variety of forms and appears under various names. **Dispute resolution** typically deals with cases in which the disputants have not yet had their grievance decided by the courts. Most of these cases involve relatively minor disputes between individuals who know one another and there is no clear-cut offender and victim. In many instances the disputing parties may be referred to mediation by the police, a prosecutor, or the criminal court. Mediation programs tend to follow very informal procedures and rules, and they rely on the voluntary participation of both parties (Garofalo and Connelly, 1980).

Many schools have implemented conflict resolution/management programs or courses. These programs typically include a strong teaching component. Key to the programs is peer mediation in which students serve as the mediators. Educators are turning to conflict resolution as a means of not only solving the immediate dispute, but also a method for teaching students alternative methods for handling confrontation. There is a recognition that staff cannot simply impose order. Rather, the students must be involved in the process of defusing situations that can lead to crime and victimization. New York City's Resolving Conflict Creatively Program (RCCP) is one well-known example of these programs. Begun in 1985, the program operates in both primary and secondary schools and deals with issues of communication, cooperation, feelings, diversity, and resolving conflicts (DeJong, 1993). The state of Ohio has initiated a number of similar projects (Ohio Commission on Dispute Resolution and Conflict Management, 1993). Both the RCCP and Ohio programs report success at reducing the level of fights and improving students' ability to resolve disputes. Bynum (1996), however, reports little impact from school-level conflict resolution programs. Unfortunately, most peer mediation programs with youths are in need of rigorous evaluation. The impact of these programs, therefore, is still not adequately known.

Summary of Victimization Responses

Juveniles can respond to victimization in a variety of ways. At the same time, many of the potential responses have negative aspects that can exacerbate problems for the youth. Fear, which may serve as a protective measure, can lead to withdrawal from other people and the community. It can also prompt a youth to stay home from school or avoid certain places at school. Still other victims may purchase and carry weapons for protection. Victimization also may drive a youth to join a gang as a means of feeling safe. While each of these may appear reasonable, they can lead to further victimization, more serious situations, and, certainly, a deterioration in the general quality of life.

THE ROLE OF FORMAL SOCIAL CONTROL AGENCIES

Various social control agencies can become involved in youthful victimization. Most social control agencies, however, focus on juvenile victims of abuse and neglect and ignore the victim status as it emerges from other forms of offending. Clearly, a juvenile who loses money due to a theft or is hurt from an assault tends to be considered a witness more so than a victim by the justice system. Assistance to these victims is relatively limited to mediation and similar programs already discussed. On the other hand, victims of abuse and neglect receive a great deal of attention by various formal control agencies, particularly child protective services and the different court systems.

Perhaps the only agency that will have contact with all forms of youthful victims will be the police. This is because they are typically the ones called whenever someone is in need of help. The police, however, are geared toward identifying offenders, making arrests, and preparing cases for prosecution. Except for initial contacts, providing immediate protection, referrals to other sources of assistance, and work with prevention programs, law enforcement officers spend little time dealing with the victim. This is true whether the victim is an adult or a juvenile. Consequently, the balance of this section looks at how other system components deal with youthful victims.

Child Protective Services

An alternative point of system entry besides the police that has been established for the purposes of protecting youths is **child protective services**. Child protective services are mandated in every state as a direct result of the Child Abuse Prevention and Treatment Act of 1974 (Wiehe, 1992). This federal act required states to set up rules for the reporting and handling of abused children. States not conforming to the Act would be denied various forms of federal funding. Because the exact nature of how a state would provide protective services was left to the state, these services appear under various state agencies such as Social Services and Departments of Human Services.

Child protective service agencies fill a variety of roles and have diverse powers in different states. First, in virtually all jurisdictions, these agencies are responsible for accepting reports of abuse and neglect cases and undertaking or coordinating the investigation of such allegations. While many investigations are done by employees of the child protective service, others may be assigned to other agencies, such as the police or prosecutor's office. A second common function of child protective services is the removal of children from suspected (or documented) abusive situations. This removal may last for only a short time or can last for an extended period, depending on the facts of the case. The protection of the child from further possible harm is the goal of any decision to remove a child from his or her parents. Child protective services often provide oversight to foster care, adoption, and other forms of custodial arrangements for the state.

Finally, child protective services focus on the preservation of the family unit. Underlying this approach is the belief that the family setting is the most appropriate for raising a child. Stabilizing the family situation, removing the problematic elements in the home, and improving the quality of life for the child guide the decisions made by the agency. Given this preoccupation with family preservation, most child protective agencies do not need court orders or sanctions to work with families. Much like diversion programs or informal probation, child protective services will work with families to solve problems without resorting to formal court procedures if all parties agree. In some cases the agency will actually provide the recommended intervention, and in others the agency may act as more of a referral source than service provider.

Child protective services, by whatever name or form, work very closely with different courts. While these agencies often generate cases for the criminal and juvenile courts, the courts also call on these services for assistance as cases work their way through the system. This referral from the courts to protective services can range from taking custody of children when parents are incarcerated for a crime to investigating allegations of abuse and neglect that emerge in the course of divorce proceedings.

Child protective services reach a large number of victims and families each year. More than 1.8 million youths were the recipients of preventive measures in 2003 (NCANDS, 2005). In addition, almost 700,000 victims received post-investigative services, and more than 600,000 youths were removed from their homes in 2003. Of those removed, 92,258 were victims of abuse or neglect (NCANDS, 2005). These figures reveal two things. First, child protective services agencies reach a substantial number of abuse and neglect victims. Second, these agencies handle many youths for an array of problems beyond just victimization.

The Juvenile Court

The juvenile court deals with a wide variety of issues related to youths. As seen earlier, the juvenile court is faced with an entire set of issues and concerns when faced with delinquent individuals. Another set of issues face the court in cases of dependency, abuse, and neglect. Rather than search for reasons why the youth acted inappropriately, in these cases, the court must consider the protection and needs of the juvenile victim, the needs of the entire family unit, and the possible sanctioning and needs of the (typically adult) offender.

Cases of abuse and neglect force the juvenile court to assume a more conflict orientation than presumed under the *parens patriae* philosophy. Because of the diverse issues in abuse and neglect cases, many juvenile courts are affiliated with (or even part of) what are more generally known as **family courts**. Larger family courts may designate certain judges to handle delinquency matters and others to deal with abuse and neglect cases. These latter cases typically follow a more rigorous set of procedural guidelines, including evidentiary safeguards, the presence of attorneys, and formal examination and cross-examination of witnesses. This is required because of the due process rights of the accused.

In every case of abuse and neglect, the primary concern of the juvenile court is the well-being of the juvenile and the family unit. Other youths in the home also become a focal point along with the individual victim, based on the assumption that they are potential victims. Because abuse and neglect cases place the interests of the child in conflict with that of an accused parent, the court typically appoints someone to be an advocate for the needs and interests of the child. Two common names for such an advocate would be a **Court-Appointed Special Advocate (CASA)** or a *guardian ad litem*. The CASA program began in Seattle in the late 1970s and has since spread to all states (Office of Juvenile Justice and Delinquency Prevention, 1987). These advocates usually serve in a voluntary capacity, although

AP Photo/The Winchester Star, Jeff Taylor

The director of the Frederick County Department of Social Services sits in a decorated child advocacy room in the department's facility in Winchester, Virginia. Child-advocacy centers are kid-friendly environments serving as way stations where abused children are interviewed for state records, and receive counseling and support.

some courts provide office space, supplies, and travel expenses. The exact role and responsibility of a CASA volunteer and a *guardian ad litem* varies across jurisdictions, although their general duty is to protect the interests of the child in virtually any legal proceeding (see Box 13.1). These individuals typically receive training in the functioning of the juvenile court, the needs of youths, the availability of resources, and how to investigate the circumstances of the case. According to the NCANDS (2005), more than 28,000 youths were appointed some form of representative in 25 states in 2003.

Court-appointed advocates often fulfill some of the same functions as other actors in the criminal and juvenile justice systems. These individuals, because of their focus on youths, can undertake a more thorough investigation of a case than can an overburdened police force. They can also spend the time to identify potential sources of treatment for the child, offender, and family that is not a role of law enforcement investigators. In some places these individuals also serve in the place of an attorney on the child's behalf. One key difference, however, between an attorney and a CASA volunteer or *guardian ad litem* involves their orientation toward the case. Whereas an attorney argues in accordance with the client's wishes, a court-appointed advocate is supposed to argue in the best interests of the child, even if that conflicts with the desires of the child (Sagatun and Edwards, 1995). These court volunteers, therefore, provide a service that may not be available in their absence.

Box 13.1 Excerpts from Ohio's Guardian ad Litem Statute

[§ 2151.28.1] § 2151.281. Guardian ad litem.

(A) The court shall appoint a guardian ad litem to protect the interest of a child in any proceeding concerning an alleged or adjudicated delinquent child or unruly child when either of the following applies:

(1) The child has no parent, guardian, or legal custodian.

(2) The court finds that there is a conflict of interest between the child and the child's parent, guardian, or legal custodian.

(B) (1) The court shall appoint a guardian ad litem to protect the interest of a child in any proceeding concerning an alleged abused or neglected child . . .

(2) The guardian ad litem appointed for an alleged or adjudicated abused or neglected child may bring a civil action against any person, who is required . . . to file a report of known or suspected child abuse or child neglect, if that person knows or suspects that the child . . . is the subject of child abuse or child neglect and does not file the required report and if the child suffers any injury or harm as a result of the known or suspected child abuse or child neglect or suffers additional injury or harm after the failure to file the report.

(I) The guardian ad litem for an alleged or adjudicated abused, neglected, or dependent child shall perform whatever functions are necessary to protect the best interest of the child, including, but not limited to, investigation, mediation, monitoring court proceedings, and monitoring the services provided the child by the public children services agency or private child placing agency that has temporary or permanent custody of the child, and shall file any motions and other court papers that are in the best interest of the child.

Source: Anderson's Ohio Online Docs. Available at: http://onlinedocs.andersonpublishing.com

---

The juvenile court can impose a variety of conditions on the child victim and the family. Among these are emergency temporary custody orders, permanent custody decisions (including adoption), individual and family counseling, mandatory treatment programs, and the incarceration of offenders. In making these decisions, the juvenile court judge must rely on information from a variety of sources. Court-appointed advocates are one source of vital information and recommendations. As in adjudication decisions in which the judge relies on probation personnel for an appropriate disposition, the judge typically follows the recommendation of court-appointed advocates in cases of abuse and neglect.

Beyond the traditional role of looking out for a youthful victim's needs, juvenile courts are beginning to be proactive in their efforts to work with youths in other settings. The ideas of conflict resolution and peer mediation are examples of programs that often receive help and guidance from the court. Another movement appearing in some courts is the attempt to build **mentoring programs** for at-risk kids. These programs are designed to couple youths who are not receiving the proper familial support (i.e., neglected youths) with adults from the community who will help nurture them. Many courts, partly due to the overcrowding, are searching for programs and solutions thaat will keep youths from becoming victims or offenders in the first place.

The Criminal Court

The criminal court holds a difficult position when faced with youthful victims, particularly abuse and neglect victims. This is because of its orientation toward determining guilt or innocence of the accused and imposing sentences on the convicted. The victim in the criminal court holds no more stature than does any witness. It is the state that is the aggrieved party and the state that is pursuing the prosecution of the offender (Doerner and Lab, 2005). As a consequence of this situation, the criminal court focuses on providing the accused with his or her due process rights. Besides the victim's role as a witness, the court's only other concern for a victim is to protect him or her from further harm.

A juvenile victim in the criminal court is especially problematic due to his or her lack of maturity. The process can be very traumatic for a child, particularly if the accused is an abusive or neglectful parent. In the past, many cases never reached trial, or the prosecution was unsuccessful due to problems with youthful victims/witnesses. Criminal courts in recent years, however, have started to make accommodations for youthful victims. For example, some jurisdictions provide victim counselors as a means of minimizing the trauma of a court appearance and assisting youths with recall problems (Burgess and Lazlo, 1976; Geiselman, Bornstein, and Saywitz, 1992). These counselors can serve in a fashion and capacity similar to CASA workers and *guardians ad litem*. Other courts have relaxed the hearsay rule (Levine and Battistoni, 1991) or allowed *in camera* **testimony** (Bjerregaard, 1989; Melton, 1980) as means of entering testimony while protecting the victim. The relaxed hearsay rule allows third-party testimony, such as from a counselor or psychiatrist. In-camera testimony entails testimony outside the courtroom, such as in a judge's chambers or by means of closed-circuit television or on tape. While these efforts are not allowed in all jurisdictions, they are gaining acceptance as a way to protect the youthful victim while still prosecuting the accused.

Two efforts to assist crime victims, both adult and juvenile, are **victim compensation** and **restitution** programs. Both of these programs primarily address victims of offenses besides abuse and neglect. Victim compensation programs are found in 49 states and federal courts (Parent, Auerbach, and Carlson, 1992). Victim compensation is a program in which the state makes monetary payments to the victims of (primarily) violent crimes. These payments are meant to offset the monetary and medical losses incurred in the criminal act (Doerner and Lab, 2005). Youthful victims can be compensated the same as an adult victim, providing the juvenile's guardian applies. The relationship between compensation and the court rests on the facts that victims must cooperate with any prosecution of an offender and that prosecutors and the police are common avenues for alerting victims about the availability of compensation. Restitution also seeks to restore a victim to a pre-crime state. Restitution, however, requires the offender to make payment to the victim. The role of the court in restitution is obvious. That is, an offender must be convicted before restitution can be imposed. The problem with both victim compensation and restitution for juvenile victims is the fact that in many cases the monetary loss is very small and may not qualify for repayment. It is also possible that a juvenile's loss will not be seen as important enough to warrant compensation or restitution.

On a final note, both juvenile and adult victims hold few rights in the criminal court. As noted earlier, there have been some accommodations made for juveniles as witnesses. Other inroads to the court appear in legislation that provides victims with rights such as the right to be informed about court proceedings, the right to protection from intimidation, and the right to address the court at the time of sentencing (Doerner and Lab, 2005). Unfortunately, there is little discussion of youthful victims in any of the arguments for these changes or in the enacting legislation.

Domestic Relations Court

A final court in which juvenile victims may find themselves is a **domestic relations court**. These are civil courts devoted to the issues involved in divorce, child support, and related matters. As with juvenile courts, domestic relations may be configured as a special court within a larger family court setting in some jurisdictions. Youthful victims appear in these courts primarily in cases in which allegations of abuse or neglect are made by one parent against another. The child does not have a separate standing in the court, despite the possibility of abuse or neglect. When such allegations are made, the court will order an investigation (often by protective services agencies) for the purpose of making a determination with regard to the question before the court (i.e., divorce, support payments, etc.). It is possible that the court will provide a CASA worker or a *guardian ad litem* to the child when such allegations are made. If evidence of abuse or neglect is uncovered in the case, those issues are turned over to the criminal or juvenile courts for action. Therefore, while youthful victimization may emerge in domestic relations courts, those problems are outside of the court's jurisdiction and will be turned over to another court.

Restorative Justice

As we discussed in the last chapter, **restorative justice** is an emerging approach for dealing with youthful offenders. At the same time, restorative justice places a great deal of attention on the victim and his or her needs. The various forms of conferencing allow the victim input to the processing of offenders and to receive assistance in becoming whole once again. Juvenile offenders and victims are common targets of restorative justice measures. There is little debate over the degree to which victims support restorative justice and the extent to which they are satisfied by the actions of most restorative justice processes. The fact that restorative justice speaks to the concerns of the victim, the offender, and the community means that it has widespread appeal and support and is gaining greater attention in the juvenile justice system.

SUMMARY: THE NEED TO RECOGNIZE THE VICTIM

Addressing children as victims of crime has long been a component of the juvenile justice system and, to a minimal extent, other courts, but this fails to garner much attention in discussions of juvenile justice. This is unfortunate because most youthful offenders prey on other youths, and significant numbers of youths are victims of abuse and neglect. While the juvenile court has long standing in the areas of abuse and neglect, youthful victims have few coping mechanisms available for dealing with other forms of victimization. This is especially true outside the juvenile justice system. To what can this anonymity of juvenile victimization be attributed? One major source of blame has to be the fact that too often the emphasis on juvenile offenders ignores the other half of the offense dyad—the juvenile victim. We have attempted to begin to rectify this shortcoming in this chapter. It is also important, however, that more emphasis be placed on research and programming for juvenile victims. Without those efforts, juvenile victims will continue to receive little attention.

Discussion Questions

1. You have recently been hired to work for an agency that deals with abused and neglected youths. Research your state statutes and report on the legal definitions of abuse and neglect, and what is mandated in terms of dealing with these victims (such as mandatory reporting, treatment, etc.). What gaps do you see in the statutes? What changes would you make?

2. You have been asked to draw up new legislation dealing with child abuse and neglect. Define the terms, outline the issues you would include in the legislation, and discuss the role you see for the juvenile court and how, if at all, it would alter the court's philosophy.

3. Discuss the responses youths make when victimized. What are the positive and negative consequences of the various responses? What types of services are available to handle victimized juveniles (not including abuse and neglect)? What services are in your town? What services would you like to see initiated?

4. Your local Parent Teacher Association (PTA) is clamoring for increased security measures at school. The PTA wants to prevent homicides and other violent crimes. What information should the PTA and the school be aware of in order to make reasonable choices?

Chapter 14

Future Directions in Juvenile Justice

INTRODUCTION

The juvenile court is in trouble. Critics point out numerous problems and suggest either change or elimination. State legislators and prosecutors have taken away many of the clients of juvenile court. New state laws mandate handling many juveniles in adult criminal court. Prosecutors today have increased authority to direct juveniles to adult court. It is likely that these trends will continue and there will be little or nothing left of juvenile court.

This chapter will examine several proposals about the future of juvenile court. One drastic proposal is to abolish juvenile court. Other proposals call for new types of courts. We will outline these proposals and assess them. This chapter will also look at some broader issues affecting the treatment of juvenile offenders. For example, we will look at the role of community and family in dealing with delinquency. We will question whether steps can be taken to improve the ways in which both community and family try to prevent delinquency.

KEY TERMS

abolishing juvenile court

capital punishment

criminalized juvenile court

divestiture

jurisdiction over status offenders

political economy

rebuilding community

restorative justice juvenile court

Roper v. Simmons

spiritual dimension in corrections

therapeutic jurisprudence

youth justice system

PROPOSALS FOR REFORMING JUVENILE COURT

Rehabilitating the Rehabilitative *Parens Patriae* Court

One approach to the problems of the juvenile court is try to return to the rehabilitative and *parens patriae* roots of the court. Reformers who support this option think that the failures of juvenile court are failures of implementation: the juvenile court has not delivered the rehabilitation that it initially promised. A major factor behind this failure of implementation is lack of funding. Legislators have not provided the money needed to help youths obtain education, counseling, family counseling, and vocational training.

If juvenile courts received adequate funding and if they followed the advice of the research on effective rehabilitation programs (see Chapters 10 and 11 for summaries of those findings), then juvenile court could be the ideal youth court envisioned by the Progressives at the beginning of the twentieth century. Juvenile court judges could act like concerned parents trying to help children.

A leader in the drive to get juvenile court to deliver rehabilitation is Lipsey (1999). Lipsey has done meta-analysis research on effective interventions. He believes that such research shows that there are effective interventions for both institutionalized and noninstitutionalized offenders. The best programs have the capability to "reduce recidivism by 40-50 percent, that is, to cut recidivism rates to very nearly half of what they would be without such programming" (Lipsey, 1999:163). Moreover, these programs "do not entail exceptional efforts or costs" (Lipsey, 1999:163); they are doable and affordable.

Krisberg uses the term "redemption" and offers the moral argument that we need to be concerned about redeeming all children:

> Moreover, it is patently clear that most of us would seek a justice system that is founded on core principles of charity and redemption if it were our own children who were in trouble. This, of course, is the key issue. If we recognize the truth that all children are our children, the search for the juvenile justice ideal is our only moral choice (Krisberg, 2005:196).

Corbett (2001) agrees with the call to implement the findings on effective interventions and adds that it is important to focus on early intervention instead of late intervention. Parent training, for example, has been shown to be effective. Another suggestion is to emphasize "the paying of just debts": "Restitution and community service programs repay and restore victims and harmed communities and counter the prevalent notion that juvenile offenders are immune from any real penalties . . ." (Corbett, 2001:149). He also suggests that probation officers should act as moral educators who help juveniles build character. He maintains that setting an example is crucial: "Every occasion where self-restraint is exercised in the face of a probationer's provo-cation, where kindness and courtesy is extended to a probationer's family in defiance of the juvenile's expectation, and every effort by the officer to insure fair treatment in dispositional and revocational proceedings are opportuni-ties for character building and moral education" (Corbett, 2001:149). His final suggestion is to attempt violence prevention through anger management skills training and similar social skills education programs.

Howell (2003) advocates both early intervention and the use of proven rehabilitation principles. He also urges the use of verified risk assessment techniques so that the court can identify and focus on youths most likely to become serious, violent, and chronic offenders, rather than wasting efforts on the least serious offenders who will not offend again. He supports grad-uated sanctions, gender-specific programming for girls, and the elimination of transfer to adult court.

Probably the most debatable point in Howell's suggestions is his call to end transfer. His rationale is that the "criminal justice system does not have the capacity to treat or protect juveniles, and incarcerating juveniles in adult facilities is not effective in deterring future crime" (Howell, 2003:309). Although Howell bases his suggestion on research evidence, it appears that the political mood is to "get tough" with juveniles, and transfer is one strategy that addresses that political mood.

None of these suggestions requires a radical reshaping of probation or the juvenile justice system. The suggestions build on the history and tradi-tion of probation as caring individuals (probation officers in the tradition of probation founder John Augustus). What Corbett proposes is that today's offi-cers utilize both social science findings (e.g., parent education and anger management training) and common sense, such as setting a character-build-ing example, to attempt to induce juveniles to become prosocial.

A Critic of the Rehabilitative Juvenile Court

Feld points out flaws with the argument that juvenile court failure is sim-ply a failure of implementation and that all that is needed is a rededication to the original rehabilitative ideals of juvenile court. Feld agrees that ade-quate funds have not been devoted to juvenile court, but he argues that funds will always be inadequate. One reason is that there is "pervasive public antipathy" to helping the poor, disadvantaged, disproportionately minority youths who are the clients of juvenile court. Another reason is that because committing a crime is the condition for receiving "help" from juvenile court, there is a built-in punishment focus. Feld argues that providing for children is a societal responsibility, not just a responsibility of juvenile court. In fact, the mere existence of juvenile court is an excuse or alibi for not providing for poor, minority youths. In Feld's words:

> A society collectively provides for the welfare of its children by supporting families, communities, schools, and social institutions that nurture all young people and not by cynically incarcerating its most disadvantaged children "for their own good" (Feld, 1999:296).

Feld also argues that juvenile court does not provide procedural fairness to children. Traditionally, some of the procedural protections of adult court, such as the right to jury trial, have been denied to children on the justification that the juvenile court was not a punitive court like adult court. Even worse than denying procedural protections, juvenile courts have treated children in similar circumstances who commit similar offenses in unequal and disparate fashion. This individualized handling was originally justified on the supposed rehabilitative foundation of juvenile court. However, because juvenile court is punitive and does not provide rehabilitation, this denial of due process safeguards makes juvenile court unfair and unjust.

In summary, Feld thinks that efforts to return the juvenile court to its rehabilitative ideal are doomed to failure: "The current juvenile court provides neither therapy nor justice *and* cannot be rehabilitated" (Feld, 1999:297).

A Criminalized Juvenile Court

A second solution to the problems of juvenile court is to "criminalize" juvenile court: to attempt to make it a scaled-down version of adult criminal court. In order to do this, two things need to be done. First, a **criminalized juvenile court** would entail providing juveniles with all the procedural protections of criminal court. Thus, children would have the right to a jury trial and would have fully adversarial defense attorneys, not attorneys who often slip into the role of a concerned parent trading off zealous advocacy for promises of treatment. A second action that needs to be taken to transform juvenile court into a criminal court for youths would be to scale down penalties out of concern for the reduced culpability of children. Sentences would be shorter in such a juvenile court compared to adult criminal court. This reform was suggested about 30 years ago by the American Bar Association and the Institute of Judicial Administration. The suggestion was published in the *Juvenile Justice Standards* (Institute of Judicial Administration–American Bar Association, 1982).

The major problem with the suggestion for a criminalized juvenile court is that it may not satisfy calls for a more punitive approach to juvenile offenders. Critics of the current juvenile justice system do not want reduced penalties; they want adult penalties for what they perceive as adult offenses: "adult crime, adult time," in the words of one governor (see Vandervort and Ladd, 2001:229). Such critics contend that violent offenses indicate culpability and should be punished with lengthy prison terms, and that is not the vision of the *Juvenile Justice Standards*.

Abolishing Juvenile Court

Feld thinks that the problems of juvenile court are too extensive and too fundamental to try to reform it. Now is the time to abandon the sinking ship of juvenile court. Because juvenile court provides neither help nor crime control, now is the time to abolish it. In its place Feld proposes adult criminal court for all, both juveniles and adults.

Adult court would mean that juveniles would receive adult procedural protections. Juveniles would have the right to a jury trial, and defense attorneys would act as zealous adversaries. In addition, Feld argues that juveniles should still get shorter sentences because shorter sentences have been a saving feature of juvenile court and they "enable most young offenders to survive the mistakes of adolescence with a semblance of their life chances intact" (Feld, 1999:304). Feld argues that adult courts could "discount" sentences for youths. Specifically, 14-year-olds would receive 25 to 33 percent of the adult penalty; 16-year-olds, 50 to 66 percent; and 18-year-old youths, the full adult penalty.

Feld fails to note that adult court sentencing for juveniles would also require some type of protection of the youth's record. The state of New York, for example, has a "youthful offender" provision that makes convictions and sentences under its provisions like juvenile court adjudications and dispositions in that they count do not count against the individual. In other words, one benefit of juvenile court is that a youth can legally say that he or she has not been "arrested" or "convicted"; instead, he or she has been "taken into custody' and "adjudicated." Such legal protections against arrest and conviction records can be extremely important if one is applying for a job, graduate school, or the military.

Vandervort and Ladd (2001) raise a serious objection to Feld's proposal. They argue that Michigan has changed its juvenile code to the point that many juveniles are now handled in adult court and the results have been harmful for juveniles. They contend that procedural rights are eroding in adult court. A juvenile transferred to adult court actually receives fewer due process protections in adult court than he or she would have in juvenile court. Juveniles are simply getting punishment in adult court, not treatment. Their conclusion is far more pessimistic than Feld's:

> Realistically, the adult criminal system has little or nothing positive to offer young people, it serves few, if any, elements of the public's interest, other than the impulse for retribution (Vandervort and Ladd, 2001:230).

One example illustrates their point. In 1997, Nathaniel Abraham, then 11 years old, was charged with murder. The juvenile court trial judge suppressed Nathaniel's confession to the police because the youth did not understand the *Miranda* warnings. The trial judge also chose a juvenile disposition; Nathaniel could only be under juvenile justice system control until age 21. The appellate court reversed the judge's ruling on understanding *Miranda* because it felt that the trial judge had placed too much emphasis on the child's youth and emotional impairment and not enough emphasis on the facts of the crime. Likewise, both the governor and other politicians criticized the judge's sentence; this is when the governor invoked the slogan "adult crime, adult time" (Vandervort and Ladd, 2001:229).

Another problem with Feld's suggestion of discounted sentencing for youths in adult court is that even discounted sentences might not be much of a bargain. Recall that Feld suggests that 16-year-olds should receive a youth discount of 50 to 66 percent. If a life sentence is equivalent to a sentence of 50 years, a 16-year-old (see the case of *LeBlanc* discussed below) processed in adult court would actually stay in prison until age 41 (half of 50 is 25 plus 16 equals age 41) or age 49 (66% of 50 plus 16). Thus, even with a youth "discount," youths processed in adult court would pay a heavy price if they left juvenile court, for which the maximum age for jurisdiction is 21.

Exemplifying the deficiencies of Feld's suggestion is the case of *In re LeBlanc*. LeBlanc was a 16-year-old who was charged with murdering his father. He had lived an exemplary life and been a good student but was immature mentally. He was waived to adult court where the likely sentence was life in prison. If he had been kept in juvenile court, he could only be confined until age 21, and he would have received high school and college education. The only possible "benefit" of adult court processing would be that the adult correctional system would teach LeBlanc a trade, but the lengthy prison sentence meant that "it would be decidedly unlikely that he would ever have been able to use that trade beyond the walls of the prison in which he would be housed" (Vandervort and Ladd, 2001:250).

Research, too, shows problems with adult court processing. Bishop and her colleagues interviewed juveniles who had been transferred to adult court in Florida. Juveniles were negative about adult court and adult corrections. They did not fully understand what transpired in adult court and perceived the process to be one of gamesmanship. They felt that criminal court judges had "little interest in them or their problems" whereas juvenile court judges "expressed interest in their problems and concern for their well-being" (Bishop, 2000:136). Similarly, the juveniles felt that juvenile correctional staff "cared for them, understood what troubled them, and believed in their potential . . .," whereas they perceived staff in adult correctional facilities as hostile, derisive, and uncaring workers who thought the juveniles were incapable of change (Bishop, 2000:144).

Kerbs (1999) notes two other problems with Feld's suggestion to switch juveniles to adult criminal court. First, politicians are not saying "discount"; they are crying out "adult crime, adult time." Politicians are mouthing a simplistic formula that suggests that they regard youthful offenders as simply younger but fully responsible offenders. Second, Kerbs fears that

African-American juveniles transferred to adult court will continue to receive unfair treatment compared to whites—"unequal justice under law" (Kerbs, 1999:120). Thus, there is reason to believe that abolishing juvenile court would not have the positive effects Feld envisions and might well produce very negative effects.

For a different interpretation of juvenile responsibility, see Box 14.1 concerning parental responsibility for juvenile misbehavior

Box 14.1 Parental Responsibility Laws

One version of the punitive trend is to hold parents criminally responsible for wrongdoing by their children. Oregon adopted an "improper supervision" statute in 1995 that imposes criminal liability on a parent whose child either "[c]ommits an act that brings the child within the jurisdiction of the juvenile court," "[v]iolates a curfew," or "[f]ails to attend school" (Oregon Revised Statute § 163.577 (3)-(4), cited in DiFonzo, 2001). A number of cities have enacted laws. For example, the City of St. Clair Shores, Michigan, mandates that parents adhere to their "continuous duty . . . to exercise reasonable control to prevent the minor from committing any delinquent act." (St. Clair Shores Ordinances § 20.563(a)). More specifically, the St. Clair Shores ordinance orders parents to ensure that their children, among other things, observe the curfew, attend school, and:

- To take the necessary precautions to prevent the minor from maliciously or wilfully destroying real, personal, or mixed property which belongs to the City of St. Clair Shores, or is located in the City of St. Clair Shores.

- To forbid the minor from keeping stolen property, illegally possessing firearms or illegal drugs, or associating with known juvenile delinquents, and to seek help from appropriate governmental authorities or private agencies in handling or controlling the minor, when necessary (St. Clair Shores Ordinances § 20.563(b); cited in DiFonzono, 2001).

Similarly, Tennessee has enacted a truancy law punishing parents for excessive truancy by their children (Tenn. Code Ann. §§ 49-6-3001 to 49-6-3009 (Supp. 2000)(cited in DiFonzo, 2001).

Penalties for some city ordinances involve both jail time and fines for the parents.

What do you think? Should parents face jail time and a fine if their child commits truancy or a delinquent act? What if a parent has done all that he or she could to prevent delinquency and the child apparently resisted the positive actions of the parent to keep the child out of trouble? What does it accomplish to have and enforce parental responsibility laws?

Creating a New Juvenile Court

Still another suggestion is to make a new juvenile court. Noriega (2000) suggests that we create a new juvenile court that has two branches: one for children and one for adolescents. The children's court would be rehabilitative and would presume that children are inculpable, that is, they do not have criminal responsibility. The adolescent court would presume partial culpability and would be more punitive than the children's court. Of course, adult court would continue to presume that adults are culpable and would be the most punitive of the three courts.

Waiver would be by judicial hearing only. There would be no prosecutorial or legislative waiver, and waiver would be only to the next step. Thus, children could only be waived to adolescent court, and only adolescents could be waived to adult court. Juveniles (children and adolescents) would not be allowed to waive their right to counsel. Noriega's reasoning for this is that children and adolescents are generally presumed not competent; they are not allowed to enter into contracts, cannot drink alcohol, and cannot vote or drive (until late adolescence).

This is an interesting proposal. Noriega disagrees with Feld that abolishing juvenile court is the best course of action. Noriega argues that abolishing juvenile court will not guarantee that adult courts treat children/adolescents properly. He argues that it will be hard to treat a juvenile as a juvenile after he has been designated an "adult" and that it will be difficult to actually give discounts, à la Feld, to juveniles in adult court "as if they were getting their sentence on sale from K-Mart" (Noriega, 2000:692-693).

An attractive feature of this proposal is that it offers a more complex and realistic view of development. Instead of assuming that one day a juvenile is a child and the next day he is an adult, it recognizes the intermediate stage of adolescence. Noriega is also probably more realistic than Feld about the actual results of abolishing juvenile court and letting adult court handle juvenile matters. Adult courts are probably not going to be as caring and protective or concerned about youth discounts as Feld hopes.

Unfortunately, Noriega just gives a sketchy outline. He says that states should have a children's court and an adolescent's court. He does not give us specific

AP Photo/Richard Sheinwald

Anthony Provenzino of St. Clair Shores, Michigan, holds hands with his wife, Susan Provenzino, while on trial under a law holding them responsible for their son. The city contended that 16-year-old Alex Provenzino got into drugs and became a burglar because his parents did not keep a close eye on him.

age limits for each. Nor does he specify punishment limits (e.g., incarceration terms) for each. Still another problem is that this could result in yet another bureaucracy—adolescent court and adolescent corrections—when the current juvenile and adult bureaucracies both have myriad problems. To note just one issue, will states be willing to create a new adolescent court and corrections system (assuming the current juvenile court becomes children's court)? Will they be willing to hire more personnel? Build more courtrooms? Build more prisons? As Garland (2000—and see below) so aptly points out, the recent trend has been to cut back the welfare state in general. Noriega's proposal goes against that trend; governmental bodies are looking to cut expenditures, not embrace new spending initiatives.

A "Youth Justice System" within Adult Criminal Court

Jeffrey Butts (2000) offers still another variation: a **youth justice system** within adult court. As we observed at the beginning of the chapter, Butts notes that the juvenile justice system is disappearing before our very eyes. Presumptive waiver provisions, mandatory waiver, blended sentencing, mandatory minimums and other sentencing guidelines, open hearings, and the use of juvenile records in adult court (e.g., to count as first or second strikes in three-strikes cases) are all nails in the coffin of the traditional juvenile court. Thus "[i]t is too late to save the traditional [juvenile justice] system because the traditional system is already gone" (Butts, 2000:52). He also notes that widespread opposition to the idea of delinquency dictates the end of delinquency cases in juvenile court. When the public hears "delinquent," they think "weak and lenient" (Butts, 2000:55).

His suggestion is to transfer all delinquency matters to adult court but to create a separate arm of adult court to deal with criminal acts allegedly committed by juveniles. He argues that adult courts are creating new specialized courts such as drug courts and mental health courts that do specialized intake and treatment. He thinks that specialized youth justice courts could do the same for juveniles. The benefit would be to stop fighting over which court—juvenile or adult—gets which offender and to start focusing "on ensuring the quality of the process used for all youth" (Butts, 2000:56). Because Butts is proposing a specialized court like drug and mental health courts, his proposal can be considered an extension of the movement called **therapeutic jurisprudence**: "an interdisciplinary perspective that urges us to consider the therapeutic and antitherapeutic consequences of legal rules, of legal procedures, and of the roles of lawyers, judges, and others acting within the legal arena" (Wexler, 2002:205).

Butts is accurate that many of the changes in juvenile court in the last 10 years have taken away many of the clientele (via some type of waiver/transfer). He is also accurate that some of the new drug courts and mental health courts (therapeutic jurisprudence) have made significant strides in dealing with their particular clients. A major question, however, is whether most jurisdictions would in fact start such courts and would devote the resources needed to allow them to carry out their mission. Creating new youth services courts in the adult system without adequate funding and resources would be a sham.

A Restorative Justice Juvenile Court

Gordon Bazemore (1999) suggests that now is the time to take the "fork in the road," to try a new path for juvenile court. As noted in Chapter 12, Bazemore is one of the main proponents for adopting a restorative justice model in the juvenile justice system.

In Pittsburgh, young offenders are involved in service projects such as home repair for the elderly and voter registration drives. In Utah, offenders are paying victim restitution out of wages from public service jobs. In Oregon, offender work crews cut firewood and deliver it to the elderly. More than 150 cities are utilizing victim–offender mediation. In Colorado and Florida, offenders work with Habitat for Humanity building homes for lower-income families. In Florida, probation officers are walking neighborhood beats to help promote local guardianship of communities. In Boston and in Florida, probation officers are helping police monitor probationers at night.

What all of these efforts have in common is a restorative justice focus that emphasizes the victim and the community. The approach is "focused less on achieving public safety by incarcerating individual offenders and more on reducing fear, building youth-adult relationships, and increasing the capacity of community groups and institutions to prevent crime and safely monitor offenders in the community" (Bazemore, 1999:98).

This represents a radical rethinking of the role of juvenile court. Instead of sanctioning and supervising offenders, the role of the **restorative justice juvenile court** would be to build community so that neighborhoods can better respond to—but also prevent—delinquency. Communities would be more involved in sentencing through community panels or conferences or dispute resolution programs. Communities would return to their role of being responsible for youths. Bazemore argues that the community must address socialization needs with "caring adults who spend time with young people not because they are paid to do so but because they share a commitment to the idea that youth development is a community responsibility" (Bazemore, 1999:101).

A positive feature of Bazemore's proposal is that it is not a hypothetical proposal; many restorative justice programs are already in place. As noted, numerous communities already are working at restorative justice. A major question, however, is how far restorative justice can go. How willing are citizens to assume the responsibilities that restorative justice would give them in deciding cases and monitoring sanctions such as community service? If people are not available to staff the restorative justice programs, they will not work. Proving that it is possible to implement such programs, Vermont has a system of 49 restorative justice boards with almost 300 volunteer board members in operation (Karp, Bazemore, and Chesire, 2004). These boards use 30- to 60-minute meetings to negotiate restorative justice contracts between victims and offenders. So it is possible to implement such programs.

A recent survey of juvenile court judges found overall support for victim involvement in the juvenile court process. For example, 60 percent of the judges agreed that victims should have input into the sanctioning and dispositional decisions of juvenile court, and 44 percent thought that victims should have input into diversion decisions. Focus group discussions with judges, however, showed some ambivalence about victim involvement. Some judges thought that involving victims in juvenile court decisions might introduce some bias into juvenile court. Some judges thought that greater victim involvement might detract from judges' attempts to remain neutral in juvenile court (Bazemore and Leip, 2000).

Zimring's Caution

Zimring (2000) adds a cautionary note to the various proposals about keeping, abolishing, or modifying juvenile court. He reminds us that even juvenile court is in the business of imposing punishment. As rehabilitative as the intentions of the founders may have been, the truth, as noted in *In re Gault,* is that juvenile court "dispositions" often deprive youths of their freedom. For Zimring, this truth of punishment means that a crucial element, even if we abolish juvenile court, is reduced punishment. In other words, even if all juveniles went to adult court, there still would be a legitimate issue of deciding on lesser punishments for such offenders. Second, Zimring points out that the United States is inconsistent about juveniles. It prohibits them from voting until age 18 and from drinking until age 21 because they are considered immature yet submits them to adult court and punishment at increasingly lower ages. Zimring agrees that youths are immature and argues that states need to address this inconsistency and not just ignore it.

Summary

Juvenile justice is at a crossroads. Critics have pointed out serious flaws with juvenile court, and many states have already removed many youths from juvenile court jurisdiction. In light of the criticisms of juvenile court and the legislation sending more juveniles to adult court, now is the time to rethink the nature and goals of juvenile court. Now is the time to consider proposals such as those delineated above and decide on the best course of action.

BROADER ISSUES

Beyond the need to make changes in juvenile court, there are additional issues that need to be addressed if American society is to help juveniles grow into mature, responsible, law-abiding adults. We will note several such issues here and show how they relate to juvenile justice. We will consider the issues of race and juvenile court, the possible decline of community and social capital, the role and needs of American families, and the **political economy**.

Race and Juvenile Court

A number of writers argue that juvenile justice must fight the influence of racism. The federal government, for example, has made the elimination of disproportionate minority confinement in juvenile correctional facilities a priority.

Feld (1999) summarizes several studies that have looked at sentencing in juvenile court. These studies indicate that legal variables—present offense and prior record—account "for virtually all the variance in juvenile court sentences that can be explained" (Feld, 1999:266). "[A]fter controlling for legal and offense variables, the individualized justice of juvenile courts produces racial disparities in the sentencing of minority offenders" (Feld, 1999:266). To give but one example, in California, African-American youths make up 8.7 percent of the youth population but 37 percent of juveniles in confinement (Feld, 1999). The existence of racial disparity is an additional reason for Feld's call to abolish juvenile court.

Ferguson (2000) contends that racism occurs prior to the juvenile justice system; it starts in school:

> Schools mirror and reinforce the practices and ideological systems of other institutions in the society. The racial bias in the punishing systems of the school reflects the practices of the criminal justice system (Ferguson, 2000:231).

Ferguson gives as evidence the remark of a vice-principal about a small 10-year-old boy: "That one has a jail cell with his name on it" (cited in Ferguson, 2000:1). Another indicator of the pervasiveness of racial prejudice and discrimination in American society is that many black kids feel that to succeed in school they must "act white": "being a "good" student is equivalent to losing one's racial cultural identity" (Ferguson, 2000:203).

Perhaps most disturbing of all is Feld's (2000) assertion that there is pervasive public antipathy to the problems of disadvantaged and minority children. If society does not really care for poor minority children, then it may not matter all that much which court—juvenile rehabilitative, juvenile criminal, or adult criminal—is designated to process juvenile delinquency. Unless society is truly committed to the problems of all youths, and especially disadvantaged youths, then youth crime will persist.

As noted in Chapter 8, a dissident voice about this issue is Tracy (2002), who contends that much of the claim for disproportionate handling of African-American juveniles in the juvenile justice system rests on flimsy evidence. Tracy's own research in Texas did *not* find "strong and consistent race and ethnic differentials in juvenile processing" (Tracy, 2002:175). Tracy thinks that there is differential minority involvement in delinquency, and this differential involvement needs to be addressed. In other words, "if a greater prevalence of minority youth commit delinquent offenses, then there will be more such youth available for processing at each point of the juvenile justice process compared to Anglo youth" (Tracy, 2002:176).

This is not the place for a thorough analysis of racism in the juvenile justice system. We simply note that many analysts see disproportionate processing of minority youths while Tracy argues that the problem is disproportionate involvement. Even Tracy would agree that it is important to eliminate any traces of racism or perceived racial inequities in juvenile court so that all youths will regard the juvenile justice system as fair. Without the perception of fair treatment, minority youths will be suspicious and resentful, and those emotions doom any hope of reclaiming problem youths.

The Need to Rebuild Community

As noted in the discussion of community policing in Chapter 7, Putnam (2000) argues that we are "bowling alone"; that is, social capital is eroding. That is, civic participation and other measures of community involvement are declining. If accurate, this decline of social capital has implications for juvenile justice.

One measure of the decline of community is religious participation. Between the 1960s and the 1990s, church membership declined by approximately 10 percent. Similarly, church attendance has declined by approximately 10-12 percent over the last quarter century, most markedly from the mid-1980s to the mid-1990s (Putnam, 2000). Participation in civic clubs has also declined. In 1975-76, about two-thirds (64%) of Americans had attended at least one club meeting in the previous year. That slipped to about 38 percent by 1999 (Putnam, 2000).

What do Americans do with their time now? One major activity is television watching. Eight out of 10 Americans now report that most evenings they watch television (Putnam, 2000). In fact, "[m]ost studies estimate that the average American now watches roughly four hours per day, very nearly the highest viewership anywhere in the world" (Putnam, 2000:222). Along with other electronic media, television has

. . . rendered our leisure more private and passive. More and more of our time and money are spent on goods and services consumed individually, rather than those consumed collectively. Americans' leisure time can increasingly be measured—as do strategic marketers—in terms of 'eyeballs,' since watching things (especially electronic screens) occupies more and more of our time, while doing things (especially with other people) occupies less and less" (Putnam, 2000:245).

As noted in Chapter 7, if community is in fact declining, then the future of community policing is not as optimistic as its proponents proclaim. Decline of community would have other repercussions as well. If community is declining and if that decline cannot be stopped, then restorative justice efforts also will face difficulties. If we want citizens to participate in restorative justice conferencing, victim-offender mediation programs, sentencing circles, and other restorative justice programs (see the earlier section on restorative justice), we need a solid community base as the foundation for those efforts. If people do not join together socially, how can we realistically expect them to come together for restorative justice initiatives?

A more fundamental issue is that the decline of community may even make delinquency worse and increase the need for juvenile justice interventions. If civic clubs are disbanding due to lack of interest and participation, we can expect reduced sponsorship of youth sports teams, scout troops, and Boys and Girls Clubs. Many civic clubs sponsor such programs for neighborhood youths. If the clubs are disappearing, either the parents will have to pick up the tab or the youth teams and programs will not survive.

There is hope, however. Putnam points out, for example, that Americans seem to want to reverse the trend of declining civic participation and social capital: "We tell pollsters that we wish we lived in a more civil, more trustworthy, more collectively caring community" (Putnam, 2000:403). He offers some steps that could be effective in restoring social capital. One is for employers to be more family- and community-friendly. Some firms, for example, offer release time to some employees to volunteer for community service such as serving on United Way campaigns. Because part-time workers participate more in community, Putnam urges employers to make greater allowance for part-time employment opportunities. He urges urban planners to design living areas that are more pedestrian-friendly and urges church leaders to revivify spiritual community. He calls for electronic entertainment that fosters community engagement rather than passive sitting in front of television sets. He suggests using the arts to foster community. He urges greater civics education and other efforts to foster political participation (Putnam, 2000).

The challenge is great. Many forces are at work to isolate us from our neighbors. Contemporary trends, such as the proliferation of personal computers, Internet usage, personal compact discs, and a TV and DVD player for each household member, are all working to drive us apart. In the 1950s, even television watching was a family activity. There was only one television set and only three major networks. Today we have multiple sets in even the poorest of households and hundreds of cable or satellite stations to choose from. Families may watch the Super Bowl together, but little else.

It is important not to idealize a past that was far from perfect. The 1950s were not idyllic for African Americans who had to sit at the back of the bus and could not get into the college of their choice. Nor were they idyllic for women who could not enter jobs and professions that they aspired to. However, it is important to note that we need to restore social capital. If we wish to prevent delinquency and to pursue new avenues such as restorative justice, then citizens must be willing to contribute to their communities. As noted above, states such as Vermont are proving that there are citizens willing to step up and serve on restorative justice boards; that is, there are people willing to do something about delinquency and victimization (Karp, Bazemore, and Chesire, 2004).

The Role of the Family

Where Putnam argues that community life is eroding, Bennett (2001) argues that the American family is in rapid decline. He points to what he considers alarming levels of divorce, births of out-of-wedlock children, single-parent families, and cohabiting couples as evidence of his claim.

Bennett believes that a decline in values is responsible for the "collapse" of the American family. He thinks that America's sense of community and religion has given way to "a radical individualistic ethos," "a fierce assault directed against marriage and the family," and "the rise of a consumerist mentality" (Bennett, 2001:16-17). He contends that the media has given much impetus to this decline. He argues, for example, that on many daytime television talk shows "indecent exposure is celebrated as a virtue, perversions are made to seem commonplace, and modesty and discretion are frowned upon" (Bennett, 2001:32). Bennett's (2001) solution is to return to family values and to resist the erosion of values.

An interesting counterpoint to Bennett's position is Mintz's argument that we are overly protective of youths, and such overprotection does not allow children the opportunities to grow and mature. He argues, for example, that binge drinking in college can be traced to not allowing children the opportunity to learn to drink responsibly. Similarly, as kids have increasingly less free time and less free space, we deny them opportunities to learn, explore, and grow.

Mintz also argues that nostalgia is no answer; there is no way to return to a Disneyland or *Music Man* version of Main Street in small-town America where the biggest threat was a pool hall coming to town:

> It is not possible to recreate a "walled garden" of childhood innocence, no matter how hard we might try. No V-chip, Internet filtering software, or CD-rating system will immunize children from

the influence of contemporary culture. Since we cannot insulate
children from all malign influences, it is essential that we prepare
them to deal responsibly with the pressures and choice they face.
That task requires knowledge, not sheltering. In a risk-filled
world, naïveté is vulnerability (Mintz, 2004:382).

So the challenge is to both protect children but at the same time give them
opportunities to explore and grow:

Our challenge is to reverse the process of age segmentation, to provide the young with challenging alternatives to a world of malls,
instant messaging, music videos, and play dates. Huck Finn was
an abused child, whose father, the town drunk, beat him for going
to school and learning to read. Who would envy Huck's battered
childhood? Yet he enjoyed something too many children are denied
and which adults can provide: opportunities to undertake odysseys
of self-discovery outside the goal-driven, overstructured realities of contemporary childhood (Mintz, 2004:383-384).

Character Education

Similar to Bennett, Christina Hoff Sommers (2000) thinks that faulty
character education is a major cause of delinquency and other problems. Sommers states that there are two approaches to educating the young, especially
boys. Aristotle argued for moral education analogous to physical training.
Just as exercise leads to muscle strength, practicing goodness leads to
moral character. Parents and schools need to discipline children to get them
to behave well.

The Rousseauian approach, on the other hand, thinks that children are
naturally good, and no external code should be imposed on the child. Teachers, therefore, should not preach to students but should allow their natural
goodness to shine forth. One recent example of this philosophy is values clarification, a program that simply tried to help children discover their own values. An even more recent example is the self-esteem movement, which
puts each student on a pedestal. Instead of studying great persons, students
are encouraged to celebrate their own wondrous gifts.

Sommers thinks that the Rousseauian approach has won out in American schools and that it is simply wrong. She thinks that most parents, however, opt for Aristotle's approach: "throughout the world, mothers and
fathers never cease to work at habituating children to the exercise of self-control, temperance, honesty, courage" (Sommers, 2000:191).

As evidence, Sommers notes that Eric Harris and Dylan Klebold, the per-
petrators of the Columbine High School violence in 1999, had written dis-
turbingly violent stories. A teacher had notified school officials but the school
took no action because there was more concern about violating free speech

than about correcting inappropriate speech. In Sommers' description, in most schools, "[i]t has become the style not to interfere with the child's self-expression and autonomy" (Sommers, 2000:200).

Character education does not mean preaching. Rather, "[w]e teach by who we are" (Tigner, 2000). The world's great teachers—Socrates, Jesus, Buddha—taught with their persons and we must do the same. Sommers makes us ask ourselves a question: Does failure to teach morality in school lead to violence such as the Columbine High School massacre? If we taught the Victorian virtues of "honesty, integrity, courage, decency, politeness" (Sommers, 2000:196), rather than pursuing the Rousseau-like path of self-expression, would delinquency decrease?

Social Support for Families

Others agree that family is critical for child and adolescent development and delinquency prevention. Many think, however, that society is not as supportive of families as it could be. The problem is not that parents are abandoning family values, but that there are social, economic, and political forces at work that weaken the ability of families to do their job. The answer is to provide more assistance to families.

Alida Merlo noted that 13 percent of American children live in conditions that are considered to make them "high-risk" children. About one-third of U.S. children live in one-parent families, about 20 percent live in a home headed by a high school dropout, about 20 percent grow up in poverty, almost 30 percent live with parents who do not have a full-time job, about 12 percent of families receive public assistance, and about 15 percent of children do not have health insurance (Merlo, 2000). In 1996, about 1,000 children died of maltreatment (abuse or neglect), yet in "all the political rhetoric about preventing youth violence, any reference to these fatalities, or the conditions that may increase their likelihood, is conspicuously absent" (Merlo, 2000:649). The proponents of tough juvenile policies also ignore the developmental stages that youths go through and instead simply assume that adolescents are completely adult in all respects. Merlo concludes that we need "a moratorium on punitive, reactionary juvenile justice reform" in favor of "a more rational, less political, more observant, more humane manner" (Merlo, 2000:658-659).

Merlo is right for two reasons. She is right because it is simply wrong to ignore these high-risk children. The second reason she is right is that there is an "emerging consensus" that "coercion causes crime and social support prevents crime" (Colvin, Cullen, and Vander Ven, 2002:19). To be more specific, the research clearly shows that childhood conduct disorders can lead to delinquency, especially for high-rate offenders. It is also clear that "supportive programs—programs that invest in at-risk children and in at-risk families—work to reduce crime" (Cullen, Wright, and Chamlin, 1999:198-199).

Social support for families includes such assistance as parent-effectiveness training, paid family leave, health care insurance, and visiting nurse programs.

In conclusion, a number of conservative and liberal writers agree that there are important problems pertaining to families and their ability to raise healthy and law-abiding children. Conservatives argue that families need to return to traditional values and character education, whereas liberals argue that families need more social and economic support to help them to do their job.

The Political Economy and Juvenile Court

Garland (2001) makes an intriguing and complex assessment of today's criminal justice policy. He argues that social, political, and economic changes in the last 30 years have had important effects on how we view and treat crime and criminals and delinquents.

First, over the last half of the twentieth century, there has been a dramatic increase in crime and delinquency. A number of changes led to this increase. One was the growth of the consumer economy with its spread of portable consumer goods. Very simply, people today have more "stuff"—stereos, TVs, cameras, laptop computers—so there are more opportunities to steal goods, whether by shoplifting or burglary. Similarly, there are more families with both spouses working, and that means that there are more empty homes to burglarize during the day. The growth of the suburbs also means more spread-out neighborhoods and fewer knowing eyes—fewer guardians—to keep a lookout on one another's homes. Finally, a questioning of traditional authority has led to less social control.

At the same time, the so-called welfare state was expanding, and government bureaucracies were growing. Then problems developed. Race riots, civil rights demonstrations, and anti-war protests caused concern. More practically, recession in the 1970s raised questions about the ability to pay for ever-expanding benefit programs. President Ronald Reagan in the United States and Prime Minister Margaret Thatcher in Britain represented "[h]ostility toward 'tax and spend' government, undeserving welfare recipients, 'soft on crime' policies, unelected trade unions who were running the country, the break-up of the family, the breakdown of law and order . . ."(Garland, 2001:97). Reagan and Thatcher both allowed market forces to take precedence in their respective economies with the same result: "the rapid collapse of industrial production and the re-emergence of structural unemployment on a massive scale not seen since the 1930s" (Garland, 2001:98). This decline of factories and factory jobs meant higher unemployment, which Garland thinks contributed to increased crime.

Crime came to be seen as a matter of individual choice and responsibility, not as something socially generated:

> Crime came to be seen instead as a problem of indiscipline, a lack of self-control or social control, a matter of wicked individuals who needed to be deterred and who deserved to be punished. Instead of indicating need or deprivation, crime was a matter of anti-social cultures or personalities, and of rational individual choice in the face of lax law enforcement and lenient punishment regimes (Garland, 2001:102).

Accompanying this was a questioning of the state's ability (via policing and corrections) to control the crime problem. Governments see the necessity of recognizing less-than-omnipotent power to control crime, yet they fear the political consequences of admitting powerlessness over crime. So for politicians the there is a perceived "need to find popular and effective measures that will not be viewed as signs of weakness or an abandonment of the state's responsibility to the public" (Garland, 2001:111). Unfortunately, the public often has unrealistic expectations and ideas about crime control, expectations that demand results at any cost. Concretely, the public demands that

> criminals should be prosecuted to the full extent of the law, the guilty should always be punished, dangerous individuals should never be released, prisoners should serve their full terms, and an offender's sentence should precisely reflect his offense. And somehow, at the same time, the innocent should always be acquitted, the rule of law upheld, and expenditure held within reasonable levels (Garland, 2001:112).

To summarize, forces such as the proliferation of consumer goods and the decline of guardianship (watchers) were increasing crime at the same time that government funds were decreasing (due to such factors as the globalization of the economy) the provision of treatment programs for delinquents and criminals. Thus, popular sentiment was developing against the poor in general and against delinquents and criminals in particular. Governments were waging war on crime and tending to incarcerate more and more and treat less and less. In juvenile court, this movement has translated into increasing transfer of youths to adult court, sentencing youthful offenders to adult corrections or blended corrections (a combination of juvenile and adult sanctions), and even use of the death penalty for juveniles.

The net result is that instead of devising initiatives to help these groups, politicians are practicing welfare reform for the poor and tough justice for youthful delinquents. These policies coincide with economic realities in twenty-first-century America (and Britain), and they also comfort the middle and upper classes with their fear of street crime—no matter how exaggerated that paranoia may be.

Garland does not have the answers to the scene he so well describes. Inattention to the real needs of youths (especially poor youths) is not a new phenomena in the United States. In the mid-nineteenth century, for example, the Children's Aid Society in New York City dealt with the urban poor by getting rid of them rather than by actually dealing with the poverty that afflicted them. Specifically, Charles Loring Brace, founder of the Children's Aid Society, began the "orphan trains" that shipped New York City youths west to farmers and whomever else would accept these youths. This practice grew, even though many of the youths suffered abuse in their new environments equal to or worse than what they had suffered at the hands of their own parents in New York. The policy was attractive because it visibly removed problem youths from New York and put them out of sight—in placements out west (O'Connor, 2001).

Part of the solution may mean a re-ordering of priorities. If the global economy means that there is only a limited amount of money available for social spending programs in our postmodern economy, perhaps we need to re-evaluate our entitlement programs. Just as Western democracies re-evaluated welfare spending in the 1990s and enacted "welfare reform," perhaps we need to re-evaluate other entitlement programs to see if we are spending enough money on programs that benefit youths.

Perhaps the easiest way to follow Garland's suggestions, however, is to use his analysis to clarify some of the true purposes of the current system. He argues that the current passion for punishment is politically generated. It coincides with many of the social and economic changes of the last 25 years and addresses much of the fear of crime generated by the proliferation of consumer goods, the reduction of guardianship in sprawling suburban housing developments spawned by the interstate highway system, the absence of anyone home during working hours due to dual-income households, and a perception that traditional values are eroding. Garland clearly shows that much of America's passion for punishment is a grasping for straws in the face of threatening changes and perceptions of high crime rates.

Reintroducing the Spiritual Dimension into Corrections

As noted above, some think that the answer to delinquency is character education. Going even further than this, Powers (2002) argues that the basic problem facing today's youths is apocalyptic nihilism. By this he means that American youths face a gnawing gap in their lives, that they seek "a community that satisfied their longing for worth-proving ritual, meaningful action in the service of a cause, and psychological intimacy" (Powers, 2002:65). Similarly, Staples (2000) argues that one explanation for school violence is the emptiness of our consumer culture, which does not satisfy the deeper longings of the heart. In Staples's words, both youths and adults possess a "fundamental yearning for significance through engagement in the processes of reflection, creativity, compassion, and the gift of self to others" (Staples, 2000:33). So Powers, Staples, and others believe that youths are searching for a deeper sense of meaning in their lives.

Instead of providing such meaning, American policy offers problem youths punishment. The answer, says Powers, is "respectful inclusion: through a reintegration of our young into the intimate circles of family and community life. We must face the fact that having ceased to exploit children as laborers, we now exploit them as consumers. We must find ways to offer them useful functions tailored to their evolving capacities" (Powers, 2002:74).

Whitehead and Braswell (2000) argue that what is needed is to re-introduce the **spiritual dimension in corrections**. This would entail efforts of corrections workers, whether prison counselors, chaplains, or probation officers, to help offenders find greater meaning in their lives.

Both residential institutions and probation can try to address the spiritual needs of juvenile offenders. Prisons and jails have always had chaplains and religious services as part of their programming. That can and should continue, but institutions and probation/parole can take additional steps to incorporate the spiritual dimension into correctional practice.

First, correctional workers—correctional counselors, probation officers, parole officers, correctional officers—can all attempt to help offenders focus on the question of meaning in their lives. In group sessions and individual reporting, these workers can encourage offenders to think about the meaning of their lives.

Second, correctional workers have the simple but potentially profound example of their own lives. They can come to work each and every day showing a sense of purpose and meaning in their lives and in their interactions with prisoners that will influence those who come in contact with them. All of us can attest to persons who show by the example of their lives that there is something that energizes them and inspires them despite the difficulties they face. This is in stark contrast to workers who exert a negative influence in the prison or in the parole office. For example, in one women's prison, some guards came in and plopped down in front of the television set to watch hours of sports programming (Girshick, 1999), and in some Canadian correctional facilities, guard supervisors were found to create an environment rife with sexual harassment (McMahon, 1999). At the very least, workers need to refrain from abuse, harassment, and anything else that detracts from prison as a place where offenders can think about the meaning of their lives.

A concrete suggestion is to adopt an intervention strategy such as the "Making Life Choices" program, which is a participatory learning strategy that focuses "on creating contexts in which young people themselves can discover their own competence for influencing the direction of their lives" (Ferrer-Wreder et al., 2002:170). The goal is "accepting control and responsibility of one's life" (Ferrer-Wreder et al., 2002:171).

One reason for raising the issue of introducing the spiritual dimension into corrections is that there is evidence that it matters. In a recent study of offenders ages 15 to 24, Benda (2002) found that religion was inversely related to carrying a weapon, violence, the use of illicit drugs, and the selling of illicit drugs. Religion was measured by church attendance, religious expressions, and forgiveness.

Recent research has shown the importance of religion in delinquency causation. In a study of boot camp inmates, Benda (2002) found that religion was clearly correlated (inversely) with crimes against persons. In fact, religion was the fifth largest correlate in the model. So the more religious the inmates, the less likely they were to be involved in violence. In addition, an analysis of the National Youth Survey found that religiosity had negative effects on adolescent use of illicit drugs (Jang and Johnson, 2001). These studies confirm the importance of religion and suggest its usefulness in preventing delinquency.

One task of corrections, then, may be to help that segment of offenders who are open to asking and seeking answers to the perennial questions about life: Why am I here? What is the meaning of life? What is happiness? Should I just seek more money and prestige, or are there other more important goals in life? Do I just consider myself, or should I think about others? Am I making moral or immoral choices? As one thinker puts it, am I seeking "significance through engagement in the processes of reflection, creativity, compassion, and the gift of self to others" (Staples, 2000:33)? None of this should lead to proselytizing or to erasing the separation of church and state. No correctional worker should impose his or her religious beliefs on inmates or probationers.

AP Photo/Stephen Morton

An inmate in Wheeler Correctional Facility reads a Bible in his bunk at the prison in Alamo, Georgia. The prison is one of 22 nationwide in which private prison operator Corrections Corporation of America has opened "faith pods," living quarters that promote reform and spiritual bonding by separating soul-searching inmates from the general population. Inmates pray and read scripture throughout the day.

Some may object that attempting to inject the spiritual into correctional practice is too ambitious a project. If corrections cannot accomplish the basic objective of keeping offenders crime-free, then how can it be expected to help offenders become better persons spiritually? However, this objection may have it backwards. Perhaps one reason that corrections has had such an uninspiring record with recidivism is that it makes no effort to help offenders in a search for meaning and purpose in their lives. If the implicit objective of corrections is that offenders only need to buy into the American Dream, and if that dream is questionable and uninspiring and one that ignores the deeper potential of human living, then it may be no surprise that probation does little to improve recidivism.

CAPITAL PUNISHMENT FOR JUVENILES

In 2003, an estimated 1,130 juveniles (youths under 18 years of age) were arrested for murder. This was a decrease of 10 percent from 2002 and a decrease of 18 percent from 1999. It is also dramatically lower than the approximately 3,800 juveniles who were arrested for murder in 1993, the peak year for murders by juveniles (Snyder, 2005). Despite this decrease, we will probably see continued media attention on juveniles who kill.

At yearend 2003, there were 67 death row inmates (out of a total of 3,374 death row inmates) who were younger than 18 at the time of their arrest for a capital offense (Bonczar and Snell, 2004). Due to a recent Supreme Court ruling (see the following discussion), these youths are no longer eligible to be executed and will be removed or have been removed from death row.

For adult murderers, capital punishment has been debated for years (see, e.g., van den Haag and Conrad, 1983, and Costanzo, 1997, for further discussion). The questions in the debate have been both philosophical and empirical. Some of the philosophical questions involve the moral issue of the state taking a human life (for viewpoints on this issue, see Boxes 14.2 and 14.3) and the morality of capital punishment in the face of the possibility of mistakes (i.e., executing someone who has been mistakenly convicted). The empirical questions include the deterrent impact of capital punishment (does it prevent individuals from committing murder because they fear being sentenced to die?) and the issue of racial or class bias (is the death penalty more likely to be imposed on minorities than on whites?). These same issues apply to the question of the appropriateness of the death penalty for juveniles.

Box 14.2. Some Arguments against Capital Punishment

Two voices against capital punishment are Mark Costanzo and Donald Cabana.

One of Costanzo's arguments is that if society considers killing to be wrong, then it is just as wrong for the state to kill as it is for an individual to kill. The only exceptions are "self-defense, imminent danger, or the protection of society" (Costanzo, 1997:135). None of these exceptions apply to the capital offender because he "has already been captured and waits in a prison cell safely isolated from the community (Costanzo, 1997:136).

Costanzo is very empathetic to the victim's family but he argues that an execution will not bring back the victim for the family. Furthermore, an execution is "a state-sanctioned killing [that] will debase us all and create a new set of victims: the murderer's family" (Costanzo, 1997:143). This is to be avoided because, for one thing, the murderer's family members are innocent of wrongdoing.

Box 14.2, *continued*

An interesting suggestion of Costanzo's is to stop trying to abolish the death penalty, at least for a period of time. Instead, opponents should try a "detour" strategy of trying to get state lawmakers to limit the death penalty to multiple or serial murder cases. There are several advantages to this strategy. First, because it would reduce the number of capital punishment cases, it would save both court trial time and appellate time. Second, it would reduce the possibility of mistakes because the evidence in multiple murder cases is "often overwhelming" (Costanzo, 1997:155). Third, it would reduce racial bias because most serial killers are white. The overall result would be that "[w]e could finally claim that only the worst of the worst are executed" (Costanzo, 1997:155).

Finally, Costanzo aptly expresses the argument of many that killing a murderer seems an extremely illogical way for society to convey the message that killing is wrong:

> Killing is an odd way to show that killing is wrong, an odd way to show that society is just and humane. . . . we also send the message that killing is an acceptable way of solving the problem of violence, that a life should be extinguished if we have the power to take it and the offender has taken a life. We lend legal authority to the dangerous idea that if someone has committed a depraved crime, we should treat him or her as a nonhuman who can be killed without remorse (Costanzo, 1997:166-167).

Donald Cabana is a former warden who carried out a number of executions in the state of Mississippi. He has written about the execution of one man, Connie Evans, whom he executed and had come to know was a changed individual:

> This was not the same cold-blooded murderer who had arrived on death row six years before. His tears were not just those of a young man fearful of what lay beyond death's door; I was convinced they were also tears of genuine sorrow and pain for the tragic hurt and sadness he had caused so many people.

Cabana argued to the governor for a stay but there were no legal grounds to do so. Cabana had to carry out the execution even though he felt that ". . . as a society we were supposed to be better than the Connie Ray Evanses of the world" (Cabana, 1996:15). Cabana eventually resigned his warden's position and went on to become a college professor.

Box 14.3   An Argument in Favor of Capital Punishment

Ernest van den Haag is one of the leading proponents of the death penalty. Here are some of his arguments in favor of the death penalty.

First, he thinks that many critics of the death penalty are cowards who are afraid to impose the penalty:

> Aware of human frailty they shudder at the gravity of the decision and refuse to make it. The irrevocability of a verdict of death is contrary to the modern spirit that likes to pretend that nothing ever is definitive, that everything is open-ended, that doubts must always be entertained and revisions made. Such an attitude may be proper for inquiring philosophers and scientists. But not for courts. They can evade decisions on life and death only by giving up their paramount duties: to do justice, to secure the lives of the citizens, and to vindicate the norms society holds inviolable (van den Haag, 1978:67-68).

Second, van den Haag argues that murder—the most serious crime—cries out for the most serious penalty—execution. Otherwise, society is failing to carry out the proper affirmation of common values:

> In all societies, the degree of social disapproval of wicked acts is expressed in the degree of punishment threatened. Thus, punishments both proclaim and enforce social values according to the importance given to them. There is no other way for society to affirm its values. To refuse to punish any crime with death, then, is to avow that the negative weight of a crime can never exceed the positive value of the life of the person who committed it. I find that proposition implausible (van den Haag, 1978:68).

Third, van den Haag is not persuaded by arguments that the death penalty is wrong because it is carried out in a discriminatory fashion. If discriminatory use of the death penalty is a problem, eliminate the discrimination, not the death penalty. Furthermore, van den Haag cautions against any unfounded cries of discrimination:

> It is true that most of those currently under sentence of death are poor and a disproportionate number are black. But most murderers (indeed, most criminals) are poor and a disproportionate number are black. (So too are a disproportionate number of murder victims.) One must expect therefore that most of our prison population, including those on death row, are poor and a disproportionate number black (van den Haag and Conrad, 1983:206-207).

Box 14.3, *continued*

Finally, van den Haag thinks that the average person favors capital punishment while the average college-educated judge opposes it. There are two reasons for this:

> First, the college-educated, including judges, usually do not move in circles in which violence, including murder, is a daily threat. Not feeling threatened by murder, they can afford to treat it leniently. . . . Second, . . . [S]tudents tend to absorb and to be victimized by the intellectual fashions of their college days. Uneducated people more often accept tradition and their own experience. . . . The idea of the criminal as a sick victim of society thrives among intellectuals. The fashion in intellectual circles for the last fifty years has been to regard criminals as victims of society, sick people who should be treated and rehabilitated. People who are executed cannot be rehabilitated (van den Haag and Conrad, 1983:159).

The Supreme Court recently ruled that the death penalty is unconstitutional for juveniles. In ***Roper v. Simmons*** (2005), writing for the majority, Justice Arthur Kennedy wrote that "[t]he Eighth and Fourteenth Amendments forbid imposition of the death penalty on offenders who were under the age of 18 when their crimes were committed." The ruling came in a case in which Christopher Simmons, age 17, with two accomplices, broke and entered a home at 2:00 A.M., took a woman captive, drove away, and threw the woman from a railroad trestle into a river.

The majority opinion reasoned that the juvenile death penalty is rejected by the majority of the states and is used infrequently in states that authorize it. This suggests that today American society views juveniles as less culpable than adults. The majority went on to cite scientific evidence that juveniles under 18 are less mature and responsible than adults, more susceptible to peer pressure, and have character that is less well formed than that of an adult. The majority recognizes that there is no perfect decision about the appropriate age for the death penalty but that a line has to be drawn somewhere. They choose age 18. "The age of 19 is the point where society draws the line for many purposes between childhood and adulthood."

Dissenting Justice Antonin Scalia argued that only 18 states actually prohibit executions for juveniles. Unlike the majority, Justice Scalia argued that one cannot reason that states without the death penalty prohibit it for juveniles; Justice Scalia contends that those states should not be considered because they have not addressed the issue of the appropriate age for the death penalty. He also notes that psychological studies about maturity and recklessness give us a picture of juveniles in general. Some particular juveniles, however, may be culpable and may commit particularly heinous crimes that merit the death penalty. He thinks that a jury can and should decide whether a particular juvenile is indeed culpable and has committed a crime that is so horrible as to deserve capital punishment. (See Box 14.4 for quotes from the majority opinion and from Justice Scalia's dissent.)

Box 14.4 Majority and Dissenting Opinions in the *Roper* Case

Justice Kennedy's Majority Opinion:

"The susceptibility of juveniles to immature and irresponsible behavior means "their irresponsible conduct is not as morally reprehensible as that of an adult." *Thompson, supra*, at 835 (plurality opinion). Their own vulnerability and comparative lack of control over their immediate surroundings mean juveniles have a greater claim than adults to be forgiven for failing to escape negative influences in their whole environment. See *Stanford*, 492 U.S., at 395 (Brennan, J. dissenting). The reality that juveniles still struggle to define their identity means it is less supportable to conclude that even a heinous crime committed by a juvenile is evidence of irretrievably depraved character. From a moral standpoint it would be misguided to equate the failings of a minor with those of an adult, for a greater possibility exists that a minor's character deficiencies will be reformed."

Justice Scalia's Dissent:

"Murder, however, is more than just risky or antisocial behavior. It is entirely consistent to believe that young people often act impetuously and lack judgment, but, at the same time, to believe that those who commit premeditated murder are—at least sometimes—just as culpable as adults. Christopher Simmons, who was only seven months shy of his 18th birthday when he murdered Shirley Crook, described to his friends *beforehand*—"[i]n chilling, callous terms,". . . the murder he planned to commit. He then broke into the home of an innocent woman, bound her with duct tape and electrical wire, and threw her off a bridge alive and conscious."

What do you think? Is Justice Kennedy correct that minors are still immature and struggling with their identity? Is there greater chance that they can be reformed? Or is Justice Scalia correct that some individual juveniles are just as culpable as adults—that some youths commit heinous crimes and should be held fully accountable for them? Do you agree with Justice Kennedy that all youths should be ineligible for the death penalty, or do you agree with Justice Scalia that some youths may deserve the death penalty?

Horowitz (2000) argues that there should be no death penalty for juveniles for several reasons. First, she claims that reasoning ability, maturity, and experience levels are lower for juveniles than for adults. Second, subjecting juveniles to the death penalty is arbitrary in that it is contrary to other laws that assume that children under 18 need protection and are not ready for certain responsibilities or privileges such as the right to vote, to sit on juries, to consent to treatment, and to marry. To subject juveniles to the death penalty but deny them these other privileges "seems hypocritical when society does not trust them with the civic responsibilities of an adult" (Horowitz, 2000:166). Horowitz also thinks that juveniles have greater potential for rehabilitation than adults. Part of this is the fact that they have a greater proportion of their lives still ahead of them. Another part of her argument is that many juveniles have not had a chance to get away from the abuse or other problems they have suffered. Society should offer them at least one chance to develop apart from a negative home environment. Finally, Horowitz contends that considerations of deterrence and retribution often do not apply to juveniles. In general, youth impulsiveness, poor judgment, and feelings of invincibility prevent them from regarding even the death penalty with the rational calculation necessary for an adequate deterrent impact. Specific problems such as history of abuse, substance abuse issues, mental illness, low intelligence, and even brain damage detract from the full capability necessary for fair deterrence or punishment.

Horowitz thinks the solution is simple: stop executing juveniles. Instead, juveniles who kill should be sentenced to prison with the possibility of parole. This would give youths who kill "the chance to reverse the violent patterns that may have been established in their lives," and it would allow us "to address the societal problems that cause them to be violent in the first place" (Horowitz, 2000:175).

Contrary to these thoughtful criticisms of the death penalty for juveniles, some voices still call for **capital punishment** for youthful offenders, particularly in multiple murder cases. For example, a recent survey of policymakers in a southern state found that 55 percent disagreed that the death penalty should not be imposed on a juvenile (Whitehead, 1998). Similarly, multiple murders like the 1998 case in Jonesboro, Arkansas, in which two children, aged 11 and 13, killed four students and a teacher and wounded 11 others (*USA Today*, 1998) make some people demand the death penalty for such apparently hardened youths. This issue will continue to stir debate.

JURISDICTION OVER STATUS OFFENSES

Also related to the fundamental issue of the philosophy and continued existence of juvenile court is the issue of **divestiture**, that is, eliminating juvenile court **jurisdiction over status offenders**. That is, assuming that a state chooses not to eliminate juvenile court completely, should it continue to exercise control over disobedient, runaway, and truant adolescents? As noted, the state of Washington has opted to continue juvenile court but to eliminate jurisdiction over status offenses. Maine has written full divestiture into law. Most states have retained jurisdiction but implemented policies of deinstitutionalization (stopped confining status offenders in state institutions). In many places, private drug treatment and mental health facilities have stepped in to fill the void that juvenile court previously occupied (Feld, 1999).

Despite such efforts, status offenses and status offenders continue to take up a considerable portion of juvenile court time and effort. In 1997, juvenile courts handled 158,500 petitioned status offense cases, an increase of more than 90 percent over 1986. Runaway, truancy, and liquor law violation cases increased more than 50 percent, while ungovernable cases increased only 14 percent. Despite more than a decade of discussion about ending juvenile court jurisdiction over status offenses, approximately 11,600 youths were adjudicated status offenders and placed in out-of-home placements in 1997 (Puzzanchero et al., 2000). (More recent national statistics are not available because the available data do not support national estimates of how the states are processing status offenders [Puzzanchero et al., 2004].) The 2001 census of juveniles in custody showed just over 5,000 youths (5,116) in custody for a status offense (Sickmund, Sladky, and Kand, 2004).

Arguments for Ending Jurisdiction

There are several arguments in favor of complete divestiture. First, it allows the juvenile court more time and resources to deal with juvenile delinquents—especially violent and chronic delinquents. Because the court does not have to process or supervise status offenders, probation officers, prosecutors, public defenders, judges, and correctional program employees are able to focus on more serious delinquents. Second, the elimination of status offense jurisdiction prevents any possible violations of the due process rights of status offenders, such as being prosecuted for very vague charges. For example, how disobedient does a child have to be before he or she is "incorrigible," or how truant before he or she is eligible for a truancy petition? Status offense statutes typically are unclear and vague. Third, elimination of this jurisdiction recognizes the reality that juvenile courts are not adequately staffed and equipped to deal with status offenders. Most probation officers often have only bachelor's degrees and are not qualified to do the social work and psychological counseling necessary to assist troubled teenagers and their families. Thus, status offenders should be diverted to private agencies with trained social workers and counselors who are better equipped to handle the complex problems of these youths and their families. Furthermore, eliminating juvenile court jurisdiction would force any intervention to be voluntary, which some argue is the proper way to deal with status offenders.

Another argument for elimination is that jurisdiction over status offenses has "weakened the responsibility of schools and agencies to arrange out-of-court interventive services and solutions" (Rubin, 1985:63). What Rubin means is that status offense laws have allowed schools to run inadequate and boring programs that promote truancy and, in turn, blame parents and children for the problem. Instead of petitioning youths to juvenile court, schools should be improving instructional programs or offering innovative approaches such as alternative schools where children attend school half a day and then work half a day for pay. In other words, prosecuting status offenders often is a blame-the-victim approach that ignores the real causes of the problems: inferior schools, ineffective parents, and insensitve communities (see Rubin, 1985, and Schur, 1973, for further discussion of this issue). (For a viewpoint of child welfare caseworkers on this issue, see Box 14.5.)

Box 14.5 Caseworker Views on the Status Offender Issue

A survey of more than 100 caseworkers and more than 100 residential program child care staff members in Nebraska produced some findings related to the issue of juvenile court jurisdiction over status offenders. On the one hand, the respondents felt that juvenile court was not effective with status offenders. On the other hand, "the caseworkers did not want responsibility for these cases" (Russel and Sedlak, 1993:23). The authors of the research report attributed workers' reluctance to take on status offense cases to high caseloads (for such problems as child abuse and neglect cases) and lack of community resources. The caseworkers also believe that dysfunctional families and problematic schools contributed to the status offense problems.

One solution would be for juvenile courts to have more power over parents, such as the authority to order treatment for parents. One specific suggestion is that juvenile courts not accept status offense cases until the family first made an attempt to undergo family therapy (Russel and Sedlak, 1993).

Chesney-Lind (1987) believes that status offenses are intricately intertwined with the place of women in American society. She questions whether the concern over maintaining jurisdiction is one of concern or control:

> What is really at stake here is not "protection" of youth so much as it is the right of young women to defy patriarchy. Such defiance by male youth is winked at, both today and in the past, but from girls such behavior is totally unacceptable (Chesney-Lind, 1987:21).

Much of the concern, therefore, about status offenders is not so much for the children as for maintaining a patriarchal society. Thus, like the critics of the child savers discussed in Chapter 2, Chesney-Lind questions the intentions of those concerned with the protection of status offenders.

Arguments for Continuing Jurisdiction

Some still think, however, that juvenile court jurisdiction over status offenses is both desirable and necessary. Proponents of continued jurisdiction contend that parents and schools need the court backing to impress adolescents with the need to obey their parents, attend school, and not run away from home. Concerning truancy, Rubin argues that repeal of status offense jurisdiction would "effectively eradicate compulsory education" and that "children will be free to roam the streets with impunity" (Rubin, 1985:65). Furthermore, such total freedom would "deny children the necessary preparation for achievement in a complex technological society (Rubin, 1985:65). Second, proponents of court jurisdiction argue that private agencies in the community will not handle (or will not be able to handle) all of the status offense cases if the juvenile court cannot intervene. Private agencies intervene only with willing clients, and many status offenders taken to such agencies simply refuse assistance. Moreover, some agencies do not provide the services they claim to provide (Schneider, 1985).

Proponents also contend that status offenders often escalate into delinquent activity, and note that truants are linked with daytime burglary and vandalism (Baker, Sigmon, and Nugent, 2001). Therefore, they claim, early intervention can prevent current and future delinquency. However, the escalation hypothesis is controversial. Some proportion of status offenders do indeed escalate or progress, but most do not (Lab, 1984; Rojek and Erickson, 1982; Shannon, 1982). Hence, it is questionable whether all status offenders should be subject to juvenile court jurisdiction. A similar argument is that many status offenders become involved in very dangerous situations that can cause serious harm to the child. For example, one study of runaways found that more than 50 percent dealt drugs and

There are differing opinions as to whether juvenile courts should continue having jurisdiction over status offenses. Status offenses, such as cigarette smoking, are forms of juvenile misbehavior that would not constitute a criminal act for an adult.

Ellen S. Boyne

about 20 percent (including 19% of the male runaways) engaged in acts of prostitution to support themselves (Miller et al., 1980). Research on street children has shown that many turn to theft, prostituting, rolling johns, and selling drugs to survive (Hagan and McCarthy, 1997). Proponents of court jurisdiction argue that courts might prevent some children from running away and becoming involved in associated dangerous behaviors. A related argument is that because states intervene "to protect adults from their own harmful conduct" (Ryan, 1987:64), they should protect juveniles from the harmful consequences of their actions

Another argument in favor of continued jurisdiction is that it prevents status offenders from being processed as delinquents. That is, where divestiture has occurred, there is some evidence of treating status offenders as minor delinquents (Schneider, 1985). Finally, there is concern that total removal of status offense jurisdiction from juvenile court "changes the character of the court and may substantially weaken attempts to consider the child status of delinquent" (Mahoney, 1987:29). In other words, Mahoney fears that removal of status offense jurisdiction, with a concentration on delinquency only, may lead to a view of the juvenile court as concerned with crime only and, hence, a belief that adult criminal courts can exercise that function. Thus, removal of status offense jurisdiction may very well be the beginning of the end of the juvenile court.

At present, the debate over divestiture has changed. In the Justice Department's research and writing on delinquency, there is little mention of status offenses as such. Instead of debate about divestiture, the Office of Juvenile Justice and Delinquency Prevention emphasizes prevention strategies that help youngsters at risk of becoming delinquent by building up protective factors. Such protective factors include caring parents who supervise their children, personal attributes such as conventional beliefs and conflict resolution skills, and schools that have caring teachers and help youths succeed in school (Coordinating Council on Juvenile Justice and Delinquency Prevention, 1996). The Coordinating Council is concerned with such programs as truancy reduction programs that have the police round up truants so that parents can be notified and come pick up their children (see also Chapter 7). Also mentioned are mentoring programs including Bigs in Blue, which matches high-risk youths with police officer mentors who try to help youths cope with peer pressure and also do well in school. Noted as well are conflict resolution programs in schools and community efforts such as community policing cooperative arrangements that attack community risk factors such as easy availability of drugs and firearms (Coordinating Council on Juvenile Justice and Delinquency Prevention, 1996; see also Baker, Sigmon, and Nugent, 2001).

Unlike a decade ago, the emphasis is not so much on the status offender as a distinct problem, but on those risk factors that can lead to serious, violent, or chronic delinquency. Attention to reducing risk factors and enhancing protective factors is considered to be the way to prevent such problematic delinquency.

Summary and Conclusion

Most of the proposals for the future of the juvenile justice system have some merit. The authors of these proposals care about juveniles and about how the juvenile court system should attempt to prevent and control delinquency.

The suggestion to get the juvenile justice system to return to its *parens patriae* roots—to attempt to get juvenile court to truly implement rehabilitation efforts based on valid empirical research findings—is a positive one. The goal is noble: genuine assistance for juveniles. Obstacles include funding problems, lack of societal commitment to the disadvantaged youths that are the clientele of juvenile court, vestiges of racism, and punitive strains in some politicians.

Bazemore's call to make a drastic change and pursue the path of restorative justice is also positive. Advantages of this proposal are that it can appeal to both liberals and conservatives. Both parties like the fact that restorative justice puts renewed emphasis on the victim. Restitution, for example, is desirable because it restores the victim to the condition he or she was in prior to the crime. Perhaps the major question about this proposal is whether citizens will commit to participate. Putnam's (2000) concerns about the decline of community in America raise the question that citizens are not as civically involved today as they were even 50 years ago. A number of communities, including the state of Vermont (Karp, Bazemore, and Chesire, 2004), have implemented restorative justice practices, though, so this does not appear to be a pipedream.

Feld's call for the end of juvenile court is controversial. His proposal is not as drastic as it seems at first hearing because he tempers it with important caveats. He would provide due process protections, such as fully adversarial attorneys, for all juveniles handled in adult court. Likewise his call for discounted sentencing would keep juveniles from serving full adult prison terms. A major concern with his proposal is the exact value of the discounts. A 10 percent discount off of a 50-year sentence—leaving 45 years for a juvenile—would be a virtually meaningless change. A 75 percent discount would be meaningful. Probably the major question about Feld's proposal is whether moving all juvenile cases to adult court would simply translate into complete abandonment of the concept of differential treatment for juveniles due to immaturity and inexperience and a very rapid track toward treating juveniles exactly like adults. Bishop's (2000) research on the experiences of youths transferred to adult court in Florida supports the probability of such abandonment of concern for children. The transferred youths she and her colleagues interviewed had negative evaluations of both adult court and adult correctional facilities while juveniles in the juvenile system felt positively about juvenile court and juvenile correctional staff.

Perhaps one way to prevent Feld's suggestion from resulting in an abandonment of the noble goals of juvenile court is to follow Butts's advice. If we are going to move all juveniles to adult court, then start a youth justice court within the confines of adult court similar to drug courts and mental health courts. These specialized courts (also known as the therapeutic jurisprudence movement [Braithwaite, 2002; Wexler, 2002]) recognize the distinctive needs of special populations. If there is only one adult court, everyone who goes to it will be treated the same. If there are specialized courts under the adult court umbrella, then there will be consideration for special needs such as drug addiction, mental illness, and youthful immaturity and reduced responsibility.

Some of the broader suggestions noted in this chapter also merit mention in this concluding section. For instance, Garland's analysis that the decline of the rehabilitative ideal is tied in with broader economic changes such as the globalizing economy and the eroding of the welfare state deserves serious attention. This analysis suggests that trying to return juvenile court to its rehabilitative roots and even trying to set up youth justice courts that address youth needs within the adult court system are both doomed to failure for the simple reason that the true problem is decreasing availability of funding. The real solution is to somehow change the economic forces that work to reduce the funds available for treatment efforts, whether in juvenile or adult court. As mentioned earlier, one issue that might be addressed is spending on the elderly (e.g., Social Security) versus spending on children. The problem is that the elderly are a significant and growing constituency. As the "baby boomers" age into senior citizen status, they will become an even greater voting bloc. Even though many senior citizens have pension plans, they are reluctant to reduce their entitlements (Social Security), which prevents those government funds from being available for delinquency prevention in particular and youth programs in general.

Character education or the reintroduction of the spiritual dimension into juvenile corrections also merits serious consideration. If Staples (2000) is correct that problems such as school violence stem, at least in part, from excessive emphasis on the consumer culture and inattention to the search for meaning, creativity, and engagement, then superficial changes in juvenile court are not critical. If such terms as "character education" or a "search for the spiritual" are simply ploys to avoid funding meaningful programs for youths in trouble, then they are hypocritical and dangerous. However, if calls for character education and the reintroduction of the spiritual dimension go along with education, job training, substance abuse counseling, and other efforts to address all the needs of problem youths, both material and spiritual, then they hold promise. Critics of our consumer culture are accurate that there is more to life than purchasing increasingly more goods.

The founders of the juvenile court had it at least half right: kids do need help. That was true back in 1899 and is as true tody in the twenty-first century. The problem is that in seeking solutions for youth problems and problem youths we prefer to ignore this truth and seek refuge in simplistic slogans like "adult time" and "Scared Straight." We are a lot like dieters seeking to lose weight; we want the easy way out. Just as persons trying to lose weight have to face the hard facts of diet and exercise, American society has to face the facts of delinquency. There is no easy solution. Whatever proposal for the future of juvenile court wins out, it will not be an answer unless it addresses the problems of youths who break the law.

Discussion Questions

1. Discuss the reform proposals for juvenile court. Which proposal(s) do you favor? Why? What might the consequences be of abolishing juvenile court?

2. How does the status of community life affect juvenile delinquency and juvenile justice? How much does reform of the juvenile justice system depend on strong communities? Is Putnam correct that community life seems to be having problems as individuals seem to turn to more solitary pursuits? Can this trend be reversed?

3. How do current political and economic events affect juvenile justice? For example, do you think that the war on terrorism will have any effects on juvenile justice?

4. Do you favor the death penalty for juveniles? Discuss this in light of the recent Supreme Court decision making the juvenile death penalty unconstitutional.

5. What role, if any, should juvenile court have with status offenders?

References

Abadinsky, H. (1989). *Drug Abuse: An Introduction*. Chicago: Nelson-Hall.

Abrahamsen, D. (1944). *Crisis and the Human Mind*. New York: Columbia University Press.

Abt Associates (1994). *Conditions of Confinement: Juvenile Detention and Corrections Facilities: Research Report*. Washington, DC: U.S. Department of Justice.

Acker, J.R., P.N. Hendrix, L. Hogan, and A. Kordzek (2001). "Building a Better Youth Court." *Law and Policy* 23:197-215.

Acoca, L. (1998). "Outside/Inside: The Violation of American Girls at Home, on the Streets, and in the Juvenile Justice System." *Crime & Delinquency* 44:561-589.

Adams, L.R. (1974). "The Adequacy of Differential Association Theory." *Journal of Research in Crime and Delinquency* 11:1-8.

Adams, K. (2003). "The Effectiveness of Juvenile Curfews at Crime Prevention." *Annals of the American Academy of Political and Social Science* 587:136-159.

Administration on Children, Youth, and Families (2005). *Child Maltreatment, 2003*. Washington, DC: U.S. Department of Health and Human Services.

Ageton, S., and D.S. Elliott (1973). "The Effects of Legal Processing on Self-concept." Mimeograph. Boulder, CO: Institute of Behavioral Science, University of Colorado.

Agnew, R. (1984). "Goal Achievement and Delinquency." *Sociology and Social Research* 68:435-451.

Agnew, R. (1992). "Foundation for a General Strain Theory of Crime and Delinquency." *Criminology* 30:47-87.

Agnew, R. (1994). "The Techniques of Neutralization and Violence." *Criminology* 32:555-580.

Agnew, R. (1997). "Stability and Change in Crime over the Life Course: A Strain Theory Explanation." In T.P. Thornberry (ed.), *Developmental Theories of Crime and Delinquency*. New Brunswick, NJ: Transaction.

Agnew, R., and A.A.R. Peters (1986). "The Techniques of Neutralization: An Analysis of Predisposing and Situational Factors." *Criminal Justice and Behavior* 13:81-97.

Agnew, R., and H.R. White (1992). "An Empirical Test of General Strain Theory." *Criminology* 30:475-499.

Aichorn, A. (1963). *Wayward Youth*. New York: Viking.

Aird, E.G. (2004). "Advertising and Marketing to Children in the United States." In P.B. Pufall and R.P. Unsworth (eds.), *Rethinking Childhood* (pp. 141-153). New Brunswick, NJ: Rutgers University Press.

Akers, R.L. (1990). "Rational Choice, Deterrence, and Social Learning Theory in Criminology: The Path Not Taken." *Journal of Criminal Law and Criminology* 81:653-676.

Akers, R.L. (1991). "Self-control as a General Theory of Crime." *Journal of Quantitative Criminology* 7:201-211.

Akers, R.L., M.K. Krohn, L. Lanza-Kaduce, and M. Radosevich (1979). "Social Learning and Deviant Behavior: A Specific Test of a General Theory." *American Sociological Review* 44:636-655.

Allen, P. (1994). *OJJDP Model Programs 1993*. Washington, DC: U.S. Deparment of Justice.

Allender, D.M. (2001). "Gangs in Middle America: Are They a Threat?" *FBI Law Enforcement Bulletin* 70(12):1-9.

Alpert, G.P., J.M. MacDonald, and R.G. Dunham (2005). "Police Suspicion and Discretionary Decision Making during Citizen Stops." *Criminology* 43:407-434.

Altschuler, D.M. (1998). "Intermediate Sanctions and Community Treatment for Serious and Violent Juvenile Offenders." In R. Loeber and D.P. Farrington (eds.), *Serious & Violent Juvenile Offenders: Risk Factors and Succssful Interventions* (pp. 367-385). Thousand Oaks, CA: Sage.

Altschuler, D., T.L. Armstrong, and D.L. MacKenzie (1999). *Reintegration, Supervised Release, and Intensive Aftercare*. Washington, DC: U.S. Department of Justice.

Altschuler, D., and P.J. Brounstein (1991). "Patterns of Drug Use, Drug Trafficking, and Other Delinquency among Inner-City Adolescent Males in Washington, DC." *Criminology* 29:589-622.

American Dietetics Association (1984). "Position Paper of the American Dietetics Association on Diet and Criminal Behavior." *Journal of the American Dietetics Association* 85:361-362.

Amir, M. (1971). *Patterns of Forcible Rape*. Chicago: University of Chicago Press.

Anderson, E. (1994). "The Code of the Streets." *Atlantic Monthly* 273(5):81-94.

Anglin, M.D. (1988). "The Efficacy of Civil Commitment in Treating Narcotics Addiction." *Journal of Drug Issues* 18:527-547.

Anglin, M.D., and Y. Hser (1990). "Treatment of Drug Abuse." In M. Tonry and J.Q. Wilson (eds.), *Drugs and Crime* (pp.393-460). Chicago: University of Chicago Press.

Anglin, M.D., and Y. Hser (1987). "Addicted Women and Crime." *Criminology* 25:359-397.

Anglin, M.D., and W.H. McGlothlin (1984). "Outcome of Narcotic Addict Treatment in California." In F.M. Tims and J.P. Ludford (eds.), *Drug Abuse Treatment Evaluation: Strategies, Progress and Prospects* (pp.106-128). Washington, DC: National Institute on Drug Abuse.

Anglin, M.D., and W.H. McGlothlin (1985). "Methadone Maintenance in California: A Decade's Experience." In L. Brill and C. Winnick (eds.), *Yearbook of Substance Use and Abuse* (pp. 219-280). New York: Human Sciences Press.

Anglin, M.D., and G. Speckhart (1986). "Narcotics Use, Property Crime, and Dealing: Structural Dynamics Across the Addiction Career." *Journal of Quantitative Criminology* 2:355-375.

Anglin, M.D., and G. Speckhart (1988). "Narcotics Use and Crime: A Multisample, Multi-method Analysis." *Criminology* 26:197-233.

Anglin, M.D., G.R. Speckhart, M.W. Booth, and T.M. Ryan (1989). "Consequences and Costs of Shutting Off Methadone." *Addictive Behaviors* 14:307-326.

Applegate, B.K., and S. Santana (2000). "Intervening with Youthful Substance Abusers: A Preliminary Analysis of a Juvenile Drug Court." *Justice System Journal* 21:281-300.

Applegate, B.K., M.G. Turner, J.B. Sanborn, E.J. Latessa, and M.M. Moon (2000). "Individualization, Criminalization, or Problem Resolution: A Factorial Survey of Juvenile Court Judges' Decisions to Incarcerate Youthful Felony Offenders." *Justice Quarterly* 17:309-331.

Aries, P. (1962). *Centuries of Childhood*. New York: Knopf.

Arrestee Drug Abuse Monitoring (2003). *Annual Report, 2000: Arrestee Drug Abuse Monitoring*. Washington, DC: National Institute of Justice.

Arrigo, B.A., and R.C. Schehr (1998). "Restoring Justice for Juveniles: A Critical Analysis of Victim-Offender Mediation," *Justice Quarterly* 15:629-666.

Ashworth, A. (2003). "Is Restorative Justice the Way Forward for Criminal Justice?" In E. McLaughlin, R. Fergusson, G. Hughes, and L. Westmarland (eds.), *Restorative Justice: Critical Issues*. Thousand Oaks, CA: Sage.

Austin, J., K.D. Johnson, and R. Weitzer (2005). *Alternatives to the Secure Detention and Confinement of Juvenile Offenders*. Washington, DC: U.S. Department of Justice.

Bailey, W.C., and R.D. Peterson (1981). "Legal versus Extra-legal Determinants of Juvenile Court Dispositions." *Juvenile and Family Court Journal* 32:41-59.

Baines, M., and C. Alder (1996). "Are Girls More Difficult to Work With? Youth Workers' Perspectives in Juvnele Justice and Related Areas." *Crime & Delinquency* 42:467-485.

Baker, M.L., J.N. Sigmon, and M.E. Nugent (2001). *Truancy Reduction: Keeping Students in School*. Washington, DC: Office of Juvenile Justice and Delinquency Prevention.

Ball, J.C., E. Corty, R. Bond, and A. Tommasello (1987). "The Reduction of Intravenous Heroin Use, Nonopiate Abuse and Crime during Methadone Maintenance Treatment—Further Findings." Paper presented at the annual meeting of the Committee on Problems on Drug Dependency, Philadelphia, PA.

Ball, J.C., J.W. Shaffer, and D.N. Nurco (1983). "The Day-to-Day Criminality of Heroin Addicts in Baltimore: A Study in the Continuity of Offense Rates." *Drug and Alcohol Dependence* 12:119-142.

Bandura, A., and R.H. Walters (1963). *Social Learning and Personality Development*. New York: Holt, Rhinehart and Winston.

Bannenberg, B., and D. Rossner (2003). "New Developments in Restorative Justice to Handle Family Violence." In E. Weitekamp and H. Kerner (eds.), *Restorative Justice in Context: International Practice and Directions*, pp. 51-79. Portland, OR: Willan.

Bannister, A.J., D.L. Carter, and J. Schafer (2001). "A National Police Survey on Juvenile Curfews." *Journal of Criminal Justice* 29:233-240.

Barnum, R. (1987). "The Development of Responsibility: Implications for Juvenile Justice." In F.X. Hartmann (ed.), *From Children to Citizens: Volume II: The Role of the Juvenile Court* (pp. 67-79). New York: Springer-Verlag.

Bartollas, C., and C.M. Sieverdes (1981). "The Victimized White in a Juvenile Correctional System." *Crime & Delinquency* 27:534-543.

Bastion, L., and B. Taylor (1991). *School Crime: A National Crime Survey Report*. Washington, DC: U.S. Department of Justice.

Bayley, D.H. (2002). "Law Enforcement and the Rule of Law: Is There a Tradeoff?" *Criminology & Public Policy* 2:133-154.

Bazemore, G. (1999). "The Fork in the Road to Juvenile Court Reform," *Annals of the American Academy of Political and Social Science* 564:81-108.

Bazemore, G., and T.J. Dicker (1994). "Explaining Detention Worker Orientation: Individual Characteristics, Occupational Conditions, and Organizational Environment." *Journal of Criminal Justice* 22:297-312.

Bazemore, G., T.J. Dicker, and R. Nyhan (1994). "Juvenile Justice Reform and the Difference it Makes: An Exploratory Study of the Impact of Policy Change on Detention Worker Attitudes." *Crime & Delinquency* 40:37-53.

Bazemore, G., and L. Leip (2000). "Victim Participation in the New Juvenile Court: Tracking Judicial Attitudes Toward Restorative Justice Reforms," *Justice System Journal* 21(2):199-226.

Bazemore, G., and D. Maloney (1994). "Rehabilitating Community Service: Toward Restorative Service Sanctions in a Balanced Justice Sytem." *Federal Probation* 58(1):24-35.

Bazemore, G., and M. Schiff (2005). *Juvenile Justice Reform and Restorative Justice: Building Theory and Policy from Practice*. Portland, OR: Willan.

Bazemore, G., and M. Umbreit (1994). *Balanced and Restorative Justice: Program Models*. Washington, DC: Office of Juvenile Justice and Delinquency Prevention.

Bazemore, G., and M. Umbreit (2001). *A Comparison of Four Restorative Conferencing Models*. Washington, DC: U.S. Department of Justice, Office of Juvenile Justice and Delinquency Prevention.

Beck, A.J., S.A. Kline, and L.A. Greenfield (1988). "Survey of Youth in Custody, 1987." *Bureau of Justice Statistics Special Report*. Washington, DC: U.S. Department of Justice.

Beldon, E. (1920). *Courts in the U.S. Hearing Children's Cases*. Washington, DC: U.S. Children's Bureau.

Belenko, S., J.A. Fagan, and T. Dumanovsky (1994). "The Effects of Legal Sanctions on Recidivism in Special Drug Courts." *Justice System Journal* 17:53-80.

Belknap, J. (1984). "The Effect of Local Policy on the Sentencing Patterns of State Wards." *Justice Quarterly* 1:549-561.

Belknap, J. (1987). "Routine Activity Theory and the Risk of Rape: Analyzing Ten Years of National Crime Survey Data." *Criminal Justice Policy Review* 2:337-356.

Bell, D., and K. Lang (1985). "The Intake Dispositions of Juvenile Offenders." *Journal of Research in Crime and Delinquency* 22:309-328.

Bellis, D.J. (1981). *Heroin and Politicians: The Failure of Public Policy to Control Addiction in America*. Westport, CT: Greenwood.

Belsky, J. (1978). "Three Theoretical Models of Child Abuse: A Critical Review." *Child Abuse & Neglect* 2:37-49.

Benda, B.B. (2002). "Religion and Violent Offenders in Boot Camp: A Structural Equation Model." *Journal of Research in Crime and Delinquency* 39:91-121.

Bennett, T. (1986). "Situational Crime Prevention from the Offender's Perspective." In K. Heal and G. Laycock (eds.), *Situational Crime Prevention: From Theory to Practice*. London: Her Majesty's Stationery Office.

Bennett, T., and R. Wright (1984a). *Burglars on Burglary*. Brookfield, VT: Gower.

Bennett, T., and R. Wright (1984b). "The Relationship Between Alcohol and Burglary." *British Journal of Addiction* 79:431-437.

Bennett, W.J. (2001). *The Broken Hearth: Reversing the Moral Collapse of the American Family*. New York: Doubleday.

Bentham, J. (1948). *An Introduction to the Principles of Morals and Legislation*. New York: Hafner.

Bilchik, S. (1998). *A Juvenile Justice System for the 21st Century*. Washington, DC: U.S. Department of Justice.

Bishop, D.M. (2000). "Juvenile Offenders in the Adult Criminal Justice System." In M. Tonry (ed.), *Crime and Justice: A Review of Research* (Vol. 27) (pp. 81-167). Chicago: University of Chicago Press.

Bishop, D.M. (2004). "Injustice and Irrationality in Contemporary Youth Policy." *Criminology & Public Policy* 3:633-644.

Bishop, D.M., and C.E. Frazier. (1996). "Race Effects in Juvenile Justice Decision-Making: Findings of a Statewide Analysis." *Journal of Criminal Law and Criminology* 86:392-414.

Bishop, D.M., C.E. Frazier, L. Lanza-Kaduce, and L. Winner (1996). "The Transfer of Juveniles to Criminal Court: Does it Make a Difference?" *Crime & Delinquency* 42:171-191.

Bjerregaard, B. (1989). "Televised Testimony as an Alternative in Child Sexual Abuse Cases." *Criminal Law Bulletin* 25:164-175.

Bjerregaard, B., and A.J. Lizotte (1995). "Gun Ownership and Gang Membership." *Journal of Criminal Law and Criminology* 86:37-58.

Bjerregaard, B., and C. Smith (1993). "Gender Differences in Gang Participation, Delinquency, and Substance Use." *Journal of Quantitative Criminology* 4:329-355.

Bloch, H.A., and A. Niederhoffer (1958). *The Gang: A Study in Adolescent Behavior*. New York: Philosophical Library.

Block, C.R., and R. Block (1992). "Street Gang Crime in Chicago." *Research in Brief*. Washington, DC: National Institute of Justice.

Bonczar, T.P., and T.C. Snell (2004). *Capital Punishment, 2003*. Washington, DC: U.S. Department of Justice.

Bonnett, P.L., and C.L. Pfeiffer (1978). "Biochemical Diagnosis for Delinquent Behavior." In L.J. Hippchen (ed.), *Ecologic-Biochemical Approaches to Treatment of Delinquents and Criminals* (pp. 183-205). New York: Van Nostrand Reinhold.

Bookin-Weiner, H., and R. Horowitz (1983). "The End of the Youth Gang: Fad or Fact?" *Criminology* 21:585-602.

Booth, A., and D.W. Osgood (1993). "The Influence of Testosterone on Deviance in Adulthood: Assessing and Explaining the Relationship." *Criminology* 31:93-118.

Bordua, D.J. (1958). "Juvenile Delinquency and 'Anomie': An Attempt at Replication." *Social Problems* 6:230-238.

Borrero, M. (2001). "The Widening Mistrust between Youth and Police." *Families in Society: The Journal of Contemporary Human Services* 82:399.

Bortner M.A., and L.M. Williams (1997). *Youth in Prison: We the People of Unit Four*. New York: Routledge.

Botvin, G.J., E. Baker, L. Dusenbury, E. Botvin, and T. Diaz (1995). "Long-term Follow-up Results of a Randomized Drug-abuse Prevention Trial in a White Middle-class Population." *Journal of the American Medical Association* 273:1106-1112.

Botvin, G.J., and L. Dusenbury (1989). "Substance Abuse Prevention and the Promotion of Competence." In L.A. Bond and B.E. Compas (eds.), *Primary Prevention and Promotion in the Schools* (pp.146-178). Newbury Park, CA: Sage.

Botvin, G., J. Epstein, E. Baker, T. Diaz, and M. Ifill-Williams (1997). "School-based Drug Abuse Prevention with Inner-city Minority Youth." *Journal of Child and Adolescent Substance Abuse* 6:5-19.

Botvin, G., K.W. Griffin, E. Paul, and A.P. Macaulay (2003). "Preventing Tobacco and Alcohol Use among Elementary School Students through Life Skills Training." *Journal of Child and Adolescent Substance Abuse* 12:1-18.

Botvin, G. J., N. Renick, and E. Baker (1983). "The Effects of Scheduling Format and Booster Sessions on a Broad Spectrum Psychological Approach to Smoking Prevention." *Journal of Behavioral Medicine* 6:359-379.

Bowker, L.H. (1980). *Prison Victimization*. New York: Elsevier.

Bowker, L.H., and M.W. Klein (1983). "The Etiology of Female Juvenile Delinquency and Gang Membership: A Test of Psychological and Social Structural Explanations." *Adolescence* 18:739-751.

Bozynski, M., and L. Szymanski (2004). *National Overviews: State Juvenile Justice Profiles*. Pittsburgh: National Center for Juvenile Justice. Online. Available at: *http://www.ncjj.org/stateprofiles/*

Bozynski, M., and L. Szymanski (2005). *National Overviews: State Juvenile Justice Profiles*. Pittsburgh: National Center for Juvenile Justice. Available at *http:www.ncjj.org/state profiles* [accessed 7/8/05]

Braga, A.A. (2001). "The Effects of Hot Spots Policing on Crime." *Annals of the American Academy of Political and Social Science* 578:104-125.

Braga, A.A., D.M. Kennedy, A.M. Piehl, and E.J. Waring (2001). *The Boston Gun Project: Impact Evaluation Findings*. Washington, DC: National Institute of Justice.

Braithwaite, J. (1989). *Crime, Shame and Reintegration*. Cambridge, England: Cambridge University Press.

Braithwaite, J. (1999). "Restorative Justice: Assessing Optimistic and Pessimistic Accounts." In M. Tonry (ed.), *Crime and Justice: A Review of Research* (Vol. 25). Chicago: University of Chicago Press.

Braithwaite, J. (2002). *Restorative Justice and Responsive Regulation*. New York: Oxford University Press.

Braithwaite, J. (2003). "Restorative Justice and a Better Future." In E. McLaughlin, R. Fergusson, G. Hughes, and L. Westmarland (eds.), *Restorative Justice: Critical Issues*. Thousand Oaks, CA: Sage.

Braswell, M., J. Fuller, and B. Lozoff (2001). *Corrections, Peace Making, and Restorative Justice*. Cincinnati: Anderson.

Brennan, P.A., S.A. Mednick, and J. Volavka (1995). "Biomedical Factors in Crime." In J.Q. Wilson and J. Petersilia (eds.), *Crime* (pp. 65-90). San Francisco: ICS Press.

Brenzel, B.M. (1983). *Daughters of the State: A Social Portrait of the First Reform School for Girls in North America, 1856-1903*. Cambridge, MA: MIT Press.

Brewster, M.P. (2001). "An Evaluation of the Chester County (PA) Drug Court Program." *Journal of Drug Issues* 31:171-206.

Bridges, G.S., and S. Steen (1998). "Racial Disparities in Official Assessments of Juvenile Offenders: Attributional Stereotypes as Mediating Mechanisms." *American Sociological Review* 63:554-570.

Brooks, K., and D. Kamine (2003). *Justice Cut Short: An Assessment of Access to Counsel and Quality of Representation in Delinquency Proceedings in Ohio*. Columbus: Ohio State Bar Association, Available at: *http://www.juvenilecoalition.org/legal_representation/ohio_report_2003/ohio_report_2003.pdf*

Brown, W.K. (1978). "Black Gangs as Family Extension." *International Journal of Offender Therapy and Comparative Criminology* 22:39-45.

Browning, S.L., F.T. Cullen, L. Cao, R. Kopache, and T.J. Stevenson (1994). "Race and Getting Hassled by the Police: A Research Note." *Police Studies* 17(1):1-11.

Brunner, H.G. (1996). "MAOA Deficiency and Abnormal Behavior. Perspectives on an Association." In G.R. Bock and J.A. Goode (eds.), *Genetics of Criminal and Antisocial Behavior* (pp. 155-163). Chichester, England: John Wiley and Sons.

Bureau of Justice Assistance (2003). *Juvenile Drug Courts: Strategies in Practice*. Washington, DC: Bureau of Justice Assistance.

Bureau of Justice Assistance (2005). *Gang Resistance Education and Training*. Washington, DC: Bureau of Justice Assistance. Available at: *http://great-online.org*

Bureau of Justice Statistics (2003). *Criminal Victimization in the United States, 2002—Statistical Tables*. Washington, DC: Bureau of Justice Statistics.

Bureau of Justice Statistics (2004). *National Crime Victimization Survey 1992-2002*. [Computer file]. Ann Arbor, MI: Inter-university Consortium for Political and Social Research.

Burgess, A.W., and A.T. Laszlo (1976). "When the Prosecutrix Is a Child: The Victim Consultant in Cases of Sexual Assault." In E.C. Viano (ed.), *Victims & Society*. Washington, DC: Visage Press.

Burgess, R.L., and R.L. Akers (1968). "Differential Association-Reinforcement Theory of Criminal Behavior." *Social Problems* 14:128-147.

Burke, M.N. (2005). "Juvenile Justice Supreme Court Provides Uniformity in Juvenile Procedure Rules." *Pennsylvania Law Weekly* 28 (17):5.

Burruss, G.W., and K. Kempf-Leonard (2002). "The Questionable Advantage of Defense Counsel in Juvenile Court." *Justice Quarterly* 19:37-68.

Bursik, R.J., and H.G. Grasmick (1993). *Neighborhoods and Crime: The Dimensions of Effective Community Control*. New York: Lexington.

Buss, E. (2000). "The Role of Lawyers in Promoting Juveniles' Competence as Defendants." In T. Grisso and R.G. Schwartz (eds.), *Youth on Trial: A Developmental Perspective on Juvenile Justice* (pp. 243-265). Chicago: University of Chicago Press.

Butts, J.A. (2000). "Can We Do Without Juvenile Justice?" *Criminal Justice* 15(1):50-57.

Butts, J.A., and J. Buck (2000). *Teen Courts: A Focus on Research*. Washington, DC: Office of Juvenile Justice and Delinquency Prevention.

Butts, J.A., J. Buck, and M.B. Coggershall (2002). *The Impact of Teen Court on Young Offenders*. Washington, DC: Urban Institute Press.

Butts, J.A., and J. Roman (2004). *Juvenile Drug Courts and Teen Substance Abuse*. Washington, DC: Urban Institute Press.Butts, J.A., and H.N. Snyder (1992). *Restitution and Juvenile Recidivism*. Washington, DC: U.S. Department of Justice.

Butts, J.A., and H.N. Snyder (1992). *Restitution and Juvenile Recidivism*. Washington, DC: U.S. Department of Justice.

Butts, J.A., J.M. Zweig, and C. Mamalian (2004). "Defining the Mission of Juvenile Drug Courts." In J.A. Butts and J. Roman (eds.), *Juvenile Drug Courts and Teen Substance Abuse* (pp. 137-184). Washington, DC: Urban Institute Press.

Bynum, T. (1996). "Reducing School Violence in Detroit." Paper presented at the National Institute of Crime Prevention Conference, Washington, DC.

Cabana, D.A. (1996). *Death at Midnight: The Confession of an Executioner*. Boston: Northeastern University Press.

Campbell, A. (1984). "Girls' Talk: The Social Representation of Aggression by Female Gang Members." *Criminal Justice and Behavior* 11:139-156.

Campbell, A. (1990). "Female Participation in Gangs." In C.R. Huff (ed.), *Gangs in America* (pp. 163-182). Newbury Park, CA: Sage.

Carpenter, C., B. Glassner, B. D. Johnson and J. Loughlin (1988). *Kids, Drugs, and Crime*. Lexington, MA: Lexington Books.

Carroll, B.P. (2001). "Major Case Management: Key Components." *FBI Law Enforcement Bulletin* 70 (6):1-4.

Cashel, M.L. (2003). "Validity of Self-Reports of Delinquency and Socio-Emotional Functioning among Youth on Probation." *Journal of Offender Rehabilitation* 37:11-23.

Cavan, R.S., and T.N. Ferdinand (1981). *Juvenile Delinquency,* 4th ed. New York: Harper and Row.

Center for Substance Abuse Prevention (1999). *Understanding Substance Abuse Prevention: Toward the 21st Century: A Primer on Effective Programs*. Rockville, MD: U.S. Department of Health and Human Services.

Chaiken, M.R. (2004). *Community Policing Beyond the Big Cities*. Washington, DC: National Institute of Justice.

Chaiken, J.M., and M.R. Chaiken (1982). *Varieties of Criminal Behavior.* Santa Monica, CA: RAND.

Charters, C.A. (1994). "Volunteer Work Assumes a New Role in Public High School: *Steirer v. Bethlehem Area School District*." *Journal of Law and Education* 23:607-613.

Chavaria, F.P. (1997). "Probation and Cognitive Skills." *Federal Probation* 61:57-60.

Chesney-Lind, M. (1977). "Judicial Paternalism and the Female Status Offender: Training Women to Know their Place." *Crime & Delinquency* 23:121-130.

Chesney-Lind, M. (1987). "Girls' Crime and Woman's Place: Toward a Feminist Model of Female Delinquency." Paper presented at the annual meeting of the American Society of Criminology.

Chesney-Lind, M. (2002). "Criminalizing Victimization: The Unintended Consequences of Pro-arrest Policies for Girls and Women," *Criminology & Public Policy* 2:81-90.

Chesney-Lind, M., and R.G. Shelden (1992). *Girls, Delinquency, and Juvenile Justice.* Pacific Grove, CA: Brooks/Cole.

Chilton, R.J. (1964). "Continuities in Delinquency Area Research: A Comparison of Studies for Baltimore, Detroit and Indianapolis." *American Sociological Review* 129:71-83.

Chin, K. (1990). *Chinese Subculture and Criminality: Nontraditional Crime Groups in America.* Westport, CT: Greenwood.

Chin, K., J. Fagan, and R.J. Kelly (1992). "Patterns of Chinese Gang Extortion." *Justice Quarterly* 9:625-646.

Christiansen, K.O. (1974). "Seriousness of Criminality and Concordance among Danish Twins." In R. Hood (ed.), *Crime, Criminology, and Public Policy.* New York: Free Press.

Chused, R. (1973). "The Juvenile Court Process: A Study of Three New Jersey Counties." *Rutgers Law Review* 26:488-615.

Clark, R.D., and S.P. Lab (1995). "The Relationship between Victimization and Offending among Junior and Senior High School Students." Paper presented at the Academy of Criminal Justice Sciences annual meeting, Boston, MA.

Clarke, J.P., and M. Felson (1993). *Routine Activities and Rational Choice.* New Brunswick, NJ: Transaction.

Clarke, J.P., and L.L. Tifft (1996). "Polygraph and Interview Validation of Self-reported Deviant Behavior." *American Sociological Review* 31:516-523.

Clarke, S.H., and G.G. Koch (1980). "Juvenile Court: Therapy or Crime Control, and Do Lawyers Make a Difference." *Law and Society Review* 14:263-308.

Clayton, R.R., A. Cattarello, and K.P. Walden (1991). "Sensation Seeking as a Potential Mediating Variable for School-based Prevention Interventions: A Two-year Follow-up of DARE." *Journal of Health Communications* 3:229-239.

Clear, T.R. (1994). *Harm in American Penology: Offenders, Victims, and Their Communities.* Albany, NY: SUNY Press.

Clear, T. R., V.B. Clear, and A.A. Braga (1997). "Correctional Alternatives for Drug Offenders in an Era of Overcrowding." In M. McShane and F. P. Williams (eds.), *Criminal Justice: Contemporary Literature in Theory and Practice* (pp. 24-44). New York: Garland.

Clear, T.R., and D.R. Karp (1998). "Community Justice: An Essay." *Corrections Management Quarterly* 2(3):49-60.

Cloward, R., and L. Ohlin (1960). *Delinquency and Opportunity: A Theory of Delinquent Gangs.* New York: Free Press.

Cohen, A.K. (1955). *Delinquent Boys: The Culture of the Gang.* Glencoe, IL: Free Press.

Cohen, B. (1969). "The Delinquency of Gangs and Spontaneous Groups." In T. Sellin and M.E. Wolfgang (eds.), *Delinquency: Selected Studies.* New York: Wiley.

Cohen, L.E., and M. Felson (1979). "Social Changes and Crime Rate Trends: A Routine Activities Approach." *American Sociological Review* 44:588-608.

Cohen, L.E., and J.R. Klugel (1978). "Determinants of Juvenile Court Dispositions: Ascriptive and Achieved Factors in Two Metropolitan Courts." *American Sociological Review* 44:588-608.

Coles, C.M., and G.L. Kelling (2002). "New Trends in Prosecutors' Approaches to Youthful Offenders." In G.S. Katzman (ed.), *Securing Our Children's Future: New Approaches to Juvenile Justice and Youth Violence* (pp. 28-83). Washington, DC: Brookings Institution Press.

Collins, J.J. (1989). "Alcohol and Interpersonal Violence: Less than Meets the Eye." In N.A. Wiener and M.E. Wolfgang (eds.), *Pathways to Criminal Violence* (pp. 49-67). Newbury Park, CA: Sage.

Collins, J.J., R.L. Hubbard, and J.V. Rachal (1985). "Expensive Drug Use and Illegal Income: A Test of Explanatory Hypotheses." *Criminology* 23:743-764.

Colvin, M., F.T. Cullen, and T. Vander Ven (2002). "Coercion, Social Support, and Crime: An Emerging Theoretical Consensus." *Criminology* 40:19-42.

Colwell, B. (2002). "Shocking the Conscience: Excessive Discipline of Elementary and Secondary Students." *School Law Reporter* 44 (1):1-3.

Colwell, B. (2003). "Student Speech at Graduation: When Does It Violate the Establishment Clause." *School Law Reporter* 45 (5):75-78.

Conger, R.D., and R.L. Simons (1997). "Life-course Contingencies in the Development of Adolescent Antisocial Behavior: A Matching Law Approach." In T.P. Thornberry (ed.), *Developmental Theories of Crime and Delinquency.* New Brunswick, NJ: Transaction.

Conley, D.J., (1994). "Adding Color to a Black and White Picture: Using Qualitative Data to Explain Racial Disproportionality in the Juvenile Justice System." *Journal of Research in Crime and Delinquency* 31(2):135-148.

Cook, P.J., M.H. Moore, and A.A. Braga (2002). "Gun Control." In J.Q. Wilson and J. Petersilia (eds.), *Crime: Public Policies for Crime Control.* Oakland, CA: ICS Press.

Cooley, C. H. (1902). *Human Nature and the Social Order.* New York: Scribner.

Coombs, R.H. (1981). "Back on the Streets: Therapeutic Communities; Impact upon Drug Abusers." *American Journal of Alcohol Abuse* 8:185-201.

Cooper, C.N. (1967). "The Chicago YMCA Detached Workers: Current Status of an Action Program." In M.W. Klein (ed.), *Juvenile Gangs in Context* (pp. 183-193). Englewood Cliffs, NJ: Prentice Hall.

Coordinating Council on Juvenile Justice and Delinquency Prevention (1996). *Combating Violence and Delinquency: The National Juvenile Justice Action Plan: Report.* Washington, DC: U.S. Department of Justice.

Corbett, R.P. (2001). "Juvenile Probation on the Eve of the Next Millenium." In J.L. Victor and J. Naughton (eds.), *Annual Edition: Criminal Justice 01/02* (pp. 141-151).

Corbett, R.P. (2002). "Reinventing Probation and Reducing Youth Violence." In G.S. Katzmann (ed.), *Securing Our Children's Future: New Approaches to Juvenile Justice and Youth Violence* (pp. 175-199). Washington, DC: Brookings Institution Press.

Cordner, G., and E.P. Biebel (2005). "Problem-Oriented Policing in Practice." *Criminology & Public Policy* 4:155-180.

Cornish, D.B., and R.V. Clarke (1986). *The Reasoning Criminal.* New York: Springer-Verlag.

Corrado, R.R., I.M. Cohen, and C. Odgers (2003). "Multi-problem Violent Youths: A Challenge for the Restorative Justice Paradigm." In E.G.M. Weitekamp and H. Kerner (eds.), *Restorative Justice in Context: International Practice and Directions.* Portland, OR: Willan.

Cortes, J.B. (1972). *Delinquency and Crime.* New York: Seminar Press.

Costanzo, M. (1997). *Just Revenge: Costs and Consequences of the Death Penalty.* New York: St. Martin's Press.

Cox, S.M., W.S. Davidson, and T.S. Bynum (1995). "A Meta-Analytic Assessment of Delinquency-Related Outcomes of Alternative Education Programs." *Crime & Delinquency* 41:219-234.

Crank, J.P., and M. Caldero (1991). "The Production of Occupational Stress in Medium-sized Police Agencies: A Survey of Line Officers in Eight Municipal Departments." *Journal of Criminal Justice* 19:339-349.

Crawford, A., and T. Newburn (2003). *Youth Offending and Restorative Justice: Implementing Reform in Youth Justice.* Portland, OR: Willan.

Cromwell, P.F., J.N. Olson, and D.W. Avary (1991). *Breaking and Entering: An Ethnographic Analysis of Burglary.* Newbury Park, CA: Sage.

Cronin, R.C. (1994). *Boot Camps for Adult and Juvenile Offenders: Overview and Update.* Washington, DC: National Institute of Justice.

Crowe, A.H. (1998). *Drug Identification and Testing in the Juvenile Justice System: Summary.* Washington, DC: Office of Juvenile Justice and Delinquency Prevention.

Crowe, A.H., and L. Sydney (2000). *Ten Steps for Implementing a Program of Controlled Substance Testing of Juveniles.* Washington, DC: Office of Juvenile Justice and Delinquency Prevention.

Crowe, RR. (1972). "The Adopted Offspring of Women Criminal Offenders." *Archives of General Psychiatry* 27:600-603.

Cullen, F.T., K.R. Blevins, J.S. Trager, and P. Gendreau (2005). "The Rise and Fall of Boot Camps: A Case Study in Common Sense Corrections." *Journal of Offender Rehabilitation* 40:53-70.

Cullen, F.T., and J.P. Wright (1995). "The Future of Corrections." In B. Maguire and P. Radosh (eds.), *The Past, Present, and Future of American Criminal Justice* (pp. 198-219). New York: General Hall.

Cullen, F.T., J.P. Wright, and B.K. Applegate (1996). "Control in the Community: The Limits of Reform." In A.T. Harland (ed.), *Choosing Correctional Options that Work: Defining the Demand and Evaluating the Supply* (pp. 69-116). Thousand Oaks, CA: Sage.

Cullen, F.T., J.P. Wright, S. Brown, M.M. Moon, M.B. Blankenship, and B.K. Applegate (1998). "Public Support for Early Intervention Programs: Implications for a Progressive Policy Agenda." *Crime & Delinquency* 44:187-204.

Cullen, F.T., J.P. Wright, and M.B. Chamlin (1999). "Social Support and Social Reform: A Progressive Crime Control Agenda." *Crime & Delinquency* 45:188-207.

Cummings, S. (1993). "Anatomy of a Wilding Gang." In S. Cummings and D.J. Monti (eds.), *Gangs: The Origins and Impact of Contemporary Youth Gangs in the United States* (pp. 305-320). Albany, NY: SUNY Press.

Cummings, S., and D.J. Monti (1993). "Public Policy and Gangs: Social Science and the Urban Underclass." In S. Cummings and D.J. Monti (eds.), *Gangs: The Origins and Impact of Contemporary Youth Gangs in the United States* (pp. 305-320). Albany, NY: SUNY Press.

Curley, T. (1997). "Easing Teens into the Driver's Seat." *USA Today* (April 21, 1997):3A.

Curry, G.D. , R.A. Ball, and S.H. Decker (1996). "Estimating the National Scope of Gang Crimes from Law Enforcement Data." *National Assessment of Law Enforcement Anti-Gang Information Resources*. Washington, DC: National Institute of Justice.

Curry, G.D., R.A. Ball, R.J. Fox, and D. Stone (1992). *National Assessment of Law Enforcement Anti-Gang Information Resources: Final Report*. Washington, DC: National Institute of Justice.

Curry, G.D., R.J. Fox, R.A. Ball, and D. Stone (1993). *National Assessment of Law Enfocement Anti-Gang Information Resources: Final Report*. Washington, DC: National Institute of Justice.

Curry, G.D., and S.H. Decker (1998). *Confronting Gangs: Crime and Community*. Los Angeles: Roxbury.

Curtis, L.A. (1974). *Criminal Violence: National Patterns and Behavior*. Lexington, MA: D.C. Heath.

Dalton, K. (1964). *The Premenstrual Syndrome*. Springfield, IL: Charles C Thomas.

Daly, K. (2002). "Restorative Justice: The Real Story." *Punishment and Society* 4:5-79.

Daly, K. (2003). "Making Variation a Virtue: Evaluating the Potential and Limits of Restorative Justice." In E.G.M. Weitekamp and H. Kerner (eds.), *Restorative Justice in Context: International Practices and Directions*. Portland, OR: Willan.

Dannefer, D., and R.K. Schutt (1982). "Race and Juvenile Justice Processing in Court and Police Agencies." *American Journal of Sociology* 87:1113-1132.

D.A.R.E. (2005). *http:/www.dare.com/IDAV/law_enforcement_kit.pdf*

Davis, R., and J. O'Donnell (2005). "Some Teenagers Call Tracking Driving an Invasion of Privacy" *USA Today*, 1B. Available at: *http://www.usatoday.com/printedition/money/20050603/1b_blackbox03.art.htm*

Davis, S.M., and M.D. Schwartz (1987). *Children's Rights and the Law*. Lexington, MA: D.C. Heath.

Davis, S.M., E.S. Scott, W. Wadlington, and C.H. Whitebread (1997). *Children in the Legal System: Cases and Materials*, 2nd ed. Westbury, NY: Foundation Press.

Decker, S.H., S. Pennel, and A. Caldwell (1997). *Illegal Firearms: Access and Use by Arrestees*. Washington, DC: National Institute of Justice.

Decker, S.H., and B. Van Winkle (1994). "Slinging Dope: The Role of Gangs and Gang Members in Drug Sales." *Justice Quarterly* 11:583-604.

Decker, S., R. Wright, and R. Logie (1993). "Perceptual Deterrence among Active Residential Burglars: A Research Note." *Criminology* 31:135-147.

DeFleur, M.L., and R. Quinney (1966). "A Reformulation of Sutherland's Differential Association Theory and a Strategy for Empirical Verification." *Journal of Research in Crime and Delinquency* 3:1-22.

DiFonzo, J.H. (2001). "Parental Responsibility for Juvenile Crime." *Oregon Law Review* 80:1-107.

DeJong, C., and K.C. Jackson (1998). "Putting Race into Context: Race, Juvenile Justice Processing, and Urbanization." *Justice Quarterly* 15:487-504.

DeJong, W. (1987). "A Short-term Evaluation of Project DARE (Drug Abuse Resistance Education): Preliminary Indications of Effectiveness." *Journal of Drug Education* 17:279-294.

DeJong, W. (1993). "Building the Peace: The Resolving Conflicts Creatively Program (RCCP)." *NIJ Program Focus*. Washington, DC: U.S. Department of Justice.

DeLeon, G. (1984). "Program-based Evaluation Research in Therapeutic Communities." In F.M. Tims and J.P. Ludford (eds.), *Drug Abuse Treatment Evaluation: Strategies, Progress and Prospects* (pp. 69-87). Washington, DC: National Institute on Drug Abuse.

DeLeon, G., and M.S. Rosenthal (1989). "Treatment in Residential Therapeutic Communities." In H. Kleber (ed.), *Treatment of Psychiatric Disorders: A Task Force Report of the American Psychiatric Association, Vol. 2*. Washington, DC: American Psychiatric Association.

DeLong, J.V. (1972). "Treatment and Rehabilitation." *Dealing with Drug Abuse: A Report to the Ford Foundation*. New York: Praeger.

DeVoe, J.F., K. Peter, P. Kaufman, A. Miller, M. Noonan, T.D. Snyder, and K. Baum (2004). *Indicators of School Crime and Safety: 2004*. Washington, DC: Bureau of Justice Statistics.

Dentler, R.A., and L.J. Monroe (1961). "Social Correlates of Early Adolescent Theft." *American Sociological Review* 26:733-743.

Doerner, W.G., and S.P. Lab (2005). *Victimology*, 4th ed. Cincinnati: Anderson.

Drug Courts Program Office (2000). *About the Drug Courts Program Office*. Washington, DC: U.S. Department of Justice.

Duffee, D.E., and B.E. Carlson (1996). "Competing Value Premises for the Provision of Drug Treatment to Probationers." *Crime & Delinquency* 42:574-592.

Dunworth, T. (2000). *National Evaluation of the Youth Firearms Initiative*. Washington, DC: U.S. Department of Justice.

Durkheim, E. (1933). *The Division of Labor in Society*. (Translated by G. Supson.) New York: Free Press.

Eck, J., and J. Maguire (2000). "Have Changes in Policing Reduced Violent Crime? An Assessment of the Evidence." In A. Blumstein and J. Wallman (eds.), *The Crime Drop in America* (pp. 207-265).

Egley, A. (2005). *Highlights of the 2002-2003 National Youth Gang Surveys.* Washington, DC: Office of Juvenile Justice and Delinquency Prevention.

Egley, A., and M. Arjunan (2002). *Highlights of the 2000 National Youth Gang Survey. OJJDP Fact Sheet* (February #4). Washington, DC: Office of Juvenile Justice and Delinquency Prevention.

Egley, A., J.C. Howell, and A.K. Major (2004). "Recent Patterns of Gang Problems in the United States: Results from the 1996-2002 National Youth Gang Survey." In F. Esbensen, S.G. Tibbetts, and L. Gaines (eds.), *American Youth Gangs at the Millennium.* Long Grove, IL: Waveland.

Egley, A., and A.K. Major (2004). "Highlights of the 2002 National Youth Gang Survey." *OJJDP Fact Sheet.* Washington, DC: Office of Juvenile Justice and Delinquency Prevention.

Ehrenkranz, J., E. Bliss, and M.H. Sheard (1974). "Plasma Testosterone: Correlation with Aggressive Behavior and Social Dominance in Man." *Psychosomatic Medicine* 36:469-475.

Eisen, M., G.L. Zellman, H.A. Massett, and D.L. Murray (2002). "Evaluating the Lions-Quest 'Skills for Adolescence' Drug Education Program: First-year Behavior Outcomes." *Addictive Behaviors* 27:619-632.

Eiser, C., and J.R. Eiser (1988). *Drug Education in Schools.* New York: Springer-Verlag.

Elliott, D.S. (1985). "The Assumption that Theories Can be Combined with Increased Explanatory Power: Theoretical Integrations." In R.F. Meier (ed.), *Theoretical Methods in Criminology* (pp.123-150). Beverly Hills: Sage.

Elliott, D.S., S.S. Ageton, and R.J. Canter (1983). *The Prevalence and Incidence of Delinquent Behavior: 1976-1980.* Boulder, CO: Behavioral Research Institute.

Elliott, D.S., and D. Huizinga (1984). *The Relationship between Delinquent Behavior and ADM Problems.* Boulder, CO: Behavioral Research Institute.

Elliott, D.S., D. Huizinga, and S.S. Ageton (1985). *Explaining Delinquency and Drug Use.* Beverly Hills: Sage.

Elliott, D.S., D.H. Huizinga, and S. Menard (1989). *Multiple Problem Youth: Delinquency, Substance Use and Mental Health Problems.* New York: Springer-Verlag.

Ellis, L. (1982). "Genetics and Criminal Behavior: Evidence Through the End of the 1970's." *Criminology* 20:42-66.

Empey, L.T. (1982). *American Delinquency: Its Meaning and Construction.* Homewood, IL: Dorsey Press.

Erickson, M.L. (1971). "The Group Context of Delinquent Behavior." *Social Problems* 19:114-129.

Erickson, M.L. (1973). "Group Violations and Official Delinquency: The Group Hazard Hypothesis." *Criminology* 11:127-160.

Erickson, M.L., and G. Jensen (1977). "Delinquency is Still Group Behavior. Toward Revitalizing the Group Premise in the Sociology of Deviance." *Journal of Criminal Law and Criminology* 68:262-273.

Erikson, E.H. (1968). *Identity, Youth and Crisis.* New York: Norton.

Esbensen, F., and D. Huizinga (1991). "Juvenile Victimization and Delinquency." *Youth and Society* 23:202-228.

Esbensen, F., D. Peterson, T.J. Taylor, A. Freng, and D.W. Osgood (2004). "Gang Prevention: A Case Study of a Primary Prevention Program." In F. Esbensen, S.G. Tibbetts, and L. Gaines (eds.), *American Youth Gangs at the Millennium* (pp. 351-274). Long Grove, IL; Waveland.

Esbensen, F., and D. Huizinga (1993). "Gangs, Drugs and Delinquency in a Survey of Urban Youth." *Criminology* 31:565-590.

Esbensen, F., and D.W. Osgood (1997). "National Evaluation of G.R.E.A.T." *NIJ Research in Brief.* Washington, DC: National Institute of Justice.

Esbensen, F., and D.W. Osgood (1999). "Gang Resistance Education and Training (G.R.E.A.T.): Results from the National Evaluation." *Journal of Research in Crime and Delinquency* 36:194-225.

Esbensen, F., D.W. Osgood, T.J. Taylor, D. Peterson, and A. Freng (2001). "How Great is G.R.E.A.T.? Results from a Longitudinal Quasi-experimental Design." *Criminology & Public Policy* 1:87-118.

Fabricant, M. (1983). *Juveniles in the Family Courts.* Lexington, MA: Lexington Books.

Fader, J.J., P.W. Harris, P.R., Jones, and M.E. Poulin (2001). "Factors Involved in Decisions on Commitment to Delinquency Programs for First-time Juvenile Offenders." *Justice Quarterly* 18:323-341.

Fagan, J. (1990). "Social Process of Delinquency and Drug Use Among Urban Gangs." In C.R. Huff (ed.), *Gangs in America* (pp. 183-219). Newbury Park, CA: Sage.

Fagan, J. (1995). "Separating the Men from the Boys: The Comparative Advantage of Juvenile versus Criminal Court Sanctions on Recidivism Among Adolescent Felony Offenders." In J.C. Howell, B. Krisberg, J.D. Hawkins, and J.J. Wilson, *A Sourcebook: Serious, Violent & Chronic Juvenile Offenders* (pp. 238-260). Thousand Oaks, CA: Sage.

Fagan, J. (2002). "Policing Guns and Youth Violence." *Children, Youth, and Gun Violence* 12:133-151.

Fagan, J., and E. Pabon (1990). "Contributions of Delinquency and Substance Use to School Dropout Among Inner-city Youths." *Youth and Society* 21:306-354.

Fagan, J., and J.G. Weis (1990). *Drug Use and Delinquency among Inner City Youth.* New York: Springer-Verlag.

Fagan, J., J.G. Weis, and Y. Cheng (1990). "Delinquency and Substance Use among Inner-city Students." *The Journal of Drug Issues* 20:351-402.

Fattah, E.A. (1993). "The Rational Choice/Opportunity Perspectives as a Vehicle for Integrating Criminological and Victimological Theories." In R.V. Clarke and M. Felson (eds.), *Routine Activity and Rational Choice* (pp. 225-258). New Brunswick, NJ: Transaction.

Faust, F.L., and P.J. Brantingham (1979). *Juvenile Justice Philosophy: Readings, Cases and Comments.* St. Paul, MN: West.

Fedders, B., R. Hertz, and S. Weymouth (2002). "The Defense Attorney's Perspective on Youth Violence." In G.S. Katzman (ed.), *Securing Our Children's Future: New Approaches to Juvenile Justice and Youth Violence* (pp. 84-117). Washington, DC: Brookings Institution Press.

Federal Bureau of Investigation (2004). *Crime in the United States, 2003*. Washington, DC: Federal Bureau of Investigation.

Feld, B.C. (1981). "Legislative Policies Toward the Serious Juvenile Offender: On the Virtues of Automatic Adulthood." *Crime & Delinquency* 27:497-521.

Feld, B.C. (1987a). "The Juvenile Court Meets the Principle of the Offense: Changing Juvenile Justice Sentencing Practices." Paper presented at the 1987 Annual Meeting of the American Society of Criminology, Montreal, Quebec.

Feld, B.C. (1987b). "The Juvenile Court Meets the Principle of the Offense: Legislative Changes in Juvenile Waiver Statutes." *The Journal of Criminal Law and Criminology* 78:471-533.

Feld, B.C. (1988). "*In re Gault* Revisited: A Cross-State Comparison of the Right to Counsel in Juvenile Court." *Crime & Delinquency* 34:393-424.

Feld, B. (1993). *Justice for Children: The Right to Counsel and the Juvenile Courts*. Boston: Northeastern University Press.

Feld, B.C. (1998). "Juvenile and Criminal Justice Systems' Responses to Youth Violence." In M. Tonry and M.H. Moore, *Youth Violence* (pp. 189-261). Chicago: University of Chicago Press.

Feld, B. (1999a). *Bad Kids: Race and the Transformation of the Juvenile Court*. New York: Oxford University Press.

Feld, B.C. (1999b). "Rehabilitation, Retribution and Restorative Justice: Alternative Conceptions of Juvenile Justice." In G. Bazemore and L. Walgrave (eds.), *Restorative Juvenile Justice: Repairing the Harm of Youth Crime*. Monsey, NY: Criminal Justice Press.

Fenwick, C.R. (1982). "Juvenile Court Intake Decisionmaking: The Importance of Family Affiliation." *Journal of Criminal Justice* 10:443-453.

Ferguson, A.A. (2000). *Bad Boys: Public Schools in the Making of Black Masculinity*. Ann Arbor, MI: University of Michigan Press.

Ferrraro, K.F. (1995). *Fear of Crime: Interpreting Victimization Risk*. Albany, NY: SUNY Press.

Ferraro, K.F., and R.L. LaGrange (1987). "The Measurement of Fear of Crime." *Sociological Inquiry* 57:70-101.

Ferrer-Wreder, L., C.C. Lorente, E. Briones, J. Bussell, S. Berman, and O. Arrufat (2002). "Promoting Identity Development in Marginalized Youth." *Journal of Adolescent Research* 17:168-187.

Feyerherm, W. (1980). "The Group Hazard Hypothesis: A Reexamination." *Journal of Research in Crime & Delinquency* 17:58-68.

Fishman, L.T. (1988). "The Vice Queens: An Ethnographic Study of Black Female Gang Behavior." Paper presented at the 1988 Annual Meeting of the American Society of Criminology, Chicago, IL.

Flanagan, T.J., and K. Maguire (1990). *Sourcebook of Criminal Justice Statistics—1989*. Washington, DC: Bureau of Justice Statistics.

Foster, J.D., S. Dinitz, and W.C. Reckless (1972). "Perceptions of Stigma Public Intervention for Delinquent Behavior." *Social Problems* 20:202-209.

Fox, J.R. (1985). "Mission Impossible? Social Work Practice with Black Urban Youth gangs." *Social Work* 30:25-31.

Franklin II, C.W., and A.P. Franklin (1976). "Victimology Revisited: A Critique and Suggestions for Future Direction." *Criminology* 14:177-214.

Frazier, C.E., and D.M. Bishop (1985). " The Pretrial Detention of Juveniles and its Impact on Case Dispositions." *Journal of Criminal Law and Criminology* 76:1132-1152.

Frazier, C.E., and D.M. Bishop (1995). "Reflections on Race Effects in Juvenile Justice." In K.K. Leonard, C.E. Pope and W.H. Feyerherm, *Minorities in Juvenile Justice* (pp. 16-46). Thousand Oaks, CA: Sage.

Fritsch, E.J., T.J. Caeti, and C. Hemmens (1996). "Spare the Needle but Not the Punishment: The Incarceration of Waived Youth in Texas Prisons." *Crime & Delinquency* 42:593-609.

Gaarder, E., and J. Belknap (2004). "Little Women: Girls in Adult Prison." *Women & Criminal Justice* 15(2):51-80.

Gaarder, E., N. Rodriguez, and M. Zatz (2004). "Criers, Liars, and Manipulators: Probation Officers' Views of Girls." *Justice Quarterly* 21:547-578.

Gallup Organization (2001). "Firefighters Top Gallup's 'Honesty and Ethics' List." *The Gallup Poll Monthly* #435 (December):46-48.

Garbarino, J., and G. Gilliam (1980). *Understanding Abusive Families*. Lexington, MA: Lexington Books.

Garfinkel, H. (1956). "Conditions of Successful Status Degradation Ceremonies." *American Journal of Sociology* 61:420-424.

Garland, D. (2001). *The Culture of Control: Crime and Social Order in Contemporary Society*. Chicago: University of Chicago Press.

Garofalo, J., and K.J. Connelly (1980). "Dispute Resolution Centers, Part I: Major Features and Processes." *Criminal Justice Abstracts* 12:416-436.

Garry, E.M. (1996). *Truancy: First Step to a Lifetime of Problems*. Washington, DC: U.S. Department of Justice.

Gates, L.B., and W.M. Rohe (1987). "Fear and Reactions to Crime: A Revised Model." *Urban Affairs Quarterly* 22:425-453.

Gay, B.W., and J.W. Marquart (1993). "Jamaican Posses: A New Form of Organized Crime." *Journal of Crime and Justice* 16:139-170.

Geary, D.P. (1983). "Nutrition, Chemicals and Criminal Behavior. Some Psychological Aspects of Anti-social Conduct." *Juvenile and Family Court Journal* 34:9-13.

Geiselman, R.E., G. Bornstein, and K.J. Saywitz (1992). *New Approach to Interviewing Children: A Test of Its Effectiveness*. Washington, DC: U.S. Department of Justice.

Geller, W.A., and H. Toch (1996). "Understanding and Controlling Police Abuse of Force." In W.A. Geller and H. Toch (eds.), *Police Violence: Understanding and Controlling Police Abuse of Force* (pp. 292-328). New Haven, CT: Yale University

Gelles, R.J. (1980). "Violence in the Family: A Review of Research in the 70's." *Journal of Marriage and the Family* 42:873-885.

Gelles, R.J., and C.P. Cornell (1990). *Intimate Violence in Families*. Beverly Hills: Sage.

Gendreau, P. (1996). "The Principles of Effective Intervention with Offenders." In A.T. Harland (ed.), *Choosing Correctional Options That Work: Defining the Demand and Evaluating the Supply* (pp. 117-130). Thousand Oaks, CA: Sage.

Gendreau, P., F.T. Cullen, and J. Bonta (1994). "Intensive Rehabilitation Supervision: The Next Generation in Community Corrections?" *Federal Probation* 58(1):72-78.

Geraghty, T.F. (1998). "Justice for Children: How Do We Get There?" *Journal of Criminal Law and Criminology* 88:190-241.

Giallombardo, R. (1974). *The Social World of Imprisoned Girls*. New York: John Wiley.

Gil, D. (1971). *Violence Against Children: Physical Child Abuse in the United States*. Cambridge, MA: Harvard University Press.

Ginsberg, C., and L. Loffredo (1993). "Violence-related Attitudes and Behaviors of High School Students—New York City 1992." *Journal of School Health* 63:438-439.

Giodano, P.C., S.A. Cernkovich, and M.D. Pugh (1986). "Friendship and Delinquency." *American Journal of Sociology* 91:1170-1202.

Girshick, L.B. (1999). *No Safe Haven: Stories of Women in Prison*. Boston: Northeastern University Press.

Glaser, D. (1956). "Criminality Theories and Behavioral Images." *American Journal of Sociology* 61:434-444.

Glaser, D. (1964). *The Effectiveness of a Prison and Parole System*. Indianapolis: Bobbs-Merrill.

Glasser, W. (1965). *Reality Therapy*. New York: Harper and Row.

Glassner, B., and J. Loughlin (1987). *Drugs in Adolescent Worlds: Burnout to Straights*. New York: St. Martin's.

Glueck, S., and E. Glueck (1956). *Physique and Delinquency*. New York: Harper.

Goddard, H.H. (1920). *Efficiency and Levels of Intelligence*. Princeton, NJ: Princeton University Press.

Goffman, E. (1961). *Asylums: Essays on the Situation of Mental Patients and Other Inmates*. Garden City, NY: Anchor Books

Gold, M. (1970). *Delinquent Behavior in an American City*. Belmont, CA: Brooks/Cole.

Goldkamp, J.S., and D. Weiland (1993). "Assessing the Impact of Dade County's Felony Drug Court." *NIJ Research in Brief*. Washington, DC: U.S. Department of Justice.

Goldman, D., J. Lappalainen, and N. Ozaki (1996). "Direct Analysis of Candidate Genes in Impulsive Behavior." In G.R. Bock and J.A. Goode (eds.), *Genetics of Criminal and Antisocial Behavior*. Chicester, UK: John Wiley and Sons.

Goldstein, A.P. (1993). "Gang Intervention: A Historical Review." In A.P. Goldstein and C.R. Huff (eds.), *The Gang Intervention Handbook* (pp. 21-51). Champaign, IL: Research Press.

Goldstein, H. (1990). *Problem-Oriented Policing*. New York: McGraw-Hill.

Goldstein, P.J. (1989). "Drugs and Violent Crime." In N.A. Weiner and M.E. Wolfgang (eds.), *Pathways to Criminal Violence* (pp. 16-48). Newbury Park, CA: Sage.

Gomme, I.M. (1988). "The Role of Experience in the Production of the Fear of Crime: A Test of a Causal Model." *Canadian Journal of Criminology* 30:67-76.

Gordon, J.A. , L.J. Moriarty, and P.H. Grant (2003). "Juvenile Correctional Officers' Perceived Fear and Risk of Victimization: Examining Individual and Collective Levels of Victimization in Two Juvenile Correctional Centers in Virginia." *Criminal Justice and Behavior* 30:62-84.

Goring, C. (1913). *The English Convict: A Statistical Study.* Montclair, NJ: Patterson Smith.

Gottfredson, D.C., and W.H. Barton (1993). "Deinstitutionalization of Juvenile Offenders." *Criminology* 31:591-611.

Gottfredson, D.M. (1987). "Prediction and Classification in Criminal Justice Decision Making." In D.M. Gottfredson and M. Tonry (eds.), *Prediction and Classification: Criminal Justice Decision Making* (pp. 1-20). Chicago: University Press of Chicago.

Gottfredson, M.R., and T. Hirschi (1990). *A General Theory of Crime.* Stanford, CA: Stanford University Press.

Gottfredson, D.C., S.S. Najaka, and B. Kearley (2003). "Effectiveness of Drug Treatment Courts: Evidence from a Randomized Trial." *Criminology & Public Policy* 2:171-198.

Gould, J.B., and S.D. Mastrofski (2004). "Suspect Searches: Assessing Police Behavior under the U.S. Constitution." *Criminology & Public Policy* 2:315-362.

Gover, A.R., and D.L. MacKenzie (2003). "Child Maltreatment and Adjustment to Juvenile Correctional Institutions." *Criminal Justice and Behavior* 30:374-396.

Graham, S., and B.S. Lowery (2004). "Priming Unconscious Racial Stereotypes about Adolescent Offenders." *Law and Human Behavior* 28:483-504.

Granfield, R., C. Eby, and T. Brewster (1998). "An Examination of the Denver Drug Court: The Impact of a Treatment-oriented Drug-offender System." *Law and Policy* 20:183-202.

Grasmick, H.G., C.R. Tittle, R.J. Bursik, and B.J. Arneklev (1993). "Testing the Core Empirical Implications of Gottfredson and Hirschi's General Theory of Crime." *Journal of Research in Crime and Delinquency* 30:5-29.

Gray, G.E., and L.K. Gray (1983). "Diet and Juvenile Delinquency." *Nutrition Today* 18:14-21.

Greenbaum, S. (1994). "Drugs, Delinquency and Other Data." *Juvenile Justice* 2(1):2-8.

Greenberg, M.T., and C. Kusche (1998). *Promoting Alternative Thinking Strategies (PATHS): Blueprints for Violence Prevention.* Boulder, CO: Institute of Behavioral Science.

Greene, J.R. (2004). "Police Youth Violence Interventions: Lessons to Improve Effectiveness." In F. Esbensen, S.G. Tibbetts, and L. Gaines, *American Youth Gangs at the Millennium* (pp. 333-350). Long Grove, IL: Waveland.

Griffin, P. (2004). *National Overviews: State Juvenile Justice Profiles.* Pittsburgh: National Center for Juvenile Justice. Available at: *http:www.ncjj.org/stateprofiles*

Griffin, P. (2005). "National Overviews." *State Juvenile Justice Profiles.* Pittsburgh: National Center for Juvenile Justice. Available at: *http://www.ncjj.org/stateprofiles/*

Griffin, P., and M. King (2005). "National Overviews." *State Juvenile Justice Profiles.* Pittsburgh: National Center for Juvenile Justice. Online. Available at: *http://www.ncjj.org/stateprofiles/*

Griffin, P., L. Szymanski, and M. King (2005). "National Overviews." *State Juvenile Justice Profiles.* Pittsburgh: National Center for Juvenile Justice. Available at: *http://www.ncjj.org/stateprofiles/*

Griffin, P., and D. Thomas (2004). "The Good News: Measuring Juvenile Outcomes at Case Closing," *Pennsylvania Progress* 10(2):1-6.

Griffin, P., and P. Torbet (2002). *Desktop Guide to Good Juvenile Probation Practice.* Pittsburgh: National Center for Juvenile Justice.

Grisso, T. (2000). "What We Know about Youths' Capacities as Trial Defendants." In T. Grisso and R.G. Schwartz, *Youth on Trial: A Developmental Perspective on Juvenile Justice* (pp. 139-171). Chicago: University of Chicago Press.

Grisso, T.P., and R.G. Schwartz (2000). *Youth on Trial: A Developmental Perspective on Juvenile Justice.* Chicago: University of Illinois Press.

Guevara, L., C. Spohn, and D. Herz (2004). "Race, Legal Representation, and Juvenile Justice: Issues and Concerns." *Crime & Delinquency* 50:344-371.

Hagan, J., and B. McCarthy, in collaboration with P. Parker and J. Climenhage (1997). *Mean Streets: Youth Crime and Homelessness.* New York: Cambridge University Press.

Hagedorn, J.M. (1988). *People and Folks: Gangs, Crime and the Underclass in a Rustbelt City.* Chicago: Lakeview Press.

Hagedorn, J.M. (1994). "Homeboys, Dope Fiends, Legits, and New Jacks." *Criminology* 32:197-220.

Hansen, W.B., C.A. Johnson, B.R. Flay, J.W. Graham, and J.L. Sobel (1988). "Affective and Social Influences Approachers to the Prevention of Multiple Substance Abuse among Seventh Grade Students: Results from Project SMART." *Preventive Medicine* 17:135-154.

Hansen, D.J. (1980). "Drug Education: Does it Work?" In F.S. Scarpitti and S.K. Datesman (eds.), *Drugs and Youth Culture* (pp. 251-282). Beverly Hills: Sage

Harcourt, B.E. (2001). *Illusion of Order: The False Promise of Broken Windows Policing.* Cambridge, MA: Harvard University Press.

Harding, R.W. (1993). "Gun Use in Crime, Rational Choice, and Social Learning Theory." In R.V. Clarke and M. Felson (eds.), *Routine Activity and Rational Choice* (pp. 85-102). New Brunswick, NJ: Transaction.

Hardt, R.H., and S. Peterson-Hardt (1977). "On Determining the Quality of Delinquency Self-report Method." *Journal of Research in Crime and Delinquency* 14:247-261.

Harp, C., M. Kuykendall, M. Cunningham, and T. Ware (2004). *Juvenile Delinquency and Community Prosecution: New Strategies for Old Problems.* Alexandria, VA: American Prosecutors Research Institute.

Harrell, A. (1998). "Drug Courts and the Role of Graduated Sanctions." *NIJ Research Preview.* Washington, DC: National Institute of Justice.

Harrell, E. (2005). "Violence by Gang Members, 1993-2003." *Crime Data Brief.* Washington, DC: Bureau of Justice Statistics.

Harris, J.A. (1999) "Review and Methodological Considerations in Research on Testosterone and Aggression." *Aggression and Violent Behavior* 4:273-291.

Harris, N. (2003). "Evaluating the Practice of Restorative Justice: The Case of Family Group Conferencing." In L. Walgrave (ed.), *Repositioning Restorative Justice.* Portland, OR: Willan.

Harvard Law Review (2005). "Juvenile Curfews and the Major Confusion over Minor Rights." *Harvard Law Review* 118:2400-2421.

Hawkins, J.D., R.F. Catalano, R. Kosterman, R. Abbott, and K.G. Hill (1999). "Preventing Adolescent Health-risk Behaviors by Strengthening Protection During Childhood." *Archives of Pediatric and Adolescent Medicine* 153:226-234.

Hayes, H., and K. Daly (2004). "Conferencing and Re-offending in Queensland." *Australian and New Zealand Journal of Criminology* 37:167-191.

Henretta, J.C., C.E. Frazier, and D.M. Bishop (1985). "Juvenile Justice Decision-making: An Analysis of the Effects of Prior Case Outcomes." Paper presented at the Annual Meeting of the American Society of Criminology, San Diego, CA.

Henretta, J.C., C.E. Frazier, and D.M. Bishop (1986). "The Effect of Prior Case Outcomes on Juvenile Justice Decision-Making." *Social Forces* 65:554-562.

Herbert, S. (2005). "POP in San Diego: A Not-So-Local Story." *Criminology & Public Policy* 4:181-86.

Herrnstein, R.J., and C. Murray (1994). *The Bell Curve: Intelligence and Class Structure in American Life.* New York: Free Press.

Hills, S.L. (1980). *Demystifying Social Deviance.* New York: McGraw-Hill.

Hindelang, M.J. (1971). "The Social versus Solitary Nature of Delinquent Involvement." *British Journal of Criminology* 11:167-175.

Hindelang, M.J. (1973). "Causes of Delinquency: A Partial Replication and Extension." *Social Problems* 20:470-487.

Hindelang, M.J. (1975). *Public Opinion Regarding Crime, Criminal Justice, and Related Topics.* Washington, DC: U.S. Department of Justice.

Hindelang, M.J., M.R. Gottfredson, and J. Garofalo (1978). *Victims of Personal Crime: An Empirical Foundation for a Theory of Personal Victimization.* Cambridge, MA: Ballinger.

Hindelang, M.J., T. Hirschi, and J. G. Weis (1981). *Measuring Delinquency.* Beverly Hills: Sage.

Hippchen, L.J. (1978). *Ecologic-Biochemical Approaches to Treatment of Delinquents and Criminals.* New York: Van Nostrand Reinhold.

Hippchen, L.J. (1981). "Some Possible Biochemical Aspects of Criminal Behavior." *International Journal of Biosocial Research* 2:37-48.

Hirschel, J.D., C.W. Dean, and D. Dumond (2001). "Juvenile Curfews and Race: A Cautionary Note." *Criminal Justice Policy Review* 12:197-214.

Hirschi, T. (1969). *Causes of Delinquency.* Berkeley: University of California Press.

Hirschi, T., and M.J. Hindelang (1977). "Intelligence and Delinquency: A Revisionist Review." *American Sociological Review* 42:572-587.

Hodges, J., N. Giulotti, and F.M. Porpotage (1994). *Improving Literacy Skills of Juvenile Detainees*. Washington, DC: U.S. Department of Justice.

Holtz, L.E. (1987). "*Miranda* in a Juvenile Setting: A Child's Right to Silence." *The Journal of Criminal Law and Criminology* 78:534-556.

Hooten, E. (1931). *Crime and Man*. Cambridge, MA: Harvard University Press.

Hope, T. (1997). "Inequality and the Future of Community Crime Prevention." In S.P. Lab (ed.), *Crime Prevention at a Crossroads* (pp. 143-158). Cincinnati: Anderson.

Horney, J. (1978). "Menstrual Cycles and Criminal Responsibility." *Law and Human Behavior* 2:25-36.

Horowitz, M.A. (2000). "Kids Who Kill: A Critique of How the American Legal System Deals with Juveniles Who Commit Homicide." *Law and Contemporary Problems* 63:133-177.

Horowitz, R. (1983). *Honor and the American Dream: Culture and Identity in a Chicano Community*. New Brunswick, NJ: Rutgers University Press.

Howell, J.C. (1997a). "Youth Gangs." OJJDP Fact Sheet #72. Washington, DC: Office of Juvenile Justice and Delinquency Prevention.

Howell, J.C. (1997b). *Youth Gang Homicides and Drug Trafficking*. Washington, DC: Office of Juvenile Justice and Delinquency Prevention.

Howell, J.C. (2000). *Youth Gang Programs and Strategies: Summary*. Washington, DC: Office of Juvenile Justice and Delinquency Prevention.

Howell, J.C. (2003). *Preventing and Reducing Juvenile Delinquency: A Comprehensive Framework*. Thousand Oaks, CA: Sage.

Howell, J.C., and J.D. Hawkins (1998). "Prevention of Youth Violence." In M. Tonry and M.H. Moore, *Youth Violence* (pp. 189-261). Chicago: University of Chicago Press.

Hser, Y., M.D. Anglin, and C. Chou (1988). "Evaluation of Drug Abuse Treatment: A Repeated Measure Design Assessing Methadone Maintenance." *Evaluation Review* 12:547-570.

Hsia, H.M., G.S. Bridges, and R. McHale (2004). *Disproportionate Minority Confinement 2002 Update: Summary*. Washington, DC: U.S. Department of Justice.

Huang, D.T. (2001). "Less Unequal Footing: State Courts' Per Se Rules for Juvenile Waivers During Interrogation and the Case for Their Implementation." *Cornell Law Review* 86:437.

Huba, G.J., and P.M. Bentler (1983). "Causal Models of the Development of Law Abidance and its Relationship to Psychosocial Factors and Drug Use." In W.S. Laufer and J.M. Day (eds.), *Personality Theory, Moral Development and Criminal Behavior* (pp. 165-215). Lexington: D.C. Health.

Hubbard, R.L., M.E. Marsden, J.V. Rachal, H.J. Harwood, E.R. Cavanaugh, and H.M. Ginzbury (1989). *Drug Abuse Treatment: A National Study of Effectiveness*. Chapel Hill, NC: University of North Carolina Press.

Huebner, B.M., J.A. Schafer, and T.S. Bynum (2004). "African American and White Perceptions of Police Services: Within- and Between-Group Variation." *Journal of Criminal Justice* 32:123-135.

Huff, C.R. (1990). "Denial, Overreaction, and Misidentification: A Postscript on Public Policy." In C.R. Huff (eds.), *Gangs in America* (pp. 310-317). Newbury Park, CA: Sage.

Huff, C.R. (1993). "Gangs in the United States." In A.P. Goldstien and C.R. Huff (eds.), *The Gang Intervention Handbook* (pp. 3-20). Champaign, IL: Research Press.

Huizinga, D.H., R. Loeber, and T. Thornberry (1994). *Urban Delinquency and Substance Abuse: Initial Findings.* Research Summary. Washington, DC: Office of Juvenile Justice and Delinquency Prevention.

Huizinga, D.H., R. Loeber, and T. Thornberry (1995). *Urban Delinquency and Substance Abuse: Research Summary.* Washington, DC: Office of Juvenile Justice and Delinquency Prevention.

Huizinga, D., S. Menard, and D. Elliot (1989). "Delinquency and Drug Use: Temporal and Developmental Patterns." *Justice Quarterly* 6:419-456.

Humes, E. (1996). *No Matter How Loud I Shout: A Year in the Life of Juvenile Court.* New York: Simon & Schuster.

Hunter, A. (1985). "Private, Parochial and Public School Orders: The Problem of Crime and Incivility in Urban Communities." In G.D. Suttles and M.N. Zald (eds.), *The Challenge of Social Control: Citizenship and Institution Building in a Modern Society* (pp. 230-242). Norwood, NJ: Ablex.

Hutchings, B., and S.A. Mednick (1977). "Criminality in Adoptees and Their Adoptive and Biological Parents: A Pilot Study." In S.A. Mednick and K.O. Christiansen (eds.), *Biosocial Bases of Criminal Behavior* (pp. 127-141). New York: Gardner Press.

Hutchinson, R., and C. Kyle (1993). "Hispanic Street Gangs in Chicago's Public Schools." In S. Cummings and D.J. Monti (eds.), *Gangs: The Origins and Impact of Contemporary Youth Gangs in the United States* (pp. 113-136). Albany, NY: SUNY Press.

Inciardi, J.A., R. Horowitz, and A.E. Pottieger (1993). *Street Kids, Street Drugs, Street Crime: An Examination of Drug Use and Serious Delinquency in Miami.* Belmont, CA Wadsworth.

Institute of Judicial Administration–American Bar Association (1980). *Juvenile Justice Standards Project: Standards Relating to Adjudication*, 2nd ed. Cambridge, MA: Ballinger.

Institute of Judicial Administration–American Bar Association (1982). *Juvenile Justice Standards Project: Standards for Juvenile Justice: A Summary and Analysis*, 2nd ed. Cambridge, MA: Ballinger.

Jang, S.J., and B.R. Johnson (2001). "Neighborhood Disorder, Individual Religiosity, and Adolescent Use of Illicit Drugs: A Test of Multilevel Hypotheses." *Criminology* 39:109-144.

Jankowski, M.S. (1991). *Islands in the Street: Gangs and American Urban Society.* Berkeley, CA: University of California Press.

Jeffery, C.R. (1965). "Criminal Behavior and Learning Theory." *Journal of Criminal Law, Criminology and Police Science* 56:294-300.

Jensen, G.F. (1972). "Delinquent and Adolescent Self-Conceptions: A Study of the Personal Relevance of Infractions." *Social Problems* 20:84-103.

Jensen, G.F., and D. Brownfield (1983). "Parents and Drugs." *Criminology* 21:543-554.

Jensen, G., and D. Brownfield (1986). "Gender, Lifestyles and Victimization: Beyond Routine Activity." *Violence and Victims* 1:85-99.

Joe, D., and N. Robinson (1980). "Chinatown's Immigrant Gangs: The New Young Warrior Class." *Criminology* 18:337-345.

Johnson, B.D., P.J. Goldstein, E. Prebel, J. Schmeidler, D.S. Lipton, B. Sprunt, and T. Miller (1985). *Taking Care of Business: The Economics of Crime by Heroin Abusers.* Lexington, MA: Lexington Books.

Johnson, B.D., E.D. Wish, J. Schmeidler, and D. Huizinga (1991). "Concentration of Delinquent Offending: Serious Drug Involvement and High Delinquency Rates." *The Journal of Drug Issues* 21:205-229.

Johnson, K. (2005). "U.S. Gang Membership May Be Higher than Reported." *USA Today* (August 3). Available at: *http://www.usatoday.com/news/nation/2005-08-03-gangs-under-estimated_x.htm*

Johnston, L.D., P.M. O'Malley, and J.G. Bachman (1987). *National Trends in Drug Use and Related Factors among American High School Students and Young Adults, 1975-1986.* Rockville, MD: National Institute on Drug Abuse.

Johnston, L.D., P.M. O'Malley, and J.G. Bachman (1996). *National Survey Results on Drug Use from the Monitoring the Future Study, 1975-1995* (Vol. 1). Washington, DC: U.S. Department of Health & Human Services.

Johnston, L.D., P.M. O'Malley, and J.G. Bachman (2002). *Monitoring the Future: National Results on Adolescent Drug Use.* Washington, DC: National Institutes of Health.

Johnston, L.D., P.M. O'Malley, and J.G. Bachman (2004). *Monitoring the Future 2004.* Washington, DC: National Institute on Drug Abuse.

Johnston, L.D., P.M. O'Malley, and L.K. Eveland (1978). "Drugs and Delinquency: A Search for Causal Connections." In D.B. Kandel (ed.), *Longitudinal Research on Drug Use: Empirical Findings and Methodological Issues* (pp. 137-156). Washington, DC: Hemisphere.

Johnstone, J.W.C. (1981). "Youth Gangs and Black Suburbs." *Pacific Sociological Review* 58:355-375.

Jones, J.B. (2004). *Access to Counsel.* Washington, DC: U.S. Department of Justice.

Josi, D.A., and Sechrest, D.K. (1999). "A Pragmatic Approach to Parole Aftercare: Evaluation of a Community Reintegration Program for High-risk Youthful Offenders." *Justice Quarterly* 16:51-80.

Juvenile Justice Update (1995). "Juveniles Subject to Warrantless Search as a Probation Condition Have No Expectation of Privacy." *Juvenile Justice Update* (April/May 1)(2):8.

Juvenile Law Center (2005). "Amicus Brief for *In Re Christopher K., a Minor.*" Available at: *http://www.jlc.org*

Kandel, D.B. (1973). "Adolescent Marijuana Use: Role of Parents and Peers." *Science* 181:1067-1070.

Kandel, D.B., O. Simcha-Fagan, and M. Davies (1986). "Risk Factors for Delinquency and Illicit Drug Use from Adolescence to Young Adulthood." *Journal of Drug Issues* 16:67-90.

Kanter, D., and W. Bennett (1968). "Orientation of Street-Corner Workers and Their Effects on Gangs." In S. Wheeler (ed.), *Controlling Delinquents*. New York: Wiley.

Kaplan, J. (1983). *The Hardest Drug: Heroin and Drug Policy*. Chicago: University of Chicago Press.

Karnowski, S. (July 6, 2005). "Prosecutor: Teen on Trial in School Shootings Upset about Being Teased." *Johnson City Press*, 7A.

Karp, D.R. (1998). "The Judicial and Judicious Use of Shame Penalties." *Crime & Delinquency* 44:277-294.

Karp, D. (2001). "The Offender/Community Encounter: Stakeholder Involvement in the Vermont Reparative Boards." In D. Karp and T. Clear (eds.), *What is Community Justice? Case Studies of Restorative Justice and Community Supervision*. Thousand Oaks, CA: Sage.

Karp, D.R., G. Bazemore, and J.D. Chesire (2004). "The Role and Attitudes of Restorative Board Members: A Case Study of Volunteers in Community Justice." *Crime & Delinquency* 50:487-515.

Karp, D.R., and K.M. Drakulish (2004). "Minor Crime in a Quaint Setting: Practices, Outcomes, and Limits of Vermont Reparative Probation Boards." *Criminology & Public Policy* 3:655-686.

Karst, G., and Frazier, J. (2000). "Reshaping the Design of Juvenile Facilities in Kansas." *Corrections Today* 62 (July):84.

Katz, J., and W.J. Chambliss (1995). "Biology and Crime." In J.F. Sheley (ed.), *Criminology: A Contemporary Handbook* (pp. 275-304). Belmont, CA: Wadsworth.

Katz, C.M., and V.J. Webb (2003). *Police Response to Gangs: A Multi-Site Study—Final Report*. Washington, DC: National Institute of Justice.

Kaufman, P., X. Chen, S.P. Choy, K.A. Chandler, C.D. Chapman, M.R. Rand, and C. Ringel (1998). *Indicators of School Crime and Safety, 1998*. Washington, DC: Office of Educational Research and Improvement and Office of Justice Programs.

Kelling, G. (1975). "Leadership in the Gang." In D.S. Cartwright, B. Tomson, and H. Schwartz (eds.), *Gang Delinquency* (pp. 111-126). Monterey: Brooks/Cole.

Kelling, G.L., and C.M. Coles (1996). *Fixing Broken Windows: Restoring Order and Reducing Crime in Our Communities*. New York: Touchstone.

Kennedy, D. (1998) "Pulling Levers: Getting Deterrence Right." *National Institute of Justice Journal* 236:2-8.

Kennedy, L.W., and D.R. Forde (1990). "Routine Activities and Crime: An Analysis of Victimization Data in Canada." *Criminology* 28:137-152.

Kerbs, J.J. (1999). "(Un)equal Justice: Juvenile Court Abolition and African Americans." *Annals of the American Academy of Political and Social Science* 564:109-125.

Kim, S. (1988). "A Short- and Long-term Evaluation of 'Here's Looking at You' Alcohol Education Program." *Journal of Drug Education* 18:235-242.

Kim, S., J.H. McLeod, and C. Shantzis (1993). "An Outcome Evaluation of Here's Looking at You 2000." *Journal of Drug Education* 23:67-81.

Kinder, B.N., N.E. Pape, and S. Walfish (1980). "Drug and Alcohol Education Programs: A Review of Outcome Studies." *International Journal of the Addictions* 15:1035-1054.

Klein, J. (2002). "The Supercop Scenario." *The New Yorker* (March 18):72-78.

Klein, M.W. (1969). "Gang Cohesiveness, Delinquency, and a Street-work Program." *Journal of Research in Crime and Delinquency* 6:135-166.

Klein, M.W. (1971). *Street Gangs and Street Workers.* Englewood Cliffs, NJ: Prentice Hall.

Klein, M.W. (1995). *The American Street Gang: Its Nature, Prevalence and Control.* New York: Oxford University Press.

Klein, M.W. (2004). *Gang Cop: The Words and Ways of Officer Paco Domingo.* Walnut Creek, CA: AltaMira.

Klein, M.W., and C.L. Maxson (1989). "Street Gang Violence." In N.A. Weiner and M.E. Wolfgang (eds.), *Violent Crime, Violent Criminals* (pp. 198-234). Newbury Park, CA: Sage.

Klein, M.W, C.L. Maxson, and L.C. Cunningham (1991). "Crack, Street Gangs, and Violence." *Criminology* 29:623-650.

Knox, G.W. (1991). *An Introduction to Gangs.* Berrien Springs, MI: Vande Vere.

Kohlberg, L. (1981). *The Philosophy of Moral Development.* San Francisco: Harper and Row.

Kopp, C.B., and A.H. Parmelee (1979). "Prenatal and Perinatal Influences on Infant Behavior." In J.D. Osofsky (ed.), *Handbook of Infant Development.* New York: Wiley.

Kornhauser, R.R. (1978). *Social Sources of Delinquency.* Chicago: University of Chicago Press.

Kretschmer, E. (1925). *Physique and Character.* London: Kegan Paul.

Kreuz, L.E., and R.M. Rose (1972). "Assessment of Aggressive Behavior and Plasma Testosterone in a Young Criminal Population." *Psychosomatic Medicine* 34:321-332.

Krisberg, B. (2005). *Juvenile Justice: Redeeming Our Children.* Thousand Oaks, CA: Sage.

Krisberg, B., and J. Austin (1993). *Reinventing Juvenile Justice.* Newbury Park, CA: Sage.

Krisberg, B., and J. Austin (1978). *The Children of Ishmael.* Palo Alto: Mayfield.

Krisberg, B., E. Currie, D. Onek, and R.G. Wiebush (1995). *Unlocking Juvenile Corrections: Evaluating the Massachusetts Department of Youth Services.* San Francisco: National Council on Crime and Delinquency.

Krisberg, B., and J.C. Howell (1998). "The Impact of the Juvenile Justice System and Prospects for Graduated Sanctions in a Comprehensive Strategy." In R. Loeber and D.P. Farringtons (eds.), *Serious & Violent Juvenile Offenders: Risk Factors and Successful Interventions* (pp. 313-345). Thousand Oaks, CA: Sage.

Kroes, W.H., B.L. Margolis, and J.J. Hurrell (1974). "Job Stress in Policemen." *Journal of Police Science and Administration* 2:145-155.

Krohn, M., and J. Massey (1980). "Social Control and Delinquent Behavior: An Examination of the Elements of the Social Bond." *Sociological Quarterly* 21:529-543.

Kurki, L. (2000). "Restorative and Community Justice in the United States." In M. Tonry, *Crime and Justice: A Review of Research* (Vol. 27) (pp. 235-303). Chicago: University of Chicago Press.

Kurlychek, M.C., and B.D. Johnson (2004). "The Juvenile Penalty: A Comparison of Juvenile and Young Adult Sentencing Outcomes in Criminal Court." *Criminology* 42:485-515.

Kurlychek, M., P.M. Torbet, and M. Bozynski (1999). *Focus on Accountability: Best Practices for Juvenile Court and Probation*. Washington, DC: U.S. Department of Justice and Delinquency Prevention.

Lab, S.P. (1984). "Patterns in Juvenile Misbehavior." *Crime & Delinquency* 30:293-308.

Lab, S.P. (1990). "Citizen Crime Prevention: Domains and Participation." *Justice Quarterly* 7:467-492.

Lab, S.P. (2004). *Crime Prevention: Approaches, Practices and Evaluation*, 5th ed. Newark, NJ: Matthew Bender.

Lab, S.P., and R.B. Allen (1984). "Self-report and Official Measures: A Further Examination of the Validity Issue." *Journal of Criminal Justice* 12:445-456.

Lab, S.P., and R.D. Clark (1994). "Gauging Crime and Control in the Schools." Paper presented at the 1994 Annual Meeting of the American Society of Criminology, Miami, FL.

Lab, S.P., and R.D. Clark (1996). *Discipline, Control and School Crime: Identifying Effective Intervention Strategies. Final Report*. Washington, DC: National Institute of Justice.

Lander, B. (1954). *Towards an Understanding of Juvenile Delinquency*. New York: Columbia University Press.

Lane, J., S. Turner, T. Fain, and A. Sehgal (2005). "Evaluating an Experimental Intensive Juvenile Probation Program: Supervision and Official Outcomes." *Crime & Delinquency* 51:26-52.

Langan, P.A., L.A. Greenfeld, S.K. Smith, M.R. Durose, and J.J. Levin (2001). *Contacts between Police and the Public: Findings from the 1999 National Survey*. Washington, DC: U.S. Department of Justice.

Lange, J.E., M.B. Johnson, and R.B. Voas (2005). "Testing the Racial Profiling Hypothesis for Seemingly Disparate Traffic Stops on the New Jersey Turnpike." *Justice Quarterly* 22:193-223.

Lattimore, P.K., C.P. Krebs. P. Graham, and A.J. Cowell (2005). *Evaluation of the Juvenile Breaking the Cycle Program—Final Report*. Washington, DC: National Institute of Justice.

Laub, J., and R.J. Sampson (1988). "Unraveling Families and Delinquency: A Reanalysis of the Gluecks' Data." *Criminology* 26:355-380. In G. Bridges, J. Weis, and R. Crutchfield (eds.), *Juvenile Delinquency*. Thousand Oaks, CA: Pine Forge Press, 1996.

Laub, J.H., and R.J. Sampson (2003). *Shared Beginning, Divergent Lives: Delinquent Boys to Age 70*. Cambridge, MA: Harvard University Press.

Lauritsen, J.L., R.J. Sampson, and J.H. Laub (1991). "The Link between Offending and Victimization among Adolescents." *Criminology* 29:265-292.

Lavrakas, P.J., and D.A. Lewis (1980). "The Conceptualization and Measurement of Citizen Crime Prevention Behaviors." *Journal of Research in Crime and Delinquency* 17(2):254-272.

LeBlanc, M. (1997). "A Generic Control Theory of the Criminal Phenomenon: The Structural Dynamic Statements of an Integrative Multilayered Control Theory." In T.P. Thornberry (ed.), *Developmental Theories of Crime and Delinquency*. New Brunswick, NJ: Transaction.

Lederman, C.S., and E.N. Brown (2000). "Entangled in the Shadows: Girls in the Juvenile Justice System." *Buffalo Law Review* 48:909-925.

Leiber, M.J., and K.Y. Mack (2003). "The Individual and Joint Effects of Race, Gender, and Family Status on Juvenile Justice Decision-Making." *Journal of Research in Crime and Delinquency* 40:34-70.

Lemert, E.M. (1951). *Social Pathology: A Systematic Approach to the Theory of Sociopathic Behavior*. New York: McGraw-Hill.

Lester, D., and M. Braswell (1987). *Correctional Counseling*. Cincinnati: Anderson.

Leitzel, J. (2001). "Race and Policing," *Society* (March/April):38-42.

Leiwand, D. (June 3, 2005). "Schools Restrict Use of Tasers," *USA Today*, 1A.

Levine, M., and L. Battistoni (1991). "The Corroboration Requirement in Child Sex Abuse Cases." *Behavioral Sciences and the Law* 9:3-20.

Leukefeld, C.G., and F.M. Tims (1988). *Compulsory Treatment of Drug Abuse: Research and Clinical Practice*. Rockville, MD: National Institute on Drug Abuse.

Levrant, S., F.T. Cullen, and J.F. Wozniak (1999). "Reconsidering Restorative Justice: The Corruption of Benevolence Revisited?" *Crime & Delinquency* 45:3-27.

Lewis, D.A., and G. Salem (1986). *Fear of Crime: Incivility and the Production of a Social Problem*. New Brunswick, NJ: Transaction.

Lilly, J.R., F.T. Cullen, and R.A. Ball (1995). *Criminological Theory: Context and Consequences*, 2nd ed. Thousand Oaks, CA: Sage.

Lindner, C. (1981). "The Utilization of Day-Evening Centers as an Alternative to Secure Detention of Juveniles." *Journal of Probation and Parole* 13:12-18.

Lindner, C., and R.L. Bonn (1996). "Probation Officer Victimization and Fieldwork Practices: Results of a National Study." *Federal Probation* 60(2):16-23.

Lipsett, P. (1968). "The Juvenile Offender's Perception." *Crime & Delinquency* 14:49-62.

Lipsey, M.W. (1992). "Juvenile Delinquency Treatment: A Meta-Analytic Inquiry into the Viability of Effects." In T. Cook, H. Cooper, D. Corday, H. Hartman, L. Hedges, R. Light, T. Louis, and F. Mosteller (eds.), *Meta-Analysis for Explanation: A Casebook* (pp. 83-127). New York: Russell Sage Foundation.

Lipsey, M.W. (1999). "Can Intervention Rehabilitate Serious Delinquents?" *Annals of the American Academy of Political and Social Science* 564:142-166.

Lipsey, M.W., and D.B. Wilson (1998). "Effective Intervention for Serious Juvenile Offenders: A Synthesis of Research." In R. Loeber and D.P. Farrington, *Serious Violent Juvenile Offenders: Risk Factors and Successful Interventions* (pp. 313-345). Thousand Oaks, CA: Sage.

Lipton, D.L. (1995). *The Effectiveness of Treatment for Drug Abusers under Criminal Justice Supervision*. Washington, DC: U.S. Department of Justice, 1995.

Listwan, S.J., J.L. Sundt, A.M. Holsinger, and E.J. Latessa (2003). "The Effects of Drug Court Programming on Recidivism: The Cincinnati Experience." *Crime & Delinquency* 49:389-411.

Lizotte, A., and D. Sheppard (2001). "Gun Use by Male Juveniles: Research and Prevention." *Juvenile Justice Bulletin*. Washington, DC: U.S. Department of Justice.

Locke, H.G. (1996). "The Color of Law and the Issue of Color: Race and the Abuse of Police Power." In W.A. Geller and H. Toch, *Police Violence: Understanding and Controlling Police Abuse of Force* (pp. 129-149). New Haven, CT: Yale University Press.

Loeber, R. (1988). "Natural Histories of Conduct Problems, Delinquency and Related Substance Abuse." In B.B. Lahey and A.E. Kazdin (eds.), *Advances in Clinical Child Psychology* (Vol. 11). New York: Plenum.

Lombroso, C. (1876). *On Criminal Man*. Milan: Hoepli.

Lowney, J. (1984). "The Wall Gang: A Study of Interpersonal Process and Deviance among Twenty-three Middle-class Youths." *Adolescence* 19:527-538.

Lozoff, B., and M. Braswell (1989). *Inner Corrections: Finding Peace and Peace Making*. Cincinnati: Anderson.

Lundman. R.J. (1993). *Prevention and Control of Juvenile Delinquency*, 2nd ed. New York: Oxford.

Lyons, M.J. (1996). "A Twin Study of Self-Reported Criminal Behavior." In G.R. Bock and J.A. Goode (eds.), *Genetics of Criminal and Antisocial Behavior* (pp. 61-69). Chichester, England: John Wiley and Sons.

MacDonald, D.I. (1984). *Drugs, Drinking, and Adolescents*. Chicago: Year Book Medical.

Mack, J.W. (1909). "The Juvenile Court." *Harvard Law Review* 23:104-119.

MacKenzie, D.L. (1994). "Results of a Multisite Study of Boot Camp Prisons." *Federal Probation* 58(2):60-66.

Maddux, J.F. (1988). "Clinical Experience in Civil Commitment." In C.G. Leukefeld and F.M. Tims (eds.), *Compulsory Treatment of Drug Abuse: Research and Clinical Practice* (pp. 35-56). Washington, DC: National Institute on Drug Abuse.

Maguire, K., and A.L. Pastore (2004). *Sourcebook of Criminal Justice Statistics, 2003*. Washington, DC: Bureau of Justice Statistics. Available at: *http://www.albany.edu/sourcebook/*

Mahoney, A.R. (1985). "Jury Trial for Juveniles: Right or Ritual?" *Justice Quarterly* 2:553-565.

Mahoney, A.R. (1987). *Juvenile Justice in Context*. Boston: Northeastern University Press.

Maitland, A.S., and R.D. Sluder (1998). "Victimization and Youthful Prison Inmates: An Empirical Analysis." *Prison Journal* 78:55-73.

Males, M.A. (2000). "Vernon, Connecticut's Juvenile Curfew: The Circumstances of Youths Cited and Effects on Crime." *Criminal Justice Policy Review* 11:254-267.

Mandel, J., and H.W. Feldman (1986). "The Social History of Teenage Drug Use." In G. Beschner and A.S. Friedman, *Teen Drug Use* (pp. 19-42). Lexington, MA: Lexington Books.

Marcos, A.L., S.J. Bahr, and R.E. Johnson (1986). "Test of a Bonding/Differential Association Theory of Adolescent Drug Use." *Social Forces* 65:135-161.

Maslach, C., and S.E. Jackson (1979). "Burned-out Cops and Their Families." *Psychology Today* 12(12):59-62.

Massey, J.L., and M.D. Krohn (1986). "A Longitudinal Examination of an Integrated Social Process Model of Deviant Behavior." *Social Forces* 65:106-134.

Matza, D. (1964). *Delinquency and Drift*. Englewood Cliffs, NJ: Prentice Hall.

Mause, L. (1974). *The History of Childhood*. New York: Psychohistory Press.

Maxson, C.L. (1995). "Street Gangs and Drug Roles in Two Suburban Cities." *NIJ Research in Brief*. Washington, DC: National Institute of Justice.

Maxson, C.L., M.A. Gordon, and M.W. Klein (1985). "Differences between Gang and Non-gang Homicides." *Criminology* 23:209-222.

Maxson, C.L., K. Woods, and M.W. Klein (1996). "Street Gang Migration: How Big a Threat?" *National Institute of Justice Journal* 230:26-31.

Mays, G.L., K. Fuller, and L.T. Winfree (1994). "Gangs and Gang Activity in Southern New Mexico: A Descriptive Look at a Growing Rural Problem." *Journal of Crime and Justice* 17:25-44.

McBride, D. (1981). "Drugs and Violence." In J.A. Inciardi (ed.), *The Drugs/Crime Connection* (pp. 105-124). Beverly Hills: Sage.

McCarthy, B.R. (1987). "Preventive Detention and Pretrial Custody in the Juvenile Court." *Journal of Criminal Justice* 15:185-200.

McCarthy, B.R., and B.L. Smith (1986). "The Conceptualization of Discrimination in the Juvenile Justice Process: The Impact of Administrative Factors and Screening Decisions on Juvenile Court Dispositions." *Criminology* 24:41-64.

McCold, P. (2003). "A Survey of Assessment Research on Mediation and Conferencing." In L. Walgrave (ed.), *Repositioning Restorative Justice*. Portland, OR: Willan.

McCold, P., and T. Wachtel (1998). *Restorative Policing Experiment: The Bethlehem, Pennsylvania, Police Family Group Conferencing Project*. Pipersville, PA: Community Service Foundation.

McCold, P., and T. Wachtel (2002). "Restorative Justice Theory Validation." In E.G.M. Weitekamp and H. Kerner (eds.), *Restorative Justice: Theoretical Foundations*. Portland, OR: Willan.

McDowall, D., C. Loftin, and B. Wiersema (2000). "The Impact of Youth Curfew Laws on Juvenile Crime Rates." *Crime & Delinquency* 46:76-91.

McElvain, J.P., and A.J. Kposowa (2004). "Police Officer Characteristics and Internal Affairs Investigations for Use of Force Allegations." *Journal of Criminal Justice* 32:265-279.

McGarrell, E.F., K. Olivares, K. Crawford, and N. Kroovand (2000). *Returning Justice to the Community: The Indianapolis Juvenile Restorative Justice Experiment*. Indianapolis: Hudson Institute.

McGlothlin, W.H., and M.D. Anglin (1981). "Shutting Off Methadone: Costs and Benefits." *Archives of General Psychiatry* 38:885-892.

McLaughlin, E., R. Fergusson, G. Hughes, and L. Westmarland (2003). "Introduction: Justice in the Round—Contextualizing Restorative Justice." In E. McLaughlin, R. Fergusson, G. Hughes, and L. Westmarland (eds.), *Restorative Justice: Critical Issues*. Thousand Oaks, CA: Sage.

McMahon, M. (1999). *Women on Guard: Discrimination and Harassment in Corrections*. Toronto, Canada: University of Toronto Press.

Mead, G.H. (1934). *Mind, Self and Society*. Chicago: University of Chicago Press.

Mears, D.P. (2000). "Assessing the Effectiveness of Juvenile Justice Reforms: A Closer Look at the Criteria and the Impacts on Diverse Stakeholders." *Law and Policy* 22:175-202.

Meehan, P.J., and P.W. O'Carroll (1992). "Gangs, Drugs, and Homicide in Los Angeles." *American Journal of Diseases of Children* 146:683-687.

Meehan, P.J., and M.C. Ponder (2002). "Race and Place: The Ecology of Racial Profiling African American Motorists." *Justice Quarterly* 18:399-430.

Megargee, E.I., and M.J. Bohn (1979). *Classifying Criminal Offenders: A New System Based on the MMPI.* Beverly Hills: Sage.

Melton, G.B. (1980). "Psychological Issues in Child Victims' Interaction with the Legal System." *Victimology* 5:275-284.

Mendel, R.A. (2001). *Guiding Lights for Reform in Juvenile Justice.* Washington, DC: American Youth Policy Forum.

Mendelsohn, B. (1956). "The Victimology." *Etudes Internationale de Psycho-sociologie Criminelle* (July):23-26.

Merlo, A.V. (2000). "Juvenile Justice at the Crossroads: Presidential Address to the Academy of Criminal Justice Sciences." *Justice Quarterly* 17:639-661.

Merton, R.K. (1938). "Social Structure and Anomie." *American Sociological Review* 3:672-682.

Miethe, T.D., L. Hong, and E. Reese (2000). "Reintegrative Shaming and Recidivism Risks in Drug Court: Explanations for Some Unexpected Findings." *Crime & Delinquency* 46:522-541.

Miethe, T.D., M.C. Stafford, and J.S. Long (1987). "Social Differentiation in Criminal Victimization: A Test of Routine Activities Lifestyle Theories." *American Sociological Review* 52:184-194.

Miller, D., D. Miller, F. Hoffman, and R. Duggan (1980). *Runaways—Illegal Aliens in Their Own Land: Implications for Service.* New York: Praeger.

Miller, J.G. (1996). *Search and Destroy: African-American Males in the Criminal Justice System.* New York: Cambridge University Press.

Miller, J. (2000). *One of the Guys? Girls, Gangs and Gender.* New York: Oxford University Press.

Miller, J.Y. (2005). "6 Aides Lose Jobs after a Boy Dies." *Atlanta Journal-Constitution* (May 14):A9-A10.

Miller, W.B. (1958). "Lower Class Culture as a Generating Milieu of Gang Delinquency." *Journal of Social Issues* 15:5-19.

Miller, W.B. (1966). "Violent Crime in City Gangs." *Annals* 343:97-112.

Miller, W.B. (1975). *Violence by Youth Gangs and Youth Groups as a Crime Problem in Major American Cities.* Washington, DC: National Institute for Juvenile Justice and Delinquency Prevention.

Miller, W.B. (1982). *Crime by Youth Gangs and Groups in the United States.* Washington, DC: Office of Juvenile Justice and Delinquency Prevention.

Miller, W.B., H. Gertz, and H.S.G. Cutter (1961). "Aggression in a Boys' Street-corner Group." *Psychiatry* 24:283-298.

Miller-Wilson, L.S., and P. Puritz (2003). *Pennsylvania: An Assessment of Access to Counsel and Quality of Representation in Delinquency Proceedings.* Washington, DC, and Philadelphia: American Bar Association Juvenile Justice Center and Juvenile Law Center in collaboration with the National Juvenile Defender Center and the Northeast Juvenile Defender Center. Available at: *http://www.jlc.org/Resources/pdfs/assess/PA%20assess.pdf*

Minor, K.I., D.J. Hartmann, and S. Terry (1997). "Predictors of Juvenile Court Actions and Recidivism." *Crime & Delinquency* 18:295-318.

Minor, W.W. (1981). "Techniques of Neutralization: A Reconceptualization and Empirical Examination." *Journal of Research in Crime and Delinquency* 18:295-318.

Mintz, S. (2004). *Huck's Raft: A History of American Childhood.* Cambridge, MA: Belknap.

Moffitt, T.E. (1997). "Adolescence-Limited and Life-Course-Persistent Offending: A Complementary Pair of Developmental Theories." In T.P. Thornberry (ed.), *Developmental Theories of Crime and Delinquency.* New Brunswick, NJ: Transaction.

Monti, D.J. (1993). "Origins and Problems of Gang Research in the United States." In S. Cummings and D.J. Monti (eds.), *Gangs: The Origins and Impact of Contemporary Youth Gangs in the United States* (pp. 3-26). Albany, NY: SUNY Press.

Moon, M.M., B.K. Applegate, and E.J. Latessa (1997). "RECLAIM Ohio: A Politically Viable Alternative to Treating Youthful Felony Offenders." *Crime & Delinquency* 43:438-456.

Moore, D., and T. O'Connell (1994). "Family Conferencing in Wagga Wagga: A Communitarian Model of Justice." In C. Adler and J. Wundersitz (eds.), *Family Conferencing and Juvenile Justice: The Way Forward or Misplaced Optimism?* Canberra: Australian Institute of Criminology.

Moore, J. (1988). "Introduction: Gangs and the Underclass: A Comparative Perspective." In J.M. Hagedorn, *People and Folks: Gangs, Crime and the Underclass in a Rustbelt City* (pp. 3-18). Chicago: Lake View Press.

Moore, J. (1991). *Going Down to the Barrio: Homeboys and Homegirls in Change.* Philadelphia: Temple University Press.

Moore, J. (1993). "Gangs, Drugs, and Violence." In S. Cummings and D.J. Monti (eds.), *Gangs: The Origins and Impact of Contemporary Youth Gangs in the United States* (pp. 27-46). Albany, NY: SUNY Press.

Moore, J., and J. Hagedorn (2001). "Female Gangs: A Focus on Research." *OJJDP Juvenile Justice Bulletin.* Washington, DC: Office of Juvenile Justice and Delinquency Prevention.

Moore, M.H. (2003). "Sizing up COMPSTAT: An Important Administrative Innovation in Policing." *Criminology & Public Policy* 2(3):469-494.

Morales, A. (1992). "A Clinical Model for the Prevention of Gang Violence and Homicide." In R.C. Cervantes (ed.), *Substance Abuse and Gang Violence* (pp. 105-118). Newbury Park, CA: Sage.

Morse, S. (1999). "Delinquency and Desert." *Annals of the American Academy of Political and Social Science* 564:56-80.

Morton, J.H., H. Addition, R.G. Addison, L. Hunt, and J.J. Sullivan (1953). "A Clinical Study of Premenstrual Tension." *American Journal of Obstetrics and Gynecology* 65:1182-1191.

Moynihan, D.P. (2005). "The Impact of Managing for Results Mandates in Corrections: Lessons from Three States." *Criminal Justice Policy Review* 16:18-37.

Nadelmann, E.A. (1997). "Thinking Seriously about Alternatives to Drug Prohibition." In M. McShane and F.P. Williams (eds.), *Criminal Justice: Drug Use and Drug Policy* (pp. 269-316). New York: Garland.

Nassi, A., and S.I. Abramowitz (1976). "From Phrenology to Psychosurgery and Back Again: Biological Studies of Criminality." *American Journal of Orthopsychiatry* 46:591-607.

National Alliance of Gang Investigators Associations (2005). *National Gang Threat Assessment.* Washington, DC: Bureau of Justice Assistance.

National Conference of State Legislatures (1993). *1993 State Legislature Summary.* Washington, DC: National Conference of State Legislatures.

National Council on Crime and Delinquency (1987). *The Impact of Juvenile Court Sanctions: A Court that Works: Executive Summary.* San Francisco: National Council on Crime and Delinquency.

National Dairy Council (1985). "Diet and Behavior." *Dairy Council Digest* 56:19-24.

National Institute of Justice (1990). *Drugs and Crime: 1989 Drug Use Forecasting Report.* Washington, DC: National Institute of Justice.

National Institute on Drug Abuse (1999). *Principles of Drug Addiction Treatment: A Research-Based Guide.* Washington, DC: National Institute on Drug Abuse.

National Institute on Drug Abuse (2004). *Lessons from Prevention Research. Info Facts.* Washington, DC: National Institute on Drug Abuse.

National Juvenile Defender Center (2004). *The Use and Abuse of Juvenile Detention: Understanding Detention and Its Uses.* Washington, DC: National Juvenile Defender Center.

National Youth Gang Center (2000). *1998 National Youth Gang Survey: Summary.* Washington, DC: Office of Juvenile Justice and Delinquency Prevention.

NCANDS (2005). *Child Maltreatment, 2003.* Washington, DC: U.S. Department of Health and Human Services.

Newcomb, M.D., and P.M. Bentler (1988). *Consequences of Adolescent Drug Use.* Newbury Park, CA: Sage.

Newman, D.J. (1986). *Introduction to Criminal Justice*, 3rd ed. New York: Random House.

Newman, H.H., F.H. Freeman, and K.J. Holzinger (1937). *Twins: A Study of Heredity and Environment.* Chicago: University of Chicago Press.

Nichol, C.G. (1999). *Community Policing, Community Justice, and Restorative Justice: Exploring the Links for the Delivery of a Balanced Approach to Public Safety.* Washington, DC: Office of Community Oriented Policing Services.

Niederhoffer, A. (1967). *Behind the Shield: The Police in Urban Society*. Garden City, NY: Anchor Books.

Noriega, C. (2000). "Stick a Fork in It: Is Juvenile Justice Done?" *New York Law School Journal of Human Rights* 16:669-698.

Novak, K.J., J. Frank, B.W., Smith, and R.S. Engel (2002). "Revisiting the Decision to Arrest: Comparing Beat and Community Officers." *Crime & Delinquency* 48:70-98.

Nugent, W.R., M.S. Umbreit, L. Wiinamaki, and J. Paddock (1999). "Participation in Victim-Offender Mediation and Severity of Subsequent Delinquent Behavior: Successful Replications?" *Journal of Research in Social Work Practice* 11:5-23.

Nurco, D.N., T.W. Kinlock, T.E. Hanlon, and J.C. Ball (1988). "Nonnarcotic Drug Use Over an Addiction Career—A Study of Heroin Addicts in Baltimore and New York City." *Comprehensive Psychiatry* 29:450-459.

O'Brien, R.M. (1985). *Crime and Victimization Data*. Beverly Hills: Sage.

O'Connor, S. (2001). *Orphan Trains: The Story of Charles Loring Brace and the Children He Saved and Failed*. Boston: Houghton Mifflin.

Office of Justice Programs (2000). *Promising Strategies to Reduce Substance Abuse*. Washington, DC: Office of Justice Programs.

Office of Justice Programs (2003). *Juvenile Family Drug Courts: Summary of Drug Court Activity by State and County*. Washington, DC: American University.

Office of Juvenile Justice and Delinquency Prevention (1999). *Promising Strategies to Reduce Gun Violence*. Washington, DC: Office of Juvenile Justice and Delinquency Prevention.

Ohio Commission on Dispute Resolution and Conflict Management (1993). *Conflict Management in Schools: Sowing Seeds for a Safer Society*. Columbus, OH: Ohio Commission on Dispute Resolution and Conflict Management.

Ott, B. (2005, July 26). "School Prayer: Teen Support Hinges on Type." *Gallup Poll Tuesday Briefing* (pp. 1-2).

Outlaw, M.C., and R.B. Ruback (1999). "Predictors and Outcomes of Victim Restitution Orders." *Justice Quarterly* 16:847-869.

Padilla, F. (1993). "The Working Gang." In S. Cummings and D.J. Monti (eds.), *Gangs: The Origins and Impact of Contemporary Youth Gangs in the United States* (pp. 173-192). Albany, NY: SUNY Press.

Pagelow, M.D. (1984). *Family Violence*. New York: Greenwood Press.

Palamar, F., F.T. Cullen, and J.C. Gersten (1986). "The Effect of Police and Mental Health Intervention of Juvenile Deviance: Specifying Contingencies in the Impact of Formal Reaction." *Journal of Health and Social Behavior* 27:90-105.

Paoline, E.A., S.M. Myers, and R.E. Worden (2000). "Police Culture, Individualism, and Community Policing: Evidence from Two Departments." *Justice Quarterly* 17:575-605.

Parent, D.G. (2003). *Correctional Boot Camps: Lessons from a Decade of Research*. Washington, DC: National Institute of Justice.

Parent, D.G., B. Auerbach, and K.E. Carlson (1992). *Compensating Crime Victims: A Summary of Policies and Practices*. Washington, DC: U.S. Department of Justice.

Parsloe, P. (1978). *Juvenile Justice in Britain and the U.S.: The Balance of Needs and Rights*. London: Routledge and Kegan Paul.

Peters, M., D. Thomas, and C. Zamberlan (1997). *Boot Camps for Juvenile Offenders: Program Summary*. Washington, DC: U.S. Department of Justice.

Petersilia, J. (2003). *When Prisoners Come Home: Parole and Prisoner Reentry*. New York: Oxford University Press.

Petersilia, J., S. Turner, J. Kahan, and J. Peterson (1985). "Executive Summary of RAND's Study, 'Granting Felons Probation: Public Risks and Alternatives.'" *Crime & Delinquency* 3:379-392.

Petersilia, J. (1997). "Probation in the United States." In M. Tonry (ed.), *Crime and Justice: A Review of Research* (Vol. 22), (pp. 149-200). Chicago: University of Chicago Press.

Peterson-Badali, M., and C.J. Koegl (2002). "Juvenile Offenders' Experiences of Incarceration: The Role of Correctional Staff in Peer-on-Peer Violence." *Journal of Criminal Justice* 30:41-49

Petit, B., and B. Western (2004). "Mass Imprisonment and the Life Course: Race and Class Inequality in U.S. Incarceration." *American Sociological Review* 69:159-169.

Pinderhughes, H. (1993). "'Down with the Program': Racial Attitude and Group Violence Among Youth in Bensonhurst and Gravesend." In S. Cummings and D.J. Monti (eds.), *Gangs: The Orgins and Impact of Contemporary Youth Gangs in the United States* (pp. 75-94). Albany, NY: SUNY Press.

Piquero, A.R., R. MacIntosh, and M. Hickman (2000). "Does Self-control Affect Survey Response?" *Criminology* 38:897-930.

Pisciotta, A.W. (1979). *The Theory and Practice of the New York House of Refuge, 1857-1935*. Unpublished Ph.D. dissertation, Florida State University.

Pisciotta, A.W. (1982). "Saving the Children: The Promise and Practice of *Parens Patriae*, 1838-98." *Crime & Delinquency* 28:410-425.

Pisciotta, A.W. (1983). "Race, Sex and Rehabilitation: A Study of Differential Treatment in the Juvenile Reformatory, 1825-1900." *Crime & Delinquency* 29:254-269.

Platt, A.M. (1977). *The Child Savers: The Invention of Delinquency*. Chicago: University of Chicago Press.

Podolsky, E. (1964). "The Chemistry of Murder." *Pakistan Medical Journal* 15:9-14.

Poole, E.D., and R.M. Regoli (1979). "Parental Support, Delinquent Friends and Delinquency." *Journal of Criminal Law and Criminology* 70:188-193.

Pope, C.E. (1994). "Racial Disparities in Juvenile Justice System." *Overcrowded Times* 5 (6):1, 5-7.

Pope, C.E. (1995). "Equity Within the Juvenile Justice System: Directions for the Future." In K.K. Leonard, C.E. Pope, and W.H. Feyerherm (eds.), *Minorities and the Juvenile Justice System* (pp.201-216). Thousand Oaks, CA: Sage.

Pope, C.E., and W. Feyerherm (1993). *Minorities and the Juvenile Justice System*. Washington, DC: U.S. Department of Justice.

Pope, C.E., and H.N. Snyder (2003). *Race as a Factor in Juvenile Arrests*. Washington, DC: U.S. Department of Justice.

Powers, R. (2002). "The Apocalypse of Adolescence." *Atlantic Monthly* (March) 89:58-74.

Prescott, P.S. (1981). *The Child Savers: Juvenile Justice Observed*. New York: Knopf.

President's Commission of Law Enforcement and Administration of Justice (1967). *Task Force Report: Juvenile Delinquency and Youth Crime*. Washington, DC: U.S. Government Printing Office.

Propper, A.M. (1982). "Make-Believe Families and Homosexuality among Imprisoned Girls." *Criminology* 20:127-138.

Puritz, P., and K. Brooks (2002). *Kentucky: Advancing Justice: An Assessment of Access to Counsel and Quality of Representation in Delinquency Proceedings*. Washington, DC: American Bar Association Juvenile Justice Center and Juvenile Law Center.

Puritz, P., S. Burrell, R. Schwartz, M. Soler, and L. Warboys (1995). *A Call for Justice: An Assessment of Access to Counsel and Quality of Representation in Delinquency Proceedings*. Washington, DC: American Bar Association Juvenile Justice Center.

Puritz, P., and M.A. Scali (1998). *Beyond the Walls: Improving Conditions of Confinement for Youth in Custody*. Washington, DC: Office of Juvenile Justice and Delinquency Prevention.

Putnam, R.D. (2000). *Bowling Alone: The Collapse and Revival of American Community*. New York: Simon & Schuster.

Puzzanchera, C., A.L. Stahl, T.A. Finnegan, N. Tierney, and H.N. Snyder (2004). *Juvenile Court Statistics 2000*. Pittsburgh: National Center for Juvenile Justice.

Quicker, J.C. (1974). "The Effect of Goal Discrepancy on Delinquency." *Social Problems* 22:76-86.

Rada, R.T., D.R. Laws, and R. Kellner (1976). "Plasma Testosterone Levels in the Rapist." *Psychosomatic Medicine* 38:257-268.

Raine, A., P.H. Venables, and M. Williams (1995). "High Autonomic Arousal and Electrodermal Orienting at Age 15 Years as Protective Factors against Criminal Behavior at Age 29 Years." *American Journal of Psychiatry* 152:1595-1600.

Rainville, G.A., and S.K. Smith (2003). *Juvenile Felony Defendants in Criminal Courts: Survey of 40 Counties, 1998*. Washington, DC: U.S. Department of Justice.

Rasmussen, A. (2004). "Teen Court Referral, Sentencing, and Subsequent Recidivism: Two Proportional Hazards Models and a Little Speculation." *Crime & Delinquency* 50:615-635.

Ray, L., P. Kestner, and L. Freedman (1986). "Dispute Resolution: From Examination to Experimentation." *Michigan Bar Journal* 65:898-903.

Reckless, W.C. (1962). "A Non-causal Explanation: Containment Theory." *Excerpta Criminologica* 1:131-134.

Reckless, W.C. (1967). *The Crime Problem*. New York: Appleton, Century, Crofts.

Reiss, A.J., and A.L. Rhodes (1961). "The Distribution of Juvenile Delinquency in the Social Class Structure." *American Sociological Review* 26:720-732.

Reiss A.J., and J.A. Roth (1993). *Understanding and Preventing Violence* (Vol. 1). Washington, DC: National Academy Press.

Rengert, G.F., and J. Wasilchick (1985). *Suburban Burglary: A Time and a Place for Everything*. Springfield, IL: Charles C Thomas.

Reppetto, T.A. (1974). *Residential Crime*. Cambridge, MA: Ballinger.

Reynolds, K.M., R. Seydlitz, and P. Jenkins (2000). "Do Juvenile Curfew Laws Work? A Time-series Analysis of the New Orleans Law." *Justice Quarterly* 17:205-230.

Rice, S.K., and A.R. Piquero (2005). "Perceptions of Discrimination and Justice in New York City." *Policing* 28:98-117.

Rich, J.M., and J.L. DeVitis (1985). *Theories of Moral Development*. Springfield, IL: Charles C Thomas.

Ringwalt, C.L., S.T. Ennett, and K.D. Holt (1991). "An Outcome Evaluation of Project D.A.R.E." *Health Education Research: Theory and Practice* 6:327-337.

Roberts, J.V. (2003). "Sentencing Juvenile Offenders in Canada: An Analysis of Recent Reform Legislation." *Journal of Contemporary Criminal Justice* 19:413-434.

Roberts, J.V. (2004). *The Virtual Prison: Community Custody and the Evolution of Imprisonment*. Cambridge, UK: Cambridge University Press.

Robin, G.D. (1967). "Gang Member Delinquency in Philadelphia." In M.W. LeKlein (ed.), *Juvenile Gangs in Context* (pp. 15-24). Englewood Cliffs, NJ: Prentice Hall.

Robin, G.D. (1982). "Juvenile Interrogations and Confessions." *Journal of Police Science and Administration* 10:224-228.

Rodriguez, N. (2005). "Restorative Justice, Communities, and Delinquency: Whom Do We Reintegrate?" *Criminology & Public Policy* 4:103-130.

Rodriguez, N., and V.J. Webb (2004). "Multiple Measures of Juvenile Drug Court Effectiveness: Results of a Quasi-Experimental Design." *Crime & Delinquency* 50:292-314.

Rojek, D.G., and M.L. Erickson (1982). "Juvenile Diversion: A Study of Community Cooperation." In D.G. Rojek and G.F. Jensen (eds.), *Readings in Juvenile Delinquency* (pp. 316-321). Lexington, MA: D.C. Heath.

Roman, J., and C. DeStefano (2004). "Drug Court Effects and the Quality of Existing Evidence." In J.A. Butts and J. Roman (eds.), *Juvenile Drug Courts and Teen Substance Abuse* (pp. 107-135). Washington, DC: Urban Institute Press.

Roncek, D.W., and P.A. Maier (1991). "Bars, Blocks, and Crimes Revisited: Linking the Theory of Routine Activities to the Empiricism of 'Hot Spots.'" *Criminology* 31:3-31.

Rose, D.R., and T.R. Clear (2003). "Incarceration, Reentry, and Social Capital: Social Networks in the Balance." In J. Travis and M. Waul, *Prisoners Once Removed: The Impact of Incarceration and Reentry on Children, Families, and Communities* (pp. 313-341). Washington, DC: Urban Institute Press.

Rosenbaum, D.P., R.L. Flewelling, S.L. Bailey, C.L. Ringwalt, and D.L. Wilkinson (1994). "Cops in the Classroom: A Longitudinal Evaluation of Drug Abuse Resistance Education (DARE)." *Journal of Research in Crime and Delinquency* 31:3-31.

Rossman, S.B., J.A. Butts, J. Roman, C. DeStefano, and R. White (2004). "What Juvenile Drug Courts Do and How They Do It." In J.A. Butts and J. Roman (eds.), *Juvenile Drug Courts and Teen Substance Abuse* (pp. 55-106). Washington, DC: Urban Institute Press.

Rossow, L.F., and J.R. Parkinson (1994a). "State Legislators React to *Jones v. Clear Creek* and *Bishop Knox* Behavior." *School Law Reporter* 36(5):1-2.

Rossow, L.F., and J.R. Parkinson (1994b). "Yet Another Student Strip Search: *Cornfield By Lewis v. Consolidated High School District No. 230.*" *School Law Reporter* 36(3):1-2.

Rossum, R.A., B.J. Koller, and C.P. Manfredi (1987). *Juvenile Justice Reform: A Model for the States.* Clairmont, CA: Rose Institute of State and Local Government and the American Legislative Exchange.

Rothman, D.J. (1971). *The Discovery of the Asylum: Social Order and Disorder in the New Republic.* Boston: Little, Brown.

Rothman, D.J. (1980). *Conscience and Convenience: The Asylum and Its Alternative in Progressive America.* Boston: Little, Brown

Roush, D.M., and M. McMillen (2000). *Construction, Operations, and Staff Training for Juvenile Confinement Facilities.* Washington, DC: Office of Juvenile Justice and Delinquency Prevention.

Rowe, D.C. (2002). *Biology and Crime.* Los Angeles: Roxbury.

Rubin, H.T. (1985). *Juvenile Justice: Policy, Practice, and Law*, 2nd ed. New York: Random House.

Russel, R., and U. Sedlak (1993). "Status Offenders: Attitudes of Child Welfare Practitioners Toward Practice and Policy Issues." *Child Welfare* 72(1):13-24.

Russell, E. (1982). "Limitations of Behavior Control Techniques." In N. Johnston and L.D. Savitz (eds.), *Legal Process and Corrections* (pp. 288-297). New York: John Wiley & Sons.

Ruth, H., and K.R. Reitz (2003). *The Challenge of Crime: Rethinking Our Response.* Cambridge, MA: Harvard University Press.

Rutter, M. (1996). "Introduction: Concepts of Antisocial Behavior, of Cause and of Genetic Influences." In G.R. Bock and J.A. Goode (eds.), *Genetics of Criminal and Antisocial Behavior* (pp. 1-14). Chichester, England: John Wiley & Sons.

Ryan, C.M. (1987). "Juvenile Court Jurisdiction: Intervention and Intrusion." In F.X. Hartmann (ed.), *From Children to Citizens: Volume II: The Role of the Juvenile Court* (pp. 56-64). New York: Springer-Verlag.

Ryerson, E. (1978). *The Best-Laid Plans: America's Juvenile Court Experiment.* New York: Hill and Wang.

Saad, L. (2001). "Fear of Crime at Record Lows." *Gallup Poll Monthly* 433:2-10.

Sagatun, I.J., and L.P. Edwards (1995). *Child Abuse and the Legal System.* Chicago: Nelson-Hall.

Sameroff, A.J., and M.J. Chandler (1975). "Reproductive Risk and the Continuum of Caretaking Causality." In F. Horowitz (ed.), *Review of Child Development Research* (Vol. 4), (pp. 187-244). Chicago: University of Chicago Press.

SAMHSA (2004). "Graduated Driver Licensing and Drinking among Young Drivers." Washington, DC: Substance Abuse and Mental Health Services Administration. Available at: *http://www.drugabusestatistics.samhsa.gov*

Sampson, R.J., and J.H. Laub (1993). *Crime in the Making: Pahtways and Turning Points Through Life.* Cambridge, MA: Harvard University Press.

Sampson, R.J., and J.L. Lauritsen (1990). "Deviant Lifestyles, Proximity to Crime, and the Offender-Victim Link in Personal Violence." *Journal of Research in Crime and Delinquency* 27:110-139.

Sampson, R.J., and S.W. Raudenbush (1999). "Systematic Social Observation of Public Spaces: A New Look at Disorder in Urban Neighborhoods. *American Journal of Sociology* 105:603-651.

Sanborn, J.B. (1994a). "Certification to Criminal Court: The Important Policy Questions of How, When, and Why." *Crime & Delinquency* 40:262-281.

Sanborn, J.B. (1994b). "Remnants of *Parens Patriae* in the Adjudicatory Hearing: Is a Fair Trial Possible in Juvenile Court?" *Crime & Delinquency* 40:599-615.

Sanborn, J. (2001). "A *Parens Patriae* Figure or Impartial Fact Finder: Policy Questions and Conflicts for the Juvenile Court Judge." *Criminal Justice Policy Review* 12:311-332.

Sanders, W.B. (1994). *Gangbangs and Drive-bys: Grounded Culture and Juvenile Gang Violence*. New York: Aldine de Gruyter.

Schaps, E.J., M. Moskowitz, J.H. Malvin, and G.A. Schaeffer (1986). "Evaluation of Seven School-based Prevention Programs: A Final Report of the Napa Project." *International Journal of the Addictions* 21:1081-1112.

Schauss, A.G. (1980). *Diet, Crime and Delinquency*. Berkeley, CA: Parker House.

Schiff, A. (1999). "The Impact of Restorative Interventions on Juvenile Offenders." In G. Bazemore and L. Walgrave (eds.), *Restorative Juvenile Justice: Repairing the Harm of Youth Crime*. Monsey, NY: Criminal Justice Press.

Schlossman, S.L. (1977). *Love and the American Delinquent: The Theory and Practice of "Progressive" Juvenile Justice, 1825-1920*. Chicago: University of Chicago Press.

Schlossman, S.L., G. Zellman, and R. Shavelson (1984). *Delinquency Prevention in South Chicago: A Fifty-Year Assessment of the Chicago Area Project*. Santa Monica: RAND.

Schlossman, S.L., and M. Sedlak (1983). *The Chicago Area Project Revisited*. Santa Monica: RAND.

Schneider, A.L. (1985). *The Impact of Deinstitutionalization on Recidivism and Secure Confinement of Status Offenders*. Washington, DC: U.S. Department of Justice.

Schneider, A.L. (1986). "Restitution and Recidivism Rates of Juvenile Offenders: Results from Four Experimental Studies." *Criminology* 24:533-552

Schneider, A.L. (1990). *Deterrence and Juvenile Crime: Results from a National Policy Experiment*. New York: Springer-Verlag.

Schneider, A.L., and P.R. Schneider (1984). "A Comparison of Programmatic and Ad Hoc Restitution in Juvenile Courts." *Justice Quarterly* 1:529-547.

Schneider, A.L., and D.D. Schram (1986). "The Washington State Juvenile Justice Reform: A Review of Findings." *Criminal Justice Policy Review* 2:211-235.

Schrag, C. (1971). *Crime and Justice: American Style*. Washington, DC: U.S. Government Printing Office.

Schuck, A.M. (2003). "The Masking of Racial and Ethnic Disparity in Police Use of Physical Force: The Effects of Gender and Custody Status." *Journal of Criminal Justice* 32:557-564.

Schulsinger, F. (1972). "Psychopathy: Heredity and Environment." *International Journal of Mental Health* 1:190-206.

Schur, E.M. (1973). *Radical Nonintervention: Rethinking the Delinquency Problem*. Englewood Cliffs, NJ: Prentice Hall.

Schwartz, I.M., G. Fishman, R. Rawson Hatfield, B.A. Krisberg, and Z. Eisikovits (1987). "Juvenile Detention: The Hidden Closets Revisited." *Justice Quarterly* 4:219-235.

Schwartz, M.D. (1989). "Family Violence as a Cause of Crime: Rethinking Our Priorities." *Criminal Justice Policy Review* 3:115-132.

Schwartz, M., and S.S. Tangri (1965). "A Note on Self-concept an Insulator Against Delinquency." *American Sociological Review* 30:922-926.

Scott, M. (2002). "Georgia Prom-goers to Face Curfew Thanks to Recent Legislation." *Johnson City Press* (May 1, 2002):6.

Sealock, M.D., D.C. Gottfredson, and C.A. Gallagher (1997). "Delinquency and Social Reform: A Radical Perspective." In L. Empey (ed.), *Juvenile Justice* (pp. 245-290). Charlottesville: University of Virginia Press.

Secret, P.E., and J.B. Johnson (1997). "The Effect of Race on Juvenile Justice Decision Making in Nebraska: Detention, Adjudication, and Disposition, 1988-1993." *Justice Quarterly* 14:445-478.

Sells, S.B., and D.D. Simpson (1979). "Evaluation of Treatment Outcomes for Youths in the Drug Abuse Reporting Program (DARP): A Follow-up Study." In G.M. Beschner and A.S. Friedman (eds.), *Youth Drug Abuse: Problems, Issues, and Treatment* (pp. 571-628). Lexington, MA: Lexington Books.

Shaffer, J.N. (2004). *The Victim-Offender Overlap: Specifying the Role of Peer Groups—Final Report*. Washington, DC: National Institute of Justice.

Shah, S.A., and L.H. Roth (1974). "Biological and Psychophysiological Factors in Criminality." In D. Gaser (ed.), *Handbook of Criminology* (pp. 101-173). New York: Rand McNally.

Shannon, L.W. (1982). *Assessing the Relationship of Adult Criminal Careers to Juvenile Careers*. Iowa City: Iowa Urban Community Research Center.

Shaw, C.R., and H.D. McKay (1942). *Juvenile Delinquency and Urban Areas*. Chicago: University of Chicago Press.

Shaw, C.R., F.M. Zorbaugh, H.D. McKay, and L.S. Cottrell (1929). *Delinquency Areas*. Chicago: University of Chicago Press.

Sheldon, W.H. (1949). *Varieties of Delinquent Youth: An Introduction to Correctional Psychiatry*. New York: Harper and Brothers.

Sheley, J.F., and J.D. Wright (1993). *Gun Acquisition and Possession in Selected Juvenile Samples*. Washington, DC: Office of Juvenile Justice and Delinquency Prevention.

Sheppard, D., H. Grant, W. Rowe, and N. Jacobs (2000). "Fighting Juvenile Gun Violence." *OJJDP Juvenile Justice Bulletin*. Washington, DC: Office of Juvenile Justice and Delinquency Prevention.

Sherman, L.W., and H. Strang (2000). *Recidivism Patterns in the Canberra Reintegrative Shaming Experiments (RISE)*. Canberra: Center for Restorative Justice, Australian National University.

Sherman, L.W., and H. Strang (2003). "Captains of Restorative Justice: Experience, Legitimacy and Recidivism by Type of Offence." In E.G.M. Weitekamp and H. Kerner (eds.), *Restorative Justice in Context: International Practice and Directions*. Portland, OR: Willan.

Shine, J., and D. Price (1992). "Prosecutors and Juvenile Justice: New Roles and Perspectives." In I.M. Schwartz (ed.), *Juvenile Justice and Public Policy: Toward a National Agenda* (pp. 101-133). New York: Lexington Books.

Short, J.F. (1960). "Differential Association as a Hypothesis: Problems of Empirical Testing." *Social Problems* 8:14-25.

Short, J.F., and I. Nye (1958). "Extent of Unrecorded Delinquency: Tentative Conclusion." *Journal of Criminal Law, Criminology and Police Science* 49:296-302.

Short, J.F., and F.L. Strodbeck (1965). *Group Process and Gang Delinquency*. Chicago: University of Chicago Press.

Sickmund, M. (2002). "Juvenile Offenders in Residential Placement: 1997-1999." *National Report Series*. Washington, DC: Office of Juvenile Justice and Delinquency Prevention.

Sickmund, M. (2004). *Juveniles in Corrections: National Report Series Bulletin*. Washington, DC: U.S. Department of Justice.

Sickmund, M., and P.J. Baunach (1986). "Children in Custody: Public Juvenile Facilities, 1985." *Bureau of Justice Statistics Bulletin*. Washington, DC: U.S. Department of Justice.

Sickmund, M., T.J. Sladky, and W. Kang (2004). "Census of Juveniles in Residential Placement Databook." Available at: *http://www.ojjdp.ncjrs.org/ojstatbb/cjrp/*

Sickmund, M., H.N. Snyder, and E. Poe-Yamagata (1997). *Juvenile Offenders and Victims: 1997 Update on Violence*. Washington, DC: Office of Juvenile Justice and Delinquency Prevention.

Sieverdes, C., and C. Bartollas (1986). "Security Level and Adjustment Patterns in Juvenile Institutions." *Journal of Criminal Justice* 14:135-145.

Silberman, C.E. (1978). *Criminal Violence, Criminal Justice*. New York: Random House.

Simons, R.L., C. Wu, C. Johnson, and R.D. Conger (1995). "A Test of Various Perspectives on the Intergenerational Transmission of Domestic Violence." *Criminology* 33:141-171.

Simpson, D.D., and S.B. Sells (1982). "Effectiveness of Treatment for Drug Abuse: An Overview of the DARP Research Program." *Advances in Alcohol and Substance Abuse* 2:7-29.

Simpson, E.L. (1974). "Moral Development Research: A Case Study of Scientific Cultural Bias." *Human Development* 17:81-106.

Singer, S.I. (1996). *Recriminalizing Delinquency: Violent Juvenile Crime and Juvenile Justice Reform*. New York: Cambridge University Press.

Skinner, B.F. (1953). *Science and Human Behavior*. New York: Macmillan.

Skogan, W.G. (1981). "On Attitudes and Behavior." In D.A. Lewis (ed.), *Reactions to Crime*. Beverly Hills: Sage.

Skogan, W.G., and S.M. Hartnett (1997). *Community Policing, Chicago Style*. New York: Oxford University Press.

Skogan, W.G., and M.G. Maxfield (1981). *Coping with Crime: Individual and Neighborhood Reactions*. Beverly Hills: Sage.

Skolnick, J.H., R. Bluthenthal, and T. Correl (1993). "Gang Organization and Migration." In S. Cummings and D.J. Monti (eds.), *Gangs: The Origins and Impact of Contemporary Youth Gangs in the United States* (pp. 193-218). Albany, NY: SUNY Press.

Smith, B. (1998). "Children in Custody: 20-year Trends in Juvenile Detention, Correctional, and Shelter Facilities." *Crime & Delinquency* 44:526-543.

Snell, T.L. (2000). *Capital Punishment 2000*. Washington, DC: U.S. Department of Justice.

Snyder, E. (1971). "The Impact of the Juvenile Court Hearing on the Child." *Crime & Delinquency* 32:97-133.

Snyder, H.N. (2000) "Juvenile Arrests 1999." *OJJDP Juvenile Justice Bulletin*. Washington, DC: Office of Juvenile Justice and Delinquency Prevention.

Snyder, H.N. (2002). "Juvenile Arrests 2000." *OJJDP Juvenile Justice Bulletin*. Washington, DC: Office of Juvenile Justice and Delinquency Prevention.

Snyder, H.N. (2005). "Juvenile Arrests 2003." *OJJDP Juvenile Justice Bulletin*. Washington, DC: Office of Juvenile Justice and Delinquency Prevention.

Sparger, J.R., and D.J. Giacopassi (1992). "Memphis Revisited: A Reexamination of Police Shootings after the *Garner* Decision." *Justice Quarterly* 9:211-225.

Spergel, I.A. (1966). *Street Gang Work: Theory and Practice*. Reading, MA: Addison-Wesley.

Spergel, I.A. (1984). "Violent Gangs in Chicago: In Search of Social Policy." *Social Service Review* 58:199-226.

Spergel, I.A. (1986). "The Violent Gang Problem in Chicago: A Local Community Approach." *Social Service Review* 60:94-131.

Spergel, I.A., and G.D. Curry (1993). "The National Youth Gang Survey: A Research and Development Process." In A.P. Goldstein and C.R. Huff (eds.), *The Gang Intervention Handbook* (pp. 359-400). Champaign, IL: Research Press.

Spergel, I.A., G.D. Curry, R. Chance, C. Kane, R. Ross, A. Alexander, E. Simmons, and S. Oh (1990). *National Youth Gang Suppression and Intervention Program: Executive Summary, Stage 1: Assessment*. Arlington, VA: National Youth Gang Information Center.

Spergel, I.A., K.M. Wa, and R.V. Sosa (2001). *Evaluation of the Bloomington-Normal Comprehensive Gang Program—Final Report*. Washington, DC: Office of Juvenile Justice and Delinquency Prevention.

Spergel, I.A., K.M. Wa, and R.V. Sosa (2002). *Evaluation of the Mesa Gang Intervention Program (MGIP)—Final Report*. Washington, DC: Office of Juvenile Justice and Delinquency Prevention.

Spergel, I.A., K.M. Wa, and R.V. Sosa (2003). *Evaluation of the Riverside Comprehensive Community-wide Approach to Gang Prevention, Intervention and Suppression—Final Report*. Washington, DC: Office of Juvenile Justice and Delinquency Prevention.

Spergel, I.A., K.M. Wa, and R.V. Sosa (2004a). *Evaluation of the Tucson Comprehensive Community-wide Approach to Gang Prevention, Intervention and Suppression—Final Report*. Washington, DC: Office of Juvenile Justice and Delinquency Prevention.

Spergel, I.A., K.M. Wa, and R.V. Sosa (2004b). *Evaluation of the San Antonio Comprehensive Community-wide Approach to Gang Prevention, Intervention and Suppression—Final Report.* Washington, DC: Office of Juvenile Justice and Delinquency Prevention.

Spohn, C., R.K. Piper, T. Martin, and E.D. Frenzel (2001). "Drug Courts and Recidivism: The Results of an Evaluation Using Two Comparison Groups and Multiple Indicators of Recidivism." *Journal of Drug Issues* 31:149-176.

Stahl, A., T. Finnegan, and W. Kang (2003). *Easy Access to Juvenile Court Statistics: 1985-2000.* Washington, DC: U.S. Department of Justice. Available at: *http://ojjdp.ncjrs.org/ojstatbb/exajcs*

Staples, J.S. (2000). "Violence in Schools: Rage against a Broken World," *Annals of the American Academy of Political and Social Science* 567:30-41.

Staples, W.G. (1987). "Law and Social Control in Juvenile Justice Dispositions." *Journal of Research in Crime and Delinquency* 24:7-22.

Starbuck, D., J.C. Howell, and D.J. Lindquist (2001). "Hybrid and Other Modern Gangs." *OJJDP Juvenile Justice Bulletin.* Washington, DC: Office of Juvenile Justice and Delinquency Prevention.

Steele, B.F., and C.B. Pollock (1974). "A Psychiatric Study of Parents Who Abuse Infants and Small Children." In R.E. Helfer and C.H. Kempe (eds.), *The Battered Child*, 2nd ed. Chicago: University of Chicago Press.

Stephens, R. C. (1987). *Mind-Altering Drugs: Use, Abuse, and Treatment.* Newbury Park, CA: Sage.

Stephens, R.D., and J.L. Arnette (2000). *From the Courthouse to the Schoolhouse: Making Successful Transitions.* Washington, DC: Office of Juvenile Justice and Delinquency Prevention.

Stoutland, S.E. (2001). "The Multiple Dimensions of Trust in Resident/Police Relations." *Journal of Research in Crime and Delinquency* 38:226-253.

Straus, M.A. (1983). "Ordinary Violence, Child Abuse, and Wife-Beating: What Do They Have in Common?" In D. Finkelhor, R.J. Gelles, G.T. Hotaling, and M.A. Straus (eds.), *The Dark Side of Families: Current Family Violence Research.* Beverly Hills: Sage.

Street, D. , R.D. Vinter, and C. Perrow (1966). *Organization for Treatment: A Comparative Study of Institutions for Delinquents.* New York: Free Press.

Strickland, R.A. (2004). *Restorative Justice.* New York: Peter Lang.

Stuart, B. (1996)."Circle Sentencing: Turning Swords into Ploughshares." In B. Galaway and J. Hudson (eds.), *Restorative Justice: International Perspectives.* Monsey, NY: Criminal Justice Press.

Studt, E. (1973). *Surveillance and Service in Parole: A Report of the Parole Action Study.* Washington DC: National Institute of Corrections.

Stuphen, R.D., and J. Ford (2001). "The Effectiveness and Enforcement of a Teen Curfew Law." *Journal of Sociology and Social Welfare* 28:55-78.

Sturgis, C. (2003). "Dismantling the School-to-Prison Pipeline." In A. Lewis (ed.), *Shaping the Future of American Youth: Youth Policy in the 21st Century.* Washington, DC: American Youth Policy Forum.

Substance Abuse and Mental Health Services Administration (2004). *Results from the 2003 National Survey on Drug Use and Health.* Washington, DC: Substance Abuse and Mental Health Services Administration.

Sullivan, C., M.Q. Grant, and J.D. Grant (1957). "The Development of Interpersonal Maturity: Applications to Delinquency." *Psychiatry* 20:373-385.

Sutherland, E.H. (1939). *Principles of Criminology*, 3rd ed. Philadelphia: Lippincott.

Sutherland, E.H., and D.R. Cressey (1974). *Criminology*, 9th ed. Philadelphia: Lippincott.

Swadi, H., and H. Zeitlin (1987). "Drug Education to School Children: Does it Really Work?" *British Journal of Addiction* 82:741-746.

Sykes, G.M., and D. Matza (1957). "Techniques of Neutralization: A Theory of Delinquency." *American Sociological Review* 22:664-670.

Szymanski, L.A. (2002). "Juvenile Delinquents' Right to a Jury Trial." *NCJJ Snapshot* 7(9). (September). Pittsburgh: National Center for Juvenile Justice.

Tanenhaus, D.S. (2004). *Juvenile Justice in the Making.* New York: Oxford University Press.

Tangri, S.S., and M. Schwartz (1967). "Delinquency Research and the Self-concept Variable." *Journal of Criminal Law, Criminology and Police Science* 58:182-190.

Tannenbaum, R. (1938). *Crime and the Community.* New York: Columbia University Press.

Taylor, M., and C. Nee (1988). "The Role of Cues in Simulated Residential Burglary." *British Journal of Criminology* 28:396-407.

Taylor, T.J., K.B. Turner, F. Esbensen, and T. Winfree (2001). "Coppin' an Attitude: Attitudinal Differences among Juveniles toward Police." *Journal of Criminal Justice* 29:295-305.

Tennenbaum, D.J. (1977). "Personality and Criminality: A Summary and Implications of the Literature." *Journal of Criminal Justice* 5:225-235.

Teplin, L.A. (2001). *Assessing Alcohol, Drug, and Mental Disorders in Juvenile Detainees.* Washington, DC: Office of Juvenile Justice and Delinquency Prevention.

Terrill, W. (2005). "Police Use of Force: A Transactional Approach." *Justice Quarterly* 22:107-138.

Thomas, C.W., and R. Cage (1977). "The Effect of Social Characteristics on Juvenile Court Dispositions." *Sociological Quarterly* 18:237-252.

Thornberry, T.P. (1973). "Race, Socioeconomic Status and Sentencing in the Juvenile Justice System" *Journal of Criminal Law and Criminology* 64:90-98.

Thornberry, T.P. (1987). "Toward an Interactional Theory of Delinquency." *Criminology* 25:863-892.

Thornberry, T.P., and J.H. Burch (1997). *Gang Members and Delinquent Behavior.* Washington, DC: Office of Juvenile Justice and Delinquency Prevention.

Thornberry, T.P., and R.L. Christenson (1984). "Unemployment and Criminal Involvement: An Investigation of Reciprocal Causal Structures." *American Sociological Review* 49:398-411.

Thornberry, T.P., A.J. Lizotte, M.D. Krohn, M. Farnworth, and S.J. Jang (1994). "Delinquent Peers, Beliefs, and Delinquent Behavior: A Longitudinal Test of Interactional Theory." *Criminology* 32:47-84.

Thornberry, T.P., M.D. Krohn, A.J. Lizotte, and D. Chard-Wierschem (1993). "The Role of Juvenile Gangs in Facilitating Delinquent Behavior." *Journal of Research in Crime and Delinquency* 30:55-87.

Thrasher, F.M. (1936). *The Gang.* Chicago: University of Chicago Press.

Thurman, Q.C. (1984). "Deviance and the Neutralization of Moral Commitment: An Empirical Analysis." *Deviant Behavior* 5:291-304.

Tigner, S.S. (2000). "Cultivating Virtue?" *Journal of Education* 182(2):11-18.

Tittle, C., W. Villemez, and D. Smith (1978). "The Myth of Social Class and Criminality: An Empirical Assessment of the Empirical Evidence." *American Sociological Review* 43:643-656.

Tobey, A., T. Grisso, and R. Schwartz (2000). "Youths' Trial Participation as Seen by Youths and Their Attorneys: An Exploration of Competence-Based Issues." In T. Grisso and R. Schwartz (eds.), *Youth on Trial: A Developmental Perspective on Juvenile Justice* (pp. 225-242). Chicago: University of Chicago Press.

Tobler, N.S. (1986). "Meta-analysis of 143 Adolescent Drug Prevention Programs: Quantitative Outcome Results of Program Participants Compared to a Control or Comparison Group." *Journal of Drug Issues* 16:537-567.

Tobler, N.S. (1997). "Meta-analysis of Adolescent Drug Prevention Programs: Results of the 1993 Meta-analysis." In W.J. Bukoski (ed.), *Meta-Analysis of Drug Abuse Prevention Programs* (pp. 5-68). Rockville, MD: National Institute on Drug Abuse.

Toennies, F. (1957). *Community and Society.* (Translated by C.P. Loomis). East Lansing: Michigan State University Press.

Tonry, M.(2004). *Thinking about Crime: Sense and Sensibility in American Penal Culture.* New York: Oxford University Press.

Torbet, P.M. (1996). *Juvenile Probation: The Workhorse of the Juvenile Justice System.* Washington, DC: U.S. Department of Justice.

Torbet, P., R. Gable, H. Hurst, I. Montgomery, L. Szymanski, and D. Thomas (1996). *State Responses to Serious and Violent Juvenile Crime.* Washington, DC: Office of Juvenile Justice and Delinquency Prevention.

Torbet, P., P. Griffin, H. Hurst, and L.R. MacKenzie (2000). *Juveniles Facing Criminal Sanctions: Three States That Changed the Rules.* Washington, DC: U.S. Department of Justice.

Toseland, R.W. (1982). "Fear of Crime: Who is Most Vulnerable?" *Journal of Criminal Justice* 10:199-210.

Toy, C. (1992). "A Short History of Asian Gangs in San Francisco." *Justice Quarterly* 9:647-666.

Tracy, P.E. (2002). *Decision Making and Juvenile Justice: An Analysis of Bias in Case Processing.* Westport, CT: Praeger.

Trasler, G. (1993). "Conscience, Opportunity, Rational Choice, and Crime." In R.V. Clarke and M. Felson (eds.), *Routine Activity and Rational Choice* (pp. 305-322). New Brunswick, NJ: Transaction.

Trebach, A.S. (1987). *The Great Drug War, and Radical Proposals That Could Make America Safe Again.* New York: Macmillan.

Trojanowicz, R., V.E. Kappeler, L.K. Gaines, and B. Bucqueroux (1998). *Community Policing: A Contemporary Perspective*, 2nd ed. Cincinnati: Anderson.

Tyler, J., R. Darville, and K. Stalnaker (1998). "Juvenile Boot Camps: A Descriptive Analysis of Program Diversity and Effectiveness." *Social Science Journal* 38:445.

Umbreit, M.S. (1997). "Victim-Offender Dialogue: From the Margins to the Mainstream Throughout the World." *The Crime Victims Report* 1:35-36, 48.

Umbreit, M. (1999). "Avoiding the Marginalization and McDonaldization of Victim Offender Mediation: A Case Study in Moving Toward the Mainstream." In G. Bazemore and L. Walgrave (eds.), *Restorative Juvenile Justice: Repairing the Harm of Youth Crime*. Monsey, NY: Criminal Justice Press.

Umbreit, M., and R.B. Coates (1992). *Victim Offender Mediation: An Analysis of Programs in Four States of the U.S.* St. Paul, MN: Center for Restorative Justice and Peacemaking.

Umbreit, M.S., and R.B. Coates (1993). "Cross-Site Analysis of Victim-Offender Mediation in Four States." *Crime & Delinquency* 39:565-585.

Umbreit, M.S., R.B. Coates, and B. Vos (2001). *Juvenile Offender Mediation in Six Oregon Counties*. Salem, OR: Oregon Dispute Resolution Commission.

Umbreit, M.S., B. Vos, R.B. Coates, and K.A. Brown (2003). *Facing Violence: The Path of Restorative Justice and Dialogue*. Monsey, NY: Criminal Justice Press.

Underwood, J. (1994). "Prayer in the Schools." *Schools and the Courts* 20 (May):1039-1050.

Urban, L.S., J.L.St. Cyr, and S.H. Decker (2003). "Goal Conflict in the Juvenile Court: The Evolution of Sentencing Practices in the United States." *Journal of Contemporary Criminal Justice* 19:454-479.

U.S. Attorney General's Task Force (1984). *Family Violence*. Washington, DC: U.S. Government Printing Office.

U.S. Department of Justice (1997). *Criminal Victimization in the United States, 1995*. Washington, DC: Bureau of Justice Statistics.

U.S. Department of Justice (2002). *Criminal Victimization in the United States, 2000*. Washington, DC: Bureau of Justice Statistics.

Valdez, A. (2000). *Gangs: A Guide to Understanding Street Gangs*, 3rd ed. San Clemente, CA: LawTech.

van den Haag, E. (1978). "In Defense of the Death Penalty: A Legal-Practical-Moral Analysis." *Criminal Law Bulletin* 14:51-68.

van den Haag, E., and P. Conrad (1983). *The Death Penalty: A Debate*. New York: Plenum.

Vandervort, F.E., and W.E. Ladd (2001). "The Worst of All Possible Worlds: Michigan's Juvenile Justice System and International Standards for the Treatment of Children." *University of Detroit Mercy Law Review* 78:202-258.

Van Kammen, W.B., and R. Loeber (1994). "Are Fluctuations in Delinquent Activities Related to the Onset and Offset in Juvenile Illegal Drug Use and Drug Dealing?" *The Journal of Drug Issues* 24:9-24.

Van Ness, D.W. (1990). "Restorative Justice." In B. Galaway and J. Hudson (eds.), *Criminal Justice, Restitution, and Reconciliation*. Monsey, NY: Criminal Justice Press.

Van Ness, D.W., and K.H. Strong (2002). *Restoring Justice*, 2nd ed. Cincinnati: Anderson.

Van Voorhis, P., M. Braswell, and D. Lester (2004). *Correctional Counseling and Rehabilitation*, 5th ed. Cincinnati: Anderson.

Veevers, J. (1989). "Pre-court Diversion for Juvenile Offenders." In M. Wright and B. Galaway (eds.), *Mediation and Criminal Justice: Victims, Offenders and Community*. Newbury Park, CA: Sage.

Vigil, J.D. (1993). "The Established Gang." In S. Cummings and D.J. Monti (eds.), *Gangs: The Origins and Impact of Contemporary Youth Gangs in the United States* (pp. 95-112). Albany, NY: SUNY Press.

Vigil, J.D. (1997). "Learning from Gangs: The Mexican American Experience." *ERIC Digest* (February).

Viljoen, J.L., J. Klaver, and R. Roesch (2005). "Legal Decisions of Preadolescent and Adolescent Defendants: Predictors of Confessions, Pleas, Communication with Attorneys, and Appeals." *Law and Human Behavior* 29: 253-277.

Vingilis, E.R., and K. DeGenova (1984). "Youth and the Forbidden Fruit: Experiences with Changes in Legal Drinking Age in North America." *Journal of Criminal Justice* 12:161-172.

Virkunen, M., D. Goldman, and M. Linnoila (1996). "Serotonin in Alcoholic Violent Offenders." In G.R. Bock and J.A. Goode (eds.), *Genetics of Criminal and Antisocial Behavior* (pp. 168-176). Chichester, England: John Wiley and Sons.

Visher, C.A. (1990). "Incorporating Drug Treatment in Criminal Sanctions." *NIJ Reports 221*. Washington, DC: National Institute of Justice.

Vold, G.B, and T.J. Bernard (1986). *Theoretical Criminology*, 3rd ed. New York: Oxford University Press.

von Hentig, H. (1941). "Remarks on the Interaction of Perpetrator and Victim." *Journal of Criminal Law, Criminology and Police Science* 31:303-309.

von Hirsch, A. (1990). "The Ethics of Community-based Sanctions." *Crime & Delinquency* 36:162-173.

Wachtel, T. (1995). "Family Group Conferencing: Restorative Justice in Practice." *Juvenile Justice Update* 1(4):1-2,13-14.

Wadlington, W., C.H. Whitebread, and S.M. Davis (1983). *Cases and Materials on Children in the Legal System*. Mineola, NY: Foundation Press.

Waldo, G.P., and S. Dinitz (1967). "Personality Attributes of the Criminal: An Analysis of Research Studies, 1950-1965." *Journal of Research in Crime and Delinquency* 4:185-202.

Walker, S. (1998). *Sense and Nonsense about Crime and Drugs*, 4th ed. Belmont, CA: West/Wadsworth.

Walker, S. (2001). *Sense and Nonsense about Crime and Drugs: A Policy Guide*, 5th ed. Belmont, CA: Wadsworth/Thomson Learning.

Walsh, W.F., and G.F. Vito (2004). "The Meaning of CompStat: Analysis and Response." *Journal of Contemporary Criminal Justice* 20:51-69.

Walters, G.D. (1992). "A Meta-analysis of the Gene-Crime Relationship." *Criminology* 30:595-613.

Watts, W.D., and L.S. Wright (1990). "The Relationship of Alcohol, Tobacco, Marijuana, and Other Illegal Drug Use to Delinquency among Mexican-American, Black, and White Adolescent Males." *Adolescence* 25:171-181.

Websdale, N. (2001). *Policing the Poor: From Slave Plantation to Public Housing.* Boston: Northeastern University Press.

Weis, K., and S.S. Borges (1973). "Victimology and Rape: The Case of the Legitimate Victim." *Issues in Criminology* 8:71-115.

Weisburd, D., S.D. Mastrofski, A.M. McNally, R. Greenspan, and J.J. Willis (2003). "Reforming to Preserve: Compstat and Strategic Problem in Solving in American Policing." *Criminology & Public Policy* 2:421-456.

Weisel, D.L., and T.O. Shelley (2004). *Specialized Gang Units: Form and Function in Community Policing—Final Report.* Washington, DC: National Institute of Justice.

Weisheit, R.A. (1983). "The Social Context of Alcohol and Drug Education: Implications for Program Evaluations." *Journal of Alcohol and Drug Education* 29:72-81.

Weitekamp, E.G.M. (1999). "The History of Restorative Justice." In G. Bazemore and L. Walgrave (eds.), *Restorative Juvenile Justice: Repairing the Harm of Youth Crime.* Monsey, NY: Criminal Justice Press.

West, W. (2002, April 2). "Confronting the Profiling Bogeyman." *Insight on the News* 17:48.

Wexler, D.B. (2002). "Some Reflections on Therapeutic Jurisprudence and the Practice of Criminal Law." *Criminal Law Bulletin* 38:205-215.

Whitaker, C., and L. Bastian (1991). *Teenage Victims: A National Crime Survey Report.* Washington, DC: U.S. Department of Justice.

White, G.F. (1990). "The Drug Use–Delinquency Connection in Adolescence." In R. Weisheit (ed.), *Drugs, Crime and the Criminal Justice System.* Cincinnati: Anderson.

White, H.R., R.J. Pandina, and R.L. LaGrange (1987). "Longitudinal Predictors of Serious Substance Use and Delinquency." *Criminology* 25:715-740.

White, J.E. (2001). "We're All Racial Profilers: Sure, Cops See Black Youths as Suspect. So Do Blacks." *Time* (April 23):157:45.

Whitehead, J.T. (1991)." The Effectiveness of Felony Probation: Results from an Eastern State." *Justice Quarterly* 8:525-543.

Whitehead, J.T., and M.C. Braswell (2000). "The Future of Probation: Reintroducing the Spiritual Dimension into Correctional Practice." *Criminal Justice Review* 25:207-233.

Wiatrowski, M., D. Griswold, and M. Roberts (1981). "Social Control Theory and Delinquency." *American Sociological Review* 46:525-541.

Widom, C.S. (1989). "Child Abuse, Neglect, and Violent Criminal Behavior." *Criminology* 27:251-271.

Widom, C.S. (1995). "Childhood Victimization and Violent Behavior." Paper presented at the Annual Conference on Criminal Justice Research and Evaluation, Washington, DC.

Wiebush, R.G., B. McNulty, and T. Le (2000). *Implementation of the Intensive Community-Based Aftercare Program.* Washington, DC: U.S. Department of Justice.

Wiebush, R.G., D. Wagner, B. McNulty, Y. Wang, and T.N. Le (2005). *Implementation and Outcome Evaluation of the Intensive Aftercare Program, Final Report*. Washington, DC: Office of Juvenile Justice and Delinquency Prevention.

Wiehe, V.R. (1992). *Working with Child Abuse and Neglect*. Itasca, IL: F.E. Peacock.

Williams, N., and S. Williams (1970). *The Moral Development of Children*. London: Macmillan.

Wilson, J.Q., and R.J. Herrnstein (1985). *Crime and Human Nature*. New York: Simon & Schuster.

Wilson, J.Q., and G.L. Kelling (1982). "Broken Windows: The Police and Neighborhood Safety." *Atlantic Monthly* 249(3):29-38.

Winner, L., L. Lanza-Kaduce, D.M. Bishop, and C.E. Frazier (1997). "The Transfer of Juveniles to Criminal Court: Reexamining Recidivism over the Long Term." *Crime & Delinquency* 43:548-63.

Wish, E.D., M.A. Toborg, and J.P. Bellassai (1988). *Indentifying Drug Users and Monitoring Them During Conditional Release*. Washington, DC: U. S. Department of Justice.

Wolfgang, M.E. (1958). *Patterns in Criminal Homicide*. Montclair, NJ: Patterson Smith. Reprinted 1975.

Wood, P.B., B. Pfefferbaum, and B.J. Arneklev (1993). "Risk-taking and Self-control: Social Psychological Correlates of Delinquency." *Journal of Crime and Justice* 16:111-130.

Wooden, K. (1976). *Weeping in the Playtime of Others: America's Incarcerated Children*. New York: McGraw-Hill.

Wooden, W.S., and R. Blazak (2001). *Renegade Kids, Suburban Outlaws: From Youth Culture to Delinquency*, 2nd ed. Belmont, CA: Wadsworth.

Worden, R.E. (1996). "The Causes of Police Brutality: Theory and Evidence on Police Use of Force." In W.A. Geller and H. Toch (eds.), *Police Violence: Understanding and Controlling Police Abuse of Force* (pp. 23-51). New Haven, CT: Yale University Press.

Wordes, M., T.S. Bynum, and C.J. Corley (1994). "Locking Up Youth: The Impact of Race on Detention Decisions." *Journal of Research in Crime and Delinquency* 31:149-165.

Wordes, M., and S.M. Jones (1998). "Trends in Juvenile Detention and Steps Toward Reform." *Crime & Delinquency* 44:544-560.

Wordes, M., B. Krisberg, and G. Berry (2001). *Facing the Future: Juvenile Detention in Alameda County*. Oakland, CA: National Council on Crime and Delinquency.

World Health Organization (1964). *WHO Expert Committee on Addiction Producing Drugs: 13th Report*. #23. Geneva: World Health Organization.

Wright, J.P., and F.T. Cullen (2000). "Juvenile Involvement in Occupational Delinquency." *Criminology* 38:863-892.

Wright, J.P, F.T. Cullen, and N. Williams (1997). "Working While in School and Delinquent Involvement: Implications for Social Policy." *Crime & Delinquency* 43:203-221.

Wright, R.T., and S.H. Decker (1994). *Burglars on the Job: Streetlife and Residential Break-ins*. Boston: Northeastern University Press.

Yablonsky, L. (1962). *The Violent Gang*. New York: Macmillan.

Zatz, M.S. (1985). "Los Cholos: Legal Processing of Chicano Gang Members." *Social Problems* 33:13-30.

Zehr, H. (1990). *Changing Lenses: A New Focus for Crime and Justice.* Scottdale, PA: Herald Press.

Zehr, H., and H. Mika (2003). "Fundamental Concepts of Restorative Justice." In E. McLaughlin, R. Fergusson, G. Hughes, and L. Westmarland (eds.), *Restorative Justice: Critical Issues.* Thousand Oaks, CA: Sage.

Zevitz, R. (1993). "Youth Gangs in a Small Midwestern City: Insider's Perspective." *Journal of Crime and Justice* 16:149-166.

Ziemer, D. (2005). "Juvenile Interrogations Must Be Recorded Rules Wisconsin Supreme Court." *Wisconsin Law Journal* (July 13, 2005).

Zimring, F.E. (1982). *The Changing Legal World of Adolescence.* New York: Free Press.

Zimring, F.E. (2000). "Penal Proportionality for the Young Offender: Notes on Immaturity, Capacity, and Diminished Responsibility." In T. Grisso and R.G. Schwartz (eds.), *Youth on Trial: A Developmental Perspective on Juvenile Justice* (pp. 271-289). Chicago: University of Chicago Press.

COURT CASES AND STATUTES

Bethel School District No. 403 v. Fraser, 478 U.S. 675, 106 S.Ct. 3159, 92 L.Ed.2d 549 (1986).

Board of Education of Independent School District No. 92 of Pottawatomie County et al. v. Lindsay Earls et al. (No. 01-332) (2002).

Breed v. Jones, 421 U.S. 519, 95 S.Ct. 1779, 44 L.Ed.2d 346 (1975).

Brown v. Gwinnet County School District, 112 F.3d 1464 (11th Cir. 1997).

Chicago v. Morales, 67 U.S.L.W. 4415 (U.S. 1999).

Commonwealth v. Fisher, 213 Pa. 48 (1905).

Cornfield by Lewis v. Consolidated High School District No. 230, 991 F.3d 1316, 1326-1327 (7th Cir. 1993).

Ex parte Crouse, 4 Wheaton (Pa.) 9 (1838).

Fare v. Michael C., 442 U.S. 707, 99 S.Ct. 2560, 61 L.Ed.2d 197 (1979).

Gonzalez v. Mailliard, Civ. No. 50424, N.D. Cal., 2/9/71/ Appeal U.S. No. 70-120, 4/9/71.

Good News Club v. Milford Central School, 533 U.S. 98 (2001).

Hazelwood School District v. Kuhlmeier, 484 U.S. 260, 107 S.Ct., 96 L.Ed.2d 694 (1988).

Ingraham v. Wright, 430 U.S. 651, 97 S.Ct. 1401, 51 L.Ed.2d 711 (1977).

In re Gault, 387 U.S. 1, 87 S.Ct. 1428, 18 L.Ed.2d 527 (1967).

In re LeBlanc, 171 Mich. App. 405, 412 (1988).

In re Tyrell, 22 Cal. Rptr. 2d33 (1994).

In re Winship, 397 U.S. 358, 90 S.Ct. 1068, 25 L.Ed.2d 368 (1970).

Johnson v. City of Opelousas, 658 F.2d 1065 (5th Cir. 1981).

Jones v. Clear Creek Independent School District, 977 F.2d 963 (5th Cir. 1992).

Kent v. United States, 383 U.S. 541, 86 S.Ct. 1045, 16 L.Ed.2d 84 (1966).

Lee v. Weisman 112 S.Ct. 2649 (1992).

New Jersey v. T.L.O., 469 U.S. 325 (1985).

Ohio Revised Code (2001) Section 2152.02. Anderson Publishing Co.

P.B. v. Koch, 96 F.3d 1298 (9th Cir. 1996).

People v. Turner, 55 Ill. 280 (1870).

Qutb v. Strauss, 11 F.3d 488 (5th Cir. 1993).

Roper v. Simmons, ___ U.S. ___, 161 L.Ed.2d (2005), 95, 01-111, 115-116.

Santa Fe Independent School District v. Doe, 530 U.S. 290 (2000).

Schall v. Martin, 467 U.S. 253, 104 S.Ct. 2403, 81 L.Ed.2d 207 (1984).

Schneckloth v. Bustamonte, 412 U.S. 218, 93 S.Ct. 2041, 36 L.Ed.2d 854 (1973).

Stanford v. Kentucky, 492 U.S. 361 (1989).

Steirer v. Bethlehem Area School District, 987 F2d 989 (3d Cir. 1994).

Tennessee v. Garner et al., 83 U.S. 1035, 105 S.Ct. 1694, 85 L.Ed.2d 1(1985).

Thompson v. Carthage School District, 87 F.3d 979 (8th Cir. 1996).

Thompson v. Oklahoma, 724 P.2d 780 (Oklahoma Criminal App. 1986), certiorari granted, 107 S.Ct. 1281 (1987).

Tinker v. Des Moines Independent Community School District, 393 U.S. 503, 89 S.Ct. 733, 21 L.Ed.2d 731 (1969).

Todd v. Rush County Schools, 133 F.3d 984 (7th Cir. 1998).

United States v. Mark James Knights, 278 F.3d 920 (9th Cir. 2002).

Vernonia School District v. Acton, 63 LW 4653 (1995).

Yarborough, Warden v. Alvarado (2004).

Glossary

A

abandonment: the permanent desertion of a child; an acceptable practice from the fourth to the thirteenth centuries when a child was an economic burden to a household.

abuse: any nonaccidental infliction of injury that seriously impairs a child's physical or mental health.

adjudication: the process of determining whether there is enough evidence to find a youth to be a delinquent, a status offender, or a dependent.

affective approach: an approach to drug use prevention that focuses attention on the individual in order to build self-esteem, self-awareness, and feelings of self-worth.

aftercare: mandatory programming for youths after release from training schools or other placements, similar to parole in adult courts.

Aggression Replacement Training (ART): a method for eliminating gang-member deficiencies in dealing with everyday situations. The three main components taught are: skillstreaming (teaching proper behavioral responses to various situations), anger control, and moral education.

anomie: Emil Durkheim's concept of the a state of normlessness in society.

atavistic: a term describing ape-like physical qualities of the head and body that were supposed by Cesare Lombroso to be indicative of the individual's developmental state.

"attack" (tough) probation: also known as "tough probation," the trend to make probation supervision stricter (tougher) by devoting less emphasis on assistance and counseling and greater attention to monitoring the conditions of probation. Attack probation can refer to intensive supervision, electronic monitoring of offender movements, and shame tactics.

avoidance: a common reaction to actual or potential victimization in which an individual stays away from particular locations where or individuals by whom victimization is anticipated.

B

balanced approach: a recent approach in juvenile corrections that places emphasis on the offender, the victim, and community safety. One aim is to restore the victim and the community, as much as possible, to his or her pre-crime status.

behavior modification: a therapeutic approach based on the work of B.F. Skinner and Hans J. Eysenck that entails the use of reinforcements to increase the probability of desired behaviors and a lack of reinforcement, or punishment stimuli, to decrease the probability of undesirable behaviors.

blended sentencing: a recent development in juvenile justice in which either the juvenile court or the adult court imposes a sentence that can involve either the juvenile or the adult correctional system or both. Blended sentencing is one example of increased punitiveness toward juvenile offenders.

bond to society (also called **social bond**):   in Travis Hirschi's control theory, the connections an individual has to the social order; the four elements of the bond are attachment, commitment, involvement, and belief.

"boob tube" therapy: the practice of allowing youths in detention homes or training schools to watch television as a way of occupying them and freeing up the time of supervising adults.

boot camp: a short-term program that resembles basic military training by emphasizing physical training and discipline; boot camps often include educational and rehabilitative components.

Breed v. Jones: U.S. Supreme Court case that ruled that double jeopardy prohibits states from first adjudicating a juvenile a delinquent and then waiving (transfer) the youth to adult court.

"broken windows" hypothesis: the belief that signs of urban decay, such as broken windows, in a neighborhood serve to make the neighborhood more conducive to crime and more fear-inducing.

burnout: See **job burnout**.

C

capital punishment: the death penalty. The Supreme Court recently ruled that capital punishment is unconstitutional for juveniles.

Chancery Court: a body concerned with property matters in feudal England; responsible for overseeing the financial affairs of orphaned juveniles who were not yet capable of handling their own matters.

Chicago School: a perspective explaining deviance as the natural outgrowth of the location in which it occurs; named for the work performed by social scientists at the University of Chicago.

child protective services: a state's method of handling child abuse cases; usually responsible for accepting and investigating reports of abuse and neglect and for removing children from potential or actual abusive situations.

child saver: Anthony Platt's term for a person involved in the development of the juvenile court.

chivalry hypothesis: the allegedly protective interaction of the police and other authorities with female offenders, leading to either harsher or more lenient treatment of female youthful offenders.

classicism: a school of thought that sees humankind as having free will, that is, humans calculate the pros and cons of an activity before choosing what to do (compare to **positivism**).

community policing: problem-oriented policing that relies on input from the public to define problems and establish police policy.

community service: the practice of having offenders perform unpaid work for government or private agencies as payment for crimes without personal victims.

CompStat policing: a management process in which police managers are held accountable for the control of crime and the enhancement of the quality of life in their areas. Statistics are collected to help pinpoint where problems are, and police managers then try to reduce crime and improve quality of life indicators in those areas.

concentric zone theory: a theory of city growth as following the natural progression of ever-increasing circles around the original city center.

conflict theory: a theory that addresses the making and enforcing of laws rather than the breaking of laws.

confrontation session: a session between adult prisoners and juveniles to deter juveniles from delinquency (e.g., Scared Straight).

congruence: genuineness on the part of a therapist.

consent search: a search in which a defendant voluntarily allows the police to search person or effects without a search warrant.

containment theory: Walter Reckless's social control theory holding that behavior is controlled through outer containment (influences of family, peers, etc.) and inner containment (strengths within an individual), working in opposition to external pushes, external pressures, and external pulls.

corporal punishment: physical punishment.

cottage system: a training school design that attempts to simulate home life more closely than would a prison-like institution; it divides the larger prison into smaller "cottages" for living.

Court-Appointed Special Advocate (CASA): a voluntary advocate for children in child abuse and neglect cases.

creaming: selectivity in accepting placements in a facility, screening out the more difficult cases.

criminalized juvenile court: a suggested reform of juvenile court that advocates providing juveniles with all the procedural protections of adult criminal court and offering reduced penalties for juvenile offenders.

culture conflict: the conflict resulting when one set of cultural or subcultural practices necessitates violating the norms of a coexisting culture.

curfew: an order that prohibits juveniles from going outside after a particular hour.

D

day-evening center: a detention alternative in which a center was formed to devote time to formal education and remedial and tutorial work in the day and recreational programs in the evening.

deadly force: police actions that have the potential to cause the death of the offender.

deinstitutionalization: the practice of avoiding any involuntary residential placements of status offenders; also, the general idea of removing any youths from institutional control.

delinquency: in general, conduct that subjects a juvenile individual to the jurisdiction of the juvenile court (for more on the various definitions comprised under this term, see Chapter 1).

detached worker program: a program designed to place system workers into the environment of the gang.

detention decision: the decision whether to keep a juvenile in custody or to allow the youth to go home while awaiting further court action.

detoxification: a treatment approach that attempts to remove an individual from an addiction by weaning him or her off drugs.

differential association: Edwin Sutherland's theory suggesting that criminal behavior is learned when an individual encounters an excess of definitions favoring deviant definitions over those that conform to the law.

differential opportunity: suggested by Cloward and Ohlin, the availability of illegitimate opportunities when legitimate opportunities are blocked.

differential reinforcement: a theory that proposes that an individual can learn from a variety of sources, both social and nonsocial, and that the differing levels of reinforcement received will help shape future behavior.

disposition: the process of determining what intervention to give a juvenile offender upon his or her adjudication as a delinquent.

dispute resolution: bringing together adversarial parties in an attempt to arrive at a mutually agreeable solution.

diversion: attempting to find alternative forms of dealing with problem youth outside of normal system processing.

divestiture: elimination of juvenile court jurisdiction over status offenses.

domestic relations court: a civil court devoted to issues involved in divorce, child support, and related matters.

double jeopardy: being tried twice for the same offense.

drift: the concept that individuals are pushed and pulled toward different modes of activity at different times in their lives (that is, a person can "drift" in and out of crime).

Drug Abuse Resistance Education (D.A.R.E.) program: a school-based, police-taught program aimed at elementary students that attempts to reduce drug use by focusing on enhancing the social skills of the individual.

drug courts: specialized courts that attempt to help drug offenders stop using drugs by providing services and judicial supervision.

Drug Use Forecasting (DUF) Program: a program that forecasts drug use through a combination of self-reports and urinalyses from arrested subjects.

E

eclectic programming: the use of multiple treatment approaches.

ecological fallacy: the fallacy of attributing results based on grouped data to the individual level.

elaboration model: a perspective that takes components of various theories in order to construct a single explanation that incorporates the best parts of the individual theories.

entitlement: a benefit or program offered by the government.

F

factor analysis: a statistical technique that isolates common dimensions on a set of variables under study.

false negative prediction: a prediction in which it is claimed that something will not happen and it does.

false positive prediction: a prediction in which it is claimed that something will happen and it does not.

family court: a court designated to deal with family matters.

Fare v. Michael C.: U.S. Supreme Court case in which the Court ruled that a juvenile can voluntarily waive his or her privilege against self-incrimination without first consulting a parent or an attorney.

focal concerns: the concerns designated by Walter Miller to represent the cultural values of the lower class; they include, trouble, toughness, smartness, excitement, fate, and autonomy.

foray: an attack, usually by two or three youths, upon one or more rival gang members (e.g., a drive-by shooting).

G

gang: in general, a group that exhibits characteristics that set them apart from other affiliations of juveniles, often involved in deviant activity (for more on the various definitions comprised under this term, see Chapter 5).

ganging: the process of developing gangs.

general strain theory: Robert Agnew's theory positing that the removal of valued stimuli or the presentation of negative stimuli can lead to strain and, perhaps, deviance.

goal confusion: the state of affairs in which judges, probation and aftercare officers, probation directors, state legislators, juvenile justice experts, and others in the system disagree about the objectives of juvenile court an community supervision.

G.R.E.A.T. (Gang Resistance Education and Training) program: a program operated by the Bureau of Alcohol, Tobacco, Firearms, and Explosives in which local police officers present a curriculum to middle-school children designed to induce them to resist the pressure to join a gang.

group hazard hypothesis: a contention that delinquency committed in groups has a greater chance of being detected and acted upon by the juvenile and criminal justice systems.

group home: a community residential facility housing delinquent youths in relatively small numbers.

guardian ad litem: an individual appointed by the court to serve as an advocate for a child in a child abuse or neglect case (also see **Court-Appointed Special Advocate**).

guided group interaction: a technique for changing delinquents into conforming youths, involving group sessions that confront delinquents with the fact that past delinquency has led to their present status as offender.

H

home detention: programs that supervise juveniles at home instead of in custody while they are awaiting further court action.

houses of refuge: early institutions for children that were designed to separate the youth from the detrimental environment of the city.

I

I-levels: See **interpersonal maturity levels.**

in camera **testimony:** testimony given outside the courtroom, often used for the testimony of children in abuse and neglect cases.

In re Gault: U.S. Supreme Court case that guaranteed certain due process rights for juveniles in delinquency hearings with the possibility of confinement.

In re Winship: U.S. Supreme Court case that established the standard of proof in both adult criminal cases and juvenile delinquency cases as guilt beyond a reasonable doubt.

Index offense: an offense included in Part I of the Uniform Crime Reports. The eight crimes included are murder, rape, robbery, aggravated assault, burglary, larceny, motor vehicle theft, and arson.

infanticide: the deliberate killing of young children, a common practice prior to the fourth century when a child was an economic burden to a household.

informal adjustment: informal handling of an offense without the filing of a petition (e.g., a probation intake officer orders the payment of restitution).

inmate code: a group of peer norms or a code of behavior among inmates that may or may not conflict with the norms expected by treatment professionals and correctional staff.

institutional life: refers to the demands of daily life in institutions such as detention centers and state training schools where all aspects of life are regulated. Inmates typically make adjustments to such institutions that often work against the objectives of staff.

intake decision: the decision whether to file a court petition of delinquent, status offense, abuse or dependency.

intelligence quotient (IQ): a test, developed by Alfred Binet. that provides a numerical representation of the mental ability of an individual [the formula is IQ = (mental age/chronological age) × 100].

intensive supervision: supervision outside of a residential faculty in which more oversight than simple probation is provided.

intermediate sanction: a sentence that is more punitive than simple probation but less severe than imprisonment.

interpersonal maturity levels (I-levels): developed by Sullivan et al., the seven levels that reflect the progressive development of social and interpersonal skills.

intraindividual theory: in explanations of child maltreatment, a theory that views child maltreatment as an internal defect of the abuser.

involuntary servitude: selling or trading a youth to another for service.

J

"Just Say No" campaign: a school- and media-based program designed to encourage children to make a personal decision to refuse any offer to use illicit drugs in the face of peer influences.

job burnout: the emotional exhaustion, cynicism, and depersonalization that can affect youth workers such as probation officers.

justice model: a model for the criminal and juvenile justice systems in which the overriding goal is to administer fair and proportional punishment.

juvenile: a minor. (The precise definition of a juvenile varies from jurisdiction to jurisdiction, currently ranging from under age 16 to under age 19.)

juvenile awareness project: interventions (such as the Scared Straight program) that involve bringing youths into the prison for presentations on prison life.

K

Kent v. United States: U.S. Supreme Court case that established minimum safeguards for waiver (transfer) hearings, including a hearing, the right to the assistance of counsel, and a statement of the reasons for transfer if so ordered.

knowledge approach: an approach to drug use prevention that entails providing youths with information on different types of drugs and the possible legal consequences of using them.

L

labeling: the contention that the fact of being labeled deviant by society leads an individual to act in accordance with that label.

legislative waiver: state laws that provide for automatic transfer of juvenile to adult court, as opposed to judicial waiver or transfer (see **waiver**).

M

maintenance program: a drug treatment program that seeks to establish a state in which the individual does not experience withdrawal systems.

maturation effect: the effect when a decrease in delinquent activity can be attributed to growing older (maturation) rather than treatment or punishment.

McKeiver v. Pennsylvania: U.S. Supreme Court case that did *not* extend the right to trial by jury for delinquency cases.

medical model: a perspective that approaches the deviant act as a symptom of a larger problem (or "disease").

mentoring program: a program for at-risk youth that is designed to bring together youths who are not receiving the proper familial support with adults in the community who will help nurture the youths.

meta-analysis: a statistical technique that uses data from a number of studies to compute a common statistic in order to compare results across studies.

minimization of penetration: keeping court processing of juveniles at the lowest possible level.

Minnesota Multiphasic Personality Inventory (MMPI): a 556-question inventory that serves as a standardized method for tapping personality traits in individuals.

modeling: a form of learning that entails copying the behavior of others.

modes of adaptation: according to Merton, the various ways of adapting to strain; the five modes of adaptation are conformity, innovation, ritualism, retreatism, and rebellion.

Monitoring the Future (MTF) survey: a self-report survey, administered annually to high school seniors, college students, and young adults, that includes both serious and less serious offenses, such as robbery, aggravated assault, hitting teachers, use of weapons, group fighting, and drug usage.

N

National Crime Victimization Survey (NCVS): a victim survey administered by the U.S. Census Bureau.

National Youth Gang Survey: a survey administered by Spergel and Curry (1993) that identified the five common gang-intervention strategies of suppression, social intervention, organization change and development, community organization, and opportunities provision.

National Youth Survey (NYS): a self-report survey administered to 11- to 17-year-old youths that taps information on Index offenses.

nature–nurture controversy: the debate as to whether intelligence is inherited (nature) or whether it is an outcome of growth in the environment (nurture).

near group: an assembly of individuals characterized by a relatively short lifetime, little formal organization, a lack of consensus between members, a small core of continuous participants, self-appointed leadership, and limited cohesion.

neglect: the failure to provide life's essentials (e.g., food, shelter, clothing, etc.) to a child.

neoclassicism: the middle ground between classicism and positivism, the contention that humankind exercises come degree of free will, but that choices are limited by a large number of factors both within and outside of the individual (also called **soft determinism**).

net-widening: the practice of handling youths (or other offenders) who normally would have been left alone.

nondirective therapy: see **person centered therapy**.

nonsecure detention: the placement of a delinquent youth in a small group home that is not as securely locked to await further court action (compare to **secure detention**).

nullification: a refusal to enforce the law or impose a punishment.

O

"once an adult, always an adult" provisions: state laws that mandate that certain juvenile offenders be processed in adult court after an initial processing in adult criminal court.

operant conditioning: the reinforcement of behavior through a complex system of rewards.

order maintenance: police intervention into behavior that disturbs or threatens to disturb the public peace.

outpatient drug-free program: a nonresidential form of drug treatment that emphasizes the provision of a supportive, highly structured, family-like atmosphere within which a patient can be helped to alter his or her personality and develop social relationships conducive to conforming behavior.

P

parens patriae: a legal doctrine under which the state is seen as a parent.

peer mediation: a program in which disputants in a matter are brought together with a third-party peer (youth) mediator in an effort to resolve the dispute to the satisfaction of both parties.

person-centered therapy: Carl Rogers's approach contending that empathic understanding, unconditional positive regard and congruence will initiate change in the individual toward self-actualization. Also called **nondirective therapy**.

petition: the document filed in juvenile court alleging that a juvenile is a delinquent, status offender, or dependent.

phrenology: the idea that the shape of the skull and facial features are linked to levels of aggression.

physiognomy: the idea that facial features are related to behavior.

plea bargaining: negotiation between the prosecutor and the defense attorney concerning the petition (charge) and/or the disposition (sentence).

police brutality: police use of excessive force.

police discretion: the authority of police to enforce or not enforce the law, or how to enforce the law.

police effectiveness: whether police are accomplishing their objectives such as controlling crime, improving the quality of life, or solving problems.

political economy: Writers such as Garland contend that both politics and economics affect the operation of the criminal and juvenile justice systems. For example, Garland argues that current political and economic pressures dictate less emphasis on rehabilitation and greater emphasis on punishment, deterrence, and incapacitation.

positivism: a school of thought based upon determinism, wherein what an individual does is determined by factors beyond the control of the individual (compare to classicism).

preventive detention: detention to prevent further delinquency while awaiting court action on an earlier charge.

primary deviance: those actions that are rationalized or otherwise dealt with as functions of a socially acceptable role (compare to secondary deviance).

probation: a type of community corrections in which an offender is under the supervision of a probation officer. The court orders the offender to follow certain rules and to report regularly to a probation officer.

problem-oriented policing: addressing the underlying causes of problems (such as delinquency) rather than simply addressing the symptoms.

professional policing: also known as the 911 model of policing, a model of policing that emphasizes rapid response to citizen calls for service. This model includes greater emphasis on police patrol in cruisers rather than foot patrol.

program effectiveness: the question of whether programs achieve their objectives.

prosecutorial waiver: a waiver or transfer by the prosecutor of a juvenile case to adult court.

punishment gap: the finding that when juveniles are tried in adult court for the first time they are usually given the same degree of leniency given to adult first offenders.

punitive model (attack probation): a philosophy of probation that emphasizes punishment such as curfew enforcement rather than a more rehabilitation-oriented model that emphasizes treatment of the underlying problems of the probationer.

Q

Quay typology: a typology suggested by Herbert Quay that identifies four personality types among delinquent youths; the four types include: neurotic-disturbed; unsocialized-psycopaths, "subcultural-socialized," and inadequate-immature.

R

racial profiling: the practice of using race as the sole indicator of suspicion of criminal activity.

radical nonintervention: the practice of leaving youths alone as much as possible in order to avoid labeling (see **labeling**).

rational choice theory: the theory that potential offenders make choices based on various factors in the physical and social environments.

rational-emotive therapy: therapy that attempts to substitute appropriate emotions for inappropriate emotions so that the individual can move on to appropriate behavior.

reality therapy: William Glasser's therapeutic approach in which the youth is taught to accept responsibility and pursue needs in a responsible manner.

reasonable doubt standard: the standard of proof used in both adult criminal cases and juvenile delinquency cases: doubt based on reason that a reasonable man or women might entertain.

regression toward the mean: the return of behavior toward its true average rate after an unusually high or low rate of behavior.

reintegration model: a model suggesting that probation personnel refer youths with problems to outside agencies that can help with integrating the youths into law-abiding society.

restitution: the practice of offenders paying for all or part of the damage inflicted on persons or property damaged by the offense.

restitution program: a program in which the offender makes monetary payment to the victim(s) of the crime he or she committed.

restorative justice: a model of justice that is concerned with repairing the damage or harm inflicted through processes of negotiation, mediation, empowerment, and reparation.

reverse waiver: the act of the adult criminal court returning certain cases received from juvenile court via waiver back to the juvenile court.

risk-control model: a model for the criminal and juvenile justice systems in which the focus is on preventing future delinquency.

role-taking: the process in which an individual (a child) assumes the role of a person or character whom they have observed (see **modeling**).

routine activities perspective: a perspective that assumes that the normal, day-to-day behavior of individuals contributes to deviant events; that is, the convergence of motivated offenders, suitable targets, and an absence of guardians allows for the commission of crime.

rumble: a gang fight.

S

Salient Factor Score: a scale that makes predictions of parole success based on items such as: no prior convictions, no prior periods of incarceration, no juvenile commitments, no commitment for auto theft, no prior parole revocation, a lack of drug dependence, a high school education, employment for at least six months over the past two years, and a place to live upon release from prison.

Schall v. Martin: U.S. Supreme Court case that ruled that a juvenile who is awaiting court action can be held in preventive detention if there is adequate concern that the juvenile would commit additional crimes while the primary case is pending further court action.

search and seizure: can include searches of persons, places, and things and actions such as taking into custody (arrest); Fourth Amendment protects against unreasonable searches and seizures.

secondary deviance: deviance that occurs when deviant behavior is used as a means of adjusting to society's reactions (compare to **primary deviance**).

secure detention: the placement of a youth in a locked facility with other youths who are awaiting either further court action or transfer to a state correctional facility.

selective incapacitation: the argument that some juveniles are high-rate offenders and as a result need special attention so as to incapacitate them from committing more delinquency.

self-control theory: Gottfredson and Hirschi's theory holding that self-control, internalized by individuals early in life, is what constrains a person from involvement in deviant behavior.

service: the various forms of assistance that the police provide to the public.

shame tactics: measures designed to embarrass offenders in order to punish them and to deter them from further delinquency. Examples include bumper stickers proclaiming one to be a drunk driver or shirts announcing one to be a shoplifter.

skills training: an approach to drug use prevention that seeks to train youths in the personal and social skills needed to resist pressures to use drugs.

social area analysis: the process of identifying geographical areas in terms of their social characteristics.

social bond: see **bond to society**.

social capital: the extent of community support that is available in a given community. Some writers argue that participation in community organizations and clubs is declining, thus reducing one type of social capital.

social disorganization: the state of a community in which the people in that community are unable to exert control over those living there.

social history investigation: an investigation performed by a probation officer into the legal and social history of a delinquent youth and his or her family, similar to a presentence investigation in adult court.

social learning approach: in explanations of child maltreatment, an approach that contends that an individual learns to be abusive or neglectful by observing past behavior of that type.

Social Prediction Table: an instrument created by Glueck and Glueck (1950) that scores youths according to the presence or absence of discipline by the father, supervision by the mother, affection by the father, affection by the mother, and family cohesiveness.

sociocultural explanation: in explanations of child maltreatment, an explanation that emphasizes the role of society and the environment in leading to deviant behavior.

soft determinism: (see **neoclassicism**).

somatotypes: physiques (e.g., ectomorph, endomorph, and mesomorph) supposedly corresponding to particular temperaments.

spiritual dimension in corrections: a suggestion that corrections should go beyond providing education and counseling to also focus on such issues as the meaning of life and the importance of personal values in one's life.

state training schools: residential placement centers for juveniles who have been adjudicated delinquent. They are youth prisons that may have a cottage structure and educational programming.

status degradation ceremony: a ceremony or ritual that moves a person to a lower social status.

status offense: an action illegal only for persons of a certain status (i.e., juveniles); an action for which only a juvenile can be held accountable (e.g., runaway behavior, truancy).

strain theory: Robert Merton's theory that deviance results from a disjuncture between the goals approved by a culture and the means approved for reaching those goals.

subculture of violence: a value system that accepts the use of violence to solve problems.

suppression effect: a decrease in the number of offenses committed after treatment or incarceration compared to the number of offense committed prior to treatment/incarceration.

symbolic interaction: the process through which an individual creates his or her self-image through interaction with the outside world.

systemic violence: violence due to factors related to the sale and marketing of drugs.

T

techniques of neutralization: techniques outlined by Sykes and Matza that allow a juvenile to accommodate deviant behavior while maintaining a positive self-image.

teen courts: a diversion option in which youths act as judge, prosecutor, defense attorney, and jury in minor cases such as status offenses and misdemeanors. The most common penalty is community service.

therapeutic community: a residential form of drug treatment that emphasizes the provision of a supportive, highly structured, family-like atmosphere within which a patient can be helped to alter their personality and develop social relationships conducive to conforming behavior.

therapeutic jurisprudence: courts that go beyond adjudicating and sentencing issues to consider the therapeutic role that the court can take. A prime example is drug courts, which attempt to use the court setting to motivate the offender and offer the offender services that will help solve his/her drug problem.

token economy: a behavior modification strategy, often used in training schools and other residential facilities, in which point or dollar values are assigned to particular behaviors and are used as a way of rewarding appropriate behavior.

Toughlove: an approach to drug use prevention that encourages the use of strong measures (e.g., filing criminal charges) by parents.

training school: an institution that houses delinquents considered to be unfit for probation or another lesser punishment.

transfer: see **waiver**.

true diversion: referral of a juvenile to a non-court agency program.

V

vicarious victimization: the phenomenon in which an individual recognizes and responds to the victimization of others.

victim-blaming: assigning some of the responsibility for a victimization to the victim.

victim compensation program: a program in which the state makes monetary payments to the victim(s) of a crime.

victim precipitation: a situation in a victimization experience in which the victim may have struck the first blow or somehow initiated the victimization.

victim survey: a survey of the general population about their experiences with being the victim of deviance.

victimization: in general, being victimized by a crime or delinquent act such as assault or theft. In reference to institutional life, victimization refers to an assault (physical or sexual) or theft experienced in a facility such as a state training school.

victim-offender reconciliation program (VORP):   a formal mediation program in which victim and offender are clearly identified and the participation of the offender is often a requirement of the court.

W

waiver: the process by which an individual who is legally a juvenile is sent to the adult criminal system for disposition and handling (also called **judicial waiver** or **transfer**).

wannabe: a juvenile who aspires to join a gang.

wilderness experience: a program in which youths undergo an outdoor experience that is designed to teach self-reliance, independence, and self-worth.

wilding gang: a middle-class gang that strikes out at what its members perceive to be inequalities and infringements on their rights by other ethnic groups.

Y

Youth Service Bureaus: common name for diversion agencies.

youth justice system: a suggestion to process juveniles in adult courts that are a type of therapeutic jurisprudence. These juvenile courts would be similar to drug courts in their emphasis on treatment within a court framework.

Z

zealous advocate role: defense attorney role that emphasizes strong tactics to prove the juvenile defendant innocent or get the least severe penalty (contrasted to the concerned adult model in which the attorney acts like a parent seeking the best treatment outcome for the youth).

Subject Index

Drug Abuse Resistance Education
    (D.A.R.E.) program, 133, 161-164
Drug courts, 165-167, 169, 213-214, 377
Due process, 241-271
    Breed v. Jones and, 246
    in curfew violations, 265-266
    in family courts, 362
    Fare v. Michael C. and, 247-248
    Kent v. United States and, 241-243
    legal drinking age and, 266-270
    McKeiver v. Pennsylvania and, 244-245
    In re Gault and, 243-244
    In re Winship and, 244
    Roper v. Simmons and, 245
    Schall v. Martin and, 248-249
    in school, 250-265
        corporal punishment and, 250-253
        freedom of speech and, 253-262
        searches and, 262-265
    in search and seizure, 249-250

Early childhood, in psychoanalysis, 64
Early intervention programs, 223
Ecological fallacy, 80
Ecological perspective, in sociological
    explanations, 76-81
Economic globalization, 182, 402
Effectiveness, 295
    of institutional programs, 281-283
    of policing, 192-193
    of probation, 308-309
    of treatment interventions, 309-314
Ego, in psychoanalysis, 63
Eighth Amendment, 394
Elaboration model, 101
Electronencephalography (EEG), 60
Electronic monitoring, 211
Elmira Reformatory, 34
Emancipation for juveniles, 269
Emotional healing, in restorative justice,
    327
Employment readiness programs, 208
Empowerment, in restorative justice, 327
Endocrine factors, delinquency and, 58-59
Entitlement programs, 388
Entrepreneurship, in gangs, 118, 121
Environmental factors, 35, 70-71
Evidence, rules of, 36
Evil, transfer of, in labeling perspective,
    98
Excessive force, 193-197, 210
Exchange theory, 326
Execution. *See* Capital punishment

Ex parte Crouse (1838), 38
Experimentation with drugs, 159
Exploitive use of juveniles, 42
External pressures to deviant behavior, 95
External pulls to deviant behavior, 95
Extortion, gangs and, 125

Fairness, in restorative justice, 328, 335-
    336
"Faith pods," 390
Family courts, 361
Family group conferencing (FGC), 331-
    332, 335, 337
Family issues, 361, 383-386
Fare v. Michael C. (1979), 247-248
Federal Bureau of Investigation (FBI), 10-
    12, 127, 172
"Feeble-mindedness" of criminals, 71
Females. *See also* Sex of juvenile offenders
    delinquency rates of, 15
    disposition and, 235
    dowries and, 28
    drug abuse of, 147, 150
    early juvenile justice and, 42
    in gangs, 117-118, 121
    in institutions, 34-35, 274, 284, 286
    intervention effectiveness with, 313
    special programming for, 371
    status offenses and, 398-399
Fifth Amendment (self-incrimination pro-
    tection), 244
Financial cutbacks, effectiveness and, 314
Financial gain, gangs and, 129
Firearms, 127-128, 132, 357-358
First Amendment, 253-254, 265
"Fleeing felon" rule, 196
Florida Parishes Juvenile Detention Center,
    337
Focal concerns of subculture, 85
Forays, as gang violence, 127
"Formalized gangs," 118
Foster care, 34, 360
Fourteenth Amendment, 394
Fourth Amendment, 241, 249-250
"Franchising" of gangs, 120
Free association (First Amendment), 265
Freedom of speech (First Amendment),
    253-262
    *Bethel School District Number 403 v.
        Fraser* and, 254-256
    censorship of school publications and,
        257

Neoclassical school of thought, 50-51, 89

Nervous system, delinquency and, 60-61

Net-widening, 169, 214, 339

Neurobiological research, Miranda rights
and, 248

Neuropsychological deficits, 102

Neurotransmitters, delinquency and, 60

Neutralization techniques, 86-87

New Jersey v. T. L. O. (1985), 262-264

New Vision Therapeutic Community program, 155

Nightwatch Program (St. Louis, MO), 176

"911 policing," 173, 177

Nonamenability, in juvenile court, 221

Nondirective therapy, 310-311

Nonsectarian prayer, 260

Nonsecure detention, 205, 210, 290

Norepinephrine, 60

Normlessness of society, 91

Nullification of laws, 29

NYGS (National Youth Gang Survey),
107, 111-112, 115, 117, 123, 128-
129, 136

NYS (National Youth Survey), 22-23, 149,
353, 390

Obscene language, freedom of speech and,
255-256

Offender responsibility, in restorative justice, 329

Offense rate, 14

Office of Juvenile Justice and Delinquency Prevention (OJJDP), 135,
176, 316, 400

Once an adult/always an adult provisions,
8-9, 216, 221, 233. *See also* Adult
courts, transfer to

Operant conditioning, as learning theory,
68, 72, 83

Operation Beat Feet (Chicago), 174

Operation Ceasefire, Boston Gun Project,
175, 185, 192

Operation Night Light (Boston), 300, 317

"Orphan trains," 388

Orthomolecular factors, delinquency and,
59-60

Outcome reporting focus, 301

Outer containment theory, 95-96

Outlaw motorcycle gangs, 126

Out-of-home placement, 229

Outpatient drug-free programs, 155-156

Overcrowding of institutions, 33-34

P. B. v. Koch (1996), 252

Paddling, 251

Parens patriae
challenges to, 44
in community corrections, 315
court jurisdiction and, 40-41
disposition stage of juvenile court and,
232
intake decision and, 212
judges and, 36
juvenile court record confidentiality
and, 234
in *Kent v. United States,* 242
as legal philosophy, 37-40
prosecutor role *versus,* 216
punishment *versus,* 211
in *In re Gault,* 243
in restorative justice, 323
return to, 401
in *In re Winship,* 244

Parents
Child Protective Services and, 360
disobeying, 3, 20
juvenile rights and, 248
lawyer confidentiality and, 227
liability for children's crimes of, 237-
238, 375
plea bargaining and, 228
single, 383, 385
status offenses and, 400
supervision by, 190
training of, 370

Parochial sources of neighborhood control, 80

Parole violations, 221. *See also* Probation

Passive speech, 254

Pat-down searches, 250

Paternalism in juvenile law, 269

Peacemaking, 305, 327, 333-334, 337

Peer mediation, 325, 358-359

Peer pressure, 43

Pennsylvania Supreme Court, 38-39, 248

People v. Turner (1870), 39

Per se rules, 247

Personality, delinquency and, 68-70

Petitions, filing (charging), 201-202

Phoenix House community for drug treatment, 154

Phrenology, delinquency and, 52

Physical appearance, delinquency and, 52-
54

Physiognomy, delinquency and, 52

PINS (person in need of supervision), 3

Punishment. *See also* Corporal punishment
 boot camps as, 281
 in classical school of thought, 49
 as community corrections model, 302-
  303
 cruel and unusual, 253
 as detention orientation, 210
 emphasis on, 232-234
 growth of, 44
 as juvenile court focus, 371
 parens patriae versus, 211
 political emphasis on, 388-389
 truth of, 379

Quasi-police, probation officer as, 298
Qutb v. Strauss (1993), 265

Race of juvenile offenders. S*ee also* Sociological explanations of delinquency
 detention decision and, 205
 disposition and, 234-237
 drug abuse and, 150
 early juvenile justice and, 42
 excessive force and, 195
 in gangs, 116-117
 in institutions, 168, 287
 intake decision and, 219
 juvenile corrections statistics on, 16-18
 juvenile justice and, 380-381
 police and, 184
 self-report statistics on, 23
 sentencing recommendations and, 297
 transfer to adult court and, 374-375
 Uniform Crime Reports data on, 11-13
 victimization and, 345-347
Racial profiling, 187-188
Ranches, as group homes, 278
Random drug testing, 264
Rape by juveniles, 12-13
Rational decisions, 49, 89
Rational emotive therapy, 299
Reactive hypoglycemia, 59
Reality therapy, 299
Rebellion, as mode of adaptation, 91-92
Rebuilding community, 381-383
Recidivism
 behavioral treatment and, 310
 boot camps and, 279-280
 drug courts and, 167, 214
 drug treatment programs and, 156
 institutions and, 40
 intensive supervision and, 298, 307,
  317

 of juveniles transferred to adult court,
  222-223
 labeling perspective and, 100
 probation and, 308, 390
 reduction strategies for, 282
 rehabilitation and, 370
 residential placements and, 293
 restitution and, 316
 restorative justice and, 336-337
Reciprocal relationship of drug use and
  delinquency, 148-149
Reciprocity, 326
Redemption, 370
Re-entry to community, 299
Reformatories, 33-34
Rehabilitation
 in boot camp, 279
 in community corrections, 315
 in detention, 210
 economic changes and, 402
 failure of, 224
 positivist school of thought and, 50-51
 in probation, 298-300, 317
 recidivism reductions by, 370
 in restorative justice, 335
Reinforcement, 68, 72, 83
Reintegration, in restorative justice, 327
Reintegrative shaming, 102, 325-326
Reintegrative Shaming Experiments
  (RISE), 337
Religion, 32, 381
Reparation, in restorative justice, 329
Residential Area Policing Program (RAPP,
  Cleveland, OH), 175, 192
Resistance skills training, to prevent drug
  abuse, 160
Resolving Conflict Creatively Program
  (RCCP, New York City), 359
Responsivity principle, 310
Restitution, 301, 315-316, 321, 333, 336,
  365, 378, 401
Restoration, in restorative justice, 327
Restorative justice, 319-341
 in balanced approach to community
  corrections, 300
 in community corrections, 304, 309,
  315-316
 community issues in, 382
 conferences for, 171, 174-175, 192
 description of, 320-322
 dispute resolution in, 323-325
 family group conferencing in, 331-332
 impacts of, 335-340

Name Index